Megaprojects for Megacities

For Bonnie, whose curiosity and love of travel inspired this work

Megaprojects for Megacities

A Comparative Casebook

Edited by

John D. Landis

Emeritus Professor of City and Regional Planning, Weitzman School of Design, University of Pennsylvania, USA

Edward **Elgar**
PUBLISHING

Cheltenham, UK • Northampton, MA, USA

Published by
Edward Elgar Publishing Limited
The Lypiatts
15 Lansdown Road
Cheltenham
Glos GL50 2JA
UK

Edward Elgar Publishing, Inc.
William Pratt House
9 Dewey Court
Northampton
Massachusetts 01060
USA

Paperback edition 2024

A catalogue record for this book
is available from the British Library

Library of Congress Control Number: 2022944524

This book is available electronically in the **Elgar**online
Geography, Planning and Tourism subject collection
http://dx.doi.org/10.4337/9781803920634

ISBN 978 1 80392 062 7 (cased)
ISBN 978 1 80392 063 4 (eBook)
ISBN 978 1 0353 4301 0 (paperback)

Printed and bound by CPI Group (UK) Ltd, Croydon, CR0 4YY

Contents

Contributors

EDITOR

John D. Landis is Professor Emeritus of City and Regional Planning at the Weitzman School of Design at the University of Pennsylvania. His current research interests focus on place and policy entrepreneurship, urban and neighborhood change, and housing policy. Landis holds a Bachelor of Science degree from MIT and a PhD in City and Regional Planning from the University of California-Berkeley, and he previously held faculty positions at the University of California-Berkeley, the Georgia Institute of Technology, and the University of Rhode Island.

CONTRIBUTING AUTHORS

Fang Bian holds a PhD in Urban Planning and Design from the University of Hong Kong, and a Master of Science Degree in Human Geography (City and Regional Planning) from Peking University.

David L. A. Gordon is Professor in the School of Urban and Regional Planning of the Department of Geography and Planning at Queen's University. David was SURP Director for over a decade and has also taught at McGill, Ryerson, Toronto, Riga, Western Australia, Harvard and Pennsylvania, where he was a Fulbright Scholar. He received degrees in Civil Engineering and Planning from Queen's and an MBA and doctorate from Harvard. Prior to becoming a full-time professor, David was a principal in an urban design firm and manager in a Toronto waterfront agency. He is Research Chair of the Council for Canadian Urbanism and a Fellow of the Canadian Institute of Planners, sharing their National Awards four times. David's books include *Town and Crown; Canadian Federalism and Infrastructure, Battery Park City, Planning Twentieth-Century Capital Cities* and *Planning Canadian Communities*. His research addresses planning history, suburbs, capital cities and waterfronts.

Mengyi Jin is a PhD student at the Department of Transportation Engineering, Shanghai Jiao Tong University.

Ziming Liu is a researcher and investor. From 2017 to 2020, she worked at the World Bank's Transport Global Practice Office in Beijing, where she provided technical assistance and support for World Bank transport lending programs in China, Central Asia, and Africa. She is the co-author of *China's High-Speed Rail (HSR) Development*, a retrospective look at China's HSR development experience, and the contributor to *Innovative China: New Drivers of Growth*, the flagship research work on China's macroeconomic policy. Ms. Liu transitioned into the private equity sector in 2020 where her current investment focus centers on renewable energy, efficient transport and logistics, environmental, social, and corporate governance (ESG), and emerging technologies. Ms. Liu holds a Bachelor of Engineering degree from the University of Hong Kong and a Master of City Planning degree from the University of Pennsylvania.

Kaifa Lu is a PhD student at the department of Urban and Regional Planning, University of Florida.

Zhong-Ren Peng is Professor of Urban and Regional Planning and Director of the International Center for Adaptation Planning and Design (iAdapt) at the College of Design, Construction and Planning, University of Florida. His major research interests include transportation planning, transportation and environment, adaptation planning for climate change, and international planning. He has been conducting extensive research about China's urbanization, urban and regional planning, and transportation planning theory and practice for the last 20 years and has first-hand experience and knowledge in understanding the process and policies of urban development, as well as the issues and challenges facing urban China.

Molly Riddle is a transportation planning consultant with Fehr & Peers in Oakland, California. She received her Master of Urban Planning, with a focus on land use and infrastructure planning, from the University of Washington. Molly previously spent seven years as a project manager and international active travel guide and holds a B.A. in Health & Societies from the University of Pennsylvania.

Oscar Serpell is the Associate Director of Academic Programming and Student Engagement at the Kleinman Center for Energy Policy at the University of Pennsylvania. He oversees student programming, alumni connections, and curriculum design. He also is a researcher, writer, and data analyst working on several research initiatives with the center on timely energy policy topics. He has held several student teaching and administrative positions in the Department of Earth and Environmental Science, the Department of Anthropology, and the Center for Excellence in Environmental Toxicology at the University of Pennsylvania. Serpell has a Master's Degree in Environmental Studies and a BA in Environmental Management, both from the University of Pennsylvania.

C. Erik Vergel-Tovar is an Assistant Professor in the Department of Architecture at Universidad de los Andes in Bogotá, Colombia. He holds a PhD in City and Regional Planning from the University of North Carolina at Chapel Hill and a Master's Degree in Urban Management and Development from Erasmus University in Rotterdam. Professor Vergel-Tovar previously worked as an urban development and housing planner and policymaker in Colombia. His current research interests involve the intersections between transport, land use, and housing policy, and urban development in Latin America, India, and the United States.

Patricia Warren is a graduate from Queen's University where she earned a Master's Degree in Urban Planning. She is currently an urban planner with Fotenn Planning + Design in Ottawa and has previously worked as a policy planner with the City of Ottawa.

Jan Whittington is an Associate Professor of the Department of Urban Design and Planning, the founding Director of the Urban Infrastructure Lab (https://uil.be.uw.edu/) at the University of Washington, Seattle, and a former strategic planner and scientist for the international infrastructure developer, Bechtel Corporation (https://urbdp.be.uw.edu/people/jan-whittington/). She is a global expert in infrastructure economics, public contracting and finance, in general and with respect to climate change. Her publications address the efficiency of public–private contractual arrangements for infrastructure, the evaluation of smart city infrastructure systems, and climate change through capital investment planning. Her PhD (2008) is in City and Regional Planning from the University of California, Berkeley, where she was advised by economic Nobel laureate Oliver Williamson. She holds bachelor degrees from the University of California, Santa Cruz (1987) and a masters from California Polytechnic State University, San Luis Obispo (1993).

Anthony G.O. Yeh is Chair Professor in the Department of Urban Planning and Design, Faculty of Architecture, the University of Hong Kong. He is a member of the Chinese Academy of Sciences and Hong Kong Academy of Sciences and a Fellow of the World Academy of Sciences (TWAS). He obtained his BA from the University of Hong Kong, MSc from the Asian Institute of Technology, Thailand, and MRP and PhD from Syracuse University, USA. His research interests are in urban development and planning in Hong Kong and China and the applications of GIS in urban planning and smart city development. He has been studying the development of the Pearl River Delta, which is now known as the Guangdong–Hong Kong–Macao Greater Bay Area, since the early 1980s. He received the UN-HABITAT Lecture Award in 2008 and Dr. Gill-Chin Lim Global Award in 2012.

Jiangping Zhou is Associate Professor in Urban Planning and Design at the University of Hong Kong (HKU). He previously served on the faculties of Iowa State University (USA) and the University of Queensland, Australia. His research focuses on transport/transit systems and land use connections and how to improve the performance of these connections.

Xinghang Zhu is a masters student at the Department of Transportation Engineering, Shanghai Jiao Tong University.

Preface

John D. Landis

The world's urban places are projected to add two billion new residents by 2040 according to the United Nations. For this amount of population growth to occur prosperously and sustainably, cities and metropolitan areas will need enormous amounts of new public infrastructure, including new roads, bridges and tunnels; new airports and seaports; new rail and bus systems; repurposed city centers and new towns; new parks and recreational facilities; new water and sewer systems; and, most of all, new clean energy generation and distribution systems. Much of this new infrastructure will be provided in the form of megaprojects—infrastructure investments costing more than $1 billion each.

This will be a challenge. The world's megaproject-building record isn't particularly good. Regardless of their type or location, today's megaprojects frequently run more than 30 percent over budget and years behind schedule. Much of the current megaproject literature seeks to identify the reasons for this poor record.

This volume takes a different approach. Acknowledging the problems with today's megaproject delivery systems, it seeks to identify the connections between good and bad megaproject planning and project management practices, and good and bad megaproject outcomes—with outcomes measured in more than just budgetary and schedule overrun terms. Specifically, we seek to understand how specific planning, design, engineering, financing and project management practices contribute to megaprojects reaching their service quality, environmental, urban development, financial and equity goals and targets.

We do this through the lens of case studies of global megaprojects completed or under construction during the last ten years. The list of case study megaprojects includes high-speed rail and metro projects, bus rapid transit systems, urban and inter-city tunnel and bridge projects, airport projects, waterfront projects, new town and smart city projects, urban park projects, and renewable energy projects. The case studies are geographically, as well as sectorally diverse, and include projects in Brazil, China, Germany, Colombia, Great Britain, India, Indonesia, Korea and the United States. This approach allows us to identify specific practices that contribute to successful project outcomes across multiple governance, planning and financing systems. Among its key takeaways are that competence and experience matter above all else; that it is indeed possible to learn from project planning and delivery experiences in other places; that design and engineering standardization can be an important source of project cost efficiency but that they can also go overboard; that senior project managers need to be held accountable on a continuous basis; that worst-case contingency planning is essential; and that the precise form of project financing is less important than having a rigorous revenue forecasting model that recognizes and incorporates uncertainty.

Undertaking megaprojects isn't quite rocket science, but it does require balancing great ambition with great humility. Hopefully, the case studies included in this volume will provide useful instruction in exactly how to do this.

Acknowledgements

Seed funding for this book was provided by the consortium of Cooperative Mobility for Competitive Megaregions (CM2), a US Department of Transportation University Transportation Center whose partners include the University of Texas at Austin, Louisiana State University, Texas Southern University, and the University of Pennsylvania. I wish to thank Professor Ming Zhang, CM2 Director at the University of Texas at Austin, and Professor Erick Guerra, CM2 Research Director at the University of Pennsylvania, for their case study and author suggestions and thoughtful comments. Additional thanks to University of Pennsylvania and CM2 staff and student researchers who provided administrative and research support, most notably Inessa Ach, Tiara Campbell, Roslynn Carter, Chris Cataldo, Sandra Ciarletta, Kate Daniel, Jessica Dejesus and Geyang Li. Thanks also to University of Pennsylvania Professors Eugenie Birch, Frederick Steiner and Susan Wachter, who encouraged me to undertake this work, and to my editors at Edward Elgar Publishing, Alan Sturmer and Katia Williford. Special thanks to my co-authors whose creative work and attention to getting things right have made this the insightful and authoritative work I hope it proves to be: Ziming Liu (Chapter 5), Professor Zhong-Ren Peng (Chapter 6), Kaifa Lu (Chapter 6), Mengyi Jin (Chapter 6), Xinghang Zhu, (Chapter 6), Professor Erik Vergel-Tovar (Chapter 7), Molly Riddle (Chapter 8), Professor Jan Whittington (Chapter 8), Professor Anthony G. O. Yeh (Chapter 9), Fian Bian (Chapter 9), Jiangping Zhou (Chapter 9), Professor David Gordon (Chapter 12), Patricia Warren (Chapter 12) and Oscar Serpell (Chapter 16).

John D. Landis
March 2022

1. The megaproject challenge

John D. Landis

MEGAPROJECTS RESURGENT

Political scientists Alan Altshuler and David Luberoff end their 2004 book, *Megaprojects: The Changing Politics of Urban Public Investments*, by concluding that "a plausible argument can be made that the age of urban megaprojects has passed" (p. 270), and that, at least in America, the place where the modern megaproject was born, the push to more fully account for the social and environmental costs of large infrastructure projects had tipped the tide of public and professional opinion firmly against them.[1]

Theirs was a distinctly American viewpoint. Had Altshuler and Luberoff been writing from the perspective of Seoul or London or Hamburg or Beijing instead of Boston, they might have come to a different conclusion. Outside of the United States, enthusiasm for undertaking very large-scale infrastructure projects was never greater. Forty minutes north of Seoul, South Korea had just completed building Incheon International Airport, soon to become the most profitable airport in the world. In Britain, transportation planners were debating how to pay for Crossrail, a new 73-mile express metro line that would halve the time it took to get from Heathrow Airport to Canary Wharf. In Germany, the city of Hamburg was beginning construction of HafenCity, the world's largest waterfront redevelopment project. And in Beijing, China's ruling State Council was one year away from approving construction of what would become the biggest transportation megaproject in history, a national high-speed rail network that, as of 2020, ran to more than 37,000 kilometers in length.

As Figure 1.1 shows, compared with the 1980s and 1990s, globally, the number of new metro system starts has increased significantly since the year 2000, as has the construction of new high-speed rail lines, long-span suspension bridges, large hydroelectric dams, underground and undersea tunnels, and large-scale airport projects. Much if not most of this increase in megaproject construction activity has occurred in China, which now boasts what is by far the world's largest high-speed rail network, seven of its ten biggest metro systems, five of its ten largest hydroelectric dams (based on generating capacity), six of its longest suspension bridges, five of its busiest international airports,[2] and four of its ten largest photovoltaic solar parks.

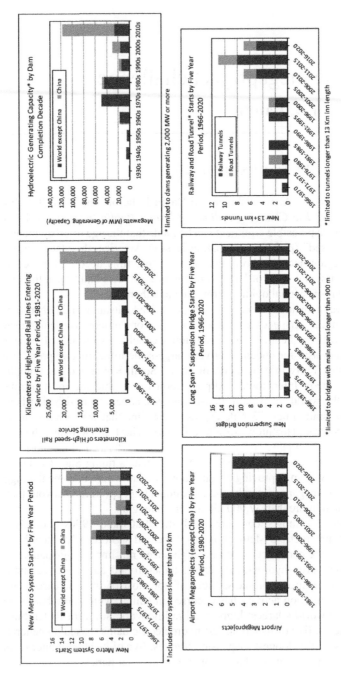

Figure 1.1   Global megaproject deliveries by project type and period

Even in the US, where megaprojects were supposedly passé, cities were gearing up for a new round of megaproject construction. Washington State was making plans to replace an elevated highway in downtown Seattle damaged in a 2001 earthquake with a new $3 billion underground tunnel. In the New York region, the Port Authority of New York and New Jersey was in the midst of major terminal building projects at both JFK and Newark Airports, and construction would soon begin on the Second Avenue Subway in Manhattan, the first entirely new subway line to be built in New York City since 1933.[3] When evaluated on a global basis, Altshuler and Luberoff weren't just slightly off about the future of large-scale infrastructure projects, they were flat-out wrong.

Altshuler and Luberoff weren't alone in their criticisms of the megaproject business. In 2003, Bent Flyvbjerg, Nils Bruzelius, and Werner Rothengatter published *Megaprojects and Risk: An Anatomy of Ambition*, the first major study to explore megaproject cost and schedule overruns on a global scale. The authors concluded that the megaproject approval process had become one in which all manner of market, financial, construction, and project management risks were systematically underestimated, and in which government megaproject planners were incentivized to overestimate project benefits and underestimate costs. Flyvbjerg would later postulate what he called the iron law of megaprojects, summarized as "over budget, over time, under benefits, and over and over again" (Flyvbjerg 2017). Megaproject best practice, Flyvbjerg went on to assert, was an outlier, and average practice was a disaster. In the same volume, Flyvbjerg also noted the need for more detailed studies connecting megaproject practice with performance, a call that was explicitly echoed by Söderlund, Sankaran and Biesenthal in their introduction to a 2017 special megaproject issue of *Project Management Journal*. The view that assessments of megaproject success or failure should not be based solely on measurements of time and cost overruns, and that a more careful accounting of how particular megaproject planning, financing, engineering and project management practices shape megaproject outcomes is the central motivation behind this book.

Before taking a closer look at recent megaproject practice, we should more precisely define what is meant by the term megaproject. According to the *Oxford Handbook of Megaproject Management* (Flyvbjerg 2017, p. 2), megaprojects are "large-scale, complex ventures that typically cost $1 billion or more, take many years to develop and build, involve multiple public and private stakeholders, generate potentially transformational impacts, and affect large numbers of people." Many but certainly not all megaprojects take the form of public-serving infrastructure such as transportation facilities, dams and powerplants, flood control projects, and very large parks and recreational facilities. Other megaprojects consist of large residential and/or commercial development projects. In rare cases, megaprojects consist of projects intended to protect and preserve the natural environment. Some analysts also include very large research and development initiatives, fossil fuel extraction and refining facilities, and high-technology and defense manufacturing plants as megaprojects—although for the purposes of this chapter, we will not do so here.

There is nothing immutable about using $1 billion as the cost threshold for distinguishing megaprojects from lesser ones; it is merely a matter of convention. Large-scale infrastructure planning and project management practices don't suddenly change whenever the $1 billion cost mark is exceeded. From a technical and planning viewpoint, building a new $2.5 billion subway line in New York City isn't all that different from building an $800 million metro line in Shenzhen, China. Similarly, the costs per megawatt of electricity of building a 1,200 MW windfarm off the English coast aren't any different from of building a 750 MW windfarm off the coast of the Netherlands. When compared at a global scale, infrastructure project costs are as much a function of local real estate prices, currency exchange rates, local environmental and labor laws, and government oversight provisions as they are a function of project size or difficulty.

HOW MANY MEGAPROJECTS?

Globally, megaprojects are a big business, but exactly how big, no one can say for sure. A 2015 pre-pandemic report by McKinsey & Company estimated that, altogether, the world's nations would need to spend upwards of US$57 trillion on infrastructure by 2030 to keep pace with expected levels of GDP growth.[4] Most of this anticipated spending will go for smaller projects but if even five percent is spent on megaprojects, that would put global megaproject spending between 2015 and 2030 at nearly $3 trillion. Including spending on non-public infrastructure items in the oil and gas, mining, aerospace, defense, ICT (information and communications technologies), and freight movement and supply chain industries, as Flyvbjerg (2017) does, adds another US$6–9 trillion dollars per year in global project spending.

A more detailed analysis of large-scale infrastructure spending is provided by the Global Infrastructure Hub (GI Hub), an infrastructure financing and best-practice information platform sponsored by the G20. In its *2021 Infrastructure Monitor Report*, the GI Hub puts annual private spending on infrastructure projects by high-income countries[5] during the 2010–2019 period at between 75 and 125 billion (US) dollars annually; and by middle-and-low-income countries at between $40 billion and $70 billion annually (p. 4). Among high-income countries, private sector lending accounts for between 50 and 60 percent of total infrastructure investment, followed by conventional bonds, and then, more recently, by so-called "green" bonds (p. 5).[6]

Worldwide, infrastructure debt continues to perform consistently better than non-infrastructure debt in terms of higher returns and lower default rates. Compared by region of the world, infrastructure debt default rates are highest in Eastern Europe and Latin America, and lowest in the Middle East and Africa. Debt incurred by infrastructure public–private partnerships (P3s) is less likely to default than debt incurred by governments (p. 48).

Counts of actual projects are more difficult to come by than spending and investment estimates. This is particularly true for megaprojects, which are not generally reported as a separate infrastructure or spending category. As of January 2022, Wikipedia, a useful if not always accurate source, counted two bridge megaprojects under construction globally, seven road and rail tunneling megaprojects, six motorway megaprojects, seven commuter and inter-city railway megaprojects, three high-speed rail megaprojects (not including the expansion of China's high-speed rail network), six light-rail megaprojects, and seven airport megaprojects. None of these counts include expansions or upgrades of existing facilities. Separate Wikipedia listings count 46 large dam projects as under construction.[7] Among the megaproject types for which there are no authoritative counts are onshore and offshore windfarms, solar parks, electricity transmission facilities, urban development and waterfront projects, event arenas, and new towns.

Other than Wikipedia, a number of entities have developed their own approaches to counting and categorizing major infrastructure projects. In North America, FMI, a built environment consulting and investment banking company, maintains an inventory of megaproject construction commitments in the US and Canada. Including private commercial and residential real estate projects and industrial, oil and gas and private utility projects as well as transportation and public infrastructure projects, it reports 320 US megaprojects as having received $718 billion in funding between 2012 and 2018.[8] The corresponding numbers for Canada are 95 megaprojects valued at $272 billion. According to FMI, public infrastructure megaprojects accounted for 32 percent of US megaproject spending awards, while transportation projects accounted for 10 percent. Following national population trends, two-thirds of all megaproject spending in the US between 2012 and 2018 occurred in the South and West.

Since 1988, the World Bank has maintained a database of all of its loans to developing countries for transport, water and sewerage, and information and communications technologies (ICT) projects. Known as the PPID, or Private Participation in Infrastructure Database, it includes loan amount and total value entries for more than 6,400 infrastructure projects undertaken since the late 1980s in 137 low- and middle-income countries.[9] Among the projects in the PPID that "reached closure" between 1990 and 2018, the average project value (in 2020 US dollars) was $238 million—an amount significantly below the $1 billion megaproject threshold. Of the PPID projects reaching closure, the most common were electricity generation and distribution projects (accounting for 48 percent of closed projects) followed by road construction projects (15 percent), and water and sewer projects (14 percent). Ranked by project value, railroad projects were by far the most expensive (with an average value of $908 million), followed distantly by road projects ($296 million), electricity projects ($245 million) and natural gas projects ($241 million). Organized by recipient region, closed projects were most commonly funded in East Asia and the Pacific region (accounting for 34 percent of projects), followed by Latin American and the Caribbean (29 percent), South Asia (18 percent), and Europe and Central Asia (12 percent). In terms of average values, projects in Latin America are the most expensive ($309 million) followed by Europe ($275 million) and South Asia ($226 million). Among cancelled projects or those under financial duress, the highest cancellation rates were among water and sewerage projects (17 percent) and railway projects (14 percent). At 12 percent, project cancellation rates were highest in Latin America and the Caribbean, followed by Sub-Saharan Africa (9 percent).

The Inter-American Development Bank (IADB) publishes a similar list of major public infrastructure, transport, energy and environmental projects undertaken in the Caribbean, Mexico, and Central and South America. Over the 2016–2020 period, the IADB approved what it refers to as "sovereign-guaranteed" funding for 41 major transport projects, 39 water and sanitation projects, 36 energy projects, and 20 environmental and disaster resilience projects.[10] The average IADB sovereign-guaranteed project during this period was valued at $128 million, putting it well below the $1 billion megaproject threshold. Unlike the World Bank, the IADB does not make available a combined database of funded projects, making it difficult to identify the share of projects which fall within different funding amount categories.

In Europe, the European Commission (EC) maintains a list of major transport, water quality, environmental improvement and economic development projects funded under its Regional and Urban Development Program. For the 2014–2020 period, the EC reported applications by 14 EU member countries for 370 projects each valued at $50 million or more, with the most applications coming from Poland, Romania, Italy and Hungary.[11] Altogether, there were 20 projects valued at between €500,000 and €1 billion, and just seven valued at more than €1 billion. These tabulations do not include private industry projects or projects not seeking EU funding. As a result, they significantly understate megaproject construction activity in Europe's wealthier countries, including Germany, France, the Netherlands, Austria, Sweden, Denmark, Norway and Belgium.

China's Belt and Road website currently identifies 42 countries in Africa and the Middle East, 21 in Central and South Asia, and 16 in the Americas that have signed Belt and Road agreements with China and have or will receive funding assistance for major infrastructure projects. The Belt and Road website does not list individual projects or funding amounts.

The lack of a single global clearinghouse for very large-scale infrastructure projects continues to complicate rigorous megaproject comparisons.

MEGAPROJECTS PRO AND CON

Economies-of-Scale and Other Megaproject Advantages

Governments and political leaders undertake large-scale infrastructure projects for many reasons. Governments may wish to showcase their technological or economic prowess. Political leaders may wish to demonstrate their leadership abilities or to reward allies and supporters. Under the right circumstances, megaproject spending can stimulate the local or regional economy, help reduce unemployment, and in some instances, improve economic and social mobility. Given their great size and durability, megaprojects serve as monuments to people or groups in power, and as focal points for societal aspirations.

Because of their sizeable costs, megaprojects should also make economic sense, meaning that their discounted benefits should exceed their discounted costs. Discounting refers to the practice of systematically reducing future project costs and benefits relative to current ones to account for inflation, investor liquidity preferences, the time value of money,[12] and the unalterable reality that the future is always less certain than the present.

The obligation to rigorously evaluate costs and benefits should apply when undertaking any major public investment, not just megaprojects. What makes large-scale infrastructure projects different is that they typically exhibit significant economies-of-scale. Economists use the term economies-of-scale to characterize processes in which each additional unit of output requires fewer and fewer inputs.[13] When applied to major infrastructure projects, economies-of-scale means that when all the expenses of planning, design, engineering, construction, financing and operation are added up, it costs less to serve each additional project user with a single large project than with several smaller ones (Stigler 1958; Ansar et al. 2014). Megaproject economies-of-scale emanate from multiple sources, including:

- *Improved planning efficiencies*: Infrastructure planning activities generally center on finding the optimal combination of project benefits and costs. In addition to exhibiting physical economies-of-scale, bigger or more extensive projects are likely to have greater spillover effects, meaning that their larger service areas enable them to capture additional economic or social benefits. This is counterbalanced on the cost side by the fact that at some point, available economies-of-scale are used up, and larger projects then begin to require more costly inputs per unit of output. The job of the infrastructure planner is to figure out which combination of project technology, size, spatial extent and phasing maximizes the difference between direct and spillover benefits and capital and operating costs. In the case of rail transit systems, for example, proposing a larger system with more lines and stations has the potential to greatly increase aggregate accessibility and environmental benefits. These additional benefits must be weighed against the difficulties of finding the additional funding necessary to build a bigger or more extensive system, as well as the additional disruptions likely to occur during construction.

- *Improved design and engineering efficiencies*: Bigger projects, it is generally believed, offer additional opportunities for sharing construction costs and for design and engineering standardization. Bigger projects also offer the possibility of designing in greater redundancy, so that when one project element breaks down or becomes congested, other project elements can pick up the slack.
- *Improved contracting, procurement and construction efficiencies*: By sharing or standardizing information and transactions costs across larger jobs, bigger projects, it is thought, have the potential to reduce contracting and procurement costs. Likewise, by sharing and standardizing construction techniques and project management practices across larger jobs, bigger projects have the potential to reduce unit construction costs.
- *Improved financing and risk-sharing efficiencies*: Bigger projects offer the opportunity to access larger amounts of capital at a lower cost. The promise of increased spillover benefits also offers the opportunity of higher returns. And by apportioning different types or levels of project revenues to different financing sources, bigger projects also offer greater risk diversification opportunities.
- *Improved project management efficiencies*: Bigger projects also offer the opportunity to develop and share improved approaches to project management. This includes opportunities for learning.
- *Expanded benefit capture and equity opportunities*: To the degree that bigger infrastructure projects have larger service or benefit areas, they offer a greater opportunity to recapture those benefits in the form of user charges or property assessments. They also offer more opportunities for well-off beneficiaries to subsidize less fortunate ones.
- *Expanded sustainability, resiliency, and redundancy benefits*: To the degree that larger projects can be efficiently designed and engineered to be more resistant to natural hazards or other adverse events, they can provide greater sustainability or resiliency benefits.
- *Expanded network effects and operations benefits*: The cost of collecting, analyzing, and acting on information is also subject to huge economies of scale. This makes it cheaper to administer and operate larger projects than smaller ones per unit of use, output, or benefit.

Exactly how each of these scale economies kicks in to lower infrastructure unit costs will vary depending on the project type and circumstances. Building larger hydroelectric dams, for example, is generally more cost-efficient than building multiple smaller ones. Likewise, if construction specifications and practices can be shared across metro lines, building a multi-line metro system all at once will be more cost-efficient than building it incrementally. In terms of financing, bigger urban development projects may be more cost-efficiently underwritten than multiple smaller projects—although this advantage may be undone by the larger project's greater risk profile. By contrast, depending on the cost of boring machines, building a single large-diameter road or rail tunnel may actually be more expensive than building two, side-by-side smaller tunnels.

The size of the potential market also plays an important role. It makes no sense to build a 50-gate airport terminal now if for the next ten years there will only be sufficient passenger demand for 30 gates. Likewise, it doesn't make sense to build a grade-separated metro line to move 5,000 passengers per hour when a bus rapid transit (BRT) system will do the same job much more cheaply and can be put in place more quickly.

Megaprojects also generate spillover costs, which, if left unaddressed, can potentially overwhelm project benefits. In the case of China's Three Gorges Dam, for example, the huge volume of impounded water behind the dam has been associated with increased landslide activity and siltation up and down the Yangtze River. In 2005, NASA scientists calculated that the shift of water mass stored by the Three Gorges Dam would increase the total length of the Earth's day by 0.06 microseconds and make the Earth slightly more round in the middle and flat on the poles! Big urban redevelopment projects can potentially displace hundreds of families and businesses, destabilizing otherwise healthy communities. Highway planners have long observed a phenomenon known as "induced demand," meaning that because bigger highway projects typically encourage drivers to shift their routes to facilities which offer additional capacity, they may actually increase traffic congestion levels. In situations where project revenues fall short of operating costs, large publicly-financed projects have the potential to undermine additional public borrowing opportunities.

Flyvbjerg's List of Megaproject Pitfalls

Whether or not they are classified as megaprojects, very large infrastructure projects also offer more opportunities for things to go awry. With this in mind, Flyvbjerg (2017, p. 2) has identified ten systemic problems that characteristically grow with project size (Table 1.1).

1. *Excessive time horizons*: The very long planning and delivery time periods typical of megaprojects exacerbate market and financial uncertainties and risks. This is particularly true for projects dependent on private-market financing or which face competition in the marketplace.

2. *Lack of relevant project management experience*: With so few megaprojects being built at any one time, it can be difficult to find senior project
personnel with suitable megaproject management experience. Nor is
all megaproject management experience equivalent. Some management
expertise transfers easily between megaproject types (e.g., managing
a bridge project involves similar skills to managing a tunneling or highway
construction project), but in other cases (e.g., urban development projects
vs. metro projects), the potential for expertise sharing is minimal.

3. *Embedded stakeholder conflicts of interest*: Public and private megaproject stakeholders may have conflicting interests that are not easily
resolved by contractual documents. Airport terminals that are planned,
financed, and built by airlines, as at New York City's Kennedy and
LaGuardia Airports, are a case in point. Whose interests come first in this
instance: the flying public or the airline that owns the terminal?

4. *Lack of learning opportunities*: Megaproject technologies and designs
are often viewed as "one-offs," a perspective that impedes learning on
experiences with prior or similar projects. Subway systems, for example,
are usually designed and engineered in a manner that makes them unique
to their cities. By contrast, the design of bus rapid transit (BRT) systems
is more generic, making it possible for the developers of later systems to
learn from the developers of earlier ones.

5. *Superficial market and financial feasibility analysis*: Many megaprojects are approved for political or aspiration reasons and may not have
undergone the rigorous market or financial feasibility analysis required to
determine whether they will attract sufficient users to repay their sponsors
and investors. This is particularly true for rail transportation and urban
development projects.

6. *Principal–agent problems and rent-seeking behavior*: The term "principal–
agent problem" applies whenever there is a conflict in priorities between
a person or group and the representative authorized to act on their behalf.
A contractor who gets paid for every change order will have an incentive
to find problems with the initial construction documents, even though the
resulting delays and cost-overruns do not serve the interests of the project
sponsor paying them. The term "rent-seeking" refers to actions by the
owner of a scarce resource to extract payments for its use far in excess of
their actual value. It is typical to find rent-seeking behavior when control
of megaproject inputs or outputs is limited to a single agent or firm.

7. *Shifting priorities*: By the time a megaproject is finally delivered, its
sponsors may have moved on to other priorities, or the need for it may
have already been met. This is particularly true of delay-prone projects
that have not undergone a rigorous market or financial feasibility analysis.

8. *Black Swan events*: As popularized by American statistician Nicholas Tassim Taleb, the term "Black Swan event" refers to a very low probability event which, if it occurs, has large system-disrupting effects. Because of their size, complexity, and long delivery times, megaprojects are thought to be more vulnerable to adverse Black Swan events than smaller projects.

9. *Inadequate contingency provisions*: With more things that can go wrong, megaproject contracts should include more extensive and liberal contingency provisions than smaller projects. This is rarely the case in practice.

10. *Unreliable information*: Because megaproject decision-making and accountability lines tend to be fragmented, there is little incentive to share accurate information on a project-wide level. This leads to situations in which internal and external misinformation may become the norm.

Table 1.1   Flyvbjerg's megaproject cost overrun list

Project	Percent cost overrun	Project	Percent cost overrun
Suez Canal	1900	Minneapolis Hiawatha Light-rail Line	190
Scottish Parliament Building	1600	Humber Bridge (UK)	180
Sydney Opera House	1400	Dublin Port Tunnel	160
Concorde Supersonic Jet	1100	Montreal Metro Laval Extension	160
Troy & Greenfield Railroad (USA)	900	Copenhagen Metro	150
Montreal Summer Olympics	720	Boston-New York-Washington Acela Service	130
Excalibur Smart Projectile (USA & Sweden)	650	Great Belt Rail Tunnel (Denmark)	120
Canadian Firearms Registry	590	London Limehouse Road Tunnel	110
Medicare Transaction System (USA)	560	Brooklyn Bridge	100
National Health Service IT System	550	Shinkansen Joetsu High-speed Rail Line (Japan)	100
Bank of Norway Headquarters Building (Norway)	440	Channel Tunnel (UK, France)	80
Lake Placid Winter Olympics (USA)	320	Karlsruhe-Bretten Light Rail (Germany)	80
Furka Base Tunnel (Switzerland)	300	London Jubilee Line Extension	80
Verrazano Narrows Bridge (USA)	280	Bangkok Metro	70
Boston Big Dig Project	220	Mexico City Metro	60
Denver International Airport	200	High-speed Rail Line South (Netherlands)	60
Panama Canal	200	Great Belt East Bridge (Denmark)	50

Source: Flyvbjerg (2017, p. 8).

Not every megaproject, Flyvbjerg is careful to emphasize, will fall into all of these traps. By the same token, simply knowing a trap exists is not enough to avoid falling into it. Instead of just hoping for the best, megaproject planners and managers should actively anticipate and prepare for the worst. This is especially hard for senior managers, who typically become the public face of their projects. Instead, managers too often become cheerleaders for their projects, both within their own organizations as well as with the public.

MEGAPROJECTS AND MEGACITIES

Much of the recent upswing in megaproject activity, especially in Asia, has been fueled by the growth of very large cities and metropolitan areas. Because they are typically characterized by significant economies of scale, very large public infrastructure projects—whether or not they exceed the $1 billion megaproject cost threshold—have the potential to provide significant increments of service capacity at an affordable cost. This is exactly what is needed to promote increased prosperity in fast-growing cities. Megaprojects also offer the potential to generate significant spillover benefits, one of which, agglomeration economies, is regarded by economists as a key driver of urban productivity growth.

The causal connection between megaprojects and city size goes the other way as well. Because of their greater size and complexity, megaprojects require a significant amount of technical and financial expertise. These qualities are usually present to a greater degree in large cosmopolitan centers. Finally, and this should not be overlooked, regardless of who is in charge, megaprojects offer tremendous patronage opportunities, the grease that drives the machinery of big city decision-making.

Globally, the number of large, very large, and hyper-large cities—those with populations of two million, five million, and ten million residents, respectively—has increased considerably in recent decades. According to data published by the United Nations, the number of global cities with populations of ten million or more residents grew from just four in 1975 to 35 in 2020 (Table 1.2). Over the same period, the number of cities with populations between five and ten million increased from 15 to 51. The growth in the number of cities with between one and five million residents is even more spectacular. In 1975, there were 22 cities around the world with populations between one and five million. By 2020, that number had increased to more than 400! Most of the recent growth in the number of very large and hyper-large cities is concentrated in Asia. Among the 50 largest cities in the world in 1975, those in Asia added 220 million new residents by 2020 while those in Europe, North America, and South America added 88 million. In China alone, cities with a million-plus residents in 1975 added another 100 million new residents by 2020, mostly as a result of rural-to-urban migration.

Table 1.2   *Global megacity growth, 1950–2020*

Number of global cities or metro areas	1950	1975	2000	2020
with a population greater than 10 million	2	4	17	35
with a population between 5 and 10 million	6	15	29	51
with a population between 2 and 5 million	13	38	52	155 [a]
with a population between 1 and 2 million	28	22	178	247 [a]
Share of the world's 25 largest cities in	1950	1975	2000	2020
Africa	0%	0%	0%	8%
Asia	36%	48%	56%	56%
Europe	24%	16%	12%	8%
Middle East	4%	4%	4%	4%
North America	20%	20%	16%	12%
South America	12%	12%	12%	12%
Other (Australia, New Zealand & Pacific Islands)	4%	0%	0%	0%

Note: [a] counts are for 2016.
Source: United Nations data.

Throughout the world, but especially in China, recent urban population growth has been accompanied by significant income growth. Based on a simple comparison of 2020 urbanization and income data collected by the World Bank, among countries with 20 million residents or more, for every 10 percent increase in the share of population living in urban areas, per capita gross domestic product rises 18 percent.[14] This powerful relationship between urban population growth and rising prosperity occurs through three reinforcing mechanisms. First, larger cities constitute bigger markets for goods and services. This creates growth opportunities for business and entrepreneurs. Second, the combination of larger markets and more businesses create additional opportunities and returns to innovation, which is the principal source of productivity and wage growth. Finally, bigger cities tend to have more risk-oriented capital looking for suitable lending and investment opportunities, whether for housing and commercial real estate development, or for starting up and growing businesses. Depending on the city and legal system, these relationships may be further fortified by population density, a relationship economists refer to as agglomeration economies.

Large and prosperous cities are more likely to have the knowledge centers, professional associations, and labor force expertise required to plan, engineer, and deliver large infrastructure projects. As cities get bigger and richer, traffic congestion invariably becomes more of a problem, encouraging city officials and business leaders to make investments in congestion-relieving infrastructure such as metro and light-rail systems and bus rapid transit (BRT). As multiple urban centers grow in concert, inter-city business transactions and trade volumes increase even faster, requiring new investments in airports, inter-city highways, passenger and freight rail service, and inter-modal port facilities. As cities increase in size and prosperity, the demand for energy also rises, requiring additional investments in energy generation and distribution capacity. As people become wealthier and have more leisure time, their demand for parks and cultural facilities typically expands. Lastly, as buildings age, they require additional investment to forestall their physical and economic obsolescence. When that investment is not forthcoming, they soon begin to deteriorate, leading ultimately to blight and abandonment. This creates both the opportunity and the incentive to undertake building and district-level redevelopment activities.

These additional infrastructure and building investments can take place incrementally in the form of smaller and more granular projects, or they can occur all at once in the form of larger and more hierarchical ones. From a purely functional and efficiency perspective, undertaking a single large project has a number of advantages over undertaking smaller and more granular ones. These include:

- Large infrastructure and urban development projects have the potential to organize future urban land uses and development patterns in a fashion that is more orderly, productive, and easier to serve than smaller projects. This is especially true for urban transportation and water megaprojects.
- To the extent that the benefits of infrastructure projects are capitalized into nearby land values, larger projects have the potential to generate greater wealth and support higher property tax payments. This is particularly true for urban transportation investments. The explicit connection between public sector infrastructure investments and higher tax revenues was first recognized by 19th-century economist Henry George, who advocated the use of "value capture" taxation to help pay for public infrastructure projects.
- As cities grow outward and upward, previously inexpensive land becomes more valuable. Forward-looking sponsors of large infrastructure and urban development projects will find it easier and less costly to acquire the sites they need *before* the next round of urban growth occurs, rather than waiting until later when such sites are in shorter supply and more expensive.
- Because they are typically planned "all of a piece," large infrastructure projects are usually better able to mitigate the adverse effects of negative

externalities such as congestion or pollution that typically worsen with city size. For the same reason, building excess capacity into larger and fewer infrastructure projects to meet future growth needs is typically less expensive than building it into many smaller projects. This is especially true for fast-growing places with weak environmental regulations and few public transportation options.

- Raising the investment capital needed to fund large infrastructure projects is typically easier because of potential economies of scale in underwriting, capital pool assembly, and risk mitigation. On the other side of the ledger, large projects may offer less opportunities for risk reduction through diversification than smaller projects.
- Because they involve more planning and coordination efforts, large projects may offer better opportunities knowledge and best practice-sharing than smaller projects.
- In the case of urban development projects, larger cities are more likely to be characterized by greater demographic, economic and consumer diversity, thereby broadening the demand for housing and commercial real estate.
- To the degree that larger projects in large cities are also more visible to high-level funding sources, they may be better able than smaller projects to assemble the financial resources they require. This is especially true in developing countries or those with primate cities that serve as migration hubs.

While larger and more prosperous cities offer more opportunities to undertake larger infrastructure and urban development projects, they may also make delivering those projects more difficult. For one, land, materials and labor are almost always more expensive in larger cities than in smaller ones. This makes it more difficult to meet project budgets. For another, there are likely to be more stakeholders involved in the project planning and construction process, each arguing that their specific requirements and issues must be addressed. This also increases project costs; and to the extent that efforts to meet stakeholder demands occur outside of legal contracts, there is also a greater potential for corruption. As noted previously, larger cities are more likely to suffer from additional congestion and transport bottlenecks, thereby slowing construction activities. Rent-seeking behavior—by which the owners of project inputs such as land and construction materials demand payments for those inputs in excess of their value—is also more common in larger places. For projects being built in populated areas, coordinating construction activities with local neighborhood and commercial activities imposes additional planning and logistical difficulties. Residents of more prosperous places may also be less willing to tolerate the daily quality of life inconveniences that go along with building large projects. These various difficulties do not lessen the appeal of big projects, but they do make their on-time and on-budget delivery more difficult.

For all the reasons listed above, the future megaproject market will be strongest in those countries and metropolitan areas experiencing significant population growth and where rising prosperity means that project capital and financing costs can be repaid out of user charges, fees, and property-based tax revenues. Figure 1.2 compares these two measures for countries with more than 20 million residents. Figure 1.2's horizontal axis identifies projected national population growth between 2020 and 2030 according to the United Nations. Its vertical axis is also based on World Bank data and indicates 2020 per capita gross domestic product, adjusted for purchasing power parity. (The size of the bubbles indicates 2020 population size.) Countries such as the US, which fall in Figure 1.2's upper right-hand quadrant, are expected to experience significant population growth by 2030 and, if they wish to do so, are also wealthy enough to pay for major infrastructure investments. Countries in the upper left-hand quadrant of Figure 1.2, such as Germany, South Korea and Japan, may not need additional infrastructure investments to accommodate their falling populations, but are nonetheless wealthy enough to undertake them for other reasons—be they to improve quality of life, deal with the effects of climate change, or to replace previous projects that are now obsolete. For China, where almost every large city will add population, the challenge will be for less wealthy interior cities to narrow the prosperity gap with their richer and coastal counterparts. India and Nigeria, which fall in Figure 1.2's lower right-hand quadrant may require additional infrastructure and urban development investments to accommodate projected population growth but will struggle to pay for them unless they can find ways to boost average income levels.[15] Similarly, unless circumstances change, shrinking countries, such as Russia in the lower left-hand quadrant of Figure 1.2, will also find it challenging to finance future large-scale infrastructure investments.

Still, as the old saying goes, demographics is not destiny. The future megaproject market—to the extent one exists—will be dominated by those cities (and countries) whose political leaders can assemble supportive stakeholder constituencies and who are able to put together financing deals that fairly share project cost burdens between the public and private sectors. By contrast, those places whose leaders cannot bring together different constituencies or who lack the expertise to put together the necessary financing packages will find the infrastructure investment game that much harder.

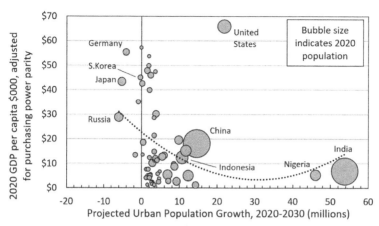

Source: Data obtained from United Nations and World Bank websites.

Figure 1.2   *A glimpse into the future megaproject market: large country comparisons of projected 2020–2030 population growth and 2020 per capita gross domestic product*

IMPROVING MEGAPROJECT PRACTICE AND PERFORMANCE—WHAT THE RESEARCH SHOWS

"Unbalanced" is perhaps the best word to describe the current state of megaproject practice research. Instead of identifying the drivers and circumstances that explain megaproject outcomes along a continuum between success and failure, much of the recent research into megaproject practice and performance is concerned with chronicling and avoiding failure. The current fascination with failure is reflected in the narratives offered by two popular books on megaprojects published in 2003 and 2004: Flyvbjerg, Bruzelius and Rothengatter's *Megaprojects and Risk: An Anatomy of Ambition* (2003), which chronicled how biases in megaproject planning and decision-making practices have caused many megaprojects to suffer horrendous cost and schedule overruns; and Altshuler and Luberoff's *Mega-projects: The Changing Politics of Urban Public Investment* (2004), which explored how the inability of many high-visibility megaprojects to deliver on their promises had undermined their political support. While these recent efforts to chronicle sources of megaproject failure may be a necessary antidote to past over-enthusiasms, they have done little to advance the current state of megaproject practice.

Methodologically speaking, the current research literature on megaproject practice and performance is composed of three types of studies: single case studies, comparative case studies, and statistical studies and meta-analyses.

Each has its own advantages and disadvantages. Single-case studies have the benefit of providing insightful project details but are difficult to generalize from because they can't easily separate project-level drivers and effects from the broader governmental or market context. Comparative case studies sacrifice detail and richness, but by examining multiple projects within a common context, enable readers to differentiate project-level relationships from more systemic ones. Statistical studies go further in the same direction of sacrificing richness in the service of generalizability by taking advantage of large numbers of cases to control for contextual factors. Meta-analyses have the potential to deliver on an even higher level of attribution by identifying key consistencies among multiple statistical studies. Starting with statistical and meta-analysis studies, this section explores what is currently known of the connection between megaproject practice and performance. It concludes with a brief agenda for future research efforts.

Statistical and Meta-analyses

Flyvbjerg, Skamris Holm, and Buhl (2003, 2004) have produced what is still the only multi-sector statistical analysis of megaproject outcomes. Drawing on project-level cost data for 258 road, rail, and bridge and tunnel megaprojects completed between 1927 and 1988, primarily in Europe and North America, they identified an average project cost overrun (i.e., the difference between forecast and actual project costs) of 28 percent. Compared by project type, cost overruns were found to be consistently larger for rail projects (45 percent) than for bridge and tunnel projects (34 percent) or road projects (20 percent). Compared geographically, rail project overruns were observed to be larger in North America than in Europe (41 percent vs. 34 percent), while road cost overruns were observed to be consistently larger in Europe than North America (22 percent vs. 8 percent). After removing a number of project outliers, the rate of cost escalation was found to increase with project cost, meaning that more expensive projects were more likely to suffer from larger percentage cost overruns than smaller projects. Comparing earlier and later projects, the authors found that cost overruns had neither increased nor decreased. This led them to conclude that project sponsors had not learned from past experiences, or that current megaproject planning and delivery practices function to incentivize rather than to discourage cost overruns. In an earlier article, the authors suggest that these results are also the product of systematic deception, and that therefore, project funding agencies "who value honest numbers should not trust the cost estimates prepared by infrastructure promoters and forecasters" (2002, p. 291). The major criticisms of this work—beyond its sometimes hyperbolic and all-encompassing conclusions—is that its comparisons are made solely on the basis of rough project type and geography, and that it doesn't distinguish among different political and decision-making regimes or between different megaproject planning and delivery approaches.

Singh (2010) tries to add some of these dimensions. Drawing on a sample of 795 projects across 17 infrastructure sectors completed in India between 1992 and 2009, Singh finds sloppy planning practices, contractual failures and construction delays to be the principal determinants of project cost overruns regardless of sector (p. 51). In a point of departure from Flyvbjerg et al., Singh finds that time delays and cost overruns decreased during later years, suggesting that the quality of practice had improved. Compared with other sectors, projects in the land-extensive transportation, urban development and power sectors experienced longer delays and bigger cost overruns than projects in the technology-oriented industrial, chemical, telecommunications and hospitals sectors. Finally, there were notable time and cost performance differences among different Indian states, suggesting that the local quality of governance and decision-making matters considerably. These last differences were unrelated to whether a state was rich or poor, or the degree to which it favored privatization over public financing.

Confirming Singh's findings that place and context matter, Cantarelli et al. (2012), explored schedule delays and cost overruns among a sample of 78 Dutch road, rail and bridge and tunnel projects undertaken between 1980 and 2010. Their main findings were that rail projects performed better than road and bridge and tunnel projects with respect to reduced cost overruns and schedule delays; that road projects were particularly vulnerable to cost overruns; that smaller projects experienced larger percentage cost overruns than larger projects; and that among all three project types, the pre-construction phase was more prone to cost overruns than actual construction. Limited as they are to projects undertaken in the Netherlands, these results are notably different than those obtained by Flyvbjerg, Bruzelius and Rothengatter (2003), providing yet another indication of the importance of geography and political context to the determination of megaproject success.

Turning from Europe to Asia, Park and Papadopoulou (2012) found a moderately positive relationship between project size and cost overruns among a group of 35 transport infrastructure projects completed between 1983 and 2010 in Bangladesh, Hong Kong, India, Malaysia, Myanmar, Pakistan, Singapore, South Korea, Sri Lanka, Taiwan, Thailand and Vietnam. Results from a complementary questionnaire pointed to automatically awarding construction contracts to the lowest bidder (as is required in many Asian countries to reduce corruption), poor quality subcontractors, and poor site management practices as notable sources of infrastructure cost overruns.

Flyvbjerg, in a separate 2007 analysis of 44 urban rail projects, found noticeably larger cost overruns among projects in Asia and Latin America than among projects in North America and Europe; and that European urban rail planners were better at correctly forecasting ridership levels than their counterparts elsewhere. Whereas ridership levels among the six European projects exceeded forecast amounts by an average of 21 percent, among the 18 non-European projects, planners overestimated actual ridership by an average of 57 percent. Drawing on Copenhagen as a case study, Flyvbjerg attributes these differences to the existence of independent audit agencies in European governments and to the use of a minimum required payback period as a criterion for project approval (p. 17).

Pivoting from transport to energy, Sovacool et al. (2014) found notably larger cost and time overruns for nuclear and hydroelectric dam projects than for fossil fuel-fired power plants, windfarms, solar facilities, and transmission lines among a sample of 401 energy projects that entered service between 1960 and 2014. Nuclear power projects experienced the largest average cost and time overruns of 117 percent and 64 percent, respectively, followed by hydroelectric dams (70 percent and 64 percent). By contrast, the average cost overrun among fossil fuel, wind, and solar power plants came to only 7 percent, while the average schedule overrun was just 6 percent. The authors attribute these differences to the fact that nuclear and hydroelectric dam projects must be custom-designed and engineered to each application, whereas fossil fuel and renewable energy power plants can make ready use of more standardized designs and technologies.

One drawback of these various studies is that, for reasons of statistical comparability, they rely on cost and time overruns as their principal measure of project performance. This understates the roles of other project objectives, which, for the decision-makers who approve megaprojects and for the everyday people who use them, may be more important than schedule and budgetary overruns. This is not to suggest that considerations of project time and cost considerations should be ignored, but rather that it is incumbent among megaproject researchers to develop and test a richer set of project performance metrics.

Because they lack a sufficient number and variety of large-sample megaproject performance studies, researchers have yet to undertake a proper meta-analysis of their results. This is not the case for public–private partnerships (P3s), a method used to finance many large-scale transportation and energy projects. In a comparison of 26 studies and publications covering P3 use in the UK, Europe and Australia, Hodge and Greve (2017) find P3 performance to be mixed in terms of providing what they call "good value-for-money." Whereas many of the P3-funded infrastructure projects studied were found to have been delivered on-time and within-budget, many others were not. Part of the difference in outcome was a function of who conducted the analysis. As might be expected, consulting reports and business case studies of individual projects tended to support P3 use more so than did multi-project comparisons prepared by academics and government reviewers. There were also notable country-based differences: assessments produced in Australia, where transport P3 are more common, mostly supported the proposition that P3-financed projects provided good value for money. By contrast, studies produced in the United Kingdom and Europe, where P3s are regarded more skeptically, found that the reason why P3s were found to have performed well meeting their delivery schedules and budgets, was because those schedules and budgets were often inflated by project sponsors.

Seeking consensus on the determinants of large-scale project management success, Crosby (2012) reviewed 29 articles published between 1976 and 2009 covering more than 2,800 infrastructure, research and development, and information technology projects. The various study results were used to identify 18 distinct "success drivers," which were then subjected to a series of pairwise comparisons using the Analytical Hierarchy Process (AHP) developed by Saaty (Coyle 2004). The result is a robust ranking of factors that is independent of order or weighting. Three success factors dominated Crosby's results: (i) the presence of formal project management control and execution systems incorporating document control and audit functions; (ii) the presence of clear and measurable project goals and objectives; and (iii) the presence of clear and effective communications mechanisms and channels, including to the general public. Two other factors, the continuing presence of an informed and engaged project sponsor, and the presence of effective benchmarking procedures, were also found to be important (p. 7).

Although it is principally focused on the Netherlands and lacks sufficient cases to be a true meta-analysis, Annema's (2013) study of the uses of cost-benefit analysis (CBA) in transport megaproject decision-making is also instructive. Briefly, Annema finds that politicians do not make use of CBA or related valuation and discounting techniques when deciding whether to undertake a project or choose among alternative projects. Annema identifies four reasons why this is so. The first is information overload: by trying to synthesize so many varied impacts into a single indicator, CBA overwhelms its audience with numbers and data. Second, no matter how often economists try to explain the workings of CBA to non-economists, it still comes across as a sort of black box. Third, whereas CBA practitioners tend to focus on costs and benefits that are measurable and monetizable, risk-averse decision-makers often focus instead on impacts that are difficult to measure or convert into monetary terms. Lastly, many political consumers of CBA see their role as explicitly providing a more qualitative counter-balancing to the narrower and more technical concerns embodied in CBA.

In a paper that is more of a synthetic literature review than a meta-analysis, Denicol et al. (2020) identify 86 papers explicitly concerned with remedying poor megaproject performance. Their review identified six practice areas needing attention: (i) decision-making behavior; (ii) strategy, governance, and procurement; (iii) risk and uncertainty; (iv) leadership and capable teams; (v) stakeholder engagement and management; and (vi) supply chain integration and coordination. In each area, the researchers identified specific "cures" for the causes of poor megaproject performance. Among the most notable such cures were improved project benchmarking (Ansar et al. 2014); identifying the different types of risks faced by project sponsors versus providers (Rose and Manley 2010); investing in standardization and modularization processes to reduce delivery complexity (Ansar et al. 2014); formalizing skill-building within and across delivery teams and organizations (Gharaibeh 2014); expanding and improving stakeholder interactions (Chang et al. 2013); and improving the usability, utility and responsiveness of multi-party project management information systems (Browning 2014).

Comparative Case Studies

Comparative case analysis involves identifying and synthesizing the similarities, differences and patterns across two or more cases that share a common purpose or context. Comparative case analyses are generally richer and more nuanced than statistical or empirical studies, even if their results are not as robust or easily generalized. The granddaddy of megaproject comparative case studies is Peter Hall's *Great Planning Disasters*. Published in 1982, *Great Planning Disasters* reviewed the planning, construction and performance histories of London's motorways and third airport, the Concorde supersonic transport, the Bay Area Rapid Transit (BART) system, and the famed Sydney Opera House. While Hall's use of the term "disasters" was admittedly hyperbolic, each of his five case studies, plus another two labeled "near disasters," suffered from three fundamental problems. The first was that their sponsors and planners had failed to understand the degree to which complex and interrelated systems (such as cities) are characterized by unknowable uncertainties. This led to an unwarranted faith in numerical forecasts that too often overestimated benefits and underestimated costs. A second problem was that different project stakeholders often had competing objectives, and that few efforts were made to get those objectives to align. Finally, Hall concluded that Western societies often put unwarranted faith in the ability of technology-based solutions to address what were intrinsically problems of equity and social justice. Hall's solutions to these myopias and shortcomings, to the extent he offered them, was for project planners to engage in rigorous rounds of alternatives and sensitivity analysis coupled with a constant questioning of any and all embedded assumptions.

In their influential book, *Megaprojects: The Changing Politics of Urban Public Investment*, Alan Altshuler and David Luberoff (2004) offer observations and conclusions based on a series of political and policy vignettes rather than true case studies. In addition to Hall's admonition that megaproject sponsors and planners should do more to address issues of uncertainty, Altshuler and Luberoff suggest they should pay greater attention to identifying the distribution of project costs and benefits across impacted communities as well as project stakeholders; and that the project decision-making process should be made more inclusive and democratic (p. 289). How exactly these changes should be implemented and whether they would make the megaproject planning and delivery process more effective as well as fairer, Altshuler and Luberoff do not say.

Case study comparisons are also at the heart of Flyvbjerg, Bruzelius and Rothengatter's (2003) book, *Megaprojects and Risk: An Anatomy of Ambition.* Drawing on detailed comparisons between the Channel Tunnel connecting the UK and France (opened in 1994), the Great Belt Link connecting East Denmark with continental Europe (opened in 1997–1998), and the Øresund Bridge and Tunnel project between Copenhagen and Malmo (opened in 2000), Flyvbjerg et al. construct what they call the "megaproject paradox." This is the observation that there is an inverse correlation between megaproject popularity and performance: as megaprojects have become bigger and more popular, their on-time and on-budget performance has continually deteriorated. The solution or correction to the megaprojects paradox, the authors go on to suggest, is for the public to demand greater accountability and transparency from decision-makers as to exactly how and why large infrastructure projects are approved; and for project sponsors and stakeholders to be much more systematic about identifying the many risks their projects face and much more thorough about adopting pro-active risk management strategies.

A more recent compilation of megaproject case studies was produced by researchers at University College London's Bartlett School of Planning as part of its multi-year OMEGA Centre project. Using a methodology that combined detailed document reviews with key informant interviews, OMEGA Centre researchers documented the planning and implementation processes of 30 transportation megaprojects (MTPs) undertaken in ten European, North American, and Asian/Oceanic countries between 1990 and 2003 (see Table 1.3). Looking beyond cost and budget overruns, the researchers identified nine "success" lessons for improving megaproject practice and performance (OMEGA Centre 2012).

Table 1.3   *Characteristics of OMEGA Centre-reviewed transportation megaprojects*

Country	Project and location	Project type	Completion date	Final cost (US$ billion)
	Channel Tunnel Rail Link	High-speed rail	2007	9.6
UK	Jubilee Line Extension	Metro rail (subway)	1999	6.8
	M6 Toll Road	Inter-urban motorway (toll)	2007	1.7
	Meteor Rail: Saint Lazare-Olympiades (Paris)	Metro rail (subway)	1998	1.8
France	TGV Med: Valence-Marseille	High-speed rail	2001	6.6
	Millau Viaduct	Motorway bridge	2004	0.5
	Rion-Antirion Bridge	Motorway bridge	2004	1.3
Greece	Athens Metro	Metro rail (subway)	2003	4.6
	Attiki Odos (Athens)	Inter-urban motorway (toll)	2004	5.4
	Neusbaustreke, Cologne-Rhine/Main	High-speed rail	2004	8.6
Germany	Tiergarten Tunnel (Berlin)	Urban motorway tunnel	2006	9
	BAB20 Motorway: Branden. to Schleswig-Holstein	Motorway	2005	2.7
	HSL Zuid	High-speed rail	2009	9.8
The Netherlands	Randstarail	Light rail and bus	2007	1.6
	Beneluxlijn	Metro rail (subway)	2002	1
	Øresund Bridge & Tunnel (Copenhagen-Malmo)	Road and rail, bridge and tunnel	2000	4.1
Sweden	Sodra Lanken Road Tunnel (Stockholm)	Urban motorway tunnel	2004	1.3
	Arlanda Rail Link (Stockholm)	Airport express rail link	1999	1.1

Country	Project and location	Project type	Completion date	Final cost (US$ billion)
USA	JFK Airport Airtrain (New York City)	Light rail link	2003	2.2
	Alameda Rail Link (Los Angeles)	Freight rail line	2002	2.8
	Big Dig Central Artery Replacement (Boston)	Urban motorway tunnel and bridges	2007	15.2
Australia	City Link (Melbourne)	Urban motorway tunnel (toll)	2000	2.5
	Metro Rail (Perth)	Inter-urban rail line	2007	1.7
	Cross City Tunnel (Sydney)	Urban motorway tunnel (toll)	2005	1.1
	Western Harbor Crossing	Urban motorway tunnel (toll)	1997	0.9
Hong Kong	HK International Airport HSR Link	Airport express rail link	1998	4.4
	KCRC West Rail Link	Urban rail line	2003	5.9
Japan	Metropolitan Expressway (Tokyo)	Urban motorway tunnel (toll)	2007	5.5
	Shinkansen HSR Link (Kagoshima-Nakata)	High-speed rail	2004	7.5
	Oedo Metro: Hokomae-Hikarigaoka (Tokyo)	Metro rail (subway)	2000	11.4

Source: OMEGA Centre 2012.

Although developed explicitly for transportation megaprojects, many OMEGA Centre lessons also apply to other megaproject types. They include:

1. Reframing MTPs as "agents of change" that generate significant spatial, economic, environmental, and social impacts beyond their intended transportation service benefits.
2. Rethinking MTPs as "open" systems in which the economic, social and institution contexts into which MTPs are inserted respond by generating concomitant and feedback effects that are as significant as the project itself.
3. Recognizing that MTPs have "organic" characteristics, meaning their functions and impacts evolve over time.
4. Explicitly recognizing measures of MTP success that go beyond on-time and on-budget criteria.
5. Understanding that decisions regarding MTPs are made within national and local political and social contexts and not solely on technical grounds.
6. Expanding MTP decision-making frameworks to explicitly include long-term sustainability criteria.
7. Engaging with non-technical project stakeholders early and often, both as a means of reducing conflicts during the MTP planning stage and improving the MTP implementation process.
8. Ensuring that essential institutional, policy, and legislative support is present throughout the MTP lifecycle, not just at its beginning.
9. Creating processes that learn and share lessons about successful MTP planning and implementation across projects and contexts.

All nine lessons are entirely observational. OMEGA Centre researchers made no attempt to develop formal models of MTP decision-making or to test how different megaproject planning and implementation procedures might have altered particular project outcomes.

One recurrent issue when comparing megaprojects across different countries and political systems involves controlling for context. Simply put, the question is whether differences in megaproject performance are the result of particular project level practices, or of government level rules and procedures? Demi Chung (2017) neatly sidesteps this problem by comparing the use of P3s to finance and deliver four Australian motorway projects during the 1990s and 2000s: The Sydney Harbour Tunnel (opened in 1992), the M2 Motorway in the Sydney suburbs (opened in 1997), Melbourne's CityLink tollway (opened sequentially in 1999 and 2000), and the Sydney Cross City Tunnel (opened in 2005). In all four cases, the private sector project sponsors (who stood to earn commissions on the deals) initially overstated projected traffic volumes and expected public sector financial returns all the while inserting contract provisions protecting their own preferred revenue streams. These practices didn't lessen over time, but the governments of Sydney, New South Wales, and Melbourne learned to expect them, and gradually improved their own abilities to apportion and mitigate project financial risks.

P3s emerged in the mid-1970s in the US as an off-budget approach to financing large-scale urban development projects. In "Megaprojects in New York, London, and Amsterdam," Susan Fainstein (2008) examines the uses of P3s in urban redevelopment megaprojects in the US, the UK, and the Netherlands to follow through on promises made by project sponsors and developers to deliver public benefits in the form of resident jobs, community facilities and affordable housing. Over time, these promises were gradually scaled back as each project faced increased competition in the marketplace. This disappointing evolution was most pronounced in the Atlantic Yards (New York) case and least pronounced in the Amsterdam South case, a result Fainstein attributes not to any fundamental weakness of the P3 funding model, but rather to the historical rootedness of each city's commitment to using private development to leverage public benefits and promote equity.

Stakeholder conflict intensity and duration are at the heart of an interesting comparative case study analysis by Lee et al. (2017) of 22 large-scale transport, defense, energy, and waste projects undertaken between 2000 and 2016 in South Korea. The authors organize each project's timeline into five sequential phases (planning, impact assessment, design, construction, and operation) using publicly-available documents to identify the sources and resolution of conflict at each stage. Regardless of when a project was started or its type or location, most stakeholder conflicts originated early in a project's lifecycle, and if not resolved, intensified as the project continued. Among public infrastructure projects, conflicts were more likely to emerge during the planning, environmental impact assessment and site selection stages than during the subsequent design, construction, and operation stages. Conflicts resolved internally by existing stakeholders were less likely to fester than conflicts resolved via government action from above.

Most comparative case studies are assembled to test or investigate a proposition. This is not the case for a portfolio of 20 European transport, energy, and cross-sectoral megaprojects identified as part of a multi-year research project supported by the European Cooperation in Science and Technology (COST) program (Brookes and Elmahroug 2013). By using a common format to trace the institutional and stakeholder relationships of all 20 projects, the researchers gained a more thorough understanding of just how organizationally complicated most megaprojects are, and of the shortcomings of modeling megaproject planning and delivery processes in the usual linear and hierarchical manner.

Best Practice Case Studies—Spotlighting the Global Infrastructure Hub

The typical case study takes the form preferred by whoever prepares it, a situation that complicates learning across multiple case studies. In order to make that task easier, the G20 group of countries has created what they call the web-based Global Infrastructure Hub (GI Hub), a common platform for exchanging information on infrastructure innovations and best practices. Participation in the GI Hub is entirely voluntary—meaning that poorly performing projects are under-represented—and so far, its megaproject case study listings include just 30 or so projects.[16] Even so, by presenting its case studies in a "problems incurred–problems solved–lessons learned" format, the GI Hub platform goes a long way toward making infrastructure delivery lessons transferable between different political and planning systems. Table 1.4 summarizes key innovation lessons and best practices from ten of the GI Hub's most notable transport, water resources and energy projects. Among its most useful observations:

- Project complexities and difficulties increase non-linearly with the number of contractors. This requires developing new approaches to project management focused on multi-party collaborative problem solving.
- The use of P3 models has focused too much on financing arrangements and should be re-oriented to facilitate improved service delivery and "value for money."
- Projects that explicitly consider risk incidence and management do better in terms of meeting their completion schedules.
- Technology is advancing so quickly that project planners and managers need to identify procedures that facilitate technological upgrades (particularly to control and information systems) after initial specifications have been determined and contracts let.
- Using standard contracting forms and procedures may be convenient and save time on the front-end, but as projects become more complicated and involve many more parties, can lead to unanticipated problems later on.
- Non-primary stakeholders (i.e., those not directly involved in project planning and delivery) have important roles to play in defining project success.

Table 1.4   Global Infrastructure Hub: selected megaproject best practices and innovations

Project sector	Challenge or issue	Project	Location	Construction period and approved cost (US$)	Notable practices and innovations
Transport	Design and contracting	Heathrow Airport Terminal 5 (T5)	United Kingdom	2002–2006; $8.5 billion	After reviewing past UK megaprojects, BAA (the project sponsor) concluded that its existing contracting and project management approaches would be inadequate for a project of T5's complexity. In response, BAA created an integrated project team involving all contractors and suppliers designed to foster positive problem-solving behaviors.
	Financing	Hyderabad Metro Rail Phase I	India	2010–2020; $2.6 billion	The project was developed using a Design–Build–Finance–Operate–Transfer (DBFOT) public–private partnership model. The private concessionaire was awarded the right to develop 1.7 million square meters of development rights above and adjacent to new metro stations.
	Engineering and contracting	Sydney Northwest Metro Line	Australia	2011–2019; $2.8 billion	The P3 procurement model adopted by the New South Wales Government for the project's OTS (Operations, Trains and Systems) component enabled bidders to incorporate innovative technology approaches in their proposals.

Project sector	Challenge or issue	Project	Location	Construction period and approved cost (US$)	Notable practices and innovations
Transport (continued)	Design and Contracting	Grand Paris Express Metrorail	France	2016–ongoing; $43 billion	In its early phases, this project was procured in the traditional French manner with 80 percent of the detailed design work produced by the sponsor before engaging a contractor. With more than 400 contracts awarded, this approach resulted in an extreme number of mid-process design and engineering changes. Subsequent changes to the project's governance and management structure produced some improvement.
	Project Scheduling and Phasing	Melbourne Metro Tunnel (twin 9-km rail tunnels under the CBD)	Australia	2016–2025; $243 million	Owing to the project's tight delivery timeframe and high-profile nature, it was divided into a site acquisition and preparation phase ("Early works") and a construction phase ("Main works").

Project sector	Challenge or issue	Project	Location	Construction period and approved cost (US$)	Notable practices and innovations
Water and Sewerage	Financing and Risk Management	Thames Tideway Tunnel	United Kingdom	2016–2025; $5.8 billion	The UK is building a 25-km "super sewer" tunnel under central London to collect sewerage and stormwater overflows (currently flowing into the Thames River) and expand the city's treatment capacity. The project is being developed using a complicated public–private partnership model that incentivizes collaboration between the government, the project sponsor and the contractors.
	Financing and Contracting	(Auckland) Watercare Enterprise Model	New Zealand	2019–2029; $3.9 billion	In September 2019, Watercare (Auckland's public water utility) entered into a 10-year agreement under a locally-developed public–private partnership model to expand and upgrade the city's water supply and treatment facilities.

Project sector	Challenge or issue	Project	Location	Construction period and approved cost (US$)	Notable practices and innovations
	Contracting	Rocky Flats Nuclear Facility Closure	Colorado (US)	1995–2005; $7 billion	After many years of delay and cost overruns, a partnership between the US Department of Energy and Kaiser-Hill (a joint venture of ICF Kaiser International and CH2M Hill) was created based on specific performance criteria and incentives.
Energy	Financing and Contracting	Ohio State University Energy Service Concession	Ohio (US)	2017–onward; $1.7 billion	In order to meet its ambitious renewable energy and climate change objectives, Ohio State University entered into a 50-year agreement with Ohio State Energy Partners (OSEP), a consortium of 2 private energy companies to handle all of its energy supply, management and renewable energy transition responsibilities.
Building Construction	Contracting	Tin Shui Wai Hospital	Hong Kong Special Administrative Region	2012–2107; $385 billion	Under its standard procurement models, the Hong Kong SAR Government was required to procure and deliver the project under a traditional and inflexible design–build contract. Instead, to promote greater design and contracting flexibility, the Government used what it called a New Engineering Contract (NEC), which allowed for more flexible and adaptive design and contracting processes.

Source: G20 Global Infrastructure Hub.

A Four-part Megaproject Research Agenda

In their introduction to a 2017 special megaproject issue of *Project Management Journal* entitled "The Past and Present of Megaprojects," Jonas Söderlund, Shankar Sankaran and Christopher Biesenthal identify four areas of inquiry they believe should guide future megaproject research. The first involves developing a richer and deeper understanding of why so many different groups and institutions continue to coalesce around large-scale infrastructure projects as a means of effecting societal change. Calling this line of inquiry "megaproject theory," Söderlund et al. suggest megaproject researchers be more outward-looking in adapting theories of individual and institutional agency developed in other fields such as economics, political science, and organization behavior.

Second, they call for increased efforts to get into the nitty-gritty of megaproject decision-making and implementation. How, for example, should megaproject managers promote increased stakeholder cooperation and coordination in situations where projects rarely proceed exactly according to plan? How should they drive innovation in circumstances where preferences for saving time and cost are pushing them toward standardization and the use of known technologies? All too often, Söderlund et al. assert, megaproject decision-making is treated as a deterministic "black box" rather than as a series of open-ended choices.

Third, researchers need to develop richer and more nuanced megaproject performance measures that go beyond simple time and cost. Once these additional performance metrics are developed, they can then be used to identify which combinations of contextual factors, organizational structures, and megaproject planning and delivery practices are most closely associated with which performance measures. Why, for example, have some countries managed to improve their megaproject decision-making, planning and delivery practices—here, the authors cite Norway as an example (p. 10)—while others have not. How much is a relevant sum for developing a metro line in one country compared with another? To what degree is the use of P3-like financing mechanisms associated with better megaproject outcomes compared with the use of conventional debt financing? These types of questions are intensely important to project decision-makers tasked with identifying the alternatives and practices that generate the highest value-for-money.

Finally, Söderlund et al. suggest that researchers pay greater attention to the question of whether and how undertaking new megaprojects will address the most pressing problems facing modern civil societies, including issues of poverty, climate change, economic inequity, and terrorism (p. 11). In some circumstances, megaprojects may indeed be an appropriate response, but in others, a portfolio of smaller and less uniform projects may be preferred.

From a methodological perspective, Söderlund, Sankaran and Biesenthal (2017) suggest that researchers apply a combination of improved performance metrics, categorical statistical models, and structured case studies to create coherent narratives—what they term, "empirical stories"—that directly connect particular practices and outcomes. Instead of just enumerating the reasons why megaprojects go wrong, the authors conclude, researchers should focus their research efforts on the harder task of identifying the "soft drivers of megaproject success" (p. 13).

APPROACH AND PLAN OF THIS BOOK

This book uses a comparative case study approach to explore the connections between contemporary megaproject practice and performance. It differs from other megaproject compendium volumes in three significant ways. First, it is more global and multi-sectoral in coverage, spanning 26 transport, bridge and tunnel, urban development, and energy megaprojects in Brazil, China, Columbia, Ecuador, Germany, India, Indonesia, Morocco, South Korea, the United States and the United Kingdom. It is also highly contemporary, with nearly all of the case study megaprojects having been started or completed within the last decade. Second, it is centrally concerned with all phases of the megaproject planning and delivery process, including project formulation, approval, design, engineering, financing, project management, construction, and operation. Third, it makes use of multiple measures of project success, not just on-time and on-schedule performance. This volume's more comprehensive geographical and sectoral coverage as well as its more multi-dimensional approach to practice and performance makes it possible to draw a fuller and more nuanced set of practice lessons from each case study project.

Four Questions

This book is written to answer four questions about contemporary megaproject practice and performance, and, in doing so, to identify a series of generalizable lessons and robust takeaways regarding global megaproject practice. The four questions are:

1. *How should megaproject performance be measured and assessed?* As the preceding discussions make clear, current megaproject outcome studies are excessively weighted toward simple determinations of on-schedule and on-budget performance. This overly narrow focus has distracted researchers and practitioners from developing and applying other measures that could provide a more complete picture of megaproject performance; and of linking those performance measures back to particular

practices. Drawing on 26 global megaproject case studies organized into 13 chapters, this book makes use of multiple measures of megaproject performance, including goal achievement measures, time and cost measures, risk management measures, environmental and social benefit and cost measures, user satisfaction measures, economic spillover and multiplier measures, and sustainability and resilience measures.

2. *Which megaproject planning, design, engineering, construction, project management and financing practices contribute most to superior megaproject performance?* Having identified a robust set of performance measures, we then explore how the different case studies perform on those measures according to how they were planned, designed and engineered, constructed, and financed. Our discussions of megaproject planning practice centers on the consideration of alternatives, the involvement of stakeholder groups, and the proper identification of project costs and benefits. Our discussion of engineering and design practices focuses on the choice of project delivery technology and tradeoffs between standardization and project-specific customization. Our discussions of construction practices include considerations of alternative project management, contracting, procurement, and reporting choices. Our discussion of financing practices centers on the uses of alternative underwriting procedures and the uses of conventional grant- and-government-based debt financing versus P3s.

3. *Are the determinants of superior project megaproject performance consistent across different project types and governance and decision-making systems?* To get at the question of type differences, we compare recent megaproject practice and performance across five different megaproject types: (i) urban and inter-city rail and bus projects; (ii) bridge and tunnel projects; (iii) airport projects; (iv) urban development and park projects; and (v) renewable energy projects. To get to issues of governance and decision-making differences, we compare projects undertaken in China, Germany, Singapore, South Korea, South America, the United Kingdom, and the United States.

4. *How different in terms of superior practices and performance are megaprojects from other large-scale infrastructure investments?* The $ 1+ billion cost threshold used to distinguish megaprojects from lesser ones is not particularly robust. A $500 million metro project undertaken in a city where land and labor are inexpensive is no less of a megaproject than a $2 billion subway project undertaken in an expensive location such as New York City or London. To get at the location and cost difference question, we compare projects of different sizes and scales, ranging from China's 37,000 km, $800 billion high-speed rail network and Seattle's $3 billion Alaskan Way Tunnel Project to New York City's $350 million Brooklyn Bridge Park.

Organization of this Book

This book is organized into three introductory chapters, 13 case study chapters
(some involving multiple cases), and a single concluding chapter. This chapter,
Chapter 1, introduces the main purposes and themes of the book, the principal
one being that improved practice should drive improved performance. Chapter
2 presents a summary history of modern megaprojects through the lens of 28
globally significant projects organized into four overlapping periods. Chapter
3 identifies the criteria used to choose the case study projects, and summarizes
each of their rationales, sponsors, completion times and costs, and financing
arrangements.

The middle chapters present the 26 case study megaprojects in detail. All
were either started or completed in the 2010–2020 period. Chapters 4 through
7 focus on rail and bus projects, beginning with Crossrail in London (Chapter
4); China's national high-speed rail network (Chapter 5); metro systems in
Beijing, Shanghai, Guangzhou and Shenzhen (Chapter 6); and six bus rapid
transit (BRT) systems in Latin America and Asia (Chapter 7). The next two
chapters explore tunnel and bridge projects: Seattle's Alaskan Way Viaduct
Replacement Tunnel (Chapter 8); and the world's longest bridge–tunnel
project, the Hong Kong–Zhuhai–Macau Bridge (Chapter 9). Airports are
the subject of Chapters 10 and 11. Chapter 10 tells the story of Singapore
Changi International Airport's new Jewel complex, an entirely new type
of airport facility. Chapter 11 compares the contrasting stories of the new
Berlin-Brandenburg International Airport and New York City's LaGuardia
Airport redevelopment program. Berlin-Brandenburg opened nine years
behind schedule and €4 billion over budget, while LaGuardia was redeveloped
on-time and on-budget all the while remaining in operation. Chapters 12
through 14 cover large-scale urban development projects. Chapter 12 updates
the story of Canary Wharf, London's second central business district, which,
35 years after it was first conceived, is still evolving. Chapter 13 focuses
on Hamburg's HafenCity, the largest and most successful waterfront urban
development project in Europe. Chapter 14 moves to South Korea to tell the
story of the new city of Songdo, a compromised project that brought together
an inexperienced sponsor with an out-of-their depth developer. With many
cities around the world converting their dilapidated industrial waterfronts
into parks and cultural areas, Brooklyn Bridge Park in New York City is the
subject of Chapter 15. Turning to renewable energy megaprojects, Chapter
16 briefly tells the stories of the UK's Walney extension offshore windfarm,
Morocco's Noor-Ouarzazate Solar Complex, India's Pavagada Solar Park, the
Bath County Hydro Storage Station in the United States, and China's efforts to
create an ultra-high voltage transmission line system. Each case study chapter

begins with a discussion of why the project it reviews is important and ends with a series of lessons and takeaways.

The final chapter in this book, Chapter 17, returns to the four core questions about practice and performance raised above. It begins by applying a 12-point performance rating system to measure each case study project's success in a manner that goes beyond issues of just schedule and cost. It also identifies the extent to which each case study project either avoided or fell into Flyvbjerg's list of megaproject pitfalls. Next, it reviews how each project performed on 27 measures of practice proficiency, including planning and design, financing, contracting, project management, risk management and mitigation, project delivery and commissioning, and operations and asset management. These practice proficiency scores are then compared with the performance scores to determine when and how improved practice is associated with project performance. Chapter 17 concludes with a summary of each case study project's key takeaways, as well as observations on common lessons and tradeoffs.

NOTES

1. Perhaps wanting it both ways, Altshuler and Luberoff (2004) later go on to conclude that the era of urban-megaprojects is likely to continue (p. 285).
2. Based on 2019 pre-pandemic passenger counts. All other rankings are current as of 2021.
3. The last new subway line built in New York City before the Second Avenue Subway was started in 2007 was the Sixth Avenue Subway, which was started in 1936.
4. https://www.mckinsey.com/business-functions/operations/our-insights/megaprojects-the-good-the-bad-and-the-better. Accessed in January 2022.
5. The World Bank defines a high-income country as one with a per capita gross national income exceeding $12,056 in 2020.
6. Green bonds are fixed-income instrument specifically earmarked to raise money for climate and environmental projects.
7. https://en.wikipedia.org/wiki/Category:Dams_under_construction.
8. Accessed on January 3, 2021, from: https://fmicorp.com/uploads/media/FMI_N -American_Megaprojects_2019.pdf.
9. The PPI Database can be accessed at https://ppi.worldbank.org/en/ppi.
10. Accessed at https://www.iadb.org/en/projects on January 7, 2022.
11. These counts were tabulated by the author from the European Commission's major projects database which can be accessed at: https://ec.europa.eu/regional _policy/en/projects/major/.
12. The concept of time-value-of-money (TVM) is based on the observation that money is worth more in the present because of its future earnings potential.
13. Economies of scale differ from economies of scope. Economies of scale refers to increasing efficiencies associated with project size or output. Economies of scope means that the production of more of one good reduces the cost of producing more of a related good.

14. Fifty-eight countries had populations of 20 million or more. Using regression analysis to compare their 2020 urbanization shares and 2020 per capita gross domestic product yields the following relationship: GDP per capita = −14,076 + (Urbanization share × 55,054). The coefficient of determination for this relationship (r-squared) is 0.47.

15. India is a special case. Some very large Indian cities, such as Mumbai (US$5,328 GDP per capita in 2015), Ahmedabad ($5,085), Bangalore ($4,874) and Pune ($4,448), are relatively wealthy by Indian standards and can afford to undertake some level of new infrastructure investment, while others such as Kolkata ($2,364) and Surat ($2,488) are too poor to do so. These estimates are drawn from a March 2020 report by Mitsui & Co. Global Strategic Studies Institute available at https://www.mitsui.com/mgssi/en/report/detail/__icsFiles/afieldfile/2020/06/ 05/2003d_suzuki_e_1.pdf.

16. Full project delivery case studies can be accessed at https://infrastructuredeli verymodels.gihub.org/case-studies/. Other GIH resources can be accessed at https://www.gihub.org/explore-our-work/.

REFERENCES

Annema, J. A. 2013. The use of CBA in decision-making on mega-projects: empirical evidence. In H. Priemus and B. van Wee (eds), *International Handbook on Mega-Projects*. Edward Elgar Publishing, pp. 291–312.

Altshuler, A., and Luberoff, D. 2004. *Mega-Projects: The Changing Politics of Urban Public Investment*. Brookings Institution Press.

Ansar, A., Flyvbjerg, B., Budzier, A., and Lunn, D. 2014. Should we build more large dams? The actual costs of hydropower megaproject development. *Energy Policy* 69: 43–56.

Brookes, N., and Elmahroug, M. 2013. *The Megaproject Portfolio* (2nd Ed.). Leeds: University of Leeds.

Browning, T. R. 2014. Managing complex project process models with a process architecture framework. *International Journal of Project Management* 32(2): 229–241.

Cantarelli, C. C., van Wee, B., Molin, E. J., and Flyvbjerg, B. 2012. Different cost performance: different determinants? The case of cost overruns in Dutch transport infrastructure projects. *Transport Policy* 22: 88–95.

Chang, A., Chih, Y.-Y., Chew, E., and Pisarski, A. 2013. Reconceptualising mega project success in Australian defence: Recognising the importance of value co-creation. *International Journal of Project Management* 31(8): 1139–1153.

Chung, D. 2017. Private provision of public services. In B. Flyvbjerg (ed.), *The Oxford Handbook of Megaproject Management*. Oxford University Press, pp. 519–538.

Coyle, G. 2004. *The Analytical Hierarchy Process (AHP) – Introduction, Practical Strategy*. Open access material. Pearson Education Limited.

Crosby, P. 2012. Key success drivers: meta-study findings applicable to large high-technology projects. *International Journal of Information Technology Project Management* 3(2): 1–20.

Denicol, J., Davies, A., and Krystallis, I. 2020. What are the causes and cures of poor megaproject performance? A systematic literature review and research agenda. *Project Management Journal* 51(3): 328–345.

Fainstein, S. S. 2008. Mega-projects in New York, London and Amsterdam. *International Journal of Urban and Regional Research* 32(4): 768–785.

Flyvbjerg, B. 2007. Cost overruns and demand shortfalls in urban rail and other infrastructure. *Transportation Planning and Technology* 30(1): 9–30.

Flyvbjerg, B. 2017. Introduction: the iron law of megaproject management. In B. Flyvbjerg (ed.), *The Oxford Handbook of Megaproject Management*. Oxford University Press.

Flyvbjerg, B., Bruzelius, N., and Rothengatter, W. 2003. *Megaprojects and Risk: An Anatomy of Ambition*. Cambridge University Press.

Flyvbjerg, B., Skamris Holm, M. K., and Buhl, S. 2002. Underestimating costs in public works projects: error or lie? *Journal of the American Planning Association* 68(3): 279–295.

Flyvbjerg, B., Skamris Holm, M. K., and Buhl, S. L. 2003. How common and how large are cost overruns in transport infrastructure projects? *Transport Reviews* 23(1): 71–88.

Flyvbjerg, B., Skamris Holm, M. K., and Buhl, S. L. 2004. What causes cost overrun in transport infrastructure projects? *Transport Reviews* 24(1): 3–18.

Gharaibeh, H. M. 2014. Cost control in mega projects using the Delphi method. *Journal of Management in Engineering* 30(5): 04014024-1–04014024-7.

Global Infrastructure Hub. 2021. Infrastructure Monitor 2021 (December). Available at https://cdn.gihub.org/umbraco/media/4306/gihub_infrastructuremonitor2021.pdf.

Hall, P. 1982. *Great Planning Disasters*. University of California Press.

Hodge, G., and Greve, C. 2013. Public–private partnership in developing and governing mega-projects. In H. Priemus and B. van Wee (eds), *International Handbook on Mega-projects*. Edward Elgar Publishing, pp. 182–208.

Lee, C., Won, J. W., Jang, W., Jung, W., Han, S. H., and Kwak, Y. H. 2017. Social conflict management framework for project viability: case studies from Korean megaprojects. *International Journal of Project Management* 35(8): 1683–1696.

OMEGA Centre. 2012. *Mega Projects: Executive Summary*. OMEGA Centre (December).

Park, Y. I., and Papadopoulou, T. C. 2012. Causes of cost overruns in transport infrastructure projects in Asia: their significance and relationship with project size. *Built Environment Project and Asset Management* 2(2): 195–216.

Rose, T., and Manley, K. 2010. Motivational misalignment on an iconic infrastructure project. *Building Research & Information* 38(2): 144–156.

Singh, R. 2010. Delays and cost overruns in infrastructure projects: extent, causes and remedies. *Economic and Political Weekly* 45(21): 43–54.

Söderlund, J., Sankaran, S., and Biesenthal, C. 2017. The past and present of megaprojects. *Project Management Journal* 48(6): 5–16.

Sovacool, B. K., Gilbert, A., and Nugent, D. 2014. An international comparative assessment of construction cost overruns for electricity infrastructure. *Energy Research & Social Science* 3: 152–160.

Stigler, G. J. 1958. The economies of scale. *The Journal of Law and Economics* 1: 54–71.

2. Megaproject milestones

John D. Landis

To better understand present-day connections between megaproject practice and performance, it helps to know something of megaproject history. When and why were megaprojects first undertaken? What was the basis for their appeal? How did they respond to the growth and economic development issues of their day? What physical and construction challenges did their designers and engineers have to overcome? How were they paid for, and by whom? How well did they meet their stated and unstated objectives, and what were their knock-on effects? Most of all, what was learned along the way about success-ful megaproject practice?

To answer these questions, this chapter explores the evolution of meg-aproject practice through the lens of 28 globally significant megaprojects completed over the last 200 years. It is organized chronologically into four overlapping eras (Table 2.1).[1] The first, spanning the years between 1825 and 1915, centered on building the great canals and railroads that opened up continental and global markets. A second megaproject era, running from the 1930s through the 1990s and largely concentrated in America, witnessed the creation of dam, bridge and highway megaprojects on an industrial scale, culminating in the creation of the US interstate highway system, arguably the most transformative megaproject in modern history. A third megaproject era, which ran from the 1960s to the early-2000s, saw megaprojects go global, as newly prosperous European, Asian and Middle Eastern countries undertook new airport, dam, tunnel, waterfront revival and rail megaprojects on a world-wide scale. The fourth and current megaproject era is dominated by China, which, since the late 1990s, has simultaneously undertaken dam, airport, and especially inter-city and urban rail megaprojects at an unprecedented rate, and for the most part, with great success. Looking ahead, with climate change and inequality now issues of worldwide concern, the obvious question is whether and how new megaproject generations will address issues of climate change mitigation, adaptation and resiliency, as well as provide all segments of society with equal access to economic and social opportunities.

Table 2.1   *Megaproject milestones*

Project (listed chronologically)	Year entered service (or approved)	Significance	Estimated cost (2020 dollars)	Principal financing sources
Erie Canal (USA)	1825	Connecting Buffalo and the Great Lakes to New York City, the 363-mile long Erie Canal reduced the costs of transporting raw materials, agricultural products, and goods by 95%.	$200 million	New York State-issued bonds
Suez Canal (France and Egypt)	1869	Built between 1859 and 1869 by the French-registered Suez Canal Company (with a concession from Sa'id Pasha, the Khedive of Egypt and Sudan), the 193 km Suez Canal connects the Mediterranean Sea to the Red Sea, allowing ships traveling between Europe and Asia to avoid circumnavigating Africa.	$5.4 billion	Private investors and the Egyptian government of the era
Transcontinental Railroad (USA)	1869	Built between 1863 and 1869 by two private railway companies on lands provided by the US government, the 3,075 km transcontinental railway connected Council Bluffs, Iowa with Sacramento, California; and reducing the per person cost of transcontinental passenger travel from $1,000 to $150.	$1.3 billion to $1.6 billion	Railroad company-issued stock and bonds backed by land grants and payments by the US government
Brooklyn Bridge (USA)	1883	Designed by innovative bridge engineer, John A. Roebling, the 6,000-foot-long Brooklyn Bridge connecting lower Manhattan with Brooklyn was the first fixed crossing of the East River and the longest suspension bridge in the world until 1909.	$400 million	New York State-issued bonds
Panama Canal (USA)	1914	Begun by the French in 1881, construction of the 82 km Panama Canal across the Isthmus of Panama connecting the Atlantic and Pacific Oceans was finally completed by the US government in 1914. The Panama Canal was returned to Panamanian ownership (by the US) on December 31, 1999.	$9.7 billion	The US government

Project (listed chronologically)	Year entered service (or approved)	Significance	Estimated cost (2020 dollars)	Principal financing sources
Trans-Siberian Railroad (Russia)	1904	Starting in Moscow and terminating in Vladivostok, the 9,289 km Trans-Siberian Railroad connects eastern and western Russia. It took roughly 25 years to complete.	$25 billion	The Russian government
Hoover Dam (USA)	1936	The 726-foot high Boulder Dam (renamed for President Herbert Hoover in 1947) was the tallest arch-gravity dam in the world when completed in 1936. Its 17 turbines generate 2,080 MW of electricity, enough for 2.4 million households.	$675 million	The US government
San Francisco–Oakland Bay Bridge and Golden Gate Bridge (USA)	1936 & 1937	Built during the same 4-year period (using 1/10th of US steel production) to link San Francisco north to Marin County and east to Oakland, the Golden Gate Bridge and Bay Bridge were the two longest suspension bridges of their era.	$2 billion	State and government authority-issued bonds
Tennessee Valley Authority Flood Control and Electrification Projects (USA)	1930s–1980s	Established in 1933 to provide electricity (and flood control) to rural Appalachia, the Tennessee Valley Authority (TVA) is a federally-owned utility providing electricity to Tennessee and parts of Alabama, Mississippi, and Kentucky. TVA currently operates 29 hydro-electric dams and three nuclear power plants (as well as additional fossil fuel plants) producing 35 GW.	$53 billion in assets	US government-backed bonds issued by the TVA
US Interstate Highway System	1956 (approved)	With 75,000-km of limited-access highways, the US Interstate Highway System connects every state and major metropolitan area in the United States. Construction of 90% of the system was completed in 17 years.	$600 billion	US government-issued bonds

Project (listed chronologically)	Year entered service (or approved)	Significance	Estimated cost (2020 dollars)	Principal financing sources
Delta Works (The Netherlands)	1958 (approved)	Built after the 1953 North Sea floods which killed 1,836 Dutch residents, the Delta Works is a series of storm barriers connecting the outer islands of the Netherland's Zeeland Province protecting the Rhine, Meuse, and Scheldt River estuaries from inundation during coastal flooding events.	$4 billon	Dutch government budget and a 400 million guilder grant from the Marshall Plan.
Tōkaidō Shinkansen (Japan)	1964	With service beginning in 1964, the 515-km Tōkaidō Shinkansen (Bullet Train) line connecting Tokyo with Osaka was the first high-speed rail line in the world. Today, the line carries about 400,000 passengers each day.	$9 billion	Japanese government loans and railroad company bonds
Battery Park City (USA)	1968 (approved)	92-acre high-density, mixed-use (residential, office, park space) community at the southwestern tip of Manhattan built atop fill excavated from the World Trade Center site.		New York State Urban Development Corporation bonds, bank loans and investor equity
Mexico City Metro System	1969	With its first line opening in 1969, Mexico was the first developing country to build a modern metro system. Today, with 12 lines in service, Mexico City's Metro is second only to the New York City subway system in size and ridership among North American metro systems.	$850 million	Mexican government grants, government-guaranteed bank loans
Bay Area Rapid Transit (BART), Washington Metropolitan Metro, Atlanta Rapid Transit Authority (MARTA);	1974 (BART), 1976 (Metro), 1979 (MARTA)	Built in the late-1960s and 1970s using similar train technologies, BART (San Francisco), Metro (Washington, DC) and MARTA (Atlanta) were the first all-new, multi-line, heavy-rail urban transit systems built in the US since 1908.	BART: $12 billion; Metro: $25 billion; MARTA: $11.8 billion	Various combinations of federal transportation grants and local tax sources

Megaprojects for megacities

Project (listed chronologically)	Year entered service (or approved)	Significance	Estimated cost (2020 dollars)	Principal financing sources
TGV—Tres à Grande Vitesse (France)	1981	2,700 km national high-speed rail network connecting Paris south to Lyon and Marseille, north to Lille and the Benelux countries, east to Nancy and Strasburg, and west to Renne and Bordeaux. In 2019, TGV lines carried 126 million passengers	$25 billion (assuming an average cost of $8 million per km)	French government budget
Canary Wharf (UK)	1986 (approved)	97-acre docklands redevelopment project five miles east of central London. Conceived of as a less expensive "back-office" district, Canary Wharf was initially developed by Canadian real estate developer Olympia and York only to go into receivership in 1993. Today, with more than 16 million square feet of office space, 300 shops and restaurants, and a growing supply of housing, Canary Wharf serves as London's second CBD.	Unknown. Current ownership interest sold for £2.6 billion ($3.5 billion) in 2015	Bank loans, investor equity and government grants (for public infrastructure)
The Big Dig (USA)	2003	2.4 km tunnel beneath central Boston replacing an elevated highway built in the 1950s. The project also includes a new bridge and a tunnel under Boston Harbor connecting downtown Boston to the airport.	$16.7 billion	US government (70%), Commonwealth of Massachusetts (30%)
Channel Tunnel (UK)	1994	The Channel Tunnel (aka the Eurotunnel or "Chunnel") is a 50.5 km railway tunnel beneath the English Channel that connects Folkestone in the UK with Coquelles in France. The tunnel has the longest underwater section of any tunnel in the world.	$38 billion	100% private sector financed

Project (listed chronologically)	Year entered service (or approved)	Significance	Estimated cost (2020 dollars)	Principal financing sources
Kansai International Airport (Japan), Hong Kong International Airport, Incheon International Airport (S. Korea)	1994 (Kansai), 1998 (Hong Kong), 2001 (Incheon)	Kansai International Airport in Osaka Bay, Hong Kong International Airport (Chek Lap Kok), and Incheon International Airport in South Korea were each constructed in the 1990s atop artificial islands to replace older airports with limited expansion opportunities. All three are design and engineering standouts. Hong Kong and Incheon have proven to be extremely popular with flyers, ranking as the 13th and 14th busiest passenger airports in the world in 2019.	Kansai: $25 billion; Hong Kong: $20 billion; Incheon $11.4 billion (not including transport access facilities)	Kansai: Japanese and Osaka Prefecture debt; Hong Kong: Airport Authority and bank debt and investor equity; Incheon: Government grants, airport authority debt, investor equity.
Akashi Kaikyo Bridge (Japan)	1998	Completed in 1998, the 3.9 km Akashi Kaikyo Bridge connects the city of Kobe on the Japanese island of Honshu to Iwaya on Awaji Island. It has the longest central span (1,991 m) of any suspension bridge in the world.	$6 billion	Japanese government bonds
Three Gorges Dam (China)	2006	Located on the Yangtze River downstream of the Three Gorges in Hubei Province in China, the Three Gorges Dam generates more electricity (22,500 MW) than any other dam in the world.	$35 billion	Loans from the China Development Bank and domestic and foreign commercial banks

Project (listed chronologically)	Year entered service (or approved)	Significance	Estimated cost (2020 dollars)	Principal financing sources
China's High-speed Rail System	2008	Less than 15 years old and still expanding, China's 37,000 km high-speed rail (HSR) system is 10 times larger than second-place Spain's and connect almost every major Chinese city. Organized by service speed (200 kph, 250 kph, and 200 kph) China's "8 by 8" network carried 2.3 billion passengers in 2019.	$800 billion	National, provincial, and city grants and loans, state-owned and private bank loans, some foreign investment
Gotthard Base Tunnel (Switzerland)	2016	With a length of 57.1 km, connecting Erstfeld in Switzerland with Ticino in Italy far below the Swiss and Italian Alps, and having taken almost 17 years to build, the Gotthard Base Tunnel is the longest and deepest railway tunnel in the world. When its predecessor, the 15 km Gotthard Tunnel was completed in 1886, it too was regarded as a civil engineering marvel.	$10.5 billion	Swiss voter-approved public financing to be repaid with revenues from the operator.

COMMERCE CONNECTIONS, 1825–1915

Megaproject Origin Story—The Erie Canal

Infrastructure historians often date the modern megaproject era from the completion of the Erie Canal in 1825 (Bernstein 2005; Guibertau 2021). The Erie Canal was built explicitly to transport bulk goods and agricultural products from the Northwest Territory states of Ohio, Indiana and Michigan to factories and consumers in New York City and beyond. Railroads were still 30 years in the future and pack animals were limited to carrying loads of 200 pounds, so the only way to move heavy or bulky shipments was by river or canal. First proposed in the 1780s, and then re-proposed in 1807, the Erie Canal extended from Lake Erie and Buffalo eastward to Albany, where it connected to the Hudson River, and ultimately, to New York City.

The Erie Canal possessed several of the characteristics we associate with modern megaprojects beyond simply size. It made use of cutting-edge technology. Where previous canals had been dug by hand, the Erie Canal made use of gunpowder to blast through rock. It required new-for-the-time approaches to project management. The innovative surveying and engineering techniques created to build the Erie Canal were soon being taught at Rensselaer Polytechnic Institute (RPI), the nation's first civil engineering school, founded in 1824. The canal was intended to serve a large and expanding market. With 124,000 residents and growing, New York City was nearly twice the size of second-place Philadelphia. And it was so big and costly—in today's dollars, the Erie Canal cost more than $200 million to complete[2]—that it could only be financed by government. Upon becoming New York's governor in 1817, DeWitt Clinton, the former mayor of New York City and an early Erie Canal backer convinced the New York State Legislature to issue bonds backed by the state's good credit to pay for the canal's construction.

Three-hundred and sixty-three miles long, 40 feet wide, and just four feet deep, it took an estimated 50,000 laborers eight years to dig the Erie Canal and build its 57 locks. Once finished, the canal quickly proved to be a transportation gamechanger. Shippers could transport goods via the Erie Canal at one-tenth the cost of shipping them over land, and by 1853, the canal was carrying three-fifths of all US trade. With a surplus of goods destined for Great Britain and Europe, New York's City's port quickly grew to eclipse its rivals in Boston, Philadelphia and New Orleans. This enabled it to later become the preferred port of entry for generations of immigrants. For the first time, manufactured goods such as furniture and clothing could be shipped in bulk to the western frontier where they had a ready market of increasingly prosperous farmers. The volume of barge traffic using the Erie Canal was so great that the investors who bought the New York State-issued bonds used to pay for the canal were fully repaid in nine years.

The success of the government-backed bond model used by New York State to finance the Erie Canal led to its adoption by other rapidly growing American cities who used it to finance new investments in roads, water systems and public buildings (Wallis 2000). Lacking the Erie Canal's robust system of user charges, many of these new civic investments turned out to be financially dubious. The result was a rise in bond defaults, which curtailed the capacity of other municipalities to undertake additional infrastructure investments. The problem of American cities chronically over-issuing municipal bonds only to have those bonds default was a systematic one and was one of the reasons so many of them were forced to turn to other sources of project finance, such as awarding transport concessions to land developers (Monkkonen 1995; Taylor 2004). States, unlike cities, did not collect property taxes, so with few independent revenue sources of their own, most stayed out of the infrastructure-building business.

A Bigger Ditch—The Suez Canal

The example of the Erie Canal was not lost on Ferdinand de Lesseps, a French diplomat, who, in 1832, while waiting in quarantine for his posting as France's vice-consul to Alexandria (Egypt), was given a memoir to read by Jacques-Marie Le Père, a French civil engineer who had worked for Napoleon in his search for a rumored 8th century canal connecting Old Cairo to the Red Sea. De Lesseps was not alone in his fascination. As trade between Europe and the Far East surged in the early 19th century, numerous engineering surveys were commissioned to identify a possible canal shortcut route that would eliminate the trip around Africa's Cape of Good Hope. All of them foundered when it was (falsely) determined that water level differences between the two seas would require building an expensive series of locks. In 1846, French social reformer Prosper Enfantin established the Société d'Études du Canal de Suez to determine once and for all whether a Suez Canal route would be technically feasible, and after several years of study by experts, word came back that it was. There was, it turned out, no sea level difference after all.

Technical feasibility was one thing, political and economic feasibility was quite another. To build a canal across Egypt would require the permission of its Ottoman Empire administrator, Sa'id Pasha, as well as the ability to assemble a syndicate of investors able to finance construction. De Lesseps, who had befriended Sa'id Pasha during his earlier Egypt posting, was the right man for both jobs. After obtaining a 99-year concession from Pasha to build and operate a potential canal in 1856, de Lesseps put together a committee of explorers and engineers to plan an exact canal route and develop the necessary engineering specifications. Based on the committee's report, de Lesseps formally established the shareholder-based Suez Canal Company (Compagnie universelle du canal maritime de Suez) in December 1858, installing himself as principal director (Karabell 2003; Roberts 2009).

Investors were initially reluctant to back the venture. British investors in particular saw the canal as a threat to Britain's dominance of existing Far Eastern trade routes, and it was only after James de Rothschild of the French House of Rothschild purchased a sizeable stake in the new company that it was able to able to attract additional investors.

Construction began in April 1859 at the Canal's Mediterranean terminus at what would later become Port Said. The initial digging was done by hand with picks and shovels wielded by forced laborers. Sources at the time put the number of laborers working on the canal in any given period at more than 30,000. Tens of thousands of workers died from recurrent cholera epidemics, leading de Lesseps to eventually replace human diggers with steam-powered shovels and dredgers imported from Europe, a technological first. When the completed Suez Canal was finally dedicated on November 17, 1869—among the European dignitaries attending the dedication ceremony were Emperor Franz Joseph I, the French Empress Eugenie, the Crown Prince of Prussia, and Prince Louis of Hesse—it was four years behind schedule and had cost more than twice the amount initially budgeted.

The Canal's narrow width and shallow depth combined with a British boycott severely limited its initial patronage. In its first full year in operation, fewer than 500 ships transited the canal. In a desperate attempt to increase canal revenues, de Lesseps instituted a unique tariff system (later known as the Suez Canal Net Tonnage System) based on each ship's maximum capacity rather than its actual cargo weight (Wilson 1939).

Shippers soon came to appreciate the Suez Canal's huge time and cost advantages, and its use skyrocketed. Even Great Britain came around, in 1875 becoming the Suez Canal Company's majority stockholder and providing the cash-strapped company with the capital it desperately needed to deepen and widen the Canal to accommodate larger ships. By 1884, 85 percent of the value of trade between the United Kingdom and India moved by way of the Suez Canal, mostly in steamships, which thanks to the Canal's preferential rate structure and faster transit times, were rapidly replacing sailing ships as the workhorses of global shipping trade (Fletcher 1958). The Suez Canal had become so important to Great Britain's global economic interests that when local unrest prompted by a surge in anti-Ottoman sentiment threatened to close it in 1882, Britain invaded and occupied Egypt, becoming its military protector and political benefactor for the next 70 years. With the discovery of oil in present-day Iran in 1908 and in Saudi Arabia in 1938, the Suez Canal's role in global commerce expanded further; and by 1955, one year before Egyptian

President Gamal Abdel Nasser announced that Egypt was terminating its lease with the Suez Canal Company and nationalizing the Suez Canal, more than 14,000 ships carrying 1,126 million tons of cargo and oil transited the canal.[3]

As far as transportation megaprojects go, the Suez Canal offers conflicting lessons (Rothengatter 2019). On the one hand, it truly transformed the world economy, even more so than its proponents and investors anticipated, while also accelerating the demise of one transportation technology (sailing ships) and the rise of another (steamships). On the other hand, it ran significantly over schedule and over budget, generated no significant local economic or social development benefits, would likely have bankrupted its original investors were it not for a timely infusion of cash from the UK in 1875, and instead of promoting greater competition among European maritime nations, ultimately ended up strengthening the already-dominant power.

Conquering a Continent—The Transcontinental Railroad

The Suez Canal was not the world's only transformative megaproject completed in 1869. With America's destiny firmly tied to its westward expansion, Congress had been debating whether to fund a railroad from the Mississippi River to the Pacific Ocean since the mid-1850s. The question was, which route should it take? One scheme had the railroad terminating at the mouth of the Columbia River in the Oregon Territories. Another had it ending in Sacramento where it could connect to the growing cities of San Francisco and Oakland. There was even a proposal for a southern route that would terminate in Los Angeles, which in 1860 had all of 5,000 residents (Bain 2000).

After much debate, Congress settled on a route that would begin in Council Bluffs in Iowa; go westward through Nebraska, Wyoming and northern Utah; and then turn southwesterly toward Sacramento, crossing the Nevada–California border just north of Lake Tahoe. In February 1860, Iowa Representative Samuel Curtis introduced a bill calling on Congress to fund the Council Bluffs to Sacramento route. Curtis' bill passed the House but died in the Senate due to opposition from southern states who preferred the southerly Kansas City to Los Angeles route. Curtis introduced his bill a second time in 1861 and again it failed. It was only after the last of the southern states seceded from the Union that Curtis' bill finally passed and was signed into law by President Abraham Lincoln as the Pacific Railroad Act of 1862.

The Act authorized the creation of two new private companies to build the railroad—the Central Pacific Railroad which would start in Sacramento and work its way east, and the Union Pacific Railroad, which would start in Council Bluffs and work its way west. To finance the project, the Act authorized the federal government to issue 30-year US government bonds at six percent interest (Duran 2013; Klein 2019). The bond proceeds would be used to pay each company $16,000 per mile (approximately $461,000 per mile today) for tracks laid on a level grade, $32,000 per mile (about $922,000 per mile today) for tracks laid in foothills, and $48,000 per mile (or about $1,383,000 per mile today) for tracks laid in the mountains. With Congress distracted by the Civil War, both companies were successfully able to insert lucrative "self-dealing" provisions into the Act which would later enable them to extract surplus profits.

To qualify for the government's construction subsidies, the two companies would have to issue large amounts of stock and debt (Ambrose 2000). The Central Pacific Railroad, which was owned by Northern California business-men C.P. Huntington, Mark Hopkins, Charles Crocker and Leland Stanford—who in 1861 would become California's governor—had no trouble raising its funding share. Things did not go as well for the Union Pacific Railroad, which was eventually forced to turn to the Church of Jesus Christ of Latter-day Saints for funding. In return for the Church's financial support, the Union Pacific promised to use Mormon workers to build the railroad's Utah sections. (The Central Pacific's workforce was disproportionately made up of Chinese immigrant laborers, many of whom didn't speak English and were severely mistreated.) To help both railroad companies raise additional capital, Congress granted each of them alternate sections of government-owned lands—6,400 acres per mile—for ten miles on both sides of the track, forming a checker-board pattern. The railroad companies were given the odd-numbered sections while the federal government retained the even-numbered sections.

The Central Pacific, which had the harder job of going up and over the Sierra Nevada Mountains, broke ground on the Transcontinental Railroad's western segment in January 1863. The Union Pacific would have to wait another two-and-a-half years until the end of the Civil War before it could begin work on the eastern segment. Using trains running on newly-completed tracks to deliver a constant supply of workers and material, both construction efforts proceeded quickly. By the time the two railroad companies' work crews met to hammer in the ceremonial golden rail spike at Promontory Summit in Utah on May 10, 1869, they had spent somewhere between $1.3 and $1.6 billion (in 2020 dollars) to build the world's longest railroad.

Five years after its completion, the Transcontinental Railroad had cut the cost of a train trip from New York City to San Francisco from $1,000 to $150. As migrants flowed west, agricultural products flowed east, slashing the cost of beef and other farm products available to eastern consumers. Just as the Erie Canal had done 50 years earlier, the first transcontinental railroad—and a second transcontinental route connecting New Orleans to Los Angeles via San Antonio and El Paso, completed in 1881—turbocharged the American economy while creating pathways for a westward population growth move-ment that continues to this day (White 2011). But whereas the Erie Canal paid back all its investors, the same could not be said for the Transcontinental Railroad. Of the Railroad's two founding companies, the California-based Central Pacific was the more fortunate. A ruthless competitor, the Central Pacific leveraged its access to eastern markets to maximize shipping rates on the lucrative (and unregulated) Sacramento-to-Oakland route, making multi-millionaires of its four founders. By contrast, with no additional lines of its own, the Nebraska-based Union Pacific could only charge what the federal government would allow. To add further economic injury, as part of the Credit Mobilier scandal, the Union Pacific's owners were called before Congress in 1872 to respond to charges that they had grossly over-billed the federal government for building their half of the Transcontinental Railway. Financially weakened, the Union Pacific was purchased in 1880 by financial speculator Jay Gould who merged it with his Kansas Pacific Railroad. The Union Pacific name would live on, but not the company itself.

Except for the owners of the Central Pacific and Southern Pacific Railroads (which merged in 1870), none of the investors in any transcontinental railroad lines prospered financially. In the absence of government regulation, competition pushed freight and passenger fares lower and lower to the point where every railroad company had to provide a rail service to remain in business, but none could make any money (Sobel 1999). As a result, investor appetites slackened for taking on national-scale transportation megaprojects. Instead, risk-minded American investors increasingly put their money into manufacturing industries such as steel, into oil exploration and production, and then later, into urban streetcar lines and property development. For now, the era of American-led megaproject development was over.

Lesser Powers, Big Ambitions

With the Suez Canal's construction delays and cost overruns still fresh in their minds, Europe's great powers were no more eager than America to take on new megaprojects. It was thus left to the Continent's lesser powers to take up the challenge. In Switzerland, the Gotthard Railway Company was established in 1871 to construct a tunnel under the Swiss Alps connecting Göschenen in Switzerland to Airolo in Italy. When attracting sufficient financing money from private investors proved problematic, the governments of Switzerland, Italy and Germany stepped in to help (Gauthier 1880). Construction on the 15 km single-bore Gotthard Tunnel, at the time, the world's longest, began in 1871 and was completed in 1882. The tunnel was initially operated by a private company, Gotthardbahn, which ran conventional steam locomotive-drawn trains between Lucerne in Switzerland and Chiasso at the Italian border. In 1909, Gotthardbahn's operations were integrated into the Swiss Federal Railways.

In Russia meanwhile, work had begun in 1891 on the 9,300 km Trans-Siberian Railroad connecting Moscow in central Russia with Vladivostok on the Pacific Ocean. To save money and avoid clashes with urban landowners, it was decided that the railroad's route should bypass existing cities, a decision which sharply limited the railroad's potential economic benefits. The route was divided into seven sections, with work commencing on all seven simultaneously. Financial support for the enterprise in the amount of £35 million (an amount equivalent to $45 billion today) was raised by French financier, Baron Henri Hottinguer (Liliopoulou et al. 2005). With a workforce of 62,000 laborers, construction activities were mostly completed by 1901 except for the section around Lake Baikal, which wasn't finished and relied on ferry transport until 1904. The new rail line quickly found a ready market, with wheat shipments from central Russia flowing west to Moscow and St. Petersburg, and peasants seeking a new life in Siberia flowing east.

America Ascendant—Completing the Panama Canal

Having completed construction of the Suez Canal to worldwide acclaim, it was understandable that Ferdinand de Lesseps might underestimate the challenges of building a canal across the much narrower Panama Isthmus separating the Atlantic and Pacific Oceans (McCullough 2001). It was 1876, and De Lesseps had recently been hired by the French limited-share company, La Société Civile Internationale du Canal Interocéanique par l'isthme du Darien, to organize French efforts to build what was already being referred to as a Panama Canal. Capitalizing on de Lesseps reputation, the Société Civile, successfully raised the equivalent of $400 million for the project, and in March 1878, obtained an exclusive 15-year concession from the Colombian government to begin construction. De Lesseps' plan, unveiled in May 1879 at the Paris-based International Congress for Study of an Interoceanic Canal, was to build a dam across the east-flowing Chagres River in Gatún on the Atlantic side, and another across the west-flowing Rio Grande River on the Pacific side. Once the two dams were completed, they would contain a mid-isthmus artificial lake that was essentially at sea level, thus negating the need for a complex lock system. This would reduce the amount of digging required, allowing the Panama project to be built economically and quickly. Engineers attending the Congress put the cost of de Lesseps' plan at $214 million and concluded it would take seven or eight years to complete. In a subsequent investor prospectus, de Lesseps reduced those figures to $120 million and six years.

Construction work on the canal began in January 1881. Of the 40,000 laborers hired for the job, 90 percent were Afro-Caribbean workers from the West Indies. With construction underway, it quickly became apparent that de Lessep's plan suffered from two significant flaws. Locks would be required after all to raise ships up and over Panama's 85-foot-high continental divide. De Lesseps had also significantly underestimated the number of canal workers tropical diseases might kill. Between the start of canal construction efforts in 1881 and their end in 1889, when the Société Civile finally exhausted its $235 million investment stake and declared bankruptcy, some 22,000 workers, including 5,000 French citizens, died from malaria and yellow fever.

Having run out of money to continue with construction, De Lesseps himself was soon to be in legal jeopardy when it was revealed that scores of French politicians had been bribed by Société Civile to publicly support the canal project. In 1893, de Lesseps was convicted of fraud and bribery and sentenced to five years in jail. His conviction was later overturned on procedural grounds and de Lesseps died in poverty in December 1894, remembered as much for his Panama Canal failures as for his Suez Canal successes.

With Société Civile bankrupt and its Panama Canal project only two-fifths complete, the company's creditors resolved to try to finish the job, emerging from receivership in 1893 with a new canal company, the Compagnie Nouvelle du Canal de Panama. After completing a new survey, engineers at the company eventually settled on a plan for a two-level, lock-based canal. Meanwhile, the Americans had begun preliminary work on a competitive canal to the north in Nicaragua, based on an 1887 plan prepared by the US Army Corps of Engineers. The competing French and American canal building efforts ended up undermining one another and both quietly closed out in 1894. Convinced that America might still finish the job started by the French, Phillippe-Jean Bunau-Varilla, a French engineer who had worked alongside de Lesseps, began publicly lobbying American lawmakers to buy and restart the French project.

Bunau-Varilla eventually found a convert in Vice-President Theodore Roosevelt, who, because of a growing American naval presence in the Philippines, was convinced that a US-controlled canal connecting the Atlantic and Pacific Oceans was essential to America's strategic interests. Having succeeded to the presidency in September 1901 following the assassination of President William McKinley, Roosevelt convinced Congress to pay $40 million to the French to acquire what remained of their Panama Canal project. The purchase price did not include the lease concession with Columbia, which had lapsed in 1894. After Congress refused to ratify a new treaty with Columbia, Roosevelt publicly offered American naval support to insurgents seeking Panamanian independence. With the backing of the Americans, the insurgents eventually prevailed, establishing the Republic of Panama on November 3, 1903. The young republic immediately named Bunau-Varilla as Envoy Extraordinary and Minister Plenipotentiary. In his new role, Bunau-Varilla negotiated the Hay–Bunau-Varilla Treaty of 1903, which provided the United States with a 10-mile-wide strip of land for the canal, and Panama with a one-time $10 million payment and an annual annuity of $250,000.

Six months later, America took official control of the canal project, naming railroad engineer John Findlay Wallace as chief project engineer. Wallace was eager to resume construction but found the French construction equipment that had been left behind rusted and unserviceable. When Congress failed to provide replacement equipment, Wallace resigned and was replaced in July 1905 by another former railroad engineer, John Frank Stevens. Stevens immediately got into a disagreement with his senior engineers who wanted to resurrect de Lesseps' original lock-less, sea level design. Stevens also disagreed with Congress' choice of Tennessee-based private contractor, William J. Oliver, who had submitted the low bid to build the canal, preferring instead to rely on the Army Corps of Engineers. Roosevelt too had originally favored using a private contractor to undertake the project, but eventually came around to agreeing with Stevens. When Stevens resigned in frustration over his lack of support from Washington, Roosevelt named his deputy, Army Major George Washington Goethals, to oversee the project.

Goethals soon proved himself to be an excellent choice, dividing the job into Atlantic, Central, and Pacific Divisions. The Atlantic Division would be responsible for building the breakwater at the entrance to Limon Bay, the Gatún locks and their 3.5-mile approach channel, and the Gatun Dam. The Pacific Division would be responsible for the Pacific entrance to the canal, including a 3-mile breakwater in Panama Bay, the approach channel, and the Miraflores and Pedro Miguel locks and their associated dams. The Central Division would be responsible for everything in between, including the Culebra Cut, which involved cutting through eight miles of rock down to a depth of 39 feet above sea level. The scale of the work was massive. Six thousand men worked in the Culebra Cut, drilling holes in which 27,000 tons of dynamite were placed to break up the rock. Landslides were frequent, but on May 20, 1913, Bucyrus steam shovels made a passage through the Culebra Cut at the level of the canal bottom. Five months later, the dike at Gamboa which had kept the Culebra Cut isolated from Gatun Lake was demolished, and on January 7, 1914, the *Alexandre La Valley*, an old French crane boat, became the first ship to make a complete Panama Canal transit under its own power. The Canal was officially dedicated on August 15, 1914. The Great War had started in Europe three weeks earlier and everyone was on edge.

Altogether, the Panama Canal cost its American sponsors $350 million ($9.7 billion in 2020 dollars) making it the most expensive construction project then undertaken in US history. The project also exacted a heavy human cost: roughly 5,600 American workers died between 1904 and 1913 because of tropical infections and accidents. Amazingly, the Panama Canal ended up costing $23 million less than had been authorized by Congress in 1907. Even more impressively, the project was carried out without any hint of scandal, corruption, or overpayment. Nor were any financial irregularities uncovered in later years.

Trade flows through the just complete Panama Canal were small during its first year, but soon picked up. During the 1914–1915 period, approximately three million tons of cargo tons passed from the Canal's Pacific Atlantic sides, with 2.5 million tons flowing in the opposite direction. Ten years later, these totals had increased to 16 million and 7 million tons, respectively (Mason and Rowlands 1938). Shipments fell during the Depression and World War II, but started growing again in 1946. Although periodically deepened to accommodate larger ships, eventually the width of the Canal's locks would prove a limit on its capacity, and in June 2016, after ten years of construction by the government of Panama (the Canal was returned to Panamanian ownership in 1999) a new higher-capacity canal with wider and longer locks was opened to shipping (Zielinski 2018). In 2019, a record 469 million tons of cargo transited the Panama Canal in both directions, up 6.2 percent from a year earlier.[4,5]

America's successful completion of the Panama Canal confirmed two important megaproject lessons. The first concerned the value of expertise and logistical might. Only after the Army Corps of Engineers, with its cadre of professional engineers and ability to mobilize resources, assumed responsibility for the job did the project move steadily ahead (Rogers 2014). The second important lesson of the Panama Canal, and also of the Erie Canal, Suez Canal, and Transcontinental Railroad (Table 2.2), is that very large-scale infrastructure investments that significantly reduce passenger and freight transportation costs quickly create huge downstream benefits and opportunities that extend well beyond the projects themselves (Stough and Haynes 1997; Rothegatter 2019).

Table 2.2   *Comparing the Erie, Suez, and Panama Canals*

	Erie Canal	Suez Canal	Panama Canal
Connects	Buffalo to Albany in New York State	Port Said, Egypt (Mediterranean Sea) to Port Suez, Egypt (Red Sea)	Port of Colon, Panama (Atlantic Ocean) to Port of Balboa, Panama (Pacific Ocean)
Original Owner/ Developer	New York State	Suez Canal Company[e]	United States Government (lease from Panama running until December 31, 1999)
Principal Engineer	Benjamin Wright	Eugène Mougel	George Washington Goethals[b]
Length	584 km	164 km	82 km
Width at narrowest point (as built)	12 m	25 m[a]	30 m
Depth (as built)	1.2 m	8 m	15 m
Elevation change	173 m	0 to 50 cm	85 m up and down
Number of Locks	36	0	3 up, 3 down
Average canal transit time	9 days	12–16 hours	8–10 hours
Largest ship size or weight	80 ft packet boat	160,000 DWT (deadweight tons)	120,000 DWT[c]
Date opened	October 1825	November 1869	August 1914
Construction time	8 years	10 years	10 years
Construction labor force	50,000	100,000+	75,000
Excavation volume	11 million cubic yards	80 million cubic yards	170 million cubic yards
Original construction cost (in 2020 dollars)	$200 million	$5.4 billion	$9.7 billion
Reduction over prior transit time	6–35 days	10–20 days	3–5 months
Shipment volume, 2019	n.a.[d]	1.2 billion metric tons	469 million tons
Operating revenues, 2019	n.a.[d]	$5.8 billion	$2.7 billion

Notes:
[a] 2015, the Egyptian government widened the canal, deepened the main waterway and opened a 35 km parallel waterway.
[b] Goethals replaced John Frank Stevens in 1907.
[c] Increased from 50,000 DWT prior to 2016.
[d] The Erie Canal was closed in 1878.
[e] A partnership between the Khedive of Egypt and an investor syndicate led by French diplomat and investor Ferdinand de Lessups.

MEGAPROJECTS ACROSS AMERICA, 1935–1995

The first era of public megaprojects centered on commerce-oriented projects such as canals and railroads. The second public megaprojects era, which began in the 1930s, was oriented around dams, bridges, and later highways and urban transit systems. Like the first, it would require significant amounts of government capital. It would also require a level of engineering expertise that the private engineering and construction companies of the era did not initially possess.

As the 20th century dawned, few areas of infrastructure construction were advancing as rapidly as suspension bridge building. Early 19th-century suspension bridges, which made use of iron suspension chains and members, were too heavy to span to major rivers. Replacing those early bridges' vertical iron trusses with lighter and stronger cables allowed bridge engineers to build longer spans, but as bridge lengths increased, so did vulnerability to wind forces and uneven loading. To solve these problems, German-born American bridge engineer John Augustus Roebling added steel reinforcing trusses to his bridge's horizontal spans, which provided additional rigidity and strength. Roebling's first suspension bridge using his new design spanned the Niagara River Gorge between New York and Canada. Completed in 1855, it featured a central span with the previously unheard-of length of 825 feet. Completed in 1866, Roebling's second major bridge, the Cincinnati–Covington Bridge crossing the Ohio River, featured an even longer 1,057-foot central span. Roebling's third bridge was his masterpiece: the 1,595-foot central span Brooklyn Bridge was completed in 1883 (McCullough 2012). Crossing the East River between Manhattan and Brooklyn, the Brooklyn Bridge was strong enough to carry elevated subway trains, which were added to the Bridge in 1906.

The same high strength steel used to build ever longer bridges was also used to frame ever taller buildings (Willis 1995). Designed by the architecture firm Burnham and Root, the world's first all-steel "skyscraper," the 148-foot-tall Rand McNally Building in Chicago, opened in 1889. It was followed in 1899 by the 390-foot-tall Park Row Building in New York City, in 1908 by the 612-foot-tall Singer Tower in New York City, and in 1909 by the 699-foot-tall Metropolitan Life Building, also in New York City. Seeking to push steel building heights to their very limit, New York City real estate developer William Reynolds hired architect William Van Alen to design a steel-framed skyscraper that would break the 1,000-foot threshold. Sold to industrialist Walter P. Chrysler before it was completed in 1930, the art-deco themed Chrysler Building topped out at 1,046 feet, making it the world's tallest building by far. Reflecting the incredible speed at which tall building design was advancing, just one year later, in 1931, that title was surrendered to the

1,250-foot Empire State Building. From beginning to end, construction of the Empire State Building took just 18 months, enabling it to open 45 days ahead of schedule. Built at a cost of $41 million ($565 million in 2020 dollars, and thus not technically a megaproject), the Empire State Building would remain the tallest building in the world for more than 40 years, until it was surpassed in 1974 by the 1,450-foot Sears Tower in Chicago.

As skyscrapers grew taller, suspension bridges grew longer. Between 1931 and 1939, bridge builders in the United States completed four new suspension bridges with central spans longer than 2,300 feet: the 3,500-foot George Washington Bridge across the Hudson River in 1931, the 4,600-foot double-span San Francisco–Oakland Bay Bridge in 1936, the 4,199-foot Golden Gate Bridge in 1937, and the 2,299-foot Bronx–Whitestone Bridge in 1939.[6]

Redefining the Possible—The Hoover Dam

As impressive as these skyscraper and bridge projects were, the Hoover Dam, also known as Boulder Canyon Dam, would be another order of magnitude altogether (Hiltzik 2010; Kwak et al. 2014). Until the Hoover Dam was completed in 1936, the tallest dam built anywhere in the world was the 430-foot-high O'Shaughnessey Dam at the entrance to California's Yosemite National Park. The Hoover Dam, at 726 feet high, would be taller by two-thirds. It would also impound what is still the largest dam-created reservoir in the United States, Lake Mead.

Located 30 miles southeast of Las Vegas on the Colorado River between Nevada and Arizona, Hoover Dam was originally conceived in 1922 by the US Bureau of Reclamation to provide electricity to the fast-growing Southern California. Created by an act of Congress and signed into law by President Calvin Coolidge in December 1928, the Boulder Canyon Project Act[7] appropriated $165 million to build Boulder Canyon Dam along with the downstream Imperial Dam and All-American Canal. Because of the narrowness of Boulder Canyon, in order to impound a sufficient volume of water to run its electricity-producing turbines year-round, the Hoover Dam would have to rise to a height of more than 700 feet. To hold back a water column of such height, the Bureau's chief design engineer, John L. Savage chose an arch-gravity design, which is straighter at the bottom and becomes more curved as it rises. At its bottom, the wedge-shaped dam would be 660 feet thick. It would taper as it rose, leaving just enough thickness at its top to accommodate a two-lane road. Before the dam could be built, the Colorado River would have to be diverted away from the construction site. This would require building four huge diversion tunnels inside the canyon walls, two on each side of Boulder Canyon. The original plan was to install 16 large turbines in the powerhouse at the dam's base, each generating 130 megawatts of electricity, but as construction progressed, the decision was made to substitute two smaller generators for one big one, bringing the total number of power-generating turbines to 17. When Lake Mead behind Hoover Dam finally filled to its full capacity in 1939, the Dam's turbines could generate 1,300 megawatts of electricity, enough to power more than a million homes for a year.

With its plans complete, the Bureau made the bid documents for Hoover Dam available to prospective contractors in January 1931. In addition to posting a $2 million bid bond, the winning bidder had to post a $5 million completion bond. The winner would have seven years to complete the project before financial penalties applied. Unable to afford the bidding and completion bonds on their own, a local contractor, the Utah Construction Company formed a joint venture with six other dam construction and engineering companies: Boise-based Morrison-Knudsen, the Pacific Bridge Company of Portland, Oregon, Henry J. Kaiser & W.A. Bechtel Company of San Francisco, MacDonald & Kahn Ltd. of Los Angeles, and the J.F. Shea Company of Portland, Oregon. Except for Morrison-Knudsen, which had completed several smaller dams on the Columbia and Snake Rivers, none of the joint venture partners were well known outside their home states. With Bechtel and Kaiser considered to be one company, the joint venture called itself Six Companies, Inc. Of the three bids submitted, the Six Companies' bid of $48,890,955 (equivalent to $860 million today) was the lowest, and they were awarded the job.

Construction began in May 1931. With its 4.4 million cubic yards of concrete and 45 million pounds of reinforced steel, Hoover Dam would be the biggest masonry structure built since the Great Pyramids of Egypt. At the peak of dam building activity in 1934, Hoover Dam's construction crew exceeded 5,000 workers, requiring the Six Companies to build a new town to house the dam's workers and their families. Efforts by the Industrial Workers of the World to unionize the dam's laborers resulted in two brief strikes but were otherwise unsuccessful. Altogether, 96 construction workers died while building the dam, a number that was not regarded as excessive given the project's size and complexity. Contrary to rumors circulating at the time, none of those who died are entombed in the dam.

The Six Companies completed the job on time and on budget, and on March 1, 1936, ownership of the new Boulder Canyon Dam was officially handed over to the US Department of the Interior. The dam had been informally dedicated nine months earlier by President Roosevelt while on a western campaign tour.

Other western states hydropower dam megaprojects would soon follow, including the 120-megawatt (MW) Parker Dam, also on the Colorado in 1938, the mile-wide 550 MW Grand Coulee Dam on the Columbia River in Washington State in 1942, and the 676 MW Shasta Dam on the Sacramento River in California in 1945. The Hoover Dam would retain its title as the US's tallest dam until 1968 when it was supplanted by the 770-foot-high Oroville

Dam on the Feather River in California. (As of 2020 there are 29 dams world-wide that are taller than the Hoover Dam; 12 are in China).

The success of the Hoover Dam provided a huge economic boost to each of the Six Companies. Morrison-Knudsen would go on to work on the San Francisco–Oakland Bay Bridge, the St. Lawrence Seaway, NASA's Kennedy Space Center, the Trans-Alaska Pipeline, and more than 100 dam projects. Henry J. Kaiser would soon establish Kaiser Shipyards, which would build Liberty ships during World War II. After the war, Kaiser founded Kaiser Aluminum and Kaiser Steel, and Kaiser Permanente to provide healthcare for Kaiser workers and their families. Bechtel would go on to become a worldwide leader in dam, powerplant, nuclear energy and mass transit engineering and project management, with projects throughout Europe, the Middle East and Asia. In addition to creating new opportunities for its contractors, Hoover Dam firmly established the United States as the place where no construction project was regarded as too big or too difficult.

Scaling Up—TVA, the Tennessee Valley Authority

The Hoover Dam demonstrated that the combination of federal funding and private sector expertise could successfully deliver on the most ambitious and complex public works projects then imaginable. The next question was, could they do so repeatedly and at scale? The answer to this question would come in the form of the Tennessee Valley Authority, better known as TVA.

Among the US regions hardest hit by the Great Depression was the Tennessee River Valley, a largely rural area that extended from the southwest-ern corner of Virginia through the entire state of Tennessee down to Alabama and Mississippi. Even by Depression standards, the Tennessee Valley was in dire economic straits. Thirty percent of its population in 1933 was affected by malaria. The average income in its rural areas was $639 per year (equivalent to $10,000 in 2020), with some families surviving on as little as $100 annually. Much of the land had been exhausted by years of poor farming practices. Crop yields were falling, further squeezing farmers. The best timber had long ago been cut, and ten percent of remaining forests were lost each year to fires. Only one percent of Tennessee farmers had indoor plumbing in 1933,[8] and fewer than one in nine had electricity.[9]

To mitigate the region's oppressive poverty, Nebraska Senator George W. Norris in 1931 introduced legislation in Congress to fund construction of a dam on the Tennessee River near Muscle Shoals, Alabama, to provide electricity for the area's rural residents and businesses. Norris' bill passed Congress but was vetoed by President Herbert Hoover, who regarded it as socialism (TVA 2021a). Norris tried again in 1933, and this time, his bill drew the support of newly-elected President Franklin Delano Roosevelt whose campaign platform had enthusiastically endorsed rural electrification. On May 18, 1933, Roosevelt signed the Tennessee Valley Authority Act into law, creating a new multi-state agency to be known as the Tennessee Valley Authority. The forward-thinking act invested TVA with the "power to acquire real estate for the construction of dams, reservoirs, transmission lines, power houses, and other structures, and navigation projects at any point along the Tennessee River, or any of its tributaries."[10]

The new authority had a huge to-do list, including building dams for floor control, improving river navigation, expanding fertilizer manufacturing, and promoting improved agricultural practices. Its foremost responsibility, however, was to supply electricity. It quickly got down to business, starting with the 126 megawatt (MW) Norris Dam completed in 1936, the 402 MW Wheeler Dam also completed in 1936, the 276 MW Pickwick Landing Dam completed in 1938, the 123 MW Guntersville Dam completed in 1939, the 172 MW Hiwassee Dam completed in 1940, the 140 MW Chickamauga Dam completed in 1940, the 196 MW Watts Bar Dam completed in 1942, the 182 MW Douglas Dam completed in 1943 in just 13 months, the 151 MW Fort Loudoun Dam completed in 1943, the 223 MW Kentucky Dam completed in 1940, and the 304 MW Fontana Dam completed in 1944, as well as numerous hydropower and flood control dams. By the end of World War II, TVA had become the largest electricity supplier in the nation, and, by 1950, TVA dams were generating 2,740 MW of electricity (TVA 2021b).

How did TVA build so many dams so quickly? In an account drawn from local press reports, TVA's website explains how the 480-foot-tall Fontana Dam, the largest of the TVA dams, was completed in less than three years:

> Construction of Fontana required an exceptional organizational effort. Because the site was in the remote mountains of western North Carolina 28 miles west of Bryson City, a railroad had to be built to transport supplies. Some joked that Fontana was the "town TVA took away from the bears." Dormitories, houses, trailers and tents for the workers and their families were erected in the wilderness almost overnight. A hospital, library, post office, and schools were established where none had been before [...] The 5,000 or so men and women who assembled at Fontana in 1942 worked in three shifts, around-the-clock, seven days a week. Because of the accelerated schedule, construction time was slashed to almost half of what it would have been in peacetime. Military marches and big band music were piped over a PA system to the camp, which featured a softball field, cafeteria, and pool halls. (TVA 1950)

TVA's dam building efforts also benefited from sharing construction methods and techniques across projects, and from developing standardized procurement and contracting approaches. It is also worth noting that TVA did not have to contend with environmental review or mitigation requirements, which might have slowed down its efforts; those would not be enacted until 1970 and the passage of the National Environmental Policy Act. Whether on the Tennessee River in the southeast or the Colorado and Columbia Rivers out west, dam building had come to be seen as a measure of American industrial prowess in the same way that building airplanes, ships, and tanks for the war effort was.

TVA itself was organized more like a for-profit company than a government agency. Section II of the TVA Act established a three-person professionally-trained board of directors whose members were not allowed to be involved with any public or private utility with which TVA might potentially compete.[11] TVA would reach its dam-building zenith under the leadership of David Lilienthal, who succeeded Harcourt Morgan as TVA chairman in 1941 (Neuse 1991). Educated and trained as a lawyer, Lilienthal was a staunch advocate of public power, and prior to taking the helm at TVA, had devoted his career to professionalizing the public utility sector. It was Lilienthal who reorganized TVA's operations to focus on its dam-building efforts. As TVA Chair, Lilienthal was centrally involved in the creation of the Oak Ridge National Laboratory, which helped build the atom bomb, and, based on that experience, was appointed by President Truman to serve as the chairman of the newly-established Atomic Energy Commission (AEC) in 1946. Lilienthal would use his passion for public power to redirect the AEC's focus away from military uses of atomic energy, and toward civilian uses, particularly power production.

The Biggest Megaproject in History—Creating the US Interstate Highway System

The dam building and project management successes of the TVA (and of the wartime Manhattan Project, which culminated in the creation of the atom bomb) imbued those thinking about America's infrastructure needs to do so systematically rather than on a project-by-project basis. This systems approach to building megaprojects would reach its apogee with the passage of the Interstate Highway Act of 1956.

The idea of building a national network of high-performance limited-access highways was not new (McNichol 2006). The US system of cities was always more equally distributed in terms of population size than Europe's, so there were good commerce and economic development reasons for wanting to connect them all with a distributed roadway network. The federal government's first efforts to put together a national highway network began with the passage of the Federal Aid Road Act of 1916 (Weingroff 1996). It provided $75 million over a five-year period in matching federal funding for states to use for building new highways. Addressing a December 1918 gathering of the State Highway Officials and Highway Industries Association, E. J. Mehren, a civil engineer and the editor of *Engineering News-Record* proposed that the states use the funding made available by the 1916 Act to collaborate in creating a 50,000-mile national highway system consisting of five east–west routes and 10 north–south routes passing through each of the 48 states. Mehran's proposal was largely ignored by the conference attendees, but would nonetheless form the conceptual basis of what would later become the US Interstate Highway system.

Fresh off its successes building the Panama Canal, the US Army was also interested in highways, and in 1919 sent a convoy of trucks across the country to evaluate the difficulties military vehicles would face should a national mobilization effort ever become necessary. Starting from the White House on July 7, it took the Army's Motor Transport Corps a total of 62 days to reach the Presidio in San Francisco, traveling an average of just 50 miles each day. Accompanying the convoy on its trip was 28-year-old Army Lieutenant Dwight Eisenhower who later recalled, "The old convoy had started me thinking about good two-lane highways... the wisdom of broader ribbons across our land" (Watson 2020).

When the 1916 Act expired after five years, Congress enacted new legislation—the Federal Aid Highway Act of 1921. The new Act once again provided for federal matching funds for road construction and improvement, allocating $75 million per year to the states for another five years. Rather than encouraging states to act individually as the 1916 Act had done, the 1921 Act targeted its funds toward the construction of a national road grid of interconnected "primary highways," encouraging states to cooperate with each other as to how they spent their allotted highway construction funds. To move states along, the Bureau of Public Roads asked the US Army to provide a list of roads that it considered necessary for national defense, and in 1922, General John J. Pershing, former head of the American Expeditionary Force in Europe during World War I, responded with a detailed map of 20,000 miles of interconnected primary highways.

Meanwhile, as often happens in America, individual states and cities were experimenting on their own. New York City, under the leadership of Robert Moses, built a series of express parkways connecting growing suburbs in Long Island and Westchester County to Manhattan. Pennsylvania started work on a limited-access east–west turnpike. Content to let states take the lead, President Franklin Roosevelt opted not to spend precious political capital on yet another national public works project, and so waited until 1938 before asking the Bureau of Public Roads to resume its previous highway planning efforts. Nor was highway building a high priority with the public. New car sales, which had finally started to recover from their Depression-era lows in 1935, slumped in 1938 and 1939.[12] They briefly recovered in 1940 and 1941 only to tumble again in 1942 as the nation's auto production capacity was converted to building airplanes and tanks. Car and truck production grew steadily following World War II, finally topping seven million in 1951. As more cars filled the nation's existing roadways, the need for newer and better highways was becoming more pressing.

Having seen firsthand the military benefits of a Germany's high-speed Reichsautobahn system during World War II, President Eisenhower in 1954 appointed Army General Lucius Clay to head a committee charged with preparing a national interstate highway plan. Clay's committee proposed a 10-year, $100 billion program to build 40,000 miles of free-of-charge divided highways linking all American cities with populations of 50,000 or more. Eisenhower personally preferred building toll roads to free ones but was convinced by Clay that charging tolls would be infeasible outside of the highly populated coastal regions (Davis 2020).

In February 1955, Eisenhower forwarded Clay's proposals to Congress where they were quickly approved by a bipartisan Senate. Worried about increasing the federal deficit, Democrats in the House were less enthusiastic. After a year of negotiations over how to pay for building a highway network, the Eisenhower Administration agreed to establish an off-budget Highway Trust Fund, to be funded by a national gasoline tax. Gas taxes were similar in principle to user charges like tolls but could be used in a way that would allow motorists in heavily-traveled urban and suburban areas to help pay for less busy rural highways. In June 1956, Eisenhower signed the Federal Aid Highway Act of 1956 into law, authorizing $25 billion in federal funds to be made available each year through 1969 for construction of a 41,000 mile inter-state highway system (Weingroff 1996). Every newly-constructed Interstate link was required to be free, have at least two lanes of travel in each direction, and have no at-grade crossings. As an inducement to get reluctant rural states to participate, the Federal Highway Administration agreed to pay 90 percent of all construction costs. Funding availability was later extended until 1972.

The program proved immediately popular. Just two months after the Highway Act's passage, $800 million in project spending had been tentatively approved, with commitments for $36 million in construction contracts ready to be distributed. States such as Pennsylvania, Missouri and Kansas, which were already building interstate-quality highways had a clear head start, but other states soon caught up.

The interstate highway program had something for everyone. As long as their design and engineering specifications met federal standards, state depart-ments of transportation were free to select their own contractors. The trucking industry and Teamsters union were especially enthusiastic since the new inter-states would allow their members to successfully compete on both time and cost with railroad companies. City officials realized they could use interstate highway funds for slum clearance and redevelopment purposes. With workers now commuting by car rather than train or streetcar, suburban homebuilders began adding attached two-car garages to their model homes.

Because building urban highways was more expensive than building rural ones, the program soon ran into funding problems (Weingroff 1996). Motorists were indeed driving more, but not yet in sufficient volumes to completely fill the Highway Trust Fund. To avoid losing momentum, Congress passed the Federal Aid Highway Act of 1958, which increased interstate funding by a total of $800 million for the next two fiscal years. By the time president Eisenhower left office in January 1961, 25 percent of the planned 41,000-mile interstate system had been completed and opened to traffic.

Despite mounting Congressional concern about the program's uneven costs—it cost six times as much to build a mile of urban interstate as a mile of rural interstate—and early rumblings of discontent in cities such as San Francisco over existing neighborhoods being bulldozed to make way for new freeways, highway construction accelerated (Weingroff 2006). By 1972, the year set by Congress for the Interstate Highway program to end, 35,000 of the system's planned 41,000 miles had been completed.[13]

Whereas Congress in 1956 had anticipated spending $25 billion per year over 12 years to complete the interstate system, for a total cost of $300 billion, by the time the system was finally declared finished in 1992, total federal spending (not including the state or local share) had exceeded $114 billion ($530 billion in 2020 dollars), making the US Interstate Highway system the biggest and most expensive public works construction program in world history.[14]

More than 60 years after its passage, opinions differ as to the wisdom of the 1956 Highway Act. Critics point to its 90 percent federal funding share as having promoted far more highway construction than needed and, aided by the pervasiveness of single-family zoning ordinances, as having encouraged excessive low-density sprawl, endless urban traffic jams, and needless auto dependency (Gutfreund 2004; Deakin 2006). Supporters of the Act cite the low cost of transporting goods throughout the US, and the ease with which Americans can travel anywhere within the country (Cox and Love 1996; Jaworski et al. 2018). Whichever side's arguments are more persuasive, the Interstate Highway Act demonstrated the power of transportation megaprojects to reorganize society on a never-before conceived scale, and to do so in a manner that would prove largely irreversible.

Reinventing Commuter Rail Service in the Automobile Era

One part of the interstate highway system did not work out as its advocates intended: instead of alleviating urban freeway congestion, the system's new highways permanently worsened it. Having permanently abandoned trains and buses for cars, and with the cost of gasoline at record lows, commuters flocked to the new freeways in droves, worsening traffic congestion and air pollution. Might providing high-speed regional rail service convince some commuters to leave their cars behind? Government officials and transportation planners in the San Francisco Bay Area, the Atlanta metro area, and Washington, DC, were determined to find out (Table 2.3).

Table 2.3   *Selected BART, Metro and MARTA rapid transit system comparisons*

	BART (San Francisco Bay Area)	Metrorail (Washington, DC)	MARTA (Atlanta)
Owner and operator	3-county San Francisco Bay Area Rapid Transit District	Washington Metropolitan Area Transit Authority (WMATA)	3-county (and City of Atlanta) Metropolitan Atlanta Regional Transit Authority
System length (at full opening)	71.5 miles	98 miles	–
Current system length	131.4 miles	117 miles	48 miles
Stations (when opened)	34		24
Current number of stations	50	91	38
Lines (when opened)	4	4	4
Current number of lines	5	6	4
Initial opening date	September 1972	March 1976	June 1979
Full system opening date	September 1974	December 1983	December 1984
Construction period	1964–1974	1969–1983	1975–1984
Initial construction cost (in 2020 dollars)	$12 billion	$25 billion (est.)[a]	$11.8 billion (est.)[b]
Major system expansions	1996, 1997, 2003 (to SF Airport), 2020	1990, 1998, 2004	1988 (to Atlanta Airport), 1992, 1993, 1996, 2000
Average weekday headways	10 mins (peak), 20–25 mins (off-peak)	4–8 mins peak; 12–20 mins off-peak	10 mins (peak), 20 mins (off-peak)
Top regular operating speed	70 mph	59 mph	60 mph
Average weekday ridership (first full year)	118,000 (1975)	375,000 (1985)	–
Average weekday ridership, 2019	411,000	643,000	231,700
Farebox recovery rate, 2019	60%	67%	40%

Notes:
[a] George Mason University Professor Zachary Schrag (2014) estimates the cost of constructing the initial Metro system at $10 billion.
[b] This is based on a 1979 MARTA Board cost estimate of $3.5 billion to complete the original system.

BART—Bay Area Rapid Transit

A decade after opening in 1936 and 1937, the San Francisco–Oakland Bay Bridge connecting San Francisco to its eastern suburbs was filling up with commuters. A 1947 joint Army–Navy Review Board traffic study concluded that building a second bridge across San Francisco Bay would only temporarily relieve worsening traffic congestion and that a better solution would be to build a high-speed train tube beneath the Bay. A follow-on commission created by the California State Legislature in 1951 took the review board's suggestion one step further, recommending the formation of a five-county rapid transit district, which would build and operate a high-speed rapid rail system linking major Bay Area job centers with suburban residential communities (BART 2021). The Legislature responded in 1957 by creating the San Francisco Bay Area Rapid Transit (BART) District, comprising the counties of Alameda, Contra Costa, Marin, San Francisco and San Mateo. To help pay for the new system, the proposed BART District would be allowed to tax property owners in the five counties a maximum of five cents per $100 of assessed property valuation. It would also have the power to levy additional property taxes as needed to support a general obligation bond issue if approved by the District's voters.

By midsummer, 1961, full-scale engineering plans had been created for a semi-automated network of high-speed trains that would run on grade-separated rights-of-way (Healy 2013). The price tag for the new built-from-scratch BART system was $996 million, or $8.5 billion in current dollars. Citing the mismatch between prospective costs and benefits, Marin and San Mateo Counties later withdrew from the proposed BART District, leaving San Francisco, Alameda and Contra Costa Counties on their own. Voters in the three counties went to the polls in November 1962, and by a sizeable margin, approved a $792 million bond issue to finance a 71.5-mile combined subway and commuter rail system serving 33 stations in 17 municipalities. To sweeten the deal, the bond issue also included undergrounding the San Francisco Municipal Railway as it ran along Market Street in San Francisco. Parsons-Brinkerhoff-Quade & Douglas, the planning and engineering firm that had prepared the 1961 BART plan, was hired as the overall project manager. Additional contracts were awarded to Tudor Engineering Company of San Francisco, and Bechtel Corporation, also of San Francisco. The team looked to be a good one: all three companies had experience delivering very large infrastructure projects.

Construction began on BART's Oakland subway lines in January 1966. Ten months later, the first of 57 giant steel and concrete sections for the 3.8-mile Transbay Tube was lowered into place at the bottom of San Francisco Bay. As more pieces of the project came together, it became apparent that completing the BART system would cost much more than originally promised. When the contract with Rohr Industries for the first 250 BART rail cars was finally signed in 1969, the cost was $80 million—$18 million more than the original cost estimate for the entire 450-car fleet. A 34th station in San Francisco was added to the original 33-station program, further increasing costs. With construction of the Transbay Tube running months behind schedule, BART Directors set September 11, 1972, as the opening date of the 28-mile East Bay line which would run from MacArthur Station in Oakland south to suburban Fremont near the border with Santa Clara County. Additional lines connecting Oakland to Walnut Creek in the east and to Richmond in the north were opened in 1973. Service on BART's Transbay line, which connected Oakland to San Francisco and Daly City, finally began in September 1974, thus completing the entire 71.5-mile system.

As later reported by Peter Hall (1982), during BART's roughly 10-year construction period, its costs escalated from the original 1962 estimate of $923 million to a final cost of $1.6 billion, an increase of nearly 75 percent. Accounts differ as to the source of the cost overruns. Hall attributed them to an unrealistic construction schedule which did not anticipate delays due to community opposition, an underestimated inflation rate, and an unrealistically small engineering contingency budget given the variety of new technologies in use. Economist Leonard Merewitz (1973) was less charitable, attributing the cost escalations to the BART District's lack of experience and its naïve confidence that the system's many technical innovations would work as promised.

Of equal importance, BART failed to live up to its initial ridership projections. Ridership estimates for 1975, the system's first year of full operation, put BART daily ridership at an average of 133,000 passengers per day, or just 51 percent of the 260,000 daily passengers initially projected by the BART District in 1965. Ridership increased steadily as Bay Area commuters grew comfortable with the service and as residential growth patterns began favoring BART-served communities in the East Bay. Average daily ridership (measured as turnstile exits) grew from 118,000 passengers in 1975 (the first full year of operation) to 241,000 in 1990 to 310,000 in 2005 to 433,000 in 2016.[15] Still, memories are long, and notwithstanding its eventual success, BART has never managed to shake its reputation for over-promising and under-delivering, and even today, longstanding plans to extend BART to downtown San Jose remain unrealized.

MARTA—The Metropolitan Atlanta Rapid Transit Authority
The BART story of grand expectations followed by cost overruns and ridership shortfalls was mirrored in Atlanta with MARTA, the Metropolitan Atlanta Rapid Transit Authority (Monroe 2012). MARTA was created in 1965 by the Georgia General Assembly to coordinate future rail transit investments across metropolitan Atlanta's five sprawling counties: Clayton, Cobb, DeKalb, Fulton, and Gwinnett. When asked to approve the Assembly's action creating MARTA, voters in four of the five counties (plus Atlanta) did so; those in Cobb County did not.

At issue were questions of race and money. Metropolitan Atlanta's outward population growth during the 1950s and 1960s was entirely fueled by white flight, and building a transit line, Cobb County voters feared, would allow Atlanta's Black residents to follow them out to their all-white suburbs. The specter of racial integration would also play a big role in Gwinnett and Clayton Counties' subsequent rejection of MARTA in 1971.

Nor was it exactly clear how MARTA would be paid for. In 1966, Georgia voters had approved a constitutional amendment allowing the state to fund ten percent of the cost of a rapid rail system in Atlanta, but the State Assembly was unwilling to appropriate any money. Two years later, in 1968, voters in MARTA's remaining counties rejected a plan to finance MARTA through an increase in local property taxes. When the property tax funding proposal came around again in 1971, voters in DeKalb and Fulton Counties approved it, but those in Clayton and Gwinnett did not. With property tax financing off the table, Atlanta's mayor Sam Massell proposed that MARTA be financed using the same sales tax surcharge mechanism being used to fund BART in the San Francisco Bay Area. To get the Georgia State Senate to go along with his sales tax proposal, Massell had to agree that no more than 50 percent of any future sales tax revenue would be used to cover operating costs. Although politically necessary, this meant that, in the future, whenever MARTA needed additional money for operating expenses, it would either have to reduce service or raise fares. After getting the Legislature's approval, Massell still had to persuade voters. He did so by promising to cut local bus fares from 60 cents per trip to 15 cents—MARTA would also take over local bus services—and by the narrowest of voter margins, MARTA rail service in Atlanta and Fulton and DeKalb Counties was approved in 1971. MARTA would go ahead after all, but with the 56-mile-long transit system presented to voters in 1971 having been whittled down to 48 miles. Eventually, the federal government would chip in $600 million to help pay for MARTA's roughly $2.5 billion construction cost.

MARTA rail service was organized into two corridors, an east–west corridor connecting the west side of Atlanta with the suburban city of Decatur, and a north–south corridor connecting Brookhaven in north Fulton County to Lakewood in south Fulton County. The two lines would connect downtown at the Five Points station. Construction of the mostly elevated East–West Line began in 1975, with service commencing four years later. Construction of the partially undergrounded North–South Line took longer, concluding in 1984. In 1988, the North–South Line was extended to Hartsfield-Jackson Atlanta International Airport, and in 1996, a new line, connecting Atlanta's Buckhead district north to Atlanta's Perimeter freeway was opened (Hurley 2021).

Atlanta commuters never quite adopted MARTA as their own. After a period of modest passenger growth accompanying MARTA's expansion during the 1980s and early 1990s, average weekday ridership eventually leveled off in the range of 135,000 to 145,000 passengers (MARTA 2012). From 2010 to 2019, MARTA's preferred ridership measure, annual passenger-miles, gradually trended downward from 490 million to 450 million per year (MARTA 2020). Meanwhile, metropolitan Atlanta's population continued growing, increasing from 4.1 million in 2010 to 4.6 million in 2019. Because MARTA's service area did not expand with its region's population, the rail system was unable to capitalize on Atlanta's growth. As a result, Atlanta in 2019 ranked 22nd among large US metro areas in terms of public transportation commute trip mode share.[16] And, at 40 percent, MARTA's farebox-recovery ratio (the share of annual operating expenses paid for out of passenger fares) is among the lowest of any urban transit system in the country.[17]

MARTA's consistently disappointing ridership performance is what happens when transit system design and siting decisions are made by voters rather than qualified transportation planners and engineers. Had MARTA been built as originally envisioned in the mid-1960s, it is likely that Atlanta's present-day settlement and travel patterns might look very different. Whether MARTA's disappointing financial performance would also have improved is more difficult to say.

Washington Metro
If the MARTA situation is what happens when rail transit projects are starved of funding, Metrorail in Washington DC was blessed with the opposite dilemma, having too much money to spend (Schrag 2014). The District of Columbia's compact size, grid-based road system, and relatively high population density meant that it was historically well-suited for rail transit; and indeed, transportation planner and engineers first suggested that Washington DC build its own subway system in 1946 (Goldchain 2017). In 1959, the first formal plan to build a Washington DC subway/commuter rail system was presented to the National Capital Planning Commission (NCPC), the agency charged by Congress with comprehensive park and infrastructure planning for the entire Washington, DC region, including suburban Maryland and Northern Virginia. The NCPC-commissioned plan identified a series of ten radial rail lines all extending outward from downtown Washington, DC. NCPC's chair at the time, renowned urban planner Harlan Bartholomew, responded coolly to the proposal, believing the region would be better served by a network of freeways that could be more readily funded under the Interstate Highway Act. Bartholomew's freeway-centric plan met fierce public opposition and was amended to include a Capital Beltway plus a series of radial rail lines. To implement the hybrid highway–rail plan, Congress created the National Capital Transportation Agency in 1960. Six years later, in 1966, Congress, the District of Columbia, and the legislatures of Virginia and Maryland agreed to co-establish the Washington Metropolitan Area Transit Authority (WMATA),

and to give it the responsibility for planning and operating the proposed Metrorail system. Among Metro's biggest backers was President Lyndon Johnson, who in a 1966 letter to the National Capital Transportation Agency, suggested that they "search worldwide for concepts and ideas that can be used to make the system attractive as well as useful. It should be designed to set an example for the Nation" (Schrag 2014, p. 32)

On March 1, 1968, WMATA unveiled its final plans for the new Metro system.[18] The plan consisted of a 97.2 mile "basic" system of five Metro lines converging at a new MetroCenter station in downtown Washington at 12th Street and G Streets. From there, things moved quickly—there were no environmental impact reporting requirements at the time and Congress could effectively self-certify the project—leading to construction getting underway in December 1969. With so much tunneling involved, progress was initially slow, with the inaugural five miles of Red Line service in downtown Washington, DC, finally opening for service in March of 1976 (Goldchain 2017). Metro service would be extended east to New Carrollton in Prince George County in 1978, west to Arlington County in 1979, north into the District's Maryland suburbs in 1978 and 1984, and south to National Airport in 1983. In October 1990, the federal government provided an addition $1.3 billion to complete the system, bringing its length to 103 miles. Subsequent additions would bring Metro's current length to just over 117 miles.

Building Metro's first five lines would cost billions of dollars, two-thirds of which were to be provided by the federal government under the auspices of the National Capital Transportation Act of 1969. The other third was provided locally by the District's government, and by the Maryland and Virginia counties served by Metro (planitmetro.com 2016). No other US transit agency had ever been given such funding carte blanche by the federal government but then again, no other city had as much tax-exempt property as Washington, DC, or was so beholden to Congress to approve its funding. While Metro was under construction, *The Washington Post* would periodically report that the job was taking longer or costing more than expected, but with the federal government picking up the tab, there was little public outcry.

Metro was always going to be expensive to build (Schrag 2014). At 98 miles in initial length, Metro was one-third longer than BART and had twice as many stations. To avoid Washington DC's mushy, unstable soils, WMATA engineers decided to dig its subway tunnels and stations deep underground. Because they were so far beneath the surface, Metro stations were designed to be tall and wide and to have a common barrel-arch design that would not require supporting columns. Extra-long platforms were required to accommodate the longer rush-hour trains. With most Metro passengers expected to live in the suburbs and arrive at their Metro station by car, large parking lots and parking structures were needed, and WMATA was empowered to condemn as much land as required. Additional land was also going to be needed to facilitate joint development, the process by which WMATA would partner with private developers to build offices, shops, and apartment buildings at suburban Metro stations. All these features cost extra money, which the federal government dutifully provided.

The care its designers took in locating, designing, and building Metro stations to maximize ridership paid off. Daily ridership in 1985, Metro's first full year in service, averaged 375,000 passengers. Over the next 25 years, Metro ridership would grow at an annual rate of nearly three percent per year, peaking at just over 750,000 riders per day in 2008. Since then, ridership has declined steadily because of employment growth outside the Metro service area and reduced service quality, falling to 644,000 average daily riders in 2019.[19] Even at that reduced patronage level, Metro still draws twice as many passengers per mile of system length as BART or MARTA.

During the first decade after Metro's completion, WMATA was regarded as the cream of the crop of US transit agencies for its superior construction management practices, its steady ridership growth, and its successful pursuit of joint development opportunities. In later decades, that leadership seems to have been lost. WMATA's newest metro line, the Silver Line, extending from East Falls Church to Dulles International Airport and now scheduled for completion in 2022, is years behind schedule and hundreds of millions of dollars over budget.[20] Many of WMATA's later joint development projects have also run into difficulties. Since peaking in 2008, daily Metro ridership has declined by 100,000 patrons. With the benefit of hindsight, the Metro experience demonstrates that infrastructure agencies can not only move up the transit learning curve, they can also fall off it.

BART, MARTA and Metro together offer several still-relevant lessons about urban transport megaprojects, especially in America. The first is that it is much more difficult to get people out of their cars and onto transit than forecasting models might suggest. It took years for BART and Metro to reach their ridership projections and MARTA never did. The second is that the more technically complex a project, the greater its planning and construction challenges, and the more expensive and time-consuming it is likely to be. BART, MARTA and Metro were far more advanced in terms of automation and train control technologies than other transit systems of their day, all of which added to their construction costs and testing times. Third, while there may be certain engineering and construction scale economies involved in building full transit systems instead of individual lines, realizing these benefits in the real world can be problematic. Finally, tunneling projects, especially when undertaken in cities, are always more complicated, time-consuming and expensive than expected. Beyond specific lessons, BART, MARTA and Metro initiated a process of reconsidering the role of megaprojects in America. In contrast to the prosperous and egalitarian future represented by the Hoover Dam and Interstate Highway system, projects such as BART, MARTA and Metro were more limited and technocratic in their ambitions—less about creating new opportunities and more about saving a few minutes of travel time for the already well off.

Battery Park City

Located at the southwestern tip of Manhattan, Battery Park City (BPC) is the largest downtown master-planned residential community in the United States and was the first to exceed the $1 billion megaproject cost threshold. Built atop 92 acres of landfill excavated during construction of the World Trade Center, Battery Park City is currently home to roughly 10,000 residents.[21] BPC was master-planned and initially financed by the Battery Park City Authority (BPCA), one of the several public development authorities created by the New York State Legislature in the late-1960s to promote new development in New York's older cities.

As was common practice for the time, BPC's development began with the creation of a detailed master plan intended to guide all future construction activity (Gordon 2012). The initial Battery Park City Master Plan, issued in April 1969, set forth plans to develop 7.2 million square feet of residential space (approximately 3,500 dwelling units) and 9.3 million square feet of commercial space (Figure 2.1). In an unheard-of luxury for the time, it also set aside 40 percent of the BPC site for parks and open space. Reflecting the social planning principles of the day, BPC was to include a diversity of family types and income groups. As such, each residential building was to include a mix of market-rate and affordable apartments, with the market-rate units helping subsidize the affordable ones.

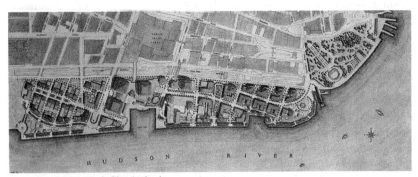

Source: Battery Park City Authority.

Figure 2.1   *1969 Battery Park City master plan diagram showing residential, commercial and public space uses*

Amidst questions about the project's proposed $1.1 billion cost and who would manage the development process on a day-to-day basis, the BPCA in 1972 named New York City real estate magnate Harry B. Helmsley to be BPC's master developer. It also arranged for the issuance of $200 million of New York State bonds to fund the first phase of BPC construction. BPCA's efforts proved ill-timed. By the time building construction was ready to begin, New York City was in the middle of the worst fiscal crisis in its history. Effectively bankrupt, New York City was unable to borrow the funds needed to provide its share of BPC funding. By the end of 1980, despite the BPCA having adopted a new and more developer-friendly master plan (Alexander Cooper and Associates 1979), just one of BPC's two-dozen planned apartment buildings was under construction and BPC bondholders were beginning to worry whether they would be repaid.

In April 1981, having terminated its agreement with Harry Helmsley, the New York State Development Corporation (the parent agency to the BPC) issued a new request for residential development proposals, ultimately selecting six companies to develop 1,800 units. That same year, the BPCA contracted with Canadian developer Olympia and York to begin construction of BPC's office project piece, to be known as World Financial Center.

By 1984, with New York City having finally emerged from state receivership and its economy rebounding, residential construction at BPC finally began to pick up. BPC added 13 new residential building during the 1980s and six more during the 1990s.[22] As an additional attraction to families, Stuyvesant High School, one of New York City's highest-performing public high schools, opened its new state-of-the art campus at BPC in 1992. By 2005, apart from a few remaining commercial sites on West Street, the development of BPC was effectively complete. Bad luck struck again on September 11, 2001, when the collapse of the nearby World Trade Center significantly damaged the World Financial Center and forced all BPC residents to evacuate their homes. Most chose to return when they could, and by 2003, BPC had fully recovered. As if to validate BPC's success, Goldman Sachs moved its world headquarters there in 2009.

From conception to build-out, BPC took 40 years to complete. During its first ten years, BPC had to contend with a series of institutional and fiscal problems not of its making, so counting just the years between 1978 and 2008, BPC's 30-years-to-full-build-out is not unusual by the standards of large master-planned communities. Since BPCA regained complete control of Battery Park City's development process in 1981, it has generally done a creditable job managing BPC's development schedule and finances—helped along of course by the boom in Manhattan real estate values.

On a less positive note, the original vision of BPC as a mixed-income community never came to pass. In 2017, according to the Census Bureau, the median income of BPC households stood at $126,771, exactly double the estimate for New York City. Just nine percent of BPC residents lived in poverty in 2017, compared with 14 percent in Manhattan and 20 percent in New York City. In 2019, Manhattan zip code 10282, which includes BPC, was determined to be the most expensive rental neighborhood in the country, with its renters paying an average monthly rent of $6,211.[23]

With so much high-valued real estate, BPC has proven to be a financial boon for New York City. Like other public benefit corporations, BPCA is exempt from paying city property taxes, but under the terms of a 1989 agreement, BPCA provides roughly $200 million per year to New York City in the form of payments-in-lieu-of-taxes.[24]

Battery Park City has in many ways proven to a megaproject success, from the quality of its master plans and open spaces, to the mix and success of its building types, to the revenues it raises for New York City, to its most recent efforts to become more sustainable. Whether BPC's success serves as a model for other urban development megaprojects requires determining how much of that success was due to the efforts of its creators and sponsors, and how much was a function of favorable timing and location.

The Big Dig and the End of an Era

Completed ten years behind schedule at a cost more than double what was promised, Boston's Central Artery and Tunnel Project (aka "The Big Dig") is frequently cited as the project that brought the megaproject era in America to a final close (Altshuler and Luberoff 2004). The Big Dig's problems were decades in the making. Like many other older American cities, Boston had made the mistake in the 1950s of building a multi-lane urban freeway right through the center of its downtown core. Completed in 1959, the Central Artery was a 3.2 mile elevated highway that connected Interstate 93 as it approached Boston from the south, to the Tobin Bridge which connected Boston to Charleston in the north. Like most urban freeways built to reduce congestion, the Central Artery had the opposite effect, turning central Boston into a sea of cars, undermining the city's established commuter rail services, and dividing Boston's historic Haymarket district area from the equally his-toric North End.

The idea of replacing the prematurely-aging Central Artery elevated struc-ture with an underground tunnel was first raised by Boston area transportation planners in the early-1970s as part of a re-evaluation of previously-approved highway projects (Commonwealth of Massachusetts 2021). With no money to pay for it, the idea was put on hold, only to be resurrected in 1978 by Massachusetts Governor Michael Dukakis as part of an even grander proposal to build a third harbor tunnel connecting Boston's downtown to its airport.

Planning for the combined Central Artery Depression/Third Harbor Tunnel project continued intermittently for another decade until 1987 when Congress finally approved partial federal funding of the $2.8 billion project. Citing what he regarded as its extreme expense and minimal benefits, President Ronald Reagan promptly vetoed the project. It would take another four years for Congress to re-approve funding, enabling construction to finally begin in 1991 (Figure 2.2). By that time, the Big Dig's cost had increased from $2.8 to $5.8 billion.

The Big Dig ran into coordination and technical problems right from the start. Because of its enormous size, the project was divided into dozens of smaller pieces, each to be undertaken by a different contractor (Greiman 2013). Presenting additional engineering and logistical problems, the new tunnel was to be constructed under the original elevated structure even as the highway remained in service. To make matters worse, the new tunnel was plagued by constant saltwater leaks from the adjacent Boston Bay.[25] With construction costs escalating by the day, the Big Dig's state government managers pointed accusatory fingers at project contractors for not having properly budgeted for contingencies. The contractors responded that the fault lay with the state, which they alleged had under-budgeted the project from its outset. In a March 2001 report to the Massachusetts Treasurer, State Inspector General Robert Cerasoli found fault with both parties, concluding that state officials had deliberately and systematically understated the Big Dig's true costs;[26] and that the project's two lead contractors, Bechtel and Parsons Brinkerhoff, had not pursued reasonable measures to control costs (Haynes 2008).

Concerns that the Big Dig had been grossly mismanaged went far beyond Boston. Although little eventually came of it, in 2001, the Securities and Exchange Commission launched an investigation into whether Massachusetts officials deliberately misled bond buyers when they failed to identify the Big Dig's potential liabilities in the bond prospectus.[27] In Washington, DC, the Federal Highway Administration issued a series of directives to its regional offices, ordering them to keep a closer eye on project spending in the wake of the Big Dig's cost overruns (Wood 2001).

In the end, there was nothing to do but finish the project. In January 2003, the new tunnel under Boston Harbor, now named for Boston Red Sox slugger Ted Williams, opened to traffic. Two months later in March 2003, the depressed Central Artery Tunnel's northbound lanes opened, followed in December 2003 by its southbound lanes. Final demolition of the original Central Artery elevated structure was completed in 2004.

Sadly, this was not the end of the Big Dig's troubled saga. In July 2006, four concrete ceiling panels and debris weighing 26 tons fell on a car entering the Ted Williams Tunnel from a northbound Central Artery ramp. The accident killed the car's passenger and fatally injured its driver. After a lengthy inves-

tigation, the National Transportation Safety Board concluded that the epoxy
used to hold the ceiling panels in place during construction was inappropriate
for permanent use.[28] In a 2007 court decision, the Big Dig's principal contractors agreed to pay more than $450 million to settle the state's construction
quality lawsuits against them and to compensate the family of the victims of
the ceiling's collapse.[29]

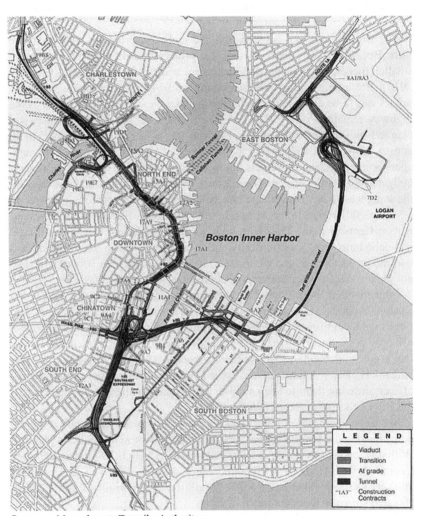

Source: Massachusetts Turnpike Authority.

Figure 2.2   Boston Big Dig project map

When finally completed in December 2007, the Big Dig was estimated to have cost $14.8 billion.[30] Seventy percent of this amount was paid for by the Federal Highway Administration with the remaining 30 percent supplied by Massachusetts taxpayers. In a subsequent 2012 audit, Massachusetts officials listed the final cost of the Big Dig project, including interest and litigation costs, at $24.3 billion, making it the most expensive single highway project in US history.[31]

What had started a century earlier at the Panama Canal with a celebration of America's unparalleled megaproject prowess ended in Boston in 2012 with an admission that when it came to building very large transportation projects, America had become the gang that couldn't shoot straight.

MEGAPROJECTS GO GLOBAL, 1964–2016

Within the US, the disappointing performance of projects such as BART and MARTA, coupled with the rise of the environmental movement and worsening inflation, all contributed to a gradual disillusionment with expensive megaprojects. Among the first things US President Jimmy Carter did upon taking office in January 1977 was to summarily kill 18 major dam and water projects then undergoing final environmental reviews. According to a report in the *New York Times*, Carter was particularly incensed about what his press secretary Jody Powell called the "sloppiness and phony figures" used by Army Corps of Engineers to justify dam projects.[32]

In many ways, Carter was just reflecting the tenor of the times, at least in the United States. Stagflation, the combination of slow economic growth and high inflation, had taken persistent hold in the US, so unless they could get the economy moving again, megaprojects were regarded as grandiose and wasteful. In 1973, German-born British economist E.F. Schumacher had published *Small is Beautiful: A Study of Economics as if People Mattered*, a collection of his essays advancing the argument that small, human-centered technologies and projects were superior to the mainstream view that "bigger is better." *Small is Beautiful* never quite became a bestseller, but in an era before social media, it generated its full share of viral quotes including, "Any intelligent fool can make things bigger, more complex, and more violent. It takes a touch of genius—and a lot of courage—to move in the opposite direction." Schumacher's critiques mirrored those of New York City writer Jane Jacobs, whose 1961 book, *The Death and Life of Great American Cities*, had warned that the deadening combination of large-scale highway and redevelopment projects was suffocating the life out of America's once dynamic cities.

A different trend was emerging outside the United States: megaprojects were gaining in popularity. Part of this was just a matter of economics. As countries in Europe and Asia emerged from the 20-year shadow of World

War II, many found they now had the financial capability to take on large infrastructure projects. Having long taken a back seat to the United States technologically and logistically, many were also eager to show off advances in their technical and engineering prowess.

The Delta Works (The Netherlands, 1958)

Often called one of the seven engineering wonders of the modern world, the Deltawerken, or Delta Works, is a series of 13 dams and storm surge barriers intended to keep the North Sea from flooding the Netherlands' Zeeland Province during severe coastal storms (Deltawerken online 2021) (Figure 2.3). The Delta Works was undertaken by the Dutch government in the aftermath of the North Sea storm of February 1, 1953, in which a combination of high tides, severe winds and strong waves led to massive dike failures, causing 1,836 deaths and 150,000 hectares of low-lying coastal land to be inundated with salt water. The response of the Dutch government to this tragedy was to create a task force (i.e., the Delta Committee) to recommend how flood-vulnerable areas along the North Sea could be better protected. The task force published five study reports, culminating in a recommendation that the Dutch government undertake construction of an elaborate series of dams, seawalls, and barriers to effectively close the Hartingvliet, Brouwershavense Gat and Eastern Scheldt River estuaries.

The largest of the 13 Delta Works projects is the 9-km-long Oosterscheldekering barrier located at the mouth of the Schelde River between Schouwen-Duiveland and Noord-Beveland islands. Originally proposed as a seawall that would have completely cut off the Schelde River estuary from the North Sea, public protests over the barrier's adverse effects on fishing and marine life led the government to change the barrier's design to include 62 operable sluice gate doors. During normal times, the doors remain open to allow salt water to replenish the estuary, but when storm surge levels rise above three meters, they can be quickly lowered into place. Since entering service in 1986, the Oosterscheldekering's storm gates have been closed 27 times.[33] A second Delta Works project, the Maeslantkering, consists of two 210-meter pivoting gates located at the entrance to Rotterdam Harbor. Completed in 1997, the Maeslantkering is one of the largest moving structures on Earth. Although it uses a different design, the Maeslantkering was the inspiration for the Thames Barrier which protects London from storm surges extending up the Thames River.

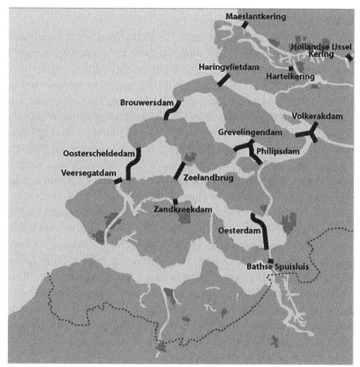

Source: Delta Works Commission.

Figure 2.3   *The Netherlands' Delta Works dam and storm surge barrier diagram*

When first approved by the Dutch Parliament in 1958, the Delta Works program was projected to be completed in 25 years and to cost 3.3 billion Dutch guilders (US$1.7 billion)—an amount then equivalent to 20 percent of Dutch GDP. Both estimates were optimistic. When the Delta Works program was finally completed in 1997, the Dutch government put its cumulative cost at 8.2 billion guilder (US$4 billion). This was later increased to 9 billion guilder (US$5 billion) to include the cost of related dike-strengthening projects necessitated by the construction of Delta Works barriers.[34] Allowing for changes to the Delta Works' scope of work—most notably the addition of operable storm gates to the Oosterscheldekering barrier—government auditors estimate the entire project to have exceeded its original cost estimates by between 15 and 30 percent. To pay for the Delta Works project, the Dutch government established a separate Delta Fund initially funded by Dutch taxpayers and a 400 million guilder contribution from the Marshall Plan. In later years, the

Delta Works was also funded out of tax revenues from offshore natural gas discoveries.

Judged solely by its original purpose, the Delta Works was hugely success-ful. Since its 1997 completion, the threat to lives and property posed by North Sea storm surges has been effectively eliminated. In addition, the Delta Works has made it possible for Dutch water quality managers to increase the volume of freshwater provided to farmers and to better regulate salt and pollution concentrations in Zeeland's estuaries. Roads built atop Delta Works barriers provide residents of Zeeland's long-isolated outer islands with ready access to the rest of the country.[35] Perhaps most important, the engineering and environ-mental knowledge gained during the Delta Works' planning and construction process has put the Netherlands at the forefront of global efforts to mitigate the effects of sea level rise caused by climate change.

Still, times and expectations change. Looking back, many researchers believe greater attention should have been paid to the Delta Works' environmental effects, and that if it had, natural alternatives to building ecologically-disruptive permanent barriers might have been considered.[36] Indeed, a 2008 revision to the government's ongoing Delta Program based on a report entitled "Room for the Rivers" advocated shifting from a strategy of using constructed barriers to contain storm surges to one of allowing controlled overflows in order restore degraded estuaries and fish and bird habitats. Subsequent studies have called for further strengthening sea and river dikes to accommodate the increased inundation threats posed by climate change.[37]

The Shinkansen Bullet Train (Japan, 1964)

The project that broke what was the US's 20th century megaproject monopoly was the Japanese bullet train. Known in Japan as the Shinkansen (or "new main line"), the first bullet trains could operate at sustained speeds of 240 kilo-meters per hour (kph), which was twice the speed of the fastest passenger trains then operating in Europe.[38] Japan's first bullet train line, the 515 km Tōkaidō Shinkansen Line connecting Tokyo, Nagoya and Osaka entered passenger service on October 1, 1964, just in time for the Tokyo Olympics.

The possibility of passenger trains that could travel faster than 200 kph was first presented by the Japanese Ministry of Railroads in the early 1930s, but it wasn't until the pre-Shinkansen Tōkaidō Line began operating at full capacity in the mid-1950s that the idea was given serious consideration (Hood 2006). Presaging what was to come, in 1957, Japan's Odakyu Electric Railway intro-duced its 90 mph 3000-series SE Romancecar train into regular commercial service. The Romancecar would later become the basis for the design of the first Shinkansen train, to be known as the 0 series (Figure 2.4).

Source: Japan National Railways.

Figure 2.4   Shinkansen Type 0 Prototype

Technical issues aside, there were many who believed that building an entirely new high-speed rail system—Japan's existing narrow-gauge railroads could not accommodate train speeds higher than 150 kph—would be a costly dead end. According to government transportation planners in the US, the future of long-distance inter-city travel belonged to roads and airplanes; passenger trains were the technology of the past. Shinji Sogō, President of Japanese National Railways (JNR), believed differently. Japan's major cities were closer together than those in the US, and combining door-to-door travel times with service frequency, high-speed trains beat airplanes every time. Sogo's view was convincing to a majority of the Japanese Parliament, which, in December 1958, approved funding for the first segment of the Tōkaidō Shinkansen Line between Tokyo and Osaka (Smith 2003). Construction of the new line began six months later. Funding for the new line, estimated at the time to cost nearly 200 billion yen (roughly $10 billion in 2020 US dollars), took the form of a government loan, sales of JNR bonds, and a low-interest loan of US$80 million from the World Bank. This would prove to be a gross underestimate, and by the time construction was completed in 1964, the Tōkaidō Line's cost had increased to 400 billion yen (Smith 2003).

Once service began, the new line proved an immediate success, reaching the 100 million passenger ridership mark in less than three years, well ahead of projections. With ridership still growing, the original 10-car Shinkansen trains were upgraded to 16-car trains in 1970, and in 1976, passenger ridership on the Tōkaidō Line exceeded one billion. The Tōkaidō Shinkansen's ridership success prompted its extension from Osaka to Fukuoka in 1975, bringing its length to over a thousand kilometers. It also led to the construction of two entirely new Shinkansen lines, the 675 km Tohoku Line, connecting Tokyo to Aomori, and the 270 km Joetsu Line connecting Tokyo to Nigata (Hood 2006).

Ridership success did not equate to financial success however, and by the early 1980s, JNR was teetering on the edge of insolvency, largely due to the cost of servicing its Shinkansen debt (Kim and Huang 2021). In 1987, with its subsidies from the Japanese Government exceeding ¥600 billion (US$6 billion), JNR was privatized, and its assets distributed among three regional operating companies. The most profitable Shinkansen trunk-line between Tokyo and Osaka was reorganized as JR Central, while the Osaka-to-Hakata Line was reorganized as JR West. The Tohoku and Joetsu Shinkansen Lines were reconstituted as JR East. Privatization brought a reduction in JNR's total workforce from 400,000 in 1980 to 191,000 in 1994, which enabled the three new regional operating companies to gradually return to profitability. In 1997, JR East and JR West jointly opened the new 345 km Hokuriku Shinkansen Line connecting Tokyo with Kanazawa in Japan's Hokuriku region. The opening of two additional Shinkansen Lines, the 257 km Kyushu Line in 2004, and the 149 km Hokkaido Line in 2016 brought the length of the Japanese Shinkansen system to its current total of 2,765 kilometers, giving Japan what is now the third-longest high-speed rail network after China and Spain. In 2018, Japan's seven Shinkansen lines carried 436 million passengers.[39]

Mexico City Metro (Mexico, 1969)

Building a new subway or metro system is so expensive that for much of the 20th century only wealthy or prestige-conscious capital cities could afford to do so. That calculus changed in 1969, when Mexico City opened its first subway line.

Mexico in the 1960s was hardly wealthy. Thanks to three decades of uninterrupted one-party rule and an inward-looking economic development policy, Mexico's per capita GDP in 1965 was just $495, one-ninth the level of its northern neighbor.[40] As Mexico's capital and largest city, Mexico City was much richer than the rest of the country, causing it to attract a continuous flow of rural migrants. With almost no planning controls in place, residential and commercial development occurred in a disorganized fashion, resulting in the highest levels of daily road congestion anywhere in the western hemisphere. Traffic congestion was so bad in Mexico City's central area that walking was often faster than driving. Urban planners had talked about building a metro system in Mexico City since the mid-1950s, but with no money budgeted to do so, and the knowledge that transit fares would be too high for most Mexico City workers, little had come of the idea.[41]

The push for Mexico City to build its own metro system is credited to Bernardo Quintana, the Mexican-born founder and politically-connected CEO of ICA (Ingenieros de Civiles Associators), Mexico's largest civil engineering company (Ulin 2017). Reviewing a plan by officials at UNAM, the National Autonomous University of Mexico, to build a monorail line serving UNAM students, Quintana proposed instead that city officials build a multi-line metro system to serve the entire city. To move his proposal along, Quintana had ICA prepare a detailed report chronicling the worsening problems of Mexico City's outmoded bus system and comparing the pros and cons of different metro systems around the world. Published in 1958, ICA's report concluded that there was no combination of bus service improvements that could keep pace with Mexico City's rapid population growth, and that the only worthwhile transit investment was a high-capacity heavy-rail subway system. ICA's efforts were not entirely publicly-motivated: given its experience and political connections, should a metro system be approved, ICA was likely to be awarded a significant share of the construction contracts (Ulin 2017, p. 6).

Quintana and ICA's proposal drew immediate condemnation from Mexico City's powerful pro-union mayor, Ernesto P. Uruchurtu, who claimed that a subway would siphon off bus ridership and cause bus drivers—almost all of whom were union members and strong Uruchurtu supporters—to lose their jobs. Worse, Uruchurtu claimed, instead of making it easier for suburban workers to travel downtown, a subway would have the opposite effect, encouraging businesses to leave Mexico City's downtown area for less expensive locations at the city's periphery. Uruchurtu also warned that a subway would cause already-soaring housing prices and rents in the city center area to rise even further, further pricing out middle-class families and small businesses (Ulin 2017, p. 7). Uruchurtu's worries, while self-serving, were hardly baseless, and when the Director of the Parisian Metro Authority—with which ICA had a business relationship—offered to provide an independent feasibility analysis of a potential Mexico City subway system, the mayor politely turned him down.

As with all politics in Mexico, what is national is local and vice versa. Having seized control of the ruling Institutional Revolutionary Party (PRI) prior to Mexico's 1964 presidential elections, Mexico City's business leaders supported the presidential candidacy of former Mexican Interior Minister Gustavo Díaz Ordaz, who had successfully negotiated Mexico City's bid for the upcoming Olympics. Díaz Ordaz won handily and upon assuming office in December 1964, directly challenged Mayor Uruchurtu's anti-metro stance, arguing that a working metro system was essential to Mexico City's Olympic hosting responsibilities (Ulin 2017, p. 8). President Díaz Ordaz's pro-metro argument was further bolstered when a strike by the Mexico City's 1,700 bus drivers in July 1965 paralyzed the city. Having splintered Uruchurtu's political coalition, President Díaz Ordaz pushed to have him removed as mayor. Under duress, Mayor Uruchurtu resigned his office on September 16, 1966, and was replaced by PRI-loyalist Alfonso Corona del Ronal, who soon announced that his administration would consider ICA's Metro proposal for funding. Without missing a beat, ICA announced it would be establishing a new subsidiary to manage all Metro-related design and planning activities (Ulin 2017, p. 9).

With Mexico's President and Mexico City's mayor both strongly in support of building the metro system, the project moved swiftly ahead. With an estimated price tag of around 2.5 billion pesos (roughly equivalent to US$850 million today), the project would require significant public and private sector financing. In addition to providing government grants, the Mexican government purchased more than 1.6 billion pesos in loans from private banks and the French government (Ulin 2017, p. 10). These funds were channeled toward contracts with ICA, which, as expected, had been granted exclusive planning and construction rights on the project. The official dedication ceremony for Mexico City's new metro system was held on June 19, 1967, less than a year after Mayor Uruchurtu's resignation. Two years later, on September 4, 1969, an orange metro train made the inaugural trip between Metro Line 1's Zaragoza and Insurgentes stations.

From a single-line system in 1969, Mexico City's Metro expanded to three lines by the end of 1970, to seven lines by 1984, and to ten lines by 1995.[42] By 2015, Mexico City's metro system included 12 lines, 195 stations, and 226 kilometers of steel-wheel and rubber-tired tracks, making it the second largest metro system in North America after New York's. With a single-ticket fare of just five Mexican pesos (about $0.25), it is also among the least expensive metro systems in the world to ride. This combination of cheap fares and a large service area has made metro service in Mexico City extremely popular. With nearly 1.7 billion passengers in 2019, Mexico City's metro system was the tenth busiest in the world.[43] Still, even with all its investments in transit service and a daily public transportation mode share of nearly 60 percent,[44] Mexico City continues to be one of the world's most congested cities.

TGV—Très à Grande Vitesse (France, 1981)

Japan built its high-speed rail (HSR) system independently and line by line. France planned its HSR system as a national network, intending to connect it to similar networks in other countries. The notion that France should build a national HSR system was first raised in the 1964, just after Japan unveiled its inaugural Shinkansen line. Having fully recovered from World War II, France was eager to reclaim its leadership role among European nations, and one way of doing so was to showcase its engineering expertise. True, the Japanese had beaten the French out of the HSR gate, but Japan had chosen to favor HSR at the expense of expanding air service and building highways. If there was a path by which HSR could compete with air and long-distance car travel on its own merits, France would find it. For the French government, HSR was to be a core national initiative rather than just another infrastructure project.

Originally, France's TGV (Très Grande Vitesse, or very high-speed) trains were to be powered by gas turbines rather than electricity (TGVWeb 2021). Gas turbines were well known for their small packaging, good power-to-weight ratio, and ability to deliver full power over an extended period, and the first TGV prototype developed by SNCF, the French national railway company, was indeed gas turbine powered. The decision to use electric power instead was made in the aftermath of the 1973 Arab Oil Embargo—France was almost totally dependent on imported oil for its gasoline supplies—and was also a good fit with the country's growing use of nuclear power to provide electricity. Nicknamed Zébulon, the first electricity-powered TGV prototype was completed in 1974, and following nearly a million kilometers of testing, was approved for full-scale production by the French train manufacturer, Alstom, in 1976.

With a working HSR train technology now in hand, the immediate question became which inter-city routes would be provided with TGV service first. Rather than build the first TGV line from Paris to France's second largest city, Marseille, the decision was made to stop at Lyon, a city half the size of Marseille, but one with tighter historical and economic linkages to Paris (Streeter 1993). After five years of construction, the 847 km Sud-Est LGV (Ligne a Grand Vitesse) line connecting Paris' Gare Lyon Station to Lyon via intermediate stops at Le Creusot and Macon opened for service on September 22, 1981. Traveling at an average speed of 260 kph (162 mph), the one-way trip took just two hours and 40 minutes. At the insistence of France's Socialist Party President, Francois Mitterrand, there was just one class of service and one fare (Meunier 2002). The route quickly became popular with travelers, attracting 6.1 million passengers in its first full year of operation. The entire Sud-Est TGV/LGV project, including land purchases, track construction, power and signaling systems and trainsets cost 13.8 billion French francs, or about US$4.7 billion in 2020 dollars (Arduin and Ni 2005).

Additional TGV routes were added from Paris to Tours in 1990, from Paris to Lille (where it would later connect to Eurostar service to London via the Channel Tunnel) in 1993, from Lyon to Marseille in 2001, and from Paris to Nancy in 2007. By 2010, France's five major TGV lines totaled 1,780 km in length (Figure 2.5). Since then, new line extensions completed in 2016 and 2017 have increased TGV network length to 2,800 km. TGV construction costs have increased along with the number of new lines. According to SYSTRA, SNCF's engineering arm, the construction cost of the initial Paris-to-Lyon line completed in 1981 was about US$4 million per kilometer. By the time the LGV line connecting Lyon to Marseille opened in 2001, construction costs were in the range of US$10 million to US$15 million per kilometer (Arduin and Ni 2005).

Source: aboutFrance.com

Figure 2.5   France's 2020 TGV system map

Until 2010, TGV patronage rose steadily with system length, reaching 30 million annual riders in 1990, 80 million in 2000, and 122 million in 2009.[45] Ridership growth has since moderated, leading French President Emmanuel Macron in 2017 to announce that his government would reassess future LGV construction plans. Even with an overall rail passenger market share of 10 percent,[46] the TGV system has never operated at a profit, and TGV-related financial losses have put its government-owned operator, SNCF, deeply in debt. To keep SNCF afloat, the French government in 2018 announced that it would directly assume €35 billion of SNCF's €47 billion debt load.[47] Worsening SNCF's debt problems, in 2021 it announced that it was committed to replacing its existing TGV rolling stock with newer trains able to accommodate 20 percent more passengers while using 20 percent less electricity.[48] Despite its ongoing financial difficulties, France's TGV system is widely regarded within France and across Europe as a success (Vickerman 1997). In France, TGV is seen as evidence that France will continue to be a global innovator. In Europe, TGV is venerated as the model for Europe's other HSR lines and networks, including Germany's InterCityExpress (ICE) system, Spain's AVE system, and the UK's cross-Channel Eurostar service.

Canary Wharf (United Kingdom, 1991)

The full significance of Canary Wharf is explored in greater detail in Chapter 12. For historical purposes, it is important to note that Canary Wharf was the first attempt by the United Kingdom or any other European country to undertake a very large-scale commercial regeneration project using a developer-led public–private partnership approach. As noted in the Battery Park case, public–private redevelopment partnerships had been in place in the US since the early 1970s. And in Europe, public sector agencies had been trying, mostly unsuccessfully, to develop business-based regeneration districts since the establishment of La Defense in Paris in 1958. What made Canary Wharf unique was that, instead of the usual approach of a city government first creating a master plan and then subsidizing developers to implement it, Canary Wharf's government sponsor, the London Docklands Development Corporation (LDDC), was willing to offer potential developers complete planning control. This was not the preferred model when London area local governments first assumed redevelopment control of the Docklands areas in the mid-1970s, but after years of failed revitalization efforts, it was very much the model envisioned by Environment Minister Michael Heseltine, when, in 1981, he rammed through Parliament legislation, creating the LDDC (Oc and Tiesdell 1991; Brownill 1999)

Having endorsed a proposal by an American financier and developer to redevelop the Docklands into back-office space for the City of London's banks and financial institutions, Heseltine and the LDDC were shaken when the Americans pulled out of the deal in 1985 (Gordon 2001). Only the personal appeal of Prime Minister Thatcher to Canadian businessman Paul Reichmann to take over the stalled project succeeded in putting it back on track. A risk taker who, through his family-owned real estate company, Olympia and York, had successfully developed First Canadian Place in Toronto in the 1970s and then the World Financial Center in New York City in the early 1980s, Reichmann was intrigued by the prospect of building an entirely new financial district entirely on speculation. One Canada Place, Olympia and York's inaugural Canary Wharf project, was completed in 1991 at a cost of £624 million (US$840 million), an amount that did not include the company's contributions to completing the Docklands Light Rail system or extending the Jubilee Underground Line from central London to Canary Wharf. Olympia and York's high-stakes gamble ultimately failed when the British economy was plunged into a deep recession just as One Canada Place was opening, but not before establishing the usefulness of the developer-led megaproject regeneration model. Canary Wharf itself eventually recovered and, today, with more than 16 million square feet of office space, 300 shops and restaurants, and a growing supply of housing, is the foremost example of how to create a new central business district in a major world city.[49]

The Channel Tunnel (United Kingdom, 1994)

Most megaprojects face design and engineering challenges or financing challenges or construction challenges. The 31.3 mile English Channel Tunnel (or "Chunnel") connecting Folkestone, England to Coquelles, France faced all three. Completed in May 1994, the Chunnel is the third-longest tunnel in the world, behind the 33.5 mile Seikan tunnel under the Tsuguru Strait in Japan and the 35.4 mile Gotthard Base Tunnel under the Swiss Alps.

Proposals to build an undersea tunnel connecting Britain and France had been around since the early 1800s, but until the 1930s were dismissed as either technically infeasible or too expensive (Gourvish 2006). Later supporters of the idea included Winston Churchill, who wrote a 1936 editorial for the *London Daily Mail* entitled "Why Not A Channel Tunnel?" Churchill's enthusiasm notwithstanding, it wasn't until a detailed geological survey was completed in 1964 that Britain and France agreed to collaborate on preparing tunnel construction plans. After ten years of planning studies, construction of a dual-bore rail tunnel carrying car and truck shuttle wagons got underway in 1974 but was cancelled by Britain's Labour Government a year later amidst concerns over rising costs.

Prime Minister Margaret Thatcher, whose Conservative Government took office in 1979, was willing to support restarting the tunnel project, but only if could be privately financed. Thatcher and French President François Mitterrand agreed to create a joint Franco-British committee to study the feasibility of a privately-financed tunnel, and when the committee concluded its work in 1982, it recommended building a conventional train tunnel capable of accommodating car and truck shuttles. In April 1985, the two countries invited would-be project sponsors to submit preliminary design and engineering proposals, eventually shortlisting four of them (Wilson and Spick 1994, pp. 14–21):

- Channel Tunnel, a rail tunnel backed by the Channel Tunnel Group/ France–Manche (CTG/FM), a consortium of 15 French and English banks and construction companies.
- Eurobridge, a 35 km bridge–tunnel hybrid made up of a series of suspension bridge spans and an undersea tunnel.
- Euroroute, a 21 km tunnel between two artificial islands connected to Britain and France by bridges: and,
- Channel Expressway, two large-diameter road tunnels with mid-channel ventilation towers.

The Channel Tunnel proposal was judged to be the least disruptive to shipping and the environment as well as the most financeable, and in January 1986, was selected to move ahead with construction. First however, Great Britain and France would each have to bless the deal. In France, which had a tradition of government-financed transportation infrastructure investments, including, most notably, the TGV, the Channel Tunnel proposal enjoyed broad support and quickly gained unanimous approval. In Britain, there was more debate about how exactly the project would be funded, and whether the British Government might have to pick up the pieces if the project went under. Ultimately, Parliament did approve the project, but only after gaining the Government's guarantee that the cross-Channel high-speed rail service, later known as HS1, would continue from Folkestone all the way to London.

The Chunnel—by 1987, everyone was calling it that—was to be delivered using a build-own-operate-transfer (BOOT) arrangement under which TransManche Link (TML), a consortium of UK and French construction companies, would design and build the tunnel, and then hand it over to Eurotunnel, a separate consortium of banks and investors who would finance and own it (Grant 1997). As security for its investment, Eurotunnel would be given an exclusive 55-year rail operating concession, later extended to 65 years. Eurotunnel wouldn't operate any trains but would instead provide British Rail and SNCF with the opportunity to use half the Chunnel's train capacity in exchange for a guaranteed share of future passenger revenues. The financing package that held the deal together was of unprecedented complexity. CTG/

FM, the bi-national consortium that had won the original contract, agreed to provide £45 million in initial equity, which it used to attract additional private and institutional investments totaling £206 million. An additional £770 million was to be raised through a public share offering. Altogether, private investment in the Chunnel totaled £2.6 billion.

With the necessary financing guarantees in place, digging commenced on the British side in December 1987 and on the French side in February 1988. Digging the two parallel rail tunnels and central service tunnel required the use of 11 tunnel boring machines (TBMs), more than had ever been used on a single project before. On December 1, 1990, three years after digging operations began, Graham Fagg from the English side and Phillippe Cozette from the French side reached through a pilot hole to officially join the English and French tunnels. Amazingly, despite having been started 30 miles apart, the two tunnels' centers were off by just 36.2 centimeters, or a bit more than a foot. Even with tunneling operations concluded, it would be another three and half years of installing and testing train equipment before rail service could begin.

When jointly dedicated by Queen Elizabeth and French President François Mitterrand on May 6, 1994, the Chunnel was 11 months late. A later audit revealed the chief cause of the delay to be a series of work slowdowns initiated in response to late construction payments by Eurotunnel and its investors. Freight service through the Channel Tunnel began on June 1, 1994, followed by Eurostar passenger service five months later.

Originally projected to cost £4.6 billion when approved in 1986, the Chunnel ended up costing £10.1 billion, a 122 percent cost increase (Goldsmith and Boeuf 2019). Less than a third of the £5.5 billion cost overrun was due to construction cost increases. Instead, most of the increase was the result of delay-related increases in interest charges and financing costs. Financed during a period of high interest rates, the extra time it took the complete the Chunnel and the HS1 high-speed rail link between Folkestone and London eventually proved devastating to the project's financial performance. For Eurotunnel and its investors, the Chunnel was an immediate financial disaster, generating four years of losses that resulted in a top-to-bottom financial restructuring in 1998. Thanks to Margaret Thatcher's insistence that the Chunnel be privately financed, English taxpayers were generally unaffected by the Chunnel's financial difficulties.

More than 25 years after it opened, opinions differ as regards the Channel Tunnel's true benefits (*The Economist* 2014). According to Getlink, the Chunnel's current operator, more than 450 million passengers have used it to travel between England and France since 1994.[50] Another 60 million cars and 30 million trucks have used the Chunnel's vehicle shuttle service, known as Le Shuttle. According to a 2017 economic analysis by the accounting firm of EY, formerly Ernst & Young, the Chunnel facilitated trade worth €138 billion between Europe and the UK in 2016, or about 27 percent of pre-Brexit UK–European trade (EY 2018).

The Great Airport Race: Kansai International Airport (Japan, 1994), Hong Kong International Airport (1998) and Incheon International Airport (2001)

When the Boeing 747 first entered commercial airline service in 1970 it had twice the passenger capacity of its predecessor, the Boeing 707, but only a bit more range. When the 747-200 was introduced two years later, it had considerably more range. 747-200 flights from east coast airports in the US to the heart of Europe, which previously required a refueling stop, could now make the trip non-stop (Bowman 2014). The 747 also required a longer runway than the 707, and the combination of needing to build bigger passenger terminals and longer runways soon initiated a new round of global airport expansion—a prior round had occurred in the early 1960s when jets replaced propeller planes—only this time there were many more airlines and many more airports.

US and European airports for the most part expanded incrementally—only two entirely new US airports opened between 1970 and 1995, Dallas-Ft. Worth in 1974 and Denver in 1995—but in the Middle East and Asia the race was on to build entirely new airports (Matsumoto and Domae 2018). First out of the gate was Singapore Changi International Airport, which opened in 1981. It was followed later that same year by King Abdulaziz International Airport in Saudi Arabia, and in 1982 by Abu Dhabi International Airport in the United Arab Emirates.

Meanwhile, Asia's economies, led by the Four Asian Tigers (South Korea, Taiwan, Singapore and Hong Kong) were booming. Between 1980 and 1990, the combined economies of the Four Tigers grew at the unheard of rate of 38 percent per year![51] Japan's economy was also surging, and thanks to the market reforms instituted by Communist Party Leader Deng Xiaoping in 1978, the Chinese economy was beginning to awaken from its 60-year slumber. One constraint faced by all six countries as they looked to further expand their economies was a lack of airport capacity. Hong Kong had the most serious problem: its Kai Tak International Airport was not only operating at the limits of its capacity, but with its mountainous landing approaches and short runways ending in Kowloon Bay, it was widely regarded as unsafe. In South Korea, Seoul's Gimpo Airport, which dated back to the Korean War, was also running out of space to expand. Itami International Airport in Osaka, Japan's third largest city, was surrounded by densely populated suburbs which limited its growth potential.

With land at a premium, all three cities followed Singapore's example and built new airports on land created out of excavated fill. Builders of Osaka's

Kansai International Airport (KIX) started first in 1987, creating an artificial island 4 km long by 2.5 km wide in Osaka Bay, five miles from the mainland.[52] KIX's seawall was completed in 1989, allowing construction of its Renzo Piano-designed terminal building to begin in 1991. To compensate for any settling, the terminal sits on adjustable columns which can be raised as needed. KIX opened to flyers on September 4, 1994. To get from KIX to central Osaka, 49 kilometers away, travelers have their choice of car, bus, express train, or local rail. The fastest train from KIX to Osaka Station takes 50 minutes and costs ¥2380 (US$21).

The total cost of building KIX, including land reclamation activities, its two terminal buildings and air cargo facilities, and a second runway completed in 2007 is estimated by the Japanese government at roughly US$25 billion (in 2020 dollars). KIX was financed by debt issued by the Japanese and Osaka Prefecture governments and was to be repaid out of landing fees, which are currently the second highest in the world after Tokyo's Narita Airport. Because of its high landing fees and the fact that until 2007 it had only one full-service runway, KIX's passenger totals have never met initial projections—as of 2018, KIX was the 30th busiest airport in Asia[53]—and from opening day, it has operated at a loss. In 2016, KIX and Osaka's Itami Airport were success-fully privatized and sold to a consortium of Vinci Airports (headquartered in France), Orix Corporation (headquartered in Tokyo) and several Osaka area investment companies.[54]

Hong Kong's Chek Lap Kok International Airport has done better (Table 2.4). Located on Lantau Island 30 km west of downtown Hong Kong, Chep Lap Kok (aka Hong Kong International Airport, or HKG) opened for passen-ger service in July 1998 after seven years of construction.[55] Planning for a new airport to replace the at-capacity and unsafe Kai Tak Airport in Kowloon had been ongoing since 1974 but was accelerated in 1988 with the completion of a consultant study recommending Lantau Island as the site of a combined airport/seaport facility. Airport construction activities began in 1991 and were originally scheduled to be completed just prior to sovereignty over Hong Kong returning to China in July 1997.

HKG was built atop a large artificial island created by flattening and leve-ling nearby Chek Lap Kok and Lam Chau Islands and reclaiming more than nine square kilometers of adjacent seabed. HKG's construction was one part of a larger Airport Core Program, which also involved the construction of new roads, bridges and a high-speed rail link connecting HKG to downtown Hong Kong. The detailed design for the new airport terminal, the largest in world when it opened in 1998, was awarded to a consortium led by project manager Mott Connell that also included Norman Foster and Partners as principal architects and the British Airports Authority as specialist designers for airport passenger facilities. Completing the full Airport Core Program, including

Table 2.4   *Kansai, Hong Kong and Incheon International Airports compared*

	Kansai International Airport (Osaka)	Hong Kong International Airport (Chek Lap Kok)	Incheon International Airport (Seoul)
IATA Code	KIX	HKG	ICN
Developer/owner	Osaka Prefecture[a]	Airport Authority of Hong Kong	Incheon International Airport Corporation
Date opened	September 1994	July 1998	March 2001
Construction time	7 years	7 years	8.5 years
Construction cost (current US$)	US$25 billion	US$25 billion	US$11.4 billion[b]
Airport site area	1,068 ha	1,255 ha	1,172 ha
Main terminal size	296,000 m² [c]	570,000 m² [c]	1,041 m² [d]
Main terminal gates	61 (Terminals 1 and 2) [c]	90 [c]	111 [d]
Distance to downtown	49 km	40 km	51 km
Rail travel time downtown	57 minutes	25 minutes	50 minutes
Car/coach travel time downtown	36 minutes	30 minutes	60 minutes
Passenger movements, 2019	28,767,000	71,541,000	71,169,516.00
Cargo shipments (metric tons), 2019	756,751	4,810,854	2,764,369

Notes:
[a] In 2016, Kansai Airport and Osaka (Itami) Airport were successfully privatized.
[b] Does not include airport groundside transportation investments.
[c] Includes Terminal 1 only.
[d] Includes Terminals 1 and 2 and central concourse.

all transport access facilities, cost US$20 billion. HKG's construction was initially financed through bond sales by the Hong Kong government-chartered Provisional Airport Authority (PAA). When supplemental funds were needed to complete the project, the PAA was reconstituted as the Airport Authority of Hong Kong (AAHK) with the Chinese government stepping in to provide additional grants and loans (Chapman and Georgoulias 2010). As in the Kansai Airport example, bondholders were to be repaid out of landing fees and other airport revenue operations.

In terms of reputation and passenger and cargo traffic, HKG has been a huge success. In 2018, HKG served 74.6 million passengers and 5.1 million tons of cargo, making it the busiest cargo airport in the world and the eighth busiest in terms of passenger movements.[56] HKG is also renowned for the design of its terminal, its high-quality passenger services, and especially for the convenience of its express rail service from the airport to downtown, a 30 km trip that takes just 24 minutes. Despite its popularity with cargo shippers and passengers—until 2020, HKG was consistently rated among the top five airports in the world by Skytrax[57]—over its more than two decades of operation, HKG has been only moderately profitable, principally because of its large debt service payments. Looking forward, HKG's future is clouded by uncertainties over how the Hong Kong economy will fare as China exerts increasing political and economic control over Hong Kong and its residents.[58]

Incheon International Airport (ICN), also known as Seoul-Incheon International Airport, is located 45 km west of Seoul on an artificial island in Incheon Bay. It is accessible to downtown Seoul by express train in 40 minutes or by car or coach in 45 minutes. Planning for a new capital city airport to replace Seoul's crowded Gimpo Airport began in the late-1980s. After less expensive land-based locations were rejected because of their distance from Seoul, the Korean government made the decision to build ICN by filling the shallow seabed between Yeongjong and Yongyu Islands off the coast of Incheon. Construction of the seawall around ICN began in November 1992.[59]

ICN's construction was planned to occur in phases. Phase I, which was scheduled to be completed in 1998, was to include ICN's two runways, its main control tower, and Terminal 1, which would have enough capacity to serve 44 million travelers annually. Phase II, which was to begin in 2002, would include a third runway, a secondary control tower, a new passenger concourse, and a 13-hectare cargo terminal to be developed as part of the new Incheon Free Trade Zone. Phase III, was to begin in 2009, would include a second terminal building boosting ICN's annual passenger capacity to 62 million, a people mover connecting Terminals 1 and 2, and additional traveler amenities such as hotels and shopping areas. (A fourth phase involving the expansion of Terminal 2 was begun in 2017.)

The Asian Financial crisis' arrival in July 1997 led to a two-year pause in ICN's construction, resulting in the airport finally opening for business three-and-a-half years late in March 2001. ICN's predecessor, Gimpo, remained in operation providing domestic and shuttle services. ICN was not immediately popular with international travelers, and for most of its first decade, annual arrivals and boardings varied between 20 and 30 million passengers.[60] Passenger traffic began to grow steadily only after 2010, reaching 71.2 million passengers in 2019 and putting it just behind Hong Kong in terms of annual passenger movements. Like HKG, Incheon is highly regarded by travelers, and in 2020, Terminal 2 was named the World's Best Airport Terminal by Skytrax. Not including the cost of new rail and roadway facilities connecting ICN to Seoul, Phase I cost $4.8 billion to complete, Phase II cost $2.6 billion, and Phase III cost $4 billion.[61] The South Korean government provided 40 percent of the costs of Phase I and II, with the Incheon International Airport Authority and various Korean companies providing the balance in the form of debt and cash contributions. The availability of government construction subsidies has enabled ICN to set its landing fees much lower than its competitors in Hong Kong, Osaka and Singapore, which has made the airport popular with airlines. Phase III was funded entirely by the ICN Authority and did not require government subsidy (Lee 2020). ICN has also made use of build–transfer–operate public–private partnerships with Korean and international freight delivery companies such as DHL to fund construction of its cargo facilities. Partly because of these arrangements, ICN's 2019 operating profit ratio of 60 percent was the highest of any major world airport.[62]

As megaprojects go, international airports face unique challenges. Because of their size and technological requirements, airports are extraordinarily expensive to build and operate, especially in fast-growing Asian cities where land is always at a premium. In recent years, they have also come to serve as projections of national and civic pride. Even so, building a new high-quality airport is no guarantee that it will be visited. Flyers use airports because they are convenient to their desired destinations, not because they are enjoyable places to spend time. Likewise, airlines fly into and out of airports because they make sense for their route structure and service areas, not because airline personnel like the facility What this means is that it is possible to spend huge amounts of money building or expanding an airport only to see that investment fail to pay off in the marketplace. Design and facility-wise, Osaka's Kansai Airport is every bit the equal of Seoul's Incheon Airport or Hong Kong's Chek Lap Kok. Yet because Osaka is not a principal international destination or airline hub, Kansai draws far fewer flyers and earns far less revenue than either Hong Kong or Incheon. These circumstances argue for building new airports incrementally, an approach that often runs up against common megaproject wisdom.

Akashi Kaikyo Bridge (Japan, 1998)

From the first Shinkansen bullet train in 1964 to world-leading manufacturing quality control practices to earthquake-resistant building construction technologies, Japan's well-deserved reputation for engineering excellence has been put to good use in the design and construction of long-span suspension bridges. Completed in 1998 after ten years of construction, the Akashi Kaikyo Bridge has the longest central span of any suspension bridge in the world. Stretching 6,532 feet from tower to tower—nearly 1,000 feet longer than the second-place Yangsigang Yangtze River Bridge in Wuhan—the Akashi Kaiyo Bridge connects the city of Kobi with Awaji Island across the Akashi Strait. Bridge design and construction are especially challenging in Japan because the country sits squarely atop the active Itoigawa–Shizuoka Tectonic Fault Line and since 1950 has experienced more than a dozen earthquakes with a Richter magnitude of 7.5 or more.[63] By comparison, California has experienced no earthquakes of magnitude 7.5 or greater since 1906, and the 1989 Loma Prieta Earthquake, which caused a cantilever section of the San Francisco–Oakland Bridge to collapse was rated at a 6.9 magnitude.

The Akashi Kaiyo Bridge was originally conceived in response to a series of storm-related passenger ferry sinkings in 1945 and 1955 that killed 472 passengers.[64] The longest suspension bridge in the world at the time was the Golden Gate Bridge in San Francisco, but at 4,200 feet, its central span was 2,500 feet shorter than what Japanese bridge engineers said would be needed to span the Akashi Strait. After wrestling with the problem for ten years, Japan's Society of Civil Engineers concluded in 1967 that building such a span was not yet technically feasible, putting further bridge planning work in limbo. Three years later, engineers at the Honshu–Shikoku Bridge Authority figured out how to construct deep water tower foundations that would allow for a central span of 5,840 feet, leading to the Akashi Kaiyo Bridge being approved for construction in 1973. Alas, world events conspired against the bridge. The Arab Oil Embargo of 1973 put construction on indefinite hold—Japan imported most of its oil from the Mideast, and the embargo sent the Japanese economy into a tailspin—and it wasn't until the early 1980s that renewed planning work for the bridge began again. The original 1973 bridge plan had called for a combined road and railway bridge, but the new plan jettisoned the rail option, which allowed for a lighter bridge with a longer central span. Construction activities began in May 1988 and remained on schedule until completed in September 1996.

Originally spaced 6,529 feet apart, the Akashi Kaiyo Bridge's two towers were moved three feet further apart by the 1995 Great Hanshin Earthquake, putting them at their current distance of 6,532 feet. In addition to being able to resist earthquakes of Richter-scale magnitudes up to 8.5, the Akashi Kaiyo Bridge was designed with a dual-hinged stiffening girder system, allowing it to withstand harsh sea currents and winds of up to 180 miles per hour.[65] The bridge also contains tuned mass dampers designed to operate at resonance frequencies that dampen wind-induced harmonic vibrations. All these safety features cost money of course, and with a 1998 price tag of US$3.6 billion, the Akashi Kaikyo Bridge is one of the most expensive bridge structures ever constructed. That cost will be eventually recovered from bridge tolls currently set at ¥2,300 (about US$20) per car. According to the Honshu-Shikoku Bridge Authority which owns and operates the Akashi Kaiyko Bridge, an average of 23,000 vehicles use it daily.[66] At that rate, it will take between 30 and 40 years for the Bridge to repay its bondholders.

The Gotthard Base Tunnel (Switzerland, 2016)[67]

In an era when megaproject leadership has shifted to China, the Gotthard Base Tunnel (GBT) in Switzerland is frequently offered as proof that Europe can still undertake ambitious megaprojects. At 35.5 miles in length, the GBT is the longest underground railway tunnel in the world, beating the Seikan Tunnel in Japan by two miles. Completed in 2016 at a cost of US$12.3 billion, the GBT connects the Swiss cantons of Uri and Ticino, at times running 2.3 km below the alpine peaks above. The GBT is one-third of the New Railway Link through the Alps (NRLA) project, which also includes the Lötschberg Base Tunnel, which opened in December 2007, and the Ceneri Base Tunnel, which opened in September 2020 (Figure 2.6). (The term *base tunnel* is used to indicate that all three projects bypass the original Gotthard railway line that opened in 1882.) All three NRLA railroad tunnels accommodate passenger as well as freight trains. For passengers traveling between Basel/Zurich in Switzerland and Lugano or Milan in Italy, the GBT reduced trip times by an hour compared with prior passenger service. With the Cenari Tunnel's completion, the freight capacity of rail lines connecting Switzerland and Italy has grown from 20 million to 50 million tons. The entire NRLA project, including all three tunnels, cost US$26.3 billion.[68]

The original rail tunnel beneath the 2,106 m Gotthard Pass separating Switzerland from Italy opened to passenger and freight traffic in 1882. An immediate success, it was followed a century later by the Gotthard Road Tunnel, which opened to automobile and truck traffic in 1980. Because of its higher elevation and steep approaches, the original rail tunnel was limited to trains of just 1,500 tons. This weight limit had the effect of diverting rail freight to trucks, which compete with cars for precious road space in the Gotthard Road Tunnel, and whose diesel exhaust led to a noticeable worsening of air quality along the road tunnel route. Intending to shift as much freight traffic as possible from trucks back to trains, Swiss voters went to the polls in 1992, and by a 64-to-36 percent margin, voted to approve the three-tunnel NRLA project. The NRLA project was jointly financed by Swiss government-issued bonds and by increased truck tolls. Even though Switzerland is not a European Union member, funding was also forthcoming from the EU because most of the trains using the GBT start or end their journey in Germany or Italy. AlpTransit Gotthard AG, a wholly-owned subsidiary of Swiss Federal Railways, was given the job of managing the GBT's construction.

After three years of survey and engineering work, construction of the GBT finally got underway in November 1999. To meet the ambitious goal of completing the GBT's tunneling work by 2010, construction began at four access sites simultaneously. Four German-built Herrenknecht Gripper tunnel boring machines were used to drill the GBT, one from each access point.

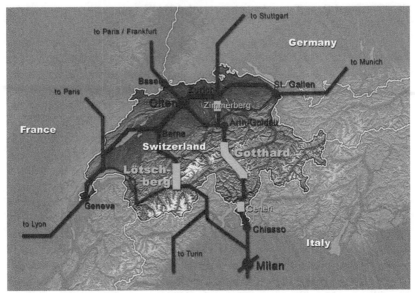

Source: Cooper.ch overlaid on Swiss topomap.

*Figure 2.6   New Railway Link through the Alps (NRLA) tunneling
               projects*

Breakthrough (the point where the two tunnel segments are joined) occurred on
the GPT's eastern tube on October 15, 2010. Six months later, the two western
segments were joined. It would take another five years to complete the tunnel's
interior surfacing and to install and test the rail track and signaling systems.
By opening day on June 1, 2016, the total cost of the GBT project exceeded
its original construction budget by 21 percent. German Prime Minister Angela
Merkel, who attended the opening ceremonies, congratulated the project's
Swiss managers for keeping its costs within reason, adding, "That's something
Germany still needs to strive for."[69]

   Since its opening, an average of between 130 and 160 trains have used the
GBT per day. This is substantially less than the original traffic projections of
200-plus daily trains (Burroughs 2019). Five months after the GBT opened for
passenger rail service in December 2016, Swiss Federal Railways reported that
an average of 9,600 passengers per day had traveled via the GBT, representing
a 30 percent increase over the number of passengers who previously used the
1882 Gotthard Pass Tunnel.

CHINA TAKES THE MEGAPROJECT REINS, 1994–PRESENT

China was a late arrival to the megaproject party but has since more than made up for lost time. Since 1999, China has built or enlarged four of the world's ten tallest dams, seven of its largest urban metro systems, three of its busiest airports, one-third of the world's photovoltaic generating capacity, and a high-speed rail network ten time longer than any other. Indeed, whereas most countries undertake one or at most two major infrastructure megaprojects at a time, China has developed the ability to simultaneously undertake dozens of very large-scale infrastructure projects over multiple sectors.

Extending into the early 1990s, China's early reluctance to make major megaproject investments was rooted in three concerns. First, as countries go, China was extremely poor: not until 2006 did its gross domestic product rise above the $2,000 per person mark.[70] Second, both of China's previous national transformative initiatives—the Great Leap Forward from 1958 to 1962, and the Cultural Revolution starting in the mid-1960—had proven to be disastrous to its economy and social cohesion. After three years of political upheavals following Mao Zedong's death in 1976, his successor as Communist Party leader, Deng Xiaoping, was more interested in having China follow the path of locally-led incremental growth rather than radical national transformation. This manifested itself in the creation of "special economic zones" (SEZs) in 1979, first in Guangdong Province and then later countrywide in which Chinese officials could experiment in creating what Deng's economic advisors euphemistically called "market socialism." Third, consistent with Deng's efforts to make China into a global manufacturing power, to the degree that the Chinese government was going to invest in large-scale infrastructure projects, it would do so in support of export-oriented manufacturers rather than on behalf of city dwellers and domestic-serving businesses. This meant investing in seaports and powerplants and dams ahead of highways, railroads, and airports. To the extent that city and provincial governments wanted to take on large-scale urban development projects themselves, they could raise the needed funds by selling or leasing state-owned land to private developers, who would then be provided with government-subsidized construction loans. This model of urban infrastructure finance worked so well that it enabled Chinese cities to add 260 million new residents between 1980 and 2000 while at the same time reducing the share of city dwellers in deep poverty[71] from 44 percent to 2 percent (Addison and Niño-Zarazúa 2012).

In 1995, after a decade-and-a-half focused on expanding its global manufacturing prowess, China's Communist Party leaders finally turned their attention to domestically-oriented infrastructure investments. They quickly found they had a lot of catching up to do. As of 1992, China's inter-city passenger trains and freight trains shared the same crowded tracks, rarely traveled at more than 50 kph (31 mph), and were frequently late.[72] With 17 million residents between them, China's two biggest cities, Beijing and Shanghai, operated just three subway lines. And with more rural residents crowding into its coastal cities every year—between 1980 and 1995, the combined populations of Shanghai, Tianjin, Guangzhou, and Shenzhen increased from 11.5 to 23.9 million—China desperately needed to invest in its urban transportation infrastructure.

Initially, China's infrastructure planners focused on expanding and modernizing the country's power grid, seaports, and highways. Improvements in China's intercity passenger rail and freight network came next, followed by a spate of airport investments. In the early 2000s, China's ruling State Council began authorizing Chinese cities to begin building metro systems, and in 2004, China's Ministry of Railroads released a 15-year master plan for what would quickly become the world's largest and most extensive high-speed rail network. Almost all these investments involved megaprojects in one form or another.

China's ability to undertake major infrastructure projects across multiple sectors on an unprecedented scale is rooted in six sets of practices. The first is a commitment to building capacity in advance of when it will be physically or economically needed. This approach is most evident in the case of China's 37,000 km high-speed rail network, which connects all of China's major cities. The second is the government's ability to direct state-owned or state-controlled banks to make large loans at favorable rates to government-approved projects without regard to those project's risks. The third is the practice by China's provincial and city government officials of advancing their careers by delivering on the development priorities identified in China's national five-year plans, which, beginning with the 10th Five-Year Plan adopted in 2001, have emphasized large-scale urban and transport infrastructure investments. Fourth, the infrastructure planning and evaluation process in China is technical in nature and excludes citizen input. This reduces the delays that characterize large infrastructure projects in countries with more democratic political systems. While Chinese decision-makers do identify negative environmental impacts when approving projects, they rarely do so on a cumulative basis, a practice that favors large projects able to mitigate their adverse impacts over smaller projects that cannot. Fifth, Chinese project planners and engineers believe strongly in achieving economies-of-scale through design, construction, and procurement standardization. Finally, while high-level favoritism is common in project decision-making, lower-level corruption and payoffs are not. This combination of standardization-based cost efficiencies, minimal public input, and the general absence of corruption has enabled Chinese government officials and contractors to deliver major infrastructure projects at costs well below their counterparts in North America or Europe.

The results have been truly impressive. Since 1999, China has built more than 30 new urban metro systems, opened six of the world's busiest international airports,[73] commissioned 20 of the world's largest hydroelectric dams,[74] built more than 30,000 km of expressways and toll highways (Sloboda and Yao 2007), completed nine of the world's 30 largest photovoltaic power stations,[75] and assembled a national high-speed rail network that is an order of magnitude larger than the next biggest. Among China's most impressive megaprojects are the Three Gorges Dam, started in 1992; Beijing Capital International Airport, which opened in 1999; Shanghai's largest-in-the-world metro system; and, of course, China's world-leading national high-speed rail network, approved for construction in 2004. Each of these megaproject exemplars is introduced in summary form below.

The Three Gorges Dam

With a total generating capacity of 22,500 megawatts—20 times that of the Hoover Dam in the US—the Three Gorges Dam on the Yangtze River in Hubei Province is the largest hydroelectric dam in the world. (The dam is named for the nearby Qutang, Wu, and Xiling Gorges on the Yangtze River.) The idea of damming the Yangtze River at the Three Gorges location to generate power was first proposed by Chinese President Sun Yat-sen in 1919.[76] Successive surveys and plans for a dam at the site were prepared by Chiang Kai-shek's Nationalist government in 1932, by occupying Japanese forces in 1939, and by consultants from the US Bureau of Reclamation following the end of World War II. After the 1949 Communist Revolution, Communist Party leader Mao Zedong indicated his support for building a hydropower dam across the Yangtze, but the dam's potential cost and the political disruptions accompanying the Great Leap Forward (1958–1962) and Cultural Revolution (1966–1976) slowed its progress. As China's economy expanded following the reforms instituted by Mao's successor Deng Xiaoping, the demand for power by China's growing cities and manufacturing industries surged, leading for urgent calls to expand China's hydroelectric capacity. Construction approval for the Three Gorges Dam project was given by the National People's Congress in 1992, with construction work beginning two years later, in December 1994. Construction of the 600-foot-high dam was completed in 2006 with installation of the Dam's 32 turbines continuing through 2012 (Figure 2.7). The final component of the project, the ship lift, was completed in December 2015. Because of record-breaking monsoon rainfalls, power production at the Three Gorges Dam in 2020 reached 112 terawatt-hours, breaking the old single-year generation record of 103 terawatts held by the Itaipu Dam on the Parana

River separating Brazil and Paraguay. Although it provides more than a tenth of China's electricity, the Three Gorges Dam remains controversial, having caused the displacement of at least 1.3 million people and the loss of more than 1,300 architectural and archaeological sites. The additional weight associated with the dam's 600-km-long reservoir has also been blamed for an increase in landslide and earthquake activity in the Three Gorges Region. All told, construction of the Three Gorges Dam is estimated to have cost US$35 billion.

Source: Wall Street Journal.

Figure 2.7   Three Gorges Dam on the Yangtze River

Beijing Capital International Airport[77]

With more than 100 million airline passengers arriving and departing from its three terminals, Beijing's Capital International Airport (IATA designation: PEK) was the world's second busiest in 2019, behind only Hartsfield-Jackson International Airport in Atlanta. Not bad for an airport that as recently as 1999 had just one under-sized terminal and didn't appear on any global airport passenger ranking lists. Beijing Airport opened to international travelers in 1958 with a single 2,500-meter runway, a small terminal able to serve just a few airplanes, and no regular international flights. Over the next 40 years, PEK would be intermittently expanded, adding a new longer runway in 1978 and a larger terminal building able to accommodate a dozen jet aircraft in 1980. In 1999, to mark the 50th anniversary of the founding of the People's Republic of China, PEK opened a new Terminal 2 while temporarily closing Terminal

1 to enlarge and modernize it. Determined to get ahead of surging passenger projections, airport officials opened a third airport runway in 2007, and a new ultra-modern Terminal 3 and rail link to downtown Beijing in February 2008, just in time for the 2008 Beijing Olympics. Unlike Terminals 1 and 2, which were domestically financed, Terminal 3 was funded by a ¥30 billion (US$300 million) loan from Japan and a €500 million (US$625 million) loan from the European Investment Bank. With just under one million square meters of floor space, when it opened, Terminal 3 was the largest man-made structure in the world. Altogether, the addition of a third runway, the construction of Terminal 3, and the completion of the downtown Beijing rail link is estimated to have cost US$3.5 billion. In 2009, PEK overtook Tokyo's Haneda Airport to become Asia's busiest, and in 2013, with passenger growth at PEK projected to exceed the airport's capacity within ten years, the Beijing's government announced it had obtained permission from China's ruling State Council to build a second and even larger airport on Beijing's south side. That airport, to be named Daxing International Airport, opened for passenger service in 2019.

Shanghai's Metro System—the Busiest in the World[78]

Shanghai is proof that adhering to best-practice megaproject planning principles produces tangible results. A metro also-ran as late as 1999, Shanghai today has world's largest metro system measured by route length. And with 2.8 billion passenger rides delivered in 2019, it also has the world's busiest. The full story of how Shanghai transformed its metro system from laggard to world leader is explored more fully in Chapter 6, but for now it is enough to note that Shanghai created its metro system using a different planning approach than Beijing's, one that emphasized traveler convenience over station connectivity, favored transport–land use integration over fixed station location rules, and has made use of innovative financing arrangements. Because of its better planned and more convenient transit service, rail transport in Shanghai accounts for nearly half of daily public transport trips, the highest share among China's major cities. The increased ease of using public transport is also the principal reason why per capita car ownership rates in Shanghai are just two-thirds of Beijing's (Gao et al. 2020). Shanghai's more flexible metro planning and financing approach has been applied with similar success in Shenzhen.

China's National High-speed Rail System[79]

Statistics alone can't do justice to China's spectacular high-speed rail (HSR) accomplishments, but they are a good place to start. Since 2005, China has built 37,000 km of new HSR track, more than the rest of the world combined. In 2019, 2.3 billion passengers traveled by HSR, more than three times as many as traveled by air. In terms of passenger-kilometers—a measure that combines the number of HSR passengers with how far they traveled—China's 774 billion HSR passenger-kilometers of travel in 2019 exceeded second-place Japan's 13 times over. Every one of China's 50 largest cities is connected to its HSR network, and more than 3,000 HSR trains depart from Chinese cities every day. Prior to the opening of the Beijing-to-Shanghai HSR route in 2011, it regularly took ten or more hours to travel by train between the two cities; today, it takes four hours. The more than $800 billion China has spent so far building its HSR network exceeds the roughly $600 billion the United States spent building its interstate highway system in the 1950s, 1960s, and 1970s. What makes these accomplishments even more amazing is that prior to 2003, outside of China's Ministry of Railroads, there was little support among senior Chinese officials for building a national HSR network, let alone the world's largest and busiest. In just five short years, from 2003 to 2008, China went from not having any HSR service to making plans to create the single biggest transport megaproject in the history of the world.

NOTES

1. Altshuler and Luberoff (2004) organize the modern megaproject era in America into four periods: (i) the pre-1950s era in which local governments received relatively little financial aid from higher levels of government; (ii) the "great mega-project era" which ran from the 1950s through the mid-1960s and involved financial partnerships between federal, state, and local government; (iii) the era of transition, which ran from the mid-1960s to early 1970s, and involved increasing grassroots resistance to federally-funded megaprojects; and (vi) the "do no harm" era, which ran from the mid-1970s through the early 2000s, and which focused on mitigating the community disruptions caused by megaprojects.
2. Calculated in 1825 dollars, the Erie Canal cost between $7 million and $8 million to build (Bernstein 2005).
3. https://www.suezcanal.gov.eg/English/Navigation/Pages/NavigationStatistics .aspx.
4. https://www.seatrade-maritime.com/americas/panama-canal-posts-62-increase -hit-record-tonnage-fy-2019
5. A Panama Canal ton is equivalent to 100 cubic feet (2.83 cubic meters) of capacity.
6. https://en.wikipedia.org/wiki/List_of_longest_suspension_bridge_spans   (sorted by construction year).
7. https://en.wikipedia.org/wiki/Hoover_Dam - cite_note-23.
8. Tennessee Encyclopedia website: https://tennesseeencyclopedia.net/entries/ tennessee-valley-authority/ (accessed December 28, 2021).
9. https://livingnewdeal.org/a-light-went-on-new-deal-rural-electrification-act/.
10. The TVA Act. TVA website: https://www.tva.com/about-tva/our-history/the-tva -act.
11. Building the World website: https://blogs.umb.edu/buildingtheworld/energy/ tennesee-valley-authority-united-states/ (accessed November 2021).

12. https://en.wikipedia.org/wiki/U.S._Automobile_Production_Figures (accessed December 28, 2021).
13. Federal Highway Administration, Urban Transport Fact Book (accessed on November 30, 2021, from http://www.publicpurpose.com/hwy-intmiles.htm).
14. In 1991, FHWA estimated the final estimate cost of the Interstate System at 128.9 billion in nominal dollars (https://www.fhwa.dot.gov/interstate/faq.cfm #question7). Depending on when particular expenditures were allocated, this puts its real cost at between $530 million and $600 million when calculated in 2020 dollars.
15. Ridership counts were accessed from the BART website at https://www.bart.gov/ about/reports/ridership on November 30, 2021.
16. Calculated from 2020 American Community Survey data (data.census.gov) accessed November 15, 2021.
17. Federal Transit Administration. The National Transit Database (https://www .transit.dot.gov/ntd) accessed November 15, 2021.
18. The name Metro was suggested by Italian designer Massimo Vignelli, who created the signage for the system as well as for the New York City Subway.
19. WMATA Metro ridership statistics. Available at https://www.wmata.com/about/ records/public-records.cfm#quarterly (accessed December 6, 2021).
20. *Washington Post.* "Why the Second Phase of Metro's Silver Line has Become More Problem-plagued than the First" (July 20, 2019).
21. https://www.city-data.com/neighborhood/Battery-Park-City-New-York-NY.html (accessed December 28, 2021).
22. Based on residential building listings in Battery Park City Wikipedia site: https:// en.wikipedia.org/wiki/Battery_Park_City#Residential (accessed December 1, 2021).
23. *The New York Times.* "New York City's Most Expensive Neighborhoods" (October 28, 2021). https://www.nytimes.com/2021/10/28/realestate/new-york -citys-most-expensive-neighborhoods.html
24. Hugh Carey Battery Park City Authority. 2020 Financial Statement. https://bpca .ny.gov/wp-content/uploads/2021/01/BPCA-Financials-10-31-2020.pdf (accessed November 20, 2021).
25. *WCVB-TV.* "Report: Even More Big Dig Leaks Found" (November 17, 2004).
26. Office of the Inspector General, Robert Cerasoli. A History of Central Artery/ Tunnel. Project Finances 1994–2001, Report to the Treasurer of the Commonwealth. Accessed on November 20, 2021, from https://www.bettertransport.info/fraud/ HistoryBigDig.pdf.
27. *The Washington Post.* "SEC Looking Into 'Big Dig' Overruns In Massachusetts" (February 13, 2000).
28. National Transportation Safety Board. "Safety Board Determines Cause of Boston's Big Dig Tunnel Ceiling Collapse Last Year." www.ntsb.gov (July 10, 2007).
29. *Boston Globe.* "Settlement Reached in Big Dig Death" (December 24, 2007).
30. "$14.8 billion later, Big Dig Finally Complete." www.nbcnews.com (December 25, 2007).
31. "State Official: Big Dig Costs Pegged At $24.3B." www.wbur.com (July 10, 2012).
32. *New York Times.* "Carter's Opposition to Water Projects Linked to '73 Veto of Georgia Dam" (June 13, 1977).

33. https://www.rijkswaterstaat.nl/nieuws/archief/2020/02/storm-en-hoogwater -zorgen-voor-drie-gesloten-stormvloedkeringen.
34. European Commission. 2018. "Case Study Report: Delta Plan/Delta Programme." p.11.
35. European Commission. 2018. "Case Study Report: Delta Plan/Delta Programme." p.20.
36. European Commission. 2018. "Case Study Report: Delta Plan/Delta Programme." p.22.
37. Henk Nijland. "Room for the Rivers Programme" (2007). Accessed at: https:// www.riob.org/IMG/pdf/roma_2007_nijland.pdf.
38. Operating speeds on later Shinkansen trains increased to 320 kph.
39. OECD Passenger transport data. https://data.oedc.org/transport/passenger -transport.htm (accessed December 28, 2021)
40. https://www.macrotrends.net/countries/MEX/mexico/gdp-per-capita
41. Urbanrail.net. "History of Mexico City Metro." http://www.urbanrail.net/am/ mexi/mex-history2.htm (accessed November 20, 2021).
42. Inauguraciones y Ampliaciones en Orden Cronológico Hasta 2000" [Inaugurations and Extensions in Chronological Order Until 2000] (in Spanish). Metro de la Ciudad de Mexico. Wikipedia: archived on August 21, 2016.
43. "Afluencia de astacin por línea 2019" (in Spanish). Metro CDMX. Wikipedia: archived on April 8, 2021.
44. OECD International Transport Forum. "Urban and suburban transport in Mexico City: Lessons learned implementing BRTs lines and suburban railways for the first time." June 2015. https://www.itf-oecd.org/sites/default/files/docs/varela_0.pdf.
45. https://ec.europa.eu/eurostat/statistics-explained/index.php.
46. https://www.autorite-transports.fr/wp-content/uploads/2018/01/bilan-ferroviaire -2015-2016-version-anglaise.pdf.
47. https://www.reuters.com/article/us-france-reform-sncf-debt-idUKKCN1IM24O.
48. https://www.railway-technology.com/features/unveiling-next-generation-french -high-speed-trains/.
49. Canary Wharf Group. https://group.canarywharf.com/portfolio-and-places/ (accessed December 28, 2021).
50. https://www.getlinkgroup.com/en/our-group/eurotunnel/activity-and -performance/ (accessed December 28, 2021).
51. Calculated from World Bank data: https://data.worldbank.org/indicator/NY.GDP .MKTP.KD.ZG (accessed November 15, 2021).
52. This discussion draws from material and data from the Kansai International Airport website, available at http://www.kansai-airports.co.jp/en/company-profile/about -airports/kix.html.
53. Based on tabulations provided by the Airports Council International Data Center available at https://en.wikipedia.org/wiki/List_of_the_busiest_airports_in_Asia (accessed December 28, 2021).
54. https://www.arup.com/projects/kansai-and-osaka-international-airports -privatisation.
55. This discussion draws from material and data from the Hong Kong International Airport website, available at https://www.hongkongairport.com/en/about-us.
56. Based on tabulations provided by the Airports Council International Data Center, available at https://en.wikipedia.org/wiki/List_of_busiest_airports_by_passenger _traffic (accessed December 28, 2021).
57. https://www.worldairportawards.com/.

58. https://www.atlanticcouncil.org/in-depth-research-reports/report/hong-kongs -future-on-edge-countering-chinas-national-security-law/ (accessed December 28, 2021).

59. This discussion draws from material and data from the Incheon International Airport website, available at https://www.airport.kr/ai_cnt/en/story/history.do.

60. 2014 Incheon International Airport Annual Report, available at https://www .airport.kr/co_file/en/file01/2014_ICN_AR_Eng.pdf.

61. Incheon Airport website (https://www.airport.kr/ai/en/cmm/cmmBbsList.do).

62. https://www.kdevelopedia.org/Development-Topics/themes/--12.

63. Based on listings published by the US Geological Survey available at https://en .wikipedia.org/wiki/Lists_of_earthquakes (accessed December 1, 2021).

64. Translated from: Hiroyuki Fujikawa. 2003. 本州四国連絡橋のはなし: 長大橋 を架ける [The story of the Honshu-Shikoku Bridge Project: How the great spans were erected]. 交通研究協会. pp. 2–5.

65. As summarized at Structurae, The International Database and Gallery of Structures, available at https://structurae.net/en/structures/akashi-kaikyo-bridge (accessed December 2, 2021).

66. https://www.jb-honshi.co.jp/english/corp_index/technology/introduction/ introduction_akashi.html.

67. This profile is assembled from material presented on the Swiss Government's Alptransit Portal website: https://www.alptransit-portal.ch/en/ (accessed November 25, 2021).

68. Swiss Federal Office of Transport. "The New Rail Link through the Alps (NRLA)." 2016.

69. *The Guardian.* "European Leaders Open World's Longest Rail Tunnel in Switzerland." June 1, 2016.

70. https://data.worldbank.org/indicator/NY.GDP.PCAP.

71. Defined by the United Nations as earning an income of $1.25 per day or less.

72. "高铁时代 中国国家地理网". Dili360.com (in Chinese). April 200, available at https://en.wikipedia.org/wiki/Campaign_to_raise_the_speed_of_railway_travel _in_China.

73. Beijing Capital International Airport, Daxing International Airport (Beijing), Shanghai Pudong International Airport, Guangzhou Baiyan International Airport, Shenzhen-Bao'an International Airport, and Kunming Changshu International Airport.

74. Based on listings reported on Wikipedia at: https://en.wikipedia.org/wiki/List_of _largest_hydroelectric_power_stations (accessed December 29, 2021).

75. Based on listings reported on Wikipedia at: https://en.wikipedia.org/wiki/List_of _photovoltaic_power_stations (accessed December 29, 2021).

76. This profile is assembled from Reuters: "Fact box: A history of China's Three Gorges project." https://www.reuters.com/article/us-china-environment-yangtze -factbox/factbox-a-history-of-chinas-three-gorges-project-id (accessed November 20, 2021).

77. This profile is assembled from Wikipedia: "Beijing Capital International Airport." https://en.wikipedia.org/wiki/Beijing_Capital_International_Airport (accessed November 20, 2021).

78. This profile summarizes material presented in Chapter 6 of this volume.

79. This profile summarizes material presented in Chapter 5 of this volume.

REFERENCES

Addison, T., and Niño-Zarazúa, M. 2012. Redefining poverty in China and India: Making growth more inclusive, Part 2. UNU-WIDER Angle, 2.

Alexander Cooper and Associates. 1979. Battery Park City draft summary report and 1979 master plan.

Altshuler, A. A., and Luberoff, D. E. 2004. *Mega-projects: The Changing Politics of Urban Public Investment*. Brookings Institution Press.

Ambrose, S. E. 2000. *Nothing Like It in the World· The Men who Built the Transcontinental Railroad 1863–1869*. Simon and Schuster.

Arduin, J. P. and Ni, J. 2005. French TGV network development. *Japan Railways and Transport Review* (March).

Bain, D. H. 2000. *Empire Express: Building the First Transcontinental Railroad*. Penguin.

BART. 2021. BART website: "A History of BART." https://www.bart.gov/about/history.

Bernstein, P. L. 2005. *Wedding of the Waters: The Erie Canal and the Making of a Great Nation*. W.W. Norton & Company.

Bowman, M. W. 2014. *Boeing 747: A History: Delivering the Dream*. Pen and Sword.

Brownill, S. 1999. Turning the East End into the West End: The lessons and legacies of the London Docklands Development Corporation. In R. Imrie and H. Thomas (eds), *British Urban Policy: An Evaluation of the Urban Development Corporations*. Sage, pp. 43–63.

Burroughs, D. 2019. 100,000[th] train travels through the Gotthard Base Tunnel. *International Railway Journal* (March).

Chapman, J., and Georgoulias, A. 2010. *Sustainable Financing for the Hong Kong International Airport*. Harvard Graduate School of Design. https://research.gsd.harvard.edu/zofnass/files/2013/05/Hong-Kong-International-Airport.pdf.

Commonwealth of Massachusetts. 2021. Mass.gov website: "The Big Dig: Project Background." https://www.mass.gov/info-details/the-big-dig-project-background.

Cox, W., and Love, J. 1996. 40 years of the US interstate highway system: An analysis of the best investment a nation ever made. Report prepared for the American Highway Users Alliance. http://www.publicpurpose.com/freeway1.htm.

Davis, J. 2020. *Federal Highway Policy under President Eisenhower, 1953 1954*. Eno Center for Transportation. https://www.enotrans.org/article/federal-highway-policy-under-president-eisenhower-1953-1954.

Deakin, E. A. 2006. The social impacts of the interstate highway system: What are the repercussions? TR News 244.

Deltawerken online. 2021. DeltaWorks.org website: "The Delta Works." http://www.deltawerken.com/Deltaworks/23.html.

Duran, X. 2013. The first US transcontinental railroad: Expected profits and government intervention. *The Journal of Economic History* 73(1): 177–200.

EY (formerly Ernst & Young). 2018. *Economic Footprint of the Channel Tunnel in the EU*. EY.

Fletcher, M. E. 1958. The Suez Canal and world shipping, 1869–1914. *The Journal of Economic History* 18(4): 556–573.

Gao, Y., Newman, P., and Kenworthy, J. 2020. The rise and decline of car use in Beijing and Shanghai. In *Sustainability in Urban Planning and Design*. IntechOpen.

Gauthier, A. 1880. The St. Gothard Tunnel. *Nature* 21: 581–586.

Goldchain, M. 2017. D.C. Metro history: A timeline—from the planning stages to the newest 7000-series cars. Curbed Washington DC. https://dc.curbed.com/2017/9/19/16330836/dc-metro-wmata-timeline.

Goldsmith, H., and Boeuf, P. 2019. Digging beneath the iron triangle: The Chunnel with 2020 hindsight. *Journal of Mega Infrastructure & Sustainable Development* 1(1): 79–93.

Gordon, D. L. 2001. The resurrection of canary wharf. *Planning Theory & Practice* 2(2):149–168.

Gordon, D. L. 2012. *Battery Park City: Politics and Planning on the New York Waterfront*. Routledge.

Gourvish, T. 2006. *The Official History of Britain and the Channel Tunnel*. Routledge.

Grant, M. 1997. Financing Eurotunnel. *Japan Railway & Transport Review* 11: 46–52.

Greiman, V. A. 2013. *Megaproject Management: Lessons on Risk and Project Management from the Big Dig*. John Wiley & Sons.

Guibertau, O. 2021. Building the Erie Canal. Megaprojects website. https://megaprojects.net/buildings/building-the-erie-canal/.

Gutfreund, O. D. 2004. *Twentieth-century Sprawl: Highways and the Reshaping of the American Landscape*. Oxford University Press.

Hall, P. 1982. *Great Planning Disasters*. University of California Press.

Haynes, W. 2008. Boston's Big Dig project: A cautionary tale. *Bridgewater Review* 27(1): 3–7.

Healy, M. C. 2013. *BART: The Dramatic History of the Bay Area Rapid Transit System*. Heyday. ORIM.

Hiltzik, M. 2010. *Colossus: Hoover Dam and the Making of the American Century*. Simon and Schuster.

Hood, C. 2006. *Shinkansen: From Bullet Train to Symbol of Modern Japan*. Routledge.

Hurley, J. 2021. Tracing a history of Atlanta's public transit. Atlanta Studies website. https://www.atlantastudies.org/2015/04/27/tracing-a-history-of-atlantas-public-transit/.

Jacobs, J. 1961. *Death and Life of Great American Cities*. Random House.

Jaworski, T., Kitchens, C. T., and Nigai, S. 2018. The interstate highway system and the development of the American economy. Unpublished manuscript, University of Colorado, Boulder. http://eh.net/eha/wp-content/uploads/2018/06/Kitschens.pdf.

Karabell, Z. 2003. *Parting the Desert: The Creation of the Suez Canal*. Knopf.

Kim, C. J., and Huang, M. C. 2021. The privatization of Japan railways and Japan post: Why, how, and now. In F. Taghizadeh-Hesary, N. Yoshino, C. J. Kim and K. Kim (eds), *Reforming State-owned Enterprises in Asia: Challenges and Solutions*. Springer, pp. 133–155.

Klein, M. 2019. *Financing the Transcontinental Railroad*. Gilder Lehrman Institute of American History,

Kwak, Y. H., Zaleski, J., Sleeper, D., and Sadatsafavi, H. 2014. What can we learn from the Hoover Dam project that influenced modern project management? *International Journal of Project Management* 32(2): 256–264.

Lee, Y. H. 2020. *Incheon International Airport: Its Success and Implications for Developing Countries*. KDI School of Public Policy and Management.

Liliopoulou, A., Roe, M., and Pasukeviciute, I. 2005. Trans-Siberian Railway: From inception to transition. *European Transport* 29: 46–56

Mason, C. Y., and Rowlands, A. 1938. Panama Canal traffic. *Economic Geography* 14(4): 325–337.

Matsumoto, H., and Domae, K. 2018. The effects of new international airports and air-freight integrator's hubs on the mobility of cities in urban hierarchies: A case study in East and Southeast Asia. *Journal of Air Transport Management* 71: 160–166.

McCullough, D. 2001. *The Path between the Seas: The Creation of the Panama Canal, 1870-1914*. Simon and Schuster.

McCullough, D. 2012. *The Great Bridge: The Epic Story of the Building of the Brooklyn Bridge*. Simon and Schuster.

McNichol, D. 2006. *The Roads that Built America: The Incredible Story of the U.S. Interstate System*. Sterling Publishing Company.

Merewitz, L. 1973. *Cost Overruns in Public Works*. Institute of Urban & Regional Development, University of California. Working paper no. 114.

Metropolitan Atlanta Regional Transit Authority. 2012. *Annual Report*.

Metropolitan Atlanta Regional Transit Authority. 2020. *Annual Comprehensive Financial Report*.

Meunier, J. 2002. *On the Fast Track: French Railway Modernization and the Origins of the TGV, 1944-1983*. Greenwood Publishing Group.

Monkkonen, E. H. 1995. *The Local State: Public Money and American Cities*. Stanford University Press.

Monroe, D. 2012. Where it all went wrong. *Atlanta Magazine* (August). https://www.atlantamagazine.com/great-reads/marta-tsplost-transportation/.

Neuse, S. 1991. David E. Lilienthal: Exemplar of public purpose. *International Journal of Public Administration* 14(6): 1099–1148.

Oc, T., and Tiesdell, S. 1991. The London Docklands Development Corporation (LDDC), 1981-1991: A perspective on the management of urban regeneration. *The Town Planning Review*: 311–330.

Planitmetro.com. 2016. *Gut Check – Funding Metro 2025*. Washington Metropolitan Area Transit Authority. https://planitmetro.com/2014/02/24/gut-check-funding -metro-2025/.

Roberts, R. 2009. *Building the Panama Canal*. Mitchell Lane Publishers, Inc.

Rogers, J. D. 2014. The American engineers that built the Panama Canal. In *Engineering the Panama Canal*. Proceedings of sessions honoring the 100th anniversary of the Panama Canal at the ASCE Global Engineering Conference, pp. 112–349.

Rothengatter, W. 2019. Megaprojects in transportation networks. *Transport Policy* 75: A1–A15.

Schrag, Z. M. 2014. *The Great Society Subway: A History of the Washington Metro*. Johns Hopkins University Press.

Schumacher, E. F. 1973. *Small is Beautiful: Economics as if People Mattered*. London: Blond & Briggs.

Sloboda, B. W., and Yao, V. W. 2007. The development of the Chinese transportation infrastructure: A case of highway development. *Business and Public Administration Studies* 2(3): 60–60.

Smith, R. A. 2003. The Japanese Shinkansen: Catalyst for the renaissance of rail. *The Journal of Transport History* 24(2): 222–237.

Sobel, R. 1999. *Panic on Wall Street: A History of America's Financial Disasters*. Beard Books.

Stough, R. R. and Haynes, K. E. 1997. Megaproject impact assessment. In *Regional Science: Perspectives for the Future*. Palgrave Macmillan, pp. 384–398.

Streeter, W. C. 1993. The French train a Grande Vitesse: Focusing on the TGV-Atlantique. *Built Environment* 19(3).

Taylor, B. D. 2004. The geography of urban transportation finance. *The Geography of Urban Transportation* 3: 294–331.

Tennessee Valley Authority (TVA). 1950. *The Fontana Project; A Comprehensive Report on the Planning, Design, Construction, and Initial Operations of the Fontana Project.* Washington, DC: US Government Printing Office

Tennessee Valley Authority (TVA). 2021a. TVA website: "Our History." https://www.tva.com/about-tva/our-history.

Tennessee Valley Authority (TVA). 2021b. TVA website: "Hydroelectric." https://www.tva.com/energy/our-power-system/hydroelectric.

TGVWeb. Website: "Early TGV History." http://www.trainweb.org/tgvpages/history.html.

The Economist. 2014. A bad project comes good – With better yet to come. London: The Economist Group (May 10).

Ulin, M. E. 2017. Ticket to the past: A political history of the Mexico City Metro, 1958–1969. *Grand Valley Journal of History* 4(2): 1–14.

Vickerman, R. 1997. High-speed rail in Europe: Experience and issues for future development. *The Annals of Regional Science* 31(1): 21–38.

Wallis, J. J. 2000. American government finance in the long run: 1790 to 1990. *Journal of Economic Perspectives* 14(1): 61–82.

Watson, B. 2020. Ike's excellent adventure. *American Heritage Magazine* 65(4).

Weingroff, R. 1996. Federal-Aid Highway Act of 1956, creating the Interstate System. *Public Roads* 60(1).

Weingroff, R. 2006. The battle of its life. *Public Roads* 69(6).

Wood, D. 2001. Learning from The Big Dig. *Public Roads* 65(1).

White, R. 2011. *Railroaded: The Transcontinentals and the Making of Modern America.* W.W. Norton & Company.

Willis, C. 1995. *Form Follows Finance: Skyscrapers and Skylines in New York and Chicago.* Princeton Architectural Press.

Wilson, A. 1939. The Suez Canal. *International Affairs* (Royal Institute of International Affairs 1931–1939) 18(3): 380–395.

Wilson, J., and Spick, J. 1994. *Eurotunnel – The Illustrated Journey.* HarperCollins.

Zielinski, K. 2018. The Panama Canal Expansion Project: A historical review and lessons learned. *Journal of Information Technology & Economic Development* 9(2).

3. Choosing the case study megaprojects

John D. Landis

This book explores the connections between megaproject practice and performance. To do so, it takes a deep dive into the planning, financing, construction, and delivery histories of a series of 14 megaproject case studies. In each case, it identifies the problem or need the project was intended to address, how it came to be proposed in the form that it was, which planning hurdles it had to jump over, how it was financed, the project management systems used to deliver it, and the unexpected challenges it encountered along the way. The megaproject case studies included in this volume were chosen for their geographic and sectoral diversity as well as for their potential to provide practical lessons for future megaproject sponsors. Unlike some previous collections which try to identify core generalities that apply to all megaprojects, this volume takes the position that what is most interesting about megaprojects is how their sponsors make key planning, design, engineering, financing, construction and project management decisions, and how those decisions shape subsequent project performance.

CASE STUDY SELECTION CRITERIA

As with any research effort organized around case studies, the validity of its results will depend on which case studies are chosen and why. To ensure that the case studies included in this volume were representative of the current state of megaproject practice and could offer useful evaluative lessons, we began by identifying a series of case study selection criteria. They include:

1. *Relevant to today's practice*: In order to identify practice lessons relevant to today's world, the case studies should be recent. That is, they should have been started or completed after 2010.
2. *Urban-oriented*: With most of the world's projected population growth expected to occur in urban and metropolitan areas, the case studies should have an urban focus.
3. *A diversity of project types*: Identifying generalizable lessons requires including a diversity of megaproject types. Based on a quick survey of recent global megaprojects, we identified six types of megaprojects to

consider in greater detail: (i) rail and bus megaprojects; (ii) bridge and tunnel megaprojects; (iii) airport megaprojects; (iv) urban development megaprojects; (v) urban park megaprojects; and (vi) renewable energy megaprojects. Among the megaproject types that this listing does not include are dams and water projects, environmental restoration projects, conventional new town projects, and projects that are undertaken entirely in the private sector.

4. *Geographically representative*: Urban megaprojects are typically undertaken in places where they generate sizeable public benefits and where their intended beneficiaries are able to pay for them. Until the close of the 20th century, this meant most megaprojects were undertaken in Europe or North America. More recently, the geographic center of megaproject activity has shifted to Southeast Asia.

5. *Iconic design or engineering features*: In addition to their functional performance, individual megaprojects may merit scrutiny because they are regarded as exemplars by experts or have captured public attention.

6. *The public sector in the lead*: Government-initiated or -funded megaprojects are more likely to generate positive spillovers and multiplier benefits than privately initiated ones. As they are likely to involve diverse stakeholders, public sector-sponsored megaprojects are also apt to be more controversial. Lastly, government-initiated megaprojects are liable to involve more diverse financing forms than private projects.

7. *Diverse financing forms*: Many megaprojects are still paid for the old-fashioned way via government spending and borrowing. At the same time, an increasing number of large projects are making use of public–private partnerships and other alternative financing forms in order to access needed capital.

8. *Available documentation and information sources*: This turned out to be the hardest criteria to meet. Many megaproject details are never made available to the public, making it difficult to connect decisions to outcomes.

9. *Good outcomes, bad outcomes, and everything in between*: Sponsors whose megaprojects do not live up to expectations are understandably reluctant to share their experiences. Yet these are precisely the projects that offer the most value in terms of useful lessons.

10. *Cause-and-effect narratives*: Sometimes megaprojects succeed (or fail) because of luck rather than careful planning and delivery. It is important when choosing megaproject case studies to be able to trace project success (and/or failure) back to prior decisions or activities, and not just luck.

11. *A diversity of takeaways*: Case studies should be chosen for their individual lessons as well as because they fit into a bigger narrative about why megaprojects succeed and fail.

Based on these criteria, we identified 14 megaprojects or sets of megaprojects to profile in greater detail (Table 3.1). Four of the case studies are rail and bus projects, two are bridge and tunnel projects, three are airport projects, three are urban development projects, one is an urban park project, and the final case study summarizes renewable energy projects in Europe, North America, North Africa and Asia. Three of the case studies involve multiple projects.

The 14 case studies are:

* London Crossrail
* China's national high-speed rail network
* China's big four metro systems
* Six Bus Rapid Transit (BRT) systems in South America and Asia
* Seattle's Alaskan Way Tunnel
* The Hong Kong–Zhuhai–Macau Bridge
* Singapore Changi Jewel Airport
* Berlin-Brandenburg International Airport
* The New LaGuardia Airport Terminal B
* Canary Wharf in London
* HafenCity Hamburg
* Songdo International Business District
* Brooklyn Bridge Park (New York City)
* Five global renewable energy projects

Not every case study meets every criteria. Two case studies, the Bus Rapid Transit (BRT) projects and Brooklyn Bridge Park, don't meet the usual $1 billion megaproject cost threshold but are included because of their size, impact and importance as global models. Except for the BRT projects, all the case studies were started or finished between 2010 and 2020 or are currently underway.

Table 3.1 Case study megaprojects and case study selection criteria

Megaproject type	Megaproject Case Study	Current: Started, underway or finished after 2010	Urban orientation	Geographic variety (location)	Iconic or emblematic case study	Public sector in the lead	Diverse financing forms	Documentation publicly available	Diversity of outcomes	Cause–effect narrative	Project-specific and generalizable takeaways
Rail and transit projects	London Crossrail	X	X	United Kingdom	X	X	X	X	X	X	X
	Beijing, Shanghai, Guangzhou and Shenzhen Metro Systems	X	X	China	X	X	X		X	X	X
	China's 37,000 km high-speed rail network	X	X	China	X	X			X	X	X
	Bus Rapid Transit (BRT) in six Latin America and Asian cities		X	Latin America and Asia	X	X		X	X	X	X
Bridge and tunnel projects	Seattle Alaska Way Tunnel	X	X	USA	X	X		X	X	X	X
	Hong Kong–Macao–Zhuhai Bridge	X	X	China/Hong Kong	X	X			X	X	X
Airport projects	The Jewel at Singapore Changi Airport	X	X	Singapore	X	X	X	X		X	X
	Berlin-Brandenburg Airport	X	X	Germany	X	X		X	X	X	X
	LaGuardia Airport Terminal B reconstruction	X	X	USA	X	X	X	X		X	X
Urban development projects	London Canary Wharf	X	X	UK	X		X	X	X	X	X
	HafenCity Hamburg	X	X	Germany	X	X	X	X	X	X	X
	Songdo International Business District	X	X	S. Korea	X	X	X		X	X	X
	Brooklyn Bridge Park (New York City)	X	X	USA	X	X	X	X	X	X	X
Other	Diverse renewable energy projects	X		Asia, Africa, UK, USA	X	X	X			X	X

As intended, the case studies are geographically diverse. Three are in China; two each are in the United States, the United Kingdom and Germany; one is in Singapore; and one is in South Korea. The BRT grouping includes projects in multiple cities in Latin America and Asia, and the renewable energy set of projects includes locations in the United Kingdom, Morocco, India, the United States and China. Except for the renewable energy projects, all the case study projects are in or connect to very large cities of global import.

Except for London's Canary Wharf, a public sector agency or publicly-chartered company was the lead sponsor for every case study. A majority of the case studies mix public and private financing sources, often-times making use of a joint venture arrangement or public–private partnership.

In terms of outcomes, except for the Hong Kong–Zhuhai–Macau Bridge and Songdo in South Korea—both of which have fallen far short of their goals— none of the case studies are complete successes or failures. A few, notably HafenCity Hamburg in Germany, LaGuardia Airport Terminal B in New York City, Singapore's Jewel Changi Airport, and China's high-speed rail network system come reasonably close to being unambiguous successes, but even they have experienced unexpected ups and downs. The majority of the case studies have had middling or slightly better-than-middling success in terms of reaching their goals and avoiding large scheduling or cost overruns. Of the projects that fall into this performance middle ground area, one, London Crossrail was only finished in May 2022, and the other, the new Berlin-Brandenburg Airport has achieved most of its goals but was grossly over budget and behind schedule. In the cases of China's high-speed rail network and its four urban metro systems, the projects as a whole have been notably successful even as individual lines or corridors have suffered from uneven performance. The final chapter of this volume goes into much greater detail regarding the determinants of each case study's successes and shortcomings.

Except for the five renewable energy projects—which are presented in summary form—all of the case study projects are characterized by strong cause–effect narratives, meaning that it is possible to trace the effects of initial project planning, financing, or project management decisions on each project's ultimate outcomes. Similarly, all of the case study projects offer useful, timely and generalizable lessons to prospective megaproject sponsors confronting comparable challenges in other locations.

Table 3.2   Selected characteristics of the case study megaprojects

		London Crossrail	UK Department for Transport (DfT) and Transport for London (TfL)	Urban congestion relief and enhanced mobility, economic development	2005 (I); 2008 (F)	13 years and counting	$26 billion and counting	Combination of government funding and value-capture business taxes.	Transit fares and business tax revenues
Rail and transit projects	Beijing, Shanghai, Guangzhou and Shenzhen Metro Systems	City governments of Beijing, Shanghai, Guangzhou and Shenzhen	Urban congestion relief and enhanced mobility	Beijing 1971; Shanghai 1993; Guangzhou 1997; Shenzhen 2004	3–4 years per metro line	$80 million to $200 million per kilometer of track	A combination of national and local government funding with a few PPP-financed lines.	Transit fares and value capture revenues (Shenzhen)
	China's 35,000 km High Speed Rail Network	China's Ministry of Railroads, superseded in 2014 by the China National Railways Administration	Improved intercity mobility, regionally balanced economic development	2004	First HSR line opened in 2008	$17 million to $21 million per kilometer (World Bank 2013)	Joint ventures formed by the China National Railways Administration, provincial governments, and some HSR operators.	Passenger fares and government subsidies
	Bus Rapid Transit (BRT) in six Latin America and Asian Cities	City governments and public transport agencies in Curitiba, Quito, Bogotá, Jakarta, Seoul and Guangzhou	Congestion relief and enhanced mobility	Curitiba 1974; Quito 1995; Bogotá 2001; Jakarta 2004; Seoul 2006; Guangzhou 2010	1–3 years per BRT corridor	$10 to $15 million per kilometer	Mixture of financing sources including national and state government grants and loans, and city and public transit agency borrowing.	Passenger fares and government subsidies

	London Crossrail	UK Department for Transport (DfT) and Transport for London (TfL)	Urban congestion relief and enhanced mobility, economic development	2005 (I); 2008 (F)	13 years and counting	$26 billion and counting	Combination of government funding and value-capture business taxes.	Transit fares and business tax revenues
Bridge and tunnel projects	Seattle Alaska Way Tunnel	Washington State Department of Transportation, City of Seattle, Port Authority of Seattle	Replace an earthquake-vulnerable viaduct with a safer and less intrusive facility	2003 (I); 2011 (A)	8 years	$3.35 billion	State funding supplemented by tolls to repay Port Authority bonds	State revenues and tolls
	Hong Kong–Macao–Zhuhai Bridge	Governments of Hong Kong and Macao Special Administrative Regions (SARs) and City of Zhuhai	Regional economic development	2009	9 years	$19.1 billion	Partnership between Hong Kong, Macau, and Guangdong Province, backed by toll revenues	Tolls

	Project	Authority	Objective	Dates	Duration	Cost	Funding	Revenue sources
	London Crossrail	UK Department for Transport (DfT) and Transport for London (TfL)	Urban congestion relief and enhanced mobility, economic development	2005 (I); 2008 (F)	13 years and counting	$26 billion and counting	Combination of government funding and value-capture business taxes.	Transit fares and business tax revenues
Airport projects	The Jewel at Singapore Changi Airport	Singapore Civil Aviation Authority (CAAS), Changi Airport Group (CAG), CapitaLand	Create a world-class experience that would cement Changi's reputation as the world's finest destination airport	2014	4.5 years	$1.4 billion	Joint venture between the government-owned Changi Airport Group (CAG) and CapitaLand	Concessionaire rents and payments; passenger service fees
	Berlin Brandenburg Airport	Flughafen Berlin Brandenburg GmbH (a partnership of the state governments of Berlin and Brandenburg (37% each), and the German government (26%).	Expand and modernize airport capacity	2003 (I); 2006 (A)	14 years	$6.5 billion	Debt and bank loans backed by the states of Berlin and Brandenburg	Gate leases, landing fees, concessionaire rents and payments, cargo revenues
	LaGuardia Airport Terminal B Reconstruction	Port Authority of New York and New Jersey, LaGuardia Gateway Partners (LGP)	Modernize and expand airport capacity	2010 (I); 2015 (A)	7 years (Terminal B remains continuously open)	$4 billion	PPP between Port Authority (debt financing) and LGP (debt and equity)	Gate leases, landing fees, concessionaire fees, and cargo revenues

			Goal	Dates (I/F)	Status	Cost	Funding	Revenue source
Urban development projects	London Crossrail	UK Department for Transport (DfT) and Transport for London (TfL)	Urban congestion relief and enhanced mobility, economic development	2005 (I); 2008 (F)	13 years and counting	$26 billion and counting	Combination of government funding and value-capture business taxes.	Transit fares and business tax revenues
	London Canary Wharf	Olympia and York (1987-1992), The Canary Wharf Group (1995–), The London Docklands Development Corporation (1981-1997)	Create a second & modern London CBD in an abandoned port area	1987	First building opens in 1991, development is ongoing		Commercial buildings are privately financed. Transportation and public realm improvements are publicly funded.	Commercial rents; transit fares for Docklands Light Rail (DLR)
	HafenCity Hamburg	HafenCity Hamburg GmbH (HHG), Hamburg City Government	Create a modern and sustainable mixed-use district in an abandoned port area	1997 (I); 1998 (F)	First building completed in 2002, development is ongoing	$2.8 billion public funding; $10 billion private funding	Combination of public funding (public infrastructure), land sales, and city-backed debt.	Property assessments
	Songdo, Korea	City of Incheon, Gale International, POSCO E&C	Develop a high-tech international business district near Incheon Airport	1997 (I); 2001 (A)	First building opens in 2005, development is ongoing	$50 billion (projected)	PPP between City of Incheon (public revenue), Gale International and POSCO E&C (private equity and debt)	Land and building sales and rental income

London Crossrail	UK Department for Transport (DfT) and Transport for London (TfL)	Urban congestion relief and enhanced mobility, economic development	2005 (I); 2008 (F)	13 years and counting	$26 billion and counting	Combination of government funding and value-capture business taxes.	Transit fares and business tax revenues
Brooklyn Bridge Park (New York City)	Brooklyn Bridge Park Development Corporation (BBPDC), New York City Mayor's Office, Brooklyn Borough President's Office	Convert abandoned docks into a financially self-sustaining park and public amenity	1997(I); 2005 (A);	10 years (Phase I); 15 years (final)	$300 million	Public development corporation able to borrow and issue debt	Commercial property rents and fees
Other Diverse Renewable Energy Projects	Various national governments and public and private energy companies	Develop a financially-beneficial renewable energy facility	various years	Projects typically take 3–5 years to complete	varies	Typically a PPP between a government entity which provides revenue guarantees and private investors who provide equity and debt.	Rate payers

THE CASE STUDIES IN BRIEF

Rail and Bus Megaprojects

Among the diverse rail and bus case studies included in this volume are Crossrail, a recently-opened high-speed metro line in London; China's 37,000 km national high speed rail network; new metro systems in Beijing, Shanghai, Guangzhou and Shenzhen; and six bus rapid transit (BRT) systems in Curitiba, Quito, Bogota, Jakarta, Seoul, and Guangzhou.

London Crossrail (aka The Elizabeth Line)

London Crossrail is a 117 km high-speed metro line connecting Heathrow Airport (and parts west) to Central London, Canary Wharf, and London's East End communities. Crossrail's eastern and western sections run on upgraded overland tracks while its 21 km central section runs deep below London in eight newly bored tunnels. Crossrail's two principal sponsors are the UK government's Department for Transport (DfT) and Transport for London (TfL), the London area government agency responsible for most of the capital region's transport network. When approved for construction by Royal Assent in 2008 at a cost of £14.8 billion, Crossrail was justified as being essential to reducing London's rising congestion levels and to cementing its future as the world's preeminent financial center. With Britain's exit from the European Union in 2020, that future is now unclear. Crossrail's financing structure is a complicated mix of government grants, supplemental fee revenue-backed bonds, contributions from property developers, and in-lieu funding from National Rail. Originally scheduled to open in 2018, Crossrail experienced numerous station construction and technology-related delays, finally opening four years late and 30 percent overbudget in May 2022.

China's national high-speed rail network

Just fourteen years old in 2022, China's 37,000 km (and growing) high-speed rail network is the world's largest and most heavily-traveled, drawing 2.3 billion riders in 2019. (In second place, Spain's AVE system extends just 3,100 km, while in terms of ridership, Japan's Shinkansen system carried 436 million passengers in 2018.) With its first high-speed rail line having opened for service only in 2008, China was a relative latecomer to offering high-speed rail service. It has since made up for lost time, and today, its 17-line high-speed rail network connects 34 of China's largest cities and carries just under a quarter of the country's long-distance inter-city passenger traffic. Originally planned and built under the auspices of China's Ministry of Railroads, China's high-speed rail network is now controlled by its successor organization, the

China National Railways Administration. As with most large-scale public works in China, planning for the country's high-speed rail network was largely a top-down affair, with funding for new lines requiring the approval of China's ruling State Council. Once approval is given, the joint-venture entities who build and operate individual lines must adhere to national design and construction standards and procedures. This focus on standardization has allowed China to build its high-speed rail network relatively inexpensively as well as quickly, and enabled it to become a major exporter of high-speed rail trains and equipment.

Four Chinese metro systems
Since the late-1990s, China's "Big Four" cities (Beijing, Shanghai, Guangzhou and Shenzhen) have each built modern multi-line metro networks that now carry billions of passengers annually. Beijing's first metro line was completed in 1971. Today, its system includes 24 lines totaling 438 miles in length and is the world's second longest. Shanghai's first metro line opened for service in 1993, and at 479 miles in length as of 2020, is today the world's largest. The first of Guangzhou's metro lines entered service in 1997, and today its 14-line system includes 330 miles of track. Shenzhen was the last of China's Big Four cities to build a metro system. Its first line entered service in 2004, and today Shenzhen's 11 lines have a total length of 255 miles. Each city planned and operates its metro system slightly differently. Beijing's metro system planners tried to standardize both their station location criteria and funding procedures. By contrast, Shanghai and Shenzhen located their metro stations to maximize access to existing commercial and residential activity centers. Shenzhen has also led in the use of a Hong Kong-style "Rail + Property" financing scheme that draws operating revenues from nearby development projects as well as passenger fares. Guangzhou has developed its own financing model that draws more heavily on city-level tax revenues. With 2.8 billion riders in 2018, Shanghai's metro system now ranks as the busiest in the world. It is followed by Guangzhou in fourth place, Beijing in fifth place, and Shenzhen in tenth place. Collectively, China's Big Four metro systems provide an excellent example of how to plan and deliver urban rail investments in a timely and cost-efficient manner.

Six Bus Rapid Transit systems
Bus Rapid Transit (BRT) is a popular and less-expensive alternative to building new subway or light-rail lines. (Because they usually cost less than "$1 billion per line to build, BRT is not always counted as true megaproject. We do so here because many cities have built multi-line BRT systems and because the rail transit alternatives to BRT do qualify as megaprojects.) Able to move up to 45,000 passengers per hour per line, BRT makes use of a dedicated

right-of-way, high-capacity buses, and station designs that permit quick vehicular access and egress. Chapter 7 looks at recent BRT experiences in three South American and three Asian cities. Curitiba (Brazil) began BRT service in 1974 and is recognized around the world for having made BRT an essential component of its long-term land use and housing planning. Quito (Ecuador) introduced BRT service in 1995 and was followed five years later by Bogotá in Colombia. Today, Curitiba has seven BRT lines, Quito has three, and Bogotá has 11. (Bogotá's BRT system is today the world's busiest, carrying more than two million passengers each weekday.)

Seeking an alternative to building expensive metro systems, many Asian cities began building BRT lines at the dawn of the new millennium. Jakarta (Indonesia) and Seoul (South Korea) both opened their first BRT corridors in 2004—today, each operates 12 BRT lines—and Guangzhou opened its one and only BRT line in 2010. (All three Asian cities also operate metro rail systems.) BRT is unusual among megaprojects in that later implementers explicitly learned from early adopters with respect to station spacing, vehicle access, and bus design. This type of planning and technology transfer was aided by the efforts of the non-profit Institute for Transport Development and Policy.

Bridge and Tunnel Megaprojects

The tunnel and bridge projects included in this volume each suffered from unforeseen problems. Seattle's Alaskan Way Viaduct replacement tunnel experienced a two-year construction delay when its tunnel boring machine broke after hitting a piece of pipe debris. Because of shifts in the regional economy, the Hong Kong-Zhuhai-Macau Bridge never came close to hitting its traffic and revenue projections.

Seattle's Alaskan Way Tunnel
The Alaskan Way Tunnel (aka SR99 Tunnel) is a 2.3 mile single-bore tunnel below Alaskan Way which runs along downtown Seattle's waterfront. Built to replace an aging elevated highway damaged in a 2001 earthquake and opened to traffic in February 2019, the Alaskan Way Tunnel took an extra two years and $250 million to complete, putting it 8 percent over budget. The delay and cost overrun were caused by the project's single tunnel boring machine unexpectedly hitting a buried pipe fragment, resulting in its internal mechanisms having to be replaced.

The planning process that led to the decision to build a tunnel instead of a surface or elevated roadway took nearly eight years owing to its initially non-collaborative nature. Once the tunnel was approved by Seattle voters in August 2011, city officials used the project as an opportunity to undertake an innovative waterfront planning and redevelopment process. The Alaskan Way Tunnel was undertaken entirely as a publicly-financed project, with funding provided by the Washington State Department of Transportation (which also served as the project manager), the City of Seattle, and the Seattle and Tacoma Port Authority.

The Hong Kong–Zhuhai–Macau Bridge

At 55 km (34 miles) in length, the Hong Kong– Zhuhai–Macau (HKZM) Bridge Project is the longest combined bridge–undersea tunnel project in the world. As its name suggest, the HKZM Bridge connects Lantau Island in Hong Kong with the 2.5 million resident city of Zhuhai across Lingdingyang Bay. In addition to its three bridge structures, the HKZM Bridge includes a 6.7 km immersed tube undersea tunnel.

Planning for the HKZM Bridge began in 2003 but it took the governments of China, Hong Kong, Macau and Guangdong Province five years to agree on an exact alignment and funding scheme. Construction of the $16.4 billion HKZM Bridge project began in December 2009 and was completed in February 2018, a year late and $2.4 billion (15%) over budget. Undertaken as an economic development project to better link the export-oriented economies of Hong Kong and Zhuhai with Macau's tourism-based economy, the HKZM Bridge has never come close to meeting its traffic projections and is today regarded as an infrastructure white elephant.

Airport Megaprojects

The three airport megaprojects included in this volume include one entirely new airport (Berlin Brandenburg International), one innovative airport terminal facility (Jewel Changi) and a re-imagined and rebuilt terminal (LaGuardia Terminal B). Jewel Changi was completed in 2019, Berlin Brandenburg in 2020, and the new LaGuardia Terminal B in 2022.

Singapore's Jewel Changi Airport

Opened in April 2019, Jewel Changi is a state-of-the-art airport passenger concourse linking Singapore Changi Airport's three main terminals and featuring a five-story waterfall, an indoor nature park, a destination shopping mall, and a 2,500-car parking garage. Jewel Changi was built at a cost of $1.3 billion to further enhance Singapore's reputation for having the world's best airport. Designed by an international team of architects and engineers led by Moshe Safdie, and completed on schedule and within its construction budget, Jewel Changi was built and financed as a public–private partnership between the Singapore Civil Aviation Authority (CAAS), the Changi Airport Group (CAG), and Singapore-based shopping center developer CapitaLand. Changi

Airport Group previously served as the airport planning and development arm of the Singapore Department of Public Works but was privatized in 2009. In its first six months of operation, Jewel Changi Airport drew 50 million visitors.

Berlin Brandenburg International Airport

Opened to the traveling public in November 2020, nine years behind schedule and $3.7 billion over budget, Berlin Brandenburg International Airport Willy Brandt (BER) is an entirely new international airport replacing three older and smaller airports (Tegel, Tempelhof and Schönefeld). Berlin Brandenburg is located just north of the Schönefeld Airport and is linked to Berlin City Center by subway and express highway. Originally planned to be financed through a public-private partnership, when no appropriate private partner could be found, Berlin Brandenburg ended up being developed by the German states of Berlin and Brandenburg. Through a specially-created authority, the two states also took on the job of managing the construction process despite having no prior expertise in that area. Many of the scheduling delays and cost overruns the project experienced can be attributed to that lack of experience.

LaGuardia Airport Terminal B

Together with JFK and Newark Airport, LaGuardia Airport is one of New York City's three principal airports. Originally completed in 1964, Terminal B, LaGuardia's principal passenger terminal had long needed to be expanded and reconfigured to deal with LaGuardia's ever-increasing passenger volumes. Managed by the Port Authority of New York and New Jersey, the $4 billion phased construction of a new LaGuardia Terminal B began in 2016 and was completed in 2022. In addition to all new terminal and concourse buildings and passenger facilities, the project involves building new taxiways and new vehicle circulation and parking facilities. A later and separately-funded phase will include building a people-mover system connecting LaGuardia to the Long Island Railroad and New York City Subway. Throughout the construction process, Terminal B remained in full operation. The project is being undertaken as a public–private partnership between the Port Authority and LaGuardia Gateway Partners, a consortium partnership assembled to redevelop Terminal B. The project is being managed by the Port Authority, which previously planned and managed the construction of new terminal buildings at both Newark Airport and JFK.

Urban Development Megaprojects

New central business districts, waterfront revitalization projects, and mixed-use/ high-technology new towns have become popular in recent years throughout Asia, Europe and North America. This volume includes one of each: Canary

Wharf, London's second financial and business district; HafenCity, an innovative waterfront and port re-use project in Hamburg, Germany; and Songdo IBD (International Business District), South Korea's first-ever effort to build a cutting edge mixed-use new town using a public–private joint venture arrangement involving American real estate developers.

London's Canary Wharf

Canary Wharf is a 97 acre docklands redevelopment project located 5 miles east of central London. Initially conceived of as a "back-office" district for London's traditional financial district, Canary Wharf was planned and developed in the late 1980s by Olympia and York, a Toronto-based real estate developer recruited by British Prime Minister Margaret Thatcher to take on the job after a previous developer-led effort fell through. Led by Paul Reichmann, Olympia and York modeled Canary Wharf after its World Financial Center project in New York City. In exchange for Transport for London providing Underground and light-rail services to Canary Wharf via the Jubilee Line Extension and Docklands Light Rail (DLR) system, Olympia and York agreed to raise all the financing for Canary Wharf itself. One Canada Square, Olympia and York's inaugural office project, was completed in 1991 in the midst of a deep property recession, and when the company was unable to pay its creditors, it was placed in administration (i.e., bankruptcy) and Canary Wharf was sold to investors. When the London office market started recovering in 1995, Canary Wharf's new owners (including Paul Reichmann) were able to continue developing the project. Today, Canary Wharf includes more than 16 million square feet of office and retail space, has a market value in excess of £10 billion, is the daytime home to more than 120,000 workers, has planning permissions in place to add another 5.5 million square feet, and is known around the world as London's second central business district.

HafenCity, Hamburg

HafenCity is a 392 acre waterfront redevelopment project involving the repurposing and physical redevelopment of Hamburg's historic Elbe River port district. Intended to be environmentally friendly and transit-and-pedestrian-oriented, HafenCity is designed around an innovative building concept that mixes different land uses vertically as well as uses horizontally. Conceived in the mid-1990s, HafenCity is the brainchild of Hamburg Mayor Henning Voscherau, who sought to redirect Hamburg's post-Cold War population growth and economic development into its largely abandoned port area, and Hamburg architect Professor Volkwin Marg, who proposed HafenCity's innovative mixed-use design principles. Rather than develop HafenCity themselves or partner with private developers to do the job, Hamburg city officials created a special purpose public land development agency and staffed it with professionals who understood the land development process. That agency, HafenCity Hamburg GmbH (HHG), was given the job of implementing the HafenCity masterplan through a multifaceted land disposition strategy that included land sales and ground leases, regulatory relief, and subsidies and financing assistance. Since beginning operations in 2001, HHG has leveraged Hamburg's roughly US$2.8 billion investment in public transport improvements and environmental amenities into more than $10 billion in additional public and private investment. HafenCity is today the preferred location of some of Germany's best-known technology companies and universities, and when its ten districts are completed in the mid-2020s, it will be home to 45,000 jobs and 12,000 residents. Even with all of its successes, HafenCity is still taking much longer to complete than when originally planned, a lesson that even in the best of circumstances, the real estate market moves at its own pace.

Songdo IBD
Songdo IBD (International Business District) is a 1,500-acre "new town" project located adjacent to the City of Incheon (South Korea), 15 minutes by car from Incheon Airport and 35 minutes from downtown Seoul. Initially conceived as an alternative to Seoul for global technology companies seeking speedy airport access and reduced rents, Songdo IBD commenced development in 2001 as a joint venture between the City of Incheon and US property developer Gale International, and was guided by a masterplan created by the New York-based design firm KPF that cleverly balanced office buildings, mixed-use retail, multiple housing types, and environmental and residential amenities. Songdo was the first large real estate project to be undertaken in South Korea following the passage of a 1998 law allowing the ownership participation of non-Korean investors. With build-out initially projected for 2015, Songdo was expected to attract $50 billion in private investment capital. Neither Gale International nor the City of Incheon quite understood what they were getting into, and from day one Songdo ran into severe land disposition, financing, tenanting and market absorption problems. Although the development of Songdo—now branded as Asia's leading smart city—continues and is expected to be completed by 2030, the Incheon–Gale joint venture was dissolved in 2010.

An Urban Park Megaproject

Following the early examples of Sydney (Australia) and Bilbao (Spain), cities around the world have been converting disinvested industrial waterfronts into a mixture of park, cultural, and residential uses. Among the largest and most watched of these efforts is Brooklyn Bridge Park in New York City.

Brooklyn Bridge Park

Brooklyn Bridge Park occupies an 85-acre site along the Brooklyn waterfront immediately under and to the south of the Brooklyn Bridge. The impetus for creating Brooklyn Bridge Park first emerged in the late 1980s when the Port Authority of New York and New Jersey announced it was moving its Brooklyn port operations to New Jersey City. Brooklyn community groups wanted all of the former port site to be used for park and cultural facilities while the Port Authority and City of New York wanted to redevelop parts of the site for commercial and residential uses to provide an operating cash flow to support the park. This conflict continued for 15 years and was only resolved in 2002 with the infusion of additional public monies and the creation of the Brooklyn Bridge Park Development Corporation. Even then, the project continued to run into legal and funding difficulties. Construction finally got underway in 2008 and was mostly completed by 2017. The full cost of the project is expected to exceed $300 million, most of which has been financed out of state and city grants and loans.

Five Renewable Energy Megaprojects

Very large-scale renewable energy projects are financially risky and, when funded by private investors and banks, typically require some form of back-up government financial guarantee. This case study (Chapter 16) looks at how five recent renewable energy megaprojects around the world were assembled and financed. They include the $2.5 billion 2050 megawatt (MW) Pavagada Solar Park in India, completed in 2019; the $2.5 billion 580 MW Noor Ourzazate Concentrated Solar Energy Facility in Morocco, completed in 2016; the $1.6 billion 659 MW Walney Extension offshore windfarm off the British coast, completed in 2018; the 3,000 MW Bath County (Virginia) pumped hydroelectric storage facility in the United States, completed in 1985; and the $5.9 billion Xinjiang-Anhui ultra-high voltage transmission line completed in 2019 in China.

4. Unfinished business—London Crossrail

John D. Landis

ABBREVIATIONS USED IN THIS CHAPTER

BCR   Benefit-cost ratio—a method for comparing project benefits and costs over time.

BRS   Business rate supplement—a supplemental yearly fee assessed on businesses in the Crossrail catchment area to help pay for Crossrail.

CRL   Crossrail Limited (aka Crossrail)—the public corporation established in 2001 to oversee construction of the Crossrail (aka Elizabeth) Line; incorporated in 2008.

DfT   The Department for Transport—the UK government agency in charge of all passenger transport modes.

GLA   The Greater London Authority—the top-tier administrative body for the Greater London region, consisting of a directly-elected executive Mayor of London and a 25-member London Assembly representing Greater London's 32 boroughs.

HMT   Her Majesty's Treasury—the UK's economic and finance ministry.

NAO   The National Audit Office—the UK's independent public spending watchdog. Reports to Parliament.

TBM   Tunnel boring machine.

TfL   Transport for London—the local government agency responsible for London's transport network.

A 117 kilometer (73 mile) express rail line connecting the Greater London region from east to west, Crossrail is the largest public infrastructure project undertaken in the United Kingdom since the Channel Tunnel opened in 1994 (Table 4.1). Approved by Parliament in July 2008 at a cost of £15.9 billion, Crossrail, now called the Elizabeth Line in honor of Queen Elizabeth, was originally scheduled to enter service in 2018. After four years of delays, Crossrail finally opened on May 31, 2022, having cost an estimated £20.7 billion, a 30 percent cost overrun. Crossrail was conceived before Brexit as an investment in maintaining London's global financial leadership. How well it will fill that role in a post-Brexit world is still very much up in the air. This chapter takes a detailed look at Crossrail's planning and construction process focusing on what went right, what went wrong, and why.

Table 4.1   *Crossrail in brief*

Description	London Crossrail is a 117 km high-speed metro line that connects Heathrow Airport (and parts west) to central London, Canary Wharf, and London's East End communities. Crossrail's eastern and western sections run on upgraded overland tracks. Its 21 km central section runs between Royal Oak and Abbey Wood in deep bore tunnels.
Lead sponsor(s)	UK Department for Transport; Transport for London
Primary rationale	(1) Relieve London area roadway and Underground congestion; (2) promote business agglomeration economies.
Primary funding sources	Government grants and loans; business and land development assessments
Regulatory/funding approval given in	2008 (after 5 years of planning)
Construction started	2009
Construction completed	2022
Schedule overrun	4 years (44%)
Initial development budget	US$20.4 billion
Final development cost	US$26.5 billion (current estimate)
Cost overrun	US$6.1 billion (30%)
Reasons for overruns	Crossrail's project management and contracting practices were overly complex and lacked adequate contractor performance requirements.
Principal takeaways	Large, complex, and spatially extensive projects such as Crossrail require experienced project managers and clear lines of authority and responsibility.

AN AMBITIOUS AND COMPLICATED RAIL PROJECT

Crossrail, also known as the Elizabeth Line in honor of Queen Elizabeth II, consists of three distinct sections. The 21 km central section runs below central London in twin-bore tunnels from Paddington Station in the west to Whitechapel in the east, with new stations at Bond Street, Tottenham Court Road, Farringdon, and Liverpool Street. West of Paddington, Crossrail takes over the Great Western main line to Hayes and Harlington Station where it divides into a southern spur serving Heathrow Airport and a northern branch that continues on to Maidenhead and Reading. Crossrail's eastern section also divides into two branches, a longer northern branch that extends from Whitechapel to Shenfield along the existing above-ground metro line, and a shorter southern branch that terminates at Abbey Wood via an underground line with stations at Canary Wharf, Custom House and Woolwich. Crossrail is tightly integrated with London's existing rail systems. Thirteen Crossrail stations, mostly in its central section, connect directly to London Underground lines while 14 stations (including Paddington, Farringdon and Liverpool Street) connect to Network Rail. Altogether, Crossrail has 41 stations, ten of which are entirely new.

Table 4.2   *Crossrail by the numbers*

Crossrail route length	117 km (each way)
Tunnel length	21 km (each way), 42 km overall
Number of stations	41
Number of new stations	10
Increase in central London rail capacity	10%
Rolling stock	9-carriage trainsets, accommodating 1,500 passengers each
Projected annual ridership in 2026	200 million passengers
Peak hour service frequency	24 trains per hour each direction
Average travel speed	140 kph
Before and after travel times, selected trips	
Paddington to Tottenham Court Road	20 minutes ▶ 4 minutes
Paddington to Canary Wharf	34 minutes ▶ 17 minutes
Bond Street to Whitechapel	24 minutes ▶ 10 minutes
Canary Wharf to Liverpool Street	21 minutes ▶ 6 minutes
Canary Wharf to Heathrow	55 minutes ▶ 39 minutes
Whitechapel to Canary Wharf	13 minutes ▶ 3 minutes
Abbey Wood to Heathrow	93 minutes ▶ 52 minutes

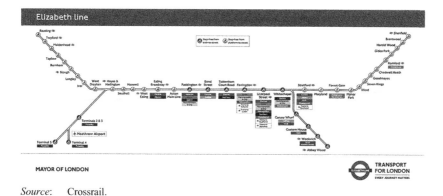

Source: Crossrail.

Figure 4.1   *Crossrail (Elizabeth Line) route map showing connections to London Underground, Docklands Light Rail and overground routes*

Crossrail is operated by Hong Kong's MTR Corporation under concession to Transport for London (TfL), the local government agency responsible for most of the London transport network. Crossrail's central section trains will run at morning and evening peak-hour speeds of up to 140 kph and frequencies up to 24 trains per hour. This will reduce trip times for passengers traveling from Paddington Station to Whitechapel from the current 39 minutes to just 13 minutes. For travelers going on to Canary Wharf, Crossrail will cut an additional 7 minutes off their trip time. Travelers to Heathrow Airport are also set to benefit. Residents of Abbey Wood in southeast London will be able to get to Heathrow Airport in 52 minutes, versus the current 93, while business travelers making the journey between Canary Wharf and Heathrow will see their travel time fall from 55 minutes to 39 minutes.

Finishing Crossrail within the originally allotted ten-year schedule and £15.9 billion budget was always going to be an engineering, funding and project management challenge. Britain's three most recent transportation megaprojects, the Channel Tunnel, the Jubilee Line Extension and Heathrow Terminal 5, were each completed late and suffered from significant cost over-runs, and Crossrail was to be bigger and more complicated than any of them. Completing Crossrail's central section twin-bore tunnels would require that its tunnel machines operate virtually non-stop for 36 months, and that the eight individually-drilled tunnels link up exactly. During peak periods, Crossrail's train signaling system would have to be capable of accommodating as many as 32 trains per hour in each direction, nearly twice the frequency of existing Underground lines. Covering Crossrail's construction cost would require assembling a financing scheme that would draw from an unprecedented number of separate funding sources, including the UK and London governments, tens of thousands of adjacent business and property-owners, various London area property development companies, and major institutions such as Heathrow Airport. Managing the more than 30 domestic and international contractors and 14,000 workers building Crossrail would require developing a matrix approach to project management that would encourage individual contractors to coordinate with each other directly, not just hierarchically through senior project managers, as is typically the case.

Initially, Crossrail's construction went much as planned. Tunnelling operations were completed on schedule in mid-2015 with significant but manageable cost over-runs. Troubles only emerged in 2017 when it became apparent that the different contractors building each of the new central segment stations were not working in sync, and when Siemens, the German company installing Crossrail's train signaling system, announced that the system would need additional testing. Once an individual contractor fell off the Crossrail critical path, delays and cost overruns quickly cascaded. Crossrail's initial £14.8 billion construction budget swelled to £15.4 billion in July 2018, to £17.8 billion in December 2018, and to more than £19 billion in August 2020, requiring continuous cash infusions from the British government. Initially scheduled to begin in mid-2018, train service on Crossrail's all-important central section between Paddington and Whitechapel finally opened for passenger service on May 31 2022, four years behind schedule.

These time and cost overruns are not extreme by the standards of other contemporary transport megaprojects, such as the Second Avenue Subway in New York City, whose 1.8 miles of length cost $4.5 billion, or the new Berlin-Brandenburg International Airport whose opening was delayed by nine years. Still, the whole point of Crossrail's much-advertised innovative project management approach was to avoid the mistakes of previous UK transport megaprojects. In the end, nothing worked out as hoped: since the beginning of construction in 2009, Crossrail Limited (CRL), the special purpose creation of the UK Department for Transport (DfT) and Transport for London (TfL) tasked with completing Crossrail, has gone through four CEOs, two chairmen, and an ever-growing number of audits.

THIRTY YEARS IN THE MAKING

The idea for a single rail line connecting all of London is hardly new (Crossrail Ltd 2021a; Hebbert 2014). It was raised first in the 1870s by the Regents Canal Company, which sought parliamentary approval to build a railway, running alongside or even replacing the Regents Canal. Parliament eventually granted permission for the scheme in the 1880s, but although efforts continued over subsequent years to identify a specific route, intense competition from other railway companies brought the idea to naught.

The idea resurfaced in 1944 as part of Sir Patrick Abercrombie's Greater London Plan. In addition to proposing a green belt circling London, Abercrombie suggested building two new underground lines to connect London's eastern and western halves (Hebbert 2014, p. 176). Although much of the Abercrombie Plan eventually came to pass, the new underground lines did not, and with Greater London losing population from 1950 to 1990, there was little government or public appetite to take on the huge financial obligations that building an entirely new underground line would entail. Instead, a succession of British governments chose to to better integrate London's underground and overland rail services.

Still, the idea of linking eastern and western London via an express rail line, something akin to what Paris was doing with its Réseau Express Régional (RER) service, wouldn't go away. In 1974, the Greater London Council and UK Department for Environment jointly published *The London Rail Study, a Blueprint for the London Rail System's Future* (Hebbert 2014, p. 180). It proposed joining British Rail's Western Region lines to its Eastern Region lines via a new central tunnel connector with stations at Paddington, Marble Arch, Bond Street, Leicester Square, Holborn and Liverpool Street. Another new tunnel would connect the Southern Region's Central Division services via stations at Victoria, Piccadilly, Leicester Square, Blackfriars, Monument and London Bridge. The visionary *London Rail Study* even saw fit to name the new line, calling it "Crossrail." Unfortunately, with an estimated cost upwards of £300 million, Crossrail was too costly an undertaking for the struggling British economy.

With London's role as a global financial center exploding in the aftermath of its "Big Bang" financial reforms, the British government in 1989 decided to look anew at the possibility of Crossrail service, commissioning a new study called the *Central London Rail Study* (Hebbert 2014, p. 184). Picking up where the 1974 study left off, the *Central London Rail Study* was more ambitious. In addition to proposing a revised Crossrail line, extending from Wimbledon (in the west) to Hackney (in the east) via Chelsea, the study proposed a north–south route crossing the Thames River to be known as Thameslink.

An altogether different study, also published in 1989, proposed extending the existing Jubilee Underground Line (which terminated at Southwark) under the Thames River east to Canary Wharf and then on to Stratford (Hebbert 2014, p. 185). With Canary Wharf developer Olympia and York offering £400 million towards the Jubilee Line Extension's £2.1 billion cost, it was quickly approved. One year later, in October 1990, the British Government gave the go-ahead to British Rail and TfL's predecessor agency, London Transport, to further develop the east–west Crossrail scheme. When the revised Crossrail scheme was submitted to Parliament in bill form in November 1991, it recommended building a new east–west connecting tunnel between Paddington and Liverpool Street at a cost of £2 billion. Prime Minister John Major's Conservative Government regarded this sum as expensive but not impossible and counseled the bill's sponsors that if they wanted their plan to go forward, its costs would have to be split between riders and property developers, the same financing scheme used for the Jubilee Line Extension. Before the revised Crossrail proposal's financing plan could be fully worked out, it was quietly scuttled by Parliament, which was still dealing with the financial after-effects of a national recession and the 1992 devaluation of the British pound (Hebbert 2014, p. 186).

Table 4.3   *Crossrail timeline*

1941–1948	First proposals for cross-London railway tunnels put forward by George Dow
1974	London Rail Study Report recommends a Paddington–Liverpool Street "Crossrail" tunnel
1989	Central London Rail Study proposes three Crossrail schemes, including an east–west Paddington/Marylebone–Liverpool Street route
1991	A private bill proposing a Paddington–Liverpool Street tunnel is submitted to Parliament by London Underground and British Rail. Amidst budgetary problems and a devalued British pound, it is rejected in 1994
2001	A new Crossrail scheme is promoted by Cross London Rail Links.
2003–2005	A series of benefit-cost analyses of Crossrail are conducted by her Majesty's Treasury, each subsequent study expanding the ways in which Crossrail's economic benefits are valued.
December 2004	The independent Montague Report is released endorsing a slightly reduced-in-scale Crossrail.
May 2005	The Crossrail Hybrid Bill is put before Parliament. It is repeatedly debated and refined over the next three years.
July 2008	Crossrail Act 2008 receives Royal Assent with an estimated construction cost of £15.9 billion. The cost estimate is later reduced to £14.8 billion. Crossrail Limited (CRL) is formally incorporated.
May 2009	Crossrail construction work begins at Canary Wharf
May 2012	Crossrail tunnelling operations begin at Royal Oak Portal. They are completed at Farringdon three years later.
2015	As scheduled, Liverpool Street–Shenfield service is transferred to TfL Rail.
2018	Two months late, Paddington–Heathrow service is transferred to TfL Rail.
July 2018	Transport Minister Jo Johnson announces that DfT and TfL have agreed to increase Crossrail funding by £600 million, bringing it to a total of £15.4 billion.
August 2018	The Government announces that Crossrail's opening has been delayed until autumn 2019 due to the need for additional equipment testing.
October 2018	The Government announces it has pumped an addition £350 million into Crossrail, bringing its total cost to £15.8 billion.
December 2018	Crossrail announces it will need another £2 billion to finish construction and that Infrastructure and Projects Authority boss Tony Meggs will replace Terry Morgan as Crossrail Chairman.
April 2019	Parliament's Public Accounts Committee says it is "unconvinced" Crossrail's £2.8 billion bailout will be enough. Crossrail CEO Mark Wild announces that service on Crossrail's central section will begin some time between October 2020 and March 2021.
September 2019	Crossrail Chair Tony Meggs admits Crossrail could be another six months late and will need a further £400 million to finish construction.
January 2020	TfL Commissioner Mike Brown says his organization expects Crossrail to be completed during the fourth quarter of 2021.
August 2020	Crossrail officials confirms the cost of finishing the project will top £19 billion and that the line will not open until the first half of 2022.
May 2022	Now known as the Elizabeth Line, Crossrail opens for passenger service along its full 73 mile length.

Parliament's decision to sideline Crossrail notwithstanding, its backers refused to concede. Assuming that Crossrail might someday rise anew, Britain's Department for Transport (DfT) moved to pre-emptively safeguard its likely route by declaring future Crossrail station sites off limits to private developers. Believing that Parliament might have acted too rashly dismissing Crossrail, London area MPs from both parties began talking with the London business community about ways to put Crossrail back on track. After months of discussions, it was announced in July 1994 that a new Crossrail feasibility study would proceed under the Transport and Works Act (TWA), which had replaced privately-sponsored bills as the procedure under which large infrastructure projects were introduced (Crossrail Ltd 2021a). The new study's results were released in early 1996 and its conclusions were not good news for Crossrail proponents: under almost every alignment and financing scenario considered, Crossrail's costs would exceed its benefits. The Government made no public comments on the study's findings, but instead asked Crossrail's sponsors, London Transport and British Rail, to quietly withdraw their TWA application (Crossrail 2021a).

Like a cat with nine lives, Crossrail refused to die. A small team of planners within the London Underground continued to safeguard its planned right-of-way, ensuring that Crossrail could proceed physically if a way could be found to pay for it. The British economy was looking up, having experienced a strong recovery from the 1994 recession. The Labour Party's victory at the polls in May 1997 also bode well, with Prime Minister Tony Blair's new government having announced a goal of increasing rail usage in Britain by 50 percent in ten years. A third factor that portended well for Crossrail was the 2000 election of Ken Livingstone as London's first executive mayor. A former socialist turned dealmaker, Livingstone viewed Crossrail as central to his efforts to have London eclipse New York City as the world's leading financial center.

Crossrail would help in two regards (Hebbert 2014, p. 187). First, by reducing travel times across central London, it would make it easier for the city's expanding banking and financial firms to recruit the workers they needed. Second, it would expand access to London's eastern boroughs where there was a surplus of land that could be redeveloped for desperately needed housing. Having publicly criticized TfL (which took over for London Transport in 2000) as too bureaucratic and not sufficiently passenger oriented, Livingstone, upon taking office in May 2000, immediately fired 27 of TfL's 30 top executives, and replaced them with a new team under leadership of former New York City transit boss Robert Kiley, whom Livingstone had recruited to rebuild and rethink London's aging transit system.[1]

With the explicit backing of both Blair and Livingstone, Secretary of State for Transport and DfT head John Prescott was directed to undertake yet another Crossrail feasibility study (Crossrail Ltd. 2021a). Released in July 2000, it again reaffirmed the need for a new deep tunnel between Paddington and Liverpool Street, and recommended that a new entity, Cross London Rail Links Limited (CLRL), be formed to take over the Crossrail planning job from British Rail and TfL. When CLRL was officially established in January 2002, it was as a joint venture of TfL and the UK's Strategic Rail Authority (later folded into the Department of Transportation), but with its own £154 million planning budget authorized by Parliament (Crossrail 2021a).

CLRL, with the help of its financial advisor, Bank of America, and Ashurst, its legal advisor, spent the next 18 months holding public hearings and preparing cost and ridership projections (Crossrail Ltd. 2021a). Despite its tremendous cost, the deep-bore tunnel between Paddington and Liverpool was less controversial whether Crossrail's east and west lines should have one or two branches each. To save money, it was decided that the eastern and western Crossrail branches would make use of Network Rail's existing rights-of-way and stations. Preliminary passenger projections indicated there would be significant ridership demand from both the northern and southern feeder line catchment areas of Crossrail's east and west branches. Given its proposed service frequency, with as many as 24 trains per hour in each direction traversing Crossrail's single tunnel segment, coordinating service on so many feeder lines was going to be a problem.

A preliminary Crossrail business case (i.e., ridership projections and an accompanying benefit-cost analysis) was presented by CLRL executives to the new Secretary of State for Transport Alistair Darling in July 2003 (Crossrail Ltd. 2021a). Darling announced that the Labour Government supported Crossrail in principle, but that with CLRL's proposal costing an estimated £10 billion, he needed to be assured that Crossrail could be fully paid for. Accordingly, Darling appointed an independent review team led by senior infrastructure advisor Sir Adrian Montague[2] to take a detailed look at every aspect of Crossrail's cost and funding structure. Montague was also given latitude to recommend eliminating possible feeder lines. Montague's review was delivered in July 2004. It confirmed CRLR's earlier £10 billion cost estimate as accurate, and to save money, recommended that the Kingston line on the western Crossrail branch be eliminated (Montague 2004). With both Darling's and Montague's endorsements, Crossrail was now further along the path to construction than ever before.

What had changed between Parliament's 1994 decision to suspend Crossrail and Darling's cautious Crossrail endorsement ten years later? For one thing the British economy, currency, and government budget were all in much sounder shape. London's reputation as a destination for investment capital and highly-educated service workers had grown steadily, generating a nascent business and property value boom (Gomez-Ibanez 2009). After a slow start, Canary Wharf was becoming an integral part of the London economy and office market, and there was an evident need for a faster connection to central London and Heathrow Airport. Despite earlier dissatisfaction over cost overruns, both the Jubilee Line Extension and the Docklands Light Rail Line had come to be regarded as worthwhile investments. And despite their ongoing personal and political differences, Prime Minister Blair and Mayor Livingstone agreed on the need to improve London's transport system: Blair for environmental reasons, and Livingstone, because he considered London's worsening traffic to be the biggest impediment to a brighter economic future (*The Guardian* 2004).

MAKING THE CROSSRAIL BUSINESS CASE

Darling and Montague's endorsements were only advisory. They carried no spending authorization. That would have to come from Parliament only after further reviews of Crossrail's business case by Her Majesty's Treasury (HMT). Making HMT's job more difficult was the fact that Crossrail was too large for the Government's standard budgeting process. Allowing for inflation, Crossrail's cost would run to £2 billion per year and account for nearly 20 percent of DfT's annual budget for all of Britain. This meant that either some other DfT transportation project would have to be removed from the budget or that Crossrail would have to be financed by issuing additional government borrowing, something that Chancellor of the Exchequer Gordon Brown had pledged not to do.

Beyond the difficulties of finding funding, HMT required all major investment projects be subject to a rigorous benefit-cost analysis in accord with the provisions of the "Green Book," its detailed manual for determining how to count, value and weight project costs and benefits. The Green Book's treatment of transportation project benefits had evolved over successive generations to go beyond travel time savings and safety improvements to also include the avoidance of social costs such as air and water pollution, and the economic effects on nearby properties.

As HMT's business case review got underway, TfL and the London Mayor's Office grew concerned that its narrow Green Book-based approach might ignore what they saw as the central argument for approving Crossrail—allowing London to better accommodate additional population and job growth (Gomez-Ibanez 2009). Recent projections produced in the Mayor's Office indicated that London's population would grow from 7.3 million in 2001 to 8 million by 2016. On the employment side, the number of London workers was forecast to increase from 4.6 million in 2001 to 5.1 million in 2016, with the bulk of the increase projected to occur in the central London and Canary Wharf areas. London' roadways were already congested, as were the Underground lines serving Central London. TfL's own projections indicated that, without Crossrail, worsening traffic congestion would cause central London to lose as many as 30,000 jobs by 2027, resulting in a £6.3 billion loss in wages and productivity.

Even when TfL's employment and economic loss scenario was included in HMT's business case analysis, its initial estimates of Crossrail's benefit-cost ratio (BCR) came in at a disappointing 1.3, far too low to be recommended for approval (Gomez-Ibanez 2009). A subsequent analysis based on the results of the Montague Report, which deleted the Kingston line, raised Crossrail's BCR to 1.8. This was better, but still on the low side of approvable projects. In response to criticism from the Mayor's Office that its analysis undercounted the economic benefits associated with potential agglomeration economies— the benefits that occur when complementary business activities locate in close proximity to one another—HMT agreed to hire London School of Economics Professor Anthony Venables to independently identify any agglomeration benefits. Venables' report, delivered in June 2003, concluded that Crossrail would indeed generate significant agglomeration benefits, but it declined to put an exact number on them. To do that, HMT hired Imperial College economics professor Daniel Graham to analyze the empirical relationships between job density and business productivity. Graham's results, presented in what became known as the *Wider Economic Benefits* reports, indicated that the higher job densities made possible by Crossrail would increase its cumulative economic benefits by another £7.1 billion, raising its BCR to 2.6 and putting it squarely within the bounds of fundable projects.[3]

On a purely practical level, HMT was also concerned about CLRL's ability to deliver Crossrail because of its TfL lineage. The last TfL-built Underground line, the Jubilee Line Extension, had become a byword for project mismanagement, having been delivered two years late and £1.4 billion over budget. And it wasn't just TfL. Other British rail projects, notably the second phase of the Channel Tunnel Rail Link connecting Folkestone to London, had done no better. A retrospective analysis of the Jubilee Line Extension's cost overruns undertaken by TfL concluded that they were principally the result of unexpected property price appreciation and a failure to budget for normal contingencies, two mistakes that TfL pledged not to repeat with Crossrail (Gomez-Ibanez 2009). HMT was unpersuaded by TfL's assurances and asked them to undertake a series of statistical simulations to better estimate the range of possible cost overruns. The results of TfL's simulations indicated that there was a 95 percent probability that Crossrail's costs would not exceed £16 billion. This became the worst-case cost estimate that HMT used in its benefit-cost analysis.

With each successive economic study, the case for Crossrail grew more robust. There was still concern over about how all the funds needed to pay for

Crossrail would be assembled, but with a draft of the *Wider Economic Benefit* report and TfL's cost simulations in hand, and with Ken Livingstone having introduced his London Congestion Charging Zone (CCZ) scheme two years earlier, making additional public transit funds available,[4] Transport Minister Alexander Darling formally presented the Crossrail Hybrid Bill to Parliament in February 2005 (Crossrail 2021a).

Thus began a three-year process of committee reviews, additional studies, bill amendments and even a June 2007 change in prime ministers from Tony Blair to Gordon Brown. Outside the halls of Parliament, TfL and DfT worked continuously to put together what would be the most complicated infrastructure funding package in British history, pulling in voluntary contributions from property developers, an increase in the business tax rate, operating credits from Network Rail, and an unprecedented £5 billion allocation from the Government (Crossrail 2021a).

An amended Crossrail Hybrid Bill finally emerged from Parliament in June 2008 and received Royal Assent a month later as the Crossrail Act of 2008. With the global economy slipping into recession, Transport Minister Andrew Adonis announced in November 2008 that Crossrail would go ahead despite the Government's worsening fiscal situation. On December 4, 2008, TfL and DfT signed the Crossrail Sponsors' Agreement, establishing a joint subsidiary, Crossrail Limited (CRL), to oversee construction and let contracts. After 35 years of on again-off again plans, Crossrail finally broke ground on May 15, 2009, at Canary Wharf, when London Mayor Boris Johnson (who had succeeded Ken Livingstone in 2008) and Transport Secretary Lord Adonis launched the first pile into the new Canary Wharf Crossrail station (Crossrail 2021a).

FILLING CROSSRAIL'S FUNDING GAP

From the outset, it was apparent to all concerned that Crossrail's size and cost would require a new funding model. Traditionally, British rail transport projects were financed from a combination of government grants and bond sales backed by user charges (i.e., passenger fare revenues). As the earlier Montague report had made clear, this would not be the case for Crossrail, noting that there was significant "doubt as to the available market capacity in the construction and financial sectors to support a project of this size" (Montague 2004, p. 2). Simply put, the Government was worried that its usual sources of finance would be insufficient to cover Crossrail's full cost. On the hopeful side, the Montague Review went on to note, "London business interests appear ready to contribute significant amounts, in the range of £2,000 million to perhaps £3,000 million NPV [net present value], to the project by way of Alternative Funding Mechanisms" (Montague 2004, p. 2). Fortunately, there was precedent for this arrangement. Fifteen years earlier, the British Government had persuaded Canary Wharf developer Olympia and York to contribute £400 million towards the completion of the Docklands Light Railway and the Jubilee Line Extension, and it hoped something similar might be possible with Crossrail.

Exactly how big was Crossrail's funding gap? An early analysis by TfL suggested it would be able to raise about £5 billion in fares from Crossrail riders, of which roughly £2 billion could be used to repay bondholders. (This assumed that Crossrail would quickly hit its ridership targets and would be able to raise fares by an average of one percent per year.) This, coupled with roughly £5 billion in DfT funding and £3 billion in fund transfers from National Rail would leave a roughly £5 billion gap that would need to be filled from tax increases and private sector contributions (Buck 2017, p. 17).

TfL's initial inclination was to try to cover most of Crossrail's funding gap using a value-capture mechanism known as tax increment financing (TIF), which was already in widespread use in US cities. Under a TIF-like scheme, owners of properties near Crossrail stations would pay an additional property tax or assessment based on the Crossrail-induced increase in the value of their properties. The resulting multi-year revenue stream could then be used to float a bond whose sale proceeds would fill the remaining funding gap.

TFL's initial value-capture proposal quickly encountered pushback. Because London had no existing property tax system of its own, the task of designing a new-from-scratch American-style property valuation system just for Crossrail was thought to be politically and administratively unrealistic. In its place, TfL officials proposed raising the current tax rate on businesses within Crossrail's immediate service area from 45 percent to 46.5 percent (Buck 2018, p. 18). So as not to unfairly burden small businesses, the tax surcharge would apply only to businesses occupying commercial properties with annual rental values in excess of £50,000. Such a scheme would exempt 87 percent of existing businesses located in the Crossrail zone, shifting the funding burden to larger office and retail businesses who stood to gain the most from the improved access Crossrail would provide for their workers and retail customers.

In the four years between the first mention of the business tax scheme and its adoption by the Greater London Authority in April 2010, the Crossrail business tax increment changed from a 1.5 percent surcharge to a £0.02 business rate supplement (BRS). In addition, the minimum property rent threshold was increased from £50,000 to £55,000, and the scheme was limited to just those properties in London west of the Maidenhead Crossrail station. With these new modifications, the Crossrail business tax increment was projected to generate between £225 million and £250 million per year, enough to support the Greater London Authority issuing bonds in the amount of approximately £4 billion

(Buck 2018, p. 18). This would make the BRS the second largest source of Crossrail funding after DfT itself. Once the bonds were fully repaid, sometime in the 2030s, the BRS levy would fall away. In addition to its businesses paying their BRS assessments, the Corporation of London pledged to contribute £250 million to Crossrail's construction on behalf of companies within the City of London (Buck 2018, p. 20).

After DfT grants and BRS-based bond financing, Crossrail's biggest source of funding would come from Network Rail, Britain's national railway. Except for its central London underground section, all of Crossrail's 117 km consisted of overland train routes previously operated by Network Rail; and as part of an earlier agreement, Network Rail executives had agreed to contribute a pro-rated share of prior line and station upgrading expenses to Crossrail if and when it took over operating responsibility for Network Rail service. The other piece of this arrangement was a regulatory protocol issued by the Office of Rail Regulation in November 2009 stipulating that £2.3 billion of Crossrail's construction costs be financed by Network Rail for possible later incorporation into the Network Rail RAB, or regulated asset base. Added together, these two provisions allowed Crossrail to count Network Rail's right-of-way and track and station contributions as a Crossrail financing source (Buck 2018, p. 21).

Even more than businesses and property owners, Crossrail stood to benefit property developers. Particular among these were the Canary Wharf Group and the Berkeley Group, each of whom owned large swaths of re-developable land immediately adjacent to proposed Crossrail stations. Early advocates for Crossrail's construction, the Canary Wharf Group agreed to contribute £150 million towards the cost of building a new Canary Wharf Crossrail station. In return, the GLA granted them exclusive rights to develop retail and leisure projects in the airspace above the station. The properties owned by the Berkeley Group were adjacent to the Woolwich-Arsenal DLR station on the south bank of the Thames. The notion of building a new Crossrail station at Woolwich had originally been rejected by CLRL as too costly and because of worries that Crossrail would cannibalize riders from the recently-completed Woolwich-Arsenal DLR extension. Undeterred, the Berkeley Group offered to contribute £150 million to CLRL if they would reinstate the Woolwich station, provided that they, like the Canary Wharf Group, would retain the air rights above the station. The CLRL assented. Between the Canary Wharf and Woolwich stations, CLRL netted £300 million for Crossrail's construction (Buck 2018, p. 19).

What of other property developers? Traditionally, developers seeking planning permission for large commercial developments provide cash contributions through proffered agreements with local boroughs. These are private agreements made between local authorities and developers under Section 106 of the Town and Country Planning Act of 1990 and are intended to compensate authorities for the additional infrastructure and social costs associated with new development. They are similar in this regard to the development impact fees assessed by local governments in the US. For Crossrail, the Government allowed the Mayor of London to assess a community infrastructure levy (CIL) on each new development project in an amount ranging between £20 and £50 per square meter, depending on the location and the Mayor's discretion. The levy for each location is set at the time of planning consent but is only payable on completion of the development. The CIL was originally budgeted to generate £300 million for Crossrail but got off to a slow start because of the lingering effects of the Global Financial Crisis. By 2016 the CIL was generating approximately £100 million per year, to be shared between Crossrail and the various local authorities (Buck 2018, p. 20).

Crossrail's construction would involve building ten new stations, many of which would require Crossrail to acquire additional private property. The 2008 Crossrail Act incorporated provisions requiring owners to sell their properties to Crossrail as needed but, amidst concerns that they might be underpaid, required CLRL to negotiate purchase agreements allowing sellers to retain partial redevelopment rights to their properties. For those properties lacking such agreements, Crossrail retained the right to resell all or part of them on the open market, generating income in the expected amount of £500 million (Buck 2018, p. 20).

As a final piece of the Crossrail funding puzzle, British Airports Authority (now Heathrow Airport Holdings), the owners of Heathrow Airport, agreed to contribute £70 million. Why so little? Because Heathrow was already served by a direct high-speed rail line to Paddington—a line that Crossrail would physically subsume—Crossrail's incremental benefit to Heathrow was deemed to be much smaller.

The composition of Crossrail's £14.8 billion financing package as of 2010 is shown in Figure 4.2. Note that it is £1.1 billion less than the £15.9 billion cost announced by Chancellor Gordon Brown in 2007. This reduction was made possible through additional value engineering and construction cost savings as well as a reduction in the value of the Network Rail assets being reassigned to Crossrail.

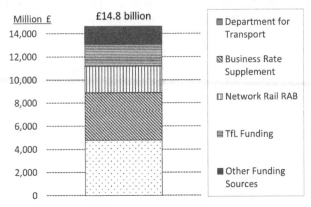

Source: Author, from Buck (2018).

Figure 4.2   Crossrail funding stack

DIGGING IN

If Crossrail was to have problems, they were expected to involve tunnel drilling operations. The amount of underground drilling required, the need to operate twin boring machines in tandem, the possibility of undocumented underground hazards, and the tight drilling tolerances—at Tottenham Court Road, the new Crossrail tunnels would be drilled to within a meter of an operating Underground platform—all combined to worry Crossrail's project managers. And it wasn't just the train tunnels. Crossrail's drilling contractors would have to dig vertical shafts at Fisher Street, Eleanor Street, Mile End, Stepney Green and Limmo Peninsula for drainage, ventilation and emergency access and egress. Altogether, Crossrail's boring and excavation activities would generate more than seven million tons of soil and other materials that would have to be transported off-site and disposed of in a sustainable manner. All told, ten percent[5] of Crossrail's £14.8 billion initial budget was reserved for tunnelling and debris removal (Figure 4.3).

London's older Underground lines were built by covering over excavated surface trenches, a method known as cut-and-cover. Newer lines, including the Jubilee Line Extension were all built using self-propelled tunnel boring machines, or TBMs. In order to meet Crossrail's ambitious tunnelling schedule, CRL purchased eight TBMs from Herrenknecht AG, a German engineering company known for its state-of-the-art TBM design (Crossrail 2021c). Weighing in at nearly 1,000 tons, each Herrenknecht TBM consisted of a 20-meter long rotating cutterhead and a 130-meter trailer section which provided locomotion. Compared with the TBMs used to drill the Jubilee Line

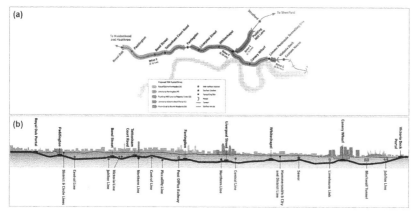

Source: Crossrail.

Figure 4.3   *(a) Tunnel locations; (b) central section tunnel depths*

Extension tunnels, the Crossrail TBMs were 2.5 m wider in diameter. Six of the Herrenknecht TBMs were designed to drill through London's clay and rock soils. The other two were engineered to bore through the chalk substrate beneath the Thames River.

In an effort to create public enthusiasm for Crossrail, CRL sponsored a newspaper contest to name its eight TBMs—British tradition stipulated that a TBM should be given a woman's name before it could begin work digging. Hundreds of entries were submitted leading to a vote to choose the final eight TBM names (Crossrail 2021c). The winning names were:

- *Ada* and *Phyllis*, named after Ada Lovelace and Phyllis Pearsall, which would dig the Royal Oak to Farringdon tunnels;
- *Victoria* and *Elizabeth*, named after Queen Victoria and Queen Elizabeth II, which would dig the Limmo Peninsula to Farringdon tunnels;
- *Mary* and *Sophia*, named after the wives of renowned English civil engineer Isambard Kingdom Brunel and his father, French civil engineer Marc Isambard Brunel, which would dig the Plumstead to North Woolwich tunnels, and;
- *Jessica* and *Ellie*, named after Jessica Ennis and Ellie Simmonds, which would dig the Pudding Mill Lane to Stepney Green and Limmo Peninsula to Victoria Dock tunnels.

Crossrail's tunnelling marathon commenced at Royal Oak Portal in May 2012 and ended three years later at Farringdon in May 2015 (Crossrail 2021c). Working in pairs, TBMs began at Royal Oak Portal in the west and the Limmo

Peninsula in the east, each bound for Farringdon Station. A third pair of TBMs worked its way west from Plumstead to North Woolwich, and a fourth pair divided its work between Pudding Mill Lane and Stepney Green Caverns; and the Victoria Dock–Limmo Peninsula extension on the main tunnel line. Each TBM was operated by its own 20-person tunnel gang running in shifts around the clock. Tunnelling progressed at an average speed of 38 meters per day, with Ellie, the TBM operating between Pudding Mill and Stepney Green, achieving the best single-day performance, advancing 72 meters in the 24 hours ending on April 16, 2014, After completing their drilling tasks, Phyllis, Ada, Victoria and Elizabeth were each dismantled. Their spent cutterheads were buried at Farringdon station (where their drilling paths had converged) while their trailer assemblies were disassembled and returned to Herrenknecht in Germany. Mary, Sophia, Jessica and Ellie were dismantled in their entirety and returned to Germany so that they might be used in subsequent projects (Crossrail 2021b).

Once excavated and stabilized, each tunnel bore had to be lined and rein-forced. This was done by assembling a series of interior rings composed of seven pre-cast concrete segments. Locked in place, each ring was then secured to the adjoining rings, creating a continuous tube structure engineered to last hundreds of years. Altogether, Crossrail's 42 km of running tunnels required more than 200,000 pre-cast arc segments.

Completed on schedule, Crossrail's excavation and tunnelling operations nonetheless went significantly over budget, with cost overruns ranging from 17 to 50 percent for digging operations, to 250 to 450 percent for civil works at the tunnel end shafts, to more than 500 percent for installing and sealing the interior tunnel rings. Initially budgeted at £1.17 billion, the final cost of Crossrail's tunnelling operations amounted to £1.76 billion according to a 2019 National Audits Office report (NAO 2019, p. 16).

AN EXPERIMENT IN OPEN INNOVATION STUMBLES

The same factors of size and complexity that required creating a new Crossrail funding model also encouraged taking a new project management approach. Dissatisfaction with the project management practices used in British mega-projects during the 1990s and early 2000s (including the Channel Tunnel, the Jubilee Line Extension, and Heathrow Terminal 5) wasn't limited to politicians and the press. It also extended to the broader engineering and project management profession, generating calls by academics and industry leaders to incorporate recent technical and organizational innovations into megaproject management practices (Egan 1998). This led to the formation of a civil engineering industry group called Movement for Innovation, which actively sought out opportunities to promote innovative project management practices into the megaproject construction process (Davies et al. 2009).

Crossrail, with its 42 km of tunnels, 10 new underground stations, 1,500-passenger trainsets and advanced technology train signaling and passenger control systems, was such an opportunity. It had two sponsors—DfT and TfL—each which had their own constituencies, interests and measures of success. Crossrail construction activities were to be organized into 17 distinct projects involving 10 principal contractors and, at their height, would employ more than 14,000 workers. Once construction was complete, the responsibility for operating Crossrail would fall to five different organizations—including Rail for London, the infrastructure manager and operator of several Crossrail stations; MTR of Hong Kong, which had won the contract to operate Crossrail train service; Network Rail, the owner and operator of most of Britain's railway infrastructure; London Underground Limited, which owns and operates London's Underground system; and Transport for London, the super-agency responsible for most components of London's transportation system—each of which had their own institutional culture and procedures.

Getting all these different players to work together was the job of Crossrail Limited (CRL), the joint venture established by TfL and DfT in 2008 to serve as the special purpose entity responsible for all Crossrail planning, engineering, construction, testing, and delivery tasks. To lead the new organization as its board chair, TfL and DfT turned to Terry Morgan, previously the CEO of Tube Lines, an asset management company with a contract to maintain and upgrade several of London's Underground lines.[6] In addition to its own staff, CRL was to be supported in its work by Transcend, a joint venture between AECOM, CH2M-Hill, and the Nichols Group, who would oversee planning and program delivery activities; and by Crossrail Central, a joint venture between Bechtel and Systra, which would manage construction activities for Crossrail's all-important central section.

With CRL firmly in charge, invitations to tender for the principal tunnelling contracts were listed in August 2009. The contract to build the 6.2 km "Tunnels West" section from Royal Oak to Farringdon via Paddington was awarded in 2010 to a consortium of BAM Nuttall, Ferrovial Agroman and Kier Construction. The contract for the three tunnel sections and launch chambers in east London, known as "Tunnels East," was also awarded in 2010 to Dragados and John Sisk & Son.[7] A third tunnelling contract, which included the tunnels under the Thames and those between Plumstead and North Woolwich, was awarded to Hochtief and J. Murphy & Sons in 2011.

With so many different tunnelling contractors involved, initial project coordination activities did not go well, leading CRL to bring in Andrew Wolstenholme as its new CEO in 2011. Wolstenholme, while serving as senior project manager for Heathrow Airport's £4.3 billion Terminal 5 project, had instituted a series of well-regarded innovations intended to speed up delivery times. Upon taking over at CRL, Wolstenholme quickly reorganized its contractor-oriented project management approach, creating what he called an Integrated Program Team consisting of 850 staff members representing every Crossrail agency, contractor and consultant. To ensure that the Integrated Program Team would be open to fresh ideas, Wolstenholme established a semi-independent Crossrail Innovation Forum (Crossrail 2021d), bringing together select CRL staff with innovation researchers from Imperial College and giving them the job of preparing an agency-wide document to be known as the Crossrail Innovation Strategy.

The core idea behind the Innovation Strategy was to create a pathway into which workers from across the Crossrail supply chain could channel their innovative ideas, assemble the resources needed to implement those ideas, and then, if they were successful, share them with the entire Crossrail delivery effort (Crossrail 2016, p. 9). The Innovation Strategy process was supported by a series of innovation teams, consisting of a program manager, two innovation coordinators, an innovation reporting assistant, and an embedded academic researcher. The job of the innovation program manager was to ensure that any new innovations furthered CRL's overall mission. The two innovation coordinators were responsible for connecting innovation project champions with each other and with groups who could implement their ideas. The innovation reporting assistant was to report the status and progress of the innovation program via CRL's intranet and publications. The job of the embedded researcher was to provide real-time feedback as to how well the innovation process was working. Collectively, the embedded researchers were responsible for implementing another Wolstenholme idea, the Crossrail Learning Legacy, which was to serve as a permanent clearinghouse for the innovation lessons learned throughout the Crossrail planning, construction and delivery process.

To support the work of its innovation teams, the Crossrail Innovation Forum created a suite of online tools to facilitate the submission of new ideas (the innovation portal); to manage, track, and report on the progress of those ideas (the innovation management system); and to communicate and share innovations across the broader Crossrail community (Crossrail 2021d).

As envisioned by Wolstenholme and the Innovation Forum, the innovation process would begin when one or more parties somewhere in the Crossrail supply chain submitted a new idea via the online innovation portal. An innovation coordinator would then be assigned to reach out to the submitting party and connect them with designated innovation champions who would "proof-of-concept" their idea. Ideas regarded as technically feasible were then moved ahead as pilot projects, gaining official sponsors and resource commitments. After six months as a pilot project, each innovation idea would be reassessed by an innovation working group composed of industry experts, contractors and senior representatives of the Innovation Program. Projects judged to have cross-agency potential would be placed on a short list, which would then go to the Crossrail Innovation Forum for final selection. By mid-2014, after three rounds of Forum recommendations, funding had been allocated to support 30 innovation projects.

CRL's approach to encouraging innovation reflected Wolstenholme's commitment to what he and innovation researchers called "open innovation" (Dodgson et al. 2015). The open innovation process encourages new ideas and innovations across organizations and stands in contrast to the more typical closed innovation process that occurs within a single organization. In theory, open innovation allows for beneficial spillovers and incremental improvements at the expense of formal idea ownership, while closed innovation is limited to promoting only those changes that advantage particular parties. To Wolstenholme, the best innovations were those that benefitted Crossrail as a whole, not the individual innovators.

How well did Wolstenholme's open innovation strategy succeed in generating measurable improvements in efficiency, cost or safety? As noted on the Crossrail website, more than 400 separate innovation ideas were brought forth during the six years of Wolstenholme's tenure, several of which resulted in significant changes (Crossrail 2021d). These included the use of thermal imaging cameras to evaluate the extent to which recently-poured concrete had cured; the reuse of grout shaft tubes as a local energy source; the pilot use of drones to continuously monitor site conditions; and the use of cloud data storage technologies rather than physical devices to share and modify digital documents. Whether these innovations would have emerged in the absence of a formal innovation strategy is difficult to say.

Beyond CRL's own public relations efforts, a preliminary assessment of the Crossrail innovation experience by University College London professor Andrew Davies and his colleagues published in 2015 identified a number of positive innovation examples with transfer potential that Davis termed "vignettes" (Davies et al. 2014; DeBarro et al. 2015). These include the widespread sharing of electronic construction documents between different contractors and the real-time digital monitoring of all tunnelling work (Davies et al. 2014, p. 34). Outside of Wolstenholme's explicit Crossrail Innovation Strategy, Davies and his colleagues also highlighted the expanding use of digital Building Information Modeling (BIM) technologies, which they regarded as likely to have significant benefit once Crossrail was finally up and running.

What Wolstenholme's Crossrail Innovation Strategy did not succeed in doing was to induce contractors who had fallen behind in their work to provide forthright explanations of their problems or reliable estimates of when those problems might be fixed. It thus seemed to government officials and the public that the greater the emphasis put on innovation, the more Crossrail fell behind.

(STILL) STRUGGLING TO THE FINISH LINE

With Crossrail's tunnelling work having been completed on schedule and without incident, and with the Liverpool Street Station-to-Shenfield overland rail service having been transferred to TfL as scheduled in 2015, no one at CRL was prepared for the announcement in late 2017 by contractors working on the new Paddington and Bond Street stations that their work had fallen seriously behind. Worse yet, from CRL's perspective was the January 2018 failure of the advanced technology train signaling and control system installed by Siemens to pass its initial tests. In a letter to TfL dated February 2018, Juergen Maier, Siemens' CEO, indicated that it might take as long as 18 months to fully diagnose and fix the system.[8] Without a working train control system and with the unfinished Bond Street station now disconnected from the rest of the project, work on Crossrail's new central and eastern section stations ground to a halt.

Simon Wright, who had recently succeeded Andrew Wolstenholme as Crossrail CEO, waited until January 2018 to notify TfL leadership that work at all nine central section stations had fallen seriously behind schedule, and that among the other new stations, work was close to being finished only at Farringdon and Woolwich. The first public indication that Crossrail's completion would be pushed back came in August 2018 when CRL officials announced that Crossrail's opening would be delayed by at least nine months until autumn 2019, citing the need "to complete the final infrastructure and extensive testing required" (Building.co.uk 2021). One month earlier, British Transport Minister Jo Johnson revealed that DfT and TfL had agreed to supplement Crossrail's construction budget by £600 million, increasing its projected construction cost from £14.8 to £15.4 billion.

Additional cash infusions and staffing changes would soon follow. In October 2018, DfT stated it would be pumping an additional £350 million into Crossrail's construction to keep the project on track. One month later, in November 2018, TFL and DfT announced that after eight months on the job, CRL CEO Simon Wright would be stepping down, and that London Underground Managing Director Mark Wild would be taking over. One month after that, in December 2018, DfT made known that Sir Terry Morgan, who had served as Crossrail's chairman since its beginning in 2008, was being ousted and would be replaced by Infrastructure and Projects Authority boss Tony Meggs. At the same press conference announcing Meggs' appointment, the Government revealed that the cost to complete Crossrail had risen by another £2 billion, and that it couldn't state with any certainty when the project might finally be finished and how much it would ultimately cost (Building. co.uk 2021).

In April 2019, new CRL CEO Mark Wild publicly indicated that Crossrail's central section would open sometime in the 18-month window between October 2019 and March 2021 (Building.co.uk 2021). In a report delivered that same month, Parliament's Public Accounts Committee said it was unconvinced that Crossrail's £2.8 billion bailout would be sufficient to complete the project.[9] Additional delays and cash infusions would be periodically announced, leading to an August 2020 public statement that the cost of finishing Crossrail would top £19 billion and that the line would not be open for full service until the middle of 2022, four years behind schedule.

As of this writing, Crossrail's final construction cost should be in the neighborhood of £19 to £20 billion. This would put Crossrail's construction five years behind schedule and £5 billion over budget.

So what went wrong? To date, the only official report on Crossrail's difficulties was published in May 2019 by Britain's National Audit Office.[10] It focused on identifying the sources of Crossrail's £2.8 billion in cost overruns since 2013, attributing them to contractor delays (37 percent), design changes (28 percent), schedule changes (13 percent), and changes to Crossrail's overall program (8 percent). In almost no case, the NAO noted, did CRL or its primary contractors have adequate contingency plans to manage cost overruns or contract changes (NAO 2019, p. 8).

Beyond putting Crossrail's many cost overruns into categories, the NAO had harsh words for CRL project managers. It concluded that CRL officials from early days onward had systematically understated the difficulties inherent in a project of Crossrail's size and complexity; that Crossrail's oft-repeated target completion date of December 2018 had always been unrealistic; that too many parallel activities were undertaken without coordination; that there were too many construction contracts to properly monitor and manage; that Crossrail project managers lacked a sufficiently detailed delivery plan against which to track their progress; and that project managers had insufficient leverage to pressure contractors when they failed to perform (NAO 2019, Summary).

Unfortunately, the NAO noted, by the time the full magnitude of these failings occurred, it was too late to do anything about them. CRL executives, the NAO noted, had spent too much time and effort touting Crossrail's benefits once it was finished, and too little effort making sure its complex systems and interrelated parts worked together as designed. Having taken contractors' exaggerated delivery promises at face value, CRL managers had not seen fit to develop any backup plans. Simply put, CRL officials had spent too much effort promoting and publicizing innovation for its own sake and not enough managing and mitigating risk. The problem wasn't just a broken system, the NAO concluded, it was also one of personnel: other than Andrew Wolstenholme, none of CRL's bosses had ever undertaken a project of Crossrail's scale or complexity, let alone completed one (NAO 2019, p. 30).

A fuller understanding of which of Crossrail's many problems could have been avoided had CRL taken a more hands-on approach to its project management responsibilities will have to await the government and industry post-mortems which will inevitably be undertaken now that Crossrail is fully up and running.

LAND VALUE AND PROPERTY DEVELOPMENT IMPACTS

Because of its dependence on business tax and real estate revenues, if Crossrail is to succeed financially, it will have to stimulate significant development activity and property value gains, especially in central London. To assess its prospects in this regard, CRL hired GVA,[11] a well-known British real estate research and appraisal company. Since 2012, GVA has undertaken three property impact studies for Crossrail. The first was a prospective study based on extrapolating recent trends. The second, a development pipeline study undertaken in 2014, tabulated the number of planning and permitting approvals within a 1 km radius of projected Crossrail stations. A third impact study, completed in 2018, combined a numerical analysis of recent construction trends, a further analysis of the permitting pipeline, and key informant surveys and interviews.

Assuming Crossrail opened as scheduled in 2018, GVA in its initial 2012 study projected that, by 2021, Crossrail would be responsible for generating an additional 3.25 million square meters of office and retail space, 57,000 new housing units, and an 18 percent (£5.5 billion) uplift in property values (GVA 2012, Executive summary). GVA's 2018 impact study was more optimistic. Still assuming a 2018 opening date for full Crossrail service, it projected that, by 2021, Crossrail would be associated with a 19 percent uplift in property values, a £10.6 billion increase in valuations, an additional 4.44 million square meters of commercial space and 90,600 new homes.

In terms of measurable construction activity, the news was also good. Compared with the number of new homes permitted, new home deliveries between 2013 and 2016 within 1 km of a Crossrail station were running at 70 percent of approvals. This compared with an average delivery rate of just 59 percent for the areas outside Crossrail station catchment zones. In terms of individual station areas, Crossrail was found to have had its biggest construction-inducing effects at the Ealing Broadway, Slough, and Southall station areas on Crossrail's western branch; at the Canary Wharf, Tottenham Court Road, Whitechapel, and Farrington station areas in Crossrail's central section; and at the Custom House, Woolwich, and Abbey Wood station areas on the Crossrail eastern branch.

The news was not quite as positive for affordable housing. GVA's analysis of planning permissions granted between 2013 and 2016 found that locations around Crossrail lines were delivering a smaller proportion of affordable housing than their corresponding boroughs. Along the entire Crossrail route, just 17 percent of newly-approved housing units between 2013 and 2016 were classified as affordable (GVA 2018, p. 72).

A bit prematurely perhaps, GVA concluded its 2018 impact study by praising Crossrail for its uplifting effects on London's property market. Within Crossrail's 1 km catchment area alone, GVA anticipated deliveries of permitted residential schemes would generate property value increases by 2026 of up to £20.1 billion, £13 billion of which was attributed to Crossrail. Similarly, deliveries of permitted office projects by 2026 would create up to £357.4 million in additional rental value, with £215 million from Crossrail-related projects. In terms of the property market expectations cited in its 2004 business case, GVA noted, Crossrail was well on track to exceed all of them.

GVA was not alone in its optimistic assessment. Another 2017 report by the UK real estate brokerage firm Knight Frank found that house prices within a 10-to-15-minute walk of Crossrail stations had outperformed their corresponding market areas by an average of 7 percent (Knight Frank 2017, p. 2). The biggest increases were in central London where, between 2008 and 2016, property values within a 10-minute walk of Crossrail stations had outperformed Knight Frank's prime central London index by 40 percent.

The single academic study undertaken of Crossrail's residential property value uplift effects is more measured in its conclusions. Focused solely on the Borough of Ealing on Crossrail's western branch, and using a difference-in-difference modeling approach—which compares home prices between affected and unaffected areas as well as before and after the announcement of a major market intervention—it found that for every kilometer closer a house was to a proposed Crossrail station, home-buyers were willing to pay a premium of between 2.4 and 2.5 percent (Comber & Arribas-Bel 2017). This was well below the 4 percent premium other housing market analysts regularly quoted.

As noted, these studies all assumed that Crossrail would open as scheduled in 2018. What happened when it didn't? Neither GVA nor Knight Frank have updated their prior studies to account for Crossrail's delayed opening. A November 2019 article in *Property Reporter* noted that despite the delay, house prices surrounding many Crossrail stations had continued to outperform the broader market during the previous year, increasing at an average rate of 2.1 percent.[12] This compared favorably with the average 1.9 percent price drop posted for neighboring areas.

Such was the Crossrail hype that Mansion Global, a property sales firm, headlined its January 2020 newsletter reporting that "It's Not Too Late For Investors to Get in on a London Crossrail Boon," even as it noted further on in the report that average sales values within 500 m of a Crossrail station had dropped significantly over the prior year.[13] A recent report on London area housing conditions published by the London Mayor's Office in March 2021 found that, as a consequence of Brexit and the Covid-19 pandemic, average asking rents in Inner London fell 12.4 percent between the fourth quarters of 2019 and 2020, while rents in Outer London were static.[14] A more recent 2021 analysis by *The Economist* magazine shows London area rents to have recovered almost to their pre-pandemic highs.[15]

Longer-term, for Crossrail's rosy property projections to be realized, Greater London will have to come close to hitting its Crossrail-boosted population and job projections. Is this likely? As of this writing, no one can say one way or another with confidence.

TWO BIG UNKNOWNS: BREXIT AND CROSSRAIL 2

Crossrail was approved in 2008 based on the argument that its presence would make the London economy more productive by promoting what economists call agglomeration economies; and that in Crossrail's absence the combination of traffic and transit congestion would lessen London's attractiveness to additional business growth. Brexit, which passed in 2016 and took Great Britain out of the European Union in 2020, calls both of these arguments into doubt.

How will the Greater London economy fare under Brexit? A 2016 report by the consulting group Oxford Economics predicted that if Brexit didn't pass, Greater London would add 800,000 additional jobs and 2.4 million additional residents by 2030. For Crossrail, Oxford Economics' 2016 forecast of consistent job growth and stronger-than-expected population growth was good news, as was its conclusion that London would need much more of the affordable and middle-class housing planned for the areas around Crossrail's eastern branch stations.

Oxford Economics' post-Brexit January 2021 addendum to its 2016 forecast was not as upbeat (Oxford Economics 2021). Without offering precise forecasts, it noted that although it was unlikely that other European financial centers would soon replace London, it was highly probable that the European Union would gradually impose tighter controls on Great Britain's access to European financial markets. Absent efforts to develop replacement markets, this would lead to a substantial slowdown in London area employment growth. On a more positive note, to the degree that London's financial sector could develop closer ties with technology companies, there might be increased opportunities for employment growth and trade connected to Asia and North

America. A more worrisome problem, Oxford Economics noted, would be the increased difficulty a post-Brexit London economy would have attracting and retaining high-quality EU-trained workers.

A January 2021 report by the London School of Economics offered a less sanguine view of Britain's—and therefore London's—post-Brexit financial future (Vaitilingam 2021). Based on a survey of 87 economists from across the UK, the US and the EU, it projected that the UK's gross domestic product in 2030 would be several percentage points smaller than if Britain had remained in the EU. Brexit's damage wouldn't be limited to Britain: the EU economy was also projected to be notably smaller. While there would undoubtedly be post-Brexit economic winners, where they might be located—whether in London or in less expensive areas of Britain—could not yet be determined. A February 2021 report by the Office of London Mayor Sadiq Kahn concurred in this general assessment, warning that in the short term, Brexit was likely to cost the London's economy £9.5 billion a year, with the region's financial and service sector employers bearing the brunt of the cost.[16]

And then there are the likely long-term effects of the Covid-19 pandemic. In London, as in cities in the US, large office employers are re-evaluating their long-term space needs to account for the wishes many of their employees have to continue working at home, even if just for a couple of days a week. Less home-to-office travel would mean fewer vehicle and transit trips, reduced traffic congestion and reduced travel time savings, all of which will adversely affect Crossrail ridership. In addition to reducing fare revenues, such a shift might also affect the Business Rate Supplement revenues Crossrail relies on for its funding. A related question is whether having to make fewer work-related trips will encourage some households to move from central London out to the suburbs, a shift that would advantage Crossrail over the London Underground and many Network Rail routes. In summary, while there is likely to be strong ridership demand for Crossrail, whether that demand generates the revenues necessary to support the service without a sizeable future fare increase is very much an open question.

Amidst all the uncertainty surrounding Brexit and Covid-19, DfT and TfL along with the London Mayor's Office are slowly moving ahead with plans for Crossrail 2, the name given to a proposed rail route that would connect London's northern and southern suburbs to its center. Like the original Crossrail proposal turned from its east–west axis to a north–south orientation, Crossrail 2 would connect two existing overland lines—the South Western Main Line in the South, and the West Anglia Main Line in the north— via a new tunnel between the Dalston Underground station in the north and the Clapham Junction Underground station in the south (Crossrail 2 2021a). In central London, Crossrail 2 would connect to Crossrail at the Tottenham Court Road station, and to the London Underground and Network Rail at

Victoria and Euston-St. Pancras. The cost of the Crossrail 2 scheme was estimated in 2014 to be in the range of £27–32 billion.[17] A more recent 2017 estimate developed by TfL put Crossrail 2's likely cost at around £45 billion (*The Guardian* 2020).

The idea for Crossrail 2 had been kicking around in one form or another since the mid-1990s, but was given a big push forward by newly-elected London Mayor Boris Johnson (Crossrail 2 2021b). In 2015, Johnson announced the formation of an independent Crossrail 2 Growth Commission to make the business and housing case for the scheme. The Commission confirmed earlier estimates that Crossrail 2 might unlock the construction of as many as 200,000 new homes in the areas around its stations while supporting the creation of up to 200,000 new jobs, mostly in central London. The current Mayor of London, Sadiq Khan, is also a strong Crossrail 2 supporter.

In March 2016, Britain's National Infrastructure Commission concluded that Crossrail 2 should go forward "as a priority" and recommended that a bill should pass through Parliament by 2019 with Crossrail 2 opening by 2033. Following up on the Infrastructure Commission's recommendation, the Treasury gave the project a green light, allocating £80 million for additional planning and economic studies with the aim of putting a Crossrail 2 hybrid bill in front of Parliament before 2020.

This was all before the June 2016 Brexit referendum. The Treasury subsequently backtracked in the wake of the Brexit vote, saying only that it would continue to work with TfL on developing fair and affordable plans for Crossrail 2 pending an independent and thorough review of its funding and financing. Subsequent Crossrail 2 planning efforts were put on indefinite hold in November 2020 as part of the £1.8 billion Covid-19 pandemic financial recovery plan agreed to by the Government and TfL. All consultancy work on Crossrail 2 ended soon thereafter although the tunnelling route and land for the proposed station sites has been safeguarded should the project pick up again (Building.co.uk 2021).

LESSONS AND TAKEAWAYS

With Crossrail so recently completed, it is still premature to try to definitively assess what went right with the project and what went wrong. Still, enough is known about Crossrail's planning, engineering, financing and delivery practices to identify a few key lessons and takeaways.

In terms of practices to emulate, the British Government's use of standardized and transparent review criteria, as embodied in its longstanding transportation Green Book evaluation procedures, ensures that transport projects will be evaluated the same way regardless of mode, location or political champion. By forcing proponents to identify project costs and benefits using a common set of measures and a common discount rate across different project types, British taxpayers can be assured that politicians have not exerted undue influence and that project benefits are likely to exceed project costs even accounting for unanticipated delays and cost overruns. This is not to say that the project construction and delivery process will always proceed as promised. What it does mean is that approved projects should produce sizable and tangible and benefits.

Notwithstanding its highly-codified nature, Britain's project assessment process is also flexible enough to permit incorporating of new evaluation criteria as appropriate. In the case of Crossrail, these included anticipated growth in business productivity, and higher wage rates and tax revenues attributable to heightened agglomeration economies. Indeed, it was the measurement and inclusion of agglomeration economy-related benefits that ultimately tipped the scales in favor of undertaking Crossrail. The use of advanced statistical procedures to establish the reliability of these estimates and their sensitivity to different sources of risk was also notable.

The Government's decision to hold the line on its financial contributions to Crossrail forced project proponents to get creative in finding new sources of financing. As a result, when Crossrail was approved by Parliament in 2008, more than one-third of its funding came from non-traditional sources, including £4.1 billion from a new tax on businesses and commercial property owners, £500 million from selling surplus properties, £400 million in contributions from real estate developers, and £70 million from Heathrow Airport. This was far more than had been raised for any previous project and required Crossrail planners to take a more entrepreneurial and real-estate-oriented approach to station area planning issues. The result was an improved quality of urban design and more careful attention to transit-oriented development opportunities, especially housing.

Crossrail's huge size and cost also required its managers to search for efficiencies in the project delivery process. For the most part, this did not turn out well. CRL's first big mistake—and the one it never recovered from—was to hire so many contractors, each of whom had their own institutional culture and procedures. This was deemed necessary at the time because of Crossrail's huge physical scale. It also reflected the later-dashed hope that the various Crossrail station construction activities would proceed in sync, enabling Crossrail's central section to be completed and tested as a single piece.

Nor did CRL executives have the requisite experience managing so many contractors. This meant that when work on the Paddington and Bond Street station fell behind in 2017, thereby delaying progress on the entire central Crossrail segment, CRL managers didn't have in place a backup plan to redeploy resources as needed to pick up the slack. In place of improving contractor coordination, CRL officials chose to focus on promoting bottom-up innovations that they hoped might be shared across contractors. This was not a bad idea, per se, but it was not a substitute for developing reporting systems capable of identifying small problems before they could turn into bigger ones, or for putting in place incentives and sanctions designed to guarantee contractor performance. The result, as later identified by the National Audit Office, was a misplaced emphasis on process over performance, and a project management system that didn't allow senior managers to see or comprehend the larger picture.

Just as it wasn't clear who the lead contractors were, it was similarly unclear who the lead client was. For the purposes of construction and eventual operation, Transport for London (TfL) was the lead client. Yet when it came to coming up with additional funding to cover cost overruns, that was the job of the Government's Department for Transport (DfT). This dual-client relationship put TfL in the unenviable position of having to approve construction changes without knowing whether DfT would appropriate money to pay for them. The fact that London's Labour Party Mayor Sadiq Khan didn't always see eye to eye with the Conservative Party governments of David Cameron, Theresa May and then Boris Johnson served to make things even more complicated.

The other big mistake CRL made was putting too much faith in new technology in the form of its Siemens-provided integrated train signaling and station control system. Siemens was indeed the global leader in manufacturing train control systems, but it had never designed and installed so large and complex a system with so little time reserved for in-place testing. So, when it turned out that the system didn't work as promised, neither Siemens nor CRL had a contingency plan to begin Crossrail service on a partial or incremental basis. What's ironic is that those in charge of planning Crossrail engaged in hundreds of simulations to ensure that the project could be financed as planned under different scenarios while those in charge of delivering Crossrail chose not to undertake any sort of meaningful contingency planning.

At the end of the day, Crossrail, like most megaprojects, was characterized by hubris and early overconfidence. With Parliament having taken three years of debate and study to finally approve Crossrail, its sponsors and planners were understandably eager to begin construction. They rationalized their speed by convincing themselves that Crossrail was as much a project management challenge as it was a construction and engineering job, and that they had fully learned the project management lessons of previous transport megaprojects. This sense of confidence was bolstered by the on-time and problem-free performance of Crossrail's tunnelling contractors, leading CRL officials to assume that subsequent tasks would also proceed smoothly. When they did not, rather than leveling with their clients and the public about their own shortcomings, CRL officials repeatedly prevaricated, offering vague assurances in place of clear timelines. This further reduced the public's confidence while allowing project contractors to escape responsibility.

NOTES

1. Kiley himself would be fired a little more than a year later for opposing the Labour Government's plans to partly privatize the network.
2. Montague was later named CEO of CLRL.
3. Graham's results are summarized in: Daniel J. Graham, Agglomeration, productivity and transport investment. *Journal of Transport Economics and Policy* 41(3): 317–343.
4. Implementation of the London congestion charging zone scheme was accompanied by the addition of 300 new buses to TfL's bus fleet.
5. A National Audit Office report on Crossrail published in May 2019 lists Crossrail's initial tunnelling budget (not including track and electrical fit out costs) at £1.5 billion. When tunnelling operations were completed in 2015, the final cost of £2.6 billion was 75% higher than the initial budget. (National Audit Office 2019).
6. Tube Lines was purchased by Transport for London in 2010.
7. https://www.crossrail.co.uk/news/articles/crossrail-awards-major-tunnelling -contracts-worth-125bn. (Accessed December 2021)
8. As reported in the *Times* of London: https://www.thetimes.co.uk/article/how -crossrail-has-hit-the-buffers-0h3njkz0s.
9. "Public Accounts Committee predicts Crossrail will continue to exceed budget." The Parliamentary Review. https://www.theparliamentaryreview.co.uk/news/ public-accounts-committee-of-mp-s-predicts-crossrail-will-continue-to-exceed -budget.
10. In April 2019, the London Assembly published its own account of Crossrail's problems. Entitled "Derailed: Getting Crossrail Back on Track" (London Assembly Transport Committee 2019) its scope was mostly limited to issues of governance and project management transparency.
11. GVA was acquired by Avison Young in 2019.
12. https://www.propertyreporter.co.uk/property/what-impact-are-the-crossrail -delays-having-on-house-price-grow.html. (Accessed December 2021)
13. https://www.mansionglobal.com/articles/its-not-too-late-for-investors-to-get-in -on-a-london-crossrail-boon-211194. (Accessed December 2021)
14. https://www.london.gov.uk/what-we-do/housing-and-land/improving-private -rented-sector/london-rents-map. (Accessed December 2021)
15. https://www.economist.com/britain/2021/12/04/britains-rental-market-is-hottest -outside-london. (Accessed December 2021)
16. https://www.london.gov.uk/press-releases/mayoral/brexit-could-cost-londons -economy-95bn-a-year. (Accessed December 2021)
17. https://crossrail2.co.uk/discover/funding/. (Accessed December 2021)

REFERENCES

Buck, M. 2017. Crossrail project: finance, funding and value capture for London's Elizabeth line. *Proceedings of the Institution of Civil Engineers-Civil Engineering.* 170(6): 15–22.

Building.co.uk. 2021. Crossrail 2 'ready to be restarted' when time is right, London's mayor promises. https://www.building.co.uk/news/crossrail-2-ready-to-be-restarted -when-time-is-right-londons-mayor-promises/5112549.article (July 2).

Building.co.uk. 2022. Crossrail: How the delay has unfolded. https://www.building.co .uk/news/crossrail-how-the-delay-has-unfolded/5096716.article (May 4).

Comber, S., & Arribas-Bel, D. 2017. "Waiting on the train": The anticipatory (causal) effects of Crossrail in easing. *Journal of Transport Geography* 64, 13–22.

Crossrail Ltd. 2016. Crossrail website: "Crossrail Innovation Strategy." https:// learninglegacy.crossrail.co.uk/wp-content/uploads/2016/04/11A_020_Innovation -Strategy.pdf.

Crossrail Ltd. 2021a. Crossrail website: "History." https://www.crossrail.co.uk/ crossrail-from-its-early-beginnings (Accessed December 22, 2021).

Crossrail Ltd. 2021b. Crossrail website: "Tunnel Boring Machines." https://www .crossrail.co.uk/project/tunnelling/meet-our-giant-tunnelling-machines/ (Accessed December 22, 2021).

Crossrail Ltd. 2021c. Crossrail website: "Main Construction." https://www.crossrail.co .uk/the-build/crossrail-the-build-main-construction (Accessed December 22, 2021).

Crossrail Ltd. 2021d. Crossrail website: "Crossrail Innovation Programme." https:// learninglegacy.crossrail.co.uk/wp-content/uploads/2016/04/11A_021_Innovation -Programme-OverviewProspectus.pdf (Accessed December 22, 2021).

Crossrail 2. 2021a. Crossrail 2 website: "The Route." https://crossrail2.co.uk/route/ (Accessed December 22, 2021).

Crossrail 2. 2021b. Crossrail 2 website: "History." https://crossrail2.co.uk/discover/ history/ (Accessed December 22, 2021).

Davies, A., Gann, D., and Douglas, T. (2009). Innovation in megaprojects: systems integration at Heathrow Terminal 5. *California Management Review* 51(2): 101–125.

Davies, A., MacAulay, S., DeBarro, T., and Thurston, M. 2014. Making innovation happen in a megaproject: London's Crossrail suburban railway system. *Project Management Journal* 45(6): 25–37.

DeBarro, T., MacAulay, S., Davies, A., Wolstenholme, A., Gann, D., and Pelton, J. 2015. Mantra to method: Lessons from managing innovation on Crossrail, UK. *Proceedings of the Institution of Civil Engineers-Civil Engineering* 168(4): 171–178.

Dodgson, M., Gann, D., MacAulay, S., and Davies, A. 2015. Innovation strategy in new transportation systems: The case of Crossrail. *Transportation Research Part A: Policy and Practice* 77: 261–275.

Egan, J. 1998. *Rethinking Construction: The Report of the Construction Industry Task Force*. UK Department of Transport.

Gomez-Ibanez, J. 2009. *Crossrail (A): The Business Case*. Harvard Kennedy School of Government Case Program. Case CR14-08-1898.0. Cambridge, MA.

GVA. 2012. *Crossrail Property Impact Study*. GVA.

GVA. 2018. *Crossrail Property Impact & Regeneration Study, 2012-2026*. GVA.

Hebbert, M. 2014. Crossrail: The slow route to London's regional express railway. *Town Planning Review*: 171–190.

Knight Frank. 2017. *Crossrail–Analyzing Property Market Performance Along the Elizabeth Line, 2017*. Knight Frank.

London Assembly Transport Committee. 2019. Derailed: Getting Crossrail back on track. (April).

Montague, A. 2004. "Crossrail Review." Report from the Crossrail review team leader. https://learninglegacy.crossrail.co.uk/wp-content/uploads/2016/02/The_Montague _Review_2004.pdf.

National Audit Office. 2019. *Completing Crossrail: Report to the Department for Transport*. (May). National Audit Office.

Oxford Economics. 2016. *Assessing the Economic Implications of Brexit*. Oxford Economics.

Oxford Economics. 2021. *Research Briefing–Cities: London as a Financial Centre, Post Brexit. Squeezed, not Crushed*. (January.) Oxford Economics.

The Guardian. 2004. "Livingstone argues Crossrail case." (March 12).

The Guardian. 2020. "Crossrail 2 plans shelved as part of £1.8bn TfL funding deal." (November 2).

Vaitilingam, R. 2021. After Brexit: The impacts on the UK and EU economies by 2030. London School of Economics. (January) https://blogs.lse.ac.uk/businessreview/ 2021/01/25/after-brexit-the-impacts-on-the-uk-and-eu-economies-by-2030/.

Venables, A. 2003. "Productivity effects of urban transport improvements." Report to the Department for Transport.

5. China bends the curve on high-speed rail

Ziming Liu and John D. Landis

ABBREVIATIONS USED IN THIS CHAPTER

CR	Conventional Railway—railway trains that travel at less than 200 kph.
CRC	China Railways Corporation—China's national railway operating company.
CRCC	China Railways Construction Corporation—China's national railway construction company.
EIA/ EMP	Environmental Impact Assessment/Environmental Management Plan—Environmental documentation required as part of the infrastructure approval process.
EMU	Electric Multiple Unit—train cars that make up an electricity-powered train.
HSR	High-speed railway—railway trains that travel at more than 200 kph.
JV	Joint Venture—financing and ownership form used to develop and operate HSR lines.
MLTRP	Medium and Long-term Railway Plan—Chinese government-approved plans denoting proposed HSR and CR routes.
MOR	Ministry of Railways—China's national railroad planning and development agency. It was eliminated in 2013.
MOT	The Ministry of Transport—China's foremost government agency responsible for road, water and air transportation.
NDRC	National Development and Reform Commission.
NRA	National Railways Administration—the successor agency to the Chinese Ministry of Railways.
RA	Regional Administrations—regional subsidiaries of the China Railways Corporation.

THE BIGGEST AND BEST HIGH-SPEED RAIL SYSTEM IN THE WORLD

Statistics alone can't do justice to China's world-leading high-speed rail (HSR) accomplishments but they are certainly a good place to start.[1] Since 2005, China has built 37,000 km of new HSR track, more than existed in the rest of the world at that time (Table 5.1). More than two billion passengers traveled by HSR within China in 2019, three times as many as traveled by air (Lawrence et al. 2019). In terms of passenger-kilometers—a measure that combines the number of HSR passengers with how far they traveled—China's 774 billion HSR passenger-kilometers of travel in 2019 exceeded second-place Japan's 13 times over.[2] Every one of China's 50 largest cities is connected to its HSR network, and more than 3,000 HSR trains depart from Chinese cities every day. China initially relied on HSR trains designed and engineered in Europe but has more recently developed its own advanced HSR train technologies and is making them available to HSR customers around the world. Measured in money terms, the more than US$630 billion[3] China has spent so far building its national HSR network exceeds the roughly $600 billion the United States spent building its interstate highway system 50 years ago.

Table 5.1   *High-speed rail system length and ridership by country*

Country	Length of HSR lines in service (km)[1]	Maximum operating speed (km/h)	High-speed rail, passengers (millions)	Passenger trip reporting year
China	35,313	350	2,300	2019
Spain	3,100	310	22.4	2019
Japan	3,041	320	365.7	2015
France	3,220	320	114.5	2010
Germany	3,038	300	73.7	2009
Sweden	1,706	205	[2]	
United Kingdom	1,377	300	20	2016
South Korea	1,104	305	59.1	2016
Italy	999	300	64	2015
Turkey	802	300	8	2019
Russia	845	205	[2]	
Finland	609	220	[2]	
Uzbekistan	600	250	[2]	
Austria	352	250	[2]	
Taiwan	354	300	67	2019
Belgium	326	300	10	2010
Poland	224	200	[2]	
The Netherlands	175	300	21	2018
Switzerland	144	250	[2]	
Luxembourg	142	320	n.a.	
Norway	64	210	1.4	2019
USA	54	240	3.5	2016

Note: High-speed rail ridership statistics are not reported separately from conventional rail.
Source: Environmental and Energy Studies Institute (downloaded January 6, 2021).

These achievements are even more impressive given how late China entered the high-speed rail game. China's first high-speed rail line, connecting Qingdao and Jinan in Shandong Province entered service only in 2008. Having previously directed its infrastructure investments toward export-oriented manufacturers, China cautiously took its time figuring out how best to upgrade its extensive passenger rail system. Should it incrementally upgrade existing passenger lines as the United States was doing or should it build an entirely new HSR network, as European countries had done? Should it use HSR train technology purchased abroad or try to develop its own? What about leapfrogging steel-wheel train technology entirely and jumping to magnetic levitation (mag-lev)? Should new HSR stations be located in city centers where they could conveniently serve business travelers or should they be located outside downtowns where they could be built quicker and less expensively? Would investing more in HSR service mean less funding would be needed for new airports? Whatever path China decided to take, it would have to do so decisively. And with more than 20 cities with populations of more than two and a half million, it would have to do so in a manner that could quickly be scaled upward.

Building on the successes of a series of campaigns undertaken during the late-1990s, which raised train speeds on selected intercity routes from 50 to 160 kph, China's Ministry of Railways announced in 2004 that it had obtained permission from China's governing State Council to begin constructing a nationwide HSR network that would be separate from China's conventional passenger rail system. The blueprint for the Ministry's HSR construction efforts was contained in its Medium- and Long-Term Railway Plan, which identified a 12,000 km HSR network comprised of four north–south routes and four east–west routes. To implement the plan, the State Council authorized expenditures of $6 billion per year. This was increased to $23 billion per year in 2007 and to $105 billion in 2010. Three years after the start of construction in 2005, the HSR line connecting Beijing and Tianjin opened in August 2008. Just as Japan had done with its Shinkansen HSR service in 1964, China used the occasion of the 2008 Summer Olympics to introduce its new HSR investments to the world. The success of the inaugural HSR line coupled with a desire to respond forcefully to the worsening Global Financial Crisis led China's leaders to commit to growing the original eight-route HSR system into a 16-route system (Lawrence et al. 2019) (Figure 5.1). This would entail building 3,000 km of new HSR track every year through 2020, bringing the total HSR network length to more than 30,000 km.

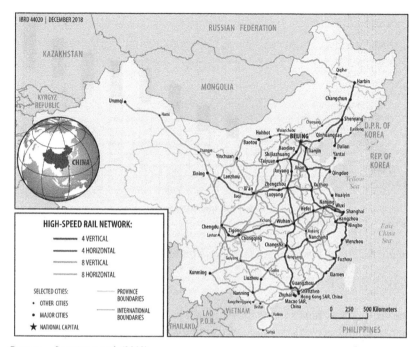

Source: Lawrence et al. (2019).

Figure 5.1   China's "8+8" high-speed rail routes

In a world in which delivery delays and bottlenecks are the norm, China's success in meeting its HSR construction goals is even more impressive. By the end of 2015, the size of China's HSR network had surpassed 20,000 km. By the end of 2019, it exceeded 35,000 km, and by the middle of 2020, it had reached 37,000 km (Figure 5.2).

China's progress in building new HSR lines enabled it to keep driving down the cost of HSR construction. According to a 2019 World Bank report (Lawrence et al. 2019), China has managed to reduce the average per-kilometer HSR construction cost to between $17 million and $21 million. This compares favorably to the $30 million per kilometer it cost Japan to extend its Hokkaido Shinkansen line in 2016.[4]

Travelers throughout China responded immediately to the new HSR routes and services, increasing the aggregate volume of HSR travel in China from 106 billion passenger-kilometers in 2011 to 777 billion passenger-kilometers in 2019.[5] By way of comparison, passenger travel on Japan's Shinkansen system in 2019 totaled 99 billion passenger kilometers.

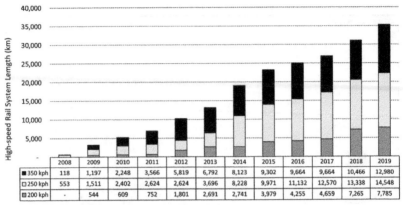

	2008	2009	2010	2011	2012	2013	2014	2015	2016	2017	2018	2019
■350 kph	118	1,197	2,248	3,566	5,819	6,792	8,123	9,302	9,664	9,664	10,466	12,980
☐250 kph	553	1,511	2,402	2,624	2,624	3,696	8,228	9,971	11,132	12,570	13,338	14,548
▨200 kph	-	544	609	752	1,801	2,691	2,741	3,979	4,255	4,659	7,265	7,785

▨200 kph ☐250 kph ■350 kph

Source: Lawrence et al. (2019).

Figure 5.2　　*China HSR system length by year*

THE SWEET SPOT

The decision by China's ruling State Council in 2004 to approve construction of a national HSR network was grounded in five objectives (Lawrence et al. 2019). The first was to enhance China's global reputation and capacity for undertaking cutting-edge infrastructure and technology projects. The second was to boost economic productivity by building a world-class passenger transportation system free from bottlenecks and delays. The third was to boost rail freight traffic volumes and speeds by shifting passenger rail traffic away from China's overburdened conventional rail routes and toward HSR. A fourth objective was to divert economic growth away from overheating coastal megacities such as Shanghai and Shenzhen and toward lagging interior cities and provinces. A fifth objective, which took on added importance in the aftermath of the Global Financial Crisis, was to further stimulate the Chinese economy by directing government investment toward high-multiplier public works projects.

Of these five objectives, the second—improving productivity by speeding domestic passenger travel—was clearly the most important. China's 20-year focus on expanding manufacturing exports had left the country with an unbalanced domestic transportation system. Except for passengers who could afford to fly, travel between China's major cities was a cumbersome and time-consuming affair. The popular 1,400 km east–west train trip between Shanghai and Chongqing took 30 hours, and trips between coastal cities and interior rural villages, where many city dwellers' families still lived, could take even longer. The problem was twofold. First, Chinese passenger trains were old and slow and, as of 1993, operating at an average systemwide speed of just 50 kph (30 mph). The second problem was that passenger and freight rail services shared the same tracks, and because passenger service had priority, freight trains had to divert to sidings while passenger trains rumbled through. The slowdown in freight service was especially problematic during peak traveling seasons, such as the Chinese New Year Holidays.

To address the train slowness problem, beginning in 1997, China's Ministry of Railways (MOR) undertook a 10-year "Speed Up" campaign[6] to triple rail speeds on high-volume passenger rail routes. Solving the passenger rail–freight rail shared track problem would be more difficult. Because freight trains are heavier than passenger trains, increasing their speeds and capacities would accelerate track wear and tear, compromising any gains in passenger train speeds. Ultimately, MOR planners deemed the shared track problem to be unsolvable, leading them to champion building a new and separate HSR passenger network.

Still to be determined were questions of how China's proposed HSR network should be configured and how fast its trains should operate. As Japanese and European HSR operators had discovered, the trip length "sweet spot" for 300 kph HSR service—the trips for which HSR service could effectively compete with airlines and car travel on the basis of door-to-door travel time—was between 250 and 600 km (Figure 5.3). Increase train speeds to 350 kph and the upper end of the sweet spot range grew to 800 km. Many city-to-city passenger trips in China fell squarely within this range, making HSR service a good match for business passengers making a one-day trip between Shenzhen and Guangzhou, or between Beijing and Tianjin, or for Nanjing residents wanting to visit their families in Wuhan during Chinese New Year. With remarkable service reliability and comfort, the sweet spot range increased to as much as 1,200 km for some popular trips, such as between Beijing and Shanghai, or Wuhan to Shenzhen. And with more than 30 Chinese cities with populations of two million or more, building a national HSR network using common track and train standards made more sense than building a few intercity lines.

Like many infrastructure investment programs in China, the HSR planning process was organized as a top-down affair. Based on the success of its conventional rail "Speed Up" campaigns, the responsibility for designing China's national HSR plan was assigned to the Ministry of Railways (MOR). MOR's plan, published as the *Medium- and Long-Term Railways Plan* (MLTRP 2004) was delivered to China's National Development and Reform Commission (NDRC) and the State Council in 2003. The Plan, known colloquially as the "4 + 4 Plan," proposed building a 12,000 km HSR network made up of four east–west (i.e., "horizontal") rail corridors and four north–south (i.e., "vertical") corridors. These eight corridors were further organized into three

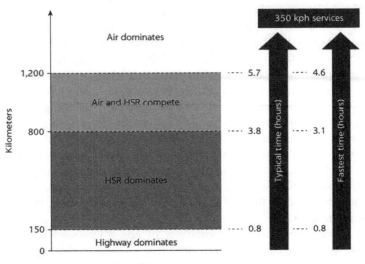

Source: Lawrence et al. (2019, p. 33).

Figure 5.3   High-speed rail distance "sweetspots"

regional clusters, connecting cities in the Pearl River Delta region in the south
to cities in the Yangtze River Delta region in the east and to cities in the Bohai
Sea Region in the northeast. Known internally as the "4+4" plan, the MLTRP's
time horizon extended to 2020.

The job of implementing the MLTRP would belong to the Railroads
Ministry, which was also responsible for planning and administering China's
integrated conventional and freight rail systems. With so many activities for
MOR to supervise, HSR construction efforts initially got off to a slow start,
but things quickly picked up as MOR planners and engineers began delivering
their detailed plans and specifications. China's first HSR line, the 156 km
Hefei–Nanjing Railway began operating on April 19, 2008, followed four
months later by the 117 km Beijing–Tianjin Intercity Railway.

A second MLTRP was released in 2008, more as a revision of the 2004 document than as an altogether new plan. The 2008 MLTRP further accelerated
China's HSR construction timetable and upped the planned size of its 2020
HSR network from 12,000 to 20,000 km. World events would soon accelerate
it further, as the Chinese government made accelerated HSR construction
a centerpiece of its economic stimulus response to the Global Financial Crisis.

A third MLTRP was published in 2016 covering the period through 2030
(NDRC 2016). The new plan was the first to be prepared by the National
Railway Administration (NRA), which had replaced the Ministry of Railways
in 2014 following a series of personnel scandals. The 2016 MLTRP further

expanded China's rapidly expanding HSR network by proposing to add four more north–south HSR corridors and four east–west corridors connecting every major Chinese city with one million resident or more. Overall, the new "8 + 8" MLTRP boosted the target size of China's HSR network to 30,000 km by 2020 and to 38,000 km by 2025. As of August 2020, China's National Railroad Administration[7] announced that construction had been completed on 36,000 km of HSR track, although not all were yet operating at full capacity.

The NRA is also charged with preparing five-year railway plans keyed to China's Five-Year National Plans. Five-year railway plans are more specific in terms of objectives and schedules than the MLTR Plan, listing the amount of HSR track to be built, the number of specific HSR projects to be undertaken, and the number of HSR trainsets to be purchased or produced. As is typical for five-year plans, each objective is then broken down into one-year increments.

In addition to the NRA's national-level MLTR and five-year railway plans, local governments in China must come up with their own rail facility construction plans. These local plans use the MLTR and five-year national plans as their jumping-off point and are intended to ensure that each local government's local railway construction and operating plans are fully aligned with national plan and priorities.

Even with an adopted plan in place, engineering and construction work on individual HSR projects only begins after the project is approved for funding by China's governing State Council. In an effort to speed up the HSR construction process, the State Council in 2015 changed its review process from evaluating individual HSR projects to evaluating groups of projects. Once funding for a specific HSR project is approved—more about how projects are funded in the next section—China's State Railway Company joins with the appropriate provincial and/or city governments to contract with one of China's eight state-sponsored Railway Design Institutes to prepare final construction plans and all required feasibility and engineering reports.

All HSR design and engineering elements must meet preset standards and specifications established by the NRA. Construction of individual HSR projects is coordinated nationally so that specialized construction equipment and labor can move from project to project as needed. In addition to ensuring that nationally identified best practices will be followed, China's insistence on standardizing engineering and construction procedures also serves to reduce HSR construction costs.

Train design and manufacturing is also standardized. The individual railway authorities that operate China's HSR lines are limited in their choice of trainset designs to those approved by China Railway Rolling Stock Corporation (CRRC), which also oversees all trainset manufacturing activities. All other HSR equipment is provided by 130 specialized manufacturing enterprises licensed by the National Railway Administration.

CHINA'S HIGH-SPEED RAIL JOINT VENTURE MODEL

The Chinese government realized early on that the only way to meet the MLTRP's ambitious construction goals would be to standardize every possible aspect of the HSR design, engineering, construction, and procurement process, starting with right-of-way and track specifications, and including bridge and tunnel designs, power supply systems, signaling and communications equipment; as well as the trainsets themselves. Rather than contract-out trainset manufacturing, the Chinese government established five HSR train manufacturing plants at Qingdao, Tangshan, Changchun, Jiangmen and Nanjing, each to be administered by yet another state-owned enterprise, the Chinese Railway Construction Corporation or CRCC. To build up HSR construction expertise, the government further stipulated that HSR construction crews should be certified and that projects be scheduled so that experienced construction crews could progress from one completed project to another.

These many standardization efforts have resulted in significant cost savings. According to a 2018 cost comparison study by the European Court of Auditors, the cost of building a 350 kph HSR line in China averaged out to about 139 million yuan (or US$20.6 million) per kilometer. Costs declined with line speed, falling to 114 million yuan ($16.9 million) per kilometer for 250 kph lines, and to 104 million yuan ($15.4 million) for 200 kph lines. Correcting for inflation and purchasing power parity, HSR construction costs in China are thought to be about 40 percent lower than in Europe (Lawrence et al. 2019).

Once a HSR project has been approved by the State Council for construction, the initiative shifts from government planners to project developers. HSR projects in China are financed using a joint venture (JV) arrangement that brings together the China Railways Corporation (CRC), one or more of the CRC's subsidiary regional administrations, various provincial or city governments, and the occasional private or social capital investor. Exactly how each JV is structured is determined on a case by case depending on the type of HSR line and on how much financing each JV partner is able to bring to the deal. The CRC and its regional subsidiaries typically have larger roles in main line JVs, while provincial and local governments usually dominate regional and intercity JVs.

The Huzhang and Huhang HSR lines provide contrasting examples of the different types of JV sponsor structures (Lawrence et al. 2019). Opened in 2017, the 287 km Zhangjiakou-to-Hohhot Huzhang line runs between Inner Mongolia and Hebei Province and is an essential link in the east–west HSR corridor connecting Beijing in the east with Lanzhou in the west. Its JV owner, the Huzhang Railway Dedicated Passenger Line Co., Ltd., is made up of the China Railway Hohhot Bureau Co., Ltd. (the CRC's designated regional railway authority), which maintains a 76 percent majority ownership share;

the Inner Mongolia Transport Investment Co., Ltd., which has a 22 percent ownership share; and the Hebei Construction Investment Transport Investment Co., Ltd., which owns the remaining two percent of shares.

The Huhang Line is a 200 km intercity line that connects Shanghai with Hangzhou, the capital city of Zhejiang Province. It has no majority owners. Thirty-six percent of its JV is owned by Shanghai Bureau Co., Ltd., a regional railway authority of the CRC; 29 percent is owned the Zhejiang Municipality's Zhejiang Transport Investment Co., Ltd.; 21 percent is owned by Shanghai Shentie Investment Co., Ltd.; and the final 14 percent is owned by Baosteel Co., Ltd., a social capital company.

Once formally incorporated, the JV sponsor officially takes over all subsequent planning, design, engineering and construction responsibilities from the NRA and CRC. The first step in the process is for the JV sponsor to prepare a draft design plan, which is followed by a preliminary design plan. Both the draft and preliminary design plans can only be undertaken by government-approved engineering and design companies, and once completed are then reviewed by the CRC. Once approved, the draft and preliminary design plans may not be further modified without going back to the CRC.

In addition to draft and preliminary design plans, the JV sponsor must also prepare a draft environmental impact assessment (EIA) plan and an environmental management (EM) plan for submission to China's Ministry of Environmental Protection. Unlike in Europe and North America, where environmental documents must be fully approved before construction can begin, in China, all that is required to begin construction is the approval of the draft EIA and EM plans. Final approval is given after a project has been completed. Its apparent complexity notwithstanding, because the CRC is both project sponsor (through its funding of HSR projects) and project reviewer (through its connections to the Ministry of Environmental Protection), the entire predevelopment planning and review process typically takes less than a year to complete.

Once draft environmental approval has been given, the JV sponsor hires a Railway Design Institute to finalize the project design; contractors, who do the actual construction work; and an engineering supervisor, who manages the day-to-day work of the contractors and ensures that all quality and safety requirements are met. JVs are required by Chinese law to use a competitive tendering process to select all contractors, suppliers, and supervising managers. In the case of main line HSR projects, the tendering process is administered by the CRC in Beijing. Bids are reviewed by an expert committee, with the JV sponsor allowed to select a final contractor from the three top-ranked bidders. The involvement of the CRC as both project sponsor and tender reviewer has both advantages and disadvantages. On the advantage side, it means that all the bidders will be technically qualified. On the disadvantage side, it also opens up issues of undue influence.

In the end, however, it is the JV sponsor that has the legal responsibility for meeting all safety and construction quality standards and for covering and construction cost overruns. Cost overruns and construction quality and scheduling problems were not uncommon during the first few years of the HSR construction system, particularly after 2008 when the government boosted HSR spending in response to the Global Financial Crisis, but these have since declined as contractors, managers, and supervisors have all gained experience working on HSR projects.

In theory, the JV sponsor also has the discretion to select the railway operator—in China as in Europe, railway owners and railway operators are legally distinct entities—but in practice, the responsibility for selecting an operating company lies with the CRC, which usually selects one of its own subsidiaries. The precise terms of the contract between the JV sponsor and the railway operator is the subject of intense negotiation based on projected passenger volumes, fare revenues, and operating costs. HSR trains are costly to operate due to their continuous electricity consumption and resistance losses, so routes that fall short of their projected passenger volumes can quickly accrue large operating deficits.

With these risks and uncertainties in mind, contracts between JV sponsors and operating railway companies usually take one of two forms (Figure 5.4). Under the ticket revenue model, passengers pay their ticket fares to the JV sponsor who then pays the operating railway all operating and maintenance costs plus any agreed-upon profit-sharing. Under the access charge model, passengers pay the operating railway for service, which then pays the JV sponsor for access to their line and usage of their equipment. Under the ticket revenue model, the JV sponsor bears most of the market risk (the likelihood that fare revenues will be below the level required to pay the operator what is owed), whereas under the access charge model, market risk is mostly borne by the operator. Most of China's HSR lines currently operate under the access charge model.[8]

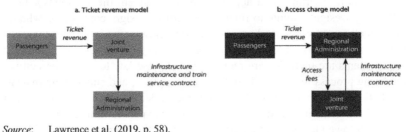

Source: Lawrence et al. (2019, p. 58).

Figure 5.4   *China high-speed rail fare revenue distribution models*

HSR ROUTE AND SERVICE CHARACTERISTICS

China's current HSR system can be categorized by speed, service category, and class. In terms of speed, the 26 types of HSR trains (also known as EMUs or electromotive units) currently in operation in China fall into two broad categories: 300–350 kph "G-class" EMUs, which are used for long-distance service and where passenger demand requires more frequent departures; and 200–250 kph "D-class" and "C-class" EMUs, which are used on shorter and lower-demand routes (China Academy of Railway Sciences 2020).[9]

In terms of service category, China's HSR system is organized into *main line* routes, such as the Beijing-to-Shanghai line, which connect large cities between provinces; *regional* routes, such as the 100 km Quizhou-to-Behai line, which connect medium-sized cities; and *intercity* routes, such as the 115 km Beijing–Tianjin line, which connect nearby large cities to one another. Because of their longer distances, mainline routes mostly rely on 350 kph "G-class" EMUs, while the shorter regional and intercity routes make greater use of "C" and "D-class" trains (China Academy of Railway Sciences 2020). The design and engineering of each HSR route is matched to the top speeds of its EMUs. Mainline routes are designed for 350 kph G-class EMUs; regional routes are designed D-class and C-class EMUs, and intercity routes are designed for C-class EMUs. Should the need for additional capacity arise, D-class and C-class EMUs can also operate on main line routes, albeit at a slower speed than G-class EMUs.

China's original "4 + 4" main line HSR routes were organized into four north–south or "vertical" corridors, and four east–west or "horizontal" corridors. Three of the original vertical corridors had their northern terminus in Beijing, and two of the original horizontal routes terminated in Shanghai. When the decision to expand from a "4 + 4" to an "8 + 8" HSR network was made in 2016, four new north–south HSR routes and four new north–south HSR routes were added. The updated system also introduced the idea of HSR "passageways," consisting of two or more HSR lines connecting the same set of cities.

Individual mainline routes may include multiple railway lines. Whereas routes and corridors are designated according to their terminus cities (e.g., Beijing-to-Guangzhou), lines are designated according to the city couples they connect and the railway companies that provide HSR service between those cities (Table 5.2). The Yangtze River Passageway, for example, which connects Shanghai in the east with the interior city of Chengdu consists of multiple HSR lines, each of which was originally developed by a separate JV company and is served by a different operator.

With individual routes averaging between 150 and 350 km in length, China's regional HSR system currently consists of seven fully-completed HSR routes, with another 11 routes listed as partially-completed or under construction. Unlike mainline routes, which may link together multiple lines, each regional route is its own line and is owned by a single company.

China's intercity HSR system currently includes 35 routes averaging 100–200 km in length.

Table 5.2   *Service characteristics of selected Chinese high-speed rail routes*

Route origin and destination cities	Route length (km)	Intermediate stops	Operating speed (kph)	Number of trains departing daily	Fastest trip	2020 1st class fare (US$)
Beijing–Guangzhou	2,324	Zhengzhou, Wuhan, Changsha	250–350	10	8–10 hours	$204
Beijing–Guilin	1,995	Shijiazhang, Zhengzhou, Wuhan, Changsha, Henyang	350	2	11 hours	$190
Guangzhou–Shanghai	1,810	Hangzhou, Nanchang, Changsha	350	4	6.5–8.5 hours	$192
Shanghai–Xi'an	1,387	Nanjiing, Zhengzhou, Luoyang	350	10	6–6.5 hours	$99 (2nd)
Beijing–Shanghai	1,318	Nanjing, Jinan	250–350	42	4–6 hours	$145
Beijing–Xi'an	1,216	Shijiazhang, Zhengzhou	250–350	20	4–6 hours	$121
Guangzhou–Wuhan	665	none	350	63	3 hrs, 45 minutes	$110
Shanghai–Nanjing	301	none	350	218	3 hours	$117 (2nd)
Shanghai–Hangzhou	169	none	160–350	150	45 min–1 hour	$20
Beijing–Tianjin	122	none	200–250	159	30 min–1 hour	$13
Guangzhou–Shenzhen	115	none	250–350	220	30 minutes	$16

Source: Assembled by the authors from China Travel Guide website.

Chinese HSR operators offer four classes of service: VIP/Business-class, first-class, second-class, and no-seat class. All mainline and regional HSR operators offer first- and second-class service on every train, while only mainline trains offer VIP/Business class seats. In terms of seat mix, 80 percent to 95 percent of train seats are typically designated as second-class, 5 percent to 15 percent are designated as first-class, and 2 percent are typically designated as VIP/Business-class. Taking the CR400AF and CRH380A(L) EMU trainsets as examples, the eight-car CR400AF has 576 seats in total with 538 second-class seats, 28 first-class seats, and 10 VIP business-class seats (China Academy of Railway Sciences 2020). The 16-CRH380A(L) EMU model has 1028 seats in total, with 838 second-class seats, 162 first-class seats, and 28 VIP business-class seats (Zhang 2012). A fourth class of service known as "no-seat class" is available on some lines during the peak holiday season, with ticket holders restricted to second-class cars.

Prior to 2016, main line train fares were determined on a nationwide basis by the National Development and Reform Committee (NDRC). Second-class seats on G-class trains were priced at 0.46 yuan per km (US\$0.069 per km), with first-class seats priced 60 percent higher. Fares on the slower D-class trains were set at 0.29 yuan per km (US\$0.043 per km) for second-class seats and at 0.35 yuan per km (US\$0.052 per km) for first-class seats.

To help attract airline passengers, fares on routes longer than 500 km were typically discounted by 50 percent (Lawrence et al. 2019). National discounts were also available for children, students and disabled veterans. Fares could be discounted by main line operators during periods of slack demand, but otherwise varied little either by line or by available capacity. In contrast to main line HSR operators, regional and intercity line operators were allowed to discount fares according to market conditions.

This fare structure made HSR travel less expensive than air travel—which was priced at 0.8 yuan per km by the NDRC—but more expensive than conventional rail and long-distance bus travel. HSR's affordability attracted a wide cross-section of riders. A 2015 survey conducted by the World Bank of passengers on four HSR lines found that 40 percent of riders had annual incomes of 4,000 yuan (US\$600) per month or less (Zhou et al. 2016).

The NRDC's national HSR fare structure worked well enough on faster and high-demand routes but left many train seats unfilled on slower and low-demand routes. In response, the power to set and alter train fares was moved in 2016 from the NDRC to the China Rail Corporation (CRC), which adopted a new fare structure that allowed fares to vary by line, seat class, and seasonal demand. The result was a 20 percent to 60 percent fare reduction on some low ridership services, such as the Xi'an to Lanzhou route, and a 20 percent to 60 percent fare increase on more popular routes and those serving affluent population centers in Southeastern China. As hoped, the adoption of seasonal discounts and a market-sensitive fares structure attracted additional riders, helping several HSR routes improve their patronage and financial performance.

Today's HSR passengers have a wide variety of fare and service choices. A VIP/business class seat on the 5-hour 300 kph "G-class" train between Beijing and Shanghai, for example, is currently priced at 1,750 yuan. A first-class seat on the same train is 935 yuan, and a second-class seat on the train costs 555 yuan. If a traveler is willing to make the trip on a 250 kph "D-class" train (in eight hours instead of five) they can buy a VIP/business class seat for 1,260 yuan, a first-class seat for 650 yuan, or a second-class seat for 410 yuan.

China's HSR operators have also improved their schedule and service quality since 2016. As a general rule, trains are scheduled so as to minimize the daily and weekly number of empty seats. Simply put, it makes no sense to add an additional train if it will depart with more empty seats than the previous train. Because domestic travel volumes in China vary by season, with many city dwellers returning to their home villages during the New Year's holiday and visiting friends and family in other cities during summer vacation months, HSR operators also routinely vary HSR service frequency by season and passenger loads.

To ensure that HSR service is competitive with airline service—and for shorter routes, with conventional rail service—HSR trains between China's biggest cities typically depart at 30-minute intervals during peak periods and at 60-minute intervals during off-peak periods (Lawrence et al. 2019). On most main line HSR lines, this translates into a minimum of about 20 trains per day. On the highest volume routes such as Beijing–Shanghai, or Shanghai–Nanjing lines, as many as 200 trains may depart daily, sometimes at intervals as short as three minutes.

HSR service in China is well regarded for its reliability and punctuality, with roughly 98 percent of trains leaving on schedule and more than 95 percent arriving on time (Lawrence et al. 2019). This gives HSR a notable reliability advantage over its airline competitors. By way of comparison, 24 percent of Chinese domestic flights in 2019 experienced departure delays of 30 minutes or more according to the VariFlight flight-tracking service (VariFlight 2019). Apart from fine-tuning their schedules, China's HSR operators continue to improve their station and on-board services, with recent additions including more on-board dining options, online ticketing, minimal-cost itinerary changes, transfer assistance, onboard device charging, and seamless Wi-Fi service.

HOW HAS HIGH-SPEED RAIL PERFORMED?

HSR Travel Volumes and Mode Shares

China's strategy of linking every major city by HSR has certainly paid off in terms of ridership. Between the launch of the HSR service in 2008 and 2019, its share of domestic passenger travel in China (measured in terms of passenger-kilometers to account for different trip lengths) has grown from 0.1 percent to 24 percent (Figure 5.5). Much of this increase has come at the expense of long-distance highway travel, which has seen its intercity passenger-kilometers decline from 1,114 billion in 2011 to 886 billion in 2019, and its passenger-kilometer mode share fall from 43 percent to 28 percent.

In contrast to highway travel, intercity air travel within China has continued to grow, albeit at a slower rate than previously. As of 2019, air travel accounted for 26 percent of intercity passenger-kilometers of travel in China. The biggest loser among travel modes, unsurprisingly, has been conventional rail, which has seen its intercity passenger-kilometer mode share decline from 44 percent in 2008 to 22 percent in 2019.

HSR has generated additional long-distance travel as well as attracted passengers from other modes. A World Bank survey of HSR passengers conducted in 2015 estimated that 15 percent of long-distance passenger-kilometers of travel were newly generated as a result of the availability of the HSR service (Lawrence et al. 2019). The liberalization of HSR fares in 2016 has also contributed to ridership gains, with the biggest year-over-year increase in the ratio of HSR travel to network length occurring between 2016 and 2017.

Although China does not report annual mode share numbers by HSR route, 2013 ridership numbers from the five segments that make up the 2,300 km Beijing–Guangzhou HSR route show that for shorter-distance trips, HSR captures between 70 percent and 80 percent of the rail market. HSR's higher rail mode shares are helped as much by its higher service frequency and convenience as by the small difference between HSR and conventional rail fares.

As rail trips get longer, HSR's mode share advantage over conventional rail starts to decline. As noted above, these mode share differences are likely to have narrowed since 2016, when HSR operators were allowed to provide additional fare discounts based on market conditions. Even so, because conventional rail travel speeds have also been increasing, there are many long-distance trips where conventional rail service is still able to compete with HSR.

This is not to say that every HSR route performs similarly. There is a wide variation in HSR trip volumes and market share among individual routes depending on their length, the population sizes of the cities they serve, and the sensitivity of rail passengers to HSR's higher fares.

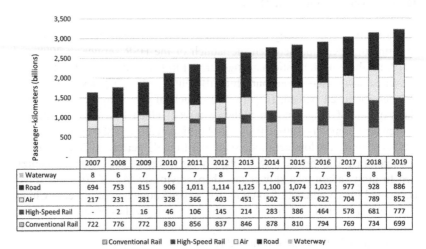

	2007	2008	2009	2010	2011	2012	2013	2014	2015	2016	2017	2018	2019
▨ Waterway	8	6	7	7	7	8	7	7	7	7	8	8	8
■ Road	694	753	815	906	1,011	1,114	1,125	1,100	1,074	1,023	977	928	886
▢ Air	217	231	281	328	366	403	451	502	557	622	704	789	852
■ High-Speed Rail	-	2	16	46	106	145	214	283	386	464	578	681	777
▨ Conventional Rail	722	776	772	830	856	837	846	878	810	794	769	734	699

▨ Conventional Rail   ■ High-Speed Rail   ▢ Air   ■ Road   ▨ Waterway

Source: Assembled by the authors from National Statistics of China (2020).

Figure 5.5   Intercity Travel in China by major mode, 2007–2019

Financial Performance

In the absence of government statistics summarizing HSR's financial performance, World Bank analysts in 2019 developed their own (Lawrence et al 2019). Using 2015 ridership counts and fares as inputs, and assuming that revenues were allocated using the access charge model, they estimated the minimum number of riders a HSR line would need to cover its operating costs, repay its interests costs, and if any revenues remained, provide their JV sponsors and investors with a return on their equity investments. (Their analysis assumes a debt-to-equity ratio of 1.0, 20-year loan terms, and a 5 percent annual interest rate.)

The results vary by line speed and repayment priority. In order to cover operating and maintenance costs but not interest or principal payments, each 300–350 kph HSR line had to attract 9 million paying passengers per year. When interest payments were added in, the minimum number of annual passengers increased to 21 million per year. And when principal repayment was included, the necessary number of passengers rose to 33 million per year. All 17 of China's 300–350 kph lines were found to have met the minimum operating and maintenance cost passenger threshold, but only eight met the additional interest cost threshold, and just five were able to cover their principal repayments.

For the 200–250 kph lines, the comparable breakeven thresholds were 21 million, 53 million, and 85 million passengers per year per line, respectively. Only five of China's sixteen 200–250 kph lines were determined to be able to cover their operating and maintenance costs, and none were able to cover their interest or principal repayment costs.

As to whether the operating railway authorities or the JV sponsors came out on top, due to the priority given to paying operators under the access charge model, regardless of line speed, the railway authorities consistently outperformed their JV sponsors (Lawrence et al. 2019).

All told, the World Bank analysts estimated the 30-year internal rate of return to be 5.5 percent for the HSR network alone, and 6.6 percent when conventional rail service was added in.[10] Adding in residual values, and the internal rate of return for the combined HSR–conventional rail system rose to 8.6 percent (Lawrence et al. 2019). This is not to say that every HSR line was equally profitable, but given the huge scale of China's HSR investments, the astounding speed with which those investments were put into place, the low cost of government-backed debt, and China's general lack of transparency in financial matters, the World Bank analysts judged the overall financial performance of China's HSR network to be satisfactory.

Freight Movement and Population Change

Recall that one of the original reasons for building a separate HSR system— rather than upgrading China's conventional rail network—was to free up space on its conventional rail lines for more frequent and additional rail freight shipments. Was this goal achieved? The evidence is mixed. On the positive side, an analysis of rail freight shipment trends since 2015 shows both tons shipped and freight shipment densities having increased by 20 percent through 2019. Even with these recent increases, however, annual rail freight shipments are still within the same overall range as they were between 2008 and 2015 (Lawrence et al. 2019). This is likely due to factors having little to do with available freight rail capacity, most notably the gradual shift in China's economy toward producing higher-value consumer goods that move by truck instead of train.

Another argument in favor of building HSR was that it would help redirect China's future urban population growth away from high-cost coastal megacities such as Beijing, Shanghai, Guangzhou, and Shenzhen, and toward lower-cost inland cities such as Chongqing and Chengdu. To the degree that such a diversion has occurred, it has been small. Between 2000 and 2010, China's largest coastal cities accounted for approximately 17 percent of the country's urban population growth. The following decade, that share rose to

Megaprojects for megacities

Table 5.3   *Coastal and inland city population totals and shares,*
             2000–2020

Province/district	Largest cities (*) indicates is served by high-speed rail)	Urban population (millions)			Urban population growth share (%) [a]		
		2000	2010	2020 (est)	2000–2010	2010–2020	Change
Coastal provinces and cities							
Guangdong	Guangzhou*, Shenzhen*, Foshan, Dongguan	25.1	35.0	40.2	27	15	–12
Shanghai	Shanghai*	16.4	20.2	26.8	11	20	9
Beijing	Beijing*	13.6	16.7	20.3	9	11	2
Zhejiang	Hangzhou*, Ningbo, Wenzhou	7.0	11.1	15.2	11	12	1
Tianjin	Tianjin*	4.7	9.6	13.5	13	12	–2
Shandong	Jinan*, Qingdao	3.8	8.2	10.9	12	8	–4
Jiangsu	Nanjing*	4.3	5.8	8.7	4	9	4
Fujian	Xiamen*, Fuzhou	4.3	6.2	7.4	5	3	–2
Liaoning	Shenyang*	4.7	5.7	7.2	3	4	2
Yunnan	Kunming*	2.7	3.4	4.4	2	3	1
Guangxi	Nanning*	1.7	2.7	3.8	3	3	1
Coastal total		88.4	124.7	158.4	17	19	2
Inland provinces and cities							
Chongqing	Chongqing*	7.9	11.2	15.9	43	44	1
Sichuan	Chengdu*	3.4	7.8	9.1	56	12	–44
Hubei	Wuhan*	4.7	7.5	8.3	36	7	29
Shaanx	Xi'an*	3.8	5.4	7.9	20	24	3
Heilongjiang	Harbin*	3.4	4.6	6.3	15	16	1
Henan	Zhengzhou*	2.0	3.7	5.3	21	15	–6
Hunan	Changsha*	2.2	3.2	4.5	13	13	0
Jilin	Changchun*	2.9	3.4	4.4	7	9	3
Xinjiang	Urumqi	2.1	2.9	4.3	10	14	4
Anhui	Hefei*	1.5	3.1	4.2	20	10	–9
Hebei	Shijiazhuang*	2.6	3.1	4.1	6	9	3
Shanxi	Taiyuan	2.5	3.2	3.9	8	7	–2
Jiangxi	Nanchang	1.9	2.6	3.6	9	9	0
Guizhou	Quiyang	1.9	2.5	3.3	8	7	–1

Province/district	Largest cities (*) indicates is served by high-speed rail)	Urban population (millions)			Urban population growth share (%) [a]		
		2000	2010	2020 (est)	2000– 2010	2010– 2020	Change
Gansu	Lanzhu*	1.9	2.4	3.1	7	6	−1
Ningxia	Yinchuan	0.6	1.0	2.3	5	12	7
Hainan	Haikou	0.9	1.5	1.9	7	4	−4
Inland total		20.9	28.9	39.5	4	6	2
Urban Population in millions (estimated)		456.0	670.0	850.0	100	100	0

Note: [a] Individual cities are compared with their regional totals; regions are compared with China's urban population total.
Source: Assembled by the authors from Chinese Statistics Bureau

19 percent. Over the same 20-year period, the share of China's urban population growth occurring in large inland cities rose from 4 percent to 6 percent. The bottom line is that population growth in China during the first 20 years of the 21st century overwhelmingly favored large and medium-sized urban places. Indeed, to the extent one might have expected absolute population growth in very large cities to have slowed due to rising congestion and land costs, investments in HSR service have likely enabled that growth to continue uninterrupted.

LESSONS AND TAKEAWAYS

China's experiences building and operating what is by far the world's largest high-speed rail system offer numerous lessons to other countries about the benefits of investing in HSR and, more broadly, about how best to undertake very-large-scale transportation megaprojects. Among the most notable megaproject planning lessons are the following.

- *Being a pioneer isn't important if you can learn from others' experiences.* China was among the last of the world's major countries to embrace HSR service, doing so only 2004. By being late, however, China was able to learn from the mistakes of countries that took the HSR plunge earlier, including Japan, France, and Spain. In addition to learning about the relative advantages of different HSR technologies—a lesson which informed China's decision to develop different HSR trainset speed classes for different lengths and types of trips—China's rail planners learned about the benefits of thinking in terms of networks rather than individual lines, as well as about the benefits of design, construction, and procurement standardization. As a result, China was able to build its HSR network at a lower cost per kilometer than similar systems in Europe as well as achieve a higher HSR market share on key intercity routes. China was also quick to learn from its own HSR experiences, improving quality control standards in the aftermath of a 2011 multi-train accident, amending its HSR planning processes in 2015 to streamline project reviews, and reforming its fare-setting practices in 2016 to better respond to route-specific market conditions.

- *There is no substitute for a long-term commitment from the top.* Once China's leaders made the decision to invest in a national HSR network, they went all in, building a national system of HSR system planners, designers, engineers, inspectors, building contractors, and equipment manufacturers. This enabled them to rapidly accumulate expertise as well as achieve construction and manufacturing economies of scale. Indeed, when many countries were pulling back financially in the immediate aftermath of the 2008–2010 Global Financial Crisis, China's leaders, realizing that borrowing costs and inflationary pressures would never be lower, accelerated their HSR construction timetable.

- *Standardization has its benefits.* China's HSR system was not inexpensive to build, averaging US$15 million to $20 million (depending on the service type) per kilometer of line length. Still, this is about 40 percent less than what it cost to build a kilometer of HSR track in Europe. The difference can be attributed to China's standardization of nearly every aspect of the HSR planning and construction process, including the use of a uniform right-of-way selection and planning process; taking a common approach to all planning, design, construction, and construction management activities; the use of uniform facility designs and standards; and a common equipment procurement process. Standardization also meant that planners, contractors and suppliers could more quickly "move up the learning curve," accumulating valuable expertise as they went along.

- *Government-sponsored joint ventures as an alternative to the PPP model.* The World Bank and other international development organizations have in recent years strongly pushed the public–private-partnership (PPP) model as a means for cash-strapped governments to access private market capital when undertaking major infrastructure projects. The PPP model does have significant advantages, but so do other financing models, including the JV model used to build new HSR lines in China. China's joint venture model brings together national and regional government infrastructure agencies with local governments and private investors to raise equity and debt capital. While it is impossible to assess the performance of individual HSR JV sponsors because of a lack of data, given the enthusiasm local governments and investors continue to have for participating in them, and the fact that none have apparently needed to be restructured even when ridership targets have not been met, it suggests that the JV model is both useful and robust. This conclusion should be taken with a grain of salt, given the overindulgent behavior of most Chinese government agencies and local governments in issuing and accessing debt, but that said, to the extent that debt is used to build long-term infrastructure for which there is a demonstrable market—something that cannot always be said of many PPP-financed projects—the Chinese model is certainly worth consideration. China's JV-centered development model has proven to be particularly useful when coupled with a competitive tendering model for choosing construction contractors and equipment suppliers.

The Chinese experience also has a lot to teach countries and governments contemplating building a HSR system:

- *When properly located, connected and priced, HSR service can quickly attract a large ridership base.* China's focus when framing its initial "4 + 4" HSR network in 2004 was on connecting cities with complementary business activities that would benefit economically from additional travel.[11] This same logic also applied to the 2015 expansion of China's HSR network to include an additional eight lines. The wisdom of this logic is evident by the fact that many HSR lines achieved a 25 percent or more (intercity) mode share within a few years of their completion. More so than almost any other country with a HSR service, China has paid close attention to capitalizing on HSR's competitive advantages when serving intercity trips between 200 and 600 km in length. China's HSR lines have not only attracted passengers from competing airline and conventional rail services, but they have also induced substantial additional travel demand.
- *Not all HSR services must operate at very high speeds.* HSR services that operate at 300 kph or more are much more expensive to build and operate than those that operate at 200–250 kph. China's HSR planners learned this lesson early on and went about designing a three-tier HSR system (main lines, regional lines, and intercity lines) in which travel speeds and service frequencies were fine-tuned to the characteristics and preference of travelers. This has enabled most Chinese HSR lines to continue to operate in the black, something that cannot be said of HSR lines is Japan, France, or Spain. According to analysts at The World Bank, Chinese lines must achieve annual passenger density levels of 20 million passenger-kilometers or more to break even. Given the large number of Chinese cities with present-day populations of two million or more, this is well within the realm of realization for almost every current HSR line.
- *Punctuality, reliability, and value-for-money are as important as connectivity.* China's HSR services have always been extremely punctual and reliable because of their exclusive-use tracks and standardized equipment

designs. This has made it easy to expand or, in some cases, contract service according to market demand. Where China's HSR operators have really made progress in recent years is in their greater use of market-based pricing strategies, which have enabled them to continually adjust their competitive positioning with respect to airline and conventional rail services.

This is not to say that every aspect of China's HSR system has worked out according to plan. Among the characteristics of China's HSR experience that other countries should think twice about emulating are:

- *A characteristic lack of transparency.* China rarely makes public all the details of its infrastructure planning, feasibility, market, or impact assessment studies; or otherwise makes them available for review outside the government. It is therefore impossible to know which (if any) HSR projects cost more than expected, fell short of ridership and revenue projections, generated unforeseen environmental impacts, or lost money for their JV partners. Had China's urbanization rate not grown so consistently, rising from 48 percent in 2009 to 60 percent in 2018 and thereby providing an expanding passenger base for its HSR services, it is likely that some or even many of its HSR lines would have experienced notable passenger and revenue shortfalls. In countries whose urban and economic growth rates have not been as favorable as China's, a similarly ambitious HSR investment program would likely have run into profound ridership and financial difficulties—difficulties that could be avoided or mitigated with a healthy level of public scrutiny.
- *Potential conflicts of interest.* The involvement of the national railway company in every aspect of the HSR planning, design, engineering, financing, and service negotiation process provides for numerous planning efficiencies, but it also creates the impression (if not the reality) of significant institutional and financial conflicts of interest. In most countries' cases, ensuring the proper safety, reliability, and financial performance of an infrastructure system as extensive and complicated as China's HSR network requires having a planning and certification process that is independent of the agency whose political and financial fortunes are dependent on it going forward.
- *Unrealized secondary benefits.* Two of China's reasons for building such an extensive HSR network were to redirect population and economic growth from its fast-growing coastal cities to its slower-growing interior cities; as well as to free-up capacity on its shared conventional rail-freight rail network in order to improve the reliability and efficiency of its freight railroads. Neither of these objectives was achieved to any significant degree. This is not a new story. In none of the European or Asian countries

that have built HSR systems has the national economic geography been affected to any significant degree. Likewise, with advanced economies increasingly shifting over to producing consumer goods that ship by road instead of rail, the additional freight rail capacity that building a separate HSR system makes available mostly goes unused.

NOTES

1. The International Union of Railways, the worldwide professional association representing the railway sector, defines high-speed rail (HSR) as any rail service that supports sustained passenger travel speeds of 250 kph or more, or rail service that operates at speeds between 200 and 250 kph but otherwise "complies with the technical and operational standards of high-speed rail." Rail services that operate at speeds below 200 kph are referred to as conventional rail (International Union of Railways 2018, 2020).
2. Erick Burgeno Salas. As reported in Statista.com (September 28, 2021)
3. China does not report its HSR capital spending. This is estimated by multiplying China's 37,000 km of HSR network by an average capital cost per kilometer of roughly $17 million as reported in the 2019 World Bank Report.
4. As reported on the International Railway Journal website (https://www.railjournal .com/in_depth/hokkaido-shinkansen-prepares-for-launch) February 16, 2016.
5. Erick Burgeno Salas. As reported in Statista.com (September 28, 2021)
6. 回顾1997第一次大提速内容. *tieliu.com.cn* (in Chinese).
7. Prior to 2013, the Chinese Ministry of Railways (MOR) served as both railway service provider and regulator. In 2013, following the release of a report blaming MOR practices for a 2011 HSR train collision that killed 40 passengers and injured another 192, the MOR was split into the National Railway Administration (NRA) under the Ministry of Transport (MOT) which serves as railway regulator; and the China Railway Corporation (CRC) in charge of all passenger railway service operations. In 2019, the CRC was renamed China Railway (China State Railway Group Co., Ltd.). We will continue to use the abbreviation CRC when referring to China Railways to avoid confusion with conventional railway (CR).
8. Some lines use both revenue models. The Beijing–Shanghai line, for example, uses the access charge model for its cross-line operations and the ticket revenue model for its main line operations.
9. Actual travel speeds are a good deal lower than listed speeds, due primarily to the effects of station "dwell times" (e.g., the increase in travel time that occurs when a train stops to pick up or discharge passengers). For example, although capable of a sustained top speed of 330 kph, after accounting for station dwell times, the "C-class" trains that operate between Beijing and Tianjin, travel at an average speed of just 226 kph.
10. HSR service reduces congestion delays on China's conventional rail system, enabling it to operate more efficiently.
11. This is the so-called network effect argument. By connecting additional nodes on a network, the total efficiency or accessibility offered by that network to existing nodes also increases (Katz and Shapiro 1994).

REFERENCES

China Academy of Railway Sciences. 2020. *"动车组介绍" Introduction to EMUs.* August 28. Retrieved from "中国铁路12306" China Railway 12306: https://www .12306.cn/index/view/station/train_intro.html.

European Court of Auditors. 2018. "A European high-speed rail network: not a reality but an ineffective patchwork." European Court of Auditors.

International Union of Railways. 2018. *High Speed Rail Fast Track to Sustainable Mobility.* International Union of Railways.

International Union of Railways. 2020. *High Speed Lines in the World (Summary) updated 27th February 2020.* International Union of Railways.

Katz, M. L., & Shapiro, C. 1994. Systems competition and network effects. *Journal of Economic Perspectives* 8(2): 93–115.

Lawrence, M., Bullock, R., and Liu, Z. 2019. *China's High Speed Rail Development.* Washington, DC: World Bank Group.

Ministry of Railways. 2004. *"铁路主要技术政策" Major Railway Technical Policies.* Ministry of Railways.

National Development and Reform Commission (NDRC). 2016. "Mid- and Long-Term Railway Network Plan." National Development and Reform Commission.

VariFlight. 2019. *"全球机场和航空公司准点率报告" International Airports and Airlines Punctuality Report.* VariFlight.

Zhang, R. 2012. "京广高铁建设贷款或近4000亿 每年利息数十亿" Beijing-Guangzhou HSR Construction Cost may be around 400 billion RMB, with several billion interests per year. *The Time Weekly.* (December 27). Retrieved from http://finance.people.com.cn/n/2012/1227/c1004-20028974.html.

Zhou, N., Bullock, R., Jin, Y., Lawrence, M., & Ollivier, G. 2016. *High-Speed Railways in China: An Update on Passenger Profiles.* Beijing: World Bank Office, Beijing.

6. China's metro explosion: lessons from China's big four cities

Zhong-Ren Peng, Kaifa Lu, Mengyi Jin, Xinghang Zhu and John D. Landis

ABBREVIATIONS USED IN THIS CHAPTER

BSC	Beijing Subway Company
CBD	Central Business District
MTR	Hong Kong Mass Transit Railway
NDRC	National Development and Reform Commission
P3	Public–private Partnership
PRC	People's Republic of China
R+P	Rail and Property Development
SMG	Shenzhen Metro Group

Few infrastructure investments epitomize the pros and cons of megaprojects better than urban metro systems. Properly implemented, metro systems can organize urban population growth in an efficient and prosperous manner while limiting adverse traffic congestion and environmental effects. At the same time, new metro lines are almost always expensive to build, are prone to construction schedule delays and cost overruns, and may not always meet their ambitious ridership targets.

No country in recent years has been more active, building more metro lines in more cities than China. Statistics hardly do China's metro-building energy justice. With only six metro lines in service as recently as 2000, China accounted for just 3.7 percent of the world's metro lines and less than 4 percent of its metro system length (Ovenden 2003). Twenty years later, with 214 metro lines operating in 41 cities, China accounts for 30 percent of the world's metro lines and 23 percent of its metro system length (UITP 2018). (For those who like to keep track of such things, India and the United States are tied for second place in the number of cities with metro systems, with 14 each.) As if this isn't enough, another 88 new metro lines are listed as scheduled to be completed by 2025.[1]

Drilling down from the national to the city level, five cities currently stand atop China's metro leader board based on system size and ridership: Shanghai, with 18 lines extending 743 km; Beijing, with 24 lines extending 703 km; Chengdu, with 12 lines extending 518 km; Guangzhou, with 13 lines extending 492 km; and Shenzhen, with 11 metro lines extending 411 km. (All of these counts are current as of 2020 and include only conventional heavy-rail transit lines). In terms of how they compare worldwide, Shanghai, Beijing, Chengdu and Guangzhou are now the top four metro systems in the world in terms of system length, while Shenzhen is number six (Table 6.1). Shanghai, with 2.8 billion passengers in 2020 is also the world's top-rated metro system in term of total ridership, followed by Guangzhou (ranked fourth with 2.4 billion passengers in 2020), Beijing (ranked fifth with 2.3 billion passengers in 2020), and Shenzhen (ranked tenth, with 1.6 billion passengers in 2020) (China Urban Rail Transit Association 2021).

Table 6.1   *Top 10 metro systems ranked by system length and ridership*

Global rank by system length	City and system name	Country	Year opened	Year of last expansion	System length (km)	Annual ridership (millions of passengers in 2018)	Global rank by annual ridership
1	SHANGHAI Metro	China	1993	2021	743	2,835	1
2	BEIJING Subway	China	1971	2020	727	2,293	5
3	GUANGZHOU Metro	China	1997	2020	531	2,416	4
4	CHENGDU Metro	China	2010	2020	519	1,220	14
5	Moscow Metro	Russia	1935	2021	412	2,561	3
6	SHENZHEN Metro	China	2004	2020	411	1,627	10
7	London Underground	UK	1863	2008	402	1,337	12
8	New York City Subway	US	1904	2017	399	1,698	7
9	NANJING Metro	China	2005	2018	378	801	17
10	CHONGQING Rail Transit	China	2005	2021	370	840	16

Source: International Association of Public Transport.

The typical Chinese metro line is between 30 and 40 kilometers in length and takes between three and five years to build. This puts it in stark contrast to recent metro lines built in the West. It took New York City ten years and more than $4 billion to build the half-mile long first phase of the Second

Avenue Subway, which finally opened in 2017. London's 16 km Jubilee Line Extension opened 20 months late in 1999 at a cost that was £1 billion over budget; and the 117 km London Crossrail Line (profiled in Chapter 4), which opened in 2022, is four years late and nearly £5 billion over-budget.

This chapter explores how China's four top-tier cities—Beijing, Shanghai, Guangzhou, and Shenzhen—have built their world-leading metro systems so quickly and with such impressive ridership results. Its conclusions suggest there are valuable lessons other global cities can learn from China's recent metro-building experiences. These include the importance of connecting local metro construction efforts to national development priorities and funding; the tradeoffs involved in standardizing metro planning processes, siting criteria and construction techniques; the dangers of ramping-up construction too quickly without allowing adequate time to take stock of past experiences; and the value of encouraging different places to undertake their own infrastructure financing approaches.

It is also important to acknowledge the limits of Chinese case studies. Like their US counterparts, Chinese cities are not required to report passenger ridership or revenue information on a line-by-line basis.[2] This makes it difficult to assess the performance of individual lines. China's economic development planning and investment decision-making processes are also notably opaque. China lists its national development priorities in its Five-Year Plans but does not make public how its two key decision-making bodies, the National Development and Reform Commission (NDRC) and the ruling State Council, decide which projects to fund and why. China's lack of decision-making transparency or use of conventional project evaluation criteria, its preference for funding infrastructure investments out of government revenues instead of borrowed capital, and, most of all, its lack of public input requirements, all mean that decision-makers elsewhere should carefully investigate China's infrastructure investment practices before necessarily adopting them as their own. Perspectives also differ regarding appropriate planning and design practices. Practices such as standardizing station spacing or siting new stations without regard to nearby land uses, which serve to reduce project delivery costs and times in China, may not produce similar benefits elsewhere.

Still, it's hard to argue with success. In the space of 20 years, Chinese cities have gone from bringing up the rear to becoming the world's undisputed leaders in terms of metro system construction and ridership; and there is much to be learned from its efforts and results.

CHINA'S METRO EVOLUTION: FROM SKEPTICISM TO ENTHUSIASM

China was a very late arrival to the business of building metro lines. As of 1990, China had just three up-and-running metro lines, two in Beijing and one in Tianjin. Until the early 1980s, most Chinese city dwellers lived in combined housing and factory projects known as *danwei*. Few residents commuted more than a mile or two to work, and most daily trips could be made by walking or bicycle. Only senior Communist Party officials owned cars, traffic congestion was non-existent, and there was little need for public transit service other than buses and the occasional taxi.

All of this changed in the mid-1980s as millions of rural residents began arriving in China's coastal cities seeking factory work. Some factory owners built dormitories for their workers, but most did not, presuming that their employees would commute from wherever they were living. Bike trips gave way to bus trips and the narrow streets of Chinese cities quickly became congested. Chinese urban planners responded to rising traffic congestion the same way their Western counterparts had a generation earlier: when existing roads became congested, build more roads. This approach worked no better to stem rising traffic congestion levels in Beijing than it had in Los Angeles. As auto ownership levels rose alongside incomes, newly-completed arterials were congested as soon as they opened. Adding to the demand for travel, the density of new residential development was also rising as four and five-story *danwei* gave way to high-rise apartment blocks. In the same way that transportation planners in Seoul, Taiwan, Hong Kong, and Singapore had turned to their national governments for help building metro systems to relieve urban traffic congestion in the 1970s and 1980s, Chinese urban planners would do so in the late 1990s.

Their requests were met with skepticism by the Chinese government. Metro systems were extremely costly to build, and China was still focused on expanding its export-oriented manufacturing industries. Unlike roads and freight rail lines, subways couldn't be used to transport goods. Instead of investing in urban transit systems, China's transportation priorities leaned toward seaports, highways, and airports. Besides, Chinese cities were constantly competing with one another for Beijing's favor, so if the government approved one city's request to build a new metro system, it would soon be besieged by similar requests from two dozen others. From the perspective of the National Reform and Development Commission, which oversees evaluating infrastructure project applications, it was better to let individual cities use their own funds to construct metro lines one at a time rather than making building new metro systems into a national priority.

Gradually, the government's reluctance to invest in new metro systems began softening. As a result of government policies encouraging rural residents to move to cities, traffic congestion was becoming a national problem. Government planners finally conceded that it would be impossible for China's cities to build their way of congestion, and instead proposed that they take a corridor-centric approach toward investing in rail transit. Helping to make their case, all four of China's top-tier cities had won the right to host major international sporting and cultural events—the Olympics in Beijing in 2008, a World Exposition in Shanghai in 2010, the Asian Games in Guangzhou in 2010, and Universiade Games in Shenzhen also in 2011—based partly on commitments by city officials to expand their public transportation systems (Jiang 2008; Zhou 2010).

With the benefit of hindsight, Chinese transportation historians divide China's metro building efforts into three distinct periods. The first occurred between 1965 and 1999 and involved a handful of high-profile Chinese cities (including Beijing, Tianjin, Shanghai and Guangzhou) each building one or two subway lines to essentially test the market for metro service (Wang et al. 2019). A second period of metro building activity extended from 2000 to 2010 and saw expanded metro construction activity in China's top-tier cities, primarily to deal with worsening traffic congestion. Metro construction activity during this second period was given a further push in 2008 as part of China's infrastructure investment response to the Global Financial Crisis.

The third and current phase of metro-building activity has seen the construction of new metro systems expand to include almost all of China's large and fast-growing cities primarily to steer factory and residential sprawl into transit corridors. Third-stage metro-building efforts follow from the ridership successes of China's second-stage metros as well as from two national policy initiatives put forth in China's 12th and 13th Five-Year Plans spanning the 2011–2020 period. The first such initiative centered on redirecting China's huge rural-to-urban migration flows away from a few high-flying coastal cities and toward lagging inland cities. The second was to reorient China's infrastructure investments toward clean energy projects that would reduce greenhouse gas emissions (Meng et al. 2012). Provided they yielded sufficient riders, building new metro lines could help accommodate both objectives. The result of metro-building efforts during this last period can be seen in Figure 6.1 and Table 6.2. Prior to 2010, metro system-building activity was concentrated in China's largest and most economically dominant cities, most notably Beijing, Shanghai, Guangzhou, and Shenzhen. Since 2010, metro construction activity has expanded to include second- and third-tier Chinese cities such as Wuhan, Qingdao, Nanjing, Hangzhou, Chongqing, Chengdu, and Xi'an.

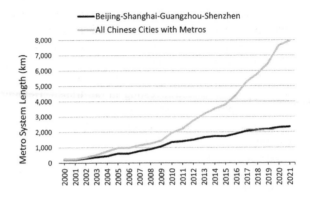

Source: Assembled by the authors from metro system websites.

Figure 6.1   *Cumulative length of Chinese metro systems, 2000–2021*

Table 6.2   *List of current Chinese metro systems, 2020*

City and metro system	Length (km)	Lines	Stations	First year of operation	Annual ridership, 2018 (millions)
Shanghai	743	18	473	1993	3,710
Beijing	727	24	428	1969	3,848
Chengdu	518	12	373	2010	1,158
Guangzhou	492	13	257	1997	3,029
Shenzhen	411	11	283	2004	1,647
Nanjing	377	10	174	2005	1,119
Chongqing	370	8	187	2004	858
Wuhan	360	9	240	2004	1,054
Hangzhou	306	7	165	2012	530
Qingdao	246	6	110	2015	154
Xi'an	245	8	171	2011	746
Tianjin	233	6	159	1984	409
Zhengzhou	213	7	151	2013	293
Suzhou	164	4	134	2012	328
Dalian	158	4	69	2002	192
Ningbo	154	5	103	2014	124
Changsha	142	5	111	2014	250
Kunming	138	5	92	2012	200
Shenyang	116	4	91	2010	330

City and metro system	Length (km)	Lines	Stations	First year of operation	Annual ridership, 2018 (millions)
Hefei	115	4	97	2016	153
Nanning	108	4	91	2016	214
Xiamen	98	3	65	2017	114
Nanchang	89	3	74	2015	142
Wuxi	89	3	69	2014	103
Jinan	84	3	40	2019	n.a.
Guiyang	76	2	55	2017	7
Changchun	68	4	59	2011	127
Shijiazhuang	62	3	51	2017	88
Fuzhou	56	2	43	2016	61
Wenzhou	54	1	18	2019	n.a.
Hohhot	49	2	44	2019	n.a.
Xuzhou	46	2	38	2019	n.a.
Foshan	40	1	25	2010	110
Dongguan	38	1	15	2016	46
Changzhou	34	1	29	2019	n.a.
Harbin	32	2	27	2013	97
Ürümqi	28	1	21	2018	2
Lanzhou	26	1	20	2019	n.a.
Luoyang	25	1	19	2021	n.a.
Taiyuan	24	1	23	2020	n.a.
Shaoxing	20	1	10	2021	n.a.
Total	7,374	212	4,704		21,243

Source: Assembled by the authors from metro system websites. Because of reporting differences, ridership total may differ from those reported to the International Association of Public Transport as reported in Table 6.1.

CHINA'S METRO PLANNING AND APPROVAL PROCESS

Infrastructure planning and investment decision-making in China is a decidedly top-down affair. While the idea of building a metro system or expanding a metro line may originate at the city level, the final authorization for doing so rests with the NDRC and the State Council. The State Council is China's principal administrative authority, functioning as both its executive branch and its parliament. The State Council draws its members from the Central Committee of China's Communist Party as well as from the ranks of local governors and mayors who have achieved prominence administering their provinces and municipalities. Technically under State Council control, the NDRC functions as a combination central bank and national economic development agency. Its primary responsibility is to prepare China's Five-Year Plans and to oversee their implementation (Cao et al. 2014). This involves reviewing infrastructure investment proposals submitted by cities as well as approving all government grants and loans provided by government-sponsored banks.

From the perspective of a city wanting to build or extend a metro line, the infrastructure planning and approval process can be divided into a preliminary planning stage and an implementation planning stage. Each involves a different level of detail and series of approvals. To kick off the preliminary planning stage, a municipality's rail transit department or agency must first develop a special urban metro transit network plan identifying proposed rail transit routes, facilities, and technologies. The proposed network plan must be consistent with the city's previously-adopted urban master plan as well as with its comprehensive transportation plan. Once a municipality's draft network plan has been prepared, it must first be approved by the city's own Department of Urban and Rural Planning, thus ensuring that it is consistent with criteria published by China's Ministry of Housing and Urban–Rural Development. From there, the plan goes to the NDRC to ensure that its goals and funding requirements are consistent with China's current national Five-Year Plan.

Assuming the NDRC recommends the proposed plan, and there is no guarantee that it will, the plan is then submitted to the State Council for funding approval and recording. Depending on the State Council's own priorities and whether there are competing plans from other cities, it is not uncommon for the State Council to partially approve a plan, meaning that only part of a proposed line may be built, or to delay approval to a subsequent year. Altogether, the preliminary planning stage typically takes two to three years, during which time conditions on the ground may change.

As cumbersome as the metro planning and approval process can be, it ensures that local proposals are consistent with national planning goals and funding resources, as well as complement local land use and development plans. It also guarantees that local projects will conform to national design, engineering, and procurement practices. This helps hold down construction and purchasing costs, as well as promotes the growth of Chinese train manufacturers and equipment providers (Zhang and Wan 2019).

Once a city's network plan has been approved, it moves on to the implementation planning stage. This involves a series of project-level approvals that include construction site approval, land pre-examination approval, land acquisition approval, land planning and design permit approval, construction project planning permit approval, and construction permit approval. These approvals generally progress as follows (Zhang and Wan 2019):

- Based on the approved network plan, municipal transit planners prepare a detailed metro construction plan which is submitted to the NDRC for project-specific funding.
- Once the NDRC approves the project's funding, the municipality's planning bureau must approve acquisition of the sites needed to accommodate the project's right-of-way, stations, and storage and equipment areas.
- Once specific sites are selected, the municipality's environmental protection bureau must certify that there are no undue adverse environmental impacts.
- Once its environmental protection bureau has weighed in, the municipality's Land Bureau can issue a construction license for the project, certifying that the project sponsor—typically the municipal transit agency—is qualified to supervise project construction.
- Once a construction license has been issued, the municipal planning bureau issues a planning permit of construction engineering which is reviewed by the municipal construction bureau, which, only then, issues a construction permit.
- With a construction permit in hand, the project sponsor must obtain a pre-evaluation report by the State Administration of Work Safety stipulating that the project can be built without risk of worker death or injury.

As complicated as this process sounds, in practice it usually progresses quickly. The two conditions that typically slow the process down are not having sufficient funding to guarantee project completion and having to pay above-market prices to acquire privately owned land.

To support their applications to the NDRC, cities frequently submit additional policy documents or plans indicating how a proposed project fits into the city's broader land use, economic development, and transportation infrastructure investment picture. With names such as "Guiding Opinions on Giving Priority to the Development of Public Transport in Beijing" or "Provisional Rules of the Shenzhen Municipality on the Administration of Metro Construction," these documents provide an important degree of planning continuity over time.

This is not to say that project approvals and funding decisions in China are devoid of local politics. Just like their congressional or parliamentary counterparts in the US or the UK, members of China's State Council continue to retain their local political loyalties, which sometimes means favoring projects in their home cities or provinces. Local government officials can also boost the likelihood that their metro projects will be approved by the NDRC and State Council by taking on greater responsibility for their funding. This is something the city of Guangzhou has done with great success (Wang and Qian 2018). Still, unlike in the US, where Congressional representatives have been known to trade approvals for each other's projects through a process known as "logrolling," in China, the fact that potential metro projects must first be approved on technical grounds by the NDRC serves to mitigate against approving projects purely on political grounds and for which there is no documented demand. As a result, completed metro projects in China usually meet their ridership forecasts.

METRO CONSTRUCTION AND OPERATING COST COMPARISONS

How much do Chinese cities spend to build and operate their metro systems? Providing precise answers to this question is complicated by the fact that construction and operating expenditures are typically reported on a systemwide rather than line-by-line basis. Nonetheless, with a little detective work, it is possible to piece together a rough picture of how and why construction and operating costs and revenues vary by place and time. Among the key comparisons, as shown in Table 6.3, and reported in both renminbi and dollars:

- *Beijing*: Opened for service in September 2009, the Beijing Subway's 28 km Line 4 cost ¥4.6 billion (US$555 million) or about $20 million per kilometer to build. As an indication of the benefits of building at scale, this was about $10 million less per kilometer than it cost to build the 4.4 km first phase of the Olympic Branch (Line 8), which opened a year earlier. Looking at the two subway lines as a pair, right-of-way acquisition and track and station construction accounted for the largest share of costs (42 percent), followed by mechanical and electrical engineering costs (16 percent), and rolling stock purchases (12 percent). Systemwide, ¥63.8 billion (US$7.7 billion) was allocated to subway construction between 2002 and 2008, with the total rising to ¥270 billion (US$43.8 billion) by 2015.

  Operating costs for the Beijing Subway in 2020 totaled ¥18.4 billion (US$2.7 billion), ¥4.7 billion (US$700 million) more than was collected in revenues. As a result, the Beijing government had to subsidize its subway system in 2020 to the amount of ¥10.5 billion (US$1.5 billion) or about ¥2.7 (US$0.39) per subway passenger. That the Beijing Subway requires continuing subsidies to operate is not atypical of cities in China or elsewhere in the world.

- *Shanghai*: Construction expenditures for Shanghai's 64 km Metro Line 2—which first entered service in 2000 and has been extended six times since—total ¥10.9 billion. This works out to about US$27 million per kilometer. Of the ¥298.3 billion (US$46.9 billion) allocated between 2018 and 2023 by the City of Shanghai to pay for new and extended metro lines, 55 percent was provided by bank loans and 45 percent from government sources. Operating costs for Shanghai's metro system in 2019 totaled ¥573 million (US$83 million), compared favorably to revenue of ¥659 million (US$94.7 million). For 2020, COVID-19 resulted in a 61.3 percent drop in operating costs compared with 2019, and a 54.3 percent revenue decline.[3]

- *Guangzhou*: Annual reports by the Guangzhou Metro differentiate between investment expenditures, which includes spending on new metro line construction; capital expenditures, which include spending on existing lines; and revenues. According to the most recent information available, investments in new metro lines in Guangzhou increased from ¥21.8 billion (US$3.3 billion) in 2017 to ¥30.7 billion (US$4.5 billion) in 2019, while other capital expenditure hardly grew at all. In 2020, the two spending categories were combined into a single category totaling ¥82.7 billion (US$12.5 billion) a remarkable year-over-year increase.

    On the revenue side, total revenues between 2017 and 2020 increased ¥6.3 billion (US$1.1 billion), with most of the increase occurring before the onset of COVID-19. Even so, Guangzhou's metro system in 2020 required subsidies totaling ¥510 million (US$76.9 million), or about ¥0.15 per metro passenger. This is a very small amount as transit subsidies go and is indicative of the Guangzhou metro system's strong financial health, which has enabled the city to continue making investments in system capacity.

- *Shenzhen*: Shenzhen's 43 km Metro Line 5, which opened for service in June 2011, cost ¥20.6 billion (US$3.2 billion) or about $75 million per kilometer to build. As an illustration of the cost savings of building at scale, Shenzhen's 6.2 km Line 1 Northwest Extension, also completed in 2011, cost $270 million per kilometer to build. Shenzhen Metro's annual investments in new metro capacity increased from ¥43.8 billion (US$6.4 billion) in 2017 to ¥57.3 billion (US$8.3 billion) in 2020.

- Operating costs for Shenzhen's metro system in 2020 totaled ¥13.3 billion (US$2.1 billion). This compared favorably with revenues of ¥20.8 billion (US$3.3 billion), which was little changed from 2019.

Table 6.3　　*Metro construction costs by system*

City	Metro lines or year	Investment (or subsidy)	Distribution of expenditures	Revenue	Additional notes
Beijing	Line 4	¥4.6 billion (US$555 million)	Investment costs were allocated as follows: civil engineering (42%); mechanical and electrical engineering (16%); train purchase (12%); and other (15%).	n.a.	A total of ¥63.8 billion (US$7.7 billion) was allocated to construction of Beijing's metro system between 2002 and 2008. By 2015, this total had risen to ¥270 billion (US$43.8 billion)
	Beijing Metro Olympic Branch Line	¥1.1 billion (US$132 million)			
	2020	Government subsidy of ¥10.5 billion (US$1.52 billion)	Annual operating costs in 2020 totaled ¥18.4 billion (US$2.7 billion)	Annual passenger revenues in 2020 totaled of ¥13.7 billion (US$2.0 billion)	
Shanghai[a]	Line 1	¥5.4 billion (US$848 million)	Cumulative funding allocation is as follows: 50–60% of funds were invested in the construction of new metro lines or extensions to existing lines; 10–15% were used for system operations and maintenance; and the balance was used to cover other potential costs.	n.a.	Of the ¥298.3 billion (US$46.9 billion) used for the third phase of Shanghai's urban rail transit construction plan (2018–2023), 55% was from bank loans and 45% was from government sources.
	Line 2	¥10.9 billion (US$1.70 billion)			
	2019[a]	n.a.	¥573 million (US$83.0 million)	¥659 million (US$95.5 million)	
	2020[a]		¥222 million (US$32.2 million)	¥301 million (US$43.6 million)	

City	Metro lines or year	Investment (or subsidy)	Distribution of expenditures	Revenue	Additional notes
Guangzhou	2017	¥21.8 billion (US$3.3 billion)	¥25.4 billion (US$3.8 billion)	¥18.2 billion (US$2.8 billion)	In Guangzhou, the payments for construction of the new lines totaled ¥25.4 billion (US$3.8 billion) in 2017; ¥31.5 billion (US$4.6 billion) in 2018; and ¥31.9 billion (US$4.6 billion) in 2019.
	2018	¥26 billion (US$3.8 billion)	¥31.5 billion (US$4.6 billion)	¥18.6 billion (US$2.7 billion)	
	2019	¥30.7 billion (US$4.5 billion)	¥31.9 billion (US$4.6 billion)	¥24.5 billion (US$3.6 billion)	
	2020	¥25.8 billion (US$3.7 billion) (Operating revenue of ¥12.9 billion (US$1.9 billion)) Government subsidy of ¥510 million (US$73.9 million)	An operating cost of ¥11.3 billion (US$1.6 billion)		

City	Metro lines or year	Investment (or subsidy)	Distribution of expenditures	Revenue	Additional notes
Shenzhen	Line 5	¥20.6 billion (US$3.2 billion)[a]	Shenzhen spent ¥60 billion in 2010 on the construction of urban metro lines (Line 1, 2 and 5) and transportation hubs; ¥11.6 billion on the operation of two metro lines; and about ¥3.2 billion on the property management and development along existing metro lines.	n.a.	Shenzhen invested about ¥20 billion (US$3.1 billion) in metro construction in 2010 to meet the deadline of the 2011 Universiade Games, including ¥12.6 billion (US$2 billion) from the city government.
	Line 1 Northwest extension	¥10.6 billion (US$1.67 billion)			
	2019	¥43.8 billion (US$6.4 billion)	An operating cost of ¥14.3 billion (US$2.1 billion)	A total revenue of ¥21.0 billion (US$3.0 billion)	
	2020	¥57.3 billion (US$8.3 billion)	An operating cost of ¥13.3 billion (US$1.9 billion)	A total revenue of ¥20.8 billion (US$3.0 billion)	

Note: [a] Shanghai estimates include only those metro lines managed by Shanghai Shentong Metro Co., Ltd.
Source: Assembled by authors from metro system websites.

METRO FINANCING MODELS

Local governments in China fund metro construction and operations using three models (Liu et al. 2016).

1. *The direct government funding model,* in which metro planning and construction costs are funded by a combination of central government tax revenues and borrowing, and local government land sales. Once a metro line is up and running, its day-to-day operating expenses are funded from passenger fares, although they are almost never enough to cover them completely. Longer-term operating costs such as maintenance and equipment upgrading/replacement are typically funded from government revenues and operator reserves, assuming they are available.

2. *The government-guaranteed loan model,* in which planning, construction and some long-term operating costs are covered by a combination of government funds and loans issued by state-owned banks and foreign financial institutions. For the most part, these loans are implicitly or explicitly guaranteed by the Chinese government. As with the government grant-based approach identified above, short-term operating costs have first claim on farebox revenues.

3. *The public–private-partnership (P3) model,* in which a municipality (with the concurrence of the central government) provides a concession to a private partner or investor to plan, construct and operate a metro line. The municipality typically provides the land for the system right-of-way and associated facilities in exchange for the private partner/investor providing all or a portion of the project financing. Passenger and land development revenues are returned to the private partner who uses them to pay operating costs and debt service and distributes whatever is left to investors. The two most common forms of P3 financing are the Build–Operate–Transfer (BOT) model in which the private partner plans, builds, finances and operates the project for an extended interval before transferring it back to public ownership (Li 2016); and the Build–Transfer (BT) model, a so-called "turn-key" approach, in which the private partner is paid a commission to plan, construct, and arrange financing for a publicly-owned project (Liu et al. 2016).

Different approaches have been tried in different cities at different times with varying degrees of success. Most Chinese metro lines approved prior to 2000 (e.g., Lines 1 and 2 in Beijing and Line 1 in Shanghai) were funded entirely out of government revenues (i.e., the direct government funding model). This was partly because Beijing and Shanghai lacked sufficient funding resources of their own, partly so that the Chinese government could keep an eye on what was going on, and partly because, at the time, Chinese local governments were locked out of international debt markets (Liu et al. 2018).

As China's coastal cities gained population and wealth, their funding base grew accordingly, enabling them to take on a larger and larger financing role. In Beijing, Line 8 (completed in 2020) and the BaTong Line (completed in 2019) were both funded using a mix of central government grants and loans, local funding, and government-guaranteed loans from foreign banks (Liu et al. 2016). This was also the funding vehicle used to pay for Shanghai's Metro Line 2, completed in 2010; and Lines 4 and 5 in Shenzhen.

The problem with infrastructure projects that are entirely government funded or backed by boundless government guarantees is that they are rarely subject to robust pre-development underwriting or to rigorous cost controls once construction is underway. Simply put, there is no way to know up front whether such projects make fundamental economic sense, or, short of stopping construction, to regulate spending once a project is underway. This is particularly problematic for cities undertaking multiple projects simultaneously. The goal becomes keeping as many funding balls in the air at the same time as possible, not keeping track of individual funding sources. At some point, this lack of financial discipline may make it difficult to access additional capital, as lenders and investors may balk at repeating past mistakes. To get around this problem, municipal and provincial governments have increasingly turned to public–private partnerships, in which private firms undertake the necessary due diligence to access private capital market to fill remaining funding gaps.

With so many new metro projects being proposed, this was the dilemma facing China's central government in the mid-2000s: how to determine which projects were worth funding and in which forms. One solution was to allow Chinese cities to create public–private partnerships to build and operate new metro lines (Yang 2016). Partnerships would form around potentially worth while projects, or at least around those thought to be able to repay investors, but not around economically dubious one. Some version of this approach was undertaken in Beijing in 2009 around the construction of Line 4; in Shanghai starting with the construction of Line 3 in 2006; and in Shenzhen with the construction of Line 4 in 2020.

This three-track approach to metro funding worked well enough until 2008, when it was superseded by a surge of government infrastructure spending in response to the Global Financial Crisis. The result was that government money flowed into all manner of approved metro projects, even those for which future demand was questionable. Fortunately, riders flocked to almost all the new lines, especially in fast-growing coastal cities where traffic congestion continued to worsen. Between 2010 and 2015, metro ridership in Beijing, Shanghai, Guangzhou, and Shenzhen increased by 80 percent, 62 percent, 137 percent, and 482 percent respectively, more than justifying the approval

Table 6.4   *Chinese metro financing models and examples*

City	Metro lines	Funding model
Beijing	Lines 1 and 2	Government-funded
	Line 8 and BaTong Line	Government-guaranteed debt financing
	Line 4 and Yi-Zhuang Line	P3: Public–Private Partnership
Shanghai	Line 1	(Local) Government-funded
	Line 2	Modified (local) government funded
	Line 3 and subsequent lines	Multiple combinations of the government-guaranteed debt financing and P3: Public–Private Partnerships
Guangzhou	All Lines	Combination of (local) government-funded and government-guaranteed
Shenzhen	Lines 1 and 2	Combination of (local) government-funded and government-guaranteed
	Line 4	P3: Public–Private Partnership (with MTR Corporation)
	Subsequent lines	P3: Public–Private Partnership (with SMG)

Source: Assembled by the authors from metro system websites.

of additional metro lines.[4] Continued government funding of new metro lines was also assured by the Chinese government's embrace of projects that would reduce greenhouse gas emissions, a national priority articulated in China's 12th Five-Year Plan, which ran from 2011 through 2015. Finally, Xi Jinping's appointment as General Secretary of the Chinese Communist Party in 2012, and then a year later as President of the People's Republic of China began a process of expanding the roles of state-owned companies and banks in China's economy at the expense of private companies and foreign investors. The result of this shift has been that many Chinese cities have taken a step backward in accessing the private sector to fund new infrastructure investments and, instead, become more dependent on government land sales.

Benefiting from their increased distance from Beijing and their proximity to Hong Kong, Guangzhou and Shenzhen are both accustomed to having greater latitude in how they pursue their economic development and infrastructure planning practices. Guangzhou in particular has relied on its export-driven prosperity to take on the job of funding new transit lines. This has provided Guangzhou city planners with additional discretion regarding the configuration of Guangzhou's transit services in general, including the establishment of a bus rapid transit line that connects to Metro Line 1, 3, 4 and 13. Half of the Guangzhou Metro's annual operating revenues are derived from ticket sales while the other half come from real estate development activities, rents, and other business activities (Guangzhou Metro Group Co., Ltd 2016–2019).

Shenzhen, has taken an altogether different approach to funding its new metro lines, using a funding model known as "Rail + Property" or "R+P" (Dou 2016). Loosely based on the value-capture model used by Hong Kong's MTR Corporation, R+P enables rail transit companies (or joint ventures between rail companies and developers) to capture the property value increases resulting from their transit investments through the sale or rental of nearby or adjacent company-owned property assets (Yan and Yang 2020). The projected cash flows are then used as security for debt issuances used to pay for construction costs. This arrangement is similar in concept to the way municipal revenue bond and tax increment financing (TIF) structures operate in the United States except for the fact that is it is real estate revenues rather than user fees or incremental taxes that are used to underwrite the debt.

R+P schemes can be divided into two categories based on the type of rail services and the spatial scale of land development (Dou 2016; Yang et al. 2020):

- *Station-level R+P*: This model is more commonly used in densely populated urban areas served by subways or light rail. Property development generally includes commercial or residential high-rise buildings directly linked to the stations themselves. A case in point is Hong Kong's R+P program in which the Hong Kong government grants additional land development rights to the MRT Corporation which, having acquired station-adjoining properties at pre-construction prices, is able to use the anticipated post-construction increase in land and building values to help cover metro construction and operating costs.
- *Corridor-level R+P*: This model is typically used around commuter rail stations or intercity train stations. Instead of focusing on single properties, it extends district-wide. A classic example is a series of new town developments along the Den-en-toshi Line in Tokyo. In that case, the Tokyo government provided the Tokyu Corporation, a private rail company, with exclusive rights to readjust adjacent land parcel boundaries to increase their development potential. The resulting increase in land value was then used as the impetus for forming joint ventures between Tokyu and private landowners, with Tokyu's share of the prospective gains used to help fund subsequent rail and station construction.

R+P schemes have both advantages and disadvantages compared with more traditional financing models. On the advantage side, they can speed up the initial stages of project implementation by lowering the financial contribution pressures on local governments. They can also be used to generate funding for related initiatives that promote sustainable development and secure social equity benefits. On the disadvantage side, R+P-based financing can add to a project's risk profile by making its funding incumbent on hitting future property appreciation targets in addition to patronage goals.

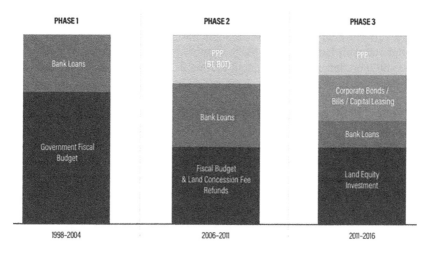

Source: Dou (2016); Yang et al. (2020).

Figure 6.2   Evolution of Shenzhen metro financing sources

Shenzhen first used the R+P model in 2004 to help finance its Longhua subway line (now Line 4), and as of 2017, had used it to help pay to build nine new metro lines (Xue and Fang 2015). With Shenzhen Metro Group (SMG), the city's municipal transit agency, initially reluctant to adopt the R+P model, Shenzhen city officials contracted directly with Hong Kong's MTR corporation to build and operate the Longhua Line. At the time, Chinese law did not allow foreign companies to own land in China, so final implementation of the scheme had to wait until the law was amended in 2009. In addition, Shenzhen city officials required MTR to rebate 50 percent of their land development profits back to the city to cover future operating subsidies (Yan and Yang 2020).

Seeing firsthand MTR's success using R+P to develop and operate the Longhua Line, SMG soon adopted it as their own and, over time, has broadened it to include additional investor-based financing beyond just the R+P operating partner. SMG does not publicly itemize individual revenue sources, so it is not possible to determine exactly how much construction funding R+P has raised for Shenzhen or the property-based cash flows it has generated. In terms of land development Xue and Fang (2015) report that Shenzhen had applied the R+P model to 285 hectares of land in 14 project areas covering 8.25 million square meters of buildable commercial or residential space. Of greater importance, Shenzhen's use of R+P has encouraged its metro system planners to look for future development synergies when identifying the locations of future metro lines and stations. This has had the beneficial effect of increasing metro ridership while also uplifting property values and property-based tax revenues. On the other side of the ledger, SMG's lack of a transparent and well-functioning corporate governance system, especially compared with Hong Kong's MTR Corporation, has hampered its ability to become more business-focused and limited its access to potential investment capital (Xue and Fang 2015).

FOUR CITIES, FOUR METRO SYSTEMS

Chinese urban researchers organize their country's cities into four prestige tiers according to their size, material affluence and leadership in the national economy. The current group of first-tier cities includes Beijing, Shanghai, Guangzhou, and Shenzhen, known colloquially as "Bei-Shang-Guang-Shen," or in Chinese, as 北上广深. Added together, Bei-Shang-Guang-Shen account for one-third of China's total metro system length and 58 percent of its metro ridership and, looking ahead, all four cities are planning major metro system expansions. This section summarizes the evolution and current state of each city's metro system and explains some of the significant design, operational, and performance differences between them (Table 6.5).

Beijing—From Pioneer to Standard Model

Beijing is the oldest, second most populous, and most politically important of China's four top tier cities. It is also the most unusual of the four in terms of its lower average population densities and extensive sprawl. This combination of factors helps explain the Beijing Subway's status as China's first metro system, its ample size and funding, and its comparatively low ridership densities.

As of 2021, the Beijing's Subway system—Beijing refers to its rail mass transit system as a subway rather than a metro—includes 19 metro lines, two airport rail links, two light-rail lines, and one maglev line: all adding up to 727 km (438 miles) of two-way track. Like all Chinese metro systems, Beijing's is relatively new: half of its current metro lines entered service after 2010. Before the Covid-19 pandemic reduced ridership levels, Beijing's metro network carried an average of more than 10.5 million passengers per day (or roughly 2.3 billion riders annually), making it the world's fifth busiest system. Most lines run near or at capacity during the morning travel peak, and metro trips currently account for between 35 and 40 percent of daily trip-making activity throughout the Beijing metropolitan area (National Bureau of Statistics of China, *China Statistical Yearbook* 2020).

As in all Chinese cities, Beijing subway lines are identified by number rather than by name, with the number designation indicating the order in which lines were planned and built. Line 1, Beijing's first subway line entered service in

Table 6.5   *Selected characteristics of metro systems in Beijing, Shanghai, Guangzhou and Shenzhen*

System characteristics	Beijing	Shanghai	Guangzhou	Shenzhen
2020 city population (millions)	21.9	24.9	18.7	17.6
2019 population density (persons/sq. mile)	3,455	10,159	6,509	22,776
2019 per capita GDP	US$23,808	US$22,779	US$22,676	US$29,498
Number of metro lines (as of 2020)	24	18	14	11
First line opened	January 1971	May 1993	June 1997	Dec. 2004
System length in miles (as of 2020)	438	479	330	255
Number of stations (as of 2020)	428	457	282	283
Average station spacing (stations per mile of system length)	0.98	0.95	0.85	1.11
Average daily ridership (millions)				
2010	5.0	5.2		0.2
2011	6.0	5.8		0.5
2012	6.7	6.2		0.8
2013	8.8	6.9		0.9
2014	9.3	7.7		1.0
2015	8.9	8.4		1.1
2016	10.0	9.3		1.3
2017	10.4	9.7		1.7
2018	10.5	10.2	8.2	1.9
2019	10.6	10.6		2.0
2020	6.3			
Daily riders per square mile	1,673	4,347	2,857	2,617
Annual ridership (billions of passengers)	3.8	3.9	3.3	1.9
Ridership growth rate (annualized), 2010–2014	13%	8%		45%
Ridership growth rate (annualized), 2015–2019	4%	5%		12%
Current metro mode share				

Source: Assembled by the authors from metro system websites.

1971 and its newest line, Line 16, began serving riders in 2016. Schematically, the Beijing subway system is organized into five north–south lines (Lines 4, 5, 8, 14 and 16), four east–west lines (Lines 1, 6, 7 and 15), inner and outer circumferential lines (Lines 2 and 10) and a northern loop line (Line 13) (Figure 6.3). Other lines function as spurs connecting the outer circumferential line to growing suburban areas and to Beijing's two international airports. This configuration maximizes the number of transfer points, so regardless of where a metro trip starts or ends, it is usually possible to complete it with a single transfer. Beijing subway system, unlike its counterparts in Shanghai, Guangzhou and Shenzhen, does not make use of transfer hubs connecting three or more lines. This makes it more difficult for passengers to cope with train delays and congestion spikes. Beijing currently has Chinese government approval to build five new subway lines and extend eight existing lines by 2025.

Source: TravelChinaGuide.com.

Figure 6.3   2020 Beijing subway system map. Note lack of hub stations

Originally built and operated by the Chinese government, since 1971 Beijing's subway system has been owned by the Municipality of Beijing through the Beijing Infrastructure Investment Co., Ltd. Fifteen of the system's current metro lines are operated by the government-owned Beijing Mass Transit Railway Operation Corporation. Four other lines, including the New Daxing Airport line, are operated by the Beijing MTR Corporation, a public–private joint venture formed in 2005 to take advantage of the development and operating expertise of Hong Kong's MTR Corporation (Lan 2014). Both Beijing Mass Transit and Beijing MTR are currently in the process of implementing automated train operation systems.

In 2014, Beijing's subway lines switched from a fixed-fare to a distance-based fare schedule on all lines except the express line to the Capital Airport. Fares start at ¥3 (about $0.50) for a trip up to 6 km, with ¥1 added for the next 6 km until the total trip distance reaches 32 km. A 40 km trip costs ¥7. Riders can also purchase single- and multi-day tickets starting at ¥20 for one day.

Beijing was China's first city to build a subway line, and, in many ways, it continues to set the subway planning and construction agenda for other Chinese cities. First proposed in 1953, just four years after the creation of the Communist Party-controlled People's Republic of China, Beijing's subway system was explicitly modeled after Moscow's in terms of having two purposes: moving workers around the city in peacetime; and moving troops around the city and sheltering the populace during wartime (Editorial Department 2010). With no subway building expertise of its own, China sent several thousand engineering students to Moscow throughout the 1950s to study the Soviet Union's subway planning and construction methods.

An early Beijing subway master plan unveiled in 1957 called for eventually building seven subway lines, one of which was to be a circular ring route tying the others together. Two lines vied for the first to be built. One was proposed to run east–west beneath Changan Avenue. The other was proposed to run north–south from the Summer Palace to Zhongshan Park. To serve their military functions, both lines were to be constructed more than 100 m below the surface. Because of Beijing's high water table and its exorbitant cost, this deep-bore proposal was eventually abandoned.

Beijing's metro planning and construction efforts were paused following the rupture of political relations between China and the Soviet Union in 1961 and wouldn't start again in earnest until the Great Leap Forward concluded in 1963. When a new iteration of Beijing's subway plan was published in 1964, the previously-approved east–west line had shifted westward so that it might be used in wartime to move troops from central Beijing to the city's western hills. Construction began in July of 1965 and was completed in October 1969, just in time to mark the PRC's 20th anniversary. The new line ran for 13 miles from Gucheng to the Beijing Railway Station and had 16 stations. A month after its dedication, a fire broke out in one of its stations, killing three and injuring more than a hundred people. Chinese Premier Zhou Enlai immediately shut down the line and ordered the People's Liberation Army to take control of it and undertake repairs. After nearly a year and a half out of operation, the line opened for a second time in January 1971. Despite frequent closures due to political turmoil, the new line proved popular, drawing nearly 30 million annual riders by 1978.

Political instability ensued throughout China but especially in Beijing following the deaths of Zhou Enlai and Mao Zedong in 1976. When order was restored in 1978 under the leadership of Deng Xiaoping, China was ready to move ahead. For Beijing, this meant finally building a second subway line. Before that could happen, control of Beijing's existing line would have to be transferred from the People's Liberation Army back to the Municipality of Beijing. It took two additional years for this to happen, but finally, in April 1981, the city-owned Beijing Subway Company (BSC) was established to take over subway operations and begin planning for a second subway line. With development extending outward in multiple directions, the new line was designed to combine with the Beijing's original line to form a loop around the downtown core. Construction of the new line began in 1981 and was completed in September 1984. The new two-line system was an immediate ridership success, drawing 300 million passengers by 1988. With subway fares set artificially low to attract riders, it was not, however, a financial success, forcing BSC to raise fares. This would set off a cycle that would be periodically repeated: new lines would open, ridership growth would exceed revenue growth, the BSC would raise fares, and ridership would temporarily decline only to eventually resume its upward trend. By 1995, with just two subway lines in operation, annual ridership exceeded 550 million passengers.

The two-line system's rising patronage notwithstanding, Beijing city officials were unsure of how many additional lines to build. To accommodate Beijing's steady outward expansion and rising auto ownership, city officials had committed to building a series of seven ring roads at increasing distances from the downtown core, and it wasn't completely clear how an expanded subway system should complement those plans. The event that eventually kick-started the expansion of Beijing's subway system was the 2001 announcement by the International Olympic Committee that the city would host the 2008 Summer Games. With Olympic events proposed to be held at locations throughout Beijing and with millions of spectators expected to attend, the only way to accommodate the influx of travelers was to accelerate the city's subway construction plans (Jiang 2008).

From 2002 to 2008, Beijing city officials committed to investing ¥63.8 billion (US$7.69 billion) to build an ambitious "three ring, four horizontal, five vertical and seven radial" subway network. Work on Lines 5 and 13, which would serve the proposed Olympic Village, began in 2000 even before a final decision to award the Games to Beijing was announced. Work on Lines

4, 8 and 10 began in 2003, and work on Line 15 began the following year. Except for Line 4, which was to be financed by the Beijing-MTR Corporation, a joint-venture with Hong Kong's MTR, all the new lines were to be funded by government-guaranteed loans from China's state-controlled "Big Four" banks: The Industrial and Commercial Bank of China, The Bank of China, The China Construction Bank, and the Agricultural Bank of China (Du et al. 2019).

Four of the new subway lines were finished in time for the Olympics and another six were completed by 2010. In the space of just ten years, the Beijing Subway had been transformed from a crowded two-line system limited to serving the city center into a truly metropolitan system linking Beijing's expanding suburbs with a growing number of downtown employment nodes. By standardizing station location and design criteria, new stations could be built quickly and inexpensively Better yet, the system's multitude of transfer stations provided needed service redundancy when trains had to be taken out of service. Daily passenger ridership rose steadily from 1.2 million daily passengers in 2000 to 3.3 million daily passengers in 2008 to just nearly six million daily passengers by 2011.

Having established a continuous planning and construction template, new subway lines could be added every year as needed, and with China's government eager to support visible infrastructure investments in the wake of the Global Financial Crisis, there was little discussion of how they should be paid for. Between 2010 and 2020, the Beijing subway system added 14 new lines, nearly 250 miles of additional track and 222 new stations—creating, in the process, the world's second largest subway system. Ridership increased right along with capacity, and in 2019, the system carried 10.6 billion passengers. Unfortunately, the growing popularity of subway travel did little to moderate the appetite of Beijing residents to own cars, and traffic congestion levels kept on climbing along with subway ridership. According to TomTom, a global provider of traffic mapping software, in 2019 Beijing ranked as the 51st most congested city in the world and the fourth most congested in China.

With new lines drawing additional riders, overcrowding continues to worsen, particularly during the morning rush hour. As of 2015, significant sections of Lines 1, 4, 5, 10, 13 and the BaTong and Changping Lines were operating over their official capacities during the morning and afternoon peaks. In response, the Beijing Mass Transit Operation Corporation has upgraded electrical, signal and yard equipment to reduce train headways and increase capacity on over-crowded lines (Xu 2019). Where possible, boarding platforms are being lengthened to accommodate 6-car and 8-car trains, and all new lines and stations will be built to handle longer trains.

The Beijing Subway's successes and challenges have much to teach subway builders in other parts of China and the world about how to plan, build and operate a metro system. Perhaps the most important lessons concern the advantages and disadvantages of standardization. On the advantage side, by standardizing station design, location and spacing criteria and construction specifications across multiple lines, Beijing has been able to plan and build new subway lines much more quickly and cheaply than if had proceeded station by station or line by line. On the disadvantage side, by not better coordinating its subway station locations and designs to current land use patterns and proposed development projects, Beijing's subway planners missed opportunities to increase ridership and property values as well as to make subway use more accessible and convenient for more riders. By a similar token, by not planning for the possibility of adding express services, planners unnecessarily limited the subway system's peak hour capacity.

A second lesson concerns the use of innovative financing mechanisms. After forming a joint venture with Hong Kong's MTR Corporation to successfully build and operate Line 4 in 2005, Beijing cut back on the use of public–private partnerships to finance new subway lines. Realizing it had lost a valuable source of finance capital and operating expertise, Beijing would later re-embrace the P3 mechanism and use it to build Lines 14, 16, 17 and 19, the Daxing and Yanfang Lines, and the city's two airport express lines.

Beijing was also slow to convert from a flat fare system which subsidized long-distance travelers to a distance-based fare system which better aligns fare revenues with operating costs. Had they done so earlier than 2014, they would have been in a better position to manage congestion on the system's more popular lines.

Shanghai—Maximizing Ridership by Design

Shanghai opened its first metro line in 1993, more than 20 years after Beijing. Shanghai city officials had considered building a metro line in the early 1960s to connect central Shanghai to Pudong but abandoned the idea when preliminary engineering surveys showed the city's soils to be too soft to support a heavy rail line (Cao 2019). The idea didn't come up again until the mid-1980s when surging population growth and the desire of city officials to reassert Shanghai's economic prominence took hold. After promising for many years to designate Shanghai as one of China's Special Economic Zones—something he had done for Shenzhen in 1980—Communist Party Leader Deng Xiaoping finally made good on his commitment in 1990, setting the stage for Pudong's emergence as Shanghai's new financial center and even faster population and economic growth (Zhao, et al. 2013). Whereas Beijing saw building new highways and promoting sprawl as a manifestation of its economic power, Shanghai officials hoped to retain their city's traditional urban form and character. This meant favoring metro construction over building highways. Lacking metro design and construction expertise of its own,

Shanghai sought assistance from two experienced European metro-building companies, Adtranz (now Bombardier), and Siemens.

As in China as a whole, Shanghai's metro-building efforts can be organized into three periods. The first, extending from 1993 to 2000, saw Shanghai develop an ambitious city-wide metro master plan but pursue it cautiously. After six years of careful planning, Line 1, a 20 km line connecting Shanghai's main railroad station in the north to Jinjiang Park in the south opened in stages between 1993 and 1996 (Liu 1995). Three years later, a second line (Line 2) opened, connecting downtown Shanghai with Pudong, thereby fulfilling Shanghai's original metro vision from the 1960s. Line 2 would later be extended to connect Hong Qiao International Airport in the west and the new Pudong International Airport in the east. A year later, in December 2000, a semi-circumferential line (Line 3) opened connecting Jingyang Road in the north to Shanghai's South Railroad Station. In the space of just five years, Shanghai had built the rudiments of its metro system (Song 2001).

Whereas Beijing's subway stations were located at regular distance intervals Shanghai's metro system planners favored an approach that maximized traveler access and thus ridership. This resulted in Shanghai's downtown metro stations being located closer together than its more distant ones and offering superior pedestrian access (Lu 2017; Zhu 2006).

Shanghai's second metro-building period extended from 2000 to 2010, and in addition to Line 3, saw the completion of eight new metro lines. Just as the run up to the 2008 Olympics had served to accelerate the pace of subway construction in Beijing, so too did Shanghai's commitment to host the 2010 Shanghai World Exposition accelerate metro construction activity in that city. The theme of the exposition, "Better City – Better Life," was meant to reinforce Shanghai's status as a world-class city and what better way to do so than to have visitors from across the world arrive at the fair via brand new metro routes (Zhou 2010). All in all, Shanghai spent $48 billion getting ready for its world's fair, which was more than Beijing spent on the 2008 Olympics, and, by the end of 2010, Shanghai had 11 metro lines in operation compared with Beijing's eight (Briginshaw 2008; Tao and Dong 2009) (Figure 6.4).

Early on, Shanghai metro planners realized the importance of maximizing connectivity among the city's metro lines to create additional travel options. This led them to configure Shanghai's metro system around a series of transit hubs located at or near each of the city's ten employment subcenters (Gu 2006; Zhu 2008).[5] Currently, there are seven Shanghai metro stations that function as hubs, including three at each of the city's railroad stations, one in downtown Shanghai, and one each at the city's two major shopping districts, Zhongshan Park and Century Avenue (Li et al. 2016; Xu 1998).

Having established an effective set of metro planning principles, Shanghai has continued to build out its metro system, adding seven additional lines

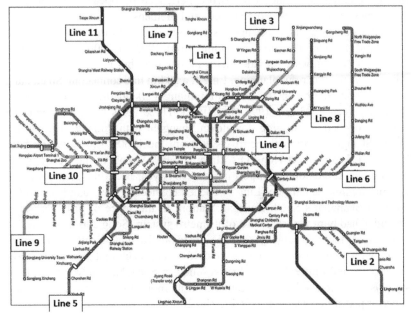

Source: TravelChinaGuide.com.

Figure 6.4   *2020 Shanghai metro system map. Note hub stations with*
                  three or more connecting lines

during its third and current phase of metro construction. Another four lines
and 117 km of extensions are scheduled to be added by 2030. This will
enable Shanghai to retain its status as having the world's largest and busiest
metro system. In 2019, Shanghai's metro system carried nearly 3.9 billion
passengers, which works out to an average of 10.6 million passengers per day.
Despite having fewer lines, Shanghai's 2019 ridership density, at 4,347 passengers per square mile, was 150 percent higher than Beijing's. This advantage
is not only reflective of Shanghai's higher residential densities, but also of the
greater attention it paid locating metro lines and stations to maximize ridership
(Shanghai Urban and Rural Construction and Transportation Development
Research Institute 2020).

Guangzhou Goes Its Own Way

Guangzhou was China's first city to consider building a metro system, having
begun preliminary planning in 1960 for what would eventually become Line
1. Currently, Guangzhou's metro system is China's fourth largest in terms

of length and third largest in terms of ridership. As of 2020, the Guangzhou Metro's 14 lines (including the Guangfo intercity line that connects to Foshan and the Zhujiang New Town Automated People Mover System) extends for 492 km. In 2019, before the Covid-19 pandemic, system ridership was running at an average of 9.1 million passengers per day (Guangzhou Metro Annual Report 2019).

The Guangzhou Metro is unique among Chinese metro systems in that its construction was municipally-financed. This has given Guangzhou transit planners and managers greater latitude in designing and operating their system (Zhu and Wen 2020). The genesis of Guangzhou's present-day metro system can be traced back to Chen Yu, the Governor of Guangdong Province from 1957 to 1967. In 1960, Yu, acting independently of Beijing, ordered that a survey of groundwater levels in and around Guangzhou be undertaken to determine whether the city's alluvial soils could support the construction of a heavy-rail underground system. The word came back that they could, but further progress was interrupted by China's tumultuous Great Leap Forward, which didn't conclude until 1962. Yu returned to the idea of building a metro system in 1965, commissioning a confidential feasibility study known at the time as "Project Nine." (Nine was the number of calligraphy strokes in the Chinese word for underground.) Yu envisioned a two-line subway and civil defense system with a north–south line and an east–west line intersecting in Guangzhou's center. The decision was made to start with the north–south line, and tunneling work beneath central Guangzhou quickly got underway. Built to military specifications, an initial subway tunnel was completed in 1966, but at just 3 m in diameter, it was too narrow to accommodate side-by-side subway tracks. Yu's successors made four more attempts over the next 15 years to revive and finish Project Nine but none panned out.

As the center of the surging Pearl River Delta manufacturing economy, Guangzhou by the early 1980s had pulled far ahead of China's other large cities in terms of its economic development and was beginning to experience some of the same problems as other booming cities, notably traffic congestion. With the responsibility for the remnants of Project Nine having been transferred from Guangzhou's Civil Defense Preparation Office to the recently-established Guagzhou Construction Commission, ample funding was now available to plan a modern subway system.

By the standards of other large Chinese cities, Guangzhou is fairly sprawling—the result of prioritizing willy-nilly factory growth over coherent land use and infrastructure planning during the early 1980s. Resolving to do better and privileged by their prosperity and political independence, Guangzhou city officials began the effort of planning a new city-wide metro system. Following the Parisian model suggested by their French consultants, Guangzhou's transit planners began by identifying current and projected high-demand travel corridors (Lin 2012). This meant that Guangzhou's new metro system would not only benefit from high ridership levels initially, but that it would continue adding new riders as it was extended outward. Seeking public input—another new-for-China approach—four preliminary design schemes were unveiled to the public in March 1988. The chosen scheme, which looked a lot like Yu's scheme from 25 years earlier, featured a north–south line and an east–west line intersecting in Guangzhou's center.

Construction of the north–south Line 1 got underway in December 1993. The project made extensive use of new-to-China subway construction techniques, including pre-cast immersed tubes and mechanized tunnel boring machines (Zhang 2015; Na et al. 2019). Outside of Guangzhou's downtown, to save money, the Line 1 project made use of traditional cut-and-cover construction techniques. This required the forced relocation of 100,000 residents, earning Guangzhou's mayor Li Ziliu the unfortunate nickname of "Li the Demolisher." The total construction budget for Line 1 was set at ¥12.75 billion (about $3.7 million in US dollars in 2020), all of which was to be provided from municipal sources. All of Line 1's rolling stock and power and signaling equipment were purchased from Germany's Siemens Corporation. The southern-most section of Line 1 opened on a trial basis in June 1997, with the full 18.8 km line entering official service exactly two years later.

Construction of the east–west Line 2 began in July 1998 and was completed in June 2003. In the interim, China's State Planning Committee directed Chinese cities building new subway lines to meet their rolling stock procurement needs from less-expensive domestic manufacturers instead of international suppliers. As a result, Line 2's equipment costs wound up being 53 percent lower than Line 1's, which had used Bombardier-manufactured trainsets.

Anticipating heavy initial ridership, Lines 1 and 2 were designed with extended platforms to accommodate longer trains. This also meant longer headways and less frequent service. When the projected number of riders was slow to materialize, subsequent metro lines were adapted to allow the use of shorter trains running at variable headways. By learning from experience and by focusing on maximizing traveler access and modal connectivity, Guangzhou transportation planners worked their way toward a series of metro planning and operating principles that would eventually enable the city's metro system to achieve three-quarters of Shanghai's passenger ridership with just two-thirds of its track length (Lin et al. 2016).

With every Chinese city of any size now racing to build a metro of its own, the Chinese government's top-down metro approvals process was soon overwhelmed, leading government officials in Beijing to tap the brakes on approving new systems. With two more metro routes (Lines 3 and 4) having already been approved, Guangzhou (along with Beijing and Shanghai) were exempted from the slowdown. Adding to the need for additional metro services, Guangzhou had agreed to host the 2010 Asian Games, the world's biggest sporting festival outside of the Summer Olympics.

Meanwhile, Guangzhou just kept growing. Between 1990 and 2005, Guangzhou added five million new residents, almost as many as China's two population growth leaders, Shanghai and Shenzhen. In 2002, Guangzhou opened the world's largest convention facility, the Guangzhou International Convention and Exhibition Center (now known as the Guangzhou Fair Complex) on Pazhou Island to serve as the permanent home of the Guangzhou Trade Fair, the world's best-attended industrial convention (Zhan 2017). With Guangzhou's economy on a roll and the city's population growth continuing unabated, huge new residential and factory developments were opening every month. To prevent the city from being overwhelmed by traffic congestion, Guangzhou city officials continued building metro lines, opening eight new lines between 2009 and 2018. An additional six metro lines are scheduled to open by 2025.

Guangzhou's approach of aggressively expanding its metro system while facilitating additional sprawl has produced mixed results. In 2019, for the first time, yearly metro ridership topped three billion, making Guangzhou's metro China's most heavily used after Beijing and Shanghai. Not all of Guangzhou's metro system measures are as positive. When compared on a passenger-per-square-mile-basis, Guangzhou's metro ridership performance puts it well below Shanghai's, reflecting its much lower population densities. In 2019, Guangzhou's ranked 38th among world cities on the TomTom traffic congestion index, well ahead of both Beijing and Shanghai.

Looking forward, Guangzhou has ambitious plans to expand its metro network by adding new lines as well as by extending existing lines to neighboring Pearl River Delta cities such as Dongguan and Huizhou (Wei 2014). Should these plans be realized, Guangzhou's present-day intra-metropolitan metro system will gradually evolve into what is likely to be the world's first true inter-metropolitan metro system (Li et al. 2016).

As other Chinese cities—most notably, nearby Shenzhen—have expanded their reliance on joint ventures and public–private partnerships to fund their metro lines, Guangzhou's go-it-alone financing approach is no longer as attractive as it once was (Qian et al. 2013; Xin and Su 2012). Although Guangzhou's metro system derives half of its net income from non-farebox sources, the city remains behind its peers in the use of value-capture and other innovative financing techniques. It will have to do better finding new financing sources if it is to follow through on its ambitious expansion plans (Wang and Qian 2018).

Shenzhen—Planning for Connections

Shenzhen is China's most prosperous, entrepreneurial, and economically vibrant city. It is also one of its best-planned. A modest fishing village on the South China Sea coast just 40 years ago, in 2020 Shenzhen's population was approaching 18 million. Established in 1980 by Communist Party Leader Deng Xiaoping as an urban economic development laboratory for the rest of the country, Shenzhen is still the place other Chinese cities look to emulate. Shenzhen's metro system is also a national model. Since its first metro line opened in 2004, Shenzhen has built ten more, giving it, as of 2020, China's fifth largest system in terms of length and fourth biggest in terms of ridership (Wang et al. 2019).

Shenzhen's unique linear shape—the city is organized into five major mixed-use districts arrayed east to west—and high densities make it especially well-suited for rail transit service (Shenzhen Metro 2019), and, like Beijing, Shanghai and Guangzhou before it, Shenzhen started planning for rail transit service long before it built its first metro line. Shenzhen's original transit plan, adopted in the early 1980s, was to build a 31 km light-rail line down the middle of Shennan Avenue extending from the Luohu district in the east to the Bo'an district in the west (Peng 2005).

With its population growing at a much faster rate than expected, Shenzhen's initial light rail plan was discarded in 1992 in favor of building a more extensive heavy-rail system consisting of nine metro lines, three of which would be converted from existing railroad lines. Construction of the initial line running beneath Shennan Avenue was scheduled to get underway in 1995 but was put on hold when China's State Council put a temporary moratorium on all impending rapid transit projects except those already approved for Beijing, Shanghai, and Guangzhou. Hoping to use the impending 1997 transfer of nearby Hong Kong back to Chinese sovereignty as am opportunity, Shenzhen's rail planners repackaged their prior metro proposal as one capable of meeting projected growth in cross-border Shenzhen–Hong Kong passenger traffic. Preliminary approval of the modified project, now with a second line connecting Shenzhen to the Hong Kong border, was forthcoming in May 1998, with final approval awarded in April 1999. Construction of the first sections of Line 1 (paralleling Shennan Avenue) and Line 4 (connecting Futian, Shenzhen's new CBD to the border) started later in the year, and the two new lines opened together for service in December 2004.

Meanwhile, Shenzhen just kept growing, adding 3.4 million new residents and 2.8 million new jobs between 2000 and 2010. Hoping to contain the city's burgeoning sprawl and concerned that building additional metro lines might make its sprawl problem worse, Shenzhen officials put the brakes on building additional metro lines, deciding instead to extend the two lines already in service. This changed in January 2007 when Shenzhen won the bidding to host the 2011 Universiade Games, an Olympics-level event for university athletes. Shenzhen was not initially regarded as a favorite to win the bidding, so, to sharpen their case, city officials committed to building three new metro lines to make it easier to move athletes and spectators to event venues distributed throughout the city. This was the same strategy Beijing had used to win the 2008 Olympic Games, and that Guangzhou had used to win the 2010 Asian Games.

Construction of the three new metro lines got off to a slower than expected start but thanks to relentless pressure from Shenzhen Mayor Xu Zongheng—not to mention Shenzhen's desire to one-up Guangzhou, which had just finished hosting the 2010 Asian Games—the three new lines were completed just in time for the Universiade Games' opening ceremonies.

With five new metro lines soon to be in operation, Shenzhen city officials pressed the case for completing their planned metro network, applying to the NDRC to build another five lines by 2020 at a cost of ¥125.6 billion (US$19.3 billion). As a key selling point, city officials made it known that they would be able to finance the new lines with locally-generated tax and real estate revenues and would not require supplemental funding from the central government. Approval was quickly forthcoming, and with the completion of phase I of Line 8 eight years later in 2020, Shenzhen had met its ambitious metro-building targets.

Shenzhen's metro system is presently 255 miles long and includes 283 stations. Of the system's 11 lines, five run essentially east–west (Lines 1, 2, 5, 7 and 9), and the other six (Lines 3, 4, 6, 8, 10 and 11) are more radial in orientation (Shenzhen Metro 2019). Four metro lines intersect at Chegongmaio Station in Futian, Shenzhen's primary transit hub. Shenzhen's metro system ridership in 2019 averaged 5.5 million passengers per day, making Shenzhen's metro the world's 10th busiest. The Shenzhen Metro's share of public transport trips currently stands at 53.9 percent, up from 38.9 percent in 2010. Helping things along is the fact that Shenzhen's highly-used Line 4 is partially owned and operated by Hong Kong's MTR Corporation, known around the world for its high-quality passenger service and transit-oriented development expertise (Yan and Yang 2020).

Shenzhen illustrates both the advantages and pitfalls of so quickly building such an extensive metro system. On the advantage side, in configuring and constructing its metro system, Shenzhen has followed a series of three well thought-out planning goals. These include: (i) using multiple metro lines to link its far-flung eastern and western districts to Futian, Shenzhen's ultra-modern business and government center; (ii) discouraging wasteful sprawl by organizing Shenzhen's fast-growing northern suburbs and factory districts into transit corridors that also connect to Futian; and (iii) maximizing opportunities for transit-oriented development. This last goal was achieved by locating proposed stations immediately beneath or adjacent to existing or planned mixed-use activity hubs. The result of this approach is that even though Shenzhen's metro stations are more distantly spaced (on average) than those in Beijing and Guangzhou, its line density and per-square kilometer passengers ridership are considerably higher. Simply put, Shenzhen's metro system is designed to fit within and reinforce the city's land use and activity patterns. The result was a metro system that filled with riders as quickly as new lines opened. From 163 million passengers in 2010, metro ridership swelled to 460 million riders in 2011, 781 million riders in 2012, 914 million riders in 2013, and over a billion riders in 2014.

Even the best planning schemes can't anticipate every eventuality. Measured on an annualized basis, metro ridership in Shenzhen grew so quickly they used up all available capacity, generating daily over-crowding problems and compromising the system's reliability and level of performance. Congestion problems were particularly severe on Line 3, which does double duty as an access line to Shenzhen's northeastern suburbs and a major east–west line connecting the Luohu and Futian districts.

LESSONS AND TAKEAWAYS

Lessons

Any way you look at it, China's metro-building performance since 2000 has been extraordinary. To restate a few of the statistics presented at the beginning of this chapter, since 2000 China has built more than 200 new metro lines in 41 separate cities spanning nearly 7,500 km of route length and more than 4,500 stations. No other country in any prior period has come close to this level of construction activity. Altogether, China's metro systems transported more than 22 billion passengers per day in 2018, which works out to a per day average of 275,000 passengers *per line*. Chinese cities currently comprise seven of the world's top ten cities in terms of metro system size and four of the top ten in terms of ridership. Given how quickly Chinese cities have rolled out new metro lines and expanded existing ones, one might expect to hear a few complaints about lower-than-expected ridership levels or construction cost overruns. Happily, this has not been the case. Judging by how quickly new metro lines have filled up with passengers, so far China's metro-building efforts must be regarded as a world-class success.

With metro ridership in China's four top-tier cities—Beijing Shanghai, Guangzhou, and Shenzhen—currently accounting for nearly 60 percent of metro passengers nationwide, what lessons do they offer about the dos and don'ts of planning, building, financing, and operating new metro systems?

And to what degree do these lessons extend beyond metro systems to other types of transportation megaprojects? Taking a further step back, what can those same experiences teach other cities and countries about how to build or perhaps how not to build transportation megaprojects in general?

Table 6.6 identifies many of the metro-building lessons Beijing, Shanghai, Guangzhou and Shenzhen have to offer, both collectively and individually. It is divided into six topic groupings: gaining and maintaining political support; system configuration and planning; station design and planning; construction; financing; and operations.

In terms of gaining and maintaining political support, all four Chinese cities benefited from the Chinese government's 2006 issuance of its "Public Transportation Priority" policy document. This policy directive identified building new metro systems as a national urban development priority, established national rolling stock and signaling procurement standards and practices, identified the level of funding the central government would make available, and set clear expectations regarding the role local officials, especially mayors, should take in implementing the policy. The issuance of this document resulted in an immediate increase in the number of metro lines being planned and constructed. Equally important, its inclusion of national design, procurement and performance standards made possible a level of standardization that drove down local construction and equipment costs as well as reduced the incidence of planning and construction delays.

In terms of improving the infrastructure approval process, China's separation of the technical evaluation process from political approvals—the former handled by the NDRC and the latter by China's ruling State Council—seems, on balance, to allow for a level of decision-making consistency and continuity not present in governmental systems where a single body evaluates both technical and political merit.

We would be remiss if we did not also call attention to the role sporting and cultural events played in leveraging government enthusiasm and funding for building new metro lines in each of China's four top-tier cities. Whether it was the 2008 Summer Olympics in Beijing, Shanghai's 2010 World Exposition, the 2010 Asian Games in Guangzhou, or the Shenzhen Universiade Games of 2011, in each case promises made to secure these events for Chinese cities included significant national and local government commitments to build new metro lines. The difference between the Chinese experience and that of Athens for example, which built a new metro line to serve spectators for the 2004 Summer Olympics, was that Chinese metro planners took care to ensure that their metro lines would be used long after the sporting and cultural events that galvanized their construction had concluded.

In terms of system design and planning, the overriding lesson is that standardizing route configurations and station placement practices across an entire

Table 6.6   Metro system lessons and takeaways from Beijing, Shanghai, Guangzhou and Shenzhen

Project planning and delivery activity	Lessons	As applied in	Applicable to other transport megaprojects?
Securing political and funding support	Helpful national legislation outlining standard models and practices	All four systems	All transport investments
	Piggyback investments on other high-prestige or economic development initiatives	All four systems	Ports and airports
	To the extent possible, separate evaluations of engineering and financial feasibility (e.g. NRDC reviews) from budgetary decisions (State Council approval)	All four systems	All transport investments
	Mayor must be a project champion	All four systems	All public transport modes
	Start with existing high traffic corridors; pre-plan to match extensions and expansions to subsequent growth	Shanghai, Guangzhou	Highways and ports
	Expanded use of multiple-line transfer hubs to better accommodate travel demand between high-volume origin and destination pairs	Shanghai, Shenzhen	Highways, inter-city rail and buses
System and planning configuration	Build in connections to complementary modes	Shanghai and Guangzhou	Highways, inter-city rail and buses
	Build in the potential to boost passenger capacity	Beijing, Guangzhou	Highways, inter-city rail and buses
	Don't rely on purported network effects: Each line or route should justify itself in terms of ridership independently of others	Shanghai, Guangzhou	All public transport modes
	Connect to local land development schemes to limit sprawl	Shanghai, Shenzhen	Highways and BRT

Project planning and delivery activity	Lessons	As applied in	Applicable to other transport megaprojects?
Station design and planning	Minimize transfer difficulties between lines and routes	Shanghai, Shenzhen	Buses and BRT
	Insure access for those with disabilities		All public transport modes
	Where possible, put stations near higher-density residential (origin) and commercial (destination) properties	Shanghai, Shenzhen	BRT
Construction	To the degree possible, standardize facility designs and construction details	All four systems	All transport modes
	Pre-certify construction contractors	All four systems	All transport modes
Financing	Government-provided or guaranteed financing must be keystone source	All four systems	
	Look for opportunities to form construction and operating joint ventures and PPPs	Beijing and Shenzhen	BRT and ports
	Test financial feasibility and structure at alternative discount rates	Shenzhen	All capital intensive investments
Operations	Distance-based fare systems are generally preferable to flat-fare systems	All four systems	Highways and BRT
	Pre-develop contingency plans to respond to congestion and service bottlenecks	Shanghai (yes), Shenzhen (no)	All transport modes
	Plan for increasing automation and digital controls over time	All four systems	All transport modes

metro system yields economies of scale benefits in terms of reducing planning and construction costs (and construction times as well), but also has significant drawbacks in terms of not being able to match metro service characteristic to the land use and economic geography conditions of individual cities. Compared with Beijing, which has taken a more extreme approach to standardizing its metro line and station siting practices, Shanghai, Guangzhou, and Shenzhen have each devoted greater effort toward matching the locations of their metro lines and stations to ground-level land uses and densities. This has enabled them to out-perform Beijing in terms of metro ridership per kilometer of line length and square kilometer of urbanized land.

Among the other notable differences among the four cities in terms of metro system planning and design practices are the following.

- Shanghai and Guangzhou have taken a more incremental approach to building out individual metro lines. Both started by building core sections to serve existing high-traffic corridors, and then extended lines outward to suburban districts to match population growth. This may have boosted overall construction costs, but it also provided for a better match between passenger demand and capacity.
- Shanghai and Shenzhen have made more extensive use of multi-line transfer hubs. This has helped shorten travel times for high-volume origin-destination pairs while also increasing each system's potential vulnerability to congestion-induced bottlenecks.
- Shanghai and Guangzhou have designed their metro lines and stations to connect to non-metro transit modes: inter-city rail service in Shanghai's case and bus rapid transit in Guangzhou's.
- Beijing and Guangzhou have both increased the length of their station platforms over time to accommodate longer trainsets and boost per-train passenger capacity.
- Lastly, Shanghai and Guangzhou have also been more attentive to matching line expansions and capacity increases to actual passenger demand rather than assuming that increased system capacity and connectivity by themselves will boost demand.

Many of these same system design lessons and tradeoffs apply to other urban transportation modes as well.

In terms of metro station location and design practices, Shanghai and Shenzhen have generally done a better job than Beijing and Guangzhou, making it easier for metro passengers to transfer between lines; as well as locating metro stations closer to high-density (and high demand) residential and employment centers. As noted previously, this has helped boost their overall ridership density.

In terms of construction practices, following national guidelines, all four systems have standardized around particular construction technologies and procurement practices. Following the same practice used to construct China's high-speed rail network, all four pre-certify contractors and suppliers to ensure that their delivery and quality control procedures are up to snuff. This has helped reduce both construction costs and delivery times.

In terms of financing practices, Beijing, Shanghai, and Shenzhen relied on funding from China's government to get their initial metro lines up and running. Once the basic financial feasibility of metro service was established—meaning that passenger revenues could cover operating costs—the different cities went their own ways in terms of financing additional lines. Beijing has continued to rely on government-provided funded sources to build its city-wide metro lines but has entered public–private partnership ventures to build its more specialized and airport connector lines. Because of its greater wealth, Guangzhou has mostly been able to self-finance its metro system. This has had the advantage of giving it greater independence from China's central government in terms of route location and station siting issues, but also (slightly) limited its financial capacity to build new lines. Befitting its more market-oriented history and land development practices, Shenzhen has made the most progress of the four cities in implementing a value-capture-based system like Hong Kong's that pays for metro facility construction costs out of tax or fee revenues generated by adjacent land development schemes. Shanghai, as with all its metro planning and development practices, has endeavored to tie the specifics of its financing sources to the funding needs and revenue-producing potential of individual lines. Amidst our focusing on the differences among the four cities in their approaches to financing new metro lines and extensions, it should not be forgotten that most metro construction funding is provided by government entities and government-controlled financial institutions. This means that Chinese cities do not underwrite their metro projects using the type of discounted cash flow analysis used in North America or Europe which considers the ability of metro-specific revenue sources, most notably passenger fares, to cover capital costs. For all their efficiency in physically constructing new metro lines, this makes it impossible to know whether China's cities are building metro lines that can be justified on economic grounds. In terms of putting together robust financing packages, so far China's cities have been more lucky than good.

Lastly, in terms of operational lessons, all four cities have transitioned from flat fare systems (in which riders pay the same fare regardless of trip length or time of day) to distance-based fare systems in which riders who make longer trips or travel during peak periods pay more. Because transit fares in China are still relatively low—compared with London or Tokyo, for example—and are not higher for peak hour travel, the benefits of this change have been limited to increasing fare revenues and have not extended to reducing congestion. To boost capacity and reliability while reducing operating costs, all four cities recently embarked on major efforts to automate their train control and passenger service systems.

Tradeoff Insights

In addition to offering relevant lessons about building urban metro lines, China's recent embrace of urban rail systems has the potential to yield new insights into the many tradeoffs involved in undertaking rail megaprojects in major urban centers.

The technology tradeoff
When developing modern technology-intensive transportation systems such as metros, should cities purchase needed technologies from global suppliers in turnkey arrangements, develop them on their own, or pursue some combination of the two approaches? The turnkey path—which was taken by Shanghai in the construction of its maglev system in 2001—is quicker but costlier and may result in difficulties adapting non-local technologies to local circumstances. The create-your-own path is likely to take longer and have more speed bumps along the way but can be far less expensive in the long-run; and in countries with large economies, can help build up domestic industries. With regard to acquiring metro trainsets, Chinese cities have mostly taken the hybrid path, initially buying equipment from leading European suppliers, and then in the case of trainsets, reverse engineering those technologies to establish a domestic supply base. This enabled Chinese cities and train manufacturers to establish sufficient technical and manufacturing expertise to rapidly reduce rolling stock procurement costs. And with so many Chinese cities building new metro lines at the same time, it allowed Chinese manufacturers to scale up their operations to become low-cost producers on a world stage. In the case of signaling systems, where technology is advancing at a rapid rate and where reliability is paramount, Chinese cities have been content to continue purchasing from European suppliers.

The standardization tradeoff
Standardizing metro planning, design, construction and procurement practices across lines greatly reduces planning and construction times and costs. It also runs the risk of perpetuating bad or locally-inappropriate practices. Different Chinese cities have tried to mediate between these two extremes in different ways. Beijing has gone all-in on standardization, especially on its city-owned metro lines. This has resulted in the creation of a highly robust and reliable system, but also one in which station locations and designs are not always well integrated with nearby activity and land use patterns. Shanghai and Shenzhen

have standardized their construction and procurement practices across different lines but not their planning and design practices. This has enabled them to locate and design stations in a manner better suited to existing urban development patterns as well as to shape future development activities in a manner that maximizes both transit ridership and property value appreciation. Guangzhou falls somewhere between Beijing and Shanghai in terms of following fixed station location criteria while also trying to maximize station area development opportunities.

The concurrent construction tradeoff
How many metro lines should a city have under construction at one time? Too few and there are no opportunities to share emerging best practices across lines. Too many and the job of coordinating so many construction activities becomes problematic and there is little opportunity to learn from prior success and failures. Overall, Chinese cities seem to have threaded this needle quite well. They have done so by hiring different contractors to build separate lines, thus ensuring that problems on one line don't spill over onto another; and by making sure that multiple lines aren't simultaneously under construction at the same locations, thereby reducing the inevitable disruptions that accompany the construction process. Simply put, metro project and construction managers in Beijing, Shanghai, Guangzhou, and Shenzhen have become very good at their jobs. At the same time, by not pausing to assess how well each new metro line has delivered on its specific goals, Chinese transportation planners have missed opportunities to learn from past experiences. This has been particularly problematic in Beijing, where the solution to mobility and congestion problems is always to build additional capacity and to do so as quickly as possible.

The tunneling tradeoff
When it comes to building or extending metro lines, tunneling is always less disruptive than surface-level construction. It is also much, much more expensive and time consuming. Given how quickly so many Chinese cities have built and extended so many metro lines, it would be useful for other metro system planners around the world to learn from the accumulated wisdom of China's metro system planners regarding when and under which circumstances tunneling is preferable to surface construction and vice versa.

The financing tradeoff
Relying too much on government funding to build capital-intensive infrastructure cannot help but elevate political desires over market preferences. This in a nutshell is the argument for using private investment capital to help fund public infrastructure projects. Primarily concerned about getting a return on their investment, private investors will always pay heed to how many riders

will willingly pay to use a facility or service. Among the cities profiled in this chapter, Shenzhen and Shanghai have done the better job matching financing structures and metro lines. And, based on the very limited data that is publicly available, their efforts seem to have paid off in terms of generating additional ridership and land development revenues. Except for specialized lines that command higher fares, Beijing and Guangzhou have tended to rely more on the Chinese government in Beijing's case, or the Guangzhou city government to provide needed construction funding. Which model is better and in which circumstances? Given the scale and variety of recent metro construction initiatives across China, it would be helpful if the Chinese government were to publish line-by-line cost and revenue information so that cities planning future metro investments might have a better sense of the benefits of alternative financing options.

NOTES

1.   This estimate is based on approved construction schedules as listed in each city and transit agency's website, as compiled by Wikipedia as of December 2021. The authors have made no effort to confirm their status.
2.   Many US transit agencies report passenger boardings and exits by station. A few also report line-by-line ridership figures.
3.   These numbers include only metro lines that are managed by Shanghai Shentong Metro Co., Ltd. Data for lines managed by other companies are not available.
4.   *China Statistical Yearbook*, 2010 and 2015
5.   With ten subcenters each, Shanghai and Shenzhen are tied as China's most polycentric cities (Li and Derudder 2020).

REFERENCES

Briginshaw, D. 2008. Shanghai metro aims to be number 1. *International Railway Journal*, 48.
Cao, G. 2019. Shanghai metros: Continuously create miracles, towards 1000 kilometers. *China Metros*, (09), 17–21. [曹刚. 2019. 上海地铁：连创多个奇迹，迈向1000公里. 城市轨道交通, (09), 17–21.]
Cao, Z. H., Xue, B. F., & Zhou, J. Z. 2014. The political constraints of China's decentralization——based on the demonstration of the subway project approval system. *Sociological Studies*, (03), 30–55+242. [曹正汉, 薛斌锋, 周杰浙. 2014. 中国地方分权的政治约束——基于地铁项目审批制度的论证. 社会学研究 (03), 30–55+242.]
China Urban Rail Transit Association. 2021. Overview of urban rail transit routes in mainland China in 2020 (https://www.camet.org.cn/tjxx/7647).
Dou, Y. 2016. Prospect of using rail-plus-property model for transit financing in China: Based on comparative case studies of Shenzhen and Hong Kong (Doctoral dissertation, Columbia University).
Du, P., Han. C., & Lin, X. 2019. Case study on 3P projects between Beijing metro line 4 and London metro. *Urban Rapid Rail Transit*, 29(5), 41–45.

Editorial Department. 2010. Review and prospect of Beijing metro in 40 years. *Modern Urban Transit*, 1, 1–3. [本刊编辑部.北京地铁40年回顾与展望. 2010. 现代城市轨道交通. 1, 1–3.]

Gu, W. H. 2006. Shanghai rail transit network construction and utilization of underground space. *Life & Disaster*, (S1), 71–72. [顾伟华. 2006. 上海轨道交通网络化建设与地下空间的开发利用. 民防苑, (S1), 71–72.]

Guangzhou Metro. 2019. *Annual Report*. Guangzhou Metro Group Co., Ltd. (https://www.gzmtr.com/ygwm/gsgk/qynb/202007/t20200708_67990.html).

Guangzhou Metro Group Co., Ltd. 2016–2019. *Annual Report*. Metro Group Co., Ltd. (http://www.gzmtr.com/ygwm/xwzx/gsxw/index_3.html).

Jiang, Y. K. 2008. Analysis on Beijing subway passenger flows during the 29th Olympics. *Journal of Transportation Systems Engineering and Information Technology*, 8(6), 46–51. [蒋玉琨. 2008. 奥运会期间北京地铁客流研究.交通运输系统工程与信息, 8(06), 46–51.]

Lan, L. 2014. The gradually integrated network of Beijing rail transit lines. *Transpo World*, (Z1), 28–31. [蓝兰. 2014. 北京市轨道交通线路逐渐密集成网.交通世界(建设.机械), (Z1), 28–31.]

Li, W., Xu, R., Luo, Q., & Jones, S. 2016. Coordination of last train transfers using automated fare collection (AFC) system data. *Journal of Advanced Transportation*, 50(8), 2209–2225.

Li, X. 2016. Research on project financing modes of BOT and 3P based on case studies. *International Conference on Logistics*. IEEE.

Li, Y., & Derudder, B. 2020. Dynamics in the polycentric development of Chinese cities, 2001–2016. *Urban Geography*, 1–21.

Lin, H., Liang, Q. S., & Fang, S. Y. 2016. Challenges and innovative solutions in urban rail transit network operations and management: China's Guangzhou metro experience. *Urban Rail Transit*, 2(1), 33–45.

Lin, J. B. 2012. The development strategy of Guangzhou Metro Corporation. South China University of Technology. [林健斌. 2012. 广州地铁总公司发展战略研究. 华南理工大学.]

Liu, J. H. 1995. Technical summary of Shanghai Metro Line 1 underground project. *Underground Engineering and Tunnels*, (3), 2–8. [刘建航. 1995. 上海地铁1号线地下工程的技术概要. 地下工程与隧道, (3), 2–8.]

Liu, M. H., Li, Q., Liu, X., et al. 2018. Ecological efficiency assessment at construction period of the metro station in Beijing based on the value influence ratio method. *Construction Science and Technology*, (13), 75–81+89. [刘明辉, 李磬, 刘萱, 贾思毅, 王海军.基于价值影响比值法的北京地铁车站建设期生态效率评估. 2018. 建设科技, (13), 75–81+89.]

Liu, Y., Yue, W., Fan, P., Peng, Y., & Zhang, Z. 2016. Financing China's suburbanization: Capital accumulation through suburban land development in Hangzhou. *International Journal of Urban and Regional Research*, 40(6), 1112–1133.

Meng, M., Niu, D., & Shang, W. 2012. CO_2 emissions and economic development: China's 12th five-year plan. *Energy Policy*, 42, 468–475.

Na, D., Fu, Y. T., Feng, X. 2019. Sustainable Construction Project Management (SCPM) evaluation—a case study of the Guangzhou metro line-7, PR China. *Sustainability*, 11(20).

National Bureau of Statistics of China. 2008–2020. *China Statistical Yearbook*. Beijing: China Statistics Press.

Ovenden, M. 2003. *Metro Maps of the World*. Middlesex: Capital Transport Publishing.

Peng, S. 2005. From 7 meters to 140 meters – Shennan Avenue width mystery. *Shenzhen Evening News* (http://gd.news.sina.com.cn/shenzhen/2005-08-22/1621517.html).

Qian, W. 2013. Research on investment and financing mode of Guangzhou rail transit. *China Market*, 22, 91–92. [钱伟. 2013. 广州市轨道交通投融资模式研究.中国市场, 22, 91–92.]

Shanghai Metro Group Co., Ltd, 2018. Metro Group Co., Ltd Annual Report. (http://download.hexun.com/ftp/all_stockdata_2009/all/120/982/1209827165.PDF https://www.chinabond.com.cn/resource/1472/1488/1505/18682/21000/18612/21280/4524155/157117187/1619769515741963296419.pdf?n=深圳市地铁集团有限公司2020年年度报告.pdf).

Shanghai Urban and Rural Construction and Transportation Development Research Institute. 2020. Shanghai Transportation Annual Report 2019. *Traffic & Transportation*, 36(3), 102–104. [上海市城乡建设和交通发展研究院. 2020. 2019年上海市综合交通运行年报. 交通与运输, 36(3), 102–104.]

Song, X. J. 2001. The sustainable development of Shanghai metros. *Urban Mass Transit*, (4), 47–50. [宋孝鋆. 2001. 上海轨道交通的可持续发展. 城市轨道交通研究, (4), 47–50.]

Tao, J., & Dong, X. L. 2009. 400 metros will be put into use during EXPO2010. *Urban Mass Transit*, 12(5), 40. [陶健, & 董晓蕾. 2009. 2010年上海世博会期间将投入400列轨道交通列车. 城市轨道交通研究, 12(5), 40.]

UITP. 2018. World Metro Figures. (https://www.uitp.org/publications/world-metro-figures/).

Wang, P., & Qian, W. 2018. Research on investment and financing mode of urban rail transit—thinking based on investment and financing mode of Guangzhou metro. *China Chief Financial Officer*, 9, 42–45. [王苹,钱伟. 2018. 城市轨道交通投融资模式研究—基于广州地铁投融资模式的思考. 中国总会计师, 9, 42–45.]

Wang, X., Tong, D., Gao, J., & Chen, Y. 2019. The reshaping of land development density through rail transit: The stories of central areas vs. suburbs in Shenzhen, China. *Cities*, 89, 35–45.

Wei, H. N. 2014. The study on the development strategy optimization of Guangzhou metro Co, Ltd. Lanzhou University. [魏海宁. 2014. 广州地铁集团公司发展战略优化问题研究[D]. 兰州大学.]

Xin, T. F., & Su, P. J. 2012. Analysis of Guangzhou metro operational efficiency. *China Economic & Trade Herald*, 26, 72–73. [辛腾飞,苏丕娟. 2012. 广州地铁运营效率浅析.中国经贸导刊, 26, 72–73.]

Xu, D. F. 1998. A review of the planning and construction process of Shanghai metro system. *Shanghai Construction Science & Technology*, (5), 3–4. [徐道钫. 1998. 深入理解、不断优化 上海轨道交通系统规划建设过程的回顾. 上海建设科技, (5), 3–4.]

Xu, D. 2019. Technical innovations in Beijing metro line 14. *Urban Rapid Rail Transit*, 32(2), 19–28. [徐东. 2019. 北京地铁14号线技术创新综述. 都市快轨交通. 32(2), 19–28.]

Xue, L., & Fang, W. 2015. Rail plus property development in China: The pilot case of Shenzhen. World Resource Institute Working Paper.

Yan, M., & Yang, L. 2020. Analysis of passenger flow growth characteristics of Shenzhen Metro network after the opening of the new line. *Urban Rapid Rail Transit*, 33(3), 63–71. [闫铭,杨良. 2020. 新线开通后深圳地铁线网客流成长特征分析.都市快轨交通. 33(3), 63–71.]

Yang, J., Zhu, L., Duan, Y., Zhou, J., & Ma, H. 2020. Developing metro-based accessibility: Three aspects of China's Rail+ Property practice. *Transportation Research Part D: Transport and Environment*, 81, 102288.

Yang, Q. 2016. Analysis on influencing factor about decision-making on concession term of 3P Beijing subway. *International Conference on Economy*.

Zhan, D. Y. 2017. Research on the evaluation system of international conference and exhibition center city competitiveness. Guangzhou University. [湛冬燕. 2017. 国际会展中心城市竞争力评价体系研究[D]. 广州大学.]

Zhang, J. J., & Wan, J. 2019. Study on the approval process of planning and construction of rail transit implementation phase. *Urbanism and Architecture*, 16(14), 162–164. 张婧婧, & 万晶. 2019. 轨道交通实施阶段规划报建审批流程的研究. 城市建筑, 16(14), 162–164.

Zhang, Z. L. 2015. Research on engineering management and technical innovation of Guangzhou's metro construction. *Guangzhou Architecture*, 43(4), 48–52. [张志良. 2015.广州地铁建设工程管理及技术创新. 广州建筑, 43(4), 48–52.]

Zhao, Z., Zhao, J., & Shen, Q. 2013. Has transportation demand of Shanghai, China, passed its peak growth? *Transportation Research Record Journal of the Transportation Research Board*, 2394(2394), 85–92.

Zhou, J. L. 2010. Exploration and practice of Shanghai metro maintenance during World Expo. *Underground Engineering and Tunnels*, 83(4), 3–7, 63. [周俊龙. 2010. 世博会期间上海轨道交通维护保障工作的探索与实践. 地下工程与隧道, 83(4), 3–7, 63.]

Zhu, H. S. 2006. Practice and countermeasures of Shanghai rail transit network construction and operation. *China Railways*, (11), 30–34. [朱沪生. 2006. 上海轨道交通网络化建设和运营的实践与对策. 中国铁路, (11), 30–34.]

Zhu, H. S. 2008. Construction of Shanghai urban rail transit network operation system. *Urban Mass Transit*, 72(10), 1–5, 15. [朱沪生. 2008. 上海城市轨道交通网络化运营体系的建设. 城市轨道交通研究, 72(10), 1–5, 15.]

Zhu, Y. T., & Wen, M. C. 2020. Guangzhou's urban rail transit industry chain achieved remarkable results. *Transportation of Guangdong*, 206(2), 48–49. [朱亚涛,温美春. 2020. 广州城市轨道交通全产业链发展成效凸显. 广东交通, 206(2), 48–49.]

7. Bus Rapid Transit—the affordable transit megaproject alternative

Erik Vergel-Tovar and John D. Landis

ABBREVIATIONS USED IN THIS CHAPTER

BRT   Bus Rapid Transit

ITDP   Institute for Transportation Development and Policy

CBD   Central Business District

CO   Carbon monoxide

NOx   Nitrogen oxides

PM10   Particulate matter smaller than 10 microns in diameter

TOD   Transit-oriented development

First implemented in its contemporary form in Curitiba, Brazil, in 1974, Bus Rapid Transit (BRT) combines the separated right-of-way, fixed stations and higher speeds of urban rail systems with the lower capital and operating costs and routing flexibility of urban buses. As of this writing, some 180 cities, primarily in Latin America and Asia, have initiated service in over 400 separate BRT corridors, with most having done so since 2000.[1] Worldwide, more than 180 cities now have BRT systems (Figure 7.1). While most individual BRT lines fall below the US$1 billion delivery cost threshold used to identify megaprojects, when considered on a city-wide basis, BRT functions as an affordable alternative to traditional megaproject investments such as metros and light-rail systems.

All modern-day BRT systems share five characteristics: (i) a dedicated right-of-way that cannot be used by other vehicles; (ii) a separate busway alignment so that conflicts with other vehicles can be minimized; (iii) an off-board fare collection system to speed passenger boarding times; (iv) priority passage at cross-streets and intersections provide for consistent travel speeds; and (v) platform-level boarding to maximize boarding convenience and access (ITDP 2017).

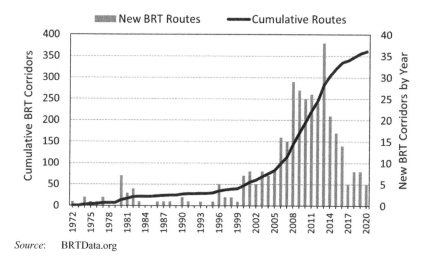

Source: BRTData.org

Figure 7.1   Number of cities with BRT systems, 1968–2020

Beyond these common features, BRT systems come in many different flavors. This has led transportation planners to create two BRT classification schemas, one based on physical characteristics and the other based on performance. In terms of physical and design attributes, *BRT-lite* systems are those in which buses enjoy priority over other vehicles but don't travel exclusively on segregated bus lanes. Examples of BRT-lite systems include the MAX system in Kansas City in the United States and the San Juan Rio Hondo Connector in Puerto Rico. *Regular BRT* systems are those with fully segregated busways, facilities for collecting fares prior to boarding and grade-separated platform stations. Segregated busways boost travel speeds while grade-separated stations and pre-boarding fare collection speed vehicle access and egress. In addition to the features that describe regular BRT lines, *Full BRT* systems such as those in Curitiba, Quito and Bogota include a fully integrated network of segregated busway lines and transfer stations (Cervero 2013) (Figure 7.2).

In terms of performance, the non-profit Institute for Transportation Development and Policy (ITDP) has created a BRT rating schema that separates individual BRT corridors into service quality classes using a 100-point scale that rewards connectivity, speed, passenger capacity, and overall user-friendliness (ITDP 2017). BRT corridors that include a dedicated right-of-way, exclusive busway alignment, off-board fare collection systems, platform-level boarding and traffic pre-emption at major intersections earn a minimum of 38 points and are classified as *Basic*. Additional points are awarded for BRT corridors that have express or passing lanes, universal

Source: ITDP (2017).

Figure 7.2   *A Curitiba BRT vehicle approaching the station platform.*
              This photo illustrates most of the features of BRT technology,
              including a dedicated right-of-way, separate bus alignments,
              the use of a pre-boarding fare payment system, and
              platform-level boarding

accessibility, multi-door boarding and egress systems, and use non-diesel or
non-petrol propulsion systems. BRT corridors that earn between 55 and 69.9
points are awarded a *Bronze* label, those that earn 70–84.9 points are labeled
Silver, and those that earn 85 to 100 points can use the *Gold* label. As of 2016,
nine BRT corridors were rated Gold, 32 corridors were rated Silver, 35 were
rated Bronze, and the balance were either classified as Basic or were unrated.[2]

With these definitions in place, we can now take a closer look at BRT practice and performance. We do so in in three sections. The first provides a brief
history of BRT, describes its principal design and operating features, explains
how it is planned and financed, and summarizes its performance and built
environment benefits. A second case study-based section compares the design
and performance of six contemporary BRT systems, including three in Latin
America and three in Asia. The three Latin American BRT case studies are
Curitiba, Brazil; Quito, Ecuador; and Bogotá, Colombia. All three are notable
BRT pioneers. The three Asian case studies include Jakarta, Indonesia; Seoul,
South Korea; and Guangzhou, China. In each of the Asian case studies, BRT

is part of a larger mass transit system that also includes metro lines. A third section concludes with a series of lessons and takeaways for city officials wondering whether BRT is the right solution for their city, and if it is, how it might be implemented.

BRT IN OVERVIEW

BRT Origins and Growth

BRT is a synthesizing technology that combines several bus system design and operating innovations into a single package designed to simultaneously increase bus operating speeds and passenger capacity. The first proposal for a BRT-like exclusive busway was put forth in the 1930s in Chicago. Similar proposals for dedicated bus right-of-way systems were incorporated into transportation plans prepared for St. Louis in the 1950s and Milwaukee in the 1970s. All three proposals were presented as being a less expensive alternative to investing in conventional subway or commuter rail systems (Levinson et al. 2003; Deng and Nelson 2011), and none were implemented. Instead, because they could move higher numbers of travelers longer distances—thus producing bigger aggregate travel time savings—federal transportation funds were directed to building urban freeways in the 1960s and heavy-rail systems and extensions in the 1970s.

The first city of note to build a properly segregated right-of-way exclusively for bus services was Lima, Peru, which opened its Via Expresa service in 1972 (Lindau et al. 2010). An innovator in 1972, by today's standards, Via Expresa would be considered a BRT-lite system since it did not include special boarding platforms at the beginning or an off-board fare prepayment system. These latter innovations were first introduced in Curitiba, Brazil, in 1974.

Rarely does the old saying that "first is best" ring truer than in the case of Curitiba and BRT. A second-tier city in terms of population size, Curitiba was wealthier, and because of its inland location, not as politically prominent among Brazilian cities as Rio de Janeiro or Sao Paulo. This provided Curitiba's leaders with more latitude to experiment. Curitiba officials had previously rejected the idea of building a conventional subway system in their city as too expensive, but with traffic congestion and urban sprawl in Curitiba continuing to worsen, the city's new mayor, Jaime Lerner, who had taken office in 1971, was determined to do something (Lindau et al. 2010). Professionally trained as an architect and urban planner, Lerner and his team realized that by coordinating BRT construction with a program to increase densities by promoting mixed-use developments along BRT corridors, Curitiba could simultaneously address its inefficient urban development and congestion problems. Further, by coupling residential density bonuses with a value-capture-based system of property taxation, it might be possible to finance other public sector initiatives such as conserving heritage buildings and building affordable housing. Curitiba undertook Lerner's BRT experiment cautiously, opening two new BRT corridors in 1974. After a few years getting established, both worked just as Lerner and his team hoped, organizing Curitiba's population growth into higher-density transit corridors, increasing property tax revenues, and by removing cars from Curitiba's downtown through the pedestrianization of several streets, making space for a much-improved public realm (Vergel-Tovar 2016).

Its successes in Lima and Curitiba notwithstanding, the BRT idea was slow to catch on elsewhere in Latin America. Widening existing arterials to accommodate exclusive busway lanes was time-consuming and expensive, and precious local tax dollars were needed just to keep existing bus services operating. International development assistance organizations such as the World Bank and Inter-American Development Bank remained committed to financing projects regarded by their North American and European-trained staffs as modern and forward-looking, such as expressways and metro systems. Gradually, the word about BRT's advantages spread among Brazil's other second-tier cities (Hidalgo and Gutiérrez 2013). Goainia, a city with a half a million residents, became Brazil's second city to begin BRT service in 1976. Recife, a city of 1.2 million residents, followed in 1982, as did Camapinas in State of Sao Paulo in 1986, and Campo Grande in the State of Mato Grosso in 1987. BRT finally penetrated Brazil's big city transportation market in 1989 when Sao Paulo initiated its "Trolebus" BRT service aimed at improving worker access to the city's southern industrial districts.

From Brazil, the BRT idea spread to Quito, Ecuador, in 1996, and to Bogotá, Colombia, in 2000 (Vergel-Tovar 2016). Quito would ultimately build five BRT corridors, while Bogotá's TransMilenio BRT system would eventually encompass 11 BRT trunk corridors. Each new BRT system improved on the prior version. Curitiba added fixed stations, fare prepayment, and a rapid access/egress door design to Lima's segregated busway design. Quito's BRT system used electric vehicles along the Trolebus corridor in place of diesel and gasoline buses, which reduced vehicle noise and air pollution. Bogotá's TransMilenio introduced an extra bus lane in each direction, making it possible to offer express service, articulated buses, and connections to feeder bus services at terminal stations (Cain et al. 2007). The cumulative effect of these later innovations was to expand BRT's passenger capacity to a level that for the first time was competitive with fixed-rail metro service.

TransMilenio's ability to inexpensively accommodate so many passengers gradually attracted the attention of transportation planners in fast-growing Asian cities including Taipei (Taiwan), Nagoya (Japan), Jakarta (Indonesia) and Seoul (Korea). In cities such as Jakarta, BRT was adopted as a less-expensive alternative to building a metro system.[3] In Taipei and Seoul, BRT lines were included as integral parts of regional public transit systems that also included metro and local bus service. With so many fast-growing cities but not enough money to build metros in every single one, China jumped aboard the BRT bandwagon in a big way in 2008, doubling the number of BRT lines in Chinese cities by 2015. Rapidly approved and built, many Chinese BRT lines were put in service without adequate planning and had subsequent difficulty attracting riders. One of the few Chinese cities that took its time carefully planning its BRT system was Guangzhou, which completed its one and only BRT line in 2010. Guangzhou's diligence paid off: as of 2016, ridership on its Zhongshan Avenue BRT line reached 27,000 passengers per hour per direction (BRTDATA.ORG 2021).

Compared with places in Latin America and Asia, cities in the US and Europe still lag well behind when it comes to building BRT systems. According to the BRTData.org website, there are currently 18 European cities with one or more BRT corridors, but in only two, Paris and Istanbul, do they carry a significant number of daily passengers. The US lags even more. While numerous cities in the US operate what they call express bus service, just 10 US cities have what might properly be termed a BRT service, and of those, only Los Angeles and Las Vegas have managed to attract noticeable daily ridership. Boston's lone BRT line is limited to connecting downtown with the airport. Among Canadian cities, only Winnipeg and Ottawa offer true BRT services.

The reluctance of US and European cities to embrace BRT as enthusiastically as their counterparts in Latin America and Asia is due partly to their lower population growth rates, partly to their higher land and property values (which makes acquiring land for BRT right-of-ways more expensive), partly to their greater concerns about potential displacement impacts, and partly to the fact that bus riders are still perceived as being of lower economic and social status than rail transit passengers (Hidalgo and Gutiérrez 2013). With this cultural reluctance in mind, urban transportation capacity-building and funding organizations such as the Institute for Transportation Development and Policy, the World Resources Institute (WRI), the World Bank and the InterAmerican Development Bank have focused their BRT promotion efforts in places where there is a strong political imperative to address worsening auto congestion problems in a speedy and cost-efficient way. This has created a knowledge network of BRT cities and operators that regularly exchanges information on BRT best practice and performance (ITDP 2017).

BRT vs. Light- and Heavy-Rail Service and Cost Comparisons

Where exactly does BRT fit within the broader spectrum of urban public transport services? Running within their own at-grade rights-of-way, BRT vehicles typically operate at speeds between 30 and 70 kilometers per hour (kph), depending on station dwell times and whether they have crossing priority at intersections. Depending on the individual city, this is double the average speed of conventional urban buses, 50 percent speedier than a typical express bus service, about the same speed as light-rail trains, and about two-thirds the speed of heavy-rail metro lines. In terms of passenger flows, BRT lines can accommodate between 5,000 and 45,000 passengers per hour (per travel direction) depending on vehicle capacity and travel headways (Cervero 2013). This is noticeably less than subway or metro lines, about the same as light-rail, and far more than express bus services. At the upper passenger capacity limit, buses on Bogotá's TransMilenio BRT system regularly operate at peak period headways of 15 seconds, providing TransMilenio lines with the potential to move nearly 50,000 passengers per hour in each direction. In Jakarta by contrast, BRT buses operate at peak-hour headways of five minutes, limiting their hourly capacity to just 3,600 passengers per direction (BRTDATA.org 2021).

BRT's biggest advantage over other public transit technologies is its lower capital costs, especially compared with its closest competitor, light-rail. Based on a sample of 42 BRT projects, 19 light rail projects, and 26 subway/metro projects, ITDP estimated the average capital cost per kilometer of a BRT line (in 2013 US dollars) at $10.1 million to $11.5 million depending on a country's level of economic development (Figure 7.3). The capital cost of a higher-quality Gold BRT line was about 50 percent more, while the cost of a Silver or Bronze BRT line was about 10 percent less. Compared on a per kilometer basis, BRT capital costs were comparable with light rail capital costs in lower-income countries, and a quarter of light-rail capital costs in upper-income ones. Depending on the level of country prosperity, the per kilometer costs of building a BRT line are between one-eighth and one-fortieth of building a fixed-rail transit line.

Depending on local labor and fuels costs, BRT lines are also typically less expensive to operate than light-rail or metro lines (Table 7.1). As reported by Deng and Nelson (2011) and based on a limited sample of transit systems for which detailed operating cost information is available, the typical BRT line costs about $4.73 (in 2000 US dollars) per vehicle revenue mile to operate. This compares with $12.22 for light-rail service and $8.54 for subway service.

While BRT usually wins out on paper over rail systems in terms of investment and per passenger operating costs, its real-world performance advantages aren't always as evident. In terms of service quality, BRT suffers in dense, built-up areas where there are frequent cross streets and where the right-of-way isn't wide enough to accommodate separate passing or express lanes. This causes station dwell times to increase, and buses to bunch up or platoon.

BRT systems can also easily become victims of their own success, especially in cases where high-than-expected ridership levels and bus overcrowding cause boarding and egress times to rise. In Bogotá, for example, passenger

Table 7.1   BRT vs. light rail and metro service comparisons

Service characteristic	Bus Rapid Transit	Express bus	Light-rail transit	Subway or metro
Right-of-way characteristics	Dedicated lanes in at-grade ROW	Shared at-grade roadway	Dedicated ROW (separate and at-grade)	Exclusive, grade-separated ROW
Maximum speed (kph)	60–70	40–50	60–80	70–99
Maximum vehicle capacity (passengers)	160–270		500–900	1,000–2,400
Minimum headway (seconds)	12–30		75–150	120–150
Maximum line capacity (passengers/direction/hour)	5,000–45,000		12,000–27,000	40,000–72,000

Source: ITDP (2017).

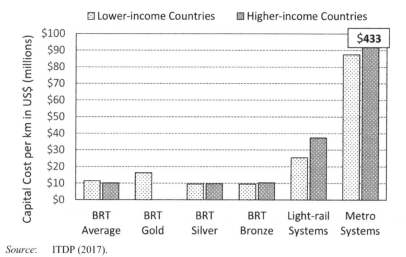

Figure 7.3   Comparison of BRT versus light-rail and metro capital costs

demand for TransMilenio service grew by 30 percent between 2005 and 2010, whereas bus capacity rose by just over 2 percent (Cervero 2013). The resulting decline in service quality and increase in crowding and crime subsequently turned off many middle-class Transmilenio riders, pushing them to other transportation modes, including heavily-polluting motorbikes (Gilbert 2008; Suzuki et al. 2013).

One unassailable advantage of BRT systems is that they can be built much more quickly—typically taking less than two years to complete—than metro or light-rail systems, and that service levels can be improved or reduced on individual BRT corridors as demand dictates without adversely affecting operations on other corridors.

Two BRT Planning Models

BRT planning processes typically follow one of two models. The first involves a government agency first undertaking a comprehensive mobility plan that identifies the travel needs of different groups and neighborhoods and proposes a mix of transit facility investments, including BRT to meet those needs. This was the planning model used by Bogotá and Jakarta in their TransMilenio and TransJakarta BRT planning processes. Curitiba, with its Agache Plan initially developed during the 1940s and then updated in the 1960s and early 2000s took this approach one step further, connecting proposed transit investments to potential growth and redevelopment areas. The advantage of the comprehensive planning model is that it offers the potential to fully integrate BRT investments with other transportation system improvements, and to better connect transit investments to land development activities. Taking a comprehensive and multi-modal rather than investment-specific approach to urban transportation planning is popular with international aid organizations such as the World Bank, and mobility advocacy/policy groups such as the ITDP and the World Resources Institute, which is one of the reasons why the comprehensive urban mobility planning model is so widely used in Latin America (Hidalgo and Graftieaux 2008; Hidalgo and Gutiérrez 2013).

A second BRT planning model involves taking a more incremental and corridor-centric approach. This usually involves city officials recommending construction of some type of high-capacity transit line as a quick and direct response to worsening automobile congestion. BRT may or may not be the best response in these situations, but it is typically the quickest, which is why the combination of rapid-response transportation planning and BRT have proven to be so popular in fast-growing cities in China and throughout Asia. In Seoul, BRT was initially seen as a corridor-specific rapid response measure, but once several BRT lines began operating, city officials pivoted toward a more comprehensive mobility planning approach that fully integrated BRT service with Seoul's metro system and citywide bus network (Hidalgo and Graftieaux 2008).

BRT Network and Route Configurations

Broadly speaking, most BRT networks are organized into one of three route configurations: (1) trunk-only service, also known as closed systems, in which BRT routes operate independently of local bus routes; (2) trunk-feeder service, in which local bus routes feed into BRT trunk lines at key points;

and (3) direct-service, also called open systems (Cervero 2013; ITDP 2017). Among the largest BRT exclusive-lane systems, trunk-only, closed systems are found in Jakarta, Ahmedabad, Beijing, Xiamen and Istanbul. Trunk-feeder systems, in which BRT buses can leave their dedicated busways and operate as their own feeders, or in which conventional buses connect peripheral areas to end-of-the-line BRT stations are more common in Latin America. Bogotá's green-color mini-buses, for example, provide free connections between informal housing settlements at the city's periphery and TransMilenio's terminal stations. Direct-line BRT routes, such as Guangzhou's, are gaining in popularity in cities where high-density apartment nodes are springing up, often around transit stations, and where jobs are decentralizing into suburban clusters. Because BRT buses can leave and return to their exclusive busway facilities on a route-by-route or even case-by-case basis, BRT is inherently better positioned than rail or even traditional fixed-route/fixed schedule buses to serve the emerging geography of urban and suburban commute trips which entail many-origin to many-destination travel.

Service Organizing Models and Financing Sources

Most BRT systems introduced to date make use of some version of the "managed competition" model (Hook 2005; Wright 2011). With this approach, control over all BRT planning, route and schedule design, fare setting and marketing is entirely in the hands of the government or public transit agency. The delivery of BRT services is then competitively tendered to the lowest bidder or bidders able to meet the government's quality-control standards while also earning a reasonable return on investment. With the managed competition model, service providers compete with one another for the entire BRT market, as it were, rather than on a line-by-line basis (Gwilliam 2002). Exceptions to the managed competition model are mostly found in the developed world, where, for coordination reasons, BRT services are often managed and delivered by regional authorities that operate other transit services. In some cases, fare collection operations are concessioned independently of bus operations (Wright 2011).

   In the rare situation in which a city government is able to pay for a new BRT corridor out of its current capital budget (or by substituting BRT service for an existing bus or transit service), adding BRT may not require additional financing. More likely, either the city's public transport agency or the BRT operator or both will have to find additional grant money or take on additional debt (ITDP 2017). In a study of BRT financing in nine countries, ITDP found on-budget funding (i.e., equity) to be the most common source of system financing, followed by commercial bank loans and loans from multi-national development agencies such as the World Bank. Of the nine countries studied, only Brazil and France made extensive use of national government loans and grants to finance their BRT systems. The US was unique among the countries studied in that its cities were able to use general-purpose municipal bond financing to fund their BRT systems. As a rule, BRT is more dependent on own-source equity and debt financing than are urban rail systems, which were more likely to receive grants and forgivable loans from national or state governments (Figure 7.4).

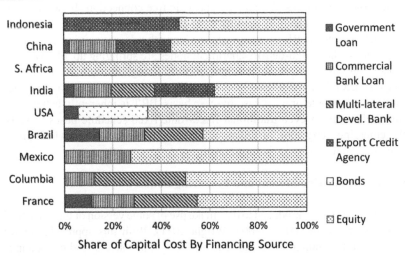

Source: ITDP (2017).

Figure 7.4   BRT debt financing sources in selected countries

Market Appeal

BRT riders are mostly commuters so how well a BRT system performs in the marketplace will depend on its relative speed advantage over other commuting modes. The huge initial demand for Bogotá's TransMilenio service, for example, was a direct result of it increasing downtown-bound trip speeds from approximately 15 kph to 26.7 kph (Cain et al. 2007). In their review of BRT systems in 11 Latin American cities, Hidalgo and Graftieaux (2008) found BRT service to have increased average travel speeds by between 14.5 and 26 kph depending on the design and quality of the busway. BRT's level boarding platforms and faster access and egress times also make it much more convenient than traditional bus and trolley services, an advantage repeatedly revealed in ridership satisfaction surveys (Deng and Nelson 2011).

In terms of ridership, BRT has generally performed best in Latin American cities, principally because of their persistent traffic congestion problems, less-than-reliable conventional bus service and monocentric urban forms that are well-served by radial rights-of-ways. Combining ridership counts with measurements of system length, Cervero (2013) found that Latin American BRT systems averaged more than 2½ times as many weekday riders (per kilometer of BRT corridor length) as Asian BRT systems, more than three times as many as BRT systems in Africa and Australia, more than five times as many as North American BRT systems, and nearly six times as many as European BRT systems.

New BRT riders come from different modes. In Asia and Latin America, most new BRT passengers previously used public or para-transit mode. In Australia, by contrast, 40 percent of new BRT commuters were previously drivers (Levinson et al. 2003; Currie 2006; Rathwell and Schijns 2002). Likewise, in Ottawa, a combination of BRT investments and driving disincentives resulted in a substantial increase in car-to-BRT diversion (Al-Dubikhi and Mees 2010). A passenger survey conducted on the Beijing Southern Axis BRT Line 1 (Deng and Nelson 2011) found that BRT primarily competed with private car use, especially during rush hour.

BRT and the Built Environment

BRT investments affect local land and real estate markets in two ways. In the short term, adding a new BRT line typically causes an "uplift" in nearby land values, housing prices, and commercial and residential rents through a mechanism known as positive capitalization. Early studies of BRT's capitalization effects focused on individual corridors but more recent studies have taken a multi-system comparative approach. In a 2020 meta-analysis of 23 BRT property value capitalization studies, Zhang and Yen found positive property effects in South American cities such as Bogotá; positive express bus capitalization effects among mid-sized US cities such as Pittsburgh and Eugene (Oregon); positive BRT uplift effects in Guangzhou, China, and Seoul, South Korea; minimal BRT capitalization effects in Beijing; and mixed property value uplift effects among Australian cities. In an earlier review of the BRT property value effects literature, Stokenberga (2014) determined that BRT-induced property value premiums were generally larger in Latin American and Asian cities than in North American ones. In a 2018 comparison of 41 BRT and rail projects in 48 countries, Ingvardson and Nielsen (2018) observed no statistically significant difference in distance-related property value capitalization effects between BRT, light-rail and heavy rail, leading them to conclude that BRT provided a larger property value uplift effect per increment of capital investment.

In the longer term, BRT investments may prompt additional residential or commercial development, although as Vergel-Tovar (2021) notes, the empirical literature on this subject is still too limited to be conclusive. The difference between BRT exerting a big versus small effect is principally a function of the presence of supportive land use policies. Unaccompanied by other public investments or regulatory changes, the impacts of new BRT investments on real estate development activity have mixed results. This changes when local government officials enact supporting changes in land use policy and zoning (Cervero 2013). Curitiba is especially illuminating in this respect. For more than 40 years, Curitiba's BRT investments have been planned in such a manner as to encourage new high-density residential development along the entire BRT corridor—and they have proven to be remarkably successful in this regard. In Quito and Bogotá by contrast, where there were fewer corridor-level development opportunities than in Curitiba, new construction activity has mostly been limited to areas immediately adjacent to BRT stations (Rodriguez et al. 2016). Study of BRT impacts on land uses and development in Bogotá and Quito shows a higher concentration of commercial land uses along phase one BRT corridors in Bogotá, few changes in already consolidated areas along BRT corridors in Bogota, while in Quito redevelopment activities were more intense along BRT corridors serving key activity nodes (Vergel-Tovar and Rodriguez 2022). The challenge of connecting BRT investments to forward-looking urban development policies is not just limited to Latin America: in Ottawa, an effort to couple BRT service with pedestrian-oriented urban design initiatives has so far met with only limited success (Al-Dubikhi and Mees 2010).

When it works as planned, the BRT investment–real estate development connection can generate a virtuous ridership cycle. A study of built environment attributes around BRT stations in seven cities in Latin America found increased BRT ridership levels among stations whose layout and use and design elements conformed to transit-oriented development (TOD) principles (Rodriguez and Vergel-Tovar 2018; Vergel-Tovar and Rodriguez 2018). Economists refer to the relationship between additional population or housing density and transit ridership as an elasticity. In Curitiba, the BRT population density–ridership elasticity was observed to be 0.26—meaning that a one percent increase in population density was associated with a 0.26 percent increase in BRT ridership—while in Bogotá, the density–ridership elasticity was found to be 0.25 (Vergel-Tovar 2019).

Environmental, Health and Equity Benefits

BRT's environmental and health benefits are principally a function of its ability to reduce air pollution emissions. By removing cars from city streets and replacing congestion-bound local bus services with free-flowing BRT services, new BRT investments should significantly reduce CO_2 and air pollution emissions as measured per passenger-kilometer of travel. Compared with traditional buses, BRT vehicles are also more easily converted to cleaner fuel sources such as compressed natural gas and electricity (Cervero 2013). Lastly, the convenient availability of BRT service may persuade some households to forego owning additional cars or motorbikes, further reducing travel volumes and vehicle pollution levels.

Whether these air pollution reduction benefits are actually achieved in practice is the subject of some debate. Most studies of the air pollution reduction benefits of BRT investments rely on computer simulation models. Among the few making use of actual field measurements, Salehi et al.'s (2016) study of pollutant levels before and after the introduction of a new BRT corridor in Tehran found corridor-level reductions of 5.8 percent for PM10, 6.7 percent for CO, 6.7 percent for NOx and 12.5 percent for SO_2. Using data from five air quality measuring stations before and after the introduction of BRT service in Jakarta, Nugroho et al. (2010) found sizeable reductions in PM10 and ozone levels, which they attributed to the modal shift of commuters from private vehicles to BRT. In a comparison of pollution emissions between BRT and light-rail in the United Kingdom, Hodgson et al. (2013) found that BRT produced lower PM10 emissions but higher NOx emissions. A study by Bel and Holst (2018) of pollution data from monitoring stations in Mexico City found post-BRT-introduction CO concentrations to have declined by between 5.5 and 7.2 percent (depending on the area), NOx emissions to have fallen by between 4.7 and 6.5 percent, and PM10 levels to have been reduced by between 7.3 and 9.2 percent. Connecting reduced transportation-related pollution levels to improved health outcomes, Hidalgo et al. (2013) estimated the health cost savings attributable to the first two phases of Bogotá's TransMilenio services at US$114 million over a 20-year period.

In terms of promoting greater economic and social equity, BRT investments have generally been found to be beneficial. In an early study of Bogotá's TransMilenio BRT system, Hildalgo and Yepes (2005) found that it generated an average of eight additional minutes of travel time savings for poor riders as compared with middle-class riders. An analysis of the mobility benefits of Mexico City's Metrobus Line 3 BRT service found that it disproportionately benefited the lowest three income quintiles (Delgado and Uniman 2011). In terms of out-of-pocket cost savings, studies of BRT systems in Jakarta (Wright 2011), Bogotá (Cervero 2005; Hildalgo and Yepes 2005) and Lagos (ITP and IBIS 2009) have all found BRT fares to be lower than for comparable trips in conventional buses. The same holds true for BRT versus private bus service (Cervero 2011).

Other BRT access studies have produced more mixed results. An analysis of BRT trunk lines in Cali (Colombia) and Lima (Peru) found them to do only a mediocre job reaching poor residents living at the urban periphery (Scholl et al. 2016). A separate review comparing BRT outcomes in Africa, Asia and Latin America found that although BRT investments do generate significant travel time savings for low-income residents, they generate even larger savings for middle-income residents (Venter et al. 2018).

BRT-related travel improvements may or may not lead to better employment outcomes. Studies of Bogotá (Cervero 2005) and Cali (Jaramillo et al.

2012) found the introduction of BRT service to have substantially improved poor workers' access to low-skill job opportunities. Looking at access to public facilities more broadly, Delmelle and Casas (2012) found BRT service disproportionately benefited poor households. In Johannesburg, by contrast, the construction of the 26 km Rea Vaya BRT did little to improve job opportunities or income levels among the poor. Combs studied the changes on travel patterns after the implementation of BRT in Bogotá, finding that the system had no substantial or significant impact in terms of meeting the travel needs for low-income households (Combs, 2017).

SIX BRT CASE STUDIES

In addition to delivering accessibility and mobility benefits (i.e., reduced travel times, improved travel convenience, better access to opportunities), transit investments have the potential to generate sizeable spillover impacts. These include increased employment and wage opportunities (with additional or higher-paying jobs now within easy commute distance); land development and property value uplift effects; health benefits through reduced injuries, improved personal safety, and reduced air pollution; and other environmental benefits such as reduced greenhouse gas emissions. All these impacts are local in nature and will therefore differ in magnitude depending on the local situation. Put simply, when it comes to estimating the costs and benefits associated with transit megaprojects, context matters as much as technology or size.

It is for this reason that our exploration of BRT's costs and benefits now turns from the general BRT case to BRT practice and performance in six specific metropolitan areas, including Curitiba, Quito, and Bogotá in Latin America; and Jakarta, Seoul and Guangzhou in Asia. Each of these BRT cases is simultaneously representative and unique. In terms of being representative, two thirds of the world's BRT systems measured by length are in Latin America or Asia. In many Latin America cities, BRT is now the backbone of public transit service. By contrast, in many Asian cities, BRT is still seen as a supplementary mode to private cars, rail transit, and local bus service. The six BRT case studies are also representative in terms of their adoption eras. Curitiba was among the very first BRT systems to be put in place back in 1974 while Guangzhou is among the most recent. All six are thoroughly modern BRT systems in terms of right-of-way and station design, vehicle design and age, fare collection procedures, and integration with other transit modes. System lengths range from Guangzhou's 22 km all the way up to Jakarta's 207 km, while daily patronage levels vary from Jakarta's 370,000 passengers to Bogotá's 2.2 million (BRTDATA.org 2021).

In terms of characteristics that make them special, Curitiba's BRT planning procedures were and still are integrated with local land use and development planning procedures to a degree unmatched anywhere else in the world. Quito matches Curitiba's BRT planning process but not its complementary land use and development management practices. Bogotá's TransMilenio improved significantly on Curitiba and Quito's BRT systems by expanding system capacity and by adding express and passing lanes. Jakarta's TransJakarta is a study in building an immense BRT system for comparatively little money. Seoul went entirely in the other direction, building what is perhaps the best planned, most expensive BRT system anywhere in the world. Finally, in China, where urban transportation investments are sometimes undertaken with the goal of enhancing a city's domestic prestige, Guangzhou's BRT system stands out as a model of efficiency and restraint.

Table 7.2   *Selected comparisons between BRT systems in Curitiba, Quito, Bogotá, Jakarta, Seoul and Guangzhou*

BRT system characteristic	Curitiba	Quito	Bogota	Jakarta	Seoul	Guangzhou
City population, 2020 (millions)	1.9	1.6	8.2	9.6	10.4	6.8
Public transport mode share (%)	46	62	59	36	n.a.	32
BRT system length (km)	74.1	71.4	112.9	207	115.3	22.9
Number of BRT corridors	7	3	11	12	12	1
Number of trunk lines	11	15	98	22	122	
Number of feeder routes	105	3	105	3	215	1
First corridor opened	1974	1995	2000	2004	2004	2010
Last corridor opened	2009	2005	2012	2013	2014	2010
BRT stations	106	126	139	240	329	
Average station spacing (m)	700	567	812	971	n.a.	880
BRT corridor scores (Gold/ Silver/Bronze/Basic)	1/6/0/0	0/0/3/0	3/5/0/3	0/1/0/11	0/0/0/5	0/1/0/0
Vehicles in BRT fleet	179	582	2006	1460	3703	989
Vehicle power source	Diesel and Biodiesel	Electricity and Diesel	Diesel	CNG and Diesel	CNG	
Standard fare (US$)	$1.30	$0.25	$0.67	$0.26	$1.17	$0.31
Average operating speed (km/hr)	28.0	17.8	25.2	19	17	24.8
Peak frequency (buses per hour)	67	140	320	40	n.a.	350
Peak load (passengers per hour per direction)	20,500	11,700	49,000	3,600	8,400	27,000
Average daily passengers	721,500	745,000	2,192,000	370,000	400,000	850,000
Annual passengers (millions)	216	223.5	658	190	120	255
Annual fare revenue (US$ millions)	196.3	39.1	308	20.89	98.3	55.3
Average revenue per passenger (US$)	$0.91	$0.17	$0.47	$0.11	$0.82	$0.22

Source: Assembled by Authors from BRTData.org

Curitiba, Brazil

Curitiba was the first city in Latin America to build a comprehensive and modern-day BRT system, opening its first two BRT corridors in 1974. Today, Curitiba's BRT system, known locally as *Rede Integrada de Transporte* or RIT, encompasses seven corridors and 74 km of segregated busways. In 2019, RIT carried an average of 721,000 passengers per day, making it one of the most successful BRT systems in the world when compared on a per capita ridership basis (BRTDATA.ORG 2021).

What makes Curitiba especially notable among cities with BRT systems is that its BRT investments were conceived and implemented as part of a broader land use–transportation mobility scheme, coupling investments in public transit with land use policies designed to encourage higher residential densities and mixed-use development forms. The result was something that was and still is rare among growing cities: a virtuous cycle in which transit investments promote complementary urban forms which in turn promote additional transit use (Cervero 1998). As of 2010, nearly half of all trips made within Curitiba were by public transport (BRTDATA.ORG 2021; Burgess and Ordiz 2010). More recently, overall public transit use in Curitiba has declined somewhat, although less so for BRT than for other public transit modes (Turbay et al. 2022).

Curitiba's BRT experience can be divided into three periods: (i) the years prior to 1972, which saw the emergence of a planning consensus favoring investments in public transportation instead of private cars; (ii) the 1972 to 1988 period during which Curitiba's RIT plan and system were gradually implemented; and (iii) the post-1988 period, in which Curitiba's continuing metropolitan growth was guided by its transit investments (Lindau et al. 2010). Like many fast-growing second-tier cities in Latin America, Curitiba's early public transit planning efforts emphasized building rail systems. When this seemed as if it would be beyond Curitiba's economic means, the city's Institute for Research and Urban Planning (Instituto de Pesquisa e Planejamento Urbano de Curitiba, or IPPUC) proposed instead that Curitiba build a system of express bus lines that would operate within the medians of downtown-bound arterials. Additional BRT features were added as the planning process moved forward, including widely-spaced stations, level boarding platforms, multiple boarding points, and a pre-boarding fare payment system. Four months after Curitiba's first two BRT lines opened in 1974, average daily ridership reached 54,000 passengers, 60 percent above initial projections.

To support the city's new BRT lines, Curitiba's Mayor Jaime Lerner pushed through two new land use planning initiatives. The first was to pedestrian-ize Curitiba's downtown core to reduce automobile congestion and make additional land available for commercial development and public space. The second involved re-zoning the parcels immediately adjacent to each BRT corridor for high-density mixed use developments. By increasing density and activity levels at both ends of the BRT trip, Lerner's approach would have a salutatory effect on system ridership.

As time went on these ideas were further systematized, eventually becoming codified as the "trinary system," which aims to increase population densities and land use intensities adjacent to BRT trunk corridors. As its name suggest, BRT corridors are divided into three arterial zones, with the BRT line running down the corridor's center, and one-way downtown express and local bus service operating on each of the adjacent arterials. Parcels fronting the BRT line are reserved for mixed-use projects with commercial uses on the first floor and residential uses on the upper floors. Parcels one block away from the central BRT right-of-way are developed at lower densities and with fewer commercial uses. Further away still, lower-density residential uses predominate. Viewed outward, the trinary forms a gentle gradient of residential densities (Figure 7.5).

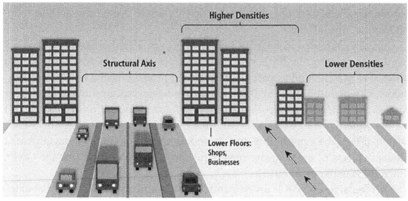

Source: Lindau et al. (2010).

Figure 7.5   *Curitiba's "trinary" BRT corridor cross-section*

A third downtown-oriented BRT corridor, Boqueirão, opened in 1977, followed in 1980 by east and west BRT corridors. Additional bus services were added as Curitiba's RIT system expanded, including inter-neighborhood circumferential routes (*interbairros*) which connected to BRT lines at terminal and midpoint stations, and feeder bus services which connected individual neighborhoods to the closest BRT corridor or express bus line. With Curitiba's population growth concentrated in its southern neighborhoods, a sixth non-radial BRT corridor known as the Green Line (Linha Verde) was opened in 2009, followed by a southern circumferential BRT line in 2013.

The positive evolution of Curitiba's RIT system was not quite as smooth as some historical chronicles make it seem. Until 1989, Curitiba mayors were prohibited by laws from serving consecutive terms. This meant that interest in BRT waxed and waned depending on who was elected to serve as Curitiba's mayor. Jaime Lerner served between 1971 and 1974, and again between 1979 and 1983. In 1986, Lerner's second-term mayoral successor, Roberto Requião, pushed to transfer operating responsibility for Curitiba's RIT system from its private concessionaires back to the city itself, citing the potential for improved coordination with a feeder bus service. With no one in city government knowledgeable about operating a BRT line, this change resulted in a steep decline in service quality and a noticeable drop in ridership (Lindau et al. 2010). Elected to a third term as Curitiba's mayor in 1989 on a pro-BRT platform, Lerner quickly sought to reinvigorate the system, replacing its aging single-carriage buses with a high-capacity bi-articulated model (developed specifically for Curitiba by Volvo) and introducing the iconic "plastic tube" station design for which Curitiba's BRT corridors would become famous. The effect of these investments was to double passenger capacity while decreasing both in-route and station dwell times.

Curitiba continued to be a BRT innovator even after Lerner completed his third mayoral term. In 2002, it converted its bus systems to an electronic fare collection system; and as part of the planning process for the Green Line corridor, which would open in 2009, adopted a value-capture financing scheme known as CEPAC (*Certificados de Potencial Adicional de Construção*), based on the experience of Sao Paulo with this innovative urban management tool, which offers the opportunity to developers to buy additional development rights in terms of more square meters for those land parcels facing the Green Corridor (Suzuki et al. 2015).

Curitiba's recent BRT investments have continued to affect its development patterns and property markets, albeit in a more limited way. A study of Curitiba's Green Line BRT corridor by Lindau et al. (2010) found the prices of nearby properties to have tripled after the city's identification of the proposed right-of-way. A later analysis by Bergman et al. (2017) found the effects of a 2015 upzoning initiative on the densities of BRT-fronting properties to have been mostly limited to blocks adjacent to the Curitiba's southern and western BRT lines.

These recent land market effects have created new challenges. As property values and rents within BRT corridors have increased, the neighborhoods along those corridors have become wealthier and, as a result, auto use has slightly increased while BRT use has slightly declined (Duarte and Ultramari 2012). In terms of business changes, a 2009 study of the Green Line corridor by Hardt and Hardt (2009) found higher value-added firms were systematically replacing smaller and less profitable businesses within Curitiba's BRT corridors. These adverse equity findings have led to a mix of new policy proposals, including inclusionary zoning requirements mandating that new residential projects in Curitiba's BRT corridors include an appropriate share of low-income housing units (Bergman et al. 2017).

So far, these trends have not substantially impacted the system's aggregate financial performance. Its strong ridership numbers (more than 700,000 daily passengers), high fares (averaging US$1.30 per rider), and enviable mode share (approximately 25 percent of daily trips in Curitiba) make it notably profitable as BRT systems go. With 2019 farebox revenues of US$216 million, Curitiba's BRT system earned roughly $0.90 per passenger, placing it among the world's most profitable BRT systems in terms of farebox revenue rates.[4]

Quito's El Trole BRT System

The capital city of Ecuador, Quito has about two-thirds of Curitiba's population, but is slightly denser and has a more linear urban form. These characteristics combine to make Quito well suited to BRT service, and indeed, Quito's average daily BRT passenger ridership is slightly higher than Curitiba's (Hidalgo and Carrigan 2010).

Known as the *El Trole*, or trolleybus, Quito's first BRT line was explicitly modeled after Curitiba's, with long corridors connecting outlying residential areas to downtown job centers. Located high in the Andes Mountains 2,600 m (8,500 feet) above sea level, Quito is prone to seasonal temperature inversions which magnify its air pollution problems. For this reason, the decision was made early on that buses on the Trole line should be powered by overhead electricity lines rather than be gas- or diesel-powered.

Quito's BRT system is organized along a north–south spine with multiple corridors (Vergel-Tovar 2016). The initial 11.2 km Trole corridor opened in three stages between December 1995 and April 1996, connecting the "La Y" district in northern Quito (and near the former Mariscal Sucre International Airport, now relocated outside the city) to the El Recreo shopping mall in the south. The Trolebus addressed the accessibility issues in the Historic Center of Quito, deemed a World Heritage Site by UNESCO, by providing stops within this historic preservation area. In 2000, the Trole line was extended further south to the Moran Valverde shopping mall area. In 2008, it was extended southward again, reaching the Quitumbe BRT terminal. Ecovia, a second 21 km bus-based corridor opened in 2002, and a third, Corredor Norte opened in 2005. Between 2010 and 2012, the Suroriental and Suroccidental BRT corridors began passenger service. Although the entire network is integrated at key BRT transfer hubs, each corridor is unique in terms of its station design themes and bus vehicles. These differences are the result of each of Quito's mayors wanting the BRT segments built during their terms to have a unique signature. Currently, Quito's BRT corridors extend for 71 km, all of which, with the exception of some segments of the Suroriental corridor, are completely segregated from adjacent rights-of-way. As of 2017, Quito's BRT network carried 745,000 daily passengers. The Trole corridor is still its only electricity-powered BRT line.

With BRT fares averaging US$0.25 (as of 2015), usage of Quito's BRT system is heavily subsidized, with each passenger contributing just $0.17 in revenues per ride, the lowest farebox revenue recovery rate of any of the six case studies.

The effects of Quito's BRT system on land development and property value uplift differ by corridor. In an analysis that compared development activity within the Trolebus, Ecovia and Corredor Norte corridors relative to nearby unserved neighborhoods, Rodriquez et al. (2016) found new apartment projects attracted to all three corridors, new single-family home construction occurring in two of the three corridors (Trole and Norte), and new office development concentrated in the Ecovia corridor. In terms of housing price increases, the Trolebus corridor performed best, followed by the Corredor Norte corridor. These property market adjustments occurred in the absence of explicit planning or public policy interventions; it wasn't until 2015 that Quito began comprehensively upzoning properties adjacent to its BRT corridors.

In terms of equity impacts, Quito is a city with more lower-income groups than Curitiba, these groups live mostly at the city's periphery in neighborhoods its BRT lines don't directly serve. Accessing central Quito where the jobs are by BRT requires that these residents begin their trips on a feeder bus or via paratransit. As a result, recent BRT investments have not benefited Quito's poorer residents as much as its middle-income and wealthier ones (Jaramillo et al. 2019). Quito did undertake a city-wide affordable housing construction program in the 1990s, but it has progressed unevenly, and the higher land values around Quito's BRT corridors, especially the Trole corridor, make it difficult to deliver affordable housing at the scale needed (Vergel-Tovar 2016).

Bogotá's TransMilenio

Bogotá's TransMilenio system is not only the world's best known BRT system, with upwards of 2.2 million daily passengers in pre-Covid pandemic times, it is also the world's most heavily used (Hidalgo et al. 2013). Built in accordance with Bogotá's 1996 Urban Transport Master Plan—which was developed with funding and technical assistance from the Japan International Cooperation Agency (JICA)—TransMilenio's construction has progressed in three phases. Phase I includes the east–west Calle 80 and north–south Caracas corridors, both of which began operating in January 2001. Three additional BRT corridors (Caracas Sur, Eje Ambiental, Autopista Norte) opened in 2002 and 2003. Phase II included four more BRT corridors (Americas, NQS Central, NQS Sur and Suba) which opened in 2005 and 2006. Phase III includes the two most recent corridors (Calle 26 and Carerra 10), both of which opened in 2012. Totaling just under 113 km in length, TransMilenio is today Latin America's fourth longest BRT system, trailing those in Sao Paulo, Rio de Janeiro and Mexico City. Conceptually, TransMilenio is organized into two north–south downtown-serving spines (comprising seven separate BRT corridors), three east–west lines (two of which terminate downtown) and a single southbound spur originating in Central Bogotá. Each of TransMilenio's 12 BRT corridors includes two lanes in each direction, and two-thirds of its vehicle fleet of 2,000 buses are of the higher-capacity articulated variety. TransMilenio's combination of four-lane rights-of-way and high-capacity buses enable each of its corridors to carry nearly 50,000 riders per hour per direction during the morning peak. No other BRT system in the world currently comes close to TransMilenio in terms of either capacity or ridership.

Because of its size and visibility, TransMilenio's impacts have been the subject of considerable empirical research. Statistical studies of TransMilenio's property value uplift effect put it between 7 percent (Rodriquez and Targa 2004) and 22 percent (Perdomo Calvo et al. 2007) depending on the property type and location. Measured in percentage terms, TransMilenio's property value uplift effects have been greater in lower-income neighborhoods than in middle- and upper-income ones (Guzman et al. 2021), a finding that has important equity implications. Rodriquez and Mojica (2009) found TransMilenio-based property value premiums to extend far beyond the usual 500-meter radius, results they attribute to TransMilenio's extensive geographic coverage and frequent service. Still, as Cervero and Dai (2014) note, with many other areas of Bogotá having experienced similar or even larger property value gains, TransMilenio's property value uplift effect has been far from uniform.

In terms of promoting redevelopment, a 2016 before-and-after study by Rodriquez et al., documented a significant increase in real estate activity around recently-opened BRT stations. A later study by Vergel-Tovar and Camargo (2019) found TransMilenio's development-promoting impacts to extend well beyond its station areas, in some cases, increasing densities around BRT terminals at urban peripheries. This result is consistent with a study of densities developed by Bocarejo et al. (2013) that found rising residential densities in peripheral locations served by BRT-connecting feeder bus services.

In Bogotá, unlike Curitiba, these effects have occurred largely in the absence of supportive land use policies and regulations. Instead, they are the result of private sector developers seeking out sites with BRT-enhanced

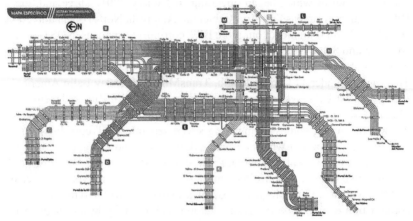

Source: City of Bogotá: Official Transmilenio Map.

Figure 7.6   *System map of Bogotá's 113 km TransMilenio network. With*
                    11 distinct BRT corridors and 139 stations, it is the largest
                    BRT system in the western hemisphere

accessibility (Vergel-Tovar and Rodriguez 2022). This finally began changing
in 2016 when Bogotá implemented new zoning codes allowing developers to
build higher density residential projects in BRT corridors. This change has not
been uncontroversial, with some critics decrying its lack of open space and
pedestrian amenity requirements, and its potential for over-building.

By providing improved access to jobs—post-TransMilenio, public transport commute times to downtown Bogotá are half of what they were
pre-TransMilenio—TransMilenio has also had beneficial labor market and
welfare effects. In a carefully done general equilibrium analysis, Tsivanidis
(2018) estimated that TransMilenio as of 2015 had increased Bogotá's gross
domestic product by 3 to 4 percent, its urban land rents by 3.5 percent, and its
workers' incomes by between 3.5 and 3.9 percent. (The higher end of each
range incorporates positive spillover effects.) In terms of equity, because
TransMilenio does a better job connecting high-skilled workers living in
Bogotá's northern neighborhoods to their downtown jobs than it does connecting lower-skilled workers to industrial jobs, Tsivanidis concluded that it
disproportionately benefits the city's wealthier residents.

A narrower cost-benefit analysis of TransMilenio undertaken by Hidalgo
et al. (2013) found that between 1998 and 2012, TransMilenio incurred
public and private costs totaling US$2 billion while generating $3.1 billion
in benefits. These estimates were calculated using a 12 percent discount
rate to compare costs and benefits occurring in different years. The biggest

public sector cost involved building TransMilenio's right-of-way and station facilities ($0.95 billion), while the biggest private cost involved day-to-day bus fleet operation ($0.41 billion). Travel time savings were valued at $1.7 billion followed by $1.2 billion in cost savings achieved by eliminating the now-redundant express bus service. Additional benefits included fewer deaths and injuries because of reduced vehicle crashes ($0.17 billion) and improvements in health due to reductions in congestion-based air pollution ($0.14 billion). The researchers also compared their *ex post* results to projections undertaken before TransMilenio opened, finding that the earlier study had substantially underestimated projected construction and operating costs while slightly over-estimating potential travel time savings.

In some ways, TransMilenio has been a victim of its own raised expectations. With station and bus capacity unable to keep pace with continually-rising demand, TransMilenio riders have grown increasingly dissatisfied with its service quality. Despite the completion of two additional TransMilenio lines in 2012, station and on-board passenger congestion levels and in-vehicle travel times continue to rise. In a 2016 poll of TransMilenio users, the system received an 86 percent disapproval rating. An earlier 2012 survey conducted by the Secretary for Women's Issues of Bogotá revealed that 64 percent of female TransMilenio riders had been victims of some form of sexual assault or harassment while using the system. TransMilenio has also diverted resources from other public transit services in Bogotá. A study by Combs (2017) found that despite recent system expansions, TransMilenio continues to lag in meeting the mobility needs of Bogotá's lower-income and lower-wealth households.

Jakarta's TransJakarta BRT

With 207 km of segregated busway divided among 13 BRT corridors, Jakarta's TransJakarta BRT system currently holds the title of the world's biggest as measured by length. As in many cities, Jakarta adopted BRT as a cost-efficient approach to dealing with worsening traffic congestion. Home to 1.5 million residents in 1950, Jakarta has grown steadily since, and today has 11 million residents. Metropolitan Jakarta is much larger still, hosting a population of between 18 million and 32 million depending on which government agency is doing the counting. As the largest city in a relatively poor country—Indonesia currently ranks 108th among nations in terms of per capita GDP according to the World Bank—Jakarta had historically underinvested in public transport. A proposed metro rail line running between Sudirman and Thamrin Streets in downtown Jakarta was debated for decades but ultimately came to naught. During the 1980s Jakarta experimented with a bus-only lane in the Sudirman–

Thamrin corridor but eliminated it after only a few years when enforcement proved too difficult (Ernst 2005).

Things started changing in November 2001 when Bogotá's former mayor, Enrique Peñalosa came to Jakarta to explain on what Bogotá had done to build its TransMilenio system. Among those in the audience for Peñalosa's presentation was Jakarta's Vice Governor Budihardjo Sukmadi who reported back favorably to Governor Sutiyoso about the possibility of Jakarta building a BRT system of its own. After visiting Bogotá to see TransMilenio firsthand, Governor Sutiyoso assigned the job of designing and building a BRT system for Jakarta to a specially-constituted task force that mixed elected officials from Jakarta's largest municipalities with professionals from its planning and infrastructure agencies (Ernst 2005).

With Governor Sutiyosa's backing and funding from international development agencies including USAID, construction of the 12.9 km north–south TransJakarta BRT Koridor 1 soon got underway, opening for passenger service in February 2004. The new BRT line proved immediately popular. After six months in operation, daily passenger volumes on Koridor 1 regularly exceeded 49,000 riders, which was about 7,000 more riders than pre-construction projections had indicated. The new BRT line also proved popular with Jakarta's politicians: when the city's other transit services were shut down by political protestors during Indonesia's 2004 presidential election campaign, officials kept Koridor 1 open. Altogether, TransJakarta Koridor 1 cost an estimated US$1 million per kilometer to build, a figure that was at the low end of BRT construction costs for the period. (A subsequent analysis revealed that Koridor 1's busway road surface and terminals had been underbuilt to meet its aggressive construction schedule, resulting in additional maintenance and construction costs later (Ernst 2005)). Construction of BRT Koridors 2 and 3 began almost immediately after Koridor 1's 2004 opening and was completed in 2006. Four additional BRT corridors (Koridors 4, 5, 6 and 7) opened for service in 2007, followed by Koridor 8 in 2009, Koridors 9 and 10 in 2011, Koridor 11 in 2012, and Koridor 12 in 2013.

No other city had ever built such a large public transit network quite so quickly or economically. The secret to Jakarta's success in this regard was its insistence on using standardized facility designs, construction techniques, and vehicle specifications. Except for Koridor 1, all of Jakarta's BRT corridors are classified as "basic" under ITDP's BRT scoring system, meaning that they meet the minimum criteria of having a dedicated right-of-way, segregated busway alignment, off-board fare collection system and platform-level boarding, but lack additional access or technology features that would boost capacity or service quality. Whether Jakarta's minimal expense approach to building its BRT lines will make them less durable and more expensive over the long run remains to be seen.

Jakarta's economical design and construction approach has enabled it to keep its BRT fares at US$0.25 per ride, the same as when Koridor 1 opened in 2004. As a result, TransJakarta ridership has grown continuously, hitting 60 million annual riders in 2007, 100 million in 2011, 150 million in 2017 and prior to the advent of the Covid-19 pandemic, 190 million in 2019. This combination of low fares and high ridership continues to stress TransJakarta's operating finances, and despite efforts to make the system more economically self-sufficient—including a change in TransJakarta's status from government agency to a city-sponsored enterprise in 2014—it continues to be heavily subsidized by Jakarta's government. According to a 2019 press report in the Indonesian online news service Temp.co, government subsidies to TransJakarta in 2019 reached 3.7 trillion rupiah (US$263 million).[5] Still, even with all its additional BRT capacity, Jakarta's traffic congestion levels steadily worsened. After many years of delay, Jakarta finally opened its first metro and light-rail lines in 2019. Both connect directly to TransJakarta BRT stations.

Because of a lack of reliable data, few authoritative studies of TransJakarta's impacts or effects have been undertaken. Those that have, have yielded conflicting results. A 2012 study by Kumar et al. found that only 20 percent of TransJakarta passengers previously used private vehicles, which why it has done so little to reduce Jakarta's challenging traffic congestion. A more recent study by Gaduh et al. (2017) found somewhat higher rates of car-to-BRT modal diversion than previously estimated as well as significant reductions in private vehicle ownership rates. These latter findings are consistent with the results of studies by Nugroho et al. (2010) and Vincent et al. (2012).

In terms of TransJakarta' property market impacts, a 2019 study by Rusadhi found average land values among Jakarta's 258 planning subdistricts to have increased an additional 20 to 30 percent (compared with citywide averages) among the 33 subdistricts newly served by TransJakarta buses after 2013. TransJakarta's potential to stimulate additional development activity has not yet been studied, although a related inquiry by Budiati et al. (2018) found the types of site conditions and planning incentives needed to support TOD-like development to be present at just three of Jakarta's 13 Metrorail (MRT) stations. This suggests that Jakarta officials have yet to fully figure out how to coordinate transit investments with land use policy.

Seoul's BRT System

The capital city of South Korea, Seoul, is part of the Seoul Metropolitan Area, the world's second largest urban conurbation with 23 million inhabitants. Having grown steadily from just over 1 million residents in 1950, the city's population peaked at 10.5 million in 1990, and has since leveled off at just under 10 million. Twice as dense as New York City, Seoul opened its first heavy-rail metro line in 1974 and has since added another 22 metro and light-rail lines, giving it one of the world's biggest metro systems as measured by route length (Cervero and Kang 2011). Even with all of Seoul's public transport investments, car ownership in the city has continued to rise, as has its evil twin, congestion. To cope with rising congestion levels, Seoul significantly expanded its curbside express bus network during the early 2000s, and then, in 2004, opened its first BRT line. The service proved instantly popular, and over the next decade, Seoul built 11 additional BRT corridors. Today, with a total system length of 115.3 km, 329 stations, 122 trunk lines and 215 feeder bus lines, Seoul's BRT network is one of the most extensive in the world. All Seoul BRT buses are powered by compressed natural gas.

Seoul's BRT network is widely used, drawing an average of 400,000 passengers per day and upwards of 120 million riders per year.[6] In terms of mode share, 28 percent of Seoul-based trips in 2011 were made by bus, which puts buses behind Seoul's subway system in terms of mode share (37.1 percent) but ahead of private cars (23.5 percent). Compared with heavily-subsidized BRT systems in Latin America and other parts of Asia, Seoul charges its BRT riders much higher fares, with the fare for a medium-length ride averaging US$1.20.

The opening of Seoul's first BRT line in 2004 coincided with a range of other public transportation changes and reforms. These included replacing the previous system of labyrinthine bus routes with a hub-and-spoke based dual system of trunk and feeder lines, the rolling out of an electronic fare card system integrated across all of Seoul's public transportation mode, and the early implementation of a real-time bus monitoring and control system, known as Topis.

Korea is better at collecting urban data than most countries, so transportation researchers have had the information they need to properly estimate the Seoul BRT system's impacts. To start with, the introduction of BRT service had an immediate effect on roadway travel speeds and congestion, increasing average travel speeds by between 15 and 60 percent depending on the corridor. This made driving for everyone less burdensome, especially in downtown Seoul. Because it was quicker for many workers to travel to their downtown destinations by BRT, the addition of BRT service precipitated an immediate shift among downtown-bound travelers from subway to BRT, which adversely affected subway patronage levels (Jun et al. 2015). In a 2018 study comparing air-pollution levels between BRT corridors and adjacent areas, Baik et al. (2018) found a measurable decrease in localized PM10 particulate concentrations after the introduction of BRT service. Differences in NO_2 pollutant concentrations were also observed although they were not determined to be statistically significant.

In terms of land and property market effects, a 2011 study by Cervero and Kang found that residential properties within 300 m of a BRT corridor sold at

5 to 10 percent premiums compared with more distant properties. For retail and non-residential properties, the BRT price premium ranged between 3 and 26 percent. Controlling for other neighborhood amenities and features, single-family properties within a half-kilometer of a BRT station were more likely to be converted to apartment use than more distant properties, but less likely to be developed as condominiums or mixed-use projects—a finding the researchers attribute to the noise and nuisance impacts of being too close to the BRT line. Apartment conversions to higher uses, however, seemed immune to this nuisance effects. A separate 2010 study by Kang found that employment densities within 500 m of a newly-opened BRT line subsequently increased by 54 percent.

In a study that looked at the effect of Seoul's BRT service on employment growth and location, Jun (2012) found that the introduction of BRT services had led to an increase in downtown employment and helped reverse prior job suburbanization trends. The advent of the BRT service was also credited with contributing to renewed population growth in central Seoul, with the biggest effect occurring in residential neighborhoods outside the CBD itself. In terms of land values and rents, Jun's results differed from Cervero and Kang's, finding no significant BRT effect on rents except among commercial properties in Seoul's CBD.

While Seoul has lagged other world cities, such as Curitiba and Portland, in promoting TOD, a study by Sun et al. (2017) identified many TOD-like urban form characteristics as being present in and around Seoul's BRT corridors, and likely functioning to increase BRT ridership. In a study comparing boarding data across different BRT station types, Rodriguez and Kang (2020) found patronage levels to be consistently higher at stations that were either centrally located or better connected to Seoul's subway lines.

Guangzhou's Zhongshan Avenue BRT Corridor

Word of the success of Seoul's BRT system quickly traveled across Asia, finding an especially receptive audience in Chinese cities where officials were struggling to come to grips with rapidly escalating auto ownership levels. Wealthy cities such as Beijing, Shanghai, and Shenzhen could afford to invest in new subway and metro lines, but poorer cities could not, and many turned to BRT. Between 2001 and 2007, 14 Chinese cities added one or more BRT corridors (Fjellstrom 2010), and five more did so between 2008 and 2012. In many of these cities, no formal BRT needs assessment or demand analysis was ever conducted, with the result that many of the newly-added BRT lines underperformed when it came to meeting ridership expectations.

One city that did take care planning its BRT system was Guangzhou. Located in China's Pearl River Delta region, Guangzhou is the capital of

Guangdong Province, the country's largest and wealthiest. Guangzhou's single BRT corridor, which opened in 2010, runs for 23 km along Zhongshan Avenue, connecting Guangzhou's eastern residential neighborhoods to the city's center. It is by far Asia's most successful BRT line, carrying upwards of 800,000 passengers each day.

The impetus for the Zhongshan Avenue BRT line was a 2003 visit by urban transport expert Karl Fjellstrom who had been invited to Guangzhou to review its World Bank funding proposal to build a curbside express bus lane.[7] In a move that must have surprised his hosts, Fjellstrom concluded that the proposed express bus scheme would provide no tangible travel time savings and recommended instead that Guangzhou consider building a BRT line based on the models of Curitiba and Bogotá. Following up on Fjellstrom's recommendation, a study group of Guangzhou officials led by Mayor Guangning Zhang traveled to Bogotá and Sao Paulo in October 2004 to investigate how BRT worked. Impressed with what he saw, Mayor Zhang asked Guangzhou's Construction Commission to assess the feasibility of building something similar in Guangzhou. The Commission recruited Fjellstrom, who had recently joined ITDP and was working in Guangzhou leading a team of city transportation engineers to identify potential BRT corridors and prepare a conceptual design scheme. In April 2005, the Construction Committee signed a memorandum of understanding with ITDP and the Guangzhou Municipal Engineering Design and Research Institute (GMEDRI) to prepare a more detailed BRT proposal. By 2006, the ITDP/GMEDR team had settled on a single BRT corridor running along Zhongshan Avenue.

Not all Guangzhou city officials were as enthused about BRT as Mayor Zhang. Guangzhou was already in the process of expanding its metro system and BRT was seen by some city officials as a less prestigious alternative. After two years of administrative dithering, construction work on the new Zhongshan Avenue BRT corridor finally got underway in November 2008. Making the job more difficult, construction of the new BRT line was to be coordinated with a city-sponsored Zhongshan Avenue urban renewal initiative. This added significantly to the Zhongshan Avenue BRT Line's construction costs and disruptive impacts and attracted highly critical media attention pointing out BRT's mixed record among Chinese cities in meeting its ridership targets.

In Guangzhou's case, the extra time and care taken to plan the Zhongshan Avenue BRT corridor paid off. Passengers flocked to the new BRT line, causing first-year average daily passenger boarding to exceed 800,000.[8] In 2011, the corridor won the IDTP's Sustainable Transport Award, the UNFCCC Lighthouse Award, and several national awards and design prizes. Led by team leader Xiaomei Duan, many of the BRT project's planners and engineers were women, and they were heralded as well, winning a Level 1 Design Prize from the China Engineering Design Association.

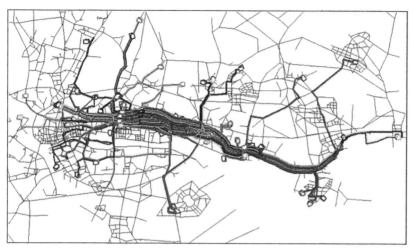

Source: Cervero (2013), from ChinaBRT.org.

Figure 7.7   *Guangzhou's Zhongshan Avenue BRT system, showing 31 different bus routes sharing a single 23 km BRT corridor*

Because of government limitations on who has access to data, independent evaluations of the impacts of Chinese infrastructure projects can be tough to undertake. The job is even tougher in Guangzhou, where researchers must disentangle the unique effects of a single BRT corridor from those of 14 metro lines. We found only two studies that successfully did so. The first is by Salon et al. (2014). Drawing on 2010 and 2011 price information on 35,000 Guangzhou apartments obtained from the Soufun Wang realty company, it found a roughly 2 percent price uplift effect for apartments located within 3 km of the Zhongshan Avenue BRT corridor. The same study also found that apartments located within the immediate BRT corridor but not next to a BRT station sold at price discounts. Being close to a BRT station added value, the authors concluded, but being too close did not. A second study of Guangzhou's Zhongshan Avenue BRT line by Cao et al. (2016) analyzed passenger satisfaction with BRT service as compared with competing metro and bus service. It found transit users to be most satisfied with the metro service, followed by BRT, then conventional bus. Comparing the different aspects of the BRT service, Zhongshan Avenue Line passengers were most satisfied with its lower cost (compared with the metro service), faster travel times (compared with the bus service) and ease of above-ground station access. They were less satisfied with vehicle comfort and crowding, customer service, and the behaviors of other passengers.

LESSONS AND TAKEAWAYS

With BRT systems currently up and running in more than 180 cities worldwide, there is ample opportunity to observe what works when it comes to
implementing BRT service, as well as to make more general observations
about the efficacy of BRT with megaproject implications. Starting with
BRT-specific takeaways.

- *BRT is a cost-efficient and locally-adaptable approach to moving large
  numbers of commuters in high travel corridors.* Depending on the market,
  BRT operating costs are between one-third and one-half of comparable
  fixed-rail systems when compared on a cost per vehicle-revenue mile basis.
  In terms of initial capital costs, the advantage is even greater, with BRT
  coming in at around US$10 to $15 million per kilometer as compared with
  $30 million per kilometer for light-rail and $100+ million per kilometer
  for heavy-rail metro systems. BRT's inherent operating cost advantages
  are somewhat offset by its lower vehicle capacities—meaning that a fully
  occupied 200-passenger BRT bus will have difficulty competing with
  a fully occupied 1000-passenger metro train—putting additional pressure
  on BRT operators to operate as close to full capacity as possible. This is
  far easier to do for BRT vehicles, which can be flexibly scheduled, dis-
  patched and routed to meet constantly changing ridership demands. Other
  BRT advantages over heavy and light-rail include the much lower costs of
  adding express lanes.
- *Crowding and congestion are BRT's Achilles heel.* The successful BRT
  service model pioneered by Curitiba in 1974, which allows for reduced
  station dwell times and much higher vehicle speeds compared with
  a conventional bus service, becomes noticeably less efficient when buses
  are overcrowded, when non-BRT vehicles linger in intersections, and
  when passing lanes are not available to smooth vehicle flow. Just as
  BRT system planners should develop contingency plans to deal with
  lower-than-expected passenger volumes, they should come up with comparable plans to deal with greater-than-expected passenger demand. This
  did not occur for in the Bogotá TransMilenio case, leading to a situation
  where hundreds of thousands of daily commuters have become dependent
  on an otherwise convenient travel model whose service quality has been
  compromised by bus overcrowding and concerns over passenger safety.
- *BRT vehicles have the advantage of leaving their busways as required.*
  This enables BRT buses to operate as their own origin and destination-end
  feeder services, providing additional routing flexibility and capacity as
  needed. Even in fully-closed BRT systems in which vehicles never leave
  their busways, transit planners can design in station and right-of-way fea-

tures that make bus-to-bus transfers easier than rail-to-bus transfers. This flexibility has its limits however, especially at peripheral stations where supporting feeder and mini-bus service is typically less reliable.

- *BRT's land development impacts are likely to be limited in scale unless accompanied by supportive land use and TOD policies and programs.* Depending on the site, the property value uplift effects accompanying BRT service can be sizeable. They are, as a rule, greater among areas adjacent to higher capacity and more frequent service, as well as areas pre-zoned for higher-density or more intense development. As to the question of whether the addition of a BRT service will promote additional land development or redevelopment activities, the answer depends on the presence of supportive planning and policies and the presence of opportunity sites adjacent to BRT facilities. Where such policies and conditions are present, as in Curitiba (and to a lesser extent, Guangzhou and more recently, Bogotá), BRT's property development stimulus effects can be significant. In places where supportive land use policies are not present or are inconsequential, as in Seoul, and Jakarta, BRT's property development stimulus effects will be reduced, and their benefits will be mostly captured by private developers. The presence of high quality pedestrian public spaces, public facilities and mixed use developments with high connectivity at BRT stations also functions to stimulate additional private investment.

Among the broader lessons that the BRT experience offers for megaproject sponsors and planners are the following.

- *Learning from recognized good practice.* Quito's BRT planners learned from Curitiba's BRT experiences, Bogotá officials learned from both Curitiba and Quito, and BRT planners in Jakarta, Seoul, and Guangzhou all learned from Bogotá. This type of learning chain is rare in the megaproject world. The more normal pattern is for each megaproject sponsor to regard their project as a unique "one-off" and therefore not subject to the accumulated wisdom generated by prior projects. What made Asian cities interested in learning from their Latin American counterparts was the fact that all were facing similar challenges: high rates of population growth, rapidly rising vehicle ownership and traffic congestion levels, poorly-performing municipal finance systems, and pressures to improve public transport service without having the financial resources to do so. These conditions are largely absent from many European and North American cities, which helps explain their collective preference for heavy-rail and light-rail investments over BRT.

- *Focus on accurately estimating demand instead of latching onto prestigious "silver bullet" technologies.* Too often when undertaking major transport investments, public officials and project sponsors latch onto technologies, delivery systems, or route alignments as constituting the "best" solution to a set of problems or challenges. BRT was never presented as the most innovative or prestigious solution to the urban congestion problem. Instead, it was presented as a cost-efficient approach to moving large numbers of transit-dependent commuters to their jobs. This forced planners to focus on the issues that truly mattered. Where did the commuters live and work? How many of them were there? How many would switch from their current mode to buses—hardly an innovative or prestigious technology—if it would cut their travel time in half? Could existing bus designs and technologies be adapted to serve additional riders? By focusing on these readily answerable questions rather than embracing the speculative promise of untested technologies, transportation planners in Latin America and Asia quickly identified BRT as the most cost-effective, flexible, and adaptable answer to their transit investment needs.

- *Flipping the megaproject service quality-price tradeoff on its head.* The usual transportation megaproject proposal promises a small but noticeable improvement in service quality for a big increase in price. BRT flips this logic on its head, offering a large improvement in service quality for a small (or no) increase in price. Put another way, by not having to pay to build an exclusive aerial or underground right-of-way, or debug an unproven new technology, BRT offers travelers a bargain. And if there's one thing that everyone likes, it's a bargain. This has enabled well-planned BRT systems to operate at or near full capacity soon after opening. Sponsors of other transportation megaprojects would be well-advised to learn from this experience. It is also important not to overstate BRT's potential benefits and to put in place procedures able to quickly respond to changes in service quality and demand. As Bogotá's TransMilenio experience suggests, megaprojects can sometimes be too successful, leaving their sponsors unprepared with plans to respond to rising congestion levels and declining service quality perceptions. The BRT experience in Latin America also makes clear the importance of paying attention to "last-mile" mobility needs in addition to trunk line service quality, especially among the least prosperous and most mobility-challenged segments of society.
- *The virtues of managed competition.* The managed competition model offers significant advantages in situations where there are established transit operators with the experience and resources to offer a new transit service. The model also has advantages in situations where new lines or services must be integrated into larger networks. The managed competition model is less advantageous when service operators must also build and finance the underlying physical infrastructure. The BRT experience also offers useful lessons about separating infrastructure planning and construc-

tion activities from day-to-day operational issues. Operators are necessarily more concerned with meeting the day-to-day service needs of their existing customers or patrons and have less incentive to consider the needs of those who are not regular users. Megaproject planners, by contrast, must take in the needs of the entire market, including those who for reasons of distance or income may be unable to take advantage of a proposed project's service benefits.

- *The importance of adaptive and entrepreneurial political leadership.* Technical professions are forward looking by nature. The transportation engineering/planning profession is no different from any other in this regard, which helps explain its historical reluctance, at least in the US and Europe, to embrace BRT, which is often perceived, incorrectly so, as just faster buses. As a result, much of the initial leadership on BRT has come mostly from politicians and elected officials feeling the heat to do something about traffic congestion. Whether it was Jaime Lerner in Curitiba or Enrique Peñalosa in Bogotá or Zhang Guangning in Guangzhou, behind most successful BRT implementation cases was a mayor who was more interested in solving problems than in pursuing the received professional wisdom. Just as politicians and elected officials would do well to emulate professionals' technical problem-solving abilities, professionals would do well to learn how to emulate the abilities of accomplished political leaders to reframe technical and resource challenges in a way that makes them solvable.

NOTES

1. BRTData.org website, accessed December 2021.
2. 2016 Corridor Rankings. Institute for Transportation and Development Policy. https://www.itdp.org/library/standards-and-guides/the-bus-rapid-transit-standard/best-practices-2016/ (retrieved December 2021).
3. Jakarta would eventually build a metro system as well, which opened in 2019.
4. URBS, Curitiba's public transport operating company does not disaggregate its operating costs by service type, making it impossible to estimate a BRT-specific farebox recovery rate.
5. https://en.tempo.co/read/1255795/budget-subsidy-for-jakarta-transportation-up-to-rp6-94tn-agency.
6. BRTData.org.
7. This material is adapted from Far East Mobility's online report, "The inside story of how BRT was implemented in Guangzhou" (https://www.fareast.mobi/en/brt/guangzhou/Guangzhou-BRT-Inside-Story).
8. https://www.itdp.org/2010/03/05/guangzhou-opens-asias-highest-capacity-brt-system/.

REFERENCES

Al-Dubikhi, S. and Mees, P. 2010. Bus rapid transit in Ottawa, 1978 to 2008: Assessing the results. *The Town Planning Review*, 81(4), 407–424.

Baik, Y. J., Kim, D. W., Kwon, H. Y., Kim, Y., and Kim, S. Y. 2018. Impact of the Exclusive median bus lane system on air pollution concentrations in Seoul, Korea. *Journal of Korean Society for Atmospheric Environment*, 344, 542–553.

Bel, G., and Holst, M. 2018. Evaluation of the impact of bus rapid transit on air pollution in Mexico City. *Transport Policy*, 63, 209 220.

Bergman, K., Franklin, J., Gadda, T., and Kozievitch, N. P. 2017. The relationship between timing of development and bus rapid transit. In *Proceedings of the 3rd ACM SIGSPATIAL Workshop on Smart Cities and Urban Analytics*, November, pp. 1–8.

Bocarejo, J. P., Portilla, I., and Pérez, M. A. 2013. Impact of Transmilenio on density, land use, and land value in Bogotá. *Research in Transportation Economics*, 401, 78–86.

BRTDATA.ORG. 2021. Global BRT Data (A public platform to share BRT systems data). Retrieved May 17 2021, from WRI & BRT Across Latitudes and Cultures http://www.brtdata.org/.

Budiati, W., Grigolon, A. B., Brussel, M. J. G., and Rachmat, S. Y. 2018. Determining the potential for Transit Oriented Development along the MRT Jakarta corridor. In *IOP Conference Series: Earth and Environmental Science*, 158(1), 012020. IOP Publishing.

Burgess, C., and Ordiz, S. 2010. Exploring the BRT Systems of Curitiba and Bogotá. Unpublished senior thesis. California Polytechnic State University-San Luis Obispo.

Cain, A., Darido, G., Baltes, M. R., Rodriguez, P., and Barrios, J. C. 2007. Applicability of TransMilenio bus rapid transit system of Bogotá, Colombia, to the United States. *Transportation Research Record*, 20341, 45–54.

Cao, J., Cao, X., Zhang, C., and Huang, X. 2016. The gaps in satisfaction with transit services among BRT, metro, and bus riders: Evidence from Guangzhou. *Journal of Transport and Land Use*, 93, 97–109.

Cervero, R. 1998. *The Transit Metropolis: A Global Inquiry*. Washington, DC: Island Press.

Cervero, R. 2005. Progressive transport and the poor: Bogotá's bold steps forward. *Access*, 27, 24–30

Cervero, R. 2011. *State Roles in Providing Affordable Mass Transport Services for Low-income Residents*. Paris: Organisation for Economic Development/International Transport Forum, Discussion Paper 2011-17.

Cervero, R. 2013. *Bus Rapid Transit BRT: An Efficient and Competitive Mode of Public Transport*. 20th ACEA Scientific Group Advisory Report.

Cervero, R., and Dai, D. 2014. BRT TOD: Leveraging transit oriented development with bus rapid transit investments. *Transport Policy*, 36, 127–138.

Cervero, R., and Kang, C. D. 2011. Bus rapid transit impacts on land uses and land values in Seoul, Korea. *Transport Policy*, 181, 102–116.

Combs, T. S. 2017. Examining changes in travel patterns among lower wealth households after BRT investment in Bogotá, Colombia. *Journal of Transport Geography*, 60, 11–20.

Currie, G. 2006. Bus transit oriented development: strengths and weaknesses relative to rail. *Journal of Public Transportation*, 9(4), 1–21.

Delgado, H. and Uniman, D. 2011. Analysis de distribucion de impacts: costs y beneficios – application Metrobus – Line 3, Centro de Transporte Sustentable de Mesico. Presented at the VII Sustainable Transport Congress, Mexico City.

Delmelle, E. C., and Casas, I. 2012. Evaluating the spatial equity of bus rapid transit-based accessibility patterns in a developing country: The case of Cali, Colombia. *Transport Policy*, 20, 36–46.

Deng, T. and Nelson, J. D. 2011. Recent Developments in Bus Rapid Transit: A review of the literature. *Transport Reviews*, 31(1), 69–96.

Duarte, F., and Ultramari, C. 2012. Making public transport and housing match: Accomplishments and failures of Curitba's BRT. *Journal of Urban Planning and Development*, 1382, 183–194.

Ernst, J. P. 2005. Initiating bus rapid transit in Jakarta, Indonesia. *Transportation Research Record*, 19031, 20–26.

Fjellstrom, K. 2010. Bus rapid transit in China. *Built Environment*, 363, 363–374.

Gaduh, A., Gracner, T., and Rothenberg, A D. 2017. Improving mobility in developing country cities: Evaluating bus rapid transit and other policies in Jakarta. Unpublished paper. Rand Corporation.

Gilbert, A. 2008. Bus rapid transit: Is Transmilenio a miracle cure? *Transport Reviews*, 28(4), 439–467.

Guzman, L. A., Enríquez, H. D., and Hessel, P. 2021. BRT system in Bogotá and urban effects: More residential land premiums? *Research in Transportation Economics*, 101039.

Gwilliam, K. 2002. *Cities on the Move*. Washington, DC: The International Bank for Reconstruction and Development/The World Bank, A World Bank Transport Strategy Review.

Hardt, C., and Hardt, L. 2009. Les interactions entre l'aménagement urbain et la planification des transports a Curitiba Brésil. In Y. Diab (ed.), *La ville durable: Urgences et utopies*. L'Ecole des Ingénieurs de la Ville de Paris, Paris, pp. 123–137 [in French].

Hidalgo, D., and Carrigan, A. 2010. BRT in Latin America high capacity and performance, rapid implementation and low cost. *Built Environment*, 363, 283–297.

Hidalgo, D. and Graftieaux, P. 2008. Bus rapid transit systems in Latin America and Asia: Results and difficulties in 11 cities. *Transportation Research Record*, 20721, 77–88.

Hidalgo, D., and Gutiérrez, L. 2013. BRT and BHLS around the world: Explosive growth, large positive impacts and many issues outstanding. *Research in Transportation Economics*, 391, 8–13.

Hidalgo, D., Pereira, L., Estupiñán, N., and Jiménez, P. L. 2013. TransMilenio BRT system in Bogotá, high performance and positive impact—main results of an ex-post evaluation. *Research in Transportation Economics*, 391, 133–138.

Hidalgo, D., and Yepes, T. 2005. January. Are bus rapid transit systems effective in poverty reduction? Experience of Bogotá's TransMilenio and lessons for other cities. In *84th TRB Annual Meeting*, CD-ROM.

Hodgson, P., Potter, S., Warren, J., and Gillingwater, D. 2013. Can bus really be the new tram? *Research in Transportation Economics*, 391, 158–166.

Hook, W. 2005. Institutional and regulatory options for BRT in developing countries: Lessons from international experiences. *Transportation Research Record*, 1939, 184–191.

Ingvardson, J. B., and Nielsen, O. A. 2018. Effects of new bus and rail rapid transit systems—an international review. *Transport Reviews*, 381, 96–116.

ITP Integrated Transport Planning Ltd and IBIS Transport Consultants Ltd. 2009. Lagos BRT-Lite: Africa's first Bus Rapid Transit scheme: Scheme evaluation and summary report.

ITDP. 2017. *The BRT Planning Guide* available online at: https://www.itdp.org/2017/11/16/the-brt-planning-guide/.

Jaramillo, C., Lizárraga, C., and Grindlay, A. 2012. Spatial disparity in transport social needs and public transport provision in Santiago de Cali, Colombia. *Journal of Transport Geography*, 2, 340–357.

Jaramillo, A. G., Philips, I., and Lucas, K. 2019. Social impact assessment: The case of Bus Rapid Transit in the city of Quito, Ecuador. In K. Lucas, K. Martens, F. Di Ciommo and A. Dupont-Kieffer (eds), *Measuring Transport Equity* (pp. 217–229). Elsevier.

Jun, M. J. 2012. Redistributive effects of bus rapid transit BRT on development patterns and property values in Seoul, Korea. *Transport Policy*, 191, 85–92.

Jun, M. J., Choi, K., Yu, J. W., and Chung, W. 2015. Bus patronage change after sustainable bus reform: A nested logit approach with the case of Seoul. *International Journal of Sustainable Transportation*, 97, 520–528.

Kang, C. D. 2010. The impact of bus rapid transit on location choice of creative industries and employment density in Seoul, Korea. *International Journal of Urban Sciences*, 142, 123–151.

Kumar, A., Zimmerman, S., and Agarwal, O. P. 2012. *International Experience in Bus Rapid Transit Implementation: Synthesis of Lessons Learned from Lagos, Johannesburg, Jakarta, Delhi, and Ahmedabad*. The World Bank.

Levinson, H. S., Zimmerman, S., Clinger, J., and Gast, J. 2003. Bus rapid transit: Synthesis of case studies. *Transportation Research Record*, 18411, 1–11.

Lindau, L. A., Hidalgo, D., and Facchini, D. 2010. Curitiba, the cradle of bus rapid transit. *Built Environment*, 363, 274–282.

Nugroho, S. B., Fujiwara, A., and Zhang, J. 2010. The influence of BRT on the ambient PM10 concentration at roadside sites of Trans Jakarta Corridors. *Procedia Environmental Sciences*, 2, 914–924.

Perdomo Calvo, J. A., Mendoza, C. A., Baquero-Ruiz, A. F., and Mendieta-Lopez, J. C. 2007. Study of the effect of the transmilenio mass transit project on the value of properties in Bogotá, Colombia. Lincoln Institute of Land Policy Working Paper No. WP07CA1.

Rathwell, S., and Schijns, S. 2002. Ottawa and Brisbane: Comparing a mature busway system with its state-of-the-art progeny. *Journal of Public Transportation*, 52, 8.

Rodríguez, D. A. 2022. Accessibility, mobility, and transportation innovations in Latin America and the Caribbean: Successes and areas for improvement. In *The Routledge Handbook of Urban Studies in Latin America and the Caribbean* (pp. 517–534). Routledge.

Rodríguez, D. A., and Kang, C. D. 2020. A typology of the built environment around rail stops in the global transit-oriented city of Seoul, Korea. *Cities*, 100, 102663. https://doi.org/10.1016/j.cities.2020.102663.

Rodríguez, D. A., and Mojica, C. H. 2009. Capitalization of BRT network expansions effects into prices of non-expansion areas. *Transportation Research Part A: Policy and Practice*, 435, 560–571.

Rodriquez, D. A., and Targa, F. 2004. Value of accessibility to Bogotá's bus rapid transit system. *Transport Reviews*, 245, 587–610.

Rodriguez, D. A., and Vergel-Tovar, C. E. 2018. Urban development around bus rapid transit stops in seven cities in Latin-America. *Journal of Urbanism: International Research on Placemaking and Urban Sustainability*, 112, 175–201.

Rodriguez, D. A., Vergel-Tovar, E., and Camargo, W. F. 2016. Land development impacts of BRT in a sample of stops in Quito and Bogotá. *Transport Policy*, 51, 4–14.

Rusadhi, E. P. 2019. The impact of Transjakarta Bus Rapid Transit on land value of Dki Jakarta province subdistricts. *Plano Madani* 8(2), 196–204.

Salehi, F., Karbassi, A. R., and Khashaypoor, M. 2016. Environmental impact assessment of bus rapid transit BRT in the Metropolitan City of Tehran. *International Journal of Human Capital in Urban Management*, 11, 47–56.

Salon, D., Wu, J., and Shewmake, S. 2014. Impact of bus rapid transit and metro rail on property values in Guangzhou, China. *Transportation Research Record*, 24521, 36–45.

Scholl, L., Bouillon, C. P., Oviedo, D., Corsetto, L., and Jansson, M. 2016. *Urban Transport and Poverty: Mobility and Accessibility Effects of IDB-supported BRT Systems in Cali and Lima*. Inter-American Development Bank.

Stokenberga, A. 2014. Does bus rapid transit influence urban land development and property values? A review of the literature. *Transport Reviews*, 343, 276–296.

Sun, S. N., Her, J., Lee, S. Y., and Lee, J. S. 2017. Meso-scale urban form elements for bus transit-oriented development: Evidence from Seoul, Republic of Korea. *Sustainability*, 99, 1516.

Suzuki, H., Cervero, R., and Iuchi, K. 2013. *Transforming Cities with Transit: Transit and Land-use Integration for Sustainable Urban Development*. Washington, DC: World Bank.

Suzuki, H., Murakami, J., Tamayose, B. C., and Hong, Y. 2015. *Financing Transit-Oriented Development with Land Values: Adapting Land Value Capture in Developing Countries*. Urban development series. Washington, DC: World Bank.

Tsivanidis, N. 2019. Evaluating the impact of urban transit infrastructure: Evidence from Bogotá's TransMilenio. Unpublished manuscript.

Turbay, A. L., Pereira, R. H., and Firmino, R. 2022. The equity implications of TOD in Curitiba. Unpublished paper. Pontificia Universidade Católica do Paraná, Brazil.

Venter, C., Jennings, G., Hidalgo, D., and Valderrama Pineda, A. F. 2018. The equity impacts of bus rapid transit: A review of the evidence and implications for sustainable transport. *International Journal of Sustainable Transportation*, 12(2), 140–152.

Vergel-Tovar, C. E. 2016. Examining the reciprocal relationship between bus rapid transit and the built environment in Latin America. (PhD Doctoral Dissertation), University of North Carolina at Chapel Hill, Chapel Hill, North Carolina, United States. Retrieved from https://cdr.lib.unc.edu/concern/dissertations/rr171x488.

Vergel-Tovar, C. E. 2019. ¿Es la densidad suficiente? Análisis de la relación entre la densidad poblacional y la demanda de pasajeros en los sistemas de transporte público masivo tipo BRT (Bus Rapid Transit) en Curitiba, Quito y Bogotá. *Medio Ambiente y Urbanizacion*, 90(1), 1–22.

Vergel-Tovar, C. E. 2021. Sustainable transit and land use in Latin America and the Caribbean: A review of recent developments and research findings. In J. Cao, J. Yang and C. Ding (eds.), *Advances in Land-use Planning from the Perspective of the Implications for Accessibility and Travel Behavior* (Vol. 9): Elsevier.

Vergel-Tovar, C. E. 2022. Sustainable transit and land use in Latin America and the Caribbean: A review of recent developments and research findings. *Journal:*

Advances in Transport Policy and Planning Urban Transport and Land Use Planning: A Synthesis of Global Knowledge, 29–73.

Vergel-Tovar, C. E., and Camargo, W. 2019. Urban development impacts of bus rapid transit in Colombia: Challenges and opportunities. In *Developing Bus Rapid Transit*. Edward Elgar Publishing.

Vergel-Tovar, C. E., and Rodriguez, D. A. 2018. The ridership performance of the built environment for BRT systems: Evidence from Latin America. *Journal of Transport Geography*, 73, 172–184.

Vergel-Tovar, C. E., & Rodriguez, D. A. 2022. Bus rapid transit impacts on land uses and development over time in Bogotá and Quito. *Journal of Transport and Land Use*, 15(1), 425–462. https://doi.org/10.5198/jtlu.2022.1888.

Vincent, W., Delmont, E., and Hughes, C. 2012. *Energy and Environmental Impacts of BRT in APEC Economies*. Breakthrough Technologies Institute.

Wright, L. 2011. Bus rapid transit: a review of recent advances. In H. Dimitriou and R. Gakenheimer (eds.), *Urban Transport in the Developing World: A Handbook of Policy and Practice*, Cheltenham, UK: Edward Elgar, pp. 421–455.

Zhang, M., and Yen, B. T. 2020. The impact of Bus Rapid Transit (BRT) on land and property values: A meta-analysis. *Land Use Policy*, 96, 104684.

8. A tunnel beneath Seattle: the megaproject to replace the Alaskan Way Viaduct

Molly Riddle and Jan Whittington

ABBREVIATIONS USED IN THIS CHAPTER

AWT	Alaskan Way Tunnel (aka SR 99 Tunnel)
AWV	Alaskan Way Viaduct
AWVRP	Alaskan Way Viaduct Replacement Program
CWC	Central Waterfront Committee
CWPC	Central Waterfront Partnerships Committee
OWPC	Seattle Office of Waterfront and Civic Projects
EIS	Environmental Impact Statement
FHWA	Federal Highway Administration
RFQ/RFP	Request for Qualifications/Request for Proposals
SR 99	State Route 99 Tunnel (aka Alaskan Way Tunnel)
STP	Seattle Tunnel Partners
TBM	Tunnel Boring Machine (i.e., "Bertha")
WSDOT	Washington State Department of Transportation

To be delivered on time and on budget, it is not enough for a megaproject to be well-managed. It must also be planned with governance structures that allow the project to emerge unscathed from a worst-case scenario. Seattle's Alaskan Way Viaduct Replacement Program, a 15-year project to replace an earthquake-damaged elevated highway running along Seattle's downtown waterfront with a single deep-bore tunnel, encountered such a scenario when about a tenth of the way into its journey, Bertha, the one-of-a-kind tunneling machine built for this project, ground to a halt.

Whereas most roadway and transit tunnels are of the double-bore variety, to save time and money, project planners in Washington State had chosen to dig a single-bore tunnel instead. This required manufacturing what would be the world's biggest, most powerful, and most expensive tunnel boring machine, or TBM. Bertha, the 328-foot long, 7,000 ton earth pressure balance TBM built by Hitachi Zosen USA, Ltd., was 57.4 feet wide, with a 2,000 ton cutter driving unit (Basetti 2020) (see Figure 8.1). In the hands of the tunnel contractor for the project, Seattle Tunnel Partners (STP, a joint venture between Tutor Perini Corp. and Dragados USA, Inc.), the TBM was meant to be run almost continuously for 9,270 feet (2,825 meters) from July 2013 to June 2014. Like all machines of its kind, however, its successful design and use ultimately depended on the ability of its operators to scrape away and pull through any and all materials that lay in the path of the TBM's massive cutterhead. Unfortunately, just six months after beginning its journey, Bertha stopped.

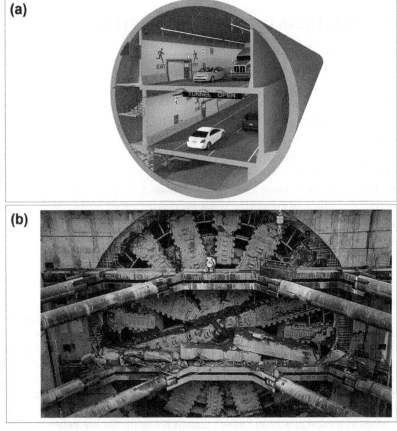

Source: WSDOT.

Figure 8.1   *(a) Cross-section of SR 99 Tunnel when completed; (b) Bertha breaks through to destination pit in South Lake Union*

Why Bertha stopped and who is responsible for the costs incurred to repair and resume operations is a hotly contested matter. At the time of writing (2021), the public cost of the overall program is $3.35 billion, which is 7 percent above the original $3.1 billion budget approved by voters in 2011, while the tunnel contract, budgeted for STP at $1.35 billion, rose 10 percent to $1.5 billion as contingencies, incentives, and taxes were paid. The actual cost to repair and reinstall Bertha's equipment is not publicly known, though claims have been made by STP against the Washington State Department of Transportation (WSDOT) and against their insurers for an additional $480 million. As these claims make their way through the Appellate and Supreme Courts of the State of Washington, all eyes are focused on the events of those days as Bertha slowed to a stop, the evidence of the cause of Bertha's decline, and the financial risks and protections afforded to each of the parties in the contracts for the project.

The Alaskan Way Tunnel opened to the public in February 2019, three years later than planned and 18 years after the earthquake that rendered the Alaskan Way Viaduct vulnerable to structural failure. This wasn't quite the 25 years it took to replace the eastern span of the San Francisco–Oakland Bay Bridge, another key transportation link damaged by an earthquake (Trapenberg-Frick 2016). Nor was this the 25 years spent on Boston's Big Dig, another tunnel built to bury the traffic from an aging elevated highway (Sigmund 2007). Still, Bertha's stall once again raised concern for the capacity of America's most productive urban centers to deliver infrastructure megaprojects.

This chapter reviews what went right and wrong with the centerpiece of the Alaskan Way Viaduct Replacement Program, the Alaskan Way Tunnel (Table 8.1). Its purpose is not to cast blame or responsibility—the events that hobbled Bertha could have happened in any major digging project anywhere in the world—but how the contractors and project managers proceeded in this case says a lot about the hubris that people attach to megaprojects, the extent to which conventional notions of megaproject success are tied to contestable outcomes, and about contemporary megaproject planning and construction practices in a democratic setting.

Before we continue, a few notes on facility and agency names. The Alaskan Way Tunnel, like the Alaskan Way Viaduct it replaced, is an integral part of Washington State Route 99 (SR 99), a multi-lane state highway which stretches from Tacoma in the south to Everett in the north. Seattleites mostly refer to the tunnel as the Alaskan Way Tunnel (AWT), occasionally even slipping the word Viaduct into the mix, but its official name is the SR 99 Tunnel, and we use both names throughout this chapter.

The ten-year planning process that culminated in the 2011 approval of the Alaskan Way Tunnel occurred in two stages. The first, which ran from 2001 to 2007 and was administered by the Washington State Department

Table 8.1   *Alaskan Way Tunnel in brief*

Description	The Alaskan Way Tunnel (aka SR 99 Tunnel) is a 2.3 mile single-bore tunnel along Seattle's waterfront. Built to replace an aging elevated highway damaged in a 2001 earthquake, the Alaskan Way Tunnel has opened up substantial land for private development and a greater program of public realm improvements.
Lead sponsor(s)	Washington State Department of Transportation, City of Seattle, and Port Authority of Seattle
Primary rationale	Replace an obsolete and vulnerable elevated highway with a safer surface or underground facility.
Regulatory/funding approval given in	2011 (after 10 years of planning and environmental review)
Primary funding sources	Federal and state government grants and revenue bonds
Construction started	2011 Tunnel; 2007 Program
Construction completed	2019 Tunnel; 2021 Program
Schedule overrun	3 years (58%) Tunnel; 3.5 years (56%) Program
Initial Development Budget	$1.35 billion Tunnel; $3.1 billion Program
Final Development Cost	$1.5 billion Tunnel; $3.35 billion Program
Cost overrun	$150 million (10%) Tunnel; $250 million (7%) Program
Reasons for overruns	Bertha, the world's largest tunnel boring machine (TBM) damaged during operations in December 2013, took three years to repair and resume tunneling.
Principal takeaways	(1) Even experienced project planners and managers should anticipate unexpected bottlenecks with adequate contingency funding and schedules. (2) The contract and enforcing judicial system matter. (3) Transportation investments can be structured to generate opportunities for creative public realm/private development projects.

of Transportation, generated two Viaduct replacement schemes that were rejected by Seattle voters, and was succeeded by the "Partnership Process," a bottom-up, stakeholder-based decision-making process. The Partnership Process, which ran from 2008 to 2011, succeeded in gaining voter and federal agency approval for the single-bore Alaskan Way Tunnel as the central feature of the larger Alaskan Way Viaduct Replacement Program (AWVRP), which included improvements to Seattle's central waterfront.

In many ways, approval could have marked the beginning of the program, which then continued for another 10 years of design and construction and centered on Bertha's progress as it carved out the new Alaskan Way Tunnel under downtown Seattle. As noted, this program was managed by WSDOT, and the contractor for the tunnel was STP, operating the TBM created by Hitachi Zosen USA, Ltd.

For the planning and redevelopment of Seattle's waterfront, there have been three agencies in charge. The first was the Central Waterfront Partnerships Committee (CWPC), a 37-member stakeholder group established in 2009 to advise Seattle's Mayor and City Council on how best to redevelop Seattle's central waterfront area. This was superseded in 2011 by the Central Waterfront Committee (CWC), which was established to oversee the preparation of a waterfront redevelopment plan. This was followed in 2014 by the Office of Waterfront and Civic Projects (OWCP), a multi-agency working group to implement the waterfront redevelopment plan. Together with the Friends of the Seattle Waterfront, a citizen advocacy group, the OWCP operated an official information hub for all waterfront planning, management and redevelopment matters (Waterfront Seattle.org).

GETTING TO NO, THEN YES

A Seismically Vulnerable Highway

Seattle sits midway along the Cascadia Subduction Zone, a 1,000 km long "megathrust" fault that extends from Northern Vancouver Island to California's Cape Mendocino and separates the Juan de Fuca and North America tectonic plates. Earthquakes along the Cascadia Subduction Zone are not as frequent as they are along California's well-known San Andreas Fault—the last severe Cascadia Zone earthquake occurred in 1700—but they can be powerful, and one was thought to be past due when the 6.8-magnitude Nisqually Earthquake occurred at 10:54 local time on the morning of February 28, 2001.[1] With its epicenter 50 miles southwest of downtown Seattle, the earthquake lasted for 40 seconds; long enough, despite its moderate magnitude, to significantly damage many of downtown Seattle's unreinforced masonry buildings as well as the air traffic control tower at Seattle–Tacoma International Airport.

The Alaskan Way Viaduct, a 2.2 mile (3.5 km) elevated highway set on a stretch of Seattle's waterfront land prone to liquefaction, was damaged by the Nisqually Earthquake. Completed in 1959, the reinforced concrete structure was split between two levels, an upper level that carried northbound traffic and a lower level that carried southbound traffic. Built above and parallel to the protective Elliott Bay Seawall on the eastern shores of Puget Sound, the Viaduct was an integral part of Washington State Route 99, and regularly carried in excess of 100,000 vehicles per day, 40,000 more than its original design capacity. Concerned that the earthquake might have done more than surface damage, WSDOT engineers shut down the Viaduct for several months to make a more thorough structural inspection and to undertake necessary repairs (Ott 2011).[2]

What really concerned WSDOT engineers about the Viaduct was its design and construction similarity to the Cypress Street Viaduct on the Nimitz Freeway in Oakland, which had catastrophically collapsed during the 6.9-magnitude Loma Prieta Earthquake in 1989, taking 42 lives. In the 1990s, the Cascadia Subduction Zone became known for its periodic magnitude 9 megaquakes (e.g., Schulz 2015; Whittington 2017), and studies comparing the Viaduct to the Nimitz showed that the facility was not up to modern standards. In 2001, the civil engineering firm T.Y. Lin reviewed assessments of the Viaduct's seismic vulnerabilities and found that by 2021 the structure would reach a 1-in-10 chance of being shut down by a seismic event (T.Y. Lin 2001, p. 20).

After the earthquake, the Viaduct shifted four more times (Ott 2011). WSDOT installed structural reinforcements along the Viaduct's columns and imposed vehicle weight restrictions. T.Y. Lin's 2001 structural review warned that the earthquake had weakened connections between the columns and the roadway decks. Additionally, the aging concrete had cracked and the structure had shifted to the east, indicating problems with the soils around the Viaduct's foundations. The study found evidence of soil liquefaction during the earthquake and warned that additional liquefaction was likely to occur during future earthquakes. The City and WSDOT's best hazard mitigation options, the report concluded, were to entirely rebuild or replace the Viaduct and the adjacent Elliott Bay Seawall.

Seattleites themselves were ambivalent about the Viaduct's future. On the one hand, it afforded northbound drivers fantastic views of the Olympic Mountains and Puget Sound to the west and downtown Seattle to the east. It was also a handy alternative route for through-bound drivers when Interstate 5, located 1/3-mile to the east, was gridlocked. On the other hand, the Viaduct was a visual and physical wall, cutting off Seattle's downtown from its active waterfront. Once celebrated, the Viaduct had become a hazard and a nuisance.

A Top-down Planning Process Fails with Voters

Recognizing the critical role the Viaduct had played in moving people and goods into, out of, and through downtown Seattle, WSDOT partnered with the City of Seattle and the US Department of Transportation Federal Highway Administration (FHWA) in mid-2001 to begin a multi-year process to identify potential Viaduct replacement schemes (WSDOT et al. 2004) (see Table 8.2).

Table 8.2   *Alaskan Way Tunnel timeline*

1959	The final section of the elevated Alaska Way Viaduct highway is completed.
February 2001	The 6.8 magnitude Nisqually Earthquake, with its epicenter 50 miles southwest of Seattle, damages the Viaduct and the adjacent Elliott Bay Seawall. Stopgap repairs cost $14.5 million.
2003–2006	After considering five Viaduct replacement schemes, a planning process led by the Washington State Department of Transportation (WSDOT) recommends two preferred alternatives: a new elevated structure and a cut-and-cover tunnel alternative.
December 2006	Washington Governor Christine Gregoire calls for a public vote on the two Viaduct replacement options.
March 2007	Seattle voters reject both Viaduct replacement options by significant margins. Washington Governor Gregoire and Seattle Mayor Greg Nickels announce they will try again with a more open and less top-down planning process. WSDOT construction begins on projects in the program that are not dependent on the form of Viaduct replacement.
2008–2009	Officials in Seattle, King County and Washington State establish the Partnership Process, a stakeholder-based planning process to identify additional Viaduct replacement options.
December 2008	The Partnership Process offered three solutions—surface roads with transit, a new viaduct, or a twin bored tunnel—but timely improvements in tunneling opened the option of a single bored tunnel. To make the tunnel fit within available funds, the Elliott Bay Seawall reconstruction was severed from the Viaduct Replacement Program.
January 2009	Governor Gregoire, King County Executive Ron Sims, Seattle Mayor Greg Nickels, and Port of Seattle CEO Tay Yoshitani signed an agreement of support for the single-bore tunnel option.
September 2009	Anticipating that the single-bore tunnel option will be approved, the WSDOT begins an RFQ/RFP process that culminates in selecting the Seattle Tunnel Partnership (STP) as the design-build tunnel contractor at a cost of $1.1 billion.
September 2010	The Seattle Planning Department hires landscape architecture firm James Corner Field Operations to prepare a public realm-oriented redevelopment plan for the Central Waterfront area, assuming the Viaduct is demolished and replaced with a tunnel.
October 2010	Despite the anti-tunnel platform of newly elected Seattle Mayor Michael McGinn, the Seattle City Council President signs the Draft Environmental Impact Statement (EIS), endorsing the single-bore tunnel option.
August 2011	Seattle voters approve the single-bore tunnel option for a total estimated program cost of $3.1 billion.
September 2011	The Final EIS is approved for the single-bore tunnel alternative, clearing the way for the Federal Highway Administration to approve its construction.
July 2012	Field Operations delivers its "Concept Design" plan for the central waterfront area. The Mayor and Seattle City Council formally adopt the plan in August 2012.
June 2013	Bertha, a huge tunnel boring machine manufactured by Japan's Hitachi Zosen USA, Ltd. begins tunneling operations from a portal area south of downtown Seattle.

December 2013	With less than 10 percent of its tunneling completed, Bertha grounds to a halt, inspection reveals damaged main bearings, and a two-year period of tunnel work stoppage and repair begins.
December 2015	Finally repaired, Bertha resumes tunneling, only to be sidelined for 3 months by a sinkhole.
April 2016	Continuous drilling resumes.
October 2016	Bertha hits the halfway point in its tunnel-drilling operations.
April 2017	Bertha emerges at the tunnel's northern portal near South Lake Union, having completed its tunneling three years behind the contracted schedule.
January 2018	Extraction of Bertha is complete, and tunnel testing and commissioning continues.
February 2019	With construction complete, the Alaska Way/SR 99 Tunnel opens to traffic three years behind schedule, and demolition begins on the old elevated viaduct structure.
November 2019	Tolling begins on the SR 99 Tunnel.

Managed by WSDOT, this process began by generating a series of Viaduct and Elliott Bay Seawall replacement alternatives. Initially, 76 viaduct and seven seawall replacement concepts were proposed; over two years these were reduced to five concepts (Figure 8.2), estimated to cost between $2.5 and $4.1 billion, published in the 2004 Draft Environmental Impact Statement (EIS) (WSDOT et al. 2004, pp. 3–28). Two of the concepts proposed replacement of the viaduct with a similar elevated structure. Another two were cut-and-cover tunnel concepts. A surface alternative proposed replacement of the Viaduct with a six-lane at-grade roadway. Each alternative included replacement of the Elliott Bay Seawall, as either a separate structure or the western wall of a new tunnel.

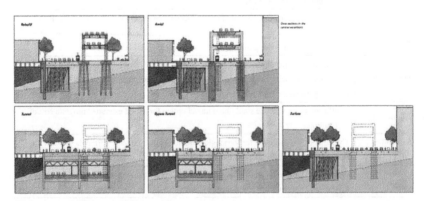

Source: WSDOT et al. (2004, p. 14).

Figure 8.2   *Five initial Alaskan Way Viaduct replacement program conceptual alternatives*

By the time of the release of the draft EIS, the program had attracted considerable attention from organizations outside of WSDOT. The People's Waterfront Coalition, for example, called for replacing the Viaduct with surface street and transit improvements (Enlow 2004). In an argument with qualities similar to San Francisco's successful replacement of the elevated Embarcadero Freeway with surface streets, municipal light rail, and streetcar lines, the People's Waterfront Coalition explained that by building a waterfront boulevard with a transit line down its median, Seattle could regain its waterfront, reduce traffic, and encourage people to move downtown to live, thus reducing sprawl. This was followed by a report from the Congress for New Urbanism which, like the People's Waterfront Coalition, argued in favor of the removal of the elevated freeway and opening of the space, much as had occurred in San Francisco.

Instead, WSDOT planners consolidated the existing five alternatives down to two, a cut-and-cover tunnel and elevated structure and published these preferences in their July 2006 Supplemental Draft EIS (WSDOT et al. 2006, pp. 40–45). The tunnel, estimated to cost $3.0 to $4.3 billion, would replace the viaduct with a stacked, three-lane tunnel, partially adjacent to the Elliott Bay coastline, capped with a ground-level lid structure. The alternative elevated structure, estimated to cost $2.0 to $2.9 billion, would replace the viaduct with a similar stacked, three-lane highway, widened in the central section to ease peak period traffic congestion and provide wide shoulders for service operations. Both alternatives included replacement of the seawall as well as surface-level adjustments to Alaskan Way and adjacent roadways, along with additional plans of work, such as enhanced multi-modal transportation connections and transit improvements. The tunnel was the FHWA's and Seattle City Council's preferred alternative. The question was how to finance this more costly structure.

In September 2006, an Expert Review Panel, called for by Washington State Governor Christine Gregoire, released its independent review of the AWVRP's finance and implementation plans, concluding that the plans needed some adjustment but were "fundamentally sound and achievable" (WSDOT 2006, p. 3). In order to garner public support and political momentum for the next phase of development, Governor Gregoire called for a public vote on the proposed designs. The Seattle City Council scheduled a referendum for March 13, 2007, for residents to issue their preference for the elevated structure or a slightly revised surface-tunnel hybrid (CSEEC 2007).

The 2007 voting ballot presented each option separately, not in comparison to one another. Voter information pamphlets presented myriad pros and cons for each design. The tunnel option was lauded for its seismic safety features, cost efficiency (relative to "mined tunnels"), transit improvements, and land use benefits anticipated from daylighting land adjacent to the waterfront

(CSEEC 2007, pp. 4–5). Arguments against the tunnel cited its expense and forewarned of cost overruns, as well as construction delays, unexamined flood risks, and "unscrupulous" waterfront land grabs. The elevated structure alternative was championed for its use of known construction techniques, its modern and capacious design, and its low cost—indicated as $2.8 billion, which was exactly the amount that had been reserved by the state to pay for the Viaduct's replacement. The opposition to the elevated structure argued it was time for Seattle to evolve past relying on big, noisy, obstructive highways that severed the connection between the waterfront and downtown.

What neither Governor Gregoire nor the Seattle City Council anticipated was that the city's voters, tired of five years of back and forth over the Viaduct, would reject both alternatives: 57 percent of those who went to the polls rejected the elevated structure and a whopping 70 percent rejected the tunnel.

Trying Again, This Time with a More Inclusive Process

For students of history, this result was not entirely unexpected: Seattle voters had a long and quirky history of rejecting and then later approving transportation funding proposals (Crowley 2002). A city-sponsored proposal to build a 47-mile regional rapid rail system introduced in the 1960s was defeated twice at the ballot box, the first time in 1968, and a second time in 1970. In 1972, Seattle voters approved a 0.3 percent sales tax increase to build a rail transit line, but then turned around and rejected the proposed right-of-way. In 1995, voters rejected a $6.7 billion plan to create a three-county transit system offering integrated commuter rail, light rail, and express bus service. One year later, they approved a $3.9 billion proposal for building a light-rail line connecting the University of Washington through downtown Seattle to SeaTac Airport. In 1997, Seattle voters approved a citizen-sponsored proposal to extend Seattle's one-mile monorail system out to the city's northern and southernmost neighborhoods. When a plan to finance the $2 billion project with a 50-year bond showed costs rising by another $9 billion in interest, residents used the referendum process to defeat the project at the polls.

In 2007, faced with resounding voter disapproval of the two viaduct replacement alternatives, Governor Gregoire, King County Executive Ron Sims and Seattle Mayor Greg Nickels regrouped. First, they issued a letter commencing "Moving Forward" projects—a slate of improvements already permitted and funded for the north and south ends of the Alaskan Way Viaduct, required for any successful replacement of the Viaduct and waterfront (WSDOT et al. 2010, p. 2). Next, WSDOT officials, together with their counterparts from King County and Seattle, signed a memorandum of agreement outlining their support for undertaking a more collaborative, bottom-up planning process.

This new and more inclusive "Partnership Process" officially launched on July 16, 2008. Under this process, an independent project management team guided design development with input from WSDOT, Seattle Department of Transportation, King County Department of Transportation leadership and management teams, and a 29-member Stakeholder Advisory Committee comprising business and nonprofit representatives interested in the effects of viaduct replacement on the economy, neighborhood character, and other public benefits (WSDOT et al. 2010, p. 3). They took a step back and broadened the study area, looking beyond the SR 99 corridor toward the city as a whole (WSDOT et al. 2011, p. 50). And they adopted new guiding principles to shape the process: "(i) improving public safety; (ii) providing for the efficient movement of people and goods; (iii) improving the city, regional, port, and state economies; (iv) enhancing Seattle's waterfront, downtown, and adjacent neighborhoods as places for people; (v) being fiscally responsible; and (vi) improving the health of the environment" (WSDOT et al. 2010, p. 3). Regarding finances, however, the parties were reluctant to agree to designs that would exceed the existing $2.8 billion in state funds secured from Washington State's 2005 Transportation Partnership Program expenditure package (RCW 48.68.290) and 2006 Washington Legislature's Engrossed Substitute Senate Bill 6103.

The Partnership Process catalyzed a second round of design development that lasted four years (2008–2011) and ultimately produced a single, widely-supported solution for Viaduct replacement. First, 170 building blocks were combined to create eight hypothetical designs, each of which reflected mixed reliance upon SR 99 as a limited-access facility (WSDOT et al. 2009, pp. 2–3). Elements from the best-performing scenarios were chosen for further study and reconstituted into three "Hybrid Scenarios": an I-5, surface, and transit hybrid; an elevated bypass hybrid (i.e., Viaduct); and a twin bored tunnel hybrid. The first two scenarios, each estimated to cost $3.5 billion, were similar to those voted down in 2007, albeit with better integration of Seattle-wide transportation improvements. The third scenario, a proposed $4.7 billion investment, would replace the viaduct with a double-bore bypass tunnel cutting diagonally beneath the city (pp. 70–72). The independent project management team and AWVRP leadership recommended the bored-tunnel for its capacity to achieve mobility objectives during and after construction and relieve the waterfront of physical obstructions. They also called for investigation into new construction techniques to see if a single-bored tunnel could provide cost savings and a more efficient timeline; no doubt, managers recalled how the 2007 voter pamphlet lambasted tunneling for its cost overruns.

Four themes identified during the Partnership Process influenced the choice of the bored tunnel design. Stakeholders unanimously agreed the state's financial contribution should be limited to $2.8 billion and the sources of any additional required funding had to be identified prior to design approval (WSDOT et al. 2011, p. 51). Additionally, all agreed the design should revive the connection between downtown and the central waterfront. Lastly, stakeholders concerned about maintaining uninterrupted freight and goods transport through Seattle pressured leadership to pursue a high-capacity tunnel bypass route. Leadership responded by convening independent tunnel experts to comment on tunnel mining techniques and options for reducing the cost of bored-tunnel construction.

The design that emerged, championed by the Seattle Chamber of Commerce, featured a large-diameter, single-bore, stacked tunnel. Influenced by the use of ever-larger TBMs for projects in Asia and Europe, evaluations of construction methods suggested that a single-bored tunnel option could be constructed on a shorter timeline than other options—5.5 years as opposed to 8.75 or 10 years for a conventional double-bored tunnel—and for less money than previously reported. Set inland, the bored tunnel design also appeared to create the possibility of separating the Seawall and a whole suite of waterfront improvements from Viaduct replacement. Decisively, from this point onward, the repair of the Elliott Bay Seawall was removed from the Viaduct replacement scope of work and made the responsibility of the City of Seattle. In one technically and politically savvy stroke, published cost estimates for Viaduct replacement fell significantly, the State was relieved of a significant financial burden, and the City received greater control over its central waterfront redevelopment.

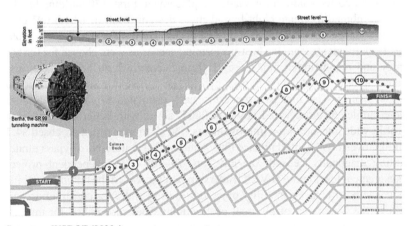

Source: WSDOT (2020c).

Figure 8.3   *Alaskan Way Tunnel route*

Absent the Elliott Bay Seawall, the AWVRP with a single-bore tunnel design was estimated to cost approximately $3.1 billion (WSDOT et al. 2010, p. 15). On January 13, 2009, Washington State, King County and the City of Seattle entered into a letter of agreement laying the groundwork for the next phase of AWVRP development. The Port of Seattle agreed to establish a funding program to supplement the state's $2.8 billion contribution and help fill the gap in project financing (WSDOT et al. 2011, p. 46). And on October 19, 2009, the Seattle City Council voted 9:0 in favor of Ordinance 123133, declaring the single-bore tunnel the preferred alternative for replacement of the Viaduct (Seattle City Council 2009) (Figure 8.3).

Approval Endgame

Although a technically feasible design had been identified, Seattle's new Mayor was opposed. In November 2009, Mayor Mike McGinn was elected to office on a platform which argued that tunnel construction was a distraction from the efforts the City should make to reduce dependence on single-occupancy vehicles. Optimistic cost estimates were a concern raised by the State's Expert Review Panel (WSDOT 2006, p. iv), but the State Legislature exacerbated tensions by including language in a bill, signed by the Governor, assigning responsibility for overruns in excess of $2.8 billion to the City. The City countered with Resolution 31235, affirming the State's responsibility for cost overruns. When lead agencies released the Supplemental Draft EIS in 2010, recommending the single-bored tunnel as the preferred option (WSDOT et al. 2011, p. 58), Mayor McGinn instructed Seattle's newly-appointed director of transportation not to sign it. Without a certified EIS, FHWA could not issue a Record of Decision, and federal funds would not be released for the tunnel (Ott 2011).

In a series of last-minute political machinations, the Seattle City Council intervened. On September 23, 2010, after extensive meetings and deliberation with Council members, staff, and legal counsel, Seattle City Council President Richard Conlin signed the Supplemental Draft EIS to authorize continuation of environmental review and project development (WSDOT et al. 2011, p. 58). On October 4, wary of further attempts to impede project development, the City Council passed Ordinance 123424 retroactively, cementing Conlin's authority to sign on behalf of the City (SCC 2010). In a striking display of solidarity, this effort received support from Council-member Mike O'Brien, a long-time supporter of Mayor McGinn's transportation policies, who recognized the need for consensus and resolution.

Having finally identified a Viaduct replacement design, project agencies started drafting agreements for its implementation. On the 10-year anniversary of the Nisqually Earthquake, February 28, 2011, the Seattle City Council adopted Ordinance 123542, entering into Viaduct replacement risk- and cost-sharing agreements with the State of Washington (SCC 2011). That summer, the Final EIS was published and the FHWA issued its Record of Decision (ROD) confirming the tolled single-bore tunnel as the preferred alternative (FHWA 2011). Shortly thereafter, on August 16, 2011, Referendum 1 was presented to Seattle voters, soliciting support for the design and associated agreements between WSDOT and the City of Seattle. This time, 58.23 percent of voters endorsed the project (King County 2011).

THE BERTHA CHRONICLES

By August of 2011, the tunnel project was already the centerpiece of many contracts underway within the $3.1 billion Alaskan Way Viaduct Replacement Program. The full program consisted of a series of projects at the terminal ends of the Viaduct, a set of projects along the waterfront of the demolished elevated highway, and a new bored tunnel (WSDOT 2020c). Several contracts were allowed to proceed as early as 2007 because their scope would not have changed regardless of the form of replacement of the Viaduct, many of which were at or below the South Portal of the new tunnel. The tunnel project could not begin construction until the Record of Decision of the Final EIS was completed in 2011. The Viaduct would remain in use until the tunnel was completed. The final stages of work included Viaduct demolition, North Portal completion, and a new Alaskan Way surface street with waterfront improvements.

WSDOT set up the tunnel project to be administered through a design-build contract—giving the contractor responsibility for completing design as well as construction. As stipulated by state law, the first step was for WSDOT to issue a Request for Qualifications, or RFQ (WSDOT 2009). When submitting a response to an RFQ, potential bidders are asked to list their technical, managerial and financial qualifications to undertake a particular job, as well as identify examples of similar projects previously undertaken. Those deemed qualified are then asked to respond to a Request for Proposals, or RFP. In the case of design-build projects, proposals include preliminary project designs, technical specifications, project management plans, contractor certifications, a proposed construction schedule, and of course, a bid price.

Published in September 2009, the RFQ, valued the project at $1 billion and stated the purpose "to expedite construction of an alternative traffic route sufficient to replace the existing through capacity of the Alaskan Way Viaduct," a capacity credited with carrying 110,000 vehicles per day (WSDOT 2009). WSDOT engineers prepared conceptual designs specifying an interior diameter of 52 feet and a length of 9,100 linear feet for the tunnel (WSDOT 2010a).[3] The interior diameter specification was understood to be a stretch—previously deep-bore tunnel widths had topped out at 45 feet—but given the SR 99 tunnel's expected traffic volumes, it was essential that both the upper and lower decks include an eight-foot service and breakdown shoulder as well as two eight-foot travel lanes.

WSDOT received submissions from four consortia of engineering, tunneling and construction companies. The four were soon whittled down to two, who were then asked to respond to a follow-up RFP by May 26, 2010. Both proposals came in at just under WSDOT's upset price of $1.09 billion—the maximum amount an agency is willing to pay—and met all associated pass/fail criteria, including a willingness to post a $500 million payment bond and a $500 million performance bond. With the minimum submittal requirements having been met, WSDOT's reviewers could focus on each bidder's technical competency and on their bid prices and terms.

Unlike some states, Washington does not require that design-build contracts be awarded to the lowest bidder. Instead, the winning proposal is the one with the smallest difference between its total technical scores and its total proposed price. Applying these criteria resulted in WSDOT awarding the tunneling contract to Seattle Tunnel Partners (STP), a joint venture of Dragados, a Spanish construction firm, and Tutor Perini, a California-based contractor and builder with projects located throughout the US. At $1.0897 billion, STP's bid price was just under the $1.09 billion upset price. STP's competition, the Seattle Tunnel Group, another Spanish–US consortium, had presented a slightly lower bid price, but earned only about half of STP's technical credits. A final contract between WSDOT and STP was signed on December 17, 2010 (WSDOT 2010b).

Because the hiring process began almost two years prior to political and public approval of the bored tunnel option, the tunneling work was divided into two scopes of work, each with a notice to proceed. Although the National Environmental Policy Act (NEPA) forbade STP from participating in decision-making, STP could begin immediately after contract signing to generate preliminary designs of the bored tunnel adequate to compare with the other alternatives considered in the Supplemental Draft and Final EIS (WSDOT et al. 2010). This early design work was also used by WSDOT to support NEPA documentation, such as regulatory compliance with the Endangered Species Act, environmental permitting, and environmental mitigation planning. Notice to proceed with final design and construction was not allowed until 2011, when the FHWA's Record of Decision and associated permits were released and approved.

As noted above, STP contracted with Hitachi Zosen, USA, Ltd. to manufacture the TBM. When it arrived by ship at the Port of Seattle on April 2, 2013, the TBM was named after Bertha Knight Landes, Seattle's first female mayor. Hitachi Zosen was on-site to train STP personnel and monitor the

TBM's performance. The TBM was assembled in two months, in a launch pit 80 feet below ground, just west of Seattle's football and baseball stadiums. This was followed by several months of testing within "safe havens" along the first 1,500 feet of the route, to determine how well Bertha would perform in Seattle soils and to see whether drilling would disrupt the damaged viaduct or neighboring historic masonry buildings (Helms 2017). Bertha passed its tests and drilling began at the South Portal on July 30, 2013. If all went according to schedule, Bertha would emerge at the North Portal in June 2014, and be disassembled and extracted by December 2015.

What Stopped Bertha?

News reports and court filings offer varying accounts of Bertha's untimely demise. WSDOT's filings document multiple periods of material clogging the TBM cutterhead, STP ceasing operations, cleaning out the material, and resuming forward movement during the first six months of operation, including one episode in which the TBM's center pipe was cracked (WSDOT v. STP 2021, p. 8). As early as November 2013, STP began deviating from the parameters specified in the TBM operating manual, reducing, for example, the use of conditioners typically needed to optimize the flow of material through the TBM (p. 9).

On December 4, 2013, the shredded steel casing of a well that had been drilled to test groundwater conditions at the site began to appear on the video feed of the conveyor belt that transported debris from Bertha's forward cutting heads out to the rear of the machine, where the excavated material would be trucked away. STP's court filings focus on this well casing, which the contractor claims to be a site condition that differs from the specifications in its contract with WSDOT, noting that the TBM was not designed to cut through steel (WSDOT v. STP 2020, p. 7). WSDOT's court filings show, however, that STP's own geotechnical engineers used the well for groundwater level readings and planned to decommission the well prior to drilling (WSDOT v. STP 2021, p. 16).

Records from the TBM on December 4 indicate that sensors on the TBM showed no unusual effects on the machine's thrust force or torque when encountering the well casing (WSDOT v. STP 2021, p. 9). By December 5, however, granite boulders began to show up on the conveyor belt of the TBM, and Bertha slowed to a crawl. What was normally a pace of 20 to 40 millimeters was reduced to 5 millimeters a minute, despite operating at maximum force.

By December 6, Bertha had only just passed through the first 10 percent of the planned tunnel area but was stopped several times due to overheating. At this point, STP had the potential to receive millions in funds offered as incentives for early completion. The TBM, however, was still under warranty by Hitachi Zosen USA, Ltd., and STP chose to press on. Overheating, stopping, cooling, and restarting, changing settings and operating further outside of TBM operating manual specifications—by the end of the day Bertha was not only stopped, it was also damaged (WSDOT v. STP 2021, p. 11). After clearing the clogged material, tests of the TBM in January of 2014 showed that the outer seal of the main bearing had been compromised (p. 12).

Bertha did not return to service for two years. It took 18 months to dig a hole from the surface, disassemble the cutting head, replace the main bearing, and reassemble and test the forward cutters. Digging operations resumed on December 22, 2015, only to be halted again less than a month later when a barge in Elliott Bay damaged nearby piers and a sinkhole opened near the project site. This led Governor Jay Inslee to briefly suspend tunneling work, citing concerns over public safety. Sustained digging finally resumed in early April 2016, after a plan by STP was approved to improve how soil is monitored around the project.

Bertha reached the halfway mark on October 2, 2016, and emerged through the North Portal to complete its journey on April 4, 2017. As Bertha advanced, the tunnel was shaped by concrete and steel tunnel rings. Installation of the tunnel's interior roadways, ventilation, and safety systems required another 22 months of work. On January 11, 2019, the Viaduct was closed to traffic so that crews could realign the highway with the new tunnel by completing the tunnel entrances and exits. On February 4, 2019, the completed tunnel was opened to traffic (WSDOT 2020b).

This project was under extraordinary time pressure. In 2011, as described by both WSDOT and the STP, construction of the tunnel project would be concluded by December 2016, with another year to demolish the Viaduct and decommission Battery Street Tunnel at the North Portal—a contract duration of just 5 years and 5 months. The assembly and operation of the TBM was to be concluded within the stunningly short period of 16 months, with another 18 months to disassemble and extract the machine by January 2016, leaving one year to finish remaining tasks. In reality, the machine was not extracted until January of 2018, commissioning took another year, and the facility opened to traffic on February 4, 2019. As a result, the full program to replace the Alaskan Way Viaduct was completed three-and-a-half years later than planned, at $250 million above the amount originally budgeted, with additional unaccounted cost and risk in the form of court claims yet to be determined.

While the tunneling contract offered a generous incentive of $25 million for on-schedule delivery, the budget for contingencies, at $40 million, was inordinately small for a contract of this size and scope—budgeted at $1.35 billion and bid at $1.09 billion. In terms of incentives and contingency, STP has been awarded $108 million, draining the tunnel budget for contingencies and drawing additional funds from savings WSDOT had conserved from the overall Alaskan Way Viaduct replacement program. When Bertha stopped working, STP stepped outside of the channels for receiving funds set aside for contingency and submitted an additional $207 million change order, requesting payment to cover the costs of repairing the TBM and any delays. Months later, when it was clear how long it would take to fix Bertha, STP submitted a second change order request for an additional $85 million. WSDOT disputed both requests, which together would have added nearly 20 percent to the cost of the project, and later went to court to have them declared invalid.

In case of a dispute, the contract between WSDOT and STP called for a hearing in front of an independent dispute resolution board. Both sides rejected this route and proceeded instead to litigation, filing suit in the Superior Court of the State of Washington for Thurston County (Judgement, No 16-2-00980-34. April 19, 2019; January 10, 2020). STP claimed that the presence of the steel pipe should have been uncovered and disclosed as part of WSDOT's initial site conditions report. WSDOT claimed that when the crushed pipe was discovered on the debris conveyor belt, Bertha's operators should have suspended operations to see if it had caused any internal damage. The trial court issued a summary judgment in favor of WSDOT, finding that regardless of the agency's actions or inactions, STP had failed in its contractual responsibilities to retain and produce the physical evidence (e.g., the pipe fragments) upon which its claim was based; and ordered STP to pay damages as stipulated in their contract with WSDOT (WSDOT v. STP 2020). At time of writing, this case reached the Appellate Courts of the State of Washington. An additional case, levied by STP against their insurers, reached the Washington State Supreme Court.

To date, results from court cases have kept cost growth to WSDOT from the tunnel boring contract relatively low, to a total paid to the contractor of $1.5 billion, which is about 10 percent above the original budgeted amount of $1.35 billion or 27 percent above the bid amount of $1.09 billion. To manage the extreme changes on the project, WSDOT's own expenses grew from $63 million to about $150 million, which brought the overall project cost to $1.65 billion, or 7.2 percent above the original budgeted estimates for WSDOT expenses and payments to the contractor. For its part, WSDOT has been ruled eligible to receive $58.1 million in liquidated damages from STP for delays during construction, which have yet to be paid.

PROJECT FUNDING SOURCES AND REVENUES

Excluding litigation costs, the AVWRP cost $3.35 billion to complete, $250 million or eight percent over its original budget of $3.1 billion (WSDOT 2020a). As noted above, the cost of the tunneling portion of the program rose

10 percent, from an initial budget from WSDOT of $1.35 to $1.5 billion, though the final amount is pending the outcome of litigation. As cost overruns go, this is small compared with other tunneling megaprojects and a testimony to WSDOT's generally sound project budgeting and management practices. In terms of individual funding sources, $2.23 billion of the AWVRP's costs were paid for by WSDOT, FHWA provided $0.78 billion, and the Port of Seattle provided the balance of $0.34 billion. All cost overruns to date have been borne by WSDOT.

The bonds issued by the Port of Seattle to pay its share of the Tunnel's construction costs are revenue bonds, meaning they are to be repaid from user charges, which in the Tunnel's case means tolls. Road tolling is relatively recent in the Pacific Northwest, and the SR 99 Tunnel is one of only five facilities in Washington State to be tolled.[4] Toll rates range from $1 during off-peak and weekend periods to $2.25 during weekday peak periods. Tolls are collected electronically in both directions. Drivers with an electronic *Good To Go!* Transponder pass always pay the minimum toll. Drivers who have a *Good To Go!* account but no transponder pay an extra 25 cents per trip. Drivers without a *Good To Go!* account pay an extra $2 per trip, with billing by mail tied to their license plate number. Tolling on the SR 99 Tunnel officially began on November 9, 2019, ten months after the Tunnel opened to motorists. There was some early concern that charging tolls for using the Tunnel might reduce its usage, but WSDOT's successful experiences with electronic tolling on bridges and high occupancy lanes recently redeveloped in the greater Seattle area helped allay those concerns.

A WATERFRONT FOR PEOPLE

Replacing a 60-foot-high elevated highway with an underground tunnel opened 26 blocks of prime Seattle waterfront land to public use and redevelopment, an opportunity lost on no one. Over the years, Seattle's mile-long waterfront had developed into a mishmash of piers, ferry terminals, maritime uses, parking lots, tourist shops, restaurants, the Seattle Art Museum, and the Seattle Aquarium. The waterfront was easily accessible by car, bus, and boat, but getting to the water's edge could be a challenge. New waterfront redevelopment plans were proposed every few years starting in the 1960s, but with the City unable to use eminent domain to acquire private land, none could ever be implemented.

The prospect of tearing down the Alaskan Way Viaduct changed all that. In the hope that the single-bore tunnel alternative would eventually be approved, the Seattle City Council in 2009 established the 37-stakeholder Central Waterfront Partnerships Committee (CWPC) to advise the Mayor and Council on how best to redevelop the central waterfront area (Waterfront Seattle.org,

2021). In September 2010, following up on the CWPC's recommendation to hire a renowned planning and landscape architecture firm to develop a waterfront redevelopment plan, the Seattle Planning Department in September 2010 hired James Corner Field Operations for the job. The firm was best known as the principal designer of High Line in New York City. To continue the work of CWPC, the City Council established the Central Waterfront Committee (CWC) in January 2011, to oversee the work.

Delivered in July 2012, the plan, known as the Waterfront Seattle Concept Design, took as its starting point six guiding principles adopted by the Mayor and City Council in 2011 (James Corner Field Operations 2012). Two of those principles stood out for their specificity: the plan should build a network of public spaces to reconnect the waterfront to Seattle's downtown and neighborhoods, and pedestrians and bicyclists should be given equal weight when making new transportation investments for motorized vehicles and freight. Among its core elements, the Concept Design proposed a continuous pedestrian promenade running along Alaskan Way on the waterfront; a continuous bike pathway; pedestrian and meeting plazas at key commercial and public facility locations; a new public park on Pier 48; new recreation and public meeting areas at Piers 62 and 63; and new improvements to all cross streets and pedestrian ways to make it easier to access the waterfront. As promised, rather than focusing on buildings and development opportunities, the Concept Design focused on public spaces. It was accompanied by a Framework Plan explaining key spatial relationships.

The Concept Design was well received as a plan for converting the existing waterfront's disorganized spaces into a coherent, functional, and pleasing public amenity that tourists and Seattleites alike could enjoy. In August 2012, on a 9–0 vote, the Mayor and City Council formally adopted the Central Waterfront Concept Design and Framework Plan as the city's official guiding document for future waterfront area capital improvements (WaterfrontSeattle. org, 2021). The plan's first big capital project, moving the Elliott Seawall 15 feet to the west and accommodating the Promenade, began in 2013 and was completed in 2017.

Changes in mayoral administrations and council elections can make it difficult for cities to follow through on long-range plans. To keep Seattle's waterfront planning focused on the public realm rather than private development, a group of stakeholders who had participated in the waterfront planning process began meeting in 2012 to form Friends of the Seattle Waterfront (the group was formally incorporated in 2014). Similarly, the City created its own separate waterfront planning unit, the Office of Waterfront and Civic Projects in 2014, bringing together key staff from the Mayor's Office and the City's Departments of Transportation, Planning and Development, and Parks and Recreation.

Even as WSDOT and STP struggled to complete the Alaskan Way Tunnel, progress on the waterfront moved forward (Waterfront Seattle.org, 2021):

- Friends of the Seattle Waterfront launched a fundraising effort to rebuild Piers 62 and 63, which would serve as major public event spaces at the Promenade's northern end.
- In late 2016, the Seattle Park District announced it would re-allocate $4.35 million in capital toward waterfront projects.
- In August 2017, the Seattle Council reaffirmed the importance of waterfront improvements, and indicated its support for the formation of a local improvement district to provide funds from fees assessed on waterfront property and business owners. The Council also gave Friends of the Seattle Waterfront responsibility for managing the waterfront's new public spaces.

Source: James Corner Field Operations (2012).

Figure 8.4   *Rendering of the new Alaskan Way surface street and Seattle Waterfront*

- In January 2019, shortly before the completion of the Alaskan Way Tunnel, the City Council dissolved the Central Waterfront Steering Committee, which had overseen the development of the original plan, and replaced it with the Central Waterfront Oversight Committee, to be staffed jointly by the City's Office of Waterfront and Civic Projects and Friends of the Seattle Waterfront.
- Once demolition of the Alaska Way Viaduct was completed in November 2019, construction began immediately on the new Alaska Way Road and on the Columbia Street transit corridor (Figure 8.4). The completion of these two projects in 2020 paved the way for the beginning of construction activity on numerous other pier renewal and public right-of-way projects, including a multi-level public access way to link Pike Place Market to the new waterfront promenade.

PROJECT EFFECTS AND IMPACTS

The Alaskan Way Tunnel was built for safety rather than economic development or congestion. This, plus the fact that it was open for just a year before the COVID-19 pandemic arrived has complicated the job of comparing its current real-world performance to initial projections. Traffic has been considerably lower than projected, but in terms of adding to property values and promoting real estate development the project is a success.

Traffic Usage and Impacts

Traffic volumes were expected to decline somewhat once tolling began in November 2019, but, even so, tunnel usage had been projected by WSDOT to be above the 80,000 that had used the Viaduct on a typical weekday. The tunnel opened in February 2019, began tolling in November, and by December, the traffic using the tunnel had dropped by 26 percent from a weekday average of 77,000 to 57,000 vehicles (WSDOT et al. 2019).

Where did the extra 23,000 vehicles—the difference between the 80,000 vehicles who had used the Viaduct and the 57,000 now using the tolled tunnel—go? A few travelers, WSDOT's surveys found out, had shifted to public transportation. Others shifted their work locations out of the downtown area. Most diverted to I-5 or to surface streets. Interestingly, because of other roadway improvements undertaken as part of the AWVRP, the newly diverted traffic did not affect downtown congestion levels (Wang et al. 2021). In terms of travel times, a January 2020 WSDOT travel time analysis found that northbound peak hour travel times for commuters using the Tunnel had decreased by 18 percent or 30 seconds (compared with travel times on the Viaduct), while southbound peak hour travel times had increased by 11 percent. Had

WSDOT compared these travel time savings to the tolls being charged, it would have found that each minute of peak hour travel time savings was costing travelers between $3 and $4. A different WSDOT survey, undertaken in December 2019, found that while most SR 99 travelers preferred the Tunnel to the Viaduct for speed and safety reasons, they disliked tolls.

WSDOT has continued to monitor Tunnel traffic during the COVID-19 pandemic, but it no longer reports hourly, daily, or weekly traffic volumes. Citing a decline in toll revenue due to COVID-19, a series of WSDOT reports published in early 2021 suggested a future toll increase of 15 percent to 25 percent might be necessary for the Tunnel to meet its debt service obligations (Craighead 2020).

Development and Real Estate Market Impacts

Real estate markets respond quickly to the creation of new development and investment opportunities. For more than 60 years, the Viaduct had separated downtown Seattle from its waterfront, creating not only a physical barrier, but adding to problems of noise and pollution. With the Viaduct to be relocated underground, not only would 26 blocks of land be opened up for redevelopment and reuse, the values of existing properties would also rise.

As noted by *Seattle Times* real estate writer Mike Rosenburg in a March 2019 article chronicling the ongoing waterfront development boom,

> The transformation of an area marked by furniture stores, parking garages and century-old buildings has already begun. In all, about two dozen major projects have launched within a quarter mile of the doomed section of the viaduct in the past five years, with more on the way.

Rosenburg's article was accompanied by two graphics, a rendering of some of the projects targeted for redevelopment, and a map identifying planned building renovations and development projects within a four block radius of the new tunnel (Figure 8.5). Although Rosenburg's report did not list the total number or value of properties planned for construction, those singled out provide a sense of the scale of the development opportunities being created:

* In 2012, less than a year after the referendum vote, Goodman Real Estate paid $9.7 million for an empty plot of land two blocks from the Viaduct in order to build the Viktoria apartment complex, reportedly at a cost of $95 million. Three years later, Goodman sold the finished project to Benedict Canyon Equities, a real estate investing firm, for $130 million.
* In 2014, Hudson Pacific Properties spent $58 million for a full block next to the elevated Viaduct, citing the chance to build a "new office building fronting the soon to be improved Alaskan Way waterfront." It quickly did

just that and spruced up other existing buildings on the site, raising the total assessed value of the block from $25 million in 2014 to $131 million.

*   Seattle developer Martin Selig, the developer of Columbia Center, Seattle's tallest building, paid $44 million to buy a century-old office building at 815 Western Avenue, one block east of Alaskan Way, so he could tear it down and build an 18-story office and apartment project in its place.

*   Next door to Selig at 911 Western Avenue, Boston-based Beacon Capital Partners spent $50 million to buy and renovate another aging office building, after persuading local gaming company Big Fish Games to move its headquarters there. Beacon Capital Partners then flipped the property for a $186 million.

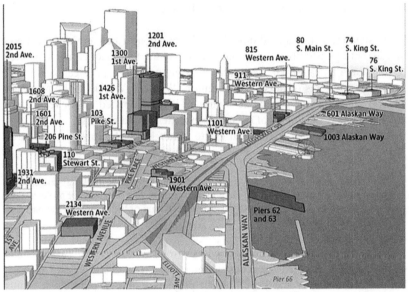

Source: Emily M. Eng, in Mike Rosenburg, *The Seattle Times* (2019).

Figure 8.5   *Seattle waterfront selected development projects as of March 2019*

Overall, according to the King County Assessor's Office, assessed values of commercial properties within a quarter-mile of the Viaduct rose 59 percent between 2011 and 2019, as compared with 38 percent in the rest of Seattle (Rosenburg 2019). Assessed values don't always match market values, but according to real estate information provider CoStar, over the 2011–2019 period, median sales prices of buildings near the Viaduct grew about twice as fast as commercial sales prices elsewhere in the city. Similarly, office and apartment rents for area properties grew faster than those in the rest of the city. Throughout the period, Seattle's downtown and inner-urban office and residential markets were consistently among the nation's strongest, making it difficult to say how much of these price and rent increases should be apportioned to the demolition of the Viaduct versus Seattle's ongoing tech boom and up-zoning efforts.

LESSONS AND TAKEAWAYS

The Alaskan Way Viaduct Replacement Program offers many important takeaways for megaproject sponsors and managers. The first is that worst-case scenarios must be part of megaproject planning and, most importantly, planning must be fit for the institutional arrangements governing project implementation. The entire program was budgeted at $3.1 billion and, though actual cost growth is yet to be determined, the fact that the cost overruns ascribed to the State of Washington have been limited to a 7 percent increase of $250 million are due to the terms of the tunnel contract implemented by WSDOT and the reliance placed on evidence within the US judicial system.

Ironically though, perhaps the next most important conclusion is that a single expensive mishap should not be the only lens through which an entire project is viewed. If the time and cost to repair the TBM could somehow be excised from the picture, the AWVRP would no doubt be considered to be a resounding success. Since it opened in February 2019, the SR 99 Tunnel has experienced no design or construction-related problems, unlike the Big Dig in Boston or the replacement of the eastern span of the San Francisco–Oakland Bay Bridge. And, importantly, the design of the project fit within a larger program giving greater access and public amenities to the Seattle waterfront.

Other takeaways from the AWVRP experience are of more practical value, and we divide them into two groups, lessons for project sponsors, and lessons for project planners and managers.

Lessons for Project Sponsors

The primacy of inclusive planning
When Seattle voters went to the polls in 2007 to choose among two Alaskan Way Viaduct replacement alternatives, they were put in the untenable position of being asked to approve projects for which they had not had the opportunity to provide substantial input. Having had ample experience seeing prior transportation investment packages voted down, WSDOT planners should have structured the initial Viaduct replacement planning process to be as inclusive

as possible. Only after this approach failed at the ballot box did elected officials intervene to ensure the participation of a broader cross-section of stakeholders.

These problems were compounded by the use of an evaluation system which focuses on identifying and mitigating adverse impacts rather than on a more balanced accounting of costs and benefits. Had the AWVRP planning process been more collaborative from the start, it would have made it possible for the different stakeholder groups to think in terms of identifying tradeoffs rather than avoiding adverse impacts or staying within narrow budgetary guidelines. Indeed, only after the alternative identification process was opened up to a broader group of stakeholders did the final single-bore tunnel alternative come to light.

Getting to yes in an era of contested decision-making.

Fiscal federalism is the idea that different levels of government should have differing responsibilities when it comes to financing major policy interventions or public sector projects. What fiscal federalism means in the US is that the federal government usually takes the lead in financing projects that have multi-state benefits, that states take the lead in financing projects that generate intra-state benefits, and that local governments lead when financing projects that generate predominantly local benefits. The initial AWVRP decision-making process assumed that because the Viaduct was an integral part of a state highway and that because Washington State would pay most of the bills for whichever replacement alternative was selected, the State should also control the decision-making process. Only when Seattle voters unexpectedly turned down both of WSDOT's chosen replacement alternatives did the agency undertake a more inclusive process, in which funding responsibilities did not automatically equate to decision-making discretion. Ultimately, the intervention of stakeholders beyond WSDOT gave the project the opportunity for a positive reception from Seattle voters. What the entire AWVRP process makes clear, with the benefit of hindsight, is that contemporary infrastructure planning and decision-making efforts must be designed in such a way as to consciously balance technical expertise, funding responsibility, and broad stakeholder representation with opportunities for innovative and out-of-the box thinking.

Lessons for Project Planners and Managers

Incrementally reclaiming the public realm

The planning process developed by the City of Seattle to reclaim and redevelop its central waterfront—a situation made possible by the demolition of the Alaska Way Viaduct—deserves praise. Three things stand out about the City's waterfront planning and implementation process. The first is that it prioritized public access and use over real estate development. Too often, megaproject planners award newly-created sites to real estate developers in order to raise revenues instead of considering how those same sites could be more appropriately used by the public. To their immense credit, none of the public agencies or stakeholder committees involved in re-planning Seattle's central waterfront fell into this trap. They were also careful to hire a planning and design consultant—James Corner Field Operations—with a strong track record of preserving and enhancing the public realm. As a result of the City's thoughtful public realm improvements, nearby private property owners have found their property values enhanced in a manner not otherwise possible. Second, the adopted waterfront plan is being implemented in an incremental fashion. This gives the City the time to allow for revenues generated from earlier projects to help pay for later ones. Third, recognizing that political administrations will likely change over the waterfront plan's extended implementation period, in order to ensure that the project is implemented as promised, city officials have welcomed the ongoing and active participation of stakeholder groups such as Friends of the Seattle Waterfront. These three characteristics of Seattle's central waterfront redevelopment process—its focus on public realm improvements, its patience, and its recognition that ongoing public support is essential—provide useful lessons to other government entities considering large-scale urban transportation investments.

Compartmentalizing risk

The high-risk single-bore tunnel—relying on what was the world's largest TBM—was one of more than 30 contracts implemented within the Alaskan Way Viaduct Replacement Program. WSDOT was able to use the design-build process to secure a qualified contractor, who then subcontracted with one of the world's pre-eminent manufacturers of TBMs, but the design-build contract and associated insurance programs had to be organized to limit WSDOT's exposure to the risks that could only be effectively addressed by those operators and manufacturers. Importantly, WSDOT further limited risk by restricting the work of the tunnel contractor to tunnel-specific tasks and distributing as many other tasks as possible to other contractors. As the TBM stalled out, WSDOT was able to adjust its numerous other project schedules to minimize cost increases, saving an additional $100 million that would be needed for tunnel cost overrun. This meant that WSDOT's own costs for program management doubled to $150 million, but in terms of the tunnel contract, the total paid to the contractor to date rose only by 10 percent, from a budget of $1.35 billion to $1.5 billion. In terms of the bid price, the cost increases have been more substantial, at 27 percent above the $1.09 billion bid.

Contingency planning

If nothing else, the two-year work stoppage caused by Bertha's breakdown indicates the importance of contingency planning for worst-case scenarios. Because of Bertha's huge size, no backup TBM could have reasonably taken over for the damaged machine. Instead, the project sponsor and contractor— WSDOT and STP in this case—should have prepared a contingency plan to reach and repair the damaged machine in case it stopped working for whatever reason. As it was, it took nearly two years to drill an access hole from the surface, for onsite inspectors to determine the reasons for the breakdown, to order replacement parts from Japan and to have them delivered, and to install them and test the repaired machine. These additional months might reasonably have been cut in half had a project engineer at WSDOT, STP or Hitachi Zosen simply asked, "What do we do if the TBM breaks down in an inaccessible location?" The fact that this didn't happen on a project of this size and complexity speaks to an unfortunate hubris all too common to megaproject planners and managers. Whether it's a giant TBM as in Seattle's case, or a fire prevention system as in the Berlin-Brandenburg Airport case, or a new train control system as in the case of Crossrail in London, new technologies must be thoroughly stress-tested before they are delivered and monitored for potential problems as they are deployed. And if they fail to perform as advertised, or are unexpectedly damaged as in Bertha's case, there should be a clearly articulated back-up plan in place to restore service as quickly as possible.

Contracting for contingencies

Even if WSDOT and STP project managers had done a better job anticipating potential problems, the $40 million set aside to cover contingencies was woefully inadequate. Real estate developers commonly set aside 10 to 15 percent of their construction budgets to cover unforeseen contingencies, but in the SR 99 Tunnel case, the $40 million set aside for shared contingencies was less than 3 percent of the tunneling project's total budget. The reasons why both parties agreed to such a low contingency were purely political: WSDOT was under pressure to bring the AWVRP's cost in under the $3.1 billion ceiling provided for by federal and state funding and Port of Seattle revenue bonds, and STP's bid price for the tunneling job had to be below the $1.09 billion set forth in the RFP. The inadequacy of the contingency was immediately apparent when Bertha broke down. Instead of accessing the project's contingency fund to cover repairs, STP filed change order requests for much larger amounts. These requests were properly contested by WSDOT, but the resulting litigation—expensive in and of itself—is still underway more than 20 years after the earthquake that shook the Viaduct.

NOTES

1. On the Modified Mercalli Intensity scale the Nisqually earthquake was rated VIII: "severe."
2. The Viaduct would ultimately require $14.5 million of repairs.
3. Bertha's diameter was 57.2 feet.
4. The other tolled roadways in Washington State are the SR 16 Tacoma Narrows Bridge, the SR 520 Bridge between Seattle and Bellevue, SR 167 HOT Lanes, and express lanes on the I-405 highway on the east side of Lake Washington.

REFERENCES

Basetti, C. (2020). *Building Seattle's State Route 99: Supertunnel.* Catherine Basetti.

CSEEC: City of Seattle Ethics and Elections Commission. (2007). *Official Local Voter's Pamphlet: Viaduct Replacement Advisory Measures 1 and 2 – Special Election All-Mail Election March 13, 2007.* n.d. Seattle.gov, www.seattle.gov/elections.

Craighead, C. (2020). Seattle's SR-520 bridge and SR-99 tunnel tolls could increase amid $72M revenue shortfall. *Seattle PI*, December 8.

Crowley, W. (2002). Seattle transportation: From trolleys to monorails, a timeline. HistoryLink.org. https://www.historylink.org/file/4005.

Enlow, C. (2004). Design perspectives: Are we better off without the viaduct? Some say the costs and benefits of tunneling the viaduct just don't make sense. *Daily Journal of Commerce*, April 14.

Federal Highway Administration. (2011). *SR 99: Alaskan Way Viaduct Replacement Project Record of Decision.* August 2011. Federal Highway Administration, Washington Division, Seattle, Washington.

Helms, L. (2017). Who killed Bertha? Why the Seattle tunnel disaster isn't what it seems, and why WSDOT is making a dangerous bet. *Seattle Business Magazine*, October 2017.

James Corner Field Operations. (2012). Waterfront Seattle concept design. https://waterfrontseattle.blob.core.windows.net/media/Default/pdf/concept_design_full.pdf.

King County. (2011). Election Results – August 16, 2011. Referendum 1 – August 30, 2011, 6:20:34 PM. Your.kingcounty.gov, https://your.kingcounty.gov/elections/elections/201108/resPage7.aspx.

Ott, J. (2011). Alaskan Way Viaduct, part 4: Replacing the viaduct. HistoryLink.org. https://www.historylink.org/file/9983.

Rosenberg, M. (2019). Viaduct gold rush: Big money flows into area around doomed Seattle highway. *Seattle Times*, March 8.

Schulz, K. (2015). The really big one. *The New Yorker*, July 20.

Seattle City Council. (2009). *Ordinance 123133: An ordinance relating to the SR 99 Alaskan Way Viaduct and Seawall Replacement Program; Stating the City's policy with respect to an alternative for replacing the present Viaduct and Seawall, and related work; and authorizing execution of a Memorandum of Agreement between the State of Washington and the City of Seattle.* September 28, 2009.

Seattle City Council. (2010). *Ordinance 123424: An ordinance relating to environmental review of the Alaskan Way Viaduct Replacement Project and ratifying and confirming certain prior acts.* September 27, 2010.

Seattle City Council. (2011). *Ordinance 123542: An ordinance accepting for general street purposes 18 deeds conveyed to the City of Seattle by the Central Puget Sound Regional Transit Authority ("Sound Transit") in connection with the Central Link Light Rail Transit Project as agreed to in a Property Acquisition and Transfer Procedures Agreement between the City of Seattle and Sound Transit ("Property Transfer Agreement")*. January 3, 2011.

Sigmund, P. (2007). Triumph, tragedy mark Boston's Big Dig Project. *Construction Equipment Guide*, June 4, 2007. https://www.constructionequipmentguide.com/redirect/8751

Superior Court of the State of Washington for Thurston County. (2019). *Washington State Department of Transportation v. Seattle Tunnel Partners*, Findings of Fact and Conclusion of Law Re Evidentiary Hearing on Spoliation, No 16-2-00980-34. April 19, 2019.

Superior Court of the State of Washington for Thurston County. (2020). *Washington State Department of Transportation v. Seattle Tunnel Partners*, Judgement, No 16-2-00980-34. January 10, 2020.

Trapenberg-Frick, K. (2016). *Remaking the San Francisco-Oakland Bay Bridge*. Routledge. https://doi.org/10.4324/9781315660905.

T.Y. Lin International. (2001). *Alaskan Way Viaduct: Report of the Structural Sufficiency Review Committee*. June 28, 2001.

Wang, F., Wang, J., Zhang, Y., Chen, C., & Ban, X. J. (2021). *Travelers' Adaptive Behaviors in Response to Seattle's Alaskan Way Viaduct Replacement No. TRBAM-21-03332*.

Washington State Department of Transportation. (2006). *The Alaskan Way Viaduct and SR 520 Bridge Projects: Report of the Expert Review Panel, Revision 1*. September 1, 2006.

Washington State Department of Transportation. (2009). *Request for Qualifications: SR-99 Bored Tunnel Project. Washington State Department of Transportation*. September 15, 2009.

Washington State Department of Transportation. (2010a). *Design-Build Contract Instructions to Proposers: SR-99 Bored Tunnel Design-Build Project*. May 26, 2010.

Washington State Department of Transportation. (2010b). *Notice of Contract Award, Contract No. 7999, Alaskan Way Viaduct SR-99 Bored Tunnel Alternative*. (Letter from Jeff Carpenter, dated December 17, 2010).

Washington State Department of Transportation, Respondent v. Seattle Tunnel Partners, et al. Appellants. (2020). No. 54425-3 Brief of Appellants (Court of Appeals for State of Washington, Division II, November 23, 2020). https://www.courts.wa.gov/appellate_trial_courts/coaBriefs/index.cfm.

Washington State Department of Transportation, Respondent v. Seattle Tunnel Partners, et al. Appellants. (2021). No. 54425-3 Brief of Respondent (Court of Appeals for State of Washington, Division II, February 10, 2021). https://www.courts.wa.gov/appellate_trial_courts/coaBriefs/index.cfm.

Washington State Department of Transportation (website). (2020a). Alaskan Way Viaduct replacement program - About. Accessed May 16, 2020. Washington State Department of Transportation, Major Project: Alaska Way Viaduct Replacement Program. https://wsdot.wa.gov/construction-planning/major-projects/alaskan-way-viaduct-replacement-program#.

Washington State Department of Transportation (website). (2020b). Alaskan Way Viaduct Replacement Program - Schedule. Accessed May 16, 2020. Washington State Department of Transportation, Major Project: Alaska Way Viaduct Replacement

Program. https://wsdot.wa.gov/construction-planning/major-projects/alaskan-way
-viaduct-replacement-program#.

Washington State Department of Transportation (website). (2020c). Alaskan Way
Viaduct Replacement Program - Media Gallery. Accessed May 16, 2020. https://
www.flickr.com/photos/wsdot/sets/72157631528692308/.

Washington State Department of Transportation, City of Seattle, and US Department
of Transportation, Federal Highway Administration. (2004). *SR 99: Alaskan Way
Viaduct & Seawall Replacement Project Draft Environmental Impact Statement.*
March 2004.

Washington State Department of Transportation, City of Seattle, and US Department
of Transportation, Federal Highway Administration. (2006). *SR 99: Alaskan Way
Viaduct & Seawall Replacement Project Supplemental Draft Environmental Impact
Statement and Section 4(f) Evaluation.* July 2006.

Washington State Department of Transportation, City of Seattle, King County and US
Department of Transportation, Federal Highway Administration. (2009). *Alaskan
Way Viaduct Replacement Project History Report.* September 2009.

Washington State Department of Transportation, City of Seattle, and US Department
of Transportation, Federal Highway Administration. (2010). *SR 99: Alaskan Way
Viaduct Replacement Project 2010 Supplemental Draft Environmental Impact
Statement and Section 4(f) Evaluation.* October 2010.

Washington State Department of Transportation, City of Seattle, and US Department
of Transportation, Federal Highway Administration. (2011). *Alaskan Way Viaduct
Replacement Project Final Environmental Impact Statement and Section 4(f)
Evaluation.* July 2011.

Washington State Department of Transportation, King County Metro, Sound Transit.
(2019). What's happened to traffic since SR 99 tunnel tolling started. WSDOTBLOG.
December 9, 2019. https://wsdotblog.blogspot.com/2019/12/traffic-since-sr-99
-tolling-started.html.

Waterfront Seattle.org. (2021). Program overview: Transforming Seattle's Waterfront
(https://waterfrontseattle.org/about/program-overview) accessed July 2021.

Whittington, J. (2017). Capital planning for high-impact earthquakes: Invest to withstand the test of time. *Washington Journal of Environmental Law and Policy*, 7(2),
444–454.

9. A bridge too far? The Hong Kong–Zhuhai–Macau Bridge and economic and regional restructuring in China's Pearl River Delta region

Anthony G.O. Yeh, Fang Bian and Jiangping Zhou

ABBREVIATIONS USED IN THIS CHAPTER

BOT	Build–Operate–Transfer (a public–private partnership delivery model)
HKZMB	Hong Kong–Zhuhai–Macau Bridge
GFC	Global Financial Crisis
OCTS	"One Country, Two Systems"
PRD	Pearl River Delta
RMB	Renminbi, or Chinese Yuan
SAR	Special Administrative Region

Bridges signify different things to different people. To geographers, they are a means for connecting topographic or riverine gaps on a map. To civil and structural engineers, they are monuments to the synthesis of form and function. To politicians and public officials, they are tangible expressions of their ability to follow through on aspirational promises. To economists, they are a way to make the economy more productive by reducing the friction of space. To travelers, they are first and foremost utilitarian devices: a faster way to get from point A to point B. The Hong Kong–Zhuhai–Macau Bridge (hereafter HKZMB), a 55 km combination of suspension bridges, viaducts, undersea tunnels and roadways that connects Hong Kong in the east with the industrial city of Zhuhai and the gambling mecca of Macau in the west, is all these things. Its technical design and engineering achievements rival those of the greatest bridges of the 20th century, including the Golden Gate Bridge in the United States, the Sydney Harbour Bridge in Australia, the Tsing Ma Bridge in Hong Kong, the Akashi-Kaikyo Bridge in Japan, the Vasco de Gama Bridge in Portugal, and the Millau Viaduct Bridge in France. Its two suspension spans are things of elegant beauty. Its six lanes of roadways, three in each direction, are the final link in a network of highways that connect the most productive manufacturing region in the world. Most importantly, as the world's longest sea crossing and longest open-sea fixed structure, it provides visible testimony to China's ability to deliver world-class infrastructure projects in a timely manner.

None of these characterizations are up for debate. What is up for debate is whether the HKZMB is economically necessary and whether it will ever generate sufficient revenue to cover its costs. Initially forecast to attract between 9,200 and 14,000 vehicles per day, average daily vehicle flows on the HKZMB in the month after its October 2018 opening barely exceeded 2,200 vehicles, a stunning shortfall in demand. A year later, according to one of the Chinese mainstream websites for English-speaking readers, ChinaDaily.com. cn,[1] average daily traffic volumes had increased to just 4,200 vehicles per day. This chapter unpacks the internal and external factors that have contributed to the HKZMB's underutilization hitherto. We begin by reviewing the specifications of the bridge itself. Next, we unravel the contentious planning processes that led to the Bridge's approval and construction and identify the sources of its cost and schedule overruns. Finally, we focus on how recent economic and regional restructuring trends in China's Pearl River Delta (PRD) region help explain why the HKZMB has fallen so far short of expectations. Together, these observations form a cautionary tale of how unchecked political and technical ambitions combined with institutional momentum can all too easily lead to white elephant megaprojects.

UP CLOSE: THE HONG KONG–ZHUHAI–MACAU BRIDGE

Like all ultra-long bridges, the HKZMB is not a single structure. Rather, it consists of three main sections, the 29.6 km (18.4 mile) Main Bridge in the middle of Lingdingyang Bay; the 12 km (7.5 mile) Hong Kong Link Road, which connects Lantau Island and Chek Lap Kok (Hong Kong) International Airport in the east to the Main Bridge; and the 13.4 km (8.3 mile) Zhuhai Link Road, which connects the Main Bridge to Zhuhai in the west. The Zhuhai Link Road further divides into a norther spur to Zhuhai and a southern spur to Macau. Traveling west-bound from Hong Kong, vehicles using the HKZMB enter the Hong Kong Link Road at Lantau Island where they must transit through the Hong Kong Boundary Crossing Station before continuing eastward through the 1 km Scenic Hill Tunnel and the 9.4 km viaduct that ends at an artificial island (White Dolphin Island) on the eastern side of Lingdingyang Bay. White Dolphin Island marks the beginning of the Main Bridge section and serves as the entrance to a 6.7 km undersea tunnel buried 45 meters below the surface of Lingdingyang Bay. The tunnel rises to its western endpoint at another artificial island (Blue Dolphin Island), where it connects to the two cable-stayed suspension bridges that form the heart of the Main Bridge section. The western anchorage of the second suspension bridge marks the beginning of the Zhuhai Link Road which continues westward as a viaduct terminating at yet another artificial island, which houses the Macau Boundary Crossing Station—since Macau and Hong Kong are both Special Administrative Regions (SARs) and not Chinese provinces or cities, visitors into and out of them is regulated. Once past the Macau Boundary Crossing Station, the Zhuhai Link Road splits into a northern spur which connects to Zhuhai, and a southern spur that connects to Macau.

Construction of the HKZMB began on the Macau side on December 15, 2009, with a dedication ceremony presided over by Chinese Vice-Premier Li Keqiang. Bridge construction on the Hong Kong side began in December 2011 after a two-year delay caused by a legal challenge regarding the Bridge's environmental impacts. Construction of the Main Bridge section was completed in July 2017, followed by the completion of the Hong Kong and Zhuhai Link Roads in February 2018 (Table 9.1, Figure 9.1).

Opened to commercial traffic on October 24, 2018, one day after its official dedication by Chinese President Xi Jinping, the six-lane (three in each direction) HKZMB cut the road travel time between Hong Kong and Zhuhai/Macau from three hours to 40–50 minutes depending on weather and traffic conditions. The HKZMB was built explicitly to accommodate commercial vehicles, typically trucks, buses, and commercial vehicles, and, for capacity reasons, use of the Bridge by private vehicles is limited to permanent and pre-arranged permit holders. Bridge tolls are levied in both directions and vary from 150 RMB (US$23.50) for private cars and taxis to 300 RMB (US$47) for shuttle buses.[2] Trucks pay lower toll rates, which vary from 60 RMB ($9.40) for dual-axle delivery trucks to 115 RMB ($18) for multi-axle container trucks. Vehicle speeds are limited to a maximum of 100 kph or 62 mph. In addition to trucks, cars, and tourist coaches, the HKZMB accommodates regularly-scheduled bus service between Hong Kong and Macau and between Hong Kong and Zhuhai. The Hong Kong–Macau bus service operates 24 hours a day at intervals of between 10 and 15 minutes; the fare for the trip is ¥58 during the day and ¥63 (roughly US$10) at night.

The entire HKZMB cost 127 billion RMB (US$19.1 billion) to build.[3] Originally scheduled for completion in late-2016, construction of the HKZMB ran US$7.7 billion over its 2009 budget allocation of 72.9 billion RMB (US$11.4 billion) and 15 months over schedule. These are significant overruns by Chinese as well as North American and European standards. Funding for the HKZMB took an unconventional tri-partite form. Hong Kong paid for the

Hong Kong Link Road, Zhuhai and Macau paid for the Zhuhai Link Road, and all three cities plus the Chinese government split the cost of the ¥51.1 billion (US$ .56 billion) Main Bridge section. Properly maintained, the HKZMB is designed and engineered to remain in service well into the 22nd century.

Table 9.1   *Hong Kong–Zhuhai–Macau Bridge in brief*

Description	At 55 km (34 miles) in length, the Hong Kong–Macau–Zhuhai (HKMZ) Bridge crossing Lingdingyang Bay at the head of the Pearl River Delta is the longest bridge–undersea tunnel project in the world. Completed in 2018, the HKMZ Bridge has drawn car, bus and truck traffic at less than half the expected levels.
Lead sponsor(s)	Governments of Hong Kong and Macau Special Administrative Regions (SARs) and Guangdong Province
Primary rationale	Promote tighter economic linkages between Hong Kong, Macau, and Zhuhai
Primary funding sources	Provincial and municipal grants and debt
Construction started	2010
Construction completed	2018
Schedule overrun	15 months (based on Hong Kong press accounts)
Initial development budget (US$)	$11.4 billion
Final development cost (US$)	$19.1 billion
Cost overrun	$7.7 billion (68%)
Reason for overruns	The HKMZ Bridge experienced higher-than-expected construction costs (and times) on every aspect of the project, most notably in trenching the undersea tunnel and building artificial island bridge anchors.
Principal takeaways	Expensive transport projects justified on regional economic grounds should undergo a robust cost-benefit (or similar) analysis incorporating worst-case scenarios.

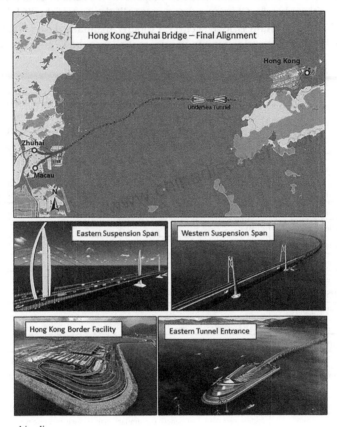

Figure 9.1   Hong Kong–Zhuhai–Macau map and photos

THE EVOLUTION OF A BRIDGE MEGAPROJECT

Bridging a Bay

The possibility of building a bridge that would span Lingdingyang Bay and connect Hong Kong to Zhuhai was first advocated in 1983 by Gordon Wu, CEO of Hopewell Holdings, Ltd, a major Hong Kong-based real estate and infrastructure developer. Great Britain and the People's Republic of China were in the midst of concluding negotiations that would return Hong Kong to Chinese control in 1997 under the concept of "one country, two systems," and Wu saw tremendous potential for linking Hong Kong's fast-growing service and export economy with the PRD's expanding manufacturing base, then centered on Guangzhou. Wu proposed building a bridge that would connect Tuen Mun in northwest Hong Kong to the village of Tangia in northeast Zhuhai with intermediate anchorages at Qi'ao Island and Neilingding Islands (Yang 2006). After visiting Zhuhai several times to gain the support of Liang Guangda, Zhuhai's then-mayor and Communist Party secretary, a proposal to build a new "Lingdingyang Bridge" was simultaneously submitted to the Chinese government in Beijing and to the British colonial government in Hong Kong. Wu's proposal was greeted with skepticism in both capitals. Hong Kong's government had its own list of infrastructure investment priorities, headed by the need to replace the over-crowded and unsafe Kai Tak International Airport in Kowloon; and, in Beijing, the Chinese government was focused on expanding export-oriented manufacturing capacity to the exclusion of all else.

The situation began changing in the mid-1990s. Hong Kong's return to Chinese control was imminent, and looking ahead, the Chinese government was eager to better integrate the Hong Kong economy with that of the larger PRD region. This led the China's State Planning Commission in 1998 to approve in concept the construction of a Lingdingyang Bridge connecting Hong Kong to Zhuhai. There was also the possibility of the same bridge connecting Hong Kong to Macau, which was due to be transferred from Portuguese to Chinese control in December 1999. The new Hong Kong SAR Government, however, remained skeptical, concerned over what it regarded as limited demand for the project, and worried that additional truck traffic would add to the region's rapidly-worsening air pollution. While Hong Kong dawdled, Macau's business community championed the idea, submitting to China's State Planning Commission a document entitled, *Comparative Research Report of the Main Proposals of the Lingdingyang Oversea Bridge across Pearl River Estuary*, which stressed the proposed bridge's importance to Macau's future economic development. Macau's argument was that it would cost next to nothing to extend the Bridge's western link an additional 10 km south from Zhuhai to Macau, thus providing tourists arriving at Hong Kong's new international airport at Chek Lap Kok with direct coach access to Macau's hotels and casinos (Yang 2006).

"Single-Y" versus "Double-Y" Alignments: Competing Visions for the Pearl River Delta

Known as the "Southern Alignment," this modification to the original Hong Kong–Zhuhai route quickly gained support from the government of Guangdong Province. Hong Kong's government remained reluctant to approve a bridge in any form, agreeing to do so only after Guangdong Province announced that if a Lingdingyang Bridge were *not* built, it would fund construction of a rail

312   *Megaprojects for megacities*

link connecting Zhuhai with the Port of Shenzhen, effectively bypassing Hong
Kong. Hoping to reclaim the initiative, in 2001, Gordon Wu proposed a bridge
scheme that came to be called the "Single-Y-Shaped Alignment," directly
connecting Hong Kong's Chek Lap Kok International Airport to Macau and
Zhuhai through a Y-shaped connecting link on the western side of the PRD.
Wu's scheme was enthusiastically received by the Hong Kong SAR government which was still struggling to recover from the 1997 Asian Financial
Crisis and was looking for ways to pay its mounting Chek Lap Kok Airport
debt service obligations. To increase the volume of truck traffic flowing over
the Bridge, Hong Kong proposed to build a container terminal on Lantau
Island adjacent to Chek Lap Kok Airport.

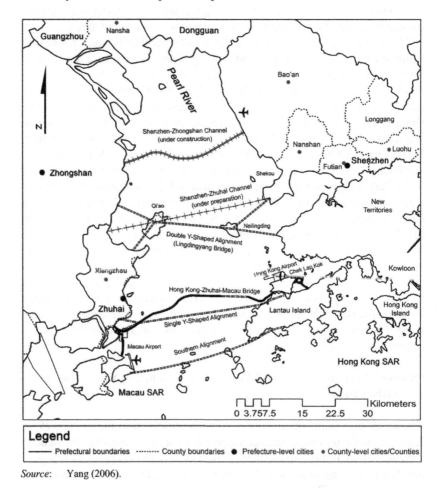

Source: Yang (2006).

Figure 9.2   Alternative Pearl River Delta crossing alignments

Wu's proposed "Single Y-shaped" alignment did not sit well with Shenzhen, Guangdong Province's other powerhouse city. In early 2004, the then-Shenzhen Mayor Li Hongzhong and Guangdong Province Vice-Governor Tang Bingquan proposed a different alignment that would move the Bridge northward and add an additional landing point in western Shenzhen (Figure 9.2). Known as the "Double Y-Shaped Bridge," this new scheme was vetoed in turn by Zhuhai, Macau and Hong Kong, all of whom argued that the extra cost of the "Double Y" alignment would be difficult to recover through bridge toll revenues. Hong Kong's motivation in rejecting the "Double Y" alignment was entirely self-serving: moving the Bridge northward and connecting it to Hong Kong in the New Territories rather than at Lantau Island would clearly weaken Lantau's role as the PRD's foremost multi-modal air and freight transport hub. For the government of Guangdong Province, the "Double Y" alignment would bring significant road connectivity benefits, enhancing Guangzhou's and Shenzhen's roles as the PRD's manufacturing and transport center all the while diminishing Hong Kong's.[4] Despite Shenzhen's intense lobbying for the "Double Y" design, Hong Kong held firm, and its importance as the project's largest financial stakeholder enabled it to prevail. As a consolation prize to Shenzhen, the Chinese government also approved construction of a proposed Shenzhen–Zhongshan Bridge, stipulating that its construction could begin only after the Lingdingyang Bridge, henceforth to be known as the Hong Kong–Zhuhai–Macau Bridge, was confirmed.

Now it was Guangdong Province's turn to get cold feet. In an echo of Hong Kong's earlier concerns over project financing, in 2002, Guangdong's then-Governor Lu Ruihua warned Beijing that the HKZMB's limited vehicle traffic and cash flows were likely to be inadequate to pay off its debts. Governor Lu's concerns were well-founded: as prosperous as Guangdong Province was, having to contribute financially to two megaprojects, the HKZMB and the Shenzhen–Zhongshan Bridge, would surely tax its financial capacity and draw funds from other projects. In the end, Governor Lu's renewed efforts on behalf of the "Double-Y" alignment proved insufficient. In August 2003, China's State Council gave its official approval to the "Single-Y" alignment. To mend political rifts and hasten the project along, the Council established the Hong Kong–Zhuhai–Macau Pre-Coordination Task Force, composed of the Hong Kong and Macau Special Administrative Regions and Guangdong Province. In 2005, the Task Force again confirmed that the HKZMB's three landing points would be in Macau, Zhuhai and Hong Kong's Lantau Island. Two years later, the State Council formally approved the HKZMB's engineering feasibility report, authorizing final design and engineering work to proceed. On December 15, 2009, the then-Chinese Vice-Premier Li Keqiang made the formal announcement that construction work on the HKZMB would soon commence.

HARDER THAN IT LOOKS: ENGINEERING AND FINANCING THE WORLD'S LONGEST BRIDGE

China's agreement that Hong Kong and Macau would each have significant political autonomy under its "one country, two systems" (OCTS) doctrine further complicated the building and financing of the HKZMB. Under OCTS, the Hong Kong and Macau SARs would retain their capitalist economic systems while China would continue its unique hybrid of socialism and state-sponsored capitalism. The three governments agreed to work together to complete the entire project with each taking construction management and financing responsibility for the sections of the project within their own respective jurisdictions. More specifically, Hong Kong SAR would be responsible for constructing the 12 km Hong Kong Road Link, Zhuhai and Guangdong Province would be responsible for building and funding the 13.4 km Zhuhai Road Link, and the central 29.6 km Main Bridge section would be built and funded by a consortium of the four local governments and Chinese central government. Macau alone would pay for the connecting link between the HKZMB's eastern anchorage and the Macau Peninsula.

Bridge projects of this scale are never easy to finance. An initial financing plan, first discussed in 2002 by the governments of Guangdong, Hong Kong and Macau, centered on creating a Build–Operate–Transfer (BOT) arrangement under which the three governments would each be responsible for building the boundary-crossing facilities, connectors and link spans within their jurisdictions, while the main bridge would be constructed by a concessionaire based on a 50-year lease period (Cheung and Chan, 2009).

Had this plan moved ahead, and the HKZMB been built using a BOT mechanism—as was preferred by Hong Kong and Macau—the financial burdens and project risks would have been mostly allocated to the private sector concessionaire. The use of the BOT arrangement was not without its own concerns. Establishing a proper bidding process to choose the private sector concessionaire would substantially prolong the project delivery period. Should the bids come in higher than expected, it would also increase potential construction costs. Finally, it would weaken the three governments' control over how bridge tolls were to be set. Hong Kong had extensive experience with BOT projects but China did not, and there were worries that weaknesses in China's legal system regarding contract enforceability might scare away potential bidders. In the end, largely because of the Chinese government's wish to maintain tight political control of the project, the BOT idea was abandoned.

The specifics of the final funding arrangements were never made public by the Chinese or Guangdong governments. According to a press briefing issued by the Hong Kong SAR government in 2008, the full expenditure of building the HKZMB was estimated to be 72.9 billion RMB, or about US$10.5 billion (HKSAR Transport and Housing Bureau 2008). This included 37 billion RMB (US$5.4 billion) for the Main Bridge section, which was to be financed by a 22 billion RMB (US$3.2 billion) loan from the Bank of China, with the balance put up by the governments of Hong Kong (7.53 billion RMB), China (5.27 billion RMB) and Macau (2.2 billion RMB). The specifics of this cost-sharing arrangement were based on estimates of how the HKZMB's economic benefits were likely to be distributed between China and the two SARs.

As is typical of megaprojects, this initial estimate proved to be far too low (Flyvbjerg et al. 2003). When completed in 2018, the total cost of constructing the HKZMB was 127 billion RMB (US$19.1 billion), with the cost overrun on the Main Bridge segment alone totaling 10 billion RMB (US$1.6 billion). Beyond basic increases in labor and materials costs, the sources of the Bridge's increased construction costs fell into three categories: construction difficulties resulting in design changes, environment controversies and "drifting" artificial island, and the "hidden" costs of building the Tuen Mun–Chek Lap Kok link road.

Construction Complications

The biggest cost overruns were not associated with the bridge structures, but with the 6.7 km long undersea tunnel built from 33 concrete tube sections prefabricated on nearby Guishan Island (Hu et al. 2015). With a length of 180 meters, a width of 38 meters, and a height of 11.4 meters, each tube section weighed 80,000 tons, roughly the same size and bulk as an aircraft carrier. Assembling the concrete tubes into a watertight tunnel posed two types of difficulties. The first, which involved properly positioning each tube, was complicated by the rough surface conditions typical of the Lingdingyang Channel. A second difficulty involved digging the proper-sized undersea trench in which the tubes were to be set. When the seabed soil foundation is rocky or composed of hard soils, the conventional process for laying tunnel sections involves digging a trench the length of the tube section, dropping each section into place, and then covering the installed section with excavated soil and rock. Instead of rock and soil, the floor of the Lingdingyang Channel is mostly composed of clay and silt. This made the tube excavation and re-covering process that much more difficult, particularly because it had to occur 45 meters below the surface (Hu et al. 2015; Zhang and Broere 2019). Figuring out how to precisely lay the tube sections became a trial-and-error process that involved frequent and extended delays as new approaches were tried and tested. All of these technical problems were eventually solved by the project's engineers, but not after adding an additional two years to the overall construction schedule.

Environmental Challenges

Criticisms about the HKZMB's environmental impacts had been voiced from the outset. The principal concern had to do with likely adverse impacts on the Chinese white dolphin population (*Sousa chinensis*), which was known to be in decline. After-construction studies of the dolphin population confirmed the merit of these concerns, noting that dolphin encounter rates in the vicinity of the HKZMB had declined 20 percent compared with pre-construction rates (Chen 2019).

More troublesome for the Bridge's construction was a lawsuit filed by a 66-year-old Hong Kong woman alleging that the Environmental Impact Report (EIR) prepared for the Bridge by the Hong Kong Department of Environmental Protection had failed to properly evaluate the project's fine particulate, sulfur dioxide, and ozone air pollution impacts. The initial ruling of the Hong Kong High Court supported her challenge, causing the EIR to be withdrawn and construction to be suspended for a year. The Hong Kong SAR government later prevailed upon appeal, but not before the legal challenge and delay had added HK$8.8 billion (US$1.1 billion) to the project cost.[5]

Complaints piled upon complaints, becoming ever more political. As anti-Mainland sentiment in Hong Kong grew in response to anti-democratic "reforms" proposed by the Chinese government, Hong Kong residents warned that the HKZMB would allow visitors from the Mainland to flood into Kowloon and Hong Kong, further pushing up housing and other living costs. Increasingly, the HKZMB came to be seen by Hong Kong residents as a link *from* China rather than *to* China.

A Drifting Island and a Hidden Road

To save money dredging and filling the seabed floor, HKZMB engineers designed the artificial island at the Bridge's eastern Hong Kong anchorage to effectively float on top of the sea bottom, the first time such a design had been tried in Hong Kong. Upon the island's completion in 2015, measurements confirmed that it had floated 6 to 7 meters from its intended position. With construction still underway, the drifting island never posed a safety problem, but it was certainly an embarrassment, prompting the Hong Kong Highway Department to publicly proclaim that the island's shifting was caused by normal subsidence activity and fell squarely within the expected range of "normal" movement (Yau and Sum 2018). Fixing the problem would end up adding another HK$5.5 billion (US$0.7 billion) to the HKZMB's construction cost.

Press reports further heightened the impression of a project whose costs were out of control when newspapers in Hong Kong incorrectly reported the Bridge's mounting costs in Hong Kong dollars instead of Chinese yuan. The media-reported cost estimates also failed to properly separate out the costs of building the Tuen Mun–Chek Lap Kok highway link, claiming that the road project's costs had been intentionally "hidden" in HKZMB's mounting construction budget. A 2016 report by the Hong Kong SAR Legislative Council subsequently corrected the record, but did little to allay citizen concerns that costs for the bridge project were out of control.

ECONOMIC RESTRUCTURING REDUCES THE DEMAND FOR THE HKZMB

Home to 70 million residents in two of China's "big four" cities—Guangzhou and Shenzhen—the 56,000 square kilometer PRD is the wealthiest and most productive of China's urban regions. The PRD's rise began in 1979 when Chinese leader Deng Xiaoping declared that it would be the focus of his government's efforts to move the Chinese economy away from its volatile past and toward a more stable and export-oriented future. Deng's plan worked better than even he could have foreseen (Vogel 1989), and with China's admission into the World Trade Organization in 2001, the PRD was on its way to cementing its position as manufacturing center of the world, with the cities of Guangzhou, Shenzhen and Zhuhai serving as its production and transport hubs (Loo 1999; Yeh and Xu 2006).

There was just one problem with this arrangement: the three cities were physically separated from each other by the Pearl River estuary and by Lingdingyang Bay. The estuary separation was easily bridged but travel from Zhuhai in the east to Shenzhen in the west by either road or rail required a much more circuitous journey. With Hong Kong taking its place in 1997 as the PRD's fourth economic pole, the physical separation problem only worsened. To promote the further economic integration of the PRD region and to enable it to get to the next level of productivity would require bridging its internal gaps between Hong Kong and Shenzhen on the east side and Zhuhai and Zhongshan on the west side (Bian and Yeh 2020; Yeung 2006).

Early opinions differed as to how those gaps should be filled, with the final arrangement, as agreed to in 2005, consisting of the Shenzhen–Zhongshan Bridge connecting Shenzhen and Zhongshan directly, and the HKZMB connecting Hong Kong and Zhuhai via Lantau Island and Hong Kong's new Chek Lap Kok airport. Looking eastward, the Bridge would facilitate the relocation of Hong Kong's remaining low-value manufacturing industries to Zhuhai, where land and labor were both still relatively cheap (Yang 2012). Looking west, the Bridge would add to Hong Kong's eastern hinterland, further cementing its status as the PRD's international gateway. Even though Macau had recently expanded its own international airport to accommodate a rising tide of visitors to its casinos, for many tourists Hong Kong was still the entry point of choice.

Predicting the future evolution of urban and regional economies is always fraught, and in the years after 2005 the economic dynamics of the PRD region changed considerably. Macau became a gambling mecca, drawing air travelers from across Southeast Asia. Shenzhen became China's foremost technology and R&D center, strengthening its financial and service ties to Hong Kong and Beijing. Guangzhou emerged as the southern terminus of China's rapidly-expanding high-speed rail network (Yeh et al. 2015).

All these changes served to economically marginalize Zhuhai, and to lessen the need for a bridge connecting Hong Kong to Zhuhai, especially if it didn't include a high-speed rail link. Forecasts of HKZMB traffic completed in 2006 projected that, by 2020, the Bridge would carry between 15,350 and 22,300 vehicles per day, with two-thirds of the traffic flowing between Hong Kong and Zhuhai, and the remaining third occurring between Hong Kong and Macau. The two travel flows would be for different purposes, with the Hong Kong–Zhuhai trips being made mostly for business and trade reasons, while the Macau-bound trips would mostly consist of leisure travelers and tourists.

Even before Covid-19 and civil unrest reduced travel into and out of Hong Kong, traffic on the HKZMB never came close to the original projections. As of January 2020, vehicular traffic on the Bridge was averaging just 3,660 vehicle per day, which was even less than a quarter of projected traffic levels. Because of Covid-19 travel restrictions, and despite temporarily halting toll collections, by March 2020 traffic flows on the HKZMB were down 59 percent over January levels. Except for truck trips, the decline in traffic was across the board, affecting private vehicle trips, coach trips, and shuttle bus trips (Figure 9.3).

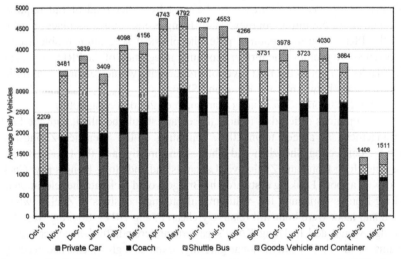

Source: Created by the authors using the monthly traffic and transport digest released by the Transport Department of the HKSAR.

Figure 9.3   *HKZMB average daily vehicular traffic, October 2018–*
March 2020

Nor did the expected growth of truck trips between Zhuhai and Hong Kong ever materialize. The 2008 Global Financial Crisis (GFC) hit China's manufacturing exporters particularly hard, hastening the decision by China's leaders to accelerate the country's shift toward expanding the role of domestic consumption and services. Rather than continuing to lead China's labor-intensive, low-tech, export-oriented manufacturing industries that fueled its economic development during the 1980s and 1990s, the Guangdong government re-oriented the PRD economy around a new *shuang lun qi dong* (i.e., "double wheels") model, shifting Guangdong's economic base toward producer services and high-value, technology-based manufacturing. These changes did not bode well for Zhuhai, which saw its status in China's economic hierarchy reduced from that of a secondary economy to a tertiary one (Cheung 2015; Fang et al. 2015). With less export-bound manufacturing output originating in Zhuhai, the number of trucks bound for Hong Kong's international air and seaport facilities gradually declined. This shift is evident from the leveling-out of the top trend line in Figure 9.4, which shows the relative decline in the once-dominant role Chinese manufacturing exports flowing through Hong Kong. Meanwhile, Shenzhen and Guangzhou have both substantially expanded their own airport and container port facilities, further reducing the flow of goods from China's interior manufacturing centers to Hong Kong (Liu et al. 2013). Since its opening in 2018, an average of just 226 trucks have rolled across the HKZMB each day.

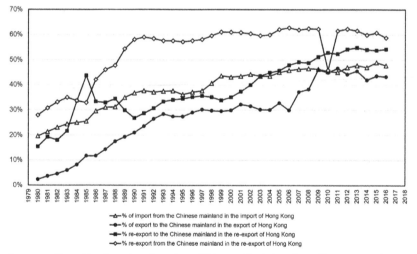

Source: Created by the authors from Annual Digest of Statistics released by Census and Statistics Department of Hong Kong SAR (1979–2018).

Figure 9.4   *Share of Cross-border Trade between Hong Kong SAR and the Chinese Mainland*

Looking ahead, the completion of the long-delayed and competing Shenzhen–Zhongshan Bridge, now scheduled for 2024, poses additional challenges for the economic viability of the HKZMB. When it comes to building large-scale surface transportation megaprojects, simply being first does not always confer durable benefits.

LESSONS AND TAKEAWAYS

Thus far into its still-brief history, the Hong Kong–Zhuhai–Macau Bridge offers at least four important lessons for planners of large and costly transportation megaprojects.

1. *Focus on the assumptions behind the projections.* No projection of megaproject demand is ever spot on. There are just too many possible variables to consider. Rather than focusing their economic feasibility studies on future truck and coach projections, HKZMB advocates should have focused on the assumptions underlying those projections. If they had, they would have quickly identified two that were questionable. The first was that regional growth trends would continue as they had in the recent past regardless of any new internal dynamics. Statisticians call this belief that the behavior of a system's elements must necessarily follow the full system's behavior the "ecological fallacy." The more likely dynamic is that small disturbances at the sub-system level add up to big system-level instabilities. Had the proponents of the HKZMB taken this into account, they would have realized that Macau's growth as a global tourist destination would inevitably lead it to expand its own airline connections and capacity, thereby lessening its dependence on Hong Kong as a gateway via the HKZMB. Similarly faulty was the presumption that Zhuhai would necessarily become the PRD's next low-cost manufacturing center and need Hong Kong as its principal export platform. History shows that Chinese cities often act in competition with each other, so the assumption that building a US$19.1 billion bridge would somehow lessen their competitive tendencies was erroneous. By reducing the potential traffic catchment area for the HKZMB, Hong Kong's rejection of the "Double-Y" configuration that would have extended a roadway link to Shenzhen also proved to be short-sighted.

2. *Scenarios and sensitivity analysis can help identify critical project vulnerabilities.* The usual practice when developing demand projections for large-scale projects is to put forth a "low" projection under which the project will clearly not be feasible, a "high projection" under which the project will be feasible but is understood by all to be wildly optimistic, and a "middle" projection which not only makes the project seem feasible,

but is clearly preferred because of its inherent reasonableness—meaning only that it is neither too high nor too low. In the case of the HKZMB, the middle projection did indeed justify the construction of the project. A more robust approach would have been to conduct a series of sensitivity analyses around several well-thought-out scenarios identifying different combinations of trip generation activity patterns, traffic volumes, and toll revenues that would have caused the HKZMB to underperform its financial targets, and then to explore the likelihood of those scenarios occurring. Had those who approved the HKZMB followed this path, they would have quickly realized that there was no reasonable combination of traffic volumes and tolls that would have rendered the HKZMB profitable using any reasonable discount rate. Raising tolls would cause traffic volumes to drop while lowering them would lead to unacceptable revenue declines. Because infrastructure projects in China are generally not evaluated in present value terms, the utility of scenarios that posit different rates and combinations of revenue growth over time is much reduced—in most cases, intentionally so. China, with its history of adventurous lending by state-owned banking institutions whose losses are covered by the government may be able to afford such laxity, but other governments are unlikely to be so lucky.

3. *Bigger isn't always more economical (especially when salt water is involved).* Chinese infrastructure designers and engineers have proven to be especially talented at assembling large infrastructure systems using highly-standardized components and construction practices. As discussed elsewhere in this volume, it was the use of such standardization practices that enabled China to build the world's most extensive high-speed rail network in a little more than a dozen years. Open sea bridge projects are more difficult to standardize than rail projects. For one thing, bottom conditions can vary greatly, as HKZMB construction crews discovered when they tried to build a 6.7 km undersea tunnel out of 180 m prefabricated concrete sections 140 feet below the surface of Lingdingyang Bay. Open sea bridges are also subject to extreme and variable force loadings, requiring that they always be overdesigned. Once completed, bridges cannot easily be shut down or taken out of service for required maintenance. And, as the engineers who designed the floating island that served as the HKM Bridge's eastern anchorage found out, new designs and technologies do not always work as expected, requiring costly retrofits. These problems are not unique to long-length open-sea bridges, but they are likely to be endemic to them, reducing any potential cost-savings benefits associated with standardization and economies of scale.

4. *When projects underperform, multi-national financing consortiums can become problematic.* Diversification may work well for individ-

ual and institutional investors, but it can be problematic for multiple governments trying to finance infrastructure megaprojects. China has used inter-governmental financing partnerships to great advantage when seeking to consolidate support for large infrastructure projects across multiple agencies and units of government. Similarly, Hong Kong has become one of the world's leaders in putting together public–private partnerships around large transportation infrastructure projects. In both situations, the projects themselves have generated significant and monetizable spinoff benefits that could then be used to pay back the project investors. The problem with a bridge, especially an ultra-long bridge in the middle of a bay, is that there is no physical or institutional "catchment area" within which any spinoff benefits can accumulate. So, instead of having the opportunity to share potential benefits, the partnership behind the HKZMB gets to share only potential risks and losses. The fact that the HKZMB was financed by a partnership that combined three semi-sovereign states with a financial institution that was effectively backed by one of those states only added to the uncertainty about how much financial liability each partner had taken on.

Of course, the big question for the HKZMB is what now? White elephant though it may be, the governments of China and Hong Kong are not about to shut it down. Is there any scenario in which it might be restored to anything approaching, if not profitability, then at least break-even status? A glimpse of hope was seen at the end of 2021 when China's State Council rolled out its 14th Five-Year Plan, which included an announcement by the government of Guangdong Province of a potential revival of the "Double-Y" Plan. If pursued, this initiative would add a new northern spur from the HKZMB's eastside artificial island to Shenzhen's Shekou district, thereby adding Shenzhen's 3.8 million licensed vehicles to this vehicle-hungry project. However, how much would such an extension cost, who would pay for it, and perhaps most importantly, will the Pearl River Delta's ever-changing economic and mobility geographies still be in sync with the project once it is finished?

ACKNOWLEDGEMENTS

We would like to acknowledge the partial funding support from Joint Programming Initiative (JPI) Urban Europe and National Natural Foundation of China (NSFC) (Grant Number: 71961137003) and the National Key R&D Program from the Ministry of Science and Technology of China (Grant number: 2019YFB1600703).

NOTES

1. https://www.chinadaily.com.cn/a/202010/26/WS5f967d8aa31024ad0ba8101c.html.
2. For purposes of comparison, the one-way private vehicle toll on the 42 km Qingdao Haiwan Bridge/Tunnel in Shandong Province is 50 RMB (US$7.9).
3. All RMB-to-dollar equivalencies in this chapter are estimated using a conversion rate of 1 RMB to US$0.157.
4. Contrary to Western perceptions, which see economic investment decisions in China occurring in an entirely top-down fashion directed from Beijing, individual provincial and city governments have tremendous discretion in how they meet their nationally-set economic development goals, and often act as vigorous rivals.
5. The original plaintiff subsequently revealed that she had filed her complaint at the request of a third party whose identity was never revealed.

REFERENCES

Bian, F. and Yeh, A. G. 2020. Spatial–economic impact of missing national highway links on China's regional economy. *Transportation Research Part D: Transport and Environment*, 84, 102377.

Chen, T. 2019. *Long-term monitoring of population dynamics of Chinese White Dolphins Sousa chinensis in Lingding Bay of the PRD Region: The second stage*. Research Report No. MEEF2018006: http://env.threerunwaysystem.com/en/meef/.

Cheung, E. and Chan, A. P. C. 2009. Is BOT the best financing model to procure infrastructure projects? A case study of the Hong Kong–Zhuhai–Macau Bridge. *Journal of Property Investment & Finance*, 27(3), 290–302.

Cheung, W. L. 2015. *Assessment of the impact and opportunities of the HK-Zhuhai-Macau Bridge to HK in the new economic situation*. Research Report No. 2013.C.003.14A: https://www.pico.gov.hk/en/research_report/report1415first_round.html.

Fang, Z., Gong, X. W. and Yang, Y. 2015. Assessment of the transport function of the Hong Kong–Zhuhai–Macau Bridge in the New Economic Situation. *Hong Kong and Macau Journal*, 4, 24–37 (in Chinese).

Flyvbjerg, B. N., Bruzelius, N. and Rothnengatter, W. 2003. *Megaprojects and Risk: An Anatomy of Ambition*. Cambridge: Cambridge University Press.

HKSAR Census and Statistics Department 1979–2018. *Annual Digest of Statistics*. Hong Kong: Government Printer.

HKSAR Transport and Housing Bureau, 2008, February 28. Press briefing by HKSAR Transport and Housing Bureau. https://www.info.gov.hk/gia/general/200802/28/P200802280261.htm.

Hu, Z. N., Xie, Y. L. and Wang, J. 2015. Challenges and strategies involved in designing and constructing a 6 km immersed tunnel: A case study of the Hong Kong–Zhuhai–Macao Bridge. *Tunnelling and Underground Space Technology*, 50, 171–177.

Liu, L., Wang, K. Y. and Yip, T. L. 2013. Development of a container port system in PRD: Path to multi-gateway ports. *Journal of Transport Geography*, 28, 30–38.

Loo, B. P. 1999. Development of a regional transport infrastructure: Some lessons from the Zhujiang Delta, Guangdong, China. *Journal of Transport Geography*, 71, 43–63.

Vogel, E. F. 1989. *One Step Ahead in China: Guangdong under Reform*. Cambridge, MA: Harvard University Press.

Yang, C. 2006. The PRD and Hong Kong: An evolving cross-boundary region under "one country, two systems". *Habitat International*, 301, 61–86.

Yang, C. 2012. Restructuring the export-oriented industrialization in the PRD, China: Institutional evolution and emerging tension. *Applied Geography*, 321, 143–157.

Yau, C. and Sum L. K. 2018. Safety concerns over artificial island at mega Hong Kong–Zhuhai–Macau Bridge dismissed. *South China Morning Post.* April 5.

Yeh, A. G. O. and Xu, J. 2006. Turning of the dragon head: Changing role of Hong Kong in the regional development of the PRD. In A. G. Yeh, V. F. Sit, G. Chen and Y. Zhou (eds.), *Developing a Competitive PRD in South China under One Country-Two systems*, pp. 63–95. Hong Kong: Hong Kong University Press.

Yeh, A. G., Yang, F. F. and Wang, J. 2015. Producer service linkages and city connectivity in the mega-city region of China: A case study of the Pearl River Delta. *Urban Studies*, 5213, 2458–2482.

Yeung, Y. M. 2006. An emerging development focus from the Pearl River Delta West to Western Guangdong: A research report. *Eurasian Geography and Economics*, 47(2), 243–250.

Zhang, X. and Broere, W. 2019. Settlements of immersed tunnel on soft ground: A case study. In D. Peila, G. Viggiani, and T. Celestino (eds.), *Proceedings of the WTC 2019 ITA-AITES World Tunnel Congress WTA 2019. Tunnels and Underground Cities. Engineering and Innovation Meet Archaeology, Architecture and Art*, pp. 1234–1241. London: CRC Press.

10. Singapore's Jewel Changi Airport— always raising the bar

John D. Landis

ABBREVIATIONS USED IN THIS CHAPTER

CAAS	Civil Aviation Authority of Singapore
CAG	Changi Airport Group
CAPE	Changi Airport Planners and Engineers
SIA	Singapore International Airlines

Ask any international frequent flier to identify their favorite airport and there is a good chance Singapore Changi Airport will top their list. In terms of passenger service quality and convenience, terminal design, and landside access, Changi defines the international airport state of the art. Since the British airline consultancy Skytrax launched its Best International Airport Award in 2000, Changi has won the award 11 times, including every year from 2013 to 2020.[1] More than just an airport, Changi has become a pre-eminent symbol of Singapore's global economic status (Chua 2011). And the pre-eminent symbol of Singapore Changi Airport is its new Jewel Terminal (Table 10.1).

In fact, the Jewel (also known as the Jewel Changi Airport or the Jewel Changi) isn't a terminal at all. It is a glass and steel-enclosed nature-themed entertainment and retail complex built atop a multi-level 2,500-car parking garage amidst Changi Airport's three main passenger terminals (Figure 10.1). Five stories tall and with a gross floor area of 1,461,000 square feet—a bit more than the Chrysler Building in New York City—the toroidal-shaped Jewel Changi includes a full-height indoor waterfall and garden; a 130-room luxury hotel; an 11-screen movie theatre; a 30-restaurant dining and shopping arcade that includes; Marks & Spencer, Muji, Zara, Uniqlo and the only airport Apple Store; as well as extensive passenger check-in and baggage-drop services (Figures 10.2 and 10.3).[2] It does not, however, include any passenger arrival or departure gates. For those, travelers must walk or take the Skytrain to Terminals 1, 2 or 3, or take a shuttle bus to Terminal 4.

Table 10.1   *Singapore's Jewel Changi in brief*

Description	Opened in 2019, Jewel Changi is a state-of-the-art airport passenger concourse linking Singapore Changi Airport's three main terminals and featuring a 5-story waterfall, an indoor nature park, a destination shopping mall, and a 2,500-car parking garage
Lead sponsor(s)	Singapore Civil Aviation Authority (CAAS), Changi Airport Group (CAG), CapitaLand (Investor)
Primary rationale	Create a unique passenger facility to bolster Singapore Changi's reputation as the world's best airport.
Primary funding sources	Government borrowing
Regulatory/funding approval given in	2014
Construction started	2015
Construction completed	2019
Development cost (US$)	$1.3 billion
Schedule and cost overrun	None
Principal takeaways	Undertaken as an image-building project to replace an outmoded surface parking lot, Jewel Changi has succeeded in meeting its visitation goals because of its unique and high-quality design and because of the planning, marketing and project management expertise of its sponsors and developers.

Developed at a cost of US$1.3 billion as a joint venture between airport oper-
ator Changi Airport Group (CAG) and property developer CapitaLand, Jewel
Changi was intended first and foremost to establish Changi as a branded traveler destination, similar in concept if not design to the Burj Khalifa in Dubai or
to the Louvre in Paris. Designed by a consortium of architects led by Moshe
Safdie, who also designed Singapore's iconic Marina Bay Sands Hotel, Jewel
Changi is a place for lingering, admiring, eating, shopping and, hopefully,
coming back to. Six months after its soft opening in April 2019, Jewel Changi
had welcomed 50 million visitors (exceeding its target for the entire year), and
prior to the Covid-19 pandemic was receiving about 300,000 visitations a day.
Those who like their buildings to occupy neat little categories aren't quite sure
what to make of Jewel Changi. It is simultaneously a passenger concourse, an
oasis for weary travelers, a shopping mall, and with the largest freestanding
indoor waterfall in the world, a structural and natural spectacle. Jewel Changi
has attracted its share of international attention, and not just for its architecture. Three years before it opened, Jewel Changi was awarded the 2016
International Architecture Award by The Chicago Athenaeum, an international
museum of architecture and design. More recently, Jewel Changi received the
Singapore Institute of Architecture's 2020 Building of the Year and Design
Award; the 2020 Prix Versailles Prize for Shopping Mall Interiors; the TEA

Thea Award for Outstanding Airport Destination Experience; a Special Jury Award from MAPIC; a global retail property developer association; and the Singapore President's Design Award.

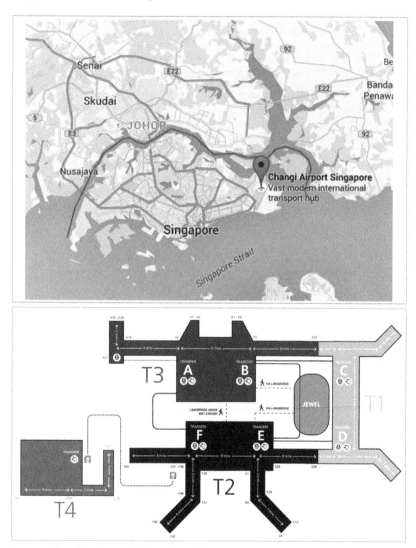

Source: Top: Googlemaps; Bottom: changiairport.com

Figure 10.1   Singapore Changi Airport locator map and site plan

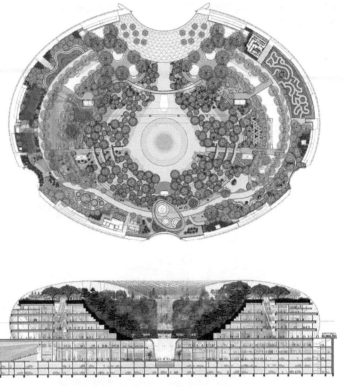

Source: Safdie Architects.

Figure 10.2   Jewel Changi section and plan view

Yet to see Jewel Changi just as a mixed-use one-off novelty—which it indeed is—is to miss the bigger and more important picture. Jewel Changi is the end result of process of continuous evolution that began with the 1981 completion of Singapore Changi Terminal 1, a rather utilitarian facility with little to distinguish it from a design or passenger service perspective (Bok 2015; Henderson 2017). Over the next 35 years, Singapore's Civil Aviation Authority (CAAS) and then later the Changi Airport Group (CAG), a public–private corporation controlled by Singapore's Ministry of Finance, continuously learned from favorable and unfavorable experiences to become the world's foremost airport owner, developer and operator (CAAS, 1994). Moreover, as with nearly everything that happens in Singapore, Changi's lessons would be shared with other government agencies, creating positive knowledge spillovers that would benefit other infrastructure system and public facility investments.

Source: traveleisure.com.

Figure 10.3   Jewel Changi interior view showing vortex waterfall

CHANGI AIRPORT TAKES SHAPE

Humble and Hurried Beginnings

Located at Singapore's eastern tip, and opened to the public on July 1, 1981, Changi International Airport was preceded by Seletar Airfield, which opened in 1930; by Kallang Airport which opened in 1937; and by Paya Lebar Airport in 1955.[3] With but a single runway, Paya Lebar was purpose-built as an international airport, serving as the hub for Singapore and Malaysia's joint national airline, Malaysian-Singapore Airlines (MSA). Eager to bolster Singapore's role in Southeast Asia following the forced 1965 dissolution of its short-lived federation with Malaysia, Singapore's ambitious Prime Minister Lee Kuan Yew quickly negotiated bilateral landing rights agreements between Singapore and many of its regional neighbors. Malaysia was slower to do the same, and by the early 1970s, four out of every five flights arriving or departing from Malaysia or Singapore were taking off or landing at Paya Lebar. This geographical imbalance contributed to the voluntary dissolution of MSA in 1972 and to the subsequent creation of Singapore Airlines.

With the Vietnam War winding down and the Japanese economy ascendant, air travel in and out of Paya Lebar during the early 1970s continued to climb. To accommodate the increase in demand, a British airport consultant hired by the Singapore government recommended building a second and longer runway at Paya Lebar. Expanding Paya Lebar was technically feasible but sure to be expensive since it would require permanently diverting the nearby Serangoon River. The alternative to expanding Paya Lebar was to construct an entirely new airport at Changi Airbase four miles to the east (Tan 2021). At just 430 hectares, Changi was too small for a two-runway international airport, but unlike Paya Lebar, it could be expanded eastward by reclaiming the shallow coastal beds off Singapore's eastern tip. Changi's other big advantage was that flights could take off and land over the water and not impact the housing estates that surrounded Paya Lebar.

Prime Minister Lee Kwan Yew, according to his later memoirs, personally favored the Changi option, but in an effort to appear impartial, gave the job of recommending whether to expand Paya Lebar or build a new airport at Changi to Howe Yoon Chong, the Chairman of Singapore's Port Authority and a political confidant (Lee 2000). Howe was well respected in Singapore's government and business community for successfully completing large infra-structure and engineering projects, especially those involving landfill opera-tions. Howe's report was delivered to Singapore's government in April 1975 while Lee Kwan Yew was visiting the United States. Howe's report projected that it would take nine years to build a second runway at Paya Lebar because of the time needed to relocate the Serangoon River. Building a new airport and runway at Changi, by contrast, would take only five or six years, and a second runway could be added a year later. The cost of the two options was essentially the same. The reason the Changi option could be completed faster was that its design and construction could be managed by engineers already working for Singapore's Department of Public Works. The Changi option's two biggest pieces, building a new passenger terminal and filling in the seabed, could be undertaken simultaneously. After reviewing Howe's report in his hotel room in Washington, DC, Lee cabled acting Prime Minister Keng Swee to proceed with the Changi alternative.

To manage Changi's construction, Lee turned to two of his most experi-enced lieutenants. The first was Howe, whose committee report had recom-mended the Changi option, and the second was Sim Kee Boon, then serving as the Permanent Secretary of Singapore's Communications Ministry. Sim knew nothing about building or operating airports, but had a reputation for being a quick learner, a thorough master of detail, and, in a project that would involve dozens of consultants and subcontractors, a firm taskmaster. Rather than take the extra time needed to assemble an international consulting team to develop a master plan for the new airport, Lee gave the job of designing and engineering Changi to the government's Public Works Department. This proved a fortuitous decision for Changi's long-term future because it meant the government would have to develop its own airport planning and engineering capabilities.

Completed in less than a year, the Draft Changi Airport Master Plan made the most of the Changi site, locating the airport's two 4,000 meter runways at its eastern and western edges, leaving plenty of space between them for terminal and cargo facilities. Changi Phase 1, which was scheduled for completion in 1981, would include a 45-gate terminal building, the first of Changi's two runways, a new 80 m tall control tower, numerous support facilities and structures, and a separate air cargo complex (Changi Airport 1980). All told, Phase 1 construction activities were expected to cost between S$1.1 billion and S$1.3 billion, or between US$1.5 billion and US$1.9 billion. Phase 2, which would be completed in 1984, would include Changi's second runway, an additional 23 aircraft gates and bays, and an expansion of Changi's air freight facilities. The overall construction budget and timeline were deemed to be tight but doable.

Construction work on Changi proceeded quickly. Seabed reclamation activities were completed in 1977, allowing runway construction work to begin months ahead of schedule. The foundation stone of Changi Terminal 1 was laid on August 1979, and the entire building was completed just two years later. Although bigger and airier than the terminal at Paya Lebar, the design of Changi Terminal 1 was more utilitarian than noteworthy. Precise estimates of the cost of completing Phase 1 are difficult to come by. The government put it at just under the S$1.1 billion mark that had originally been budgeted. Independent observers put the cost at closer to S$1.3 billion—still an impressive achievement in a realm where 50 percent cost overruns were not uncommon.

With just one runway in operation, Changi was initially limited with respect to the number of flights it could accommodate. Compared with Paya Lebar, Changi's longer runway could oblige more wide-body planes, so even though the number of flights into and out of Changi was initially less than at Paya Lebar, total passenger counts were higher. Following the opening of Changi's second runway in 1984, the number of inbound and outbound flights also started rising, and in 1986, for the first time, annual passenger movements in and out of Changi exceeded 10 million.

From the beginning, the relationship between Changi Airport and Singapore International Airlines (SIA) was mutually beneficial. Not wanting to compete for regional travelers with other Southeast Asia airlines, SIA branded itself as a premium international carrier; and to expand its business, aggressively pursued reciprocal takeoff and landing rights between Changi and airports in Europe and North America.[4] This arrangement enabled SIA to efficiently standardize its airplane fleet around the Boeing 747 jumbo jet, which first entered service with SIA in 1973.

In addition to destinations in Europe and North America, SIA, through Prime Minister Lee Kwan Yew, also kept an eye open for potential opportunities in China (Lee 2000). Lee had a ready partner in Chinese Communist Party leader Deng Xiaoping, who, after taking a few years to consolidate his political power following the 1976 death of Mao Zedong, was eager to expand China's economic and trade relations with the rest of the world. Deng's first trip abroad in 1978 after being named China's Communist Party leader was to Singapore where he insistently queried Lee Kwan Yew as to how Singapore had achieved so much economic progress in so short a time. Lee generously offered Deng his thoughts and advice, but among the things he asked for in return was a commitment to expanding air travel between Singapore and China. A year later, SIA signed an agreement with China's Civil Aviation Administration, establishing regularly scheduled air service between Changi and Beijing. Flight traffic between Singapore and China rose continuously over the ensuing 40 years, and by 2020, ten different Chinese airlines were flying in and out of Changi on a daily basis.

In addition to actively seeking out new trade partners, Lee was constantly measuring Singapore's economic progress against Hong Kong's, its chief regional rival. Believing that Hong Kong regarded Singapore in a similar manner, Lee was especially puzzled why Hong Kong's leaders were dragging approval of construction of their own new airport to replace the obsolete and dangerous Kai Tak Airport in Kowloon. Hong Kong would eventually have to act, but until they did, Lee was determined to continue to press Singapore's airport advantage (Lee 2000).

On the Expansion Path

Lee Kuan Yew was a fervent believer in the "if you build it, they will come" school of infrastructure investment, and, from the beginning, Changi was sized for expansion. The 1976 Master Plan had envisioned adding a second Changi terminal sometime in the late 1980s and, right on schedule, construction of Changi Terminal 2 began in 1986 (CAAS 1989). The new Terminal 2 was 50 percent larger than Terminal 1, and befitting Singapore's rising status in the world, much more luxurious. Located immediately to the south of Terminal 1 and connected by a new automated Skytrain service, Changi Terminal 2 opened to the flying public in November 1990, quickly becoming the center of SIA's international flights, including its new non-stop 747-400 service to Los Angeles. With Changi's terminal capacity having more than doubled, annual passenger counts began rising at double-digit rates, exceeding 20 million in 1994 and 25 million in 1997 (Figure 10.4).[5] This put Changi on par for the first time with Hong Kong's Kai Tak Airport, which Hong Kong, after years of delay, was finally replacing with a new international airport on Chek Lap Kok Island.

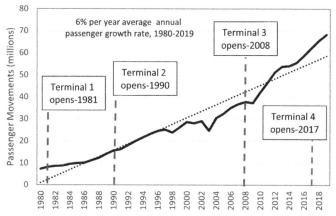

Source: Changi Airport Group

Figure 10.4   Singapore Changi Airport passenger volumes, 1980–2019

Lee Kuan Yew stepped down as prime minister in November 1990, but his view that Singapore should continue to invest in infrastructure capacity in advance of demand remained very much in favor. Although Changi's 1976 master plan had envisioned just two passenger terminals, it had presciently left sufficient space for a third terminal that would mirror Terminal 2 in size and configuration. Planning for Terminal 3 began in earnest in late 1996, and despite the economic uncertainties associated with the 1997 Asian Financial Crisis, continued at a steady clip. Unlike Terminals 1 and 2, whose utilitarian designs promoted function over form, Terminal 3 would be much more passenger-oriented and luxurious. The job of designing the new terminal was again given to Singapore's Public Works Department, but for the first time an experienced international airport design firm, Skidmore, Owings and Merrill, was brought in to help (Kuang 2009). The final design for Terminal 3 would feature a unique roof structure as well as an immediately adjacent nine-story Crowne Plaza Hotel.

Construction of Changi Terminal 3 began in 1999 with an estimated construction budget of S$1.75 billion. Befitting the new terminal's new features as well as the need to keep both Terminals 1 and 2 in operation, construction was planned to take six years, with an opening date scheduled for 2006. Construction paused following the SARS outbreak in 2003, causing Terminal 3's original opening date to be pushed back an additional two years. When Terminal 3 was officially dedicated on July 1, 2008, it included a traveler amenity no other airport terminal in the world had: a tropical butterfly garden featuring a 6-meter grotto waterfall and 40 species of butterflies. The idea of building a garden in the terminal was a natural extension of Lee Kwan Yew's having branded Singapore as "the city in the garden," and immediately garnered international attention and numerous awards. Over the next ten years, seven additional garden areas would be added to Changi's main three terminals, culminating in the 2019 opening of the garden-centric Changi Jewel.

The completion of Terminal 3 boosted Changi's annual capacity from 44 million to 66 million passengers per year. In 2006, two years before Terminal 3 opened, Changi won Skytrax's "World's Best Airport Award," for the first time, breaking the new Hong Kong airport's five-year winning streak. Changi would win the award again in 2010, and then every year from 2013 to 2020. Even though it is now more than ten years old, Terminal 3 is still frequently cited by travelers as their favorite airport terminal in the world. More important than awards, Changi airline passenger visits kept climbing, passing 40 million in 2010 and 50 million in 2012.[6]

Rare Missteps

Changi officials were not immune from occasional missteps. To add to Singapore's international prestige—and despite a raft of consultant studies recommending that Singapore build an island-wide express bus system instead of a metro system—Lee Kuan Yew and his government were intent on building a modern subway system, and after many years of planning, construction finally began on Singapore's two-line MRT (Mass Rapid Transit) system in 1982. The 15-station North–South MRT Line would bring riders downtown from the northern part of the island, while the 26-station East–West MRT Line would bring them downtown from housing estates in the east and west.

Initially at least, neither the North–South nor East–West Lines were intended to connect directly to Changi Airport. Instead, Changi passengers could travel between the airport and downtown Singapore by taking an express bus which connected to the East–West Line at the Tanah-Merah MRT station. The entire trip, including transfers, took between 30 and 45 minutes. This was longer than traveling by car or airport shuttle, but shorter than by local bus. The extra time it took to transfer at the Tanah-Merah station was deemed by travelers as burdensome, especially when compared with Hong Kong's planned express train service connecting central Hong Kong to its new airport on Lantau Island. This led to proposals in Singapore to build an East–West Line extension terminating at Changi, thereby eliminating the need for a transfer at Tanah-Merah. The final scheme, unveiled by Deputy Prime Minister Lee Hsien Loong in 1996, called for constructing a new underground MRT subway station midway between Terminal 2 and the newly-approved Terminal 3 that would connect to the East–West Line (later renamed the Green Line) at the Expo MRT station (*The Business Times* 1996). Construction of the new Changi spur (and additional switching and siding facilities at Tanah-Merah to permit direct service between Changi and downtown Singapore) was completed in 2001, and service began in early 2002.

Despite its convenience and relatively low cost, the new subway service failed to meet its ridership forecasts and was quietly discontinued a year after its opening. This was a rare comeuppance for Singapore transportation planners whose belief that demand would always materialize to take advantage of new transportation investments had proved unerring in the past.

The other misstep Changi officials made was to build a budget airlines terminal. This was less an outright mistake than a matter of being swept up in the trends of the day (Min 2006). With the dramatic rise of the Four Asian Tiger economies (Singapore, Taiwan, South Korea and Hong Kong) in the early 1990s, and following the budget airline example then being set in the United States by Southwest Airlines and in the UK by RyanAir and EasyJet in Europe, a rush of investors had entered the Asian airline passenger market offering leisure travelers frequent service at rock bottom fares. Among the leaders of this new generation of budget airlines were AirAsia in Malaysia, Thai Smile Airlines in Thailand, and Tiger Airways and Jetstar Asia in Singapore.

The formula was usually the same (Hirsch 2017). To save on operating costs, budget airlines would fly a single airplane, usually a Boeing 737 or Airbus A320. Labor costs were kept low by hiring young pilots just out of the military or flying school and providing minimal inflight service. Regular maintenance activities were contracted out. To lower landing fees, airlines agreed to board passengers on the tarmac rather than from terminal airbridges. Instead of paying commissions to travel agents, passengers were expected to book their own tickets, first by phone or fax, and then later over the internet. Travelers responded in droves, and the number of leisure flyers skyrocketed. To handle the increased passenger volume, airport authorities started opening up budget-airline-only passenger terminals, usually located some distance from the main terminal. With AirAsia as its principal carrier, Kuala Lumpur was the first to do so in January 2006, building an entirely new low-cost carrier airport 20 km from its international facilities.

Changi quickly followed Kuala Lumpur's lead, opening its own budget airline terminal three months later in March 2006. Physically separate from Terminals 1 and 2 (and the soon to be completed Terminal 3), budget fliers could access the new Budget Terminal—the descriptive but bland sounding name was chosen through a public naming competition— only from a shuttle bus stop in the basement of Terminal 2. Despite its inconvenient location and access, fliers flocked to the new facility, requiring Changi officials to enlarge it in 2008.

In retrospect, Changi's timing could not have been worse. Singapore was the first Asian country to be impacted by the Global Financial Crisis emanating from America and Europe at the end of 2007. Following a 5.7 percent contraction during the second quarter of 2008, Singapore's economy declined by an additional 6.3 percent during the third quarter of 2008. Air freight shipments into and out of Changi took the biggest hit, declining 15.3 percent between 2008 and 2009. Airline passenger traffic also fell, with leisure travel-oriented budget airlines experiencing the biggest losses.

The new Budget Terminal had also compromised Changi's ever-expanding efforts to brand itself as a travel experience instead of an airport (Henderson 2017). These efforts were embodied in Changi Airport official's plans to include unique passenger amenities in each terminal, starting with Terminal 3's Butterfly Garden. Needing the land under the Budget Terminal to eventually accommodate a new full-service Terminal 4, Changi's budget terminal experiment ended abruptly in September 2012 when, with little fanfare, all Budget Terminal flights were moved to Terminal 2.[7] With a new business strategy and renewed confidence in its future, Changi was preparing to redefine the airport state of the art and, in light of what was being planned, a budget airline terminal presented the wrong image.

STATE OF THE ART

Singapore recovered quickly from the Global Financial Crisis, as did Changi. Changi passenger and freight volumes in 2010 were each up more than 10 percent compared with 2009, and the airport's own planning projections suggested that the number of Changi passengers could potentially reach 70 million by 2020.[8] To accommodate this new increment of growth, Changi would need yet another new passenger terminal, its fourth.

Change was also coming to Changi's organizational structure. Since its opening in 1981, Changi had been run by Singapore's Civil Aviation Authority (CAAS). This arrangement proved advantageous during Changi's early years by enabling CAAS to take advantage of the government's low borrowing costs and construction management expertise, but as time went on, CAAS, like many government agencies, had become increasingly bureaucratic. What was needed, or so officials believed, were government agencies that were nimble and entrepreneurial and run more like private businesses. With this goal in mind, operational responsibility for Changi Airport was shifted in 2009 from CAAS to a new publicly-chartered company, the Changi Airport Group (CAG). CAG's charge was simple: it was to make Changi the world's pre-eminent airport in terms of air carrier efficiency and passenger and cargo service (Changi Airport Group 2010). CAG also took over Changi Airports International (CAI), an airport management consulting group established within CAAS in 2004 to market Singapore's airport management expertise internationally.

As CAG executives looked ahead to 2020, they found themselves confronting a rapidly changing air travel market. With the rapid growth of China's urban middle-class, more and more of Changi's airplane traffic was coming from or bound for China. Load factors, the share of occupied seats on each plane, were also on the rise, which meant that airline boarding, disembarking, baggage, and ground transportation operations would have to become more efficient. After the 2001 terrorist attacks on New York City and the 2003 SARS outbreak, safety and security issues had also become much more important. Increased airline competition meant lower margins, which meant that carriers were looking for additional ways to save money by shifting personnel and service costs from airlines to airports. The hassle of flying had increased along with the convenience of flying, which meant that airports such as Changi that had cultivated a reputation for superior service had to continuously up their service quality game. Even though Changi had been privatized, which implied that any new airport facilities would have to pass a financial rate-of-return test, Singapore's government officials continued to regard Changi's success and excellent reputation as a reflection of their own.

Looking to accommodate an additional 40 million airline passengers by 2020 while also elevating the level of terminal amenities, CAG's first major decision was to replace the near-capacity Budget Terminal with a larger and more luxurious facility. To meet passenger projections, the new Terminal 4 would need to accommodate 16 million additional passengers annually in a physical footprint that was half the size of the existing Terminal 2. This would require designing a much more space-efficient facility. Whereas Terminals 1,2 and 3 had all been designed by Singapore's Department of Public Works, the responsibility of leading the design team for Terminal 4 was given to Singapore-based SAA Architects, who, while well regarded locally, had never designed an airport terminal. To compensate for SAA's lack of expertise, the other design team members were selected on the basis of their airport design and engineering experience. They included Benoy Ltd., AECOM, and Beca Carter Hollings & Ferner.[9] CAG would serve as the developer and project manager with most of Terminal 4's nearly US$1 billion cost financed by Singapore banks and financial institutions, albeit it backed by government loan guarantees.

The Terminal 4 design team faced several problems. With the construction of Terminal 3 having taken nine years (partly because of SARS-related delays), CAG wanted to finish Terminal 4 in three years or less. Bounded by Runway 2 to the east, a taxiway to the north, the airport circulation road to the west, and the Taneh-Merah Country Club and Golf Course to the south, Terminal 4's building footprint would have to be much smaller than the footprints of Terminals 1, 2 or 3. This need for increased space efficiency put a premium on maximizing gate efficiency and internal circulation. With more passenger gates per square meter than either Terminals 2 or 3, Terminal 4 would have to accommodate passengers and their baggage more efficiently. Terminal 4 would also have a higher share of its floorspace devoted to retail uses; and, building on the garden theme pioneered in Terminal 3, would have its own dedicated recreation areas. Last, Terminal 4's height would be limited to five stories in order not to block runway views from Changi's air traffic control tower adjacent to Terminal 1. All told, the design team developed 70 preliminary floorplans for Terminal 4 before settling on one that maximized space use vertically as well as horizontally. This was done by stacking retailers and restaurants one atop another and by maximizing the use of automated ticketing and information kiosks for departing and arriving passengers.

With a final design in hand, construction of Terminal 4 got underway in early 2014 and was completed in December 2016. After nearly a year testing its new automated passenger and baggage-handling systems, Terminal 4 officially opened in October 2017.[10]

Terminal 4 continued the theme begun with Terminal 3 of mixing function and fun. Among its passenger-oriented amenities were a 4-story rope playground in the shape of a double-helix known as the "Chandelier"; a 3-story digital wall mural depicting shop facades from Singapore's colonial-era Peranakan Shophouse district; the Immersive Wall, a 70 m × 5 m LED screen with constantly changing video shows; and a modern tea room where passengers could participate in free tea tastings. Whereas many other international airports had art displays and entertaining visuals for passengers to see, with the features now included in Terminals 3 and 4, Changi also had things for them to do. Since it opened, Terminal 4 has won numerous design honors, including the 2018 Prix Versailles Architectural Award for South Asia and the Pacific.

The Crown Jewel

From its utilitarian start in 1981, by 2014 Changi was evolving into the world's first true destination airport (Table 10.2), a place for travelers and their families to experience rather than to simply endure. Jewel Changi was intended to be the next step in this evolution (Lohmann et al. 2009). The idea for Jewel Changi emerged out of a combination of necessity and the changes in the long-distance flying market. In terms of necessity, Changi Airport was running out of parking spaces, and the airport's updated master plan called for replacing its open air parking lot nestled between Terminals 1, 2, and 3 with a much larger parking structure. In terms of market changes, global carriers such as Emirates, Qatar Airways, and Turkish Airlines were increasingly selling their home airports in Dubai, Doha and Istanbul as destination hubs. This was the market niche Singapore Airlines and Changi had pioneered 20 years earlier but now found themselves falling behind in. With a single building, Singapore and

Table 10.2   Singapore Jewel Changi timeline

1955	Singapore's Paya Lebar International Airport opens.
1975	Singapore Prime Minister Lee Kuan Yew approves construction of Changi International Airport at a projected cost of S$1 billion to replace a soon-to-be-at capacity Paya Lebar. Landfill and seabed reclamation activities begin immediately.
1977	Airport land reclamation activities are completed, enlarging Changi's footprint from 430 to 1300 hectares.
1979	Construction begins on Terminal 1. Singapore negotiates landing rights for SIA in China.
1981	Construction of Terminal 1 is completed.
1986	Construction of Changi Terminal 2 begins. *Annual passenger volume at Changi exceeds 10 million.*
1990	Terminal 2 opens in November bringing Changi's passenger capacity to 48 million.
1996	Planning begins for the construction of Terminal 3 immediately opposite Terminal 2. The lead responsibility for designing Terminal 3 and managing its construction is again given to Singapore's Public Works Department, with Skidmore, Owings and Merrill (SOM) as a design consultant. *Annual passenger volume at Changi exceeds 24 million.*
2000	Construction begins on Terminal 3. It is delayed for 18 months following the SARS outbreak, and takes 8 years to complete.
2002	Subway service directly linking Changi to downtown Singapore begins. It is discontinued a year later due to a lack of demand.
2006	A new Budget Terminal opens to accommodate an increasing number of low-cost carrier flights. *Changi's annual passenger volume tops 35 million.*
2008	After multiple delays, Terminal 3 with its unique Butterfly Garden finally opens, expanding Changi's new emphasis on a convenient and world-class passenger experience. The 2-year old Budget Terminal is expanded.
2009	Changi Airport is privatized, with all responsibilities for operating and expanding the airport transferred from Singapore's Civil Aviation Authority (CAAS) to the Changi Airport Group (CAG).
2010	Fully recovered from the effects of the Global Financial Crisis, *Changi passenger volume exceeds 42 million.*
2012	Less than six years old, the Budget Terminal is demolished to make room for Terminal 4. *Annual passenger volume exceeds 50 million.*
2014	Construction begins on Terminal 4, the first Changi terminal to be developed by CAG and not to be designed and developed by the Singapore Public Works Department. CAG and LandCapital agree to jointly develop the mixed-use hub that will become the Jewel. A design team headed by architect Moshe Safdie is later hired to design the Jewel.
2017	Terminal 4 with its many passenger amenities opens in October, bringing Changi's annual capacity to 82 million passengers. *Annual passenger volumes top 62 million.*
2019	Jewel Changi Airport opens in April to worldwide acclaim, and receives 50 million visitors in its first six months. Changi wins its seventh consecutive Skytrax Best Airport Award.

CAG saw an opportunity to leapfrog their Middle Eastern competition. Instead of an above-ground parking structure, CAG would build an even bigger underground parking structure and top it with a combination shopping mall and multi-story nature park that extended the tropical garden theme originally developed for Changi Terminals 3 and 4.

The idea for the Jewel is sometimes credited to Singapore's Prime Minister Lee Hsien Loong, who, like his father Lee Kuan Yew, viewed large-scale infrastructure investments as a manifestation of Singapore's global economic and cultural aspirations. With just five-and-a-half million residents, Singapore would never rival China's still-growing southern megacities like Shenzhen and Guangzhou in terms of size, but it could set the agenda for how cities deploy large-scale infrastructure investments to promote sustainable urban development. In his National Rally Day speech in 2013, Prime Minister Lee Hsien Loong called on CAG to double Changi's capacity by 2030 but do so in a manner consistent with the "city in the garden" vision his father had established for Singapore back in 1967. [11] Judged by the Prime Minister's high-flying rhetoric, the request for proposals (RFP) issued by CAG in 2014 for the combined parking structure–pedestrian concourse–shopping mall was a good deal more down to earth. It called for a shopping mall, airport services that included early check-in facilities and baggage storage, plus an unspecified "attraction." In a first for Changi, the new structure was to be built by a partnership between CAG and a qualified property developer.

The favorite to win the contract was Israeli–Canadian–American architect Moshe Safdie. Safdie was the lead architect for the iconic three-tower Marina Bay Sands complex in Singapore that opened in 2010 to international acclaim. For the still-unnamed Jewel project, Safdie proposed building a six-story torus around a vertical garden that would leave ample floorspace for retail and airport uses. Emanating from the center of the torus's glass roof would be a circular waterfall that tapered inward as it fell to ground six stories below. [12] The central waterfall would be ringed by a series of gardens, forming a multi-story green amphitheater. The torus's outer rings would be devoted to shops and services, which would be separated from the central waterfall and gardens save for a series of radial "canyons" (Safdie Architects 2020). Principal access to the building would be through Terminal 1, but it would also connect to Terminals 2 and 3 through a series of above-ground pedestrian bridges.

Safdie's design was greeted with universal acclaim for the way it extended Singapore's blue-green, water-garden, "city in the garden" motif into three dimensions as well as for its clever use of space. [13] Because of its many innovative design features and complex environmental systems, the project—now named the "Jewel" because it was to be the jewel in Changi's crown—would not be inexpensive. Preliminary estimates put its cost at US$1.5 billion.

While Safdie and his team—which also included Singapore-based RSP Architects Planners & Engineers (executive architects), Peter Walker and Partners (landscape architecture), Benoy (interior designers), BuroHappold Engineering (façade structure), Lighting Planners Associates (lighting), and WET Design (water features)—worked to turn his design into construction plans, CAG was busy lining up a development partner. The group they settled on was CapitaLand, a Singapore-based property development and management company with a portfolio of projects that included shopping malls, offices, homes, and mixed-use development projects in Singapore, Malaysia, China and Japan. As is typical of Singapore real estate projects, the financial details of the CAG/CapitaLand deal have never been made public beyond acknowledging that CAG owns a controlling 51 percent share of the joint venture. When one of Singapore's opposition political parties claimed in June 2020 that the "government has also seen it fit to splash billions of dollars of taxpayers' dollars on extravagant public projects, including Jewel Changi Airport," the Singapore Ministry of Finance was quick to respond that no government funds or taxpayer monies were involved in Jewel Changi's development.[14]

After four-and-a-half years of construction, Jewel Changi opened to travelers and the public on April 17, 2019. Six months prior to its opening, CapitaLand announced that it had already leased 90 percent of the building's available retail space.[15]

The Never-Finished Airport

Even as it was finishing construction on Terminal 4 and Jewel Changi, CAG was already busy planning Changi's further expansion. In March 2018, CAG and CPG (the privatized entity that was previously the Singapore Department of Public Works) unveiled plans to develop Changi East, a 1,080 hectare expansion of Changi Airport that will eventually add a fifth passenger terminal, a third runway, 40 km of new taxiways, and additional air cargo facilities to be developed as part of a new Changi East Industrial Zone.[16] If completed as planned in the early 2030s, Changi East will bring Changi's passenger capacity to 140 million passengers and its annual air freight capacity to 5.4 million tons. Initial contracts for building Changi's third runway were signed in 2015 and construction began in 2018. Based on a design created by the Singapore office of KPF Architecture, construction of the new Terminal 5 is expected to begin sometime in the early-to-mid 2020s. To help pay the more than S$10 billion cost of developing Changi East, Singapore's Civil Aviation Authority announced that beginning in July 2018, it would be levying an additional S$10.80 surcharge on all passengers arriving or departing from Changi Airport. Even with the additional surcharge revenue, questions remain about how the full Changi East project will ultimately be financed and whether it will require government subsidies.

LESSONS AND TAKEAWAYS

The one critical question whenever Singapore is used as a case study is whether the resulting findings can be usefully generalized to other places and situations. This is certainly the case with Jewel Changi. Jewel Changi is not just an atypical airport project; it is located in an atypical country.

Singapore is a prime example of what political economists refer to as a "developmental state," meaning that the full range of the government's planning, investment, and regulatory powers are used in concert to promote national economic development imperatives (Thurbon and Weiss 2016; Woo 2018). Once a particular goal or priority is identified by government officials, all relevant public and private sector actors are mobilized to achieve it. Developmental states need not be entirely autocratic—there is typically some space within their political processes to debate which economic development goals or projects are to be pursued—but they are almost always technocratic. Because decision-makers in developmental states like Singapore and South Korea adhere to a common technocratic and hierarchical implementation model, getting things done, particularly when it comes to undertaking major public infrastructure investments like roads, transit systems, and airports, is generally easier than in places with more pluralistic governing models. Infrastructure projects undertaken by developmental states can certainly run into difficulties, but they usually occur as a result of unanticipated events or external constraints, and not because of a lack of stakeholder alignment.

There is no doubt that Jewel Changi was expertly planned and executed. Its construction was scheduled to take four-and-a-half years and to cost US$1.4 billion, and that's what it took. The site was clean and free of encumbrances, the project design was thoroughly reviewed, the appropriate engineering and building partners were all assembled, the required government financing was made available, and the construction managers and contractors diligently did their jobs. The Changi Airport Group, Jewel Changi's corporatized government sponsor had successfully and successfully completed Changi Terminal 4 using a comparable contracting and delivery model. Jewel Changi was more complicated structurally and financially than Terminal 4, but it was not terra incognita. Prior to the Covid-19 pandemic's arrival, passenger and tourist visitations to Jewel Changi were running well ahead of projections.

Would another country, province or city lacking Singapore's developmental state ideology or successful infrastructure investment track record have been able to perform as well? Probably not, but we should nonetheless take a deeper look at the factors that contributed to Jewel Changi's success, being sure to note how they might or might not be applied outside of Singapore. Five such factors are especially important.

- *A longstanding commitment to transformative infrastructure investments.* Even before its establishment as an independent country in 1965, Singapore's one-party government—largely as a result of the technocratic biases of its Prime Minister, Lee Kuan Yew—was committed to undertaking transformative infrastructure investments. These started in the early 1960s with investments in public housing and coastal landfill projects to create industrial development sites. They continued throughout the 1970s and 1980s as a series of transportation investments, including new national road and public transport networks, as well as major seaport and airport facilities. They continued further during the 1990s as human capital investments in parks and universities. They broadened again in the early 2000s, to include major ecological and environmental investments. In each case, these investments have yielded promised economic or quality-of-life returns. This is partly because Singapore is an island economy, enabling it to capture most multiplier benefits and positive externalities; partly because its economic development and physical development ministries operate in a highly coordinated manner, and partly because Singapore's single-party government has been smart about anticipating and responding to its citizen's wants and needs. The result has been the creation of a national political culture that is forward-looking, used to undertaking action, and which embraces major public investments as the principal vehicle for creating private and public prosperity. Jewel Changi fits right into this favorable investment narrative: it accelerated Changi's lead over competing airports in Dubai, Doha, Istanbul and Hong Kong while also reinforcing Singapore's brand as the only place in Asia able to seamlessly integrate global commerce, cosmopolitan living, and the natural environment in equal proportions. Countries or cities with more pluralistic decision-making systems are likely to find it difficult to maintain this level of commitment.
- *Investing in public sector expertise.* Lee Kuan Yew's 1975 insistence on giving the job of designing Changi Airport to Singapore's Public Works Department— rather than the prevailing practice of hiring contractors from the US or UK —began a 30-year process of building public sector airport planning expertise. This intentional capacity-building approach yielded significant benefits when it later came to designing and building Changi Terminals 2 and 3; and it continued to pay off when the corporatized Changi Airport Group assumed the responsibility for planning and developing Terminal 4 and Jewel Changi. No other country in Asia has gone as far as Singapore in investing in its own technical expertise, and much of

CAG's success to date is due to the fact that it was assembled out of highly qualified personnel from existing public agencies.

- *Benchmarking everything.* Much of the secret to Singapore's 60-year history of economic growth and success lies in the fact that it is continually benchmarking itself against competitors big and small, looking for any advantage. Every Singapore public agency is constantly comparing its performance to recognized leaders in the US, Europe, and Asia, looking for ways to improve. Where other national governments favor home-grown solutions to technical problems, Singapore is all too happy to adapt other countries' best practices. This approach of constant and honest benchmarking has had huge payoffs. In the 25 years between Singapore's independence in 1965 and Lee Kuan Yew's retirement as prime minister in 1990, Singapore went from one of Asia's poorest countries to its richest. It developed a world-class port, chemical industry and university; achieved a 95 percent literacy rate and 80 percent homeownership rate; and built what are among the best-functioning airports and rapid transit systems in the world. Singapore never rests on its laurels. Changi Airport Terminal 4 was designed and engineered to be measurably better and more efficient than Terminal 3, just as Terminal 3 was designed to be measurably better than Terminal 2. Jewel Changi continues that practice. Beyond its spectacle-like design qualities, Jewel Changi was engineered to achieve measurable improvements in check-in practices and security, baggage handling and reliability, passenger circulation and comfort, and, not unimportantly for its bottom line, in-terminal traveler spending. Outside of Singapore, benchmarking is much more common in the private sector than in the public sector.
- *Incremental privatization.* Hoping to make its public ministries and agencies more entrepreneurial, Singapore's government undertook a major privatization effort in the late 1990s. In most instances, this took the form of corporatizing existing government departments to make them leaner and better able to compete for work outside Singapore. In the case of Changi Airport, privatization involved spinning off the Changi Airport Group from Singapore's Civil Aviation Authority. The Singapore Department of Public Work's airport design and engineering unit was likewise spun off as Changi Airport Planners and Engineers (CAPE), and then later made a division of CAG. Initially, CAPE and CAG continued doing most of their work at Changi for the Singapore government, but over time, both have broadened their client lists. Today, CAPE and CAG (through their Changi Airports International subsidiary) are doing work at airports in over 20 countries, including, most notably China, India and Brazil. Privatization has not only enabled Singapore to bring its airport planning, development and operations expertise to the world, it has also allowed Changi to keep

an eye out for new practices to bring back home. Most countries and cities that have privatized governmental functions have done so for budgetary reasons and not for the purpose of creating more entrepreneurial service delivery systems.

* *Quality-of-life-enhancing infrastructure investments.* Many airports are designed for the benefit of the large air carriers who fly in and out of them. This is especially true in the United States where nearly every commercial airport is dominated by one or two domestic carriers. Changi is different: its focus is first and foremost on passenger experience. This is partly an extension of Singapore Airlines' superior customer service brand, and partly a reflection of the fact that Singapore itself is organized to compete. When Changi first opened in 1981, competing meant having the most modern airplanes and flying to the most destinations. Over time, airlines and airports started competing on price, airlines by offering lower fares, and airports by building terminals for low-cost carriers. As flying itself became more commoditized, airports began competing by providing passenger amenities, including frequent flyer club space, stores and restaurants, and a more seamless check-in experience. Changi was an early leader in all these areas, but as other airports caught up, Changi differentiated itself by providing a unique traveler experience. This was the motivation behind Changi management's decision in the early 2000s to add themed gardens to each terminal. Gardens offer different attractions to different travelers. To kids, they offer a glimpse of a non-urban environment and a sense of adventure. For families, they offer something that can be done together. And for travel-weary adults, they offer the possibility of a peaceful respite. The result, when coupled with Jewel Changi's state-of-the-art circulation and check-in and baggage services, is a physical environment that puts the customer first while relegating the operational concerns of the airlines to the background. Jewel Changi explicitly takes this traveler experience emphasis to the next level by combining a unique building design, a nowhere-else-in-the-world waterfall and garden space, a carefully-curated variety of globally-branded shops and eateries, and an easy-to-navigate circulation system. None of these have anything to do with flying, per se. Instead, they read as thoughtfulness and attention to what the traveler wants. Jewel Changi reminds infrastructure planners that megaproject investments should be as much about responding to human aspirations as they are about achieving greater efficiency and economies of scale.

NOTES

1. Available on the Skytrax website (https://skytraxratings.com/about-world-airport-rating).
2. https://www.jewelchangiairport.com/en.html (current as of December 2021).
3. The history of Changi Airport is presented in summary form at the Changi Airport Group (CAG) website: https://www.changiairport.com/corporate/about-us/our-story.html (current as of December 2021).
4. The history of Singapore International Airlines (SIA) is presented in summary form at the SIA website: https://www.singaporeair.com/en_UK/us/flying-withus/our-story/our-heritage/ (current as of December 2021).
5. "1990-1999 Singapore Changi Airport Passenger Movements". Department of Statistics, Singapore.
6. "2012 Singapore Changi Airport Statistics". Changi Airport Group. January 31, 2013.
7. Changi Airport Group. (2012). "Changi Airport's Budget Terminal to be closed." March 1, 2012.
8. Changi Airport Group. (2011). "2010 Singapore Changi Airport Statistics." January 20, 2011.
9. https://www.airport-technology.com/projects/terminal-4-changi-international-airport-singapore/.
10. https://www.forbes.com/sites/christinaliao/2017/10/31/singapore-changi-airport-terminal-4-now-open-for-business/?sh=4ab7a8cc4fc6.
11. "Expanding Changi Airport for 2030 and Beyond - National Day Rally 2013". govsingapore YouTube channel uploaded August 22, 2013.
12. "Safdie reveals greenhouse for Singapore's Changi airport". *Dezeen*. December 5, 2014.
13. "Changi Airport proves it is the jewel of the world". *TheDesignAir*. March 14, 2015.
14. https://www.gov.sg/article/clarification-on-funding-of-jewel-changi-airport.
15. https://www.capitaland.com/international/en/about-capitaland/newsroom/news-releases/international/2018/oct/jewel-leasing-announcement.html.
16. https://www.changiairport.com/corporate/our-expertise/changi-east.html.

REFERENCES

Unless otherwise noted, all websites were accessed in November 2021.
Bok, R. 2015. Airports on the move? The policy mobilities of Singapore Changi Airport at home and abroad. *Urban Studies* 5214: 2724–2740.
Business Times. 1996. Changi Airport MRT line details. December 12.
Changi Airport. 1980. *Changi Airport: Singapore*. Singapore: Ministry of Communication; Changi Airport Development Division: Public Works Department: Department of Civil Aviation.
Changi Airport Group. 2010. *2009–2010 Annual Report: A Fresh Perspective*. https://www.changiairport.com/content/dam/cacorp/publications/Annual%20Reports/2010/Changi_Airport_Group_AR_0910_Full.pdf.
Civil Aviation Authority of Singapore. 1989. *Singapore Changi Airport Terminal 2: Phase II Development*. Singapore: Imprint Singapore.

Civil Aviation Authority of Singapore. 1994. *Singapore Changi Airport: Providing the Best, Always*. Singapore: Imprint Singapore.

Chua, B. H. 2011. Singapore as model: Planning innovations, knowledge experts. *Worlding Cities: Asian Experiments and the Art of being Global* 31: 29–54.

Henderson, J. 2017. Airport roles: Pushing the boundaries at Singapore's Changi Airport. *Asian Journal of Tourism Research* 23: 1–24.

Hirsh, M. 2017. Emerging infrastructures of low-cost aviation in Southeast Asia. *Mobilities* 122: 259–276.

Kuang, K. L. 2009. Changi Airport Terminal 3, Singapore. *Structural Engineering International* 191: 28–32.

Lee, K. Y. 2000. *From Third World to First: The Singapore Story 1965*. New York: HarperCollins.

Lohmann, G., Albers, S., Koch, B., and Pavlovich, K. 2009. From hub to tourist destination–An explorative study of Singapore and Dubai's aviation-based transformation. *Journal of Air Transport Management* 155: 205–211.

Min, F. S. 2006. A budget terminal for budget airlines. *International Airport Review* 102.

Tan, R. 2021. How Changi Airport came to be. *BiblioAsia* Oct–Dec.

Thurbon, E., and Weiss, L. 2016. The developmental state in the late twentieth century. In *Handbook of Alternative Theories of Economic Development*. Edward Elgar Publishing.

Safdie Architects. 2020. *Jewel Changi Airport*. New York: Images Publishing.

Woo, J. J. 2018. *The Evolution of the Asian Developmental State: Hong Kong and Singapore*. Routledge.

11. Epic fail and cautious success—Berlin Brandenburg Airport and New York LaGuardia Terminal B

John D. Landis

ABBREVIATIONS USED IN THIS CHAPTER

BBF	Berlin Brandenburg Flughafen Holding GmbH
BBI	Berlin Brandenburg Airport Willy Brandt (early name abbreviation)
BER	Berlin Brandenburg Airport Willy Brandt (later name abbreviation)
FBB	Flughafen Berlin Brandenburg GmbH
LGA	LaGuardia Airport
LGP	LaGuardia Gateway Partnership
P3	Public–Private Partnership
RFQ	Request for Qualifications
RFP	Request for Proposals
TUV	(Brandenburg State) Technical Inspection Association

Big infrastructure projects don't always turn out the way we expect. If a Las Vegas casino was taking bets that New York City's rebuilt LaGuardia Airport would open on budget and schedule, but that the new Berlin Brandenburg International Airport would take an additional €4 billion and nine years to complete, they might put the odds of such an outcome at one in a thousand. Germans, after all, pride themselves on their precision and ability to work through difficult technical problems. New Yorkers, by contrast, are not known for always carrying through on their boastful aspirations. Circumstances also favored Berlin Brandenburg: the airport was to be new and an entirely clean sheet design, unencumbered by physical or economic limitations. The new LaGuardia terminal, by contrast, would have to be shoe-horned into a slice of land between an existing highway and a bay and would have to remain fully operational throughout the construction process.

Why did things go right at LaGuardia but wrong at Berlin Brandenburg? The short answer is that LaGuardia's owners, the Port Authority of New York and New Jersey, understood the challenges they were facing and hired experienced consultants and contractors to help meet them. The governments of the states of Berlin and Brandenburg (neither of which had previously managed an airport construction job) naively assumed they could manage the construction process themselves, hired inexperienced contractors, and when things started going wrong, issued vague assurances rather than acting to correct underlying problems. The longer answer, as discussed at length in this chapter, is that building (or in LaGuardia's case, rebuilding) a modern airport is a difficult job requiring experienced designers and managers, clear delineations of responsibility, carefully managed expectations, a realistic construction budget and financing plan, partners who are committed to a successful outcome, and not a small amount of luck. LaGuardia was fortunate to have had all of these things. Berlin Brandenburg, as it turns out, had none of them.

LAGUARDIA AND BERLIN TEGEL—UNPOPULAR BIRDS OF A FEATHER

The opening years of the 21st century presented Berlin's Tegel Airport (Berlin Brandenburg's predecessor) and New York City's LaGuardia Airport with similar challenges. Both airports were old, overcrowded, and unpopular with passengers. LaGuardia was the older of the two, having opened to commercial flights as New York Municipal Airport in 1939. (The airport was renamed for New York City Mayor Fiorello LaGuardia when the New York Port Authority took over its ownership in 1948.) LaGuardia was the second of New York City's three major airports to open: Newark Airport across the Hudson River in New Jersey had opened in 1928, and JFK, then known as Idlewild, wouldn't open until 1948.

Until 1983, LaGuardia had two passenger terminals, Marine Air Terminal A, which originally served passengers flying to Europe overnight by planes known as "flying boats," and Central Terminal B which served as LaGuardia's main domestic flight terminal. The original Terminal B building was demolished in 1963 and replaced by a new $36 million facility able to accommodate jet plane service. Six-blocks long and four-stories high, the new Terminal B included a quarter-circle arrivals and departure hall and four concourse areas with 40 aircraft gates, all wedged between the Grand Central Parkway, LaGuardia's three large airplane hangars, and Flushing Bay. Terminal B was given a modest upgrade in 1983 after Delta Air Lines departed for its own purpose-built terminal. It received a more extensive modernization in 1994 when US Airways moved to its own terminal (Stoff 2008).

With the Port Authority having lengthened LaGuardia's runways in 1979 to accommodate larger planes, passenger traffic in and out of LaGuardia rose slowly but steadily from 17.1 million passengers in 1979 to 19.7 million passengers in 1991.[1] The increase would have been greater but for LaGuardia's constrained taxiway capacity, which limited the number of planes able to queue for takeoff, and complaints from nearby residential neighborhoods about night-time and weekend flight noise. In response, the Port Authority instituted a Sunday-thru-Friday perimeter rule in 1984, which banned nonstop flights between LaGuardia and airports located more than 1,500 miles away. Passenger travel to and from LaGuardia kept rising nonetheless, leading the Federal Aviation Administration in 2001 and 2007 to impose its own restrictions on the number and type of LaGuardia-bound flights. These did little to reduce underlying demand and, in 2000, the number of LaGuardia airline passengers exceeded 25 million for the first time. Transit access to LaGuardia is also limited, with most outbound passengers arriving at the airport by car or shuttle. Getting to LaGuardia by subway requires transferring at the Jackson-Roosevelt Heights subway station for a three-mile bus ride to the airport terminal. For inbound business travelers continuing on to midtown Manhattan, the trip typically takes 45 minutes to an hour depending on the time of day.

LaGuardia's combination of flight and passenger congestion, small gates and taxiways, lack of terminal amenities, old and unreliable baggage facilities, poor transit access, and frequent flight delays had earned it the scorn of generations of air travelers; and it consistently ranked at or near the top of lists of least favorite US airports. In its 2015 airport satisfaction survey, J.D. Power ranked LaGuardia last among large and medium-sized US airports.[2] Readers of the *Wall Street Journal* were no kinder, giving LaGuardia a 2019 grade of "D+," and calling it the worst airport in America.[3] For years, New York City real estate magnate and later US President Donald Trump had delighted in publicly criticizing La Guardia as a "third world airport," a sentiment famously echoed by then Vice-President Joe Biden in 2015.[4] New York City public officials, including those at the Port Authority, had long agreed that major improvements at LaGuardia were needed, but other regional transportation investment priorities always seemed to take priority.

A Berliner visiting the US and reading about LaGuardia's shortcomings might easily imagine substituting Berlin's Tegel Airport for LaGuardia. The two airports were comparable in size, configuration, passenger volumes and lack of traveler appreciation. Built in the 1930s as a Nazi rocket test site, Tegel was pressed into service during the Berlin Airlift to supplement relief flights landing at Tempelhof, then West Berlin's main airport. Following the conclusion of Airlift operations in 1949, Tegel became a French air force base, and then, in 1960, the terminus for Air France flights from Paris. As propeller planes gave way to jets in the 1960s, Tegel's longer runways made it an attractive destination for British European Airways and for American air carrier Pan Am. Following British European's lead, Britain's premier air carrier British Airways shifted its daily London–Berlin service from Tempelhof to Tegel in 1975.[5] To accommodate increased airline passenger traffic, a much-needed new passenger terminal was constructed at Tegel in 1965. The new terminal was designed by German architects Meinhard von Gerkan and Volkwin Marg, and its innovative hexagonal shape quickly attracted worldwide attention.

With the area surrounding Berlin under Communist East German control, airline travel in and out Berlin grew steadily but slowly. (Schönefeld Airport, Berlin's third airport, was located in East Berlin and was inaccessible to Western air carriers until 1990.) Following the fall of the Berlin Wall in October 1989 and the subsequent announcement that Berlin would replace Bonn as the newly-reunified Germany's capital, the country's flag carrier Lufthansa began Tegel passenger service, eventually taking over Pan Am's Berlin-to-New York flights. In 1990, discount air carrier Air Berlin moved its operations hub to Tegel. Other air carriers soon followed, and in 2000, the number of Tegel passengers exceeded 10 million for the first time. As Berlin's international reputation for business and cultural innovation grew, so too did number of Tegel airline passengers, reaching 20 million in 2014.[6]

Tegel's deficiencies grew more apparent as its passenger volume increased. The airport's once-lauded state-of-the-art hexagonal terminal was now under-sized and couldn't easily be enlarged. Its crowded departure areas lacked the space to fit post-9/11 security facilities and the shops and restaurants sought by passengers. Many of Tegel's gates were too narrow to accommodate wide-body aircraft. Tegel's runways were long enough to serve jumbo-sized Airbus A380s and Boeing 747s, but when flights were delayed, it, like LaGuardia, quickly ran out of aircraft queuing space. With traffic congestion worsening on Berlin's surface streets, the lack of a direct subway connection between Tegel and downtown Berlin was also becoming more irksome. As at LaGuardia, these problems revealed themselves through worsening ratings. Skytrax, the global airline and airport survey company, ranked Tegel 90th in terms of passenger satisfaction on its 2013 list of the world's 100 largest airports.[7] Subsequent surveys would see further declines in Tegel's ratings, and in 2019, its last full year in operation, Tegel was awarded just two out of ten stars in Skytrax's customer satisfaction survey.[8] In the years since German reunification, Berlin had become a world-class city. What it needed now was a world-class airport.

Table 11.1   *Berlin Brandenburg and LaGuardia Airport comparisons at*
                a glance

	Berlin Brandenburg (replacing Tegel Airport)	LaGuardia Airport
Metro area population (2010)	3.5 million	18.4 million
Primary metropolitan airports	Tegel International Airport (closed in 2020), Schönefeld International Airport (incorporated into Berlin-Brandenburg)	JFK International, Newark Liberty International, LaGuardia
Passenger traffic—all metro airports (2015)	29.5 million	124 million
Passenger traffic (2015)	21 million (Tegel)	28.4 million
Non-stop passenger destinations (2018)	94 (Tegel)	86
Share of metro area airport passenger traffic (2015)	71% (Tegel)	23%
Passenger traffic growth rate, 2002–2015	6.0%	2.0%
Leading flight destinations	Munich, Frankfurt, Zurich	Chicago, Boston, Atlanta
Airport development entity	Government corporation	Public–private partnership
Airport owner and operator	Flughafen Berlin Brandenburg GmbH	Port Authority of New York and New Jersey
Terminal size	360,000 square meters (Terminal 1)	78,000 square meters (Terminal B)
Number of gates	41 (Terminal 1)	38 (Terminal B)
Runways	2	2
Annual passenger capacity when completed	45 million (all terminals)	17.5 million (Terminal B)
Construction begins	September 2006	2016
Initially announced terminal opening date	October 2010	2021
Actual terminal opening date	October 2020	November 2018
Full and final completion date	October 2020	2025 or 2026
Initially approved construction cost	€2.2 billion	$4 billion (Terminal B)
Final construction cost	€8.2 billion	$4 billion (Terminal B)
Percent increase in construction cost	270%	0%
Rail or subway travel time to CBD	35–45 minutes	45–60 minutes

BERLIN BRANDENBURG—ANATOMY OF A FIASCO

Berlin's need for additional airport capacity was apparent well before the fall of the Berlin Wall (Alberts et al. 2009). Passenger volumes were on the rise at both Tegel and Tempelhof and neither had space to expand. With Berlin set to completely replace Bonn as Germany's capital by 1999, the race was on to find a location for a new international airport. As a first step, in May 1991, the German states of Berlin and Brandenburg agreed to form Berlin Brandenburg Flughafen Holding GmbH (BBF), a jointly-owned public airport development corporation. Berlin and Brandenburg would each own 37 percent of the new corporation, and the German government would own the balance. A second step involved establishing a study group composed of planners and former public officials from East and West Berlin to identify potential airport sites. After evaluating 53 alternative locations, the study group whittled the list down to three finalists: the two existing airfields at Sperenberg and Jüterbog, and the area immediately south of Schönefeld Airport in the former East Berlin.[9] The more distant Sperenberg and Jüterbog sites did better on the criteria of expandability and managing adverse noise impacts, but Schönefeld was much closer to Berlin and was already well-served by road and rail links. After several months of back and forth, government officials announced in May 1996 that they had reached a consensus decision in favor of the Schönefeld site (Figure 11.1). To help hold down construction costs, the new Berlin-Schönefeld International Airport could reuse Schönfeld's southern runway and some of its existing aircraft service facilities.

A Privatization Effort Comes Up Short

With Germany's federal and state governments weighed down for the foreseeable future by the costs of reunification, BBF officials hoped that the new airport could be built and financed by private investors through a public–private partnership (P3). P3s were being actively encouraged by the European Union and World Bank as a means of financing needed infrastructure projects while keeping construction costs off public sector balance sheets. Berlin and Brandenburg would provide the land and existing facilities through a 50-year land lease, and a suitable investor group would be assembled to provide equity and arrange for private financing. The investor group would own and manage the airport for the term of the land lease, at which point, the Berlin and Brandenburg governments would have the option of buying it back (Fiedler and Wendler 2016, p. 106).

To get the PPP process moving, BBF in 1999 issued a call for proposals from potential private partners. It produced just two responses. The first was

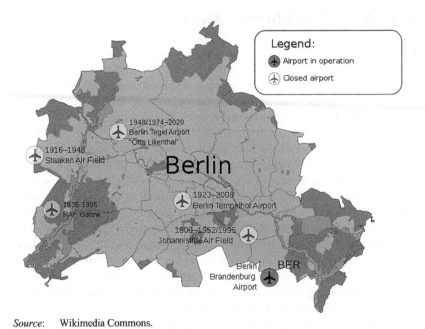

Figure 11.1   *Map showing locations of Tempelhof, Tegel, Schönefeld and*
                 Berlin Brandenburg Airports

from a consortium of Hochtief Construction; the infrastructure technology
company ABB; Fraport AG, a German airport operations and management
company; and banking giant Bankengesellschaft Berlin (now Landesbank
Berlin Holding). The other response came from an investor group consisting of IVG, Flughafen Wien AG, Dorsch-Consult, Commerzbank, and Cais
se des Dépôts. In September 1998, BBF announced that it had selected the
Hochtief-led consortium, and that pending the outcome of further negotiations,
they would be granted a 50-year concession to build and operate the new Berlin
Brandenburg airport. The IVG-led group promptly protested the BBF's decision, contending that Hochtief had been unfairly provided with advance details
of the selection process. In an August 1999 ruling, the Brandenburg Regional
Court agreed with the IVG group's complaint and voided BBF's contract
with Hochtief. After two years of further back and forth, the IVG group was
convinced to join Hochtief in submitting a new joint bid, only to have BBF
officials reject it as too expensive. Five years into its work to replace Tegel
with a new international airport, the government's efforts were back to square
one.

With a private-sector-led approach having failed in two attempts, Berlin Mayor Klaus Wowereit and Brandenburg Minister-President Matthias Platzeck stepped in to take public control of the project (Fiedler and Wendler 2016, p. 106). Declaring that they would build the new airport themselves, BBF reconstituted itself (with the same ownership shares as previously) as a government-owned airport development and operating corporation named Flughafen Berlin Brandenburg GmbH (FBB). In August 2004, the new corporation was granted approval by the Brandenburg Ministry for Infrastructure and Regional Policy to begin planning and permitting work on the new airport, now to be officially known as Berlin Brandenburg International Airport, or BBI. To protect their investment and minimize controversy over the choice of the Schönefeld site, the Berlin and Brandenburg governments announced that Tempelhof and Tegel would close, Tempelhof in 2008, and Tegel when the new airport was completed. Citizens groups would later qualify ballot initiatives to try to keep both airports open.

Going It Alone

Recognizing that it lacked the necessary expertise to plan and develop a major airport, FBB in 2004 hired Thomas Weyer to serve as its supervising project manager (Fiedler and Wendler 2016, p. 107). As was normal practice, Weyer, who had supervised preparation of the Hochtief bids several years earlier, announced that FBB would be hiring a single contractor to coordinate all future airport planning and construction activities. Following Weyer's advice, FBB selected Planungsgemeinschaft Berlin Brandenburg International (pg.bbi) to serve as BBI's general planner and architect. Pg.bbi was a joint venture of two well-regarded German architecture firms, Gerkan, Marg und Partner, and JSK Architekten. Heading the new airport's design team, it was announced, would be 70-year-old Meinhard von Gerkan, who 30 years earlier had overseen the team that had come up with Tegel's innovative hexagonal design. The terminal design for Berlin Brandenburg was to be far more traditional, consisting of a single arrivals and departure hall connected by a pedestrian bridge to the main flight concourse. Viewed from the air, the terminal shape looked like a huge "C." This open-ended design would allow for the subsequent construction of additional terminal areas and concourses as demand rose. All told, the new terminal facility would include 200,000 square meters of space, making it a bit more than half the size of Heathrow Airport's new state-of-the-art Terminal 5.

Pg.bbi's initial airport and terminal design plan was approved by Berlin and Brandenburg officials in 2005. For reasons never made public, FBB's leadership decided against having pg.bbi serve as overall project manager, preferring instead to keep that role for themselves. Pg.bbi personnel would continue to be involved, but in the reduced role of contractor liaison and quality control monitor (Fiedler and Wendler 2016, p. 108). After nearly 15 years of anticipation, preliminary construction work on the new airport finally got underway in September 2006. All told, the job was expected to take five years, leading FBB officials to confidently predict that the new facility would open to the flying public in October 2011 (Ernst & Young 2012).

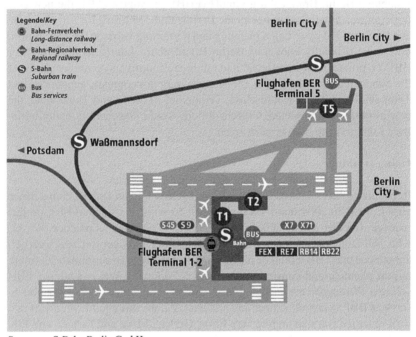

Source: S-Bahn Berlin GmbH.

Figure 11.2   Berlin Brandenburg site map

With Berlin's economy and airport passenger numbers growing faster than expected, FBB planners concluded that the size of Berlin Brandenburg's BBI main terminal should increase from 200,000 square meters to 340,000 square meters. This would require significant changes to the approved terminal design, including, most notably, the addition of a pier connected to the southern end of the flight concourse. The airport's original "C" shape would grow an extended foot (Figure 11.2). Among FBB staff, there was a general acknowledgement that these changes would raise the airport's construction cost and extend its delivery schedule, but publicly, FBB officials continued to maintain that the airport would still be completed by the end of 2011 (Fiedler and Wendler 2016, p. 117).

Its enlarged terminal design in hand, FBB officials put the job of building the new terminal and related facilities out to tender, drawing four bids, including one from Hochtief. All four were rejected as too expensive. The bidders countered that the additional costs were entirely due to the FBB's having increased the scope of the job to reflect the now-larger terminal and were not due to excessive pricing on their part. Regardless, FBB officials held firm in their rejection of the bids and announced that they themselves would serve as the overall construction manager. The actual construction work would be divided into seven subcontracts, each to be bid separately. This was a positive development, FBB officials assured the public, one that would reduce airport construction costs by €350 million while having no effect on the schedule airport delivery and opening date.

Others were not so sure. Having lost a third consecutive Berlin Airport tender process, Hochtief sued the FBB, arguing that it had knowingly understated the construction budget to force potential bidders to reduce their tenders. Hochtief would eventually lose its challenge, but not before presciently warning that the FBB's inexperience and fragmented management approach would almost certainly extend the airport's opening date and raise its construction costs (Fiedler and Wendler 2016, p. 110) (Table 11.2).

Table 11.2   Berlin Brandenburg Airport timeline

June 1996	After several years of study, the German states of Berlin and Brandenburg announce a "consensus decision" to build a new Berlin-Brandenburg International Airport (BBI) immediately south of the existing Schönefeld Airport, replacing it and Tegel and Tempelhof Airports.
March 1997	A first attempt to create a public–private partnership to develop BBI is undertaken. After years of legal challenge, it ends unsuccessfully in 2001.
August 2002	A second attempt to create a BBI public–private partnership is undertaken; it too ends unsuccessfully.
October 2003	Berlin Brandenburg Flughafen Holdings is merged with two subsidiaries, creating a new public airport development entity, Flughafen Berlin Schönefeld GmbH (FBB).
January 2004	FBB hires Planungsgemeinschaft Berlin Brandenburg International (pg.bbi), a joint venture of two airport German architecture firms, Gerkan, Marg und Partner, and JSK Architekten, to serve as BBI's general planner and architect. An airport opening date of October 2010 is announced.
August 2004	FBB officials and pg.bbi officials unveil their plans for BBI's new terminals and runways.
September 2006	BBI construction begins.
November 2006	With only a single bidder, the tender for the BBI terminal building (T1) fails.

October 2007	A second tender for T1 fails, leading to a decision that FBB will served as project construction manager and general contractor.
June 2008	FBB finally awards construction contracts for T1, including hiring Drees and Sommer as construction managers. T1 construction begins soon thereafter.
Early 2009	Following the dismissal of Drees and Sommer, the FBB divides the T1 construction job into 35 separate subcontracts.
June 2009	A BBI financing package of €2.83 billion is announced; BBI's name is officially changed to Berlin Brandenburg Airport Willy Brandt (BER).
June 2010	Because of numerous design changes, FBB announces BER's opening will be delayed until June 2012.
October 2011	Construction of the BER rail link and station is completed on schedule.
May 2012	After the new T1 terminal fails its smoke and fire control tests, a new BER opening date of March 2013 is announced.
January 2013	Following a series of senior staff changes and €1.2 billion in additional financing (bringing BER's construction budget to over €4 billion), the airport opening date is again delayed.
June 2014	More staff changes follow, together with another €1.1 billion in financing.
December 2015	FBB CEO Karsten Muhlenfeld announces BER will open in the second half of 2017
March 2017	Berlin Secretary of State Englebert Lütke-Daldrup is appointed to replace Karsten Muhlendfeld as FBB CEO.
November 2017	An audit by Germany's technical supervision service TÜV uncovers significant lapses in BER's fire and emergency systems, further delaying the airport opening
June 2018	Berlin's legislative assembly forms a committee of inquiry to investigate delays and cost overruns at BER. Notwithstanding the October 2017 bankruptcy of its principal tenant, Air Berlin, plans to construct a second €200 million terminal (T2) for discount air carriers are announced.
May 2018	Continuing problems with BER's electrical and wirings systems cause it to fail a mandatory TUV acceptance test. Lütke-Daltrip announces BER won't open until 2019 or 2020.
January 2019	New inspections reveal continuing wiring and structural problems at both terminals, requiring FBB to apply for a building permit continuation. T2's construction budget is cut to €100 million.
May 2020	After TÜV approves BER's emergency and safety systems, construction is finally declared complete.
November 2020	BER finally opens without incident, ten years behind schedule. All airport operations are moved from Tegel to BER; Schönefeld Airport's refurbished terminal opens as BER Terminal 5.

Unforced Errors Accumulate

In order to keep to their October 2011 completion deadline, FBB officials decided to issue the subcontracting tenders even as pg.bbi was finishing up the terminal redesign. This was a major error and one that would repeatedly come back to haunt the FBB in the form of frequent change orders, building permit resubmissions, and ultimately, failed inspection tests. The FBB's efforts were not helped by the departure of Thomas Weyer, who, having had enough of the increasingly chaotic Berlin airport construction job, resigned in March 2008 to become the general manager of Munich Airport.

With Weyer gone, FBB officials realized they would need outside expertise to bolster their own limited project management capabilities and turned to the construction management firm of Drees and Sommer for help. The arrangement didn't last long. According to later press accounts, when Drees and Sommer reported back to FBB executives in November 2008 that their planned opening date of October 2011 was completely unrealistic, and that the new terminal would cost much more than had previously been announced, they were terminated and replaced as construction managers by a different company, WSP/CBP. Before their termination, Drees and Sommer had recommended reconfiguring the terminal scope of work from seven subcontracts to 35, a change which, although extending the airport's completion date by 12 to 18 months, would also result in significant cost savings (Fiedler and Wendler 2016, p. 110). The FBB decided to follow Drees and Sommer's advice regarding reallocating the construction workload, but, publicly at least, stuck with their projected October 2011 opening date. Having pushed pg.bbi, and now their construction manager, WSP/CBP, into lesser roles, FBB staff found themselves managing the overall design process as well as 35 construction contractors.

While all this drama was unfolding, the airport had gained a new name. Starting in June 2009, Berlin Brandenburg International Airport would be officially known as Berlin Brandenburg *Willy Brandt* International in honor of West Berlin Mayor and German Chancellor Willy Brandt, whose efforts to engage East Germany during the 1970s under the "realpolitik" rubric had helped lay the foundation for Germany's eventual reunification. Adding the names of distinguished historical figures to German airports was not an uncommon practice: in 1988, Tegel Airport had been renamed Berlin Tegel Otto Lilienthal Airport in honor of the German aviation pioneer. The new airport also gained a new airport code designation, BER, when it was discovered that the original BBI designation officially belonged to India's Biju Patnaik Airport.

False Starts

In June 2010, with construction of the terminal building lagging, FBB officials finally acknowledged that Berlin Brandenburg's opening would be delayed, most likely until late 2011. Publicly, the delay was blamed on the bankruptcy of IGK-IGR, one of pg.bbi's subsidiaries. Behind the scenes, the airport was years away from being operational. Initial testing of the new terminal's check-in, security screening, boarding and baggage claim service began in November 2011 and the results were terrible, with the airport's overall readiness rated at just 56.2 percent, far below the required standard (Fiedler and Wendler 2016, p. 118). An even bigger problem emerged in May 2012 when the terminal's fire protection system failed a basic test, forcing the FBB to push back the airport's prospective opening date to March 2012. This was later pushed back further to June 2012.

Problems and delays at new airports are not uncommon, and by international standards, Berlin's performance was not yet overly worrisome. Denver International Airport, the last new airport built in the US, was three years late when it finally opened in March 1995. Originally scheduled to open in the summer of 1997, Hong Kong's new Chek Lap Kok International Airport didn't officially open until July 1998. Months after London-Heathrow Terminal 5's official opening in March 2008, its baggage management system still didn't work reliably.

As Berlin Brandenburg's promised June 2012 opening date drew nearer, airlines operating out of Tegel and Schönefeld finalized their plans to shift operations to the new airport, as per the original agreement authorizing its construction (Fiedler and Wendler 2016, p. 118). Once the last flights from Tegel departed in the early evening of June 2, all Tegel's support vehicles and equipment would be transported by road to Berlin Brandenburg where they would be available to service the new airport's inaugural flight at 6:00 am the next morning. On May 8, just 26 days before the scheduled move, the FBB again postponed Berlin Brandenburg's opening date, citing unresolved technical difficulties with the airport's fire safety and smoke exhaust systems. After replacing several senior executives, the FBB announced a new opening date of March 17, 2013. In what was becoming a regular occurrence, this was subsequently pushed back to October 2013.

Stormclouds on the Financial Horizon

Berlin Brandenburg's original construction budget as approved in 2006 by the Berlin and Brandenburg state governments was set at €2.2 billion. By the time construction of the terminal building got underway in 2008, the construction budget had grown to just over €2.8 billion. Of this total, €2.4 billion was to be provided by bank loans backed by government guarantees with the balance coming from FBB's own funds (Fiedler and Wendler 2016, p. 114). The fact that the loans were entirely government guaranteed made them essentially risk free. As a result, none of the banks financing Berlin Brandenburg undertook their initial due diligence or later construction monitoring efforts with anything approaching the level of care normally required for large construction projects. This lack of basic checks and balances between project sponsor and project lenders would repeatedly come back to haunt both the FBB and the airport's state sponsors.

Few in the FBB or the states of Berlin and Brandenburg or even the German government worried about whether the bank loans would be repaid. Air traffic in and out of Tegel Airport had grown 30 percent between 2000 and 2007,[10] and with the rising popularity of discount air carriers like Berlin-based Air Berlin, passenger volumes and airport revenues were projected to keep growing. Air travelers worldwide were also spending increasing amounts at in-airport shops and restaurants—facilities that both Tegel and Schönefeld lacked—and the accompanying growth in retail rents was adding significantly to many airport owners' bottom lines.

This glowing state of affairs did not last. By 2012, Berlin Brandenburg's overall construction budget had increased to €4.3 billion, with all of the additional cost paid for by FBB's government shareholders. Things were also looking shakier on the revenue front. In spite of the Global Financial Crisis, overall airline passenger traffic in and out of Berlin had continued growing, but the number of high-revenue business travelers was down and the discount airline market was becoming saturated. Air Berlin, which was slated to become the new airport's largest airline operator, was in particular trouble. Airport operators across the EU and especially in Germany were facing increased legal action over excessive aircraft noise, requiring them to spend more on legal settlements and noise abatement. The FBB's bankers were also becoming more wary, announcing that they wouldn't extend it any additional loans unless they were co-signed by the German government.

Who's in Charge?

With uncertainties mounting about when Berlin Brandenburg would finally open and how it would be paid for, senior personnel changes at the FBB were in the offing. In January 2013, the FBB announced that the new airport wouldn't open until sometime in 2014 and that both its CEO and the chair of its supervisory board were departing. Questions were also arising as to whether the new terminal would be large enough to accommodate the increases in airline passenger traffic now occurring at both Tegel and Schönefeld. Meanwhile, Berlin Brandenburg was no closer to completion. In his October 2014 testimony in a special commission established by the Brandenburg Parliament to investigate construction delays at the new airport, recently-appointed FBB CEO Hartmut Mehdorn pointed to sometime in 2017 or 2018 for the airport's most likely opening.[11] This did not go down well with commission members.

Berlin Brandenburg's most serious problems continued to center on its exhaust and smoke control system. The initial design, known as "the monster" to construction workers, had called for a single ventilation and smoke control system. When the additional terminal pier was added and engineering simulations revealed that the original single system would be inadequate, the design was changed to include multiple and redundant systems, all of which would be controlled by an upgraded wiring system to be engineered by Siemens, Germany's foremost engineering and technology company. With a busy backlog of its own, Siemens announced that it wouldn't get to the job until well into 2014.

Technology-caused delays weren't the only problem facing the FBB. In October 2014, the airport's former technical director, Jochen Grossmann, was found guilty of bribery, having admitted to demanding €500,000 from a potential contractor to help fix the airport's malfunctioning smoke extraction system. During Grossmann's trial, it was revealed that Alfredo di Mauro, the engineer in charge of designing and installing the airport's fire protection system, was not in fact a qualified engineer but an engineering draftsman.

As these and other lapses became public knowledge, Brandenburg state officials stepped up their monitoring and inspection efforts, soon finding additional technical and safety issues. In an attempt to get a handle on their problems, FBB officials sought permission from Brandenburg's Technical Inspection Association, or TUV, to open the terminal's north pier for interim airline and passenger use as a test case while they worked out other issues. This too did not go as hoped. In its preliminary safety evaluation inspection of the north pier's facilities, TUV inspectors found that required lightning rods were missing and that the back-up generator needed to pressurize the sprinkler system in case of a power outage was not powerful enough to do its job. As one TUV inspector put it, "What the airport ordered was sufficient for a circus tent, but [if power fails] not for the dimensions of the terminal."

2015 would prove no better. Facing questions from another investigative commission, this one convened by Berlin's Parliament, FBB CEO Mehdorn was unable to offer a firm date for the airport's eventual opening. Soon thereafter Mehdorn resigned citing health reasons.[12] His replacement, Karsten Mühlenfeld, the former head of Rolls Royce Germany, quickly came into conflict with his boss, Berlin Mayor Michael Müller, who had been appointed as head of the FBB's supervisory board. When Mühlenfeld declined to commit to a firm airport opening date, Müller publicly contradicted him, announcing that the airport would open for certain in 2017.

In August of 2015, the German subsidiary of (Dutch) Royal Imtech, the company that had the contract to re-engineer and rebuild the airport's malfunctioning fire control and exhaust system announced it was filing for bankruptcy.[13] Days later, its parent company in the Netherlands also declared bankruptcy, leading FBB and Brandenburg state officials to concede that a 2017 opening was unlikely. With Tempelhof having closed in 2008 and with Tegel's operating permit set to expire at the end of 2017—having already been extended once—this would leave Berlin with just Schönefeld to meet all of its airport needs. Faced with such a disastrous possibility, the FBB requested that Tegel's operating permit be extended for another three years.

2016 was supposed to be the year FBB officials finally caught a break. Within the FBB, the timetable for Berlin Brandenburg's opening had been pushed back to 2018, leaving contractors with sufficient time to finish their work. Or so they thought. An April inspection of the main terminal's redesigned smoke exhaust system found new problems. Subsequent testing of the airport's underground railway station, which had been fully certified in 2011, found that it too suffered from ventilation problems, which, in the case of an emergency, could cause smoke to build up within the station area. Also in April, press spokesman Daniel Abbou was fired after admitting in an on-the-record interview that billions of euros had been squandered on airport construction jobs, and that only someone "dependent on medication" could provide firm guarantees as to when the airport would eventually open.[14] In August 2016, a former FBB department head admitted in court to taking €150,000 in bribes five years earlier from the now bankrupt Imtech.[15]

Later the same month, Brandenburg TUV inspectors announced that permissions for the next phase of airport construction would not be issued because of the FBB's inability to remedy multiple open problems. An October 2016 TUV report found that motors which opened and closed the terminal's windows would not operate at temperatures above 30°C (86°F). In case of fire, as many as 80 percent of the terminal's automated doors might not open or close reliably. Unable to accommodate sufficient water flow to the sprinkler system, the water pipes in the south tier would have to be replaced, necessitating the removal and reinstallation of the entire ceiling. Most worrisome of all, the main construction permit for the terminal was set to expire on November 23, 2016, requiring Berlin authorities to quickly pass a law extending it for ongoing projects.[16]

Slow Walking to the Finish Line

No one, it seemed, could say authoritatively when Berlin Brandenburg Airport would be completed or would finally open. In March 2017, with polls showing public confidence in the airport project declining, the FBB replaced

Karsten Mühlenfeld as its CEO with Berlin Secretary of State Englebert Lütke-Daldrup.[17] Criticized in some quarters as "Berlin's man," Lütke-Daldrup quickly proved to be the right man for the job (Müller 2020). An urban planner and experienced public servant, Lütke-Daldrup viewed his most important task as one of restoring the FBB's public credibility. Instead of promising that the airport would open as soon as the engineering problem of the moment could be solved, Lütke-Daldrup admitted that Berlin-Brandenburg's opening date would likely have to be pushed back until 2019, or even 2020. This was not good news in and of itself, but it established that the FBB finally had someone credible at its helm. Lütke-Daltrup also benefited from former CEO Hartmut Mehdorn's decision to recruit Jörg Marks as the FBB's new technical director. Marks had been a senior manager for Siemens and was eminently knowledgeable about the intricacies and deficiencies of fire protection and smoke extraction systems.

While Lütke-Daltrup was putting the FBB's messaging in order and Marks was getting its contractors to deliver, others in the FBB were worrying about the construction budget. In August 2017, after the *Berliner Zeitung* newspaper reported that the airport's construction financing would run out in 2018, the FBB was forced to appeal to the German government for additional funds. After months of back and forth between private lenders, the FBB and the European Union about how additional credit infusions should be secured, a consortium of seven German banks agreed to provide €2.4 billion[18] in additional government-secured loans (Lykotrafiti 2017). Among the banks' concerns in making the new loans were whether they would be fully repaid. In August 2017, Air Berlin, the discount air carrier that had leased the largest block of airport gates announced it would be ceasing operations after its majority shareholder, Etihad Airways, declined to extend the credit it needed to keep flying.[19]

Lufthansa agreed to take over some of Air Berlin's soon-to-be abandoned routes but refused to commit to making Berlin an international hub like Frankfurt or Munich. If the airport was not going to operate as a transfer hub, why then did it need to be so far away from Berlin? Berlin Brandenburg's suddenly diminished status led to public calls for Tegel Airport to remain open and serve as a commuter airport for time-sensitive business travelers in much the same way as London City Airport complemented Heathrow. When a majority of Berlin voters in a non-binding referendum cast ballots to keep Tegel open,[20] Berlin's Parliament and the FBB were put in the unenviable position of having to reject the will of the voters.

Even as its mechanical systems were redesigned and fixed, defects continued to pop up in the airport's wiring system.[21] An all-around test of Berlin Brandenburg's electrical and software systems was planned for September 2018 but had to be postponed for nearly a year because different sub-systems would not properly connect with one another. In May of 2018, Siemens testified before the Berlin Senate's Airport Committee that FBB officials had not yet delivered the paperwork necessary for them to properly test the terminal's smoke control software. Adding to the FBB's worries, a citizen suit claiming that noise from night flights in and out of Berlin Brandenburg would cause discomfort and adverse health effects, had made its way to Germany's Supreme Court. (The claim was later determined to be without merit.) In June 2018, Berlin's Parliament formed yet another investigative committee to get to the bottom of the airport's continuing delays.

Further heightening the FBB's embarrassment, construction work on a second airport terminal, known as T2, had progressed without difficulty. Intended exclusively for use by discount airlines, T2 was smaller and more basic than the main terminal. Initially planned to cost €200 million, the airport's exploding construction costs had made it necessary to cut T2's construction budget to €100 million. This engendered a drive to find design and construction cost efficiencies that would ultimately enable T2's contractor, Zechbau Bremen, to deliver the completed terminal in just ten months. Citing the successes of the T2 experience, FBB CEO Lütke-Daldrup cautiously predicted that Berlin Brandenburg might finally be able to open by August 2020—a position from which he later had to walk back.[22]

However useful from a public relations perspective, the FBB's new openness policy provided an unsparing window into Berlin Brandenburg's continuing construction problems. A software update for the fire alarm system scheduled for March 2019 was delayed until May. The sand-lime bricks used for the airport's foundation were determined to be unable to carry their specified weight loads, requiring the construction of additional concrete reinforcing beams. Flooding of the conduit ducts next to the airport's southern runway necessitated replacing more than 700 km of cable wiring. In a June 2019 interview with the *Berlin Morgenpost*, Christian Gräff, a deputy in Germany's ruling Christian Democratic Union party, went so far as to suggest that Tegel and Schönefeld airports should be renovated and that construction of Berlin Brandenburg be abandoned. [23]

Out of the gaze of the media, airport contractors made slow but steady progress. After five years of re-engineering work, Terminal 1's smoke removal system was certified by the TUV in April 2019. In early 2020, the airport successfully completed testing of all of its major passenger service systems; and in May 2020, the airport finally received its official operating license. On October 25, 2020, the one Schönefeld Airport terminal that would remain in operation as part of the new airport was officially redesignated BER Terminal 5. Six days later, early in the morning on October 31, 2020, a special service EasyJet flight from Tegel Airport landed on Runway 1, officially opening Berlin Brandenburg Airport Willy Brandt.[24] As an indication of just how tired government officials were of dealing with the airport's problems, German Transport Minister Andreas Scheuer was the lone federal dignitary to attend the opening.

Prescient Pre-mortems

Even before its completion, Berlin Brandenburg's slow-motion progress provided observers with opportunities to assess what had gone wrong. These were summarized in a 2015 presentation by Berlin School of Economics and Law Professor Jurgen Mueller as part of a research project undertaken by the German Airport Performance (GAP) group, as well as in a 2016 book chapter on large German infrastructure projects by Jobst Fiedler and Alexander Wendler of the Hertie School of Governance in Berlin. Among the prescient judgements rendered by the three authors were the following.

*   The Berlin Brandenburg Airport's government ownership structure—with the states of Berlin and Brandenburg each having a 37 percent ownership share and the German federal government owning the balance—was inherently unstable, with the different entities at times pursuing competing political objectives. In spite of its greater political, financial, and regulatory powers, the German federal government was too timid in exercising needed project oversight.
*   Because all of their loans were completely government-guaranteed, the airport's private lenders exercised only marginal oversight on how the monies were being used.
*   The FBB's lack of airport construction management experience, coupled with their repeated mistakes bidding the project, created a situation in which no single contractor or staff could properly coordinate the entire construction job. This situation worsened after the departure of Thomas Weyer in 2008 and the FBB's inability to replace him with someone of comparable expertise. With pg.bbi providing some coordination and oversight, the situation was at least manageable until 2012, but it worsened as FBB officials took on project management responsibilities for which they had insufficient training.
*   Particularly troubling was the fact that the FBB's supervisory board—the equivalent of a board of directors in a private corporation—had virtually no development or construction management experience. Eight of the ten supervisory board members as of December 2013 were politicians of cabinet minister or state secretary level. The remaining two were a hotel and gastronomy consultant and the manager of the chamber of industry and commerce of Cottbus, a small city in Brandenburg.
*   By hiring too many subcontractors—50 at one count—and no overall supervisory contractor, the FBB ensured that there would be an excessive

number of expensive program and design changes as well as contractor quality control problems. The lack of a single project supervisor also made it difficult to control costs or stay on budget.

- Until the appointment of Englebert Lütke-Daldrup as FBB CEO in 2017, the FBB's practice of not leveling with the public about the airport's construction problems and opening date served to undermine public confidence.
- The FBB's failure to anticipate and plan for the adoption of more stringent airport safety codes after 2010 led to additional construction delays and cost overruns.
- Because Berlin Brandenburg took so long to complete, it was unusually vulnerable to shifts in the airline industry and passenger demand. This led to a situation in which the airport construction program continually lagged behind unfolding industry and passenger trends. This increased the number of in-process design changes as well as threatened the airport's projected cash flows when Air Berlin (the airport's dominant air carrier) declared bankruptcy in 2017.

THE PROFESSIONALS TAKE CHARGE: REBUILDING LAGUARDIA AIRPORT'S TERMINAL B

Lauded as cutting-edge and contemporary when it opened to the public in 1939, people have been complaining about New York's LaGuardia Airport since the dawn of the jet age. New York City's crowded expressways meant it took too long to get there. There was no subway service. The terminals were too small and run-down. The security and waiting areas were inadequate. Its short taxiways exacerbated aircraft congestion and ground delays. Birds were drawn to LaGuardia's runways—a problem given national attention after a bird strike forced US Airways Flight 1549 to ditch in the Hudson River, fortunately with no fatalities thanks to the quick thinking of its pilot and crew.[25]

Its many annoyances notwithstanding, LaGuardia is conveniently located for many New Yorkers, making it a frequently-used if not necessarily popular airport (Figure 11.3). Because its passenger gates are so tightly spaced, planes with wingspans longer than a Boeing 767's cannot use LaGuardia. This includes most widebody aircraft. The combination of high passenger demand and limitations on aircraft size means that LaGuardia is always crowded with passengers and planes. Depending on the weather, aircraft landing at LaGuardia sometimes descend over Queen's more highly-populated neighborhoods. To mitigate these problems, in 1984, the Port Authority instituted a Sunday-thru-Friday "perimeter rule" banning nonstop flights from LaGuardia to cities more than 1,500 miles away. When this locally-imposed rule didn't do enough to reduce crowding at LaGuardia, the FAA stepped in in 2007 to impose its own flight operations limits.[26]

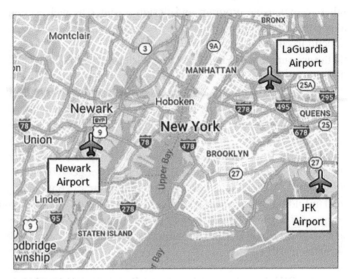

Source: Google Maps.

Figure 11.3   New York City airports locator map

Even with these restrictions, the number of airline passengers using LaGuardia continued growing, reaching 25 million in 2000 and 28 million in 2015.[27] The construction of two additional terminal buildings in 1983 and 1992 helped alleviate congestion in its terminals, but with the New York City metro area having added 2+ million new residents since 1990, LaGuardia was constantly bumping up against its capacity limits. In 2011, Delta Air Lines announced that it would be making LaGuardia Airport one of its major domestic hubs, increasing incoming Delta flights by 60 percent and outgoing ones by 75 percent. By the summer of 2013, Delta was offering 264 daily flights between LaGuardia and 60 cities, more than any other airline at LaGuardia.

After years of favoring the higher-profile JFK and Newark Airports over LaGuardia, by 2010 the Port Authority was finally ready to do something about LaGuardia's worsening capacity and congestion problems.

In April 2010, Port Authority Director Christopher Ward announced that the agency had hired consultants to explore a full rethink of LaGuardia Airport.[28] The rebuilding job was projected to be a difficult one, not only because of its cost, expected to be in the range of $2.4 billion, but because there was no possibility of physically expanding the airport's footprint. It was also understood that the airport would have to remain fully operational throughout any reconstruction process. Complicating the process further, of LaGuardia's four terminals, the Port Authority controlled just Terminals A and B; Terminals C and D were controlled by Delta Airlines.

The Port Authority consultant's rethinking report was never made public. Nonetheless, in 2012, it issued a draft Request for Qualifications (RFQ) covering the demolition and replacement of LaGuardia's Terminal B building and related parking and access facilities (Port Authority 2012). Along with a list of design and programmatic requirements, the Port Authority's draft RFQ (and subsequent Request for Proposals) included a solicitation for potential partners who could provide construction financing for the project in exchange for an agreement to maintain, operate, and potentially own the rebuilt terminal once completed. This type of public–private partnership (P3) arrangement was becoming increasingly popular among airport authorities, and the Port Authority itself had used it in 2012 to renovate LaGuardia's Terminals C and D for Delta Airlines.

Enter Governor Cuomo

Among the stakeholders the Port Authority had neglected to consult when developing its LaGuardia reconstruction scheme was New York Governor Andrew Cuomo. The eldest son and political confidante of three-time New York Governor Mario Cuomo, Andrew Cuomo had served in the Clinton Administration as Secretary of Housing and Urban Development. While there, he had developed a reputation for an abrasive management style that was none-theless effective at cutting through government bureaucracy. Cuomo returned to New York in 2002 to run unsuccessfully for governor. In 2010, after four years as New York State's high-profile attorney general, Cuomo ran again for Governor, this time successfully. From the outset, Cuomo saw himself as a transformational figure whose take-no-prisoners style would enable him to break through Albany's partisan gridlock to get things done (Cuomo 2014). Governing as a pro-growth, pro-business Democrat, Cuomo quickly focused on upgrading New York's aging public infrastructure.

Whereas other Democratic governors saw infrastructure as competing with social programs for limited tax revenues, Cuomo was comfortable raising tolls and user charges to pay for needed infrastructure investments. Cuomo's first big infrastructure push came with his environmental fast-tracking of a replacement bridge for the 60-year old Tappan Zee Bridge that carried the New York Thruway across the Hudson River north of New York City. When a replacement Tappan Zee Bridge was initially approved for construction by the New York Metropolitan Transportation Council in August 2012, knowl-edgeable observers thought it might take three or four years to line up all the environmental and construction permits. Instead, with Cuomo's pushing to speed things up, the final environmental permit was forthcoming in just ten months. Building on his experiences in successfully advancing the Tappan

Zee Bridge, Cuomo wondered if he could use a similar approach to speed up rebuilding LaGuardia Airport. (Plotch 2015)

Always seeking to safeguard his own prerogatives, Cuomo used his January 2014 "State-of-the-State Address" to announce his own plans for the future of LaGuardia Airport, one in which the State of New York and not the Port Authority or some yet-to-be-constituted public–private partnership would have principal responsibility for rebuilding the airport.[29] There was just one problem with Cuomo's announced LaGuardia plan: it contained no actual plan, at least not yet. To create one, Cuomo assembled an advisory panel to be led by Dan Tishman, Vice-President of the infrastructure giant AECOM and former head of the Tishman-Speyer construction firm. Other panel members included former New York City Planning Commission head Amanda Burden, Manhattan real estate developer John Zuccotti, Harvard infrastructure economist Jose Gomez-Ibanez, Queens Borough President Melinda Katz, Clarkson University President Tony Collins, and Jackie Snyder, Governor Cuomo's Special Infrastructure Advisor.

Determined not to reinvent the proverbial wheel, Cuomo's panel wisely took its starting point as the Port Authority's LaGuardia rebuilding plan as well as the results of a 2014 LaGuardia design competition. With Vice-President Joe Biden at his side—it was at this announcement that the Vice-President compared LaGuardia to a third-world airport—Governor Cuomo released his advisory panel's recommendations on June 27, 2015, noting that fully implementing them would cost in the neighborhood of $4 billion.[30] Among the plan's key recommendations were to (LaGuardia Airport Advisory Panel 2015, p. 2):

- Demolish the existing Central Terminal (i.e., Terminal B) structure and thoroughly redevelop Terminals C and D to create a unified terminal structure that would provide an efficient and appealing passenger experience;
- Move the new unified terminal closer to the Grand Central Parkway (i.e., the access roadway serving LaGuardia) to free up nearly two miles of additional aircraft taxiways in order to improve aircraft circulation and reduce gate delays;
- Design the new Central Terminal building to have high ceilings, expansive natural lighting, and best-in-class passenger amenities;
- Build an Airport People Mover (APM) system to quickly move passengers between the airport terminals and facilities;
- Include integrated business and conference center capabilities to meet the needs of business travelers, as well as leave room to build additional hotel and hospitality facilities;
- Better integrate the existing LaGuardia Marine Air Terminal (MAT) with other terminal facilities via an automated tram or some other form of reliable and convenient mode of transportation, and

- Work with the Port Authority, the MTA, and neighboring communities to conduct the necessary evaluation and planning to determine the best method and route for a rail service to LaGuardia that minimizes community impacts.

To build what was now being referred to as the New LaGuardia, the Governor's advisory panel recommended continuing the Port Authority's public–private partnership approach which had preliminarily identified a LaGuardia reconstruction team composed of HOK and Parsons Brinckerhoff, which would design the new facility; Skanska and Walsh Construction, which would build it; and Vantage Airport Group, which would operate it. Financing would be provided by a partnership entity to be called the LaGuardia Gateway Partnership (LGP). LGP would be responsible for designing, building, financing, operating, and maintaining the new terminal as part of a 35-year lease. Lost on no one who attended the Governor's June 27 announcement was the understanding that the Port Authority, by allowing Governor Cuomo to take credit for what was essentially its plan, had converted a so-so supporter into a vigorous ally.

In previous years, the New Jersey appointees to the Port Authority Board might have balked at such a New York City-centric undertaking, but with Governor Cuomo politically ascendant and New Jersey Governor Chris Christie weakened by the "Bridgegate" scandal[31] and due to be termed out of office in January 2018, the Port Authority Board quickly lined up behind Cuomo's proposal. Besides, plans were also in the works to eventually rebuild Newark Liberty Airport in New Jersey.

Making matters easier was the fact that the Port Authority and the participants in LGP were all highly regarded in the business and financial community and that, among themselves, they had years of continuous experience building and operating airport facilities. This was a far cry from the Berlin situation in which the FBB and many of its contractors were all newcomers to the airport building business. It also helped that LaGuardia was a known commodity to New Yorkers and that the suggested changes to the airport's circulation and access features represented a clear improvement. The situation was very different in Berlin where the new Berlin Brandenburg Airport was a clean-sheet design.

New York City's two nationally influential newspapers, the *New York Times* and *The Wall Street Journal*, both of which had harped about LaGuardia's deficiencies for years, quickly lined up behind the Cuomo–Port Authority plan, as did the Regional Plan Association and just about every labor, business, and tourist organization in the city. With all of New York City's institutional and financial heavyweights in agreement that the time to rebuild LaGuardia was now, things moved ahead quickly. And because it was replacing an existing terminal structure within what was essentially the same footprint, the rebuilt Central Terminal would not require an environmental impact statement.

Table 11.3   LaGuardia Airport timeline

October 1939	LaGuardia Airport opens as New York Municipal Airport on the site of the old Glenn Curtis Airfield. It is renamed LaGuardia Airport (after New York City Mayor Fiorello LaGuardia) in 1948 when the New York City Port Authority assumes ownership.
April 1964	A new and larger Central Terminal Building (CTB) opens, better suited to jet passengers and flights.
1983 and 1992	Delta Air Lines moves its LaGuardia gates from the CTB to its own purpose-built Terminals C and D.
1984	With air traffic in and out of LaGuardia (and nearby JFK) rising, the Port Authority institutes a Sunday-thru-Friday "perimeter rule" banning nonstop flights from LaGuardia to cities more than 1,500 miles away. Additional restrictions are imposed later by the FAA.
1994	For the first time, passenger traffic in and out of LaGuardia exceeds 20 million. It will be another 24 years before it reaches 30 million.
April 2010	The NY-NJ Port Authority announces that it has hired consultants to plan the rebuilding of LaGuardia's Central Terminal, and that the project will likely be financed through a public–private-partnership (P3).
December 2011	Delta Air Lines announces plans to open a new domestic hub at LaGuardia, the airport's largest expansion since 1964.
January 2014	Pre-empting the Port Authority's ongoing planning process, NY State Governor Andrew Cuomo announces the state will oversee planning and construction of a new Central Terminal and related facilities. To guide the state's efforts, Cuomo announces the appointment of his own advisory committee.
May 2015	The Port Authority selects LaGuardia Gateway Partners (LGP) as its preferred bidder to redevelop and operate what it calls "The New LaGuardia."
July 2015	Following the advice of his advisory committee, Governor Cuomo announces a $4 billion plan to rebuild the Central Terminal. The project will be undertaken by LaGuardia Gateway Partners.
Spring 2016	LGP takes over existing operations at Terminal B. Construction begins on the Central Terminal reconstruction project, with final completion scheduled for 2022.
July 2018	Delta Airlines announces it will spend $3.6 billion to replace Terminals C and D with a new four-concourse single terminal.
December 2018	Terminal B's new Eastern Concourse is partially opened to passengers.
June 2020	Terminal B's new Arrivals and Departure Hall is opened to passengers. The Western Concourse is partially opened, with completion expected in 2021.
Late 2021	Construction begins on LaGuardia's new AirTrain system, connecting the airport to the Willits Point subway and Long Island Railroad Station.

A Complicated Building and Financing Program Takes Shape

LaGuardia's ten-year rebuilding program is so complicated and has so many moving parts that keeping track of them all requires a scorecard (Table 11.3).[32] Making the job more complicated still is the fact that the project involves two separate owners—the Port Authority and Delta Airlines—each of which was bound and determined to keep all of their flight and passenger operations up and running throughout the construction period.

Conceptually, the entire LaGuardia rebuilding project is organized into two phases, each costing roughly $4 billion. Phase I, which began in 2016 and is scheduled for completion in 2022, is organized around rebuilding LaGuardia's Central Terminal B. Whereas the original Central Terminal was organized into a four-story central section, two three-story wings and four concourses (A, B, C, and D), the new Central Terminal—which will be half-again as large as the old one—will have eastern and western concourses joined by a headhouse and a common arrivals and departure hall. The new terminal would have 38 gates (18 in the eastern concourse and 20 in the western concourse) and more than 200 check-in desks and kiosks. Opened to passengers in stages in 2018 and 2019, the new eastern concourse, which will include gates 40 to 59, was built first. A new Terminal B West Parking Garage with room for 3,100 cars also opened in 2018 (Figure 11.4). Demolition of the 50 year-old LaGuardia

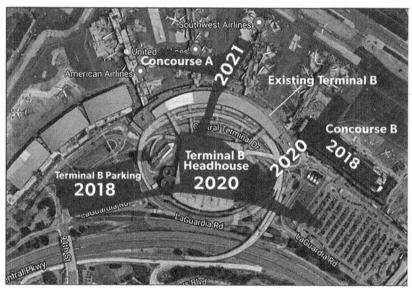

Source: Image by Mike Arnot from New York YIMBY.

Figure 11.4   LaGuardia Airport old and new Terminal B configurations

Terminal B facilities began in December 2016 and progressed in sections to allow continued access to available airline gates. The new Arrivals and Departures Hall, which is closer to the street, wider, and more modern in every respect, opened in June 2020. The western concourse is also being opened in sections, with the final section having been opened in December 2021.[33]

Of the $4 billion that Phase I will cost, $2.4 billion is being provided by the Port Authority. The balance is being funded by LaGuardia Gateway Partners, the P3 investor group composed of Vantage Airport Group, Skanska Construction, JLC Infrastructure, and Meridiam, a Paris-based infrastructure investment fund. In exchange for its funding commitment, LGP was given a 35-year lease by the Port Authority to operate the entire Central Terminal complex.[34] Beyond these rather vague provisions, the precise details of the deal between the Port Authority and LGP have never been made public. Although the Port Authority is a public corporation, it is not required to publish the details of its financing arrangements with third parties such as the LGP.

While the Port Authority was overseeing Phase I of LaGuardia's reconstruction, work has also progressed on Phase II, which involves combining the current Delta Airlines-owned Terminals C and D into a single structure. Like Phase I, Phase II is being completed in sections in order keep current flight and passenger operations up and running. The first of four new concourses opened in November 2019, with subsequent concourse openings projected at two-year intervals. Delta currently anticipates completing Phase II sometime in 2026 at an estimated cost of $3.6 billion (Figure 11.5).[35]

Ironically, more is known about the details of Delta's financing deal than the Port Authority's. To help fund its rebuilding of Terminals C and D, Delta, through its financial partner, the Mellon Bank of New York, purchased New York State Transportation Development Corp. (TDC) special facilities revenue bonds from the Empire State Development Corporation, a TDC subsidiary. The cash then flowed to Delta as a $1.38 billion building loan leasehold mortgage and a $4 million project loan leasehold mortgage. Goldman Sachs served as Delta's original leasehold mortgager, but when they subsequently withdrew in 2017, the Port Authority stepped in to assume the debt.[36]

Beyond the rebuilt and expanded terminals and new parking structures, the other big piece of the LaGuardia rebuilding program involves the construction of a new AirTrain people mover system connecting LaGuardia to the combined New York City Subway and Long Island Railroad station at Willets Point near Citi Field, home of the Mets baseball team. The 1.5-mile system will use technology similar to that of the AirTrain system that connects JFK Airport's terminals to the Jamaica and Howard Beach subway and LIRR stations. Projected to cost upward of $2 billion, the proposed AirTrain system has attracted both advocates and opponents. AirTrain supporters, who include the Port Authority, all of LaGuardia's major airlines, and most Queens and

Source: Image from A Whole New LGA (www.anewlga.com).

*Figure 11.5   Rendering of completed reconstruction of Terminals B
(Phase I) and C–D (Phase II)*

Manhattan business and labor organizations, echo Governor Cuomo's con-
tention that the system will significantly improve subway and rail access to
LaGuardia, and help alleviate traffic congestion and air pollution levels in and
around the East Elmhurst community.[37] Opponents of the AirTrain scheme
question whether it will offer any real travel time savings over existing subway
and bus routes while adding further to congestion on the already-packed No.
7 subway line.[38] In a city with other pressing public transportation needs, they
also question its cost. In March 2021, the Federal Aviation Administration
released its final AirTrain Environmental Impact Statement which counted
the creation of 3,000 construction jobs and $500 million in contracting oppor-
tunities for minority- and women-owned businesses as among the system's
proposed benefits.[39] After gaining FAA approval, AirTrain construction began
in late 2021, with an opening date scheduled for 2024 or 2025.

Promises (So Far) Delivered

Although the entire LaGuardia rebuilding project is only two-thirds complete
as of this writing, so far it has kept to its original opening schedule and budget.

• With space for 3,100 vehicles and a covered connection to Terminal B,
  LaGuardia's new West Parking Garage opened in February 2018.

- Eleven passenger gates at Terminal B's new Eastern Concourse opened in December 2018. Five additional gates opened seven months later. The final two Eastern Concourse gates opened in 2020.
- In November of 2019, Delta Airlines opened the first of four new concourses at its Terminal C and D complex.
- On June 11, 2020, Governor Andrew M. Cuomo cut the ribbon on the brand-new Terminal B Arrivals and Departures Hall. Two days later, the new hall opened to the public along with the new connector to the Eastern Concourse at LaGuardia Airport.
- In August 2020, seven gates in the new Western Concourse opened. The remaining ten Western Concourse gates are scheduled to open in the fall of 2021.
- With the final demolition of the Central Terminal's Concourse C in March 2021, the demolition of the original Central Terminal facility was declared complete.
- Even with all this construction activity going on, until the onset of the Covid-19 pandemic, the number of passengers using LaGuardia airport continued to grow, rising from 29.8 million in 2016 to 31.1 million in 2019.

Although full reviews of the new Central Terminal building will have to await its final fit-out, so far, the commentaries have mostly been positive. The headline of a June 2020 column by *New York Times* travel correspondent Patrick McGeehan characterized LaGuardia's transformation as "From Disgraceful to Breathtaking."[40] Thomas Pallini, transportation correspondent for the *Business Insider* website wrote of the new Terminal B in June 2020, "I flew out of the new LaGuardia Airport terminal 2 weeks after it opened and couldn't believe it was the same airport I hated."[41] Thepointsguy.com, a website that advises air travelers on how to maximize their frequent flyer points, wrote of the new Terminal B in June 2020, "It's hard to believe you're at LaGuardia."[42] Whether these and other reviewers will still be quite as positive once passenger volumes at LaGuardia return to their pre-Covid levels remains to be seen, but for now, the word on the street about the rebuilt LaGuardia is encouraging.

Among the reasons the LaGuardia rebuilding project has progressed so well is that its major design, engineering and construction contractors are all highly experienced. HOK, the lead project architect, had successfully completed terminal rebuilding projects at the nation's two busiest airports, O'Hare in Chicago, and Hartsfield-Jackson in Atlanta. WSP, the prime engineering contractor, had successfully designed and engineered the baggage-handling and terminal operations systems at the new JetBlue terminal at nearby JFK airport, which is also operated by the Port Authority. With operations throughout the US and Europe, Skanska, the lead construction contractor, had developed a highly successful practice redeveloping airport terminals while maintaining flight operations at full capacity. Started in Vancouver in 1994, Vantage Airport Group specialized in medium-sized airport asset management and operations. Perhaps most importantly, for all of its well-known difficulties managing its real estate assets and serving its dual political masters in Albany and Trenton, the Port Authority of New York and New Jersey is a top-notch airport owner and operator, having profitably managed three of the nation's busiest airports through floods, recessions, security threats, and a constantly changing airline industry. If any organization could successfully structure a P3 with financial staying power, it is the Port Authority.

LESSONS AND TAKEAWAYS

The side-by-side comparisons presented in this chapter between Berlin Brandenburg International Willy Brandt Airport in Berlin and LaGuardia Airport in New York City offer a unique opportunity to identify good and bad contemporary airport megaproject planning and construction practices. At the risk of oversimplifying, Flughafen Berlin Schönefeld GmbH (a.k.a. FBB), the government corporation created to build and operate Berlin Brandenburg, made just about every mistake there was to make in the megaproject playbook. It:

- *Never developed a clear understanding of the how Berlin Brandenburg's design and project parameters had shifted since the initial airport construction program was approved in 2006.* As a result, the FBB was always playing catch-up with respect to Berlin Brandenburg's size and capacity, and was unprepared when a major airline tenant, Air Berlin, declared bankruptcy in 2017. In contrast to the FBB's lack of foresight, LaGuardia Airport's owner, the Port Authority of New York and New Jersey, periodically engaged in a sophisticated strategic planning process that evaluated LaGuardia's competitive position within New York City's three airport system as well as within the broader domestic and international air travel and air cargo markets.
- *Was overly reliant on its public sector sponsors to access needed financing.* A creature of the governments of the states of Berlin and Brandenburg, and with nearly unlimited access to government-provided loan guarantees and revenues, the FBB never undertook a proper financial feasibility or risk analysis of its airport financing plan. Instead, it assumed it would always be able to cover whatever cost overruns it incurred. The Port Authority, by contrast, not only had to justify LaGuardia's financing plan to the governors of New York and New Jersey, its use of a P3 arrangement to access private capital to finance Terminal 2's complete reconstruction

required it to document how much debt could reasonably be supported by
the Airport's future cash flows.

* *Never developed an effective set of contracting and project management
  practices.* This was perhaps the FBB's most egregious error. When it was
  initially unable to hire a suitable overall contractor, rather than go back and
  revise its construction program and bidding procedures, the FBB divided
  the job into seven separate subcontracts. When it was unable to find qualified subcontractors, it made the same mistake again, dividing the job into
  35 subcontracts. The result was a hydra of uncoordinated contracts and job
  specifications for which no single entity was accountable. In New York,
  by contrast, the Port Authority midwifed the creation of a special-purpose
  development team composed of experienced construction managers, contractors, and financiers.
* *Never developed sufficient in-house project management expertise to properly manage the project.* Not hiring an overall project manager or supervisor is not the end of the world if you can develop that expertise in-house.
  Unfortunately, the FBB never did so, preferring to create a revolving door
  of CEOs and technical supervisors, none of whom, except for Thomas
  Weyer, had actual experience managing an airport construction job.
  Indeed, as was revealed later, some of the FBB's project engineers were
  not qualified for the jobs they were given. In the LaGuardia case, not only
  did the Port Authority have years of in-house project management and
  contracting experience, so too did the members of the development team,
  some of whom had worked together on previous airport projects.
* *Never instituted a robust system of cost and delay controls.* This omission
  was similarly egregious. Having encountered significant coordination,
  accountability and delivery problems three years into the project—which
  resulted in an announcement delaying the airport's opening date by an
  initial two years—one would think the FBB would have developed robust
  procedures for controlling construction costs and monitoring contractor
  progress. This never happened. Instead of incentivizing contractors to
  work together to solve newly-found problems, the different parties would
  point fingers at each other as to who was to blame. In the LaGuardia airport
  case, the partnership between the Port Authority's and LaGuardia Gateway
  Partners (LGP) assigned most of the delay and cost overrun risk to LGP.
* *Provided vague updates about the project's progress and didn't level with
  the public or other stakeholders about the nature and sources of delays and
  cost increases.* After the airport failed to meet its revised June 2012 opening
  target date, it became apparent to anyone familiar with the project that the
  FBB had no capability to accurately plan ahead. So, rather than level with
  its governmental sponsors and the public about the sources of its problems,
  the FBB issued a succession of vague and unrealistic promises about future

completion dates. This went on for four years until the appointment of Englebert Lütke-Daldrup as FBB CEO. Lütke-Daldrup instituted a policy of public transparency, which, when coupled with positive staff changes went a long way toward re-establishing the FBB's credibility. Rather than focus on a single completion date, the LaGuardia reconstruction project was scheduled in a manner that allowed the Port Authority (and the Governor of New York) to publicly meet a series of intermediate target dates. So, instead of apologizing for what wasn't finished, the LaGuardia team could brag about what had been completed.

This is not to say that everything about the Berlin Brandenburg Airport development process went badly and that everything about the LaGuardia process turned out well. LaGuardia is not yet fully finished as of this writing and new problems may emerge before it is. Since its opening, Berlin Brandenburg has had no problems of note—as indicated by the lack of public nostalgia for Tegel—and its design is well suited to later incremental expansion. Whether LaGuardia's AirTrain system will prove a suitable substitute for direct subway service remains to be seen. Despite huge declines in passengers and ticket revenues, the US and German airline industries seem to have weathered the Covid-19 pandemic reasonably intact, although whether and how the pandemic will permanently alter business and tourism travel patterns in the US and Europe is still uncertain. Environmental activists in both the US and Germany are pushing to accelerate cuts in greenhouse gas emissions of which airline travel is a significant contributor.

NOTES

1. Port Authority of New York and New Jersey. Annual Airport Traffic Reports. Various years. (2000–2020 monthly statistics can be downloaded from: https://www.panynj.gov/airports/en/statistics-general-info/Monthly_Airport_Activities.html).
2. https://www.jdpower.com/business/press-releases/2015-north-america-airport-satisfaction-study.
3. https://www.wsj.com/articles/new-york-airports-the-best-at-being-the-worst-11573658995.
4. https://time.com/5318/joe-biden-laguardia-airport/.
5. https://www.key.aero/article/history-berlins-airports.
6. Historical airport passenger statistics for Berlin can be retrieved from: https://www.adv.aero/service/downloadbibliothek/.
7. https://www.worldairportawards.com/the-worlds-top-100-airports-2013/.
8. https://www.worldairportawards.com/worlds-best-airports-announced-2019/.
9. [The Schönefeld Act – 1989–1996]. *Der Tagesspiegel* (https://www.tagesspiegel.de/berlin/flughafen-ber-die-akte-schonefeld-1989-bis-1996/5916252.html).
10. https://www.adv.aero/service/downloadbibliothek/.

11. https://www.tagesspiegel.de/berlin/bericht-des-untersuchungsausschusses
    -ueberall-verfehlungen-das-ber-drama-auf-ueber-1000-seiten/13735612.html.
12. "Hartmut Mehdorn tritt als Airport-Chef zurück" [Hartmut Mehdorn resigns as
    chief Airport]. *Bild*. December 15, 2014.
13. "Imtech files for bankruptcy protection in NL—Imtech beantragt in Niederlanden
    Gläubigerschutz". *Die Welt*. August 11, 2015.
14. "Troubled German airport's PR man 'sacked for straight-talking interview'".
    PRWeek. April 15, 2016.
15. "Geständnis zu Prozessbeginn: Ex-BER-Bereichsleiter nahm Schmiergeld an".
    n-tv. August 23, 2016.
16. "HauptstadtFlughafen-Ministerium plant Lex BER". *Focus*. May 24, 2015.
17. "Lütke-Daldrup soll es nun richten" [Lütke-Daldrup is now supposed to get
    a grip]. March 6, 2017.
18. "Die nächsten BER-Milliarden können fließen" [Now BER Millions Can Flow].
    Der Tagesspiegel. February 13, 2017.
19. "Air Berlin Files for Insolvency as Etihad Pulls Funding Plug". *Bloomberg*.
    August 15, 2017.
20. https://www.dw.com/en/berlin-votes-to-keep-tegel-airport-open/a-40667155.
21. "Keine Betriebssicherheit – BER fällt durch TÜV" [no sustained operation – BER
    fails TUV test]. May 21, 2018.
22. "Naechster BER Eroeffnungstermin wackelt" [Yet another opening date is shaky].
    May 10, 2019.
23. "CDU-Politiker empfiehlt Plan B für BER". *Berlin Morgenpost*. June 30, 2019.
24. "Easyjet landete zuerst: Die Baustelle BER ist endlich ein Flughafen" [Easyjet
    landed first: The construction site BER is finally an airport]. *Der Tagesspiegel*.
    October 31, 2020.
25. https://www.forbes.com/sites/jeremybogaisky/2019/01/14/blood-in-the-sky-10
    -years-after-the-miracle-on-the-hudson-bird-strikes-remain-an-unsolved-danger
    -for-aviation/.
26. https://www.faa.gov/regulations_policies/rulemaking/recently_published/media/
    LGA%20order.pdf.
27. https://www.panynj.gov/airports/en/statistics-general-info/Monthly_Airport
    _Activities.html.
28. Queens Gazette. "Rebuild LaGuardia Airport?" May 5, 2010. https://www
    .qgazette.com/articles/rebuild-laguardia-airport/.
29. WNYC. "Cuomo Asks Public for LGA and JFK Makeover Plans". October 20,
    2014.
30. *The Observer*. "We Need to Tear It Down'—Cuomo Announces Plans for New
    LaGuardia Airport". July 27, 2015.
31. *The Christian Science Monitor*. "Bridge-gate: Key figure says Chris Christie knew
    about lane closures". January 31, 2013.
32. The "A New LaGuardia" website (https://www.anewlga.com/explore/
    redevelopment-milestones/) provides a year-by-year timeline of major Terminal
    B reconstruction activities.
33. https://centreforaviation.com/news/new-york-laguardia-airport-opens-phase-ii-of
    -western-concourse-in-terminal-b-1109135.
34. *US News & World Report*. "$4 billion redevelopment of aging LaGuardia Airport
    approved". September 2, 2017.

35. https://www.forbes.com/sites/willhorton1/2020/05/22/delta-could-finish-laguardia-construction-much-much-sooner-as-coronavirus-reduces-airport-complexity/.
36. https://www.constructiondive.com/news/delta-gets-14b-loan-for-4b-laguardia-terminal-construction/523522/.
37. https://www.abetterwaytolga.com/.
38. https://www.amny.com/news/queens-community-groups-voice-opposition-to-laguardia-airtrain-project-and-review-process/.
39. https://www.lgaaccesseis.com/.
40. https://www.nytimes.com/2020/06/10/nyregion/new-la-guardia-airport-terminal.html.
41. https://www.businessinsider.com/laguardia-airport-new-terminal-b-tour-behind-the-scenes-2020-6.
42. https://thepointsguy.com/news/flying-from-lga-new-terminal-b/.

REFERENCES

Alberts, H. C., Bowen Jr, J. T., & Cidell, J. L. 2009. Missed opportunities: The restructuring of Berlin's airport system and the city's position in international airline networks. *Regional Studies*, 43(5), 739–758.

Cuomo, A. M. 2014. *All Things Possible: Setbacks and Success in Politics and Life.* Harper Collins.

Ernst & Young. 2012, April 27. Sachverhaltsdarstellung zu Störungen des Projektablaufes und deren Auswirkungen, Report an Planungsgemeinschaft Flughafen Berlin-Brandenburg International pg.bbi.

Fiedler, J., and Wendler, A. 2016. Berlin Brandenburg Airport. In *Large Infrastructure Projects in Germany*, pp. 87–145. Cham: Palgrave Macmillan.

LaGuardia Airport Advisory Panel. 2015. *21st Century Airport for the State of New York: The New LaGuardia.* July 27, 2015.

Lykotrafiti, A. 2017. The white elephant in the room... *European State Aid Law Quarterly*, 16(2), 299–309.

Müller, J. 2020. A case study of the politics of airport construction: The new Berlin Airport. In *Air Transport and Regional Development Policies*, pp. 240–267. Routledge.

Plotch, P. M. 2015. *Politics across the Hudson.* Rutgers University Press.

Port Authority of New York and New Jersey. 2012. Request for Qualifications-LaGuardia Airport Central Terminal Building Replacement Project RFQ #31224. October 26, 2012.

Stoff, J. 2008. *LaGuardia Airport.* Arcadia Publishing.

12. Canary Wharf's transformation from "planning disaster" to London's second business district

David Gordon and Patricia Warren

ABBREVIATIONS USED IN THIS CHAPTER

CWG	Canary Wharf Group
CBD	Central Business District
DLR	Docklands Light Rail
EZ	Enterprise Zone
JLE	Jubilee Line Extension
LDDC	London Docklands Development Corporation
O&Y	Olympia & York Development Company
P3	Public–private Partnership
SOM	Skidmore Owings and Merrill
UDC	Urban Development Corporations

When newly-elected Prime Minister Tony Blair hosted French President Jacques Chirac at One Canada Square in 1997, he cited the building as a symbol of the "New Britain" (Drohan 1997). Setting the meeting in Europe's tallest skyscraper signaled Britain's policies to encourage London to surpass Paris and Frankfurt and become a global trading center. The building was also the centerpiece of Canary Wharf, the brash new business district developing on abandoned docklands in East London.

Blair's choice of Canary Wharf also highlighted the central role of urban development corporations in the New Labour domestic policies. Canary Wharf's sponsor, the London Docklands Development Corporation (LDDC), was reviled by local Labour politicians and discredited by most academic observers (Brownill 1990; Thornley 1991; Ambrose 1994). Even worse, Canary Wharf had been a pet project of Margaret Thatcher, the divisive former

Table 12.1   Canary Wharf in brief

Description	Canary Wharf is a 97-acre docklands redevelopment project located 5 miles east of central London. Initially conceived of as a "back-office" district for the City of London, Canary Wharf was initially developed in the late 1980s by Olympia and York, a Canadian real estate developer. Canary Wharf opened in 1991 amidst a severe economic downturn, sending Olympia and York into bankruptcy. Served by the Docklands Light Rail (DLR) system and the Jubilee Underground Line, Canary Wharf recovered, and today, with more than 16 million square feet of office space, and 300 shops and restaurants, Canary Wharf is recognized as London's second CBD.
Lead sponsor(s)	Olympia and York (1987–1992), The Canary Wharf Group (1995–), The London Docklands Development Corporation (1981–1997)
Primary rationale	Canary Wharf was conceived in the mid-1980s as a modern and lower-rent alternative to the City of London, London's financial district; with the government-funded construction of the Docklands Light Rail (DLR) system linking the two business districts.
Primary funding sources	Bank loans, government grants (for public infrastructure)
Regulatory/funding approval given in	1986
Construction started in	1987
Construction completed	One Canada Square, Canary Wharf's first and largest office building, was completed on schedule in 1991 in the midst of a severe recession. It would take another five years for the market to recover. With over 16 million square feet of office space as of 2020, commercial and residential construction at Canary Wharf is ongoing.
Cumulative investment	The 8 million square feet of office and retail space owned by the Canary Wharf Group is currently valued at about £5 billion (US$6.8 billion).
Principal takeaways	Timing is all important: having been brought into the deal by British Prime Minister Margaret Thatcher in 1986, Canary Wharf developer Olympia and York pursued an aggressive, over-leveraged financing strategy, which, although having worked in Toronto and New York City previously, was ill-suited to uncertain economic times. In terms of planning, design, and construction management issues, Canary Wharf has been well carried out.

Conservative Prime Minister. Canary Wharf's 1993 financial collapse was widely regarded as proof that the neo-liberal public–private partnership (P3) model was as bankrupt as Canary Wharf's Canadian developer, Olympia and York (Brownill 1990; Fainstein 1994).

Rather than disband the state-owned urban development corporations such as the LDDC, Blair commissioned more of them and ordered the agencies to focus on social regeneration with the same entrepreneurial zeal that they had pursued physical redevelopment of abandoned docklands and post-industrial landscapes such as Canary Wharf under the Thatcher regime. This was a startling policy shift that focused renewed attention on Canary Wharf, which quickly developed into London's second business district in the years ahead.

Canary Wharf merits attention as a mega-project because it demonstrated the possibility of developing a second central business district (CBD) within a global metropolis. With over 17 million square feet of commercial space, 40 buildings and more than 120,000 employees (Canary Wharf Group 2019), it was in the same league as the original CBD in the historic City of London or the government node in Westminster by 2020. Canary Wharf is also a prominent example of urban regeneration, rising from abandoned docklands in one of England's most distressed communities (Figure 12.1) and an illustration of a mega-project rebounding from what appeared to be a disaster in 1991 (Table 12.1).

Source: Alamy Photos.

Figure 12.1   *Abandoned West India Docks in 1987, crossed by the Docklands Light Railway*

ORIGINS AND DEVELOPMENT HISTORY

The Canary Wharf site was part of the West India Docks, built in 1802 and considered an engineering marvel in their day. The enclosed docks in the East End helped position London as the world's leading port by 1900 (Hein and Schubert 2020). The East End was heavily damaged by bombing in World War II, but the docks were rapidly repaired, so that the Port was still dominant in 1960, with local dockworkers unloading a record freight cargo. Unfortunately, the Port of London was rendered obsolete by the global adoption of containerized shipping in the 1960s. Strikes and delays in constructing downstream container terminals deflected most European trade to Rotterdam and Hamburg. London's historic docks, constructed for the age of sail and steamships, were all closed between 1967 and 1976 (Hein and Schubert 2020).

The East End was devastated, with high unemployment rates and thousands of acres of abandoned docks and industrial buildings. Redevelopment plans were stalled by the UK's 1976 financial crisis (Ledgerwood 1985; Brownill 1990). Margaret Thatcher's 1979 Conservative government brought dramatic and controversial change to the Docklands. Environment Minister Michael Heseltine was appalled by the extent of the dereliction in Liverpool and London's docklands and the inaction of the local authorities. He proposed that the Liverpool and London docklands be placed in the hands of independent urban development corporations (UDCs) with broad powers to facilitate development (Heseltine 1987).

The London Docklands Development Corporation (LDDC) was established in 1981 with authority over 5,000 acres (2,200 hectares) in three local boroughs, all controlled by Labour. The LDDC imported the public–private partnership (P3) model for waterfront redevelopment that had been pioneered in Baltimore, Boston and Toronto (Wrenn 1983). The North American agencies used flexible "development frameworks" and design guidelines instead of master plans (Harbourfront Corporation 1978). The LDDC quickly demonstrated an ability to put shovels into the ground, getting suburban developers to start construction on new private housing in the eastern docks within three months (LDDC 1998).

The local Boroughs and Greater London Council were outraged that their planning and development authority were usurped by the central government (Colenutt 1992). The LDDC took unprecedented powers away from the local and metropolitan governments, who vehemently resisted the corporation's activities with demonstrations, billboards (Figure 12.2), and by disrupting events such as the ground-breaking ceremonies for Canary Wharf (DCC 1992; SPLASH 1993). When local political resistance became widespread, Thatcher abolished the GLC in 1986, placing the metropolitan region directly under the control of the central government.

The LDDC issued development frameworks and design guidelines for many docks, encouraging a broad range of private development opportunities (LDDC 1982). This design guidance was radically different from the earlier statutory plans that guided public investment into social housing and public transit in the Boroughs (DJC 1976). However, even these new permissive planning guidelines attracted few proposals for the most difficult sites in the West Indies Docks of the Isle of Dogs, an isolated peninsula created by a bend in the River Thames.

*Figure 12.2   Billboard erected by project opponents outside the Canary
Wharf sales office.*

Although the LDDC was able to mobilize private investment in some parts
of the Docklands, there was little initial interest in the Isle of Dogs area that
included Canary Wharf. In 1982, the central government created further incentives to encourage development by declaring the Canary Wharf area to be an
Enterprise Zone (EZ). This designation included a greatly simplified approvals
process and granted significant business and property tax concessions to attract
private investment (Hall 1998; LDDC 1982).

Not much happened for a few years. Although development was booming
on the other docks, all that could be attracted to the area around Canary Wharf
was a fish market, some industrial studios and a few low-rise offices.

The Isle of Dogs was initially deemed a weak development site because it
was isolated and inaccessible to the traditional CBD in the City of London.
Although Canary Wharf was only five kilometers east of the Bank of England
as the crow flies, there were no direct road or public transit connections, due
to the meandering river. London's famous Underground system did not serve
the Isle of Dogs and the earliest buses in the area could not get workers to an
office in Westminster, or vice versa. This was not a problem in the 1960s, since
the dockers lived in public housing projects adjacent to the docks and walked
to work. After the docks closed, unemployed residents had little access to the
wider London labor market, and the abandoned docklands had limited appeal

to business investors, since access to the City was difficult and Heathrow Airport was almost impossible to reach.

The LDDC quickly improved both problems, creating a light rail network and a new airport. The Docklands Light Railway (DLR) connected abandoned railway viaducts that crossed the site using the elevated guideway and auto-mated trams from the Vancouver SkyTrain system. It was derided as a "toy train" when first proposed, but the LDDC had the DLR planned, funded and under construction in three years, which was warp speed by British transit planning standards of the day. The DLR opened in 1987, providing service to the edge of the City of London in 10 minutes (Hostettler 1987; LDDC 1997a; Hickman and Hall 2008).

The London City Airport also opened in 1987 in the abandoned Royal Docks, immediately east of Canary Wharf. Following the model of Toronto's waterfront airport, it uses short takeoff and landing (STOL) aircraft to provide 90-minute access to European financial centers—less time than the journey to Heathrow Airport (LDDC 1997a).

Canary Wharf's prospects began to change in February 1985, when Credit Suisse First Boston investigated the dock warehouse as a site for the bank's back office operations, assisted by American developer Ware Travelstead. Within a month, Travelstead proposed Canary Wharf as a location for the head offices of financial corporations. This was a truly radical proposal to attract massive private investment and generate thousands of jobs, just the sort of idea that an Enterprise Zone is supposed to encourage.

In April 1985, the LDDC granted Travelstead and Credit Suisse an option to lease 20 acres on Canary Wharf for 200 years at £400,000 per acre (land values in the Docklands were so low that they were sold by the acre). By September 1985, the agency had approved Skidmore Owings and Merrill's master plan, calling for three high-rise buildings containing over 10 million square feet of commercial development. The LDDC optimistically held a ground-breaking in 1986, but there was a problem—Travelstead had not been able to sign up any big financial corporations to move to Canary Wharf.

In 1987, Travelstead's option on Canary Wharf was taken over by Olympia and York (O&Y), a private firm owned by Toronto's Reichmann family. O&Y brought instant credibility to the project, since they were the world's largest developer of commercial offices, with a reputation for rapid construction of high-quality, large-floorplate buildings suitable for the computerized financial industry (Bianco 1997; Foster 1986, 1993; Stewart 1993). The O&Y team had just completed the World Financial Center in Battery Park City, a waterfront site in Lower Manhattan, leasing over five million sq. feet to major financial institutions such as Merrill Lynch, Dow Jones, Oppenheimer and American Express (Gordon 1997).

Paul Reichmann became the principal champion of Canary Wharf, expanding Travelstead's idea of a corporate office park to London's second financial district and committing his family's entire financial fortune to its construction. When the project collapsed in the 1992 recession, it bankrupted the Reichmann family, who lost over $10 billion (Bianco 1997). Yet, in one of the boldest moves in 20th century real estate, Reichmann assembled a consortium that bought the project back from the bankruptcy trustees in 1994–1995 and completed Canary Wharf according to his plans (Gordon 2001) (Table 12.2).

Table 12.2   Canary Wharf timeline

1802	The West India Docks opens on the Isle of Dogs, admired as England's greatest engineering structure of its day.
1961	Shipping traffic in and out of the Docklands peaks at 60 million tons of cargo
1967	As a result of increasing shipping containerization, East India Docks are closed, followed by the London and St. Katherine Docks in 1968, and the Surrey Docks in 1970.
1979	Parliament passes the Local Government Planning and Land Act, giving itself the authority to set up and oversee private-sector-oriented local development corporations.
1980	The three West India Docks and the Millwall Docks on the Isle of Dogs are closed.
1981	The London Docklands Development Corporation (LDDC) is established as the first local development corporation under the oversight of Secretary of State for the Environment, Michael Heseltine. The LDDC adopts a commercial development regeneration framework for Canary Wharf.
1982	The Isle of Dogs becomes an Enterprise Zone, offering liberal tax allowances to investors and developers.
1985	A consortium of American investors led by Credit Suisse First Boston proposes to build 10 million sq. ft of office space at Canary Wharf, making it London's second financial downtown.
1987	Development rights to Canary Wharf are acquired by the Canadian firm of Olympia and York. Docklands Light Rail (DLR) connecting the Docklands to the City, and London City Airport open for service.
1988	Construction of One Canada Square at Canary Wharf begins.
1991	Construction of One Canada Square is completed. Leasing grounds to a halt as the British economy enters a steep recession.
1992	Unable to find tenants and pay its creditors, Olympia and York is forced into bankruptcy.
1993	Olympia and York' s Canary Wharf assets are acquired by a consortium of creditors
1995	The sale of Canary Wharf to an international consortium (headed by Paul Reichmann) is completed. The British economy enters an extended growth period, favoring financial services and Canary Wharf.
1996	Citibank signs a deal for a new 560,000 square foot Canary Wharf office building.
1998	HSBC announces plans to move its London headquarters to a 1.1 million square foot office building at Canary Wharf.
1999	The Jubilee Line opens for service, directly connecting Canary Wharf to the West End and City of London.
2004	Paul Reichmann loses control of Canary Wharf to Songbird Estates, a consortium led by US investment bank Morgan Stanley. Canary Wharf recognized as London's second CBD in Greater London Authority's London Plan
2009	After Songbird nearly collapses under the weight of its debts, the Qatari Investment Authority and China's sovereign wealth fund become the company's controlling owners.
2014	Canary Wharf expands eastward with plans for 30 new buildings.

THE LONDON OFFICE MARKET

Paul Reichmann and Ware Travelstead saw an opportunity for Canary Wharf to serve an emerging market for high-quality large-floorplate office space in central London. There was a market for this type of space caused by Britain's "Big Bang"—the 1986 de-regulation of the financial sector. Institutions located in the UK were permitted greater latitude in the services that they could offer, including electronic trading. These changes made London an attractive location for international investment banks that wished also to serve the European market from a sophisticated English-speaking city (LORP 1996; Marsh 1997).

The traditional location for British financial institutions was the City of London, the historic square mile within the Roman walls. By historical accident, the City was a small, independent municipality with a Lord Mayor, providing local government for London's CBD and only 6,000 residents. The Bank of England, most commercial banks and investment houses had their headquarters in small historic buildings within the City, supported by a centuries-old social network of private clubs and guilds. Heritage preservation regulations and the maze of small blocks complicated large redevelopment projects, so it was not uncommon for British institutions to be spread out among 10 or even 20 buildings across central London (LORP 1996).

Office vacancy rates were low and rents were the highest in the world when Olympia and York entered the London market in July 1987, offering to supply modern, large-floorplate structures that could accommodate a firm's entire staff in one new building, at half the rent in the nearby City (Gordon 2001). This pitch was attractive to O&Y's New York tenants and other foreign firms. However, O&Y could not entice British firms to establish their headquarters at Canary Wharf for at least three reasons: class bias, social networks and competing projects. Tower Hamlets abuts the eastern edge of the City and Canary Wharf may only be three miles away, but it was not in the same league in terms of social prestige in 1988. An office in the City was the pinnacle of British financial success, while Tower Hamlets was a working-class borough that led England's "league tables' of social and economic deprivation in the early 1990s (Edwards and Flatley 1996).

Second, these class divisions were reinforced by the City's social network. If a Bank relocated to Canary Wharf, how would the CEO get to his private club for lunch and trade gossip? These were significant concerns, since the City was a classic example of a successful industry cluster, with a dense network that facilitated the exchange of ideas and people.

Finally, Canary Wharf faced competition from new developments at the edges of the City of London. Travelstead's brash announcement that he expected to attract banks to his new office node shook the City out of its complacent torpor (Cassidy 1997; Lett 1997). Heritage guidelines were altered to permit "groundscrapers"—low-rise buildings that covered entire blocks (Williams 1992). Several large sites were assembled at the edges of the City, such as Broadgate, London Bridge City and Spitalfields Market. These projects were more expensive than Canary Wharf but proved competitive for British firms that wanted modern offices close to the historic core.

O&Y timed its New York market entry perfectly in the early 1980s, but got it drastically wrong in London, entering a few months before the 1987 stock market crash, leasing during the 1991 recession, and completing the first phase on schedule in 1992, at perhaps the worst point of the downturn (Gordon 2001). The O&Y team leased almost six million square feet in four years, better than their Battery Park City project. But Paul Reichmann had insisted that Canary Wharf's first phase be ten million square feet to give it "critical mass" (Bianco 1997; Solskone 1997). Building four million square feet of vacant office space can bankrupt even the largest developers quite quickly.

GAINING POLITICAL AND REGULATORY APPROVALS

Political and regulatory approvals to construct the Canary Wharf buildings were simple and fast because the UK government had designated the area as an Enterprise Zone. Almost anything was permitted, with the only constraint on height set by the adjacent airport flight path. Travelstead submitted a proposal for a complex of office buildings, including Europe's tallest skyscraper on September 20, 1985, only five months after optioning the site. The LDDC Board gave approval-in-principle to the Canary Wharf master plan only 27 days later (Brownill 1990). Similar approvals under the regular planning system would take years, if not a decade.

The buildings were approved, but how would thousands of office workers reach Canary Wharf? The Dockland Light Railway was under construction, but its initial capacity would not be adequate for a new CBD and it did not connect to the London Underground system. The LDDC modified the DLR design on the fly to increase train capacity and reduce headways. The agency also lobbied the national government for permission to build a tunnel connecting the DLR directly to the Bank Underground station in the heart of the City. Parliament approved the extension in late 1986 but negotiations over funding broke down. O&Y stepped into the breach in 1987, guaranteeing £140 million for the DLR Bank Extension and construction of the Canary Wharf DLR station. The Bank Extension opened on schedule in 1991, just in time to serve the first tenants of Canary Wharf (Hickman and Hall 2008).

However, opening just in time for the first tenants added to Canary Wharf's leasing problems. The new rail system suffered the usual teething problems during its run-in period, which were covered in great detail and glee by the London media, who continuously ridiculed the LDDC's "toy train." More seriously, potential tenants were occasionally stuck on trips to the sales office and site, with unimpressive views of Tower Hamlets' distressed housing estates (Picardi 1993). Although the DLR rapidly became London Transport's most reliable system after its official opening (LDDC 1992), by then it was too late. The teething problems during the run-in period and the adverse media coverage gave an impression of unreliable service that deterred tenants during leasing.

The DLR Bank extension provided enough capacity for the first phase of Canary Wharf, but an Underground service would be required for subsequent phases. The obvious choice was the Jubilee Line Extension (JLE) from Westminster, London's government office node. The JLE was cancelled in the 1980 austerity budget, but O&Y offered a breathtaking £400 million contribution (about 40 percent of its 1980 initial estimated cost) for its connection to Canary Wharf. In contrast to the DLR, which was planned, managed and built by the LDDC, the JLE went through the "normal" London transit process of the 1990s. It was only approved by Parliament in March 1992, a few weeks before O&Y went bankrupt. The JLE project was put on hold once again, but after another 18 months of drama and negotiation, construction finally began in December 1993, far too late for O&Y.

The JLE was plagued by variable route planning, poor project management, substantial cost over-runs and numerous schedule delays (Dimitriou et al. 2011). It finally opened in December 1999, 12 years after it was proposed by O&Y. Although the JLE was mired in controversy throughout its planning, with the benefit of a couple of decades of hindsight, it might now be regarded as a heavily-used link in the London Underground network. The Jubilee Line provides a 12-minute connection to the Westminster node and finally gave Isle of Dogs residents a high-speed transit service and connection to the greater London job market (Cervero et al. 2017).

One of the reasons that the JLE encountered such resistance was that the CrossRail project (Chapter 4) was always considered a more important element in regional transportation plans. Despite the City's opposition, Canary Wharf was finally acknowledged as a second business district in the 2004 *London Plan*, prepared by the new Greater London Authority. A Canary Wharf station was also added to the CrossRail plan. CrossRail started construction in 2009 and the top four levels of the Canary Wharf station opened as retail in 2015, although completion of the line was continuously delayed. When CrossRail is finally operating as the Elizabeth Line (May 2022) it will provide a 17-minute access from Canary Wharf to Paddington Station and a 38-minute service to Heathrow.

DESIGN AND CONSTRUCTION

The Isle of Dogs has seen a lot of planning over the past half-century. Matthew Carmona's comprehensive review of the design strategies identified four development waves, five planning models and 12 plans from the 1970s into the new millennium (Carmona 2009). Plans from the 1970s were largely two-dimensional land use schemes with little design content (Travers Morgan 1973; DJC 1976). These plans were largely ignored as Britain's late 1970s financial crisis halted all public investment (Hebbert 1992; Brownill and O'Hara 2015).

The four development waves that followed took different approaches to urban design (Carmona 2009):

1. LDDC and the *Isle of Dogs Design Guide* (1981–1985);
2. Canary Wharf arrives with SOM's master plan (1985–1991);
3. Canary Wharf flies again, with more contemporary architecture (1991–2002);
4. The *London Plan* and return of local planning (2002+).

Development on the Isle of Dogs was initially guided by a LDDC framework (1982) prepared with Gordon Cullen, one of Britain's most influential urban designers. Cullen's beautifully-illustrated guidelines provided minimum guidance for development in the Enterprise Zone, except for a focus on small-scale industrial interventions and a recommendation to preserve the waterscapes by limiting filling of the docks. These guidelines shaped some of the earliest industrial–commercial buildings surrounding Canary Wharf but were largely abandoned following Travelstead's proposals for a head office complex (Shaw 1992).

The second phase brought the most influential design guidance, but surprisingly it came from the private sector. The Enterprise Zone regulations allowed almost anything to be built, but the Canary Wharf developers prepared their own strict master plans to guide growth. Travelstead retained Chicago's Skidmore Owings and Merrill (SOM) to prepare the Canary Wharf Master Plan (see Figure 12.3). SOM brought their international experience with high-rise office buildings to the plan, proposing Europe's tallest tower as the centerpiece of the project. O&Y kept SOM on the project, but awarded individual buildings to several different architects, with detailed design guidelines so that the designers and tenants of early buildings would know the context for future projects (SOM 1987; Kapoor 1992; Turner 1992).

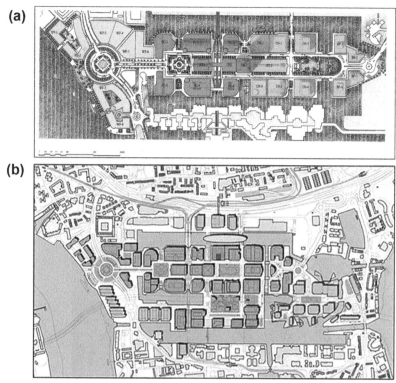

Figure 12.3   *Canary Wharf Master Plan 1987 (top) and 2020 (bottom), by Skidmore Owings and Merrill*

When private developers impose strong urban design guidelines upon themselves (and follow them) planners should take notice. O&Y placed constraints upon themselves (and their architects) because the LDDC design guidance was too weak to protect their massive investment to create a new CBD (Solskone 1997). The Reichmanns were committing their entire fortune to create a first-class business precinct, so they could not risk having low-quality development depress the value of their investment.

The centerpiece 50-storey tower, One Canada Square, was designed by Cesar Pelli, the design architect for O&Y's World Financial Centre in New York. It had the Reichmann's favorite floorplate (from Toronto) topped with Pelli's signature pyramid from Manhattan. Other first-phase buildings were designed by large American firms that had built high-rise corporate offices, such as Kohn Petersen Fox and SOM. Only one building had a British architect, igniting another storm of complaints from designers and critics (including Prince Charles) that the post-modern buildings did not respect London's scale or aesthetics (Charles 1989).

Later buildings followed the built-form guidelines but were designed in a more contemporary style, including some leading British architects. Lord Foster designed two office buildings and a truly monumental Jubilee Line station (Figure 12.4).

Source: Foster + Partners.

Figure 12.4   *Canary Wharf Jubilee Line Station, designed by Foster + Partners*

The open spaces between the buildings were built with high-quality materials and are impeccably maintained by the Canary Wharf Group, but they are private, not public, spaces. The first phase spaces faced inward to avoid views of dereliction across the water. They were dull because the building ground floors were corporate office lobbies. Later phases were activated by more retail at grade and better orientation to the waterfront (Sheppard 1997). North–south connections were improved after the adjacent Heron Quays were developed, offering hope that Canary Wharf and the rest of the Isle of Dogs would eventually be stitched together (Carmona 2009). Similarly, although urban design in the Isle of Dogs was incoherent in 1993 (Buchanan 1989; Edwards 1992), rehabilitation of some Modernist housing estates and infill with urban villages has helped repair some of the urban fabric (Tait 2003).

After the LDDC was wound up in 1998, development approvals were returned to the local governments, so the London Borough of Tower Hamlets found itself in charge of the development of the second half of a regional CBD (Henry 1997). Most of the development was previously approved by the LDDC, and Tower Hamlets and the Greater London Authority finally included Canary Wharf as a new office node in their statutory plans. New proposals outside the Canary Wharf estate now go through the regular development approval process (Tower Hamlets 1997) and offer the opportunity for planning gain agreements with the Borough.

FINANCING CANARY WHARF

The standard, low-risk method to finance an office building is to option land, prepare plans and find tenants who will sign leases to occupy the building. Once most of the building is leased, banks will give a loan to construct the building, while other institutions (pension funds, insurance companies, financial tenants) will provide a long-term mortgage or buy the fully-occupied building. Travelstead could not sign enough tenants to fill a first building, so he had to sell his option to O&Y and walk away (Bianco 1997). It is difficult to get the first tenants to commit to a new CBD when it consists of abandoned docks and derelict buildings.

The Reichmann family did not follow the standard financing model. They built and held Class A office buildings in major cities, developing the world's largest private portfolio of commercial office buildings. O&Y offered its own commercial bonds, secured by the cash-flow of these fully-leased trophy properties (McNish et al. 1992). The cash-flow from the bonds and other rents was poured into construction of the next project.

O&Y started construction on the entire World Financial Center in Manhattan in 1981 using their own cash flows. The firm did not take out a construction loan until 1983 (Gordon 1997). The Reichmanns committed the income from their entire family fortune to build the world's largest office project in New York, leased it, finished construction on schedule, re-financed the project and moved their team to London to do it again on an even-larger scale.

Paul Reichmann's financial plan for Canary Wharf was the same as the World Financial Center—use O&Y's cash flow to build a critical mass of buildings that irretrievably established the new business district. Rather than build a single office building, O&Y started construction on the entire first phase of ten million square feet, including the DLR station, piped infrastructure, streets, parks and waterfront walkways (O&Y 1992).

O&Y's leasing staff could point to a tower rising into the sky and ask a potential tenant how many floors of new space would they like to occupy in 18 months? Or did they need a complete building to accommodate their entire staff in one location? They could offer as much modern space as any financial institution could need, at half the rent in the City, with reduced property and business taxes from the Enterprise Zone (Gordon 2001).

O&Y was left holding four million square feet. The family first sold other assets to fund construction, but when institutional investors would not roll over O&Y's commercial bonds in 1992, they ran out of cash. Their entire portfolio of office towers (worth perhaps $15 billion) was lost to creditors in the ensuing bankruptcy (McNish 1992; Foster 1993; Bianco 1997).

The Reichmanns appealed to their friends in Thatcher's government to lease a building or two for government offices, as the State of New York had done to save the New York Port Authority's World Trade Center when it stood half empty in the 1970s recession. O&Y's appeals fell on deaf ears, since the Thatcher government did not bail out bankrupt companies (Pelling 1992; Sorensen 1997).

O&Y's failure and the collapse of the Canary Wharf project was viewed by most academic observers as proof that the P3 financing model was ineffective or corrupt (Brownill 1990; Fainstein 1994; Brownill and O'Hara 2015). The development industry was equally pessimistic and there was little interest in purchasing Canary Wharf's buildings from the bankruptcy trustees after the creditors were paid off.

Once again, Paul Reichmann saw an opportunity that others did not. While other developers saw a failed office park, he saw a new central business district with completed buildings, an Underground line in construction, first-class offices waiting to be leased and planning approvals in place for another ten million square feet. He committed his family's last $150 million as a minority share in a consortium of New York and Saudi investors that bought the project from the trustees in 1995, just as the British economy began to emerge from the recession.

The new company, Canary Wharf Limited (CWL), operated with more conventional financing techniques, leasing the remaining 70 percent of the project within three years and starting new buildings with standard construction loans only after tenants were secured. The new tenants flooded in during the next decade, including major banks from China, Hong Kong, the USA, Canada and Europe. British institutions finally followed, with BZW (1995) and the Barclay's Bank headquarters (2001). In a major vote of confidence from the new British government, the new Financial Services Authority (1997) and London Underground Limited (1999) leased buildings in Canary Wharf.

Having proven the concept with high-risk private capital to build critical mass, the remainder of Canary Wharf has been financed with conventional real estate techniques. Canary Wharf Limited was so successful in leasing during the 1990s that they almost ran out of building sites. The company purchased the adjacent Heron Quays and Shed 35 parcels. Canary Wharf Limited's prospects were so lucrative that Paul Reichmann's partners forced him out in the 2004 re-structuring that created Canary Wharf Group plc (CWG).

Canary Wharf's initial architecture may have been mundane, but there was nothing pedestrian about Olympia and York's construction methods. The firm built a high-quality office building significantly faster than their competitors using innovative project management techniques to complete complex projects such as Toronto's First Canadian Place (Foster 1986; Bianco 1997, pp. 349–350) and Manhattan's World Financial Center. The firm's construction management was an important component of its corporate strategy, especially in complicated waterfront sites such as Battery Park City or Canary Wharf. O&Y would finish the lobby and move tenants into the lower floors, even before the structure was completed, bringing in rent earlier (Foster 1993; Stewart 1993).

Source: Alamy photos.

Figure 12.5   *Olympia and York President Paul Reichmann discusses new plans for Canary Wharf with Prime Minister Margaret Thatcher in 1987*

Constructing office buildings in Central London was a difficult and slow process. O&Y made extraordinary innovations to build Canary Wharf's first phase. Truck access to the Isle of Dogs was difficult, so a floating concrete plant was moored next to the docks and construction materials were delivered by barge from the downstream container port—all coordinated by a sophisticated computer system. Credit Suisse and Texaco moved into their buildings in 1991 only three years after Margaret Thatcher drove the first pile (Figure 12.5). Although construction of the first phase finished on schedule and only 1 percent over budget, it was too late to save O&Y (Solskone 1997).

Construction management continued as a competitive strength of the new Canary Wharf Limited in the period after the first phase leased up. For example, Citibank signed agreements for a new office building in December 1996; construction started February 1997, the 18-storey building topped-out in May 1998, and the bank moved in a few months later. Canary Wharf could deliver new space much faster than developers in the City and at a substantial rent discount, so some major tenants such as HSBC and Citibank commissioned multiple buildings from the firm.

OPERATING A NEW BUSINESS DISTRICT

Although Canary Wharf Group and O&Y constructed most of the buildings in the district, CWG only retained ownership of One Canada Square, the retail complex and a few smaller office buildings. However, the company owns and manages the retail, parking and ground level of the 97-acre estate. CWG kept control of the site for two major reasons: quality control and security. Tower Hamlets could not possibly afford to maintain the streets and open spaces at Canary Wharf to the standard expected of a CBD of a major city, especially since the Borough receives little to no property taxes from the Enterprise Zone. Expecting Tower Hamlets to spend public funds on manicuring Canary Wharf when the Borough is battling severe social issues would be unjust (Keith 1997).

Security has been a major concern in the Canary Wharf area since the beginning of its redevelopment as an office node. The project's close identification with the polarizing Thatcher regime made it a target for the Irish Republican Army (IRA) during its war with the UK government. IRA truck bombs were discovered on the Canary Wharf site in 1992 and office buildings in South Quay, adjacent to Canary Wharf, were destroyed by another IRA bomb in 1996. Other truck bombs destroyed the Baltic Exchange in the City of London (1992), and most of Manchester's CBD (1996), killing or injuring hundreds of civilians and causing enormous damage. The City responded with a "Ring of Steel" security and access system, while the 2001 attack on New York's World Trade Center only heightened concerns about terrorist attacks against global financial centers. Canary Wharf Group employs a large private security force, deploys numerous CCTV cameras and controls vehicular access to the streets and parking of the estate (Imrie and Sakai 2007).

As a result of these security features, Canary Wharf cannot act as a true downtown for East London, since access to the streets and open spaces are controlled and public assembly and protests are not permitted. These privately-owned public spaces (POPS) will likely remain as extensions of the corporate ownership of Canary Wharf for years to come.

Environmental sustainability was another missed opportunity in the development of Canary Wharf. This large, master-planned complex might have supported a district energy system, similar to those found in many institutional districts and a few CBDs. Green buildings arrived later in the development cycle at Canary Wharf and attention to sustainability seems somewhat superficial (CWG 2019).

SOCIAL REGENERATION

The Isle of Dogs saw little benefit from the regeneration of the Canary Wharf area in the early days, leading to hostility and obstruction. O&Y made some initial moves to fund local schools and job retraining (Johns 1992; Bensley 1997; Wade 1997). Blair's New Labour government directed the UDCs to engage in social regeneration, so the LDDC established a Community Services Department that funded rehabilitation of 2,500 housing units in distressed council estates on the Isle of Dogs and construction of 423 new units of non-profit housing. In addition, the LDDC invested £33 million in social and community projects on the Isle of Dogs, including construction of a new school, healthcare center, job training and curriculum support (LDDC 1997b, 1998).

After the LDDC was wound up in 1997, CWG continued supporting local initiatives, including small business start-ups, skills gaps and training programs, education funds, sponsorships, and funding transportation connections. CWG's Local Business Liaison Office and East London Business Place (ELBP) project has helped generate over £1.59 billion of business for East London companies. CWG also established partnerships with local authorities to ensure that the residents of Tower Hamlets can benefit from the employment and economic opportunities at Canary Wharf. In addition to these job creation and educational supports, CWG funded over 150 local sport and community groups with £15 million from 2010–2018 (CWG 2018).

Finally, Tower Hamlets has been able to extract considerable social benefits from the new projects outside the original Canary Wharf approvals through separately negotiated "planning gain" agreements. For example, the Riverside South agreement included approximately £21 million of funding for social benefits such as community facilities, social/community and environmental works, a library, rent reductions, and upgrades to the DLR and bus system (Carmona 2009, pp. 130–132).

These are all relatively minor concessions made as huge fortunes were poured into Canary Wharf with little local benefit for one of Britain's most distressed communities. Although Tower Hamlets has seen some improvements over the past 40 years, it still is a severely distressed borough that requires action to specifically address the difficulties that Isle of Dogs residents face. Regrettably, this situation is unlikely to change significantly, unless Britain's central government agrees to release some of the property taxes back to the local governments in the future.

LESSONS AND TAKEAWAYS

Canary Wharf demonstrates many of the advantages of mega-project development and some glaring disadvantages. The project certainly took advantage of *planning, engineering and construction economies of scale* to build London's second business district with remarkable speed and at a much lower cost than new buildings in the City. After the first phase was built, Canary Wharf had excellent *capacity flexibility*, demonstrating the ability to construct and commission new office buildings in record time on the many serviced sites in later phases.

These advantages allowed London to rapidly expand its financial sector after the "Big Bang" deregulation. In addition, Canary Wharf's tenants reaped productivity benefits by consolidation of their operations in one location and access to the large electronic trading floors that revolutionized late 20th century financial services. As a result, London drew away from Paris and Frankfurt to become Europe's leading financial center and rivalled New York for global domination as the "capital of capital" prior to Brexit (Z/Yen Partners 2020).

Canary Wharf certainly benefited from a *streamlined approval process* in the LDDC's Enterprise Zone, obtaining planning approvals in days that would have taken years elsewhere. However, the LDDC's regulatory regime was not sufficient to protect O&Y's investment in a first-class business district, so the developer imposed its own, stricter design guidelines. In addition, the project's lack of official status in other London plans led to poor land use/transportation planning co-ordination (Church 1990) and little protection for CW's proponent when the City deliberately encouraged competing projects.

Similarly, it is not clear if Canary Wharf benefits from *reduced operating costs*. Certainly, the developer benefited from the EZ's holiday on property and business taxes, but CWG must also bear the additional cost of maintaining all publicly-accessible spaces and a high level of private security. Also missing are potential network savings through a district energy system or smart building efficiencies that might be available if all the office buildings were operated collaboratively.

Canary Wharf clearly did not benefit from *financing economies of scale and scope* or the *greater re-distributive potential* seen in other megaprojects. Infrastructure megaprojects often use sophisticated financial structures to spread risk and uncertainty to parties that can best absorb them. The Reichmann family's strategy was to concentrate risk upon themselves to increase control and concentrate rewards. When it worked in Toronto and New York, this strategy made them billionaires, but in London it made them bankrupt. The Reichmanns' modest demeanor and dress fooled many people, since they were among the most daring financial gamblers the real estate industry had seen. It is unlikely that a private firm will try their financial risk concentration strategy on a megaproject again (Leung and Hui 2005).

Construction of a second CBD in the middle of a low-income municipality had the potential to shower benefits on the surrounding community, but this did not happen in Canary Wharf's early days due to the Thatcher government's neo-liberal stance, the LDDC's restricted mandate, the Enterprise Zone tax holidays and Travelstead's tone-deafness to local concerns. As a result, Canary Wharf's early phases attracted mountains of opposition from the GLC, municipal governments, academics and community associations (DCC 1992; SPLASH 1993) that delayed its launch and soured potential British tenants. In addition, there was not much "trickle-down" from Canary Wharf's early phases other than the opportunity for younger residents to participate in the broader London labor market after the Jubilee Line Extension opened in 1999. The image of the glittering new office towers dumped into England's most distressed community without local benefits was simply unpalatable and unjust (see Figure 12.6). The reputational damage was not undone until Blair's "New Labour" government ordered the urban development corporations to pursue social regeneration as vigorously as economic revitalization.

Canary Wharf's early phases encountered many of the dangerous disadvantages of megaprojects, but O&Y largely avoided problems with *unproven technologies and construction methods*, since they were experienced industry leaders in constructing office buildings. Canary Wharf had many other problems, but even its first phase was completed on time, within budget and at a high standard of quality. In contrast, O&Y radically *misestimated the market potential* in the short-term, creating a critical mass of buildings that just could not be leased in time due to the 1991 recession, increased competition from the City and faced the initial indifference of British tenants (Gordon 2001).

Paul Reichmann's belief in the project's long-term potential was rewarded after his consortium bought the project back, but it was not enough to save his family from bankruptcy. This financial catastrophe demonstrated *increased risks that translated into higher required yields* for funding future office buildings. Canary Wharf Group used conventional real estate financing and

Source: Getty Images.

Figure 12.6   Canary Wharf adjacent to Robin Hood Gardens, a distressed
council housing estate that was demolished in 2017

rarely started construction on a new office building without a major tenant under contract.

O&Y avoided problems with *consortiums that don't work well together* in the initial stages, but they might have benefited from a British development partner. The consortium that Paul Reichmann put together to buy the project out of administration eventually fractured and cut him out of the big profits in the early 2000s, but CWG was careful to maintain the quality and construction speed that gave the project a competitive advantage.

Transportation planning for CW *demonstrated streamlining that didn't speed up construction*. The LDDC's DLR project management was good, except that it later proved necessary to have transit fully functional for the leasing period, not just for the opening of the building. All new transit systems have teething problems, and delays during the run-in period damaged the leasing process. In comparison, placing the Jubilee Line Extension into the hands of the London Regional Transport created endless debates over route options and years of delay (Dimitriou et al. 2011). CrossRail encountered similar trials, as noted in Chapter 4 earlier.

The Thatcher government's abandonment of O&Y to bankruptcy was a classic example of *blame avoidance*. The government allowed the private company to suffer the financial disaster rather than accept additional political risk by bailing them out by leasing government offices. Ironically, the Blair government later leased two buildings at higher rents.

Constructing a new business district is an unusual type of megaproject, with few precedents for comparisons. Paris' La Défense built the high-capacity transportation systems early but was slower than Canary Wharf to develop a critical mass of employment. However, La Défense has performed well as a pressure release valve for historic central Paris, acting as a wild game preserve for the excesses of Modern architecture better than London. Wren's churches no longer define London's skyline between the City and St. Paul's, which has been littered by shards, scalpels, gherkins, cheese-graters and other strange objects. Prince Charles now suggests Canary Wharf as the proper place for London's skyscrapers (Charles 2008).

Dubai and Canary Wharf demonstrate the limits of private finance and the need for good physical planning. Building a new business district will take decades and span several financial cycles, so some mechanisms to backstop private partners may be useful during the inevitable recessions.

Finally, skilled and powerful development corporations can accelerate urban regeneration, as we saw with the LDDC and New York's Battery Park City Authority, but these agencies should also have a mandate for distributing local benefits (Brownill 2010; Brownill and O'Hara 2015; Gordon 1998). A role in redistribution is not just a matter of social justice; it is also good project implementation practice to increase local support for publicly sponsored megaprojects.

REFERENCES

Ambrose, P. 1994. *Urban Process and Power*. London: Routledge.
Bensley, R. 1997. (Association of Island Communities) interview August 2, 1997.
Bianco, A. 1997. *The Reichmanns: Family, Faith, Fortune and the Empire of Olympia & York*. New York: Random House.
Brownill, S. 1990. *Developing London's Docklands: Another Great Planning Disaster?* London: Paul Chapman Publishing.
Brownill, S. 2010. London Docklands revisited: The dynamics of waterfront development. In G. Desfor, J. Laidley, Q. Stevens and D. Schubert (eds), *Transforming Urban Waterfronts: Fixity and Flow*. London: Routledge, pp. 121–142.
Brownill, S. and O'Hara, G. 2015. From planning to opportunism? Re-examining the creation of the London Docklands Development Corporation. *Planning Perspectives*, 30(4), 537–570.
Buchanan, P. 1989. Quays to design. *The Architectural Review*, April, 36–46.
Canary Wharf Group plc. 2018. *30 Years of Canary Wharf: Local Impact Report*. Retrieved from https://group.canarywharf.com/corporate-responsibility/30-years -canary-wharf-local-impact-report/.
Canary Wharf Group plc. 2019. *Canary Wharf Fact Sheet*, December 2019.

Carmona, M. 2009. The Isle of Dogs: Four development waves, five planning models, twelve plans, thirty-five years, and a renaissance of sorts. *Progress in Planning*, 71(3), 87–151.

Cassidy, M. 1997. (Councilor, City of London) interview August 20, 1997.

Cervero, R., Guerra, E., and Al, S. 2017. *Urban Transformations. Beyond Mobility: Planning Cities for People and Places*. Washington. DC: Island Press, pp. 67–86.

Charles, Prince of Wales. 1989. *A Vision of Britain: A Personal View of Architecture*. London: Doubleday, 160 pp.

Charles, Prince of Wales. 2008. Opinion – new London skyscrapers. *Architects Journal*, 6 February.

Church, A. 1990. Transport and urban regeneration in London Docklands: A victim of success or a failure to plan? *Cities*, November, 289–303.

Colenutt, R. 1992. (Docklands Consultative Committee, former Southwark councilor) interview July 14, 1992.

Dimitriou, H.T., Wright, P.G., and Ward, E.J. 2011. *Mega Projects and Mega Risks: Lessons for Decision-makers through a Comparative Analysis of Selected Large-scale Transport Infrastructure Projects in Europe, USA and Asia Pacific, Volume 3*. London: University College London OMEGA Centre.

Docklands Consultative Committee. 1992. *All That Glitters is Not Gold: A Critical Assessment of Canary Wharf*. London: DCC, May 1992.

Docklands Joint Committee. 1976. *London Docklands Strategic Plan*. London: DJC.

Drohan, M. 1997. Blair working on new image for nation. *Toronto Globe & Mail*, 8 November 1997, p. A16.

Edwards, B. 1992. *London Docklands: Urban Design in an Age of Deregulation*. Oxford, UK: Butterworth Architecture.

Edwards, P. and Flatley, J. (eds). 1996. *The Capital Divided: Mapping Poverty and Social Exclusion in London*. London: London Research Centre.

Fainstein, S.S. 1994. *The City Builders: Property, Politics & Planning in London and New York*. Oxford, UK: Basil Blackwell.

Foster, P. 1986. *The Master Builders: How the Reichmanns Reached for an Empire*. Toronto: Key Porter Books.

Foster, P. 1993. *Towers of Debt: The Rise and Fall of the Reichmanns*. Toronto: Key Porter Books.

Gordon, D.L.A. 1997. *Battery Park City: Politics and Planning on the New York Waterfront*. New York: Gordon and Breach.

Gordon, D.L.A. 1998. Canary Wharf & Battery Park City: Implementation lessons for the new millennium. *Rising East*, 2(2), 160–188.

Gordon, D.L.A. 2001. The resurrection of Canary Wharf. *Planning Theory & Practice*, 2(2), 149–168

Greater London Authority. 2004. *The London Plan*.

Hall, P.G. 1998. *Cities in Civilization*. New York: Pantheon. 1169 pp. esp. Chapter 28, "The city of capitalism rampant," pp. 888–931.

Harbourfront Corporation. 1978. *Harbourfront Development Framework*. Toronto, ON: Harbourfront Corporation, October 1978.

Hebbert, M. 1992. One 'planning disaster' after another: London Docklands 1970–1992. *The London Journal*, 17(2), 115–134.

Hein, C., and Schubert, D. 2020. Resilience and path dependence: A comparative study of the port cities of London, Hamburg, and Philadelphia. *Journal of Urban History*, July 2020, early release.

Henry, O. 1997. (Head of the Built Environment, London Borough of Tower Hamlets) interview August 19, 1997.

Heseltine, M. 1987. *Where There's a Will*. London: Arrow Books.

Hickman, R. and Hall, P. 2008. Moving the city east: Explorations into contextual public transport-orientated development. *Planning Practice & Research*, 23(3), 323–339.

Hostettler, E. (ed.). 1987. *Traveling Light*. London: LDDC.

Imrie, R. and Sakai, A. 2007. Governance in private-public spaces. *Town & Country Planning*, 76(12), 228–450.

Johns, T. 1992. (Former LBTH Councilor; local resident) interview July 17, 1992.

Kapoor, V. 1992. (Vice President, Olympia & York Developments) interview July 17, 1992.

Keith, M. 1997. (Council Leader, London Borough of Tower Hamlets) interview August 15 and 29, 1997.

Ledgerwood, G. 1985. *Urban Innovation*. Aldershot: Gower.

Lett, J. 1997. (Assistant Chief Planner, LPAC; later Chief Planner GLA) interview 20 August.

Leung, B.Y.P. and Hui, E.C.M. 2005. Evaluation approach on public-private partnership (PPP) urban redevelopments. *International Journal of Strategic Property Management*, 9(1), 1–16.

London Docklands Development Corporation. 1982. *Isle of Dogs: A Guide to Design and Development Opportunities*, London: LDDC 1982.

London Docklands Development Corporation. 1992. DLR consolidates reliability. *Keep The Traffic Moving*, No. 67, July 15, 1992.

London Docklands Development Corporation. 1997a. *Starting From Scratch: The Development of Transport in London Docklands*. London: LDDC.

London Docklands Development Corporation. 1997b. *Isle of Dogs Completion Booklet*. London: LDDC.

London Docklands Development Corporation. 1998. *Housing in the Renewed London Docklands*. London: LDDC.

London Office Review Panel (LOPR). 1996. *1996 Report*. London: London Planning.

Marsh, G. 1997. (Principal, London Property Research) interview August 19, 1997.

McNish, J., Philip, M., and Milner, B. 1992. Olympia and York's hard times stem from shift to short-term debt. *Toronto Globe and Mail*, April 4, 1992, p. B1.

Olympia & York Developments. 1992. Canary Wharf. London: O&Y. Marketing brochure.

Pelling, A. 1992. (Under Secretary Department of the Environment) interview July 29, 1992.

Picardi, C. 1993. (Vice-President, Olympia & York Developments) interview June 1993.

Shaw, B. 1992. (Former LDDC Head of Urban Design) interview July 8 and 30, 1992.

Sheppard, H. 1997. (Director, City Design & Planning, LDDC) interviews August 14, 1997; July 10, 1992.

Skidmore Owings and Merrill. 1987. *Canary Wharf Design Guidelines*. London: Olympia & York Developments, 13 November.

Solskone, R. 1997. (Developer, former VP, O&Y) interviews October 15, 1997; July 2 and August 12, 1992.

Sorensen, E. 1997. (Chief Executive, Millennium Commission, former LDDC CEO, former DoE Staff) interviews August 14, 1997; July 22, 1992

SPLASH. 1993. *The Other Side of Docklands*. London: South Poplar and Limehouse
    Action for Secure Housing and the Environment, 172 East India Dock Road, London
    E14.
Stewart, W. 1993. *Too Big to Fail: Olympia & York: The Story behind the Headlines*.
    Toronto: McClelland and Stewart.
Tait, M. 2003. Urban villages as self-sufficient, integrated communities: A case study
    in London's Docklands. *Urban Design International*, 8, 37–52.
Thornley, A. 1991. *Urban Planning under Thatcherism: The Challenge of the Market*.
    London: Routledge.
Tower Hamlets, London Borough. 1997. *Planning Implications of LDDC Exit (Isle of
    Dogs)*. Report to Planning & Environment Committee, 31 July 1997.
Travers Morgan. 1973. *Docklands: Redevelopment Proposals for East London*.
    London: London Docklands Study Team.
Turner, R. 1992. (Director, Skidmore Owings & Merrill) interview July 28, 1992.
Wade, P. 1997. (Canary Wharf PLC; former AIC president) interview August 13, 1997.
Williams, S. 1992. The coming of the groundscrapers. In L. Budd and S. Whimster
    (eds), *Global Finance and Urban Living: A Study of Metropolitan Change*. London:
    Routledge, pp. 246–259.
Wrenn, D. 1983. *Urban Waterfront Development*. Washington, DC: Urban Land
    Institute.
Z/Yen Partners. 2020. *The Global Financial Centres Index 27*. London: Z/Yen Partners
    and China Development Institute, March 2020.

13. Urban regeneration meets sustainability—HafenCity, Hamburg

John D. Landis

ABBREVIATIONS USED IN THIS CHAPTER

FAR	Floor area ratio: The ratio of building floor area to lot area; a measure of density
HHG	HafenCity Hamburg GmbH: The public corporation charged with developing HafenCity

Conceived in 1996 as an urban waterfront regeneration initiative, HafenCity Hamburg (in English, Port City) is currently Europe's largest urban redevelopment project. Located along the northern banks of the Elbe River adjacent to Hamburg's historic Speicherstadt quarter, HafenCity is built atop two irregularly-shaped islands constructed out of landfill between the 15th and 19th centuries. Four kilometers long, one kilometer wide, and with a land area of 157 hectares (390 acres), when fully built-out, HafenCity will be home to 15,000 residents and up to 45,000 jobs (HafenCity 2017, p. 84).[1] Planning-wise, HafenCity is organized into ten distinct neighborhoods known as quarters, each with its own mix of land uses and, to a lesser degree, public facilities. All are connected by a network of parks and pedestrian ways. Within Hamburg, HafenCity is known as the hub of the city's new information-based economy. Beyond Hamburg, HafenCity is best known for the Elphilarmonie Concert Hall designed by the noted Swiss design firm Herzog & de Meuron. Completed in 2017 after a decade under construction, the Elphilarmonie sits atop an old warehouse building and is currently Hamburg's tallest occupied building.

Although HafenCity has many of the scale and financial characteristics of a megaproject, it was not originally conceived as such (Table 13.1). Instead, it was presented as an effort to reclaim Hamburg's historical waterfront and in a manner as economically productive, technologically modern, and environmentally sustainable as possible. To a notable degree, it has succeeded. HafenCity office buildings are currently home to 750 companies, including

45 with 50 or more employees.[2] Among the list of global and European corporations with headquarters in HafenCity are the international shipping leader
Kühne & Nagel, the German publishing giant the Spiegel Group, and Unilever,
the global consumer goods conglomerate. HafenCity is also on the cutting
edge in terms of energy efficiency and reduced consumption. All buildings in
western HafenCity are connected to a cogeneration-powered district heating
network which is supplemented by 1,800 square meters of on-site solar
thermal facilities. Thanks to its decentralized and modular heating system,
eastern HafenCity has been able to attain a CO_2 emission rate that is less than
one-third of the European Union average.[3] To protect against periodic storm
surges—which with climate change are projected to increase in frequency
and severity—all new HafenCity buildings stand on base structures eight
feet above sea level. Each HafenCity neighborhood has proscribed land use
mix goals intended to make it easy for residents and workers to walk, bike,
and take public transportation to their daily activities. To promote greater
social diversity, a minimum of 30 percent of HafenCity's housing units must
be rented to families with children younger than 18 years old. Recognizing
the potential for gentrification, HafenCity planners put in place a variety of
housing subsidy and assistance programs intended to ensure that one-third
of the district's housing units are affordable to low and moderate income
households (HafenCity 2017, p. 72). Largely because of HafenCity's progress

Table 13.1   HafenCity in brief

Description	Organized around an innovative vertical mixed-use concept and intended to be pedestrian-oriented and environmentally sustainable, HafenCity's 10 neighborhood "quarters" will eventually be home to 45,000 jobs and 12,000 residents.
Lead sponsor(s)	HafenCity Hamburg GmbH (HHG), Hamburg City Government.
Primary rationale	Reclaim an abandoned port facility as an economically-productive and environmentally-sustainable mixed-use district.
Primary funding sources	Combination of public infrastructure grant, land sales, and city-backed debt.
Regulatory/funding approval given in	1997
Construction started	1998
Construction completed	Rough build-out of all 10 HafenCity districts is now expected sometime in the mid-to-late 2020s.
Initial development budget (US$)	$2.8 billion (public funding); $10 billion in initial private financing
Principal takeaways	HafenCity demonstrates how with the right leadership, it is possible to combine an innovative and market savvy redevelopment plan with a sophisticated land disposition strategy and financing plan to create an economically successful and environmentally sustainable mixed-use district.

meeting its environmental goals, Hamburg was awarded the European Union's second annual Green Capital City Award in 2011.

A DERELICT WATERFRONT BECOMES A MASTER-PLANNED URBAN REGENERATION DISTRICT

The waterfront district now called HafenCity has been central to Hamburg's history since the 13th century when it became the preferred port for the newly-established Hanseatic League, a free trading union between the German and Baltic city-states lining the Baltic Sea (HafenCity 2021a). For five centuries, Hamburg's growth and prosperity were tied to its status as a free port where shippers could escape the high tariffs assessed at other European ports. Upon joining the German Empire in 1871, Hamburg reluctantly agreed to relinquish its city-wide free port status in exchange for allowing its port district to remain tariff-free. Determined to take advantage of this concession, Hamburg embarked on a port-centered building boom, one which, by the turn of the 20th century, had made Hamburg into Germany's second largest city after Berlin.

With its free trade-bias, Hamburg had always tried to stay out of Europe's wars, something it could not do as part of Germany. Shipping operations into and out of Hamburg's ports ceased almost entirely during World War I, picked up modestly following the War's end, but then fell again with the onset of the Great Depression. Business continued at a reduced level throughout the 1930s as Britain, France and the Low Countries began to isolate an increasingly militaristic Nazi Germany. In March 1933, the entire Hamburg Senate resigned to protest Adolf Hitler's selection as German Chancellor. This brought on five years of political marginalization, followed by the German Reichstag's decision in 1938 to suspend Hamburg's constitution, dissolve its Senate, and abolish the Mayor's office. Once World War II began, Hamburg's many factories and munition plants made it a favored target for Allied bombers. In July 1943, in a series of bombing raids known as Operation Gomorrah, allied bombers undertook what was until then the most intensive bombing campaign of the War. Lasting for eight straight days, Operation Gomorrah left 42,000 civilians dead and Hamburg's port facilities entirely in ruins.

Following the end of the war, Hamburg languished under British control until 1949. Funds to rebuild Hamburg's port were scarce, and many of the city's prior trading partners were now isolated behind the Iron Curtain. With much of Northern Europe's shipping traffic having moved to Rotterdam, Hamburg's rebuilt port facilities went only half-used. Additional building demolitions followed the 1962 adoption of a modernist zoning code intended to replace the city's older buildings with new superblock apartment projects.

After rising briefly during the 1950s, Hamburg's population fell throughout the 1960s and 1970s, reaching a post-War low of 1,580,000 in 1985. Hamburg's future and that of its abandoned dock district looked dim.

Like many German cities, Hamburg's prospects changed following the fall of the Berlin Wall and German reunification. Before reunification, Hamburg was a regional port city on the eastern edge of a Europe whose population growth, economic energy, and trading activity were concentrated in its western realms. After reunification, Hamburg suddenly found itself at the heart of a continent growing eastward as well as westward, and in possession of a deep-water port with the potential to rival Rotterdam as Europe's largest

In 1994, hoping to get ahead of events, Hamburg First Mayor Henning Voscherau commissioned an unofficial study to explore how to best reuse Hamburg's historic port district (HafenCity 2021b). Instead of renovating the city's existing piers on the north side of the Elbe River, the study recommended building an entirely new container port along the Elbe's southern bank, an area which already had good rail and truck connections. This scheme would leave Hamburg's traditional port areas available for redevelopment and re-use. Discretion was imperative: if the study recommendations were made public too early, Mayor Voscherau feared Hamburg's existing shipping companies would fight the move, causing land costs to rise on both sides of the Elbe. So, under a cloak of secrecy, Voscherau created a city-owned entity, Hamburger Hafen und Lagerhausgesellschaft mbH (later renamed HHLA Hafen und Logistik AG) to execute a land swap, giving Hamburg shipping companies land on the south bank of the Elbe for the new container port in exchange for Hamburg assuming ownership of the two north bank islands soon to be known as HafenCity.

Once Hamburg had gained sufficient waterfront site control, Mayor Voscherau commissioned Hamburg architect Volkwin Marg to develop a confidential port reuse and regeneration study. Marg, who was a professor of town planning on the Faculty of Architecture at RWTH Aachen and a former president of the Association of German Architects, had years of experience creating district masterplans. Marg's draft recommendations, which were presented to Hamburg officials in a December 1996 confidential session, laid out many of the land use and development principles that would guide HafenCity's eventual redevelopment. Foremost among these were avoiding superblocks in favor of short street blocks, limiting on-street and off-street parking to encourage more walking and public transportation use, and requiring that buildings as well as blocks mix land uses. With less land needed to accommodate cars, additional space could be devoted to parks, public spaces, and environmental features. It was this new urban form, Marg believed, that would be most attractive to innovative companies and their creative class workers.

Six months later, in May 1997, Voscherau released the results of Marg's study to the public as *Vision HafenCity* (HafenCity 2021c). The public response was enthusiastic, leading Hamburg's Bürgerschaft (City Council) to approve further planning efforts. This work would proceed along two tracks. The first would be to develop Marg's largely conceptual scheme into a detailed masterplan. Along these lines, the Hamburg Senate and Mayor's Office announced in December 1998 that the city would sponsor an international competition to select a design and planning team to create HafenCity's new masterplan.

The second planning track was intended to ensure that the city would have the financial and executive capacity to implement whatever masterplan was produced. Accordingly, in January 1998, the Hamburg Senate established a special purpose public entity, GHS Gesellschaft für Hafen- und Standortentwicklung mbH, (renamed HafenCity Hamburg GmbH in 2004) which would inherit ownership of all land in HafenCity, have the legal authority to issue bonds and sell them to investors, and be able to enter into subsequent land, development, and construction contracts. In nature if not in name, HafenCity was becoming a megaproject (Table 13.2).

Table 13.2   HafenCity timeline

1995	Hamburg Mayor Henning Voscherau approves the creation of Hamburger Hafen und Lagerhausgesellschaft GmbH (later renamed HHLA Hafen und Logistik AG) to execute a land swap giving Hamburg's shipping companies land on the Elbe's south bank for a new container port in exchange for the city assuming ownership of Hamburg's historical port areas.
1996	Hamburg architect Professor Volkwin Marg presents his first study for the redevelopment of what will become HafenCity.
1997	Hamburg Mayor Voscherau makes the first public presentation of Professor Marg's design concepts as *Vision HafenCity*. In August, the Hamburg City Council (Burgerschaft) gives the go-ahead for the project.
1998	Development control of HafenCity is given to GHS Gesellschaft für Hafen- und Standortentwicklung mbH—today's HafenCity Hamburg GmbH (HHG)—which is empowered to raise needed revenues through land sales.
1999	The international competition to develop a masterplan for HafenCity (based on Professor Marg's planning principles) is won by the Dutch-German design team, Kees/Chrisiaanse/ASTOC.
2000	The HafenCity Masterplan is approved by the Hamburg Senate.
2000	Business software giant SAP commits to building its regional headquarters on Grosser Grasbrook in HafenCity.
2001	Construction begins on the Kibbelsteg bridges linking HafenCity to central Hamburg. The bridges are completed in April 2002.

2002	HHG sells its first residential sites, to be used by cooperative housing corporations.
2003	The Hamburg Senate approves construction of the new U-4 subway line connecting HafenCity to central Hamburg.
2003	The groundbreaking for HafenCity's second neighborhood, Sandtorkai, takes place.
2003	Hamburg's city government approves the construction of a new concert hall (later named Elbphilharmonie) atop HafenCity's historic Kaispeicher A warehouse.
2004	The Hamburg Senate approves a zoning plan for HafenCity.
2005	A Dutch-German consortium of investors wins the right to develop the entire Überseequartier neighborhood.
2006	Global consumer goods giant Unilever announces it will build its new German headquarters with offices for 1,100 employees in the Strandkai neighborhood.
2006	The Barcelona-based firm BB + GG Arquitectes wins the competition to design HafenCity's central park and the connecting east–west promenades.
2007	Construction of HafenCity's first primary school is approved. Construction of the U-4 subway line begins.
2007	HafenCity introduces the Ecolabel sustainability certification process.
2007	Storm surge and flooding protection barrier construction is completed in HafenCity's west-side quarters.
2008	The International Maritime Museum Hamburg opens in the renovated Kaispecher B warehouse.
2009	Energy producer Dalkia wins the competition to provide supply energy to eastern HafenCity with a promise to reduce CO_2 emissions to 89 g/kWhr.
2010	A revised HafenCity Masterplan, focusing on the eastern neighborhoods is released.
2011	HafenCity's first public park opens.
2012	The U-4 subway line opens for service.
2025–2030	Construction of all planned HafenCity developments is expected to be completed.

The winner of the masterplan competition, the Dutch-German team of Kees Christiaansee/ASTOC, was announced in October 1999 (HafenCity 2021d). Among the winning entry's features that most impressed the competition jury were the way it opened HafenCity to the adjacent Speicherstadt warehouse district, the variety of place and urban typologies presented in the plan, the clever partitioning of the project area into discrete neighborhoods, and the plan's openness to later changes. With city officials anxious to get development underway, the new HafenCity masterplan was approved in February 2000, just five months after the competition's conclusion.

The freshly-minted HafenCity masterplan identified 11 mixed-use districts (later expanded to 13 in 2002 and then reduced back to 10 in 2010) to be developed west to east (Figure 13.1). When fully completed in 2030, HafenCity would be home to 12,000 new residents and 40,000 jobs and would require public and private investments totaling €10.4 billion. The largest share of land uses, 40 percent, was to be reserved for publicly-accessible open spaces, followed by building footprints (31 percent) and traffic and circulation areas (25 percent).[4] Almost every large building was to include a mix of land uses and activities. Ground floors were to be reserved for retail, cultural, and public uses, while the upper floors would be occupied by residential and office uses. Office and commercial uses would dominate HafenCity's central districts, with residential uses getting priority along its waterfront areas. Overall, the HafenCity plan called for its 13 neighborhoods to accommodate 2.4 million square meters of building area (Bruns-Berentelg 2017; HafenCity 2017, p. 85).

Source: HafenCity: Themes, Quarters, Projects (2017).

Figure 13.1   *Aerial photos showing HafenCity prior to redevelopment in 1998 (top) and location of planned HafenCity quarters (bottom)*

Because the plan reserved so much land for public use, the remaining privately-owned land would have to be developed at higher-than-typical densities. As specified in the plan, proposed floor area ratios (FARs), the numerical ratio of total building area to lot area, would vary within a relatively narrow range of 3.1 to 5.6 (Figure 13.2). Would there be enough market demand for all this additional density? No one could say for sure.

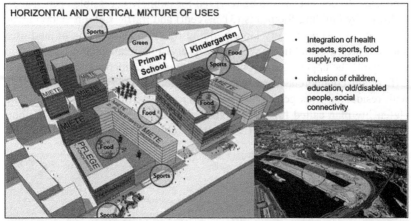

Source: HafenCity 2000 Masterplan.

Figure 13.2   HafenCity vertical and horizontal mixed use block archetypes

Three new streetcar lines would provide internal circulation within HafenCity as well as connect it to Hamburg's central Alstadt district and to the nearby Speicherstadt warehouse district. To discourage private auto use, the number of non-residential parking spaces in HafenCity would be strictly limited. Unless otherwise necessary, every new HafenCity structure would rely on district heating, and commercial buildings would make use of district cooling. All energy provision contracts would be negotiated by HafenCity Hamburg GmbH with an eye toward maximizing the use of renewable energy sources. Developers seeking building permission would be required to make maximum use of energy conservation features.

Implementing the new masterplan would require connecting appropriate sites with capable developers. This was to be the job of HafenCity Hamburg GmbH (HHG) and it could do so in three ways (Gödtel 2015; HafenCity 2021e). The first way to lease or sell parcels to private owners who agreed to develop them as proscribed by the masterplan. This approach had the advantage of speed but sacrificed public input into the final project design. Alternately, it could offer an option to a developer, giving itself and the developer more time to come up with an appropriate building program, site plan and design. Third, HHG could initiate a competition for a project-level development plan. This last approach was intended for large, multi-parcel sites. It would enable HHG to entertain multiple designs from different developers and to select the combined project-developer deemed most appropriate for a given site or situation. Competition winners would not automatically be granted needed development approvals, but they would have an edge in securing financing.

As the new millennium dawned, HafenCity was well on its way. It had a forward-looking master plan, an implementing agency with a clear mission, and the unanimous backing of both of Hamburg's political and governing institutions. Construction on the first HafenCity project, the Kibbelsteg pedestrian bridge connecting HafenCity to the Speicherstadt historic district broke ground in April 2001. Altogether, it had taken less than 18 months from selecting the HafenCity master planning team to the first HafenCity project groundbreaking, an impressively quick period.

PROJECT FINANCE: A SHIFTING URBAN ECONOMY FUELS STRONG LAND SALES

Urban development megaprojects face many of the same challenges and risks faced by transportation megaprojects. Both must gain regulatory and environmental approvals. Both must be able to generate sufficient revenues to cover initial infrastructure development costs and subsequent debt service payments. Both must have contingency plans to deal with potential construction delays and cost overruns.

Both also face market-based risks, but they are typically of different types. In the transportation case, what's at issue is not whether a particular facility is needed, but what price those who would use it are willing to pay. In the urban development case, the issues are less about pricing—housing and commercial real estate prices are constantly adjusting up and down—and more about whether there is sufficient demand to fill the available space. The sources of demand depend on the type of space. The demand for new office and industrial space is mostly driven by job growth. New housing demand is formed from household growth and the desire of current residents for a nicer home or neighborhood. Retail demand is more complicated still: it is influenced by the number of shoppers, their lifestyle and income, and their preferences for particular brands.

What's common to all forms of real estate demand is growth, something that was mostly absent from Hamburg during the 1980s and early 1990s. Between 1980 and 1990, Hamburg's population grew by just 7,000 people, or by 0.04 percent per year.[5] Hamburg's population growth picked up following the fall of the Berlin Wall—the city added 55,000 new residents between 1990 and 1995—but even so, during the final few months of 1999, as Hamburg's governing Senate body debated whether or not to approve the HafenCity masterplan, the question of how long it might take to fill all of HafenCity's new apartments and office buildings was foremost on everyone's mind. The answer they were given by HHG officials was atypically honest: somewhere between 25 and 30 years.

Coupling HafenCity's lengthy build-out period with its huge upfront infrastructure costs effectively ruled out using private financing. Given the combination of an uncertain market and a 25-year absorption schedule, HafenCity was just too risky to attract private investment capital. If the City of Hamburg wanted to build HafenCity, it would have to pay for it with public funding. From the beginning, this was understood by all.

Fortunately, Hamburg was well positioned to take on HafenCity's potential market and financing risks. As the closest of Germany's big cities (along with Berlin) to the old East Germany, Hamburg would continue to attract population from behind the former Iron Curtin. Hamburg's economic base was also poised for growth. Between 2004 and 2013, Airbus Industries, Hamburg's largest employer, saw its inflation-adjusted sales grow by 54 percent.[6] Other growing companies with headquarters or major operations in Hamburg included Asklepios Kliniken GmbH (healthcare), Lufthansa AG (aviation), Otto GmbH & Co. KG (technology) and Deutsche Bank (banking).

The economics of cities were also changing in ways that favored HafenCity. Responding to their employees' growing preferences for urban living and to the competitive advantages of co-locating near other related businesses—the attractive force economists call agglomeration economies—major corporations were increasingly eschewing suburban business parks for downtown locations. Suburban office vacancy rates were rising while downtown rates were falling. If HafenCity could offer the parcels capable of accommodating mid-sized office buildings, it would have little trouble attracting corporate office tenants. This was confirmed in June 2000 when, well before HafenCity's first public groundbreaking, global software giant SAP announced that it would be locating its northern German headquarters in HafenCity (HafenCity 2019). Six months later, in January 2001, eight European architectural firms announced they would be collaborating on the design and construction of a series of new mixed-use office buildings in HafenCity's Dalmannkai district.

HafenCity Hamburg GmbH's biggest advantage was that all of HafenCity's land was publicly owned, having been acquired in a land swap with Hamburg's Port Authority in the early 1990s. Free land is the holy grail of real estate development, and with so much of it in hand, HHG could take its time selecting the combinations of building proposals, tenants, and developers that best served HafenCity's long-term prospects for success. In addition to controlling the land supply pipeline, HHG also administered the development review and approval process. This combination of ready-to-build sites and entitlement certainty was appealing not only to developers and prospective tenants, but also to construction and mortgage lenders, making it easier to put together timely development deals. These market and financing advantages were immediately capitalized into land value premiums, allowing HHG to charge top euro for HafenCity sites. This method of selling pre-approved publicly-owned parcels to developers is widely used in Chinese cities to raise infrastructure investment capital but had not previously been used in Europe. As of October 2019, HHG has either sold or leased sufficient land to accommodate 2 million square meters (about 20 million square feet) of building area (HafenCity 2019). With about half of HafenCity's 127 hectares of developable land available for sale, HHG projects that HafenCity land sales will ultimately generate upwards of €10 billion in private investment.

Proceeds from land sales are used by HHG to pay for HafenCity's transportation, environmental and public realm infrastructure, including roads, bridges, promenades, parks, and waterfront facilities. To prevent infrastructure spending from getting too far ahead of land sales revenues, HHG has been careful to phase HafenCity's development. Consistent with its 2000 and 2010 masterplans, HafenCity has mostly developed west to east (HafenCity 2017). The first of HafenCity's ten districts to be developed was the largely residential Sandtorkai/Dalmannkai quarter (Figure 13.3). This was followed by the more commercially-oriented Sandtorpark/Grasbrook quarter, the waterfront Strandkai quarter, and the core area Uberseequartier.

Source: HafenCity: Themes, Quarters, Projects (2017).

Figure 13.3   HafenCity Sandtorkai/Dalmannkai Quarter in 2011 with partially-constructed Elbphilharmonie Concert Hall in the foreground

Not everything went according to HafenCity's masterplan. As the number of workers walking or biking to HafenCity rose, concerns mounted that passenger ridership on the still-to-be-built tram system might not meet expectations, so plans for its construction were abandoned in favor of extending the U-2 subway line from Hamburg's city center to HafenCity (with additional trains added to the U-2 line, the extended subway line was renamed the U-4).[7] Nor had the original masterplan included provisions and financing to build the Elbphilharmonie Concert Hall in the Am/Sandtorkai quarter.

Neither the U-4 subway line nor the Elbphilharmonie Concert Hall could be financed out of internal land sales. Both would require substantial outside funding. Completed in 2012, the U-4 subway line carries commuters each day into HafenCity from Hamburg's northern suburbs. Funded out of Hamburg's city budget and with federal grants. The other major HafenCity project funded from city revenues was the Elbphilharmonie Concert Hall. Started in 2007, and projected to cost €241 million and take three years to complete, Elbphilharmonie Hall ended up taking an extra seven years and €548 million to finish.[8]

Even so, HafenCity had clearly hit a sweet spot in the real estate market. In March 2006, global consumer giant Unilever announced it would build its new 1,100 employee German headquarters in HafenCity's Strandkai quarter.[9] Four months later, in June 2006, HafenCity was chosen as the site of HafenCity University Hamburg, a new 1,500-student public university focusing on architecture, civil engineering, and urban planning.[10] In November 2008, construction began in HafenCity's Brooktorkai/Ericus quarter on a new headquarters building for Spiegel Publishing House, the publisher of *Der Spiegel*, Germany's largest weekly news magazine. In April 2009, HHG announced that there were no building sites still available in HafenCity's west-side Dalmannkai district.

Overall, Hamburg's bet on HafenCity's future appears to have paid off. As of 2019, Hamburg was ranked fourth in the European Cities Regions of the Future[11] competition (behind London, Dublin and Paris), and was listed in the top ten of the 2018 Digital Economy of the Future ranking. In the EU's 2018 European Capital of Innovation ratings, Hamburg was rated sixth.[12] Not including the Elbphilharmonie Concert Hall, Hamburg's total investment in HafenCity's infrastructure and public realm is expected to run about €2.2 billion (HafenCity 2017, p. 84). Assuming HHG's €10 billion private investment estimate is accurate, this corresponds to a 20-year annual return-on-investment of just under 8 percent.

PIVOTING TOWARD CULTURE AND SUSTAINABILITY

The demand for commercial sites in HafenCity was sufficiently robust that by 2005, HHG could begin pivoting away from its initial focus on infrastructure development and commercial land sales, and toward broader community building and sustainability concerns (HafenCity 2017). This pivot took several forms, the most notable being the HHG's 2003 donation of the former Kaispeicher A warehouse to serve as the future home of the Hamburg Philharmonic Orchestra in what would later become the Elbphilharmonie Concert Hall. Two years later, in 2005, the HHG would make the nearby Kaispeicher B warehouse available for use as the International Maritime Museum Hamburg. Renovating the Kaispeicher B warehouse for a maritime museum proved an easier challenge than building a new concert hall atop the Kaispeicher A warehouse, allowing the International Maritime Museum to open its doors in 2008, nine years before the Elbphilharmonie Concert Hall. Plans were also underway to build a combined science museum and aquarium to be located in the Überseequartier. As conceived by an international design team led by Dutch architect Rem Koolhaas, the proposed science museum–aquarium was shaped like a cubist-style, upward-standing ring, and was to combine interactive exhibits with working lab space. Projected to cost €50 million when it was unveiled in 2006, the Koolhaas' design failed to attract sufficient funding and has yet to be built.

HafenCity's central location, innovative reputation and available building sites also proved to be a draw for universities and graduate schools, especially business and technical programs. In September 2010, three private graduate universities opened their HafenCity doors to students for the first time: Kuehne Logistics University (KLU), Medical School Hamburg (MSH), and the Hamburg branch of the International School of Management (ISM). KLU and MSM had each purchased sites some years earlier and constructed their own purpose-built facilities—MSH would later expand to four buildings—while the ISM made do with leased space. Another private business school, the Frankfurt School of Finance and Management, opened its Hamburg branch in HafenCity in 2011. HafenCity got its first public university in 2014 when HafenCity University Hamburg, with programs specializing in architecture, civil engineering and urban planning, enrolled its first student class. By 2015, some 5,000 full-time university students were studying in HafenCity, adding to the demand for housing, restaurants, and sports facilities (HafenCity 2017, p. 85).

HafenCity's biggest push was in the area of sustainability, with HHG using every regulatory and contracting arrow in its quiver to reduce energy consumption and greenhouse gas emissions (Huang-Lachmann et al. 2016; HafenCity 2021f). On the energy supply side, HHG employed the same competitive bidding process it used with land sales to find suppliers who would meet its energy and emissions targets. In its 2005 request for proposals for a company to provide energy for HafenCity's new district heating plant—heating and cooling services were previously supplied by a plant in central Hamburg— HHG stipulated that the winning contractor would have to compete on CO_2 emissions as well as on reliability and price, specifying an emissions target that was 27 percent below the level required of current energy suppliers.

On the energy consumption side, HHG encouraged all HafenCity developers and building owners to make use of best-practice sustainable development technologies. This was accomplished through the use of an energy conservation certification process known as Ecolabel. Similar to the US EPA's EnergyStar label, but more extensive in its coverage, Ecolabel was created by the European Union in 1992 to help consumers identify appliances and products with reduced environmental impacts (Lavallée and Plouffe 2004). HafenCity took the Ecolabel idea one step further in 2007, extending it to buildings as well as furnishings and appliances. As implemented in HafenCity, new buildings could earn a "gold" Ecolabel rating if they excelled in at least three of five sustainability categories, including: reduced energy and water use; reduced automobile use; using building materials determined not to be ecologically harmful; meeting indoor air quality and thermal and acoustic comfort targets; and ensuring that buildings will continue to meet their performance targets after construction completion (HafenCity Hamburg 2010). Preliminary Ecolabel certification may be awarded on the basis of building plans, but final certification must wait until a project is completed and occupied. Although HHG does not mandate that HafenCity developers apply for Ecolabel certification, it strongly encourages them to do so. According to the HafenCity website, as of 2018, more than 50 HafenCity projects, including 42 residential buildings, had either received or were projected to receive a gold Ecolabel rating (HafenCity 2021f).

HafenCity's pedestrian and bicycle facility requirements have also paid dividends. Where pedestrian paths and bikeways traverse private property, property owners are required to maintain them and ensure access. To ensure greater pedestrian and bicyclist safety, 70 percent of HafenCity's pedestrian walkways and bike paths are physically separated from adjacent roadways (HafenCity 2021g). The rest are located in residential areas, where additional access control and traffic calming methods are used to reduce vehicle volumes and speeds. Thanks largely to HafenCity's extensive bicycle facilities, in 2013 Hamburg was added to Copenhagenize Design Company's biannual list of the world's 20 most bike-friendly cities.

Completed HafenCity projects regularly drew praise, first from within Germany, and then later, internationally. In December 2005, Am Sandtorkai 54, a residential building designed by Jan Störmer Architekten, was awarded the Hamburg German Architecture Association Chapter's First Prize. In 2007, the HafenCity's Shanghai Pedestrian Bridge was designated building of the year by the Hamburg Architects and Engineers Association. The same award was won the following year by the Museum Bridge. In October 2008, the annual publication, *Architecture in Hamburg* selected five Sandtorkai buildings for inclusion on its "1989-2008 Best Projects" list.

These local awards were soon complemented by international ones. At the October 2009 World Architecture Festival Awards in Barcelona, HafenCity's Unilever Building was selected as the world's best office building. One month later, the nearby Marco Polo Tower won the European Property Award in the "best high-rise development" category (Figure 13.4). In 2011, largely in recognition of initiatives started in HafenCity, Hamburg was awarded the second European Green Capital Award by the European Commission.

Marco Polo Tower

Elbphilharmonie Concert Hall

Lohsepark (Central Park)

Unilever Building

Figure 13.4   Notable HafenCity buildings: (top left) Marco Polo Tower (photo credit: Roland Halbe); (top right) Elbphilharmonie Concert Hall (photo credit: HafenCity Hamburg); (bottom left) Lohsepark (photo credit: HafenCity Hamburg); (bottom right) Unilever Building in foreground (photo credit: Siegfried Kuttig)

A REVISED MASTERPLAN UPS THE ANTE

HafenCity's growing international recognition did not distract HHG from its core mission: providing a timely supply of development sites to blue-chip companies and institutions willing to spend money and help HafenCity meet its sustainability and equity goals. Like cascading dominoes, as property sales were completed in one HafenCity neighborhood, another would be promptly opened up. The first HafenCity neighborhood to be listed as "being completed"—that is to have no remaining land parcels available for sale or development—was the Sandtorkai/Dalmannkai quarter in 2009. By 2012, the Sandortorpark/Grassbrook quarter was essentially complete, as was the Uberseequartier neighborhood in 2015.

For HHG, the successful completion of the Sandorkai/Dalmannkai quarter meant it was time to revisit HafenCity's original masterplan. Not wanting to stray too far from the principles responsible for its success, HHG hired the same team that had put together the 2000 HafenCity Masterplan, Kees, Christiaanse/ASTOC, to produce a 2010 update. Conceptually, the new masterplan would depart from the original one in three ways (HafenCity 2021d). Whereas the original plan had approached HafenCity's development as being separate and distinct from that of downtown Hamburg, the updated plan would focus on connecting HafenCity with Hamburg's central district. The new masterplan would also focus on intensifying development around HafenCity's two U-4 subway stations, which were scheduled to open in 2012. Lastly, because of rising concerns over the effects of climate change, the revised masterplan would focus on additional efforts to reduce greenhouse gas emissions.

From a development perspective, the new plan's biggest change had to do with maximum densities. Whereas the original masterplan had foreseen floor area ratios (FARs) ranging from 3.1 to 5.6 depending on the neighborhood, the revised plan increased the FAR ceiling to 6.5 (HafenCity 2021d). The practical effect of this change was to increase HafenCity's gross floor area at build-out from 1.5 million square meters to 2.3 million square meters, and to increase the number of jobs HafenCity was ultimately expected to accommodate from 40,000 to 45,000.

The shift to higher FARs and taller buildings left additional land available for open space. To make use of the additional land, Lohsepark, HafenCity's "Central Park" was extended to the Elbe where it connected to HafenCity's riverfront promenade. In addition, the promenade would be extended to HafenCity's eastern tip. Altogether, the amount of public open space in HafenCity was increased from 24 hectares in the 2000 plan to 28 hectares in the 2010 plan revision.

HafenCity's environmental standards were likewise elevated from their prior levels. In its request for proposals to supply HafenCity's eastern district heating energy needs, HHG required prospective bidders to meet a CO_2 emissions standard of 125 grams/kWh, down from the 175 grams/kWh standard required of west-side bidders six years earlier. The winning bidder, Dalkia Energie, went further still, promising to deliver energy based on a CO_2 emissions target of just 89 grams/kWh (HafenCity 2017, p. 57).

Not every proposed change was a progressive one. Discouraged by the slower-than-expected pace of new market-rate residential construction—which it attributed to having to give priority to building government-subsidized social housing—HHG would henceforth open up the residential bidding process to additional private builders and public–private joint ventures. To accommodate additional market-rate housing, HafenCity's ultimate housing unit inventory would grow from 5,500 dwelling units to more than 6,000. To increase their market appeal, homes built after 2012 could also be larger than homes built previously (HafenCity 2017, p. 72).

Having established the physical feasibility and market appeal of HafenCity's vertical mixed-use organizing principle, the 2010 masterplan revision set about giving HafenCity's three eastern subdistricts their own neighborhood identities: new developments in the Am Baakenhafen neighborhood would focus on living and leisure; the Oberhafen neighborhood would become the east-side's creative and cultural quarter; and the Elbbrücken neighborhood would be reserved for business and housing (HafenCity 2017, pp. 43–55). The 2010 masterplan also combined HafenCity's ten existing west-side neighborhoods into seven, leaving the total number of HafenCity neighborhoods unchanged.

Independently of the plan revision, HHG committed itself to experimenting with new and innovative energy technologies, including hydrogen fuel cells for heating, and using geothermal energy to dehumidify room air (HafenCity 2017, p. 57). In 2012, a hydrogen filling station was constructed at HafenCity's Oberbaum Bridge entrance to provide fuel for Hamburg's expanding fleet of hydrogen-power buses. On the energy consumption side, the 2010 plan revision specified that all new buildings would henceforth be required to meet Ecolabel gold energy standards.

LESSONS AND TAKEAWAYS

Usually regarded as an urban regeneration initiative, HafenCity also scores extremely well as a megaproject. It has done well in meeting its original goals and objectives in a timely manner. HafenCity Hamburg GmbH, HafenCity's sponsor, has done a noteworthy job developing and staying within its original construction budget. It also developed and implemented a robust financing and revenue model able to endure the stresses posed by the Global Financial Crisis. Thanks to the City of Hamburg's farsightedness in gaining complete site control, HafenCity's development has been able to proceed without significant legal or environmental challenge. By applying best-practice environmental planning methods and technologies, HafenCity has become a globally-recognized leader in the field of sustainable development.

HHG has also done a laudable job incorporating equity goals into HafenCity's development program, especially those focusing on affordable housing. HHG has promoted the use of innovative energy, environmental, construction and transportation technologies, but at the same time, kept a close eye on controlling costs. It has also implemented sound operations and asset management practices that have enabled HafenCity properties and facilities to gain financial and market value over time. Perhaps most impressively, it has done all of this without having to fall back on government bailouts. And when circumstances changed—as they did around the construction of the U-4 subway line and the potential to build more densely than originally planned—HafenCity planners responded quickly and flexibly.

Some of HafenCity's success was the result of fortunate circumstance. Following the fall of the Berlin Wall and German reunification, Germany's population was growing again—something it hadn't done consistently since the early 1970s—and both spatially and economically, Hamburg was well positioned to take advantage of the country's resurgence. The HafenCity site was centrally located, well-served by public transportation, and didn't require much environmental mediation. Hamburg's shipping companies and labor unions, which in other cities had fought hard to keep waterfront sites in maritime and industrial use, were content to move to Hamburg's new container port along the opposite bank of the Elbe River. After two decades of favoring suburban office parks with highway access, major employers in Europe and North America, especially those in innovative industries, were again looking to relocate in downtowns.

Serendipity notwithstanding, HafenCity's key lesson is about the importance of civic vision, political will, and managerial and financial competence. Had Hamburg's First Mayor, Henning Voscherau, not recognized HafenCity's potential as a mixed-use urban innovation district and moved forcefully to relocate its remaining maritime uses elsewhere; had initial HafenCity designer Volkwin Marg not rejected a superblock-based design in favor of a granular mixed-use concept; had Mayor Voscherau not persuaded the Hamburg Senate to approve Marg's initial concept (and the resulting masterplan); and had the City of Hamburg elected not to place the responsibility for overseeing HafenCity's development in a semi-independent organization that understood how to link progressive urban design principles with market-based financial realities—had these things not all come together in the manner they did—it is doubtful that HafenCity would have attained its current level of success.

What lessons does HafenCity offer other places thinking about undertaking comparable urban regeneration megaprojects? Three spring to mind. The first concerns the importance of having complete site control. The second involves the importance of having a realistic and robust infrastructure financing model.

And the third pertains to not being afraid to push on conventional wisdoms about market demand and environmental performance.

• *The critical role of full and complete site control.* Experienced developers know there is nothing more important than establishing early and complete control of any development site. Having complete site control involves having physical site control, legal site control, and regulatory site control. Having physical site control means being able to access the site for any reason, including physical and environmental inventorying, and undertaking any and all construction activities. Having legal site control means ensuring that no other parties can make a legal claim against the owner or site that will impinge upon its development potential; and that the owner can dispose of all or part of the site as they see fit. Having regulatory site control means that there is a reasonable, fair, and timely process for resolving any statutory, administrative or discretionary limitations on the use of the site, most notably those involving prospective land uses and development densities.

The fact that Hamburg's municipal government and its sub-entities— first Hamburger Hafen und Lagerhausgesellschaft GmbH, and then later, HafenCity Hamburg GmbH (HHG)—was initially able to acquire complete physical, legal and regulatory site control over the entire HafenCity site greatly simplified and sped up HafenCity's master planning and site preparation timeline. It also made it possible for HafenCity Hamburg GmbH to create an efficient process for selling fully-entitled sites to prospective developers in a manner that maximized sales revenues and potential public benefits. Because these entitlements were fully transferrable to all site purchasers, developers had the confidence that they would be able to meet their construction and occupancy schedules. This, in turn, enabled HHG to meet its west-to-east goal of sequentially developing complete neighborhoods in which the quality and pace of private construction matched the rate and type of public infrastructure improvements.

• *Phasing and brand-building without over-spending.* Regardless of whether they are publicly or privately developed, most large-scale urban development projects face significant financing challenges early on in their development cycle. This is because their sponsors typically underestimate the up-front costs of providing essential infrastructure while overestimating sales and absorption rates. Simply put, most large development projects don't take in enough revenue early in their lives to pay for all their up-front infrastructure needs. This problem is less severe for publicly-financed projects (in which the project sponsor can request additional public financing or debt relief) than for privately-financed projects in which the project may have to negotiate an entirely new (and usually less advantageous) financing package.

To its immense credit, HHG avoided both of these pitfalls. It didn't over-spend up-front on unneeded infrastructure, and its projections of land sales rates (and prices) were always conservative and well-considered. With hind-sight, these results were achieved by pursuing successful cost-minimization and branding strategies. First, by developing HafenCity's neighborhood quarters sequentially from west to east, and by building necessary trans-portation and environmental infrastructure only as it was needed, HHG was able to keep its development budget under control. Second, and in a related vein, by promoting walking and discouraging car use, HHG was able to minimize its road construction and parking facility costs; as well as make additional development sites for sale. Third, by metering the supply of entitled sites available for purchase, HHG was able to maximize its land sales revenue, even during the Global Financial Crisis. Likewise, by focusing its initial land sales and development activity on daytime activi-ties such as office buildings and educational institutions, HHG created the sense that HafenCity was part of downtown Hamburg rather than a sep-arate community. And by cutting deals with companies known as global leaders and innovators (as well as with business and engineering graduate programs), HHG was successfully able to establish HafenCity's brand as a forward-looking innovation hub—a brand that could then be extended to HafenCity's residential projects. Finally, instead of building residen-tial amenities such as parks and schools beforehand as an (expensive) inducement to potential residents, HHG waited to build them until after the neighborhood had been established.

• *Focusing on preference shifts rather than relying on trend projections.* Apple co-founder Steve Jobs is famous for saying that Apple never under-took advance market research for any of its products because he believed that people didn't really know what they wanted until someone gave it to them. This is a questionable approach when applied to expensive urban megaprojects, but it does contain a grain of truth: when asked about what they might be willing to pay for an entirely new product, most people cannot come up with a reliable answer. As Hamburg prepared to replace its historical waterfront district with a series of new mixed use neighborhoods, it had many more questions than answers. Who would live there? Like the rest of Germany, Hamburg's population was not growing. Where would the new jobs come from? Munich, not Hamburg, was Germany's innova-tion center. And perhaps most crucially, in a country just coming to grips with the impending costs of reunification, how much would it cost and who would pay for it? To someone looking just at numbers and trends, nothing about HafenCity would have seemed favorable.

In fact, consumer and business preferences were changing, and not necessarily in the ways a closer look at market statistics would have revealed. After decades of decline, Hamburg's population was finally growing again, and that growth was concentrated among the young. Pushed by agglomeration economies, especially among information-intensive businesses, companies were locating many of their new and formerly suburban operations in downtown locations. An increasing number of younger and better-educated workers were also looking to live in urban neighborhoods where they wouldn't need a car on a daily basis. And with a growing share of their expenditures going to labor, companies were willing to pay the higher office rents required for buildings and locations desired by their employees. These shifts were occurring across North America and Europe, not just in Hamburg, but as architect and town planner Professor Volkwin Marg realized when given the job to come up with the concept plan for HafenCity, they could be harnessed to work to Hamburg and HafenCity's advantage.

This is not to say everything about HafenCity went smoothly or according to the initial plan. While business space absorption in HafenCity has mostly occurred faster than expected, residential absorption has occurred more slowly. Whereas HafenCity's pivot from light-rail to a new subway line occurred smoothly, construction of the iconic Elbphilharmonie Concert Hall was plagued by delays and cost overruns.

NOTES

1. As of 2019, roughly half of HafenCity's planned 140 building projects had been completed, including 3,000 residential units and working space for 15,000 employees.
2. https://www.hafencity.com/en/overview/facts-figures.
3. https://www.hafencity.com/en/urban-development/sustainability.
4. https://www.hafencity.com/en/overview/facts-figures.
5. https://www.macrotrends.net/cities/204341/hamburg/population.
6. https://www.airbus.com/sites/g/files/jlcbta136/files/2021-06/eads-airbus-group -fy2013-presentation.pdf.
7. "Historie der Hochbahn" [History of the U-Bahn] (in German). Hamburger Hochbahn. 2013.
8. The Local.de. "€700m over budget, Hamburg concert hall finally finished." November 1, 2016.
9. https://www.archdaily.com/41761/unilever-headquarters-behnisch-architekten.
10. https://www.hcu-hamburg.de/en/university/.
11. https://www.fdiintelligence.com/article/70906.
12. https://www.hafen-hamburg.de/en/press/news/-hamburg-nominated-for-european -capital-of-innovation-award-35939/.

REFERENCES

Unless otherwise noted, all website information retrieved in June 2021.

ASTOC Architects and Planners. *HafenCity Masterplan*. Retrieved on December 20, 2021, from: https://www.world-architects.com/en/astoc-architects-and-planners -koln/projects.

Bruns-Berentelg, J. 2017. HafenCity, 21st century, urban development, continuity & transformation. [PowerPoint presentation.]

Gödtel, T. 2015. HafenCity Hamburg – From harbour space to a sustainable new downtown and the planning structure behind. [PowerPoint presentation.]

HafenCity. 2017. *Themes, Quarters, Projects*. [English version.]

HafenCity. 2019. *Buildings in HafenCity*.

HafenCity. 2021a. History of the site. HafenCity website. Retrieved June 2021, from: https://www.hafencity.com/en/overview/history.

HafenCity. 2021b. Genesis of an idea. HafenCity website. Retrieved June 2021, from: https://www.hafencity.com/en/overview/genesis-of-idea.

HafenCity. 2021c. Chronology. HafenCity website. Retrieved June 2021, from: https:// www.hafencity.com/en/overview/chronology.

HafenCity. 2021d. Masterplan. HafenCity website. Retrieved June 2021, from: https:// www.hafencity.com/en/overview/masterplan.

HafenCity. 2021e. HafenCity Hamburg GmbH. HafenCity website. Retrieved June 2021, from: https://www.hafencity.com/en/hafen-city-hamburg-gmbh/hafencity -hamburg-gmbh.

HafenCity. 2021f. Sustainability. HafenCity website. Retrieved June 2021, from: https://www.hafencity.com/en/urban-development/sustainability.

HafenCity. 2021g. Mobility. HafenCity website. Retrieved June 2021, from: https:// www.hafencity.com/en/urban-development/smart-mobility.

HafenCity Hamburg. 2010. Sustainable construction in HafenCity: HafenCity Ecolabel. https://epub.sub.uni-hamburg.de/epub/volltexte/2017/74579/pdf/Sustainable _Construction_1.4.pdf.

Huang-Lachmann, J. T., and Lovett, J. C. 2016. How cities prepare for climate change: Comparing Hamburg and Rotterdam. *Cities*, 54, 36–44.

Lavallée, S., and Plouffe, S. 2004. The ecolabel and sustainable development. *The International Journal of Life Cycle Assessment*, 9(6), 349–354.

14. A case of hubris—Songdo International Business District

John D. Landis

ABBREVIATIONS USED IN THIS CHAPTER

DUP   District Unit Plan—the approved land use and zoning plan for new development projects indicating allowable densities and land uses.

IFEZ   Incheon Free Economy Zone—the agency created by the South Korean government to administer preferential economic development activities in the Incheon region.

ISCC   Incheon Smart City Corporation—the partnership between Incheon and Cisco to develop a data sharing and collaborative decision-making tool for Songdo and Incheon.

LSA   Land Supply Agreement—the agreement between the City of Incheon and NSCD specifying the delivery schedule and pricing for New Songdo City land parcels.

NSC   New Songdo City—the initial name of the 1500-acre master-planned development at the center of Songdo City.

NSCD   New Songdo City Development LLC—the partnership between Gale International and POSCO E&C charged with developing New Songdo City.

NSCID   New Songdo International City Development LLC—the new name of the NSCD partnership as of 2007.

P3   Public–private Partnership

SIBD   Songdo International Business District—the later name of New Songdo City designed to call attention to its status as an international business hub.

U-City Ubiquitous City—a designation indicating that a city was participating in the Korean government's smart city embedded ICT program.

Songdo International Business District (SIBD) in Incheon, Korea, is a city of multiple identities. Now projected to cost upward of US$50 billion by the time it is finally completed in the mid-to-late 2020s, Songdo is the single development project in modern history. It is also the largest mixed-use master-planned community in the world, and one of the largest public–private partnership projects ever undertaken (Table 14.1). Thanks to its energy and water-saving design, Songdo is widely touted as one of the world's greenest cities, and because of the ubiquity of its sensors and digital control systems, one of its smartest cities as well. Last but not least, because of its proximity to Incheon International Airport, Songdo has been called an aerotropolis. Labels aside, how well has Songdo performed in the real world? Has it earned its developers and financial sponsors a reasonable financial return? Do Songdo's carefully planned buildings, streets and public spaces make it a good place for its corporate residents to do business and for its citizens to live? As master-planned cities go, in which ways should it be considered a model for similar urban megaprojects around the world?

Of its different identities, Songdo is foremost a master-planned community or MPC. This means that its mix of land uses, buildings, and public facilities are designed in such a fashion as to maximize the quality of life for its residents and the productivity of its businesses, and are developed in a manner that takes maximum advantage of construction and financing economies of scale. Developing MPCs is a risky proposition. Because they include multiple land uses and product types, MPCs must hit several real estate sub-markets spot on at once. Because of their higher amenity levels and densities, they are more expensive to build. Because they require so much new and expensive infrastructure to be built before any buyers or tenants arrive, they are more difficult to finance. And because they lack an established image or brand, MPCs are more difficult to market. In theory, these higher costs and greater risks may be offset by efficiencies that can be realized by designing and building everything as a piece, but in practice these advantages rarely materialize.

MPCs also face huge marketing and pricing challenges. Because they are new and untested and lack a market brand, an MPC's initial phases must sell or lease at a discount in order to build market interest. To compensate for the reduced cash flows in an MPC's early years, its developers plan to charge premium prices in later years. The problem with this incremental pricing strategy is that it hardly ever succeeds: competition is ever-present, project identities fail to take hold, and there is always something newer and shinier to attract a prospective buyer or tenant.

Songdo is also organized as a public–private partnership (P3), the first real estate P3 in Korea's history. Real estate P3s are different from infrastructure P3s in a couple of ways. In the latter, a government entity gives a private concessionaire an exclusive right to develop and operate a roadway or metro line or water system in exchange for the private partner designing, building, financing, and operating the facility. The private partner gets to set prices and keep the cash flows, while the public partner typically gets an up-front licensing fee and the ability to keep the project off its balance sheet. In a real estate P3, the public partner, typically a local government, agrees to sell the site to their private partner at a much reduced price, assist with any needed entitlements, build supporting public infrastructure, and provide some level of project financing. The private partner brings design, construction, marketing

Table 14.1   *Songdo International Business District in brief*

Description	Songdo IBD (International Business District) is a 1500-acre "new town" 35 minutes from Seoul and 12 minutes from Incheon Airport by car. Developed as a joint venture by the City of Incheon and Gale International, a US-based developer, Songdo IBD includes a balanced mix of offices, housing types, retail space, parks, schools, and residential amenities, making it Korea's first true master-planned community. After running into repeated market and financial problems, the joint venture was dissolved in 2010.
Lead sponsor(s)	City of Incheon, Gale International, and POSCO E&C
Primary rationale	Taking advantage of Songdo's proximity to Incheon Airport, Incheon and Gale International sought to attract global technology companies and their "creative-class" workers by providing high-quality amenities and services at a much lower office and residential occupancy cost than Seoul.
Primary funding sources	Bank loans, government grants (for public infrastructure)
Regulatory/funding approval given in	1997 (preliminary)
Construction started	2001
Construction completed	Songdo's market absorption has been much slower than projected and build-out isn't currently expected until the mid-to-late-2020s.
Cumulative investment at build-out (US$)	$50 billion (projected)
Principal takeaways	Songdo is what happens when a municipality with no partnering experience with developers enters into a real estate joint venture with a contextually-ignorant foreign development company. Both partners based their participation on unrealistic "best-case" market and financing assumptions, and neither was prepared for slower-than-expected market absorption.

and operating expertise, as well as agrees to assemble a project financing package. As shown in Table 14.2, this was the situation both parties in the Songdo project thought they were involved in, but because of the project's size and complexity and both parties' inexperience with P3s, from its first day, the arrangement never worked out as anticipated.

Last, Songdo is a megaproject, and like any megaproject, it faces significant pitfalls. These include accurately estimating construction costs and timelines, projecting the size of the market, identifying and mitigating multiple risk sources, managing multiple contractors, and dealing with the political and financial aftermath if the project doesn't deliver as promised. In Songdo's case, all parties initially treated it as just a bigger version of a conventional real estate project rather than trying to understand the heightened difficulties and risks inherent in megaprojects.

Table 14.2   New Songdo City public–private partnership roles

Partner and type	Brings to the deal	New Songdo City case specifics
Public partner: Incheon Free Economic Zone	Developable land	1,500 acre development-ready site
	Supporting infrastructure and public facilities	Bridge to Incheon International Airport and metro extension
	Development approvals	Quick approval of District Unit Plan (DUP)
	Preferential financing	Public sector financing; preferential relationships with Korean banks
	Other capabilities	Designation of Incheon Free Economy Zone (FEZ) tax incentives
Private partner: Gale International	Development expertise	Office buildings in Boston and New York City
	Market knowledge	Knowledge of corporate tenant needs and preferences
	Access to private financing sources	Relationships with US commercial and investment banks
	Tenanting and sales expertise	Relationships with US technology companies as prospective tenants
	Other capabilities	Risk management skills

Songdo has garnered considerable attention in recent years as an example of the successes and failures of government-based spatial development programs (Shin 2016); and because of its status as a "smart city," a place where embedded systems of sensors and computer networking technologies handle routine building and public facility management tasks (Rugkhapan and Murray 2019; Kuecker and Hartley 2020). Except in passing, this chapter is not centrally concerned with either of these themes. Instead, we are focused on Songdo's economic and financial performance as a mega-scale urban real estate project. This involves tracing its development history from conception to completion. This is complicated by the fact that Songdo is still only about half complete and by the lack of publicly-available information regarding Songdo's market and financial performance.

SONGDO IN A NUTSHELL

Songdo has had several names over its 20-plus year existence. Having started out as New Songdo City in 2001, Songdo's name was officially changed to Songdo International Business District (SIBD) in 2003 to reflect its updated market positioning. Whatever Songdo City's official name, for brevity's sake we will henceforth refer to it simply as Songdo. Along with the Incheon International Airport and the nearby City of Cheongna, Songdo is located in the Incheon Free Economy Zone (IFEZ), a special administrative district created in 2003 by the

Korean government to extend tax breaks to international companies locating in the Incheon area. Songdo is connected to Incheon by a roadway and subway line, and to the Incheon International Airport by a 12 km causeway and bridge. Driving from Songdo to downtown Seoul takes about 35 minutes.

Songdo was planned and developed by a P3 between Gale International, a New York-based real estate company; POSCO Engineering & Construction (POSCO E&C), a subsidiary of one of South Korea's largest steel companies; and the Incheon Metropolitan City, a governmental entity which includes the Municipality of Incheon and the Incheon Free Economy Zone. In 2001, Gale International and POSCO E&C came together to form New Songdo City Development LLC (NSCD), a joint venture partnership, with Gale owning 70.1 percent of the company and POSCO E&C owning the remaining share (Segel 2006, p. 4). In 2007, NSCD reconstituted itself as New Songdo International City Development LLC (NSICD). Songdo was originally planned for completion in 2015, but with office absorption currently running years behind schedule, current estimates are that Songdo will be finally completed sometime in the mid-to-late 2020s.

Songdo is built atop a 1,415 acre site that was reclaimed from the sea off the Incheon coast during the 1990s (Figure 14.1). Area wise, Songdo IBD is about the size of downtown Boston. Songdo IBD serves as the commercial and residential center of a larger 13,000 acre new town project known as Songdo City that is ultimately expected to have 300,000 residents. At build-out, Songdo will accommodate approximately 65,000 residents and 30,000 jobs (Songdo IBD 2021a). The New Songdo City Masterplan, which was created in 2003 by the US firm of Kohn Pederson Fox, projects that Songdo will ultimately include 40 million square feet of office space, 35 million square feet of residential buildings, 10 million square feet of retail space, 5 million square feet of hotel and hospitality space, and 9 million square feet of public space.[1] With a population density of roughly 25,000 persons per square mile, Songdo is about as dense as New York City and half as dense as Seoul.

Forty percent of Songdo's land area is to be permanently preserved as park and green space, a huge percentage compared to the typical Korean new town (Songdo IBD 2021a). Songdo's three districts are arrayed around a 100-acre park—named after New York City's Central Park—with an artificial creek at its center that flows west into Songdo Lake. Songdo Lake, also a man-made feature, forms Songdo's waterfront. Additional park areas include a community park at Songdo's northwestern corner and an 18-hole Jack Nicklaus-designed golf course at its southern edge. In addition to a generous supply of recreation spaces, Songdo is home to two American university satellite campuses, two international schools, a hospital, a convention center and a cultural and performing arts center. Measured on a per capita basis, this is an impressive level of community services and amenities.

Source: Kim and Choi 2018.

Figure 14.1   Songdo City locator map

Each of Songdo's three districts has its own identity (Songdo IBD 2021a). The northern district features a series of high-rise residential towers arrayed around the K-12 Chadwick International School, with shops at its southern edge. The southern district, also a mostly residential district, faces westward toward Songdo Lake Park. The central district runs diagonally along Incheon Tower Blvd, and when completed, will be dominated by high-rise office buildings and ground floor retail uses. Songdo's convention center as well as its tallest building, the Northeast Asia Trade Tower, are located at the eastern end of Central Park. To ensure that the maximum amount of land is reserved for greenspace, all parking is underground except for along Songdo's retail-fronted streets. With regards to sustainability, Songdo currently has over 20 million square feet of LEED-certified space—"the highest concentration of LEED-certified projects in the world," according to the official Songdo website—and 40 percent of all such space in South Korea (Songdo IBD 2021b). When fully occupied, according to its designers, Songdo IBD will emit 70 percent fewer greenhouse gases than a similarly-sized conventional project. Songdo's smart city initiatives are run by the public–private Incheon Smart City Corporation (ISCC), which hosts a unified data platform and operating system for Songdo's transportation, public safety, disaster prevention, environmental management, and business development services.

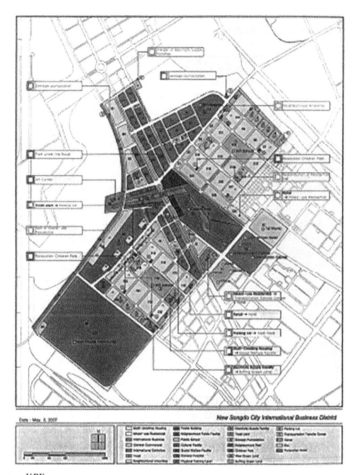

Source: KPF.

Figure 14.2   Songdo amended DUP land use map

The performance of Songdo's commercial real estate market has also fallen short of expectations. Songdo has so far managed to attract a number of high-visibility NGO office tenants, including the Green Climate Fund, the World Bank Korea, the Global Green Growth Institute, and the UN Office for Sustainable Development,[2] but collectively, these organizations do not lease very much office space. With most US technology companies having elected to keep their Korean headquarters in Seoul, Songdo's office rental rates are about one-third those of Seoul's. According to the Korean Real Estate Board, office vacancy rates in the Incheon/Songdo market in 2019 were in the range or 35 to 40 percent, more than three times the level in Seoul.[3] Part of the problem is Songdo's poor transit access: getting from Songdo to Incheon International

Airport by subway takes an average of 80 minutes, twice as long as it takes to get from the Airport to Seoul.

AN AMBITIOUS PLAN TAKES SHAPE

The idea of reclaiming the sea around Songdo Island off Korea's west coast to create an entirely new city—hence the origin of the name Songdo City—was first suggested in 1962 by Woojin Mulsan, a Korean construction company that proposed to undertake the project entirely on its own (Shin 2016). The idea knocked around in different forms without result until April 1988, when, on a visit to Incheon by South Korean President Roh Tae-Woo, city officials raised it anew, this time proposing to reclaim 48 km^2 around Songdo Island to build an international trade and information technology business hub (Shin 2016). President Roh listened with interest. South Korea's economy was still expanding at a world-leading 10 percent annual rate,[4] but most of the country's economic and population growth was concentrated in and around Seoul. Between 1968 and 1988 Seoul's population had swelled from 4.4 to 10 million,[5] and with a greenbelt that limited its physical expansion, Seoul had become choked by traffic congestion and expensive.[6] Singapore and Hong Kong, South Korea's two regional rivals, were each building or enlarging international airports with passenger capacities that would dwarf Seoul's Gimpo Airport. More worrisome still, after decades of stagnation, China's economy was now growing at the same rate as South Korea's and would soon surpass it in size. Based on the success of its Shenzhen Special Economic Zone, China was getting ready to designate another special economic zone in Shanghai, and if that happened, foreign investment that would otherwise flow to Seoul might be diverted to Shanghai instead (Segel 2006, p. 6). In the eyes of government planners, the best way to maintain South Korea's economic leadership was to promote the construction of a series of new high-technology and business hubs linked to Seoul by highway and high-speed rail service. With this decentralized growth model in mind, South Korea's government announced in 1990 that it would build a giant new airport of its own on reclaimed land between Yeongjong and Youngyu islands just off the Incheon coast (Yun 2015).

With the new Incheon airport sure to generate economic spinoffs, Incheon officials revised their Songdo Island land reclamation plan to accommodate a new city of 300,000 residents with a built-from-scratch trade and technology hub at its center. Approvals were gained from the Ministry of Construction, and land reclamation activities around Songdo Island began in September 1994 (Kim and Choi 2018). Bolstering Incheon's growth hopes, Korean officials announced that they would consider designating Incheon as a potential Free Economic Zone (FEZ), which would provide business tenants of the new city with sizeable tax breaks. In December 1997, Incheon announced that it had signed a memorandum of understanding with a consortium of 17 private companies to build a 3.5 km^2 "knowledge information industrial complex" to accommodate global IT firms and create a Korean version of California's Silicon Valley (Shin 2016). To finance the project, Incheon officials announced they would increase the size of the new Songdo business district to 6.8 km² and begin leasing or selling land parcels to prospective developers.

Incheon's financing model may or may not have been sound, but its timing was terrible. The arrival of the Asian Financial Crisis in July 1997 sent Korean financial and real estate markets into a tailspin and mooted Incheon's piece-meal development plans for Songdo. Instead, city officials decided to develop Songdo as a public–private megaproject and began searching for a capable private developer with which to partner. The outline of the deal would be roughly as follows: Incheon would provide the necessary land at a subsidized price and pay to build a metro connection and other transportation infra-structure linking Songdo to the new airport; the Korean government would designate the area around Songdo and pay for half of any new infrastructure improvements; and the yet-to-be-identified private developer would create the project master plan, supervise development and marketing activities, and secure all the necessary equity and debt financing (Kim and Choi 2018).

Although not uncommon in the United States, this type of real estate deal would have been unthinkable in South Korea just a few years earlier. Korea was a proud and relatively insular country, and its Alien Land Acquisition Act had long prohib-ited foreign companies from owning Korean real estate. In a nod to International Monetary Fund pressure to open up its economy in the aftermath of the Asian Financial Crisis, the Korean government amended the Alien Land Act to enable foreign investors and developers to buy and own land. The New Songdo City deal would be the first to take advantage of those changes (Kim and Choi 2018).

In terms of finding a developer, Incheon and South Korean officials were especially keen on securing the involvement of an American company. A US-based developer, they reasoned, was more likely to have the mixed-use development and public–private partnership experience they were looking for, as well as have ready access to Wall Street investors and lenders. In the interim and so as not to lose momentum, Incheon city officials hired POSCO E&C, the development subsidiary of the Korean Steel giant POSCO to serve as Songdo's temporary developer (Segel 2006, p. 4). With no American connections of their own, POSCO E&C hired Jay Kim, a semiretired Korean-American real estate developer to help them find a US partner. Kim in turn reached out to John B. Hynes, III, the President of Gale International, based in New York City. Hynes, along with his boss Stan Gale, had recently completed One Lincoln Street in Boston, one of the biggest financing deals in America in recent years, and both men were looking for fresh development opportunities. Intrigued by the possibility of creating an entirely new city from scratch, Gale and Hynes flew to Korea in early 2001 to take a look at the project site. As Hynes later recalled:

> We spent three days poking around trying to understand the dynamics and potential of the deal. We saw that the central government, the city government, and POSCO

were serious about the project. So it was really a government-sponsored initiative more than anything else, and it was only going to work as an international business center if it could attract corporate interests and provide them with some comfort that they were truly dealing with a non-Korean authority (Segel 2006, p. 5)

Convinced that the Korean government would backstop the project financially if need be, Hynes returned to Korea in early July 2001 on behalf of Gale International to sign a memorandum of understanding with POSCO E&C to develop what was now being called New Songdo City. The partnership, named New Songdo City Development LLC (NSCD) was set up as a 70/30 joint venture with Gale International having the controlling interest. Gale would serve as the project developer and POSCO E&C would be the construction manager (Segel 2006, p. 4). In return, POSCO would earn an additional 3 percent contractors fee and would be solely responsible for all completion guarantees (Lee and Oh 2008). Later the same month, the new NSCD partnership signed a formal Land Supply Agreement (LSA) with Incheon. The LSA identified the roles and responsibilities of the public sector and private developer and set forth a projected land supply and price schedule and a preliminary site development program. In return for Incheon agreeing to sell NSCD the 1,500-acre Songdo site at a reduced price, and lobbying the Korean government to designate Songdo as a Free Economy Zone, Gale and POSCO committed to securing US technology companies as tenants and to raising US$12.7 billion of investor equity and debt to fund all development activities (Lee and Oh 2008, p. 17). The full cost of developing New Songdo City was projected to be US$18.4 billion (KRW 24.4 trillion), 98 percent of which would be raised by NSCD. For their parts, Incheon and the Korean government agreed to provide $8 billion worth of transportation and infrastructure improvements.

In announcing the LSA, Incheon Mayor Ki-Sun Choi remarked,

> We believe that New Songdo Intelligent City will elevate the republic of Korea as a leader of world trade and business ... We are very pleased to have developed what we see as an innovative private–sector partnership with the first-ever US–Korean real estate joint venture of this kind. Together, government and the private sector hand in hand, we will make history and build one of the finest urban centers in the world. (*Site Selection Magazine* 2002)

Although Gale and the NSCD were technically in charge, the Incheon and Korean governments would both continue to have major roles. There was still the matter of getting FEZ designation, which was essential if potential corporate tenants were to take advantage of any promised tax breaks. There was also the matter of who would approve the final development plans. Until the FEZ was established, that role would fall to the Municipality of Incheon. After the FEZ was created, the role of land use regulator would transition to it. There was also the open question of how much NSCD would be paid for any public facilities it built.

Much has been made of New Songdo City as an example of how Asian governments like South Korea operate as "developmental states." That is, of their efforts to nurture human capital, discipline the work force, subordinate social policies, and secure land and investment capital on behalf of private economic interests (Woo-Cummings 1999; Shin et al. 2015). This was true to some extent in the New Songdo City case, but the bigger story was of Incheon's desire to promote its own prestige and wealth, and of its efforts to secure and work with an American real estate developer for that purpose.

DESIGNING A NEW CITY FROM SCRATCH

To help NSCD develop a land use program and master plan, Gale hired Kohn Pederson Fox (KPF), the New York City-based architecture firm best known in Asia for its supertall office projects in China and Hong Kong. NSCD would need KPF's high-rise expertise: with the South Korean government talking about Songdo as a future "eco-city" and stipulating that as much as possible of the city's land area should be reserved for parks and open space, physically accommodating Songdo's planned 65,000 residents was going to be a challenge.

An even more difficult challenge would be getting Songdo's land use mix and phasing just right. In the US, commercial real estate projects such as office buildings typically occupy the top rung of the real estate prestige ladder. This is less the case in Korea, where, because office buildings are typically owned by the companies that occupy them, speculative office projects such as those planned for Songdo are regarded by many Korean real estate investors as less attractive than for-sale residential projects. The lack of speculative office market also means that reliable real estate market data is more difficult to obtain in South Korea, especially outside of Seoul. Another difference between US and Korean real estate markets is that US investors and lenders are comfortable underwriting projects based on their anticipated cash flows. This is not the case in South Korea, where commercial real estate loans are underwritten based on the value of the underlying land and typically require a supplemental letter of credit from the general contractor, which in the case of Songdo, would have to be provided by POSCO E&C.

With these considerations in mind, Gale and Hynes started by projecting the 15-year revenue potential of Songdo's for-sale housing market (Segel 2006, p. 8). This enabled them to determine how much land they should acquire at any one time, how much they would be willing to pay for that land and how much revenue would be available from home sales to fund the office and retail portions of the project.

For Hynes, whose prior experience was mostly limited to commercial real estate and whose job it was to work with KPF to develop the New Songdo City master plan, this required a new way of thinking about the connections between different land uses. Instead of inserting a single building into an existing urban context, as Hynes and Gale had done with One Lincoln Street in Boston, New Songdo City would involve creating an entirely new urban fabric, one that would have to appeal to its prospective residents as much as to its commercial tenants. This would require paying more attention to residential amenities such as parks, waterways, pedestrian walkways, and neighborhood shopping opportunities—features Hynes would refer to as "quality of life" improvements—than either Gale or the Korean government had done previously (Segel 2006, p. 5).

After several months of studying urban mixed-use communities around the world, KPF designers identified two organizing principles for the new city (Gale International and KPF 2008). The first was that New Songdo City would be organized into a series of mixed-use districts arranged around a central park, which would serve as the city's hub. Second, in an effort to create a unique identity, each district's mix of land uses, densities, and building configurations would be different, an approach the planners at KPF referred to as "planned heterogeneity." This was very different from the typical Korean new town model which featured homogeneous residential blocks arrayed around a central retail core.

The central park hub/heterogeneous district scheme had both advantages and disadvantages. On the advantage side, it would enable NSCD to charge homebuyers higher prices since they would be getting additional residential amenities and a unique neighborhood design. On the disadvantage side, building all those amenities up front would be extremely expensive, and breaking the project up into distinct districts or neighborhoods would entail a more complicated and lengthy project review process.

After a year of research and design work, KPF unveiled its New Songdo City Masterplan in mid-2002. The plan featured a 100-acre central park at its core named after Central Park in New York City, a man-made creek that flowed from the park to Songdo's waterfront lake, and a wide boulevard that bisected the city diagonally. The two residential districts, one to the north of Central Park and the other to its south, would each include a mixture of high-rise towers and mid-rise apartment blocks and be centered on elite neighborhood schools. A third district primarily devoted to residential and high-rise office towers would front Songdo Lake. The streets separating the districts would be lined with retail shops. Street parking would be allowed on the retail streets, but elsewhere all parking would be underground. Not having to provide surface parking meant that additional land would be available for parks and open spaces which, counting Central Park, a new community park in the north, and a new golf course in the south, would account for an impressive 40 percent of Songdo's total land area (Gale International and KPF 2008). Looking to add global expertise to Songdo's brand, Gale turned to the Harvard Advisory Group to design an international curriculum for Songdo's new schools, to Philadelphia International Medicine to design and administer its new hospital, and to the Jack Nicklaus Company to design its new 18-hole golf course. A new cultural center adjacent to Central Park would include a fine arts museum, a world-class aquarium, and a performing arts center modeled on the Sydney Opera House (Segel 2006, p. 7).

Source: KPF.

Figure 14.3   *3D eastward view rendering of KPF's Songdo master plan*

KPF's New Songdo City Masterplan was conditionally approved by Incheon city officials in November 2002. Ten months later, in August 2003, New Songdo City was formally designated by the South Korean government as part of the Incheon Free Economy Zone, which would henceforth handle all development approvals (Kim and Choi 2018). To better differentiate their 1,500-acre project site from the 13,170 acre New Songdo City also approved as part of the IFEZ, NSCD formally changed the name of their project from New Songdo City to Songdo International Business District, or Songdo IBD.

The KPF Masterplan was understood by all to be as much an aspirational document as a strict blueprint. The more important document was the District Unit Plan or DUP, which, like a zoning map in the US, set out parcel-level land uses and densities (Segel 2006, p. 8). IFEZ officials approved an initial Songdo DUP in October 2003 but it was based on the lower residential densities that predated the KPF Masterplan. Up-zoning the site to allow for denser and thus more profitable residential development would require that IFEZ regulators approve a follow-on DUP amendment. NSCD filed for the DUP amendment in June of 2004 and was given assurances that it would be quickly approved. These assurances proved premature. As it turned out, IFEZ had inherited a lawsuit filed by the environmental group Birds Korea challenging the entire Songdo project over its lack of an environmental impact analysis of potential bird habitat losses. It would take until early 2005 to resolve the lawsuit to allow the project to go ahead. Preliminary approval of the DUP amendment was finally granted in June 2005, enabling construction to begin on Songdo IBD's initial residential towers, with final approval following five months later (Lee and Oh 2008, p. 25). The journey had taken longer than expected due to IFEZ official's inexperience, but going forward, things looked bright.

A FINANCING PLAN WITH NO ROOM FOR ERROR

For NSCD, purchasing the entire 1500-acre New Songdo IBD site from IFEZ, even at a discount, would have been prohibitively expensive. Instead, Gale planned to acquire the site as a series of five separate land parcels, appropriately numbered I through V (Segel 2006, p. 9; Lee and Oh 2008, p. 22). This would enable NSCD to use the revenues from Parcel I residential presales as collateral for a loan to buy Parcel II, and so on. By combining presale revenue with borrowing, Gale figured he would have just enough working capital to begin building the signature office towers that would provide Songdo IBD with its international identity. The key to successfully executing this strategy would be to match residential completions and sales with land purchases. If Gale let his land acquisition and predevelopment costs get too far ahead of residential sales, his financing gap and interest costs would balloon upward. If he erred in the other direction and was too slow in acquiring land, he would run the risk of missing the market. There was also pressure from the Korean government, which wanted NSCD to begin office construction as soon as possible.

NSCD purchased the 94-acre Parcel I from IFEZ in October 2003 for $60 million (Segel 2006, p. 9). To help raise the financing he needed, Gale turned to Morgan Stanley, with whom he had worked on the One Lincoln Square deal in Boston. Notwithstanding the Korean government's preference for a US investor or lender, Gale's initial $50 million round of financing came mostly from two Korean banks, Woori Bank and the state-run Industrial Bank of Korea. A second tranche of first-round financing totaling $40 million was provided by a multi-investor consortium that included Morgan Stanley, ABM Amaro, and the Bank of Nova Scotia (Segel 2006, p. 9). All told, NSCD's first round of financing came to $90 million, enough to buy Parcel I and still leave $30 million for working capital.

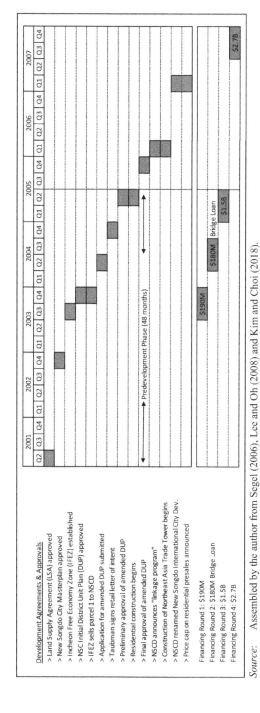

Source: Assembled by the author from Segel (2006), Lee and Oh (2008) and Kim and Choi (2018).

Figure 14.4   Songdo development and financing timeline

While Gale arranged Songdo IBD's financing, Hynes looked for prospective commercial tenants, ultimately reaching out to more than 2,000 companies (Segel 2006, p. 5). Many were aware of Gale's Songdo plans, but most wanted to wait until construction was underway before signing a lease or letter of intent. Hynes persistence finally paid off in November 2004, when the Michigan-based real estate investment trust, Taubman Shopping Centers, agreed to a deal to form a joint venture with Morgan Stanley and Gale giving Taubman exclusive rights to develop Songdo's retail facilities (Lee and Oh 2008, p. 22). Other blue-chip tenants would prove harder to find. Cisco Systems, the computer networking company whose preliminary interest in Songdo in 2001 had helped get the project going, remained a notable holdout.

With approval of the DUP amendment taking longer than anticipated and his initial $90 million loan package coming due, Gale was forced to take out a $180 bridge loan from Woori Bank, ABN Amaro, and Morgan Stanley to tide NSCD over. Worryingly for NSCD's cash flow situation, this new loan carried an interest rate of 9 percent (Segel 2006, p. 9).

By spring 2005, the $180 million bridge loan had been fully drawn down and NSCD was starting to run out of cash. Fortunately, IFEZ's approval of the Parcel I DUP amendment was forthcoming in May 2005, enabling NSCD to finally begin construction. With the amended DUP approval in hand, Gale and Hynes immediately began pursuing a bigger loan with a lower interest rate to replace the $180 million bridge loan (Lee and Oh 2008, p. 25). They soon found themselves subject to competing pressures. The Korean government strongly preferred that Gale find US lenders who would fund the construction of new office and commercial projects. When no American banks were willing to do so, Gale went back to Woori Bank and ABN Amaro, and added a $1.5 billion loan from Kookmin Bank (another Korean Bank) at a 7.4 percent interest rate to be underwritten based on residential sales and retail leasing revenues. Any new office construction would have to wait until tenants could be found.

With this new $1.5 billion loan secure, NSCD was able to negotiate firm purchase prices for Parcels II through IV and an option on Parcel V, effectively bringing all of Songdo IBD under its control (Lee and Oh 2008, p. 26). Although no residential units would be delivered before early 2006, NSCD anticipated generating $500 million in income from residential presales during the final six months of 2005. When this amount was added to the $1.37 billion in anticipated revenues for 2006, and with subsequent revenues projected to grow at a modest 2 to 3 percent per year through 2015, NSCD anticipated that it would be able to fully fund additional infrastructure and buildings valued at $13.2 billion. In a best-case scenario, this would allow NCSD to take on additional debt in the amount of $2.1 billion in 2007 or 2008 (Lee and Oh 2008, p. 29). The two loans, one for $1.5 billion and the other for $2.1 billion, would be paid back between 2007 and 2012, leaving NSCD with an accrued profit of $1.8 billion when construction was fully completed in 2015 or 2016.

Unfortunately for all concerned, this best case scenario never came to pass. With office development continuing to lag, NSCD in early 2006 introduced a new development "linkage program," which granted residential development rights to individual investors willing to help fund new commercial projects; previously, only NSCD had actual development rights (Kim and Choi 2018, p. 47). When the first linkage program partnership proved successful, NSCD followed it up with seven more. This did not go down well with either IFEZ or POSCO E&C. IFEZ did not regard linkage funding as constituting foreign direct investment, which was what Gale had been brought on board to attract. For its part, POSCO E&C was unhappy about the prospect of having to share construction fee contracts with other developers. To reassure his two partners, Gale announced that he would work with Morgan Stanley Real Estate to fund $350 million in new foreign investment to serve as the financial foundation for an additional $3 billion in financing to jumpstart construction of the 300-meter Northeast Asia Trade Tower (NEATT). Designed by KPF as Songdo's signature building, the 68-story mixed-use NEATT center would be the fourth tallest building in Korea and the tallest building outside of Seoul. Construction began in 2006 and wouldn't be completed until 2011.

As in the game of Whac-a-Mole, just as NSCD would find a way to solve one problem, another would pop up. In January 2007, amid concerns over a potential housing price bubble, the Korean government announced that it would be enacting a cap on residential presale prices (Kim and Choi 2018, p. 47). Previously, developers and construction companies could freely set presale prices based on their costs and what the market would bear. With the new regulation, the government capped presale prices based on a cost index keyed to nationwide land prices and construction costs. This adversely affected Songdo in two ways. First, because it was located on compacted land fill and boasted better quality construction, its construction costs were much higher than was typical for other parts of Korea. Second, because NSCD was so dependent on presales for revenue, capping presale prices meant a sharp drop in prospective cash flows. The combined effect of these changes was to limit how much NSCD could finance based on its residential build-out schedule. Adding to Songdo's problems, IFEZ had fallen several years behind building the highway and transit links needed to connect Songdo to Seoul and other parts of the greater Incheon region (Kim and Choi 2018, p. 48). Without preferred access, the higher residential prices and commercial rents NSCD was asking for made little sense.

In November 2007, in what was the largest real estate financing deal in Korean history, NSCD—newly renamed as New Songdo International City Development (NSICD)—concluded a $2.7 billion financing agreement with

Source: H.G. Esch.

*Figure 14.5   Looking eastward over Songdo Central Park toward the
                  Northeast Asia Trade Tower, the fourth tallest building in Korea*

Korea's second largest bank, Shinhan Bank, and a consortium of twelve
other Korean lenders. The additional funding was used to purchase two of the
remaining three land parcels, to begin construction of additional commercial
projects, and to consolidate and repay prior loans. The year 2007 also marked
the first year NSICD generated cash flow from completed residential projects
(Kim and Choi 2018, p. 47).

   The arrival of the Global Financial Crisis (as the Great Recession was
known in Asia) in Korea in October 2008 upended all of Gale's finely-tuned
financial plans. New home sales collapsed and many who had pre-bought
homes demanded their money back. NSICD's lenders announced their willingness to forego loan repayments until the crisis eased but, starting in 2010,
began aggressively demanding that Gale restructure the project's financing.
Everyone, it seemed, was stuck. NSICD cash flows had slowed to a trickle.
With construction at a standstill, POSCO E&C wasn't making any money in
fees. Given the times, even if Gale's lenders had foreclosed, it was unclear

they would be able to find a developer to finish Songdo. In return for guaranteeing a larger share of the outstanding Shinhan Bank loan and extending its maturity date from 2014 to 2016, Gale granted POSCO E&C exclusive construction rights for all of Songdo's remaining residential buildings (Kim and Choi 2018, p. 47). On the equity side, Gale and POSCO E&C were forced to give 50 percent of any future profits back to Incheon. In blessing the deal, the Korean government agreed to allow NSICD to continue building homes ahead of unwanted office space. Beyond these barest of details, neither NSICD nor their lenders nor any government agency was required to publicly disclose the details of the restructuring. Frustrated over Gale's rapidly diminishing role in developing Songdo, John Hynes stepped down as Gale International's CEO in 2010. In 2011, the Korean government announced that it was revising its FEZ-enabling laws to enable it to cancel the development rights of any private partner it deemed had failed to perform in the required time frame (Kim and Choi 2018, p. 48).

With POSCO having guaranteed most of Songdo's financing and the residential market still slow to recover, tensions rose between Gale and POSCO. In September 2018, with no Songdo completion schedule in sight, POSCO unilaterally ended the NSCID partnership and sold Gale's majority share to two Hong Kong companies. Gale responded in March 2019 by filing a breach of contract lawsuit against POSCO in a US District Court in New York City, alleging the POSCO had overcharged the partnership more than $300 million in construction costs and improperly seized and sold Gale's stake in the project (*Wall Street Journal* 2019). In June 2019, Gale filed a $2 billion lawsuit against the government of South Korea with the International Centre for Settlement of Investment Disputes, alleging that South Korea had expropriated a substantial portion of Gale's investment. As of September 2020, both of Gale's legal actions were still pending. Meanwhile, construction activities in Songdo continue, with final completion now expected for some time in the mid-to-late 2020s.

REBRANDING MEETS MARKET REALITY

As first conceived in the 1990s, Songdo was to be a free-trade technology hub whose combination of corporate tax incentives, proximity to the new Incheon International Airport, low office rents, and built-from-scratch efficiency would make it appealing to global technology companies eager to escape Seoul's high rents and unrelenting traffic congestion (Kim and Choi 2018, p. 45). When Gale International and KPF entered the picture in 2001, they quickly realized that the global companies most likely to be interested in Songdo were less concerned about airport proximity and office rents than about providing a high-quality living environment for their workers and reinforcing their reputation for being on the environmental cutting edge (Segel 2006, p. 5). This led KPF to reorient Songdo's design away from economic efficiency and toward environmental and worker amenities. The amount of parkland and greenspace was increased, vehicle parking was banished underground, block dimensions were reduced to improve pedestrian circulation, leading US educational and medical institutions were recruited to run Songdo's schools and hospitals, and buildings were designed from the ground up to conserve energy and water (Gale International and KPF 2008). Songdo's brand as a green or eco-city would become especially noteworthy after the 2008 election of President Lee Myung-bak. Having served as Seoul's mayor and championed replacing the Cheonggyecheon Expressway with a reclaimed urban stream, Lee was eager to demonstrate Korea's credentials as a global environmental leader.

Gale and KPF's green city design and branding efforts proved moderately successful in catering to the residential market. Right from the start, Songdo appealed to creative class workers and their families, partly because of its high level of environmental and community amenities and partly because its apartments and condominiums were much more affordable than Seoul's. Songdo's green design and features were also hit with environmental NGOs, several of whom—including the Green Climate Fund, the Global Green Growth Institute, and the UN Office for Sustainable Development—chose to locate their Asian headquarters in Songdo.

Global technology and financial companies proved to be a much harder sell. Korea's post-1997 efforts to open itself up to foreign investors and companies notwithstanding, the Korean economy continued to be dominated by domestic conglomerates such as Samsung, Hyundai Motor, SK, and LG (Park and Yuhn 2012). For US technology companies and financial institutions hoping to expand into the Korean market, being near the center of political and economic power in Seoul was far more important than Songdo's low office rents and energy-efficient buildings. With so many prime building sites awaiting development and with so few daytime workers crowding its streets, the overall impression Songdo gave to visitors was one of emptiness. Business journalists regularly traveled to Songdo expecting to report on Asia's most forward-looking city only to find the city half-built and empty (Bloomberg City Lab 2018).

If Songdo were to regain its initial buzz, it would need to bolster its global image. One path forward was capitalize on the growing global interest in using digital technologies to improve and personalize urban services (Kuecker and Hartley 2020). This was an area where Songdo already had a head start, having long billed itself as Asia's leading "smart city." Thousands of miles of high-bandwidth fiber optic cable already lay beneath Songdo's streets, and internet use by Songdo residents and businesses was among the world's highest. As far back as the 1990s, Korea's government had identified investing in information and communication technologies as a priority for maintaining the country's productivity growth. The policy initiative that emerged from the government's deliberations was known as "ubiquitous city" or "U-city".[7] After an early government program funding cities to undertake local U-city initiatives ended in disappointment, the Korean government enacted the Construction of Ubiquitous City Act of 2008, which provided funding to Korean cities to form smart cities partnerships with domestic and global technology leaders (Shwayri 2013).

IFEZ got out of the U-city gate earlier than other Korean cities, having formed a partnership with US networking giant Cisco Systems in 2007 to design and implement its own U-city system (Incheon Smart City Corporation 2021). Cisco itself had little experience creating smart city systems, but its early interest in Songdo and its reputation as a global technology leader made it an attractive partner. In 2011, the IFEZ–Cisco partnership received $275 million from the Korean government to implement a U-city system in Songdo, Yeongjong and Cheongna, with most of the money earmarked for Songdo. A year later, IFEZ and Cisco formed the Incheon Smart City Corporation (ISCC) to develop internet-based tools that would integrate data and decision-making across Songdo's transportation, public safety, disaster prevention, and environmental agencies. Cisco expanded its own research and development efforts and in 2013 opened up one of its nine Global Innovation Centers in Songdo. While the ISCC U-city initiative added to Songdo's reputation as global technology leader, in terms of attracting corporate office tenants, its benefits have been modest. More recently, Songdo's top-down and hardware-based approach to smart cities has been criticized as being out of step with a digital ecosystem increasingly dominated by open-source software, cloud-computing, real-time benchmarking, and smartphone applications (Carvalho 2015; Glasmeier and Christopherson 2015).

LESSONS AND TAKEAWAYS

The story of Songdo is much like the tale of Rashomon; depending on the perspective of the teller, it can signify something altogether different. To urban designers and environmental planners, Songdo's significance lies in its granular mixed-use morphology, pedestrian orientation, and clever operationalization of green city planning principles. To urban planners, Songdo's significance lies in it careful balancing of land uses, multiple mobility options, and high level of residential amenities. To economic geographers, Songdo's importance stems from how it serves as a physical manifestation of Korea's national economic development policies. To technologists and urban futurists, Songdo is emblematic of how advanced information and communication technologies can make urban services more efficient and responsive. And to Korean government officials, Songdo represents the success of their post-Asian Financial Crisis efforts to open up the economy to global investors and businesses.

The reality of Songdo is more mundane and disappointing. Conceived as a master-planned city of the future to be developed by a public–private partnership between an experienced developer and a forward-looking government agency, Songdo wound up falling into every trap in the book of bad development case studies. Songdo's many failures as a large-scale development projects include:

- The initiating public agency, the City of Incheon, lacked a clear set of objectives and development program.
- The search for a US development partner was ad hoc and didn't account for Gale International's lack of experience developing mixed-use and master-planned projects.
- There was no initial market study of the demand for Songdo commercial space. Instead, the four project partners (Gale International, POSCO E&C, the Incheon Free Economy Zone, and the Korean government) all chose to believe their own marketing hype.
- To the degree there was any financial underwriting, it was based entirely on inflated estimates of the underlying land value and the presumed creditworthiness of the developers.
- The contributions and responsibilities of the different development partners were never laid out in a concrete and contingent fashion.
- The Incheon government and IFEZ underestimated the importance to potential business tenants of a high-quality rail connection between Songdo and Seoul, and to the Incheon International Airport.
- Korean government agencies had no understanding of how speculative real estate development projects are financed. The development partnership of Gale International and POSCO E&C failed to carry out proper market and financial risk analysis.
- There was no robust phasing or contingency plan that connected market absorption and pricing to subsequent construction.

To be fair, these failings are hardly unique to Songdo. To one degree or another they characterize most large-scale urban development initiatives that bring together inexperienced local governments and developers who believe their projects are somehow exempt from having to do a proper market study or financial risk analysis. Other recent examples of very large-scale, cutting-edge new town development projects that have failed in a similar manner include Masdar in Abu Dhabi, Lavasa in India, Ordos in China, and Santander in Spain.[8]

Notwithstanding its failures as a development enterprise, Songdo has acquitted itself quite well in its design and planning. KPF's original Songdo Masterplan was well-researched, thoughtful, and broke new ground in terms of how it mixed land uses and building types, incorporated residential and pedestrian amenities into every element of its fabric, and was engineered from the bottom-up to reduce energy and water use. Had it been informed by a credible market study and phasing plan, it is quite possible that the original Songdo Masterplan could have been implemented as designed. Other aspects of the Songdo planning and design process that have drawn favorable reviews are the ways in which sensor technologies were incorporated into public facilities, the de-emphasis of the automobile at the street level, and the careful programming of recreation areas.[9] Gale's original structuring of the sequence of land parcel takedowns was also notable, if overly optimistic.

What lessons does Songdo offer as a real estate development or public–private megaproject? The first and most obvious is that projects of the size and complexity of Songdo should not be developed as single-deal projects or via a single partnership. The greater-than-anticipated time it always takes to finish real estate megaprojects and the market uncertainties that are sure to arise within that time are simply too great for one developer or one development partnership to bear. Had Songdo been developed as a smaller series of projects and through a series of partnerships, its inherent risks would have been easier to manage. Second, the infrastructure planning and construction scale economies that characterize large real estate megaprojects rarely translate into cost savings: the tendency to want to build every piece of infrastructure to the highest possible (and most costly) standard is just too great. Third, government agencies should not get involved as financial partners in large-scale commercial real estate deals unless they are willing to guarantee project occupancy or wait out the real estate cycle. Office and retail markets are by their nature competitive and ever-changing, so building a lot of office or retail space at any one time is a necessarily risky endeavor. To the degree that government agencies wish to promote office or retail development, they should only do so by subsidizing the underlying land cost, paying for supportive infrastructure, or providing favorable bridge financing. Finally, to the extent that real estate megaprojects are developed as public–private partnership deals, they should be subject to rigorous risk and contingency analysis to evaluate how the project and the partnership is likely to perform under different market and financial scenarios.

NOTES

1.   https://www.kpf.com/projects/new-songdo-city.
2.   http://songdo.com/work/ (retrieved December 21, 2020).

3. Korean Real Estate Board R-One Real Estate Statistics Viewer (https://www.reb .or.kr/r-one/statistics/statistics).
4. https://data.worldbank.org/indicator/NY.GDP.MKTP.KD.ZG.
5. https://www.macrotrends.net/cities/21758/seoul/population.
6. South Korea House Prices Growth, 1987 – 2021 | CEIC Data.
7. The term ubiquitous refers to the idea that digital technologies make it possible to deliver urban services to anyone, anywhere, and at any time (Shin 2009).
8. https://tomorrow.city/a/smart-cities-that-failed-along-the-way/.
9. AIA Architect. July 25, 2008 (https://info.aia.org/aiarchitect/thisweek08/0725/ 0725d_songdo.htm).

REFERENCES

Unless otherwise indicated, website materials were retrieved in December 2021.

Bloomberg City Lab. 2018. Sleepy in Songdo, Korea's smartest city. June 22, 2018.

Carvalho, L. 2015. Smart cities from scratch? A socio-technical perspective. *Cambridge Journal of Regions, Economy and Society*, 8(1), 43–60.

Gale International and KPF. 2008. *New Songdo Green City*.

Glasmeier, A., and Christopherson, S. 2015. Thinking about smart cities. *Cambridge Journal of Regions, Economy and Society*, 8(1), 3–12.

Incheon Smart City Corporation. 2021. ISCC Website: "History." https://www .incheonsmartcity.com/default/mp4/mp4_sub2.php (retrieved December 21, 2021).

Kim, Y. J., and Choi, M. J. 2018. Contracting-out public-private partnerships in mega-scale developments: The case of New Songdo City in Korea. *Cities*, 72, 43–50.

Kuecker, G. D., and Hartley, K. 2020. How smart cities became the urban norm: Power and knowledge in New Songdo City. *Annals of the American Association of Geographers*, 110(2), 516–524.

Lee, J., and Oh, J. 2008. New Songdo City and the value of flexibility: A case study of implementation and analysis of a mega-scale project. Unpublished Master's thesis.

Park, S. R., and Yuhn, K. H. 2012. Has the Korean chaebol model succeeded? *Journal of Economic Studies*, 39(2), 260–274.

Rugkhapan, N. T., and Murray, M. J. 2019. Songdo IBD (International Business District): Experimental prototype for the city of tomorrow? *International Planning Studies*, 24(3-4), 272–292.

Segel, A. 2006. *New Songdo City: A Harvard Business School Case Study*. Harvard University.

Shin, D. H. 2009. Ubiquitous city: Urban technologies, urban infrastructure and urban informatics. *Journal of Information Science*, 35(5), 515–526.

Shin, H. B. 2016. Envisioned by the state: Entrepreneurial urbanism and the making of Songdo City, South Korea. In A. Datta and Abdul S. (eds), *Mega-Urbanization in the Global South* (pp. 95–112). Routledge.

Shin, H., Park, S. H., and Soon, J. W. 2015. The emergence of a multiscalar growth regime and scalar tension: The politics of urban development in Songdo New City, South Korea. *Environment and Planning C: Government and Policy*, 33(6), 1618–1638.

Shwayri, S. 2013. A model Korean ubiquitous eco-city? The politics of making Songdo. *Journal of Urban Technology*, 20(1), 39–55.

Site Selection Magazine. 2002. "Gale Co. Tapped as JV Partner in $12.5B Korean 'Intelligent City'." April 15, 2002.

Songdo IBD. 2021a. Songdo IBD Website: "Masterplan." http://songdo.com/about/#masterplan (retrieved December 21, 2021).

Songdo IBD. 2021b. Songdo IBD Website: "Green." http://songdo.com/about/green (retrieved December 21, 2021).

Wall Street Journal. 2019. "Developer feuds with Korean partner over busted 'smart' city." June 11, 2019.

Woo-Cummings, M. (ed.). 2019. *The Developmental State.* Cornell University Press.

Yun, J. 2015. A new city prototype? Songdo International City as an airport city. *Journal of Asian Architecture and Building Engineering*, 14(3), 549–556.

15. Who is in charge here? Brooklyn Bridge Park

John D. Landis

ABBREVIATIONS USED IN THIS CHAPTER

BBPC   Brooklyn Bridge Park Corporation—the non-profit organization established in 2002 to plan, maintain, and operate Brooklyn Bridge Park

BBPDC   Brooklyn Bridge Park Development Corporation—the public agency established in 2002 charged with development planning and financing for Brooklyn Bridge Park.

ESDC   Empire State Development Corporation—the state-level parent organization of the Brooklyn Bridge Park Development Corporation

HR&A   Hamilton, Rabinowitz & Alschuler—the consultant hired to advise the BBPDC on financial matters.

LDC   Brooklyn Waterfront Local Development Corporation—the non-profit organization established in 1998 to undertake initial planning and design activities for Brooklyn Bridge Park.

With a final bill expected to be in the neighborhood of $350 to $375 million,[1] New York City's Brooklyn Bridge Park is too small to be included on most megaproject lists. There are however considerations beyond cost that recommend its inclusion in this volume. Foremost among them is size: at 85 acres, Brooklyn Bridge Park (BBP) is one of the largest parks to be constructed in the midst of a major US city since World War II (Table 15.1). Brooklyn Bridge Park is also a pre-eminent example of how an obsolete industrial waterfront can be repurposed as a regional amenity supporting the resurgence of nearby residential neighborhoods. Brooklyn Bridge Park is also notable for how it is being financed. A substantial share of BBP's construction and operating expenditures are and will be derived from on-site land sales for development (i.e., "development in the park") as well as from supplementary tax assessments. This type of mechanism is commonly used to finance urban development and transportation projects but, until the 1980s, was rarely used to finance public parks.

Lastly, as we shall see, BBP offers a powerful and cautionary tale of the problems that ensue when multiple governmental and community stakeholders fail to get on the same page around a megaproject's purpose or program. Since its inception as a public park in 1988, it has taken more than 30 years to get to a point where BBP's completion is in sight. To the degree that Brooklyn Bridge Park may be considered as a megaproject failure, it is not for the usual reasons of over-promised benefits, under-estimated costs, or a poorly specified program (Flyvbjerg 2014). Rather, it is because Brooklyn Bridge Park was conceived and implemented within a contentious public decision-making process that provided too many openings for stakeholders to put their individual agendas above the common goal of delivering a broadly beneficial project in a timely way. To the extent that Brooklyn Bridge Park might someday be regarded as a megaproject success, it will be because its underlying program and design are sufficiently flexible to allow future generations to enjoy using the park in a manner that works best for them. To understand how Brooklyn Bridge Park can be both a megaproject success and a megaproject failure requires telling the Park's convoluted story in greater detail. To help do so, we are fortunate to be able to rely on two carefully documented Brooklyn Bridge Park histories, Nancy Webster and David Shirley's *A History of Brooklyn Bridge Park*, published in 2018; and Joanne Witty and David Krogius' 2016 volume, *Brooklyn Bridge Park – A Dying Waterfront Transformed.*

Brooklyn Bridge Park occupies an 85-acre dogleg-shaped site along the Brooklyn waterfront between the Manhattan Bridge and Atlantic Avenue. Befitting its name, BBP houses the base of the eastern tower of the Brooklyn Bridge, which is located at the crook in BBP's dog-leg shape. The park lies immediately to the west of and below Brooklyn Heights, one of New York City's oldest and wealthiest residential neighborhoods. Brooklyn Heights is also New York City's oldest historic district, having gained that designation in 1965. South of the Brooklyn Bridge, the Park consists mainly of six former shipping piers that are today used for recreational and cultural purposes. North of the Brooklyn Bridge, the park includes a series of three small embankment areas hosting recreation and meeting facilities. The piers and embankment areas are connected to each other (as well as to BBP's north and south entrances) by a meandering series of pedestrian pathways. The park also includes six private development sites, the largest of which are: One Brooklyn Bridge Park, a historic warehouse converted to condominium use in 2008; Pier 1, a mixed-use project located adjacent to the park's northern-most pier that includes a 200-room hotel and 100 residential units; and Empire Stores, a complex of late 19th century shipping warehouses converted into a retail–restaurant–office project. The Park's three smaller development sites are all designated for residential development.

Table 15.1   *Brooklyn Bridge Park in brief*

Description	The $300 million Brooklyn Bridge Park occupies an 85-acre site along the Brooklyn waterfront. The main (southern) part of the Park consists of six former shipping piers converted to a variety of recreational and cultural purposes. The Park also encompasses six private development sites which generate rental revenues used to cover ongoing Park operations and programming costs.
Lead sponsor(s)	Brooklyn Bridge Park Development Corporation (BBPDC), New York City Mayor's Office, Brooklyn Borough President's Office.
Primary rationale	Having moved its cargo operations to New Jersey in 1983, the Port Authority of New York and New Jersey sought to sell its Brooklyn docklands to a private developer. In response, Brooklyn preservationists organized to preserve the site as a public park. The argument over how much of the park should be used for recreation versus development continued for nearly 15 years, finally culminating in the 2002 creation of the Brooklyn Bridge Park Development Corporation.
Primary funding sources	State and city grants and loans.
Regulatory/funding approval given In	1997 (preliminary); 2005 (final)
Construction started	2008
Construction completed in	2017 (construction was delayed by a series of development-related lawsuits and by the need to update the park master plan in the aftermath of Superstorm Sandy in 2012).
Cumulative investment	$350 million–$375 million (projected)
Principal takeaways	Brooklyn Bridge Park offers several cautionary takeaways about how not to structure a very large-scale public preservation and development process; the most important one being the need to prevent junior stakeholders from exercising veto power over the actions of senior stakeholders.

TECHNOLOGICAL CHANGE UNDERMINES A ONCE-THRIVING PORT

For most of the 19th century, the Brooklyn waterfront served as New York City's primary cargo port (Brooklyn Bridge Park Corporation 2021b). Prior to 1800, Brooklyn was mostly a farming area providing daily and weekly foodstuffs to Manhattan, located just across the East River. Robert Fulton's introduction of a steam-powered ferry service between lower Manhattan and Brooklyn's Fulton Street (located at the present-day base of the Brooklyn Bridge) quickly led to Brooklyn's rapid growth as the nation's first commuter suburb—albeit one served by boats instead of trains. The waterfront ferry service was joined in the 1820s by an increasing volume of cargo ships carrying industrial and consumer goods (including grains, whiskey, coffee, molasses, sugar, leather goods, and coal) up and down the US east coast as well as across the Atlantic to England and Europe. As the number of arriving and departing ships grew in size and capacity, Brooklyn's waterfront filled with newly-built warehouses. Like other fast-growing American industries during the 1890s and 1890s, New York City's maritime businesses were largely unregulated, and thus prone to periods of over- and under-investment. This boom-bust dynamic enabled larger businesses to buy up smaller ones, and by the early 20th century, most of Brooklyn's waterfront piers and warehouses were owned by a single maritime conglomerate, the New York Dock Company. When it was completed in 1928, the New York Dock Company's ten-story, million-square foot warehouse at the base of Furman Street was the largest in the world. While all this was happening along Brooklyn's waterfront, New York City was opening up the rest of Brooklyn to residential and commercial development, completing the Brooklyn Bridge in 1883 and the Manhattan Bridge in 1912.

Source: Shorpy.com.

Figure 15.1   Brooklyn waterfront finger piers looking east to Manhattan circa 1900

Brooklyn's industrial waterfront was able to hold its own amidst two world wars and the Great Depression, but the arrival of the expressway in the 1940s and shipping containerization in the 1960s heralded its gradual decline. When first released in 1943, New York City master builder Robert Moses' plan for a circumferential expressway along the Brooklyn and Queens waterfront cut through the heart of Brooklyn Heights, leaving Brooklyn's piers and warehouses largely unaffected. Moses' plan did not go down well with Brooklyn Height's politically-connected residents, who forced him to opt for a more-expensive cantilevered structure built into the side of the bluff separating Brooklyn Heights from the Brooklyn waterfront. (The top of the structure supports the Brooklyn Heights promenade, made famous in Woody Allen movies for its views of lower Manhattan).[2](It is the top of that structure that supports the Brooklyn Heights Promenade, made famous in movies by Woody Allen and others). When finally completed in 1954, the Brooklyn–Queens Expressway isolated the Brooklyn waterfront from the rest of the borough.

The second shoe, containerization, dropped 15 years later (Stiles 2012). Using the construction of the Brooklyn–Queens Expressway as a wartime pretext to expand its domain, the Port Authority of New York and New Jersey acquired most of Brooklyn's waterfront piers from the New York Dock Company in the early 1940s. As it looked ahead to converting its operations from break-bulk service to containerization in the early 1960s, the Port Authority was initially inclined to divide its new container facilities between Brooklyn in New York City and Bayonne in New Jersey. The pier designs for the two locations differed, however. In Brooklyn, the Port Authority replaced most of the old and narrow "finger" piers that jutted out into the East River with wider finger piers. In New Jersey, the Port Authority built in-line facilities. With each year bringing a new generation of longer and wider containerships, Brooklyn's finger piers lost competitive ground to Bayonne's in-line piers, leading the Port Authority to transfer ever more of its container operations from Brooklyn to Bayonne; and in 1983, the Port Authority finally shut down all of its Brooklyn shipping facilities.

With no potential uses of its own for Brooklyn's waterfront piers and warehouses, the Port Authority began actively planning to sell them. Recognizing that such a move would be politically fraught in a union town like New York City, the Port Authority reached out to city officials in 1984 about co-sponsoring a working group to discuss the waterfront's future (Webster and Shirley 2018). Simultaneously, the Port Authority contacted the nearby Brooklyn Heights Association to solicit their input. With memories still fresh of how the Port Authority had opposed the 1965 creation of the Brooklyn Heights Historic District, the Association was disinclined to support the Port Authority's sale-to-the-highest bidder strategy, and instead proposed its own reuse set of priorities. These included safeguarding the world-famous views from the Brooklyn Promenade, mixing park and recreation activities for the benefit of Brooklyn area residents, promoting still-feasible maritime uses, and minimizing the sorts of high-rise development that could endanger the still-fragile historic district. For its part, the Port Authority was not opposed to using parts of the waterfront for public purposes, but it was also counting on potential commercial development to raise the market value of its remaining waterfront assets. This view, which was embodied in a 1985 Port Authority consultant report recommending that the piers be intensively redeveloped, was greeted angrily by the Brooklyn Heights Association (Halcyon 1985).

PLANS AND MORE PLANS

Hoping to identify common ground between itself and the Port Authority, the Brooklyn Heights Association's leadership hired its own consultant to come up with what it termed a consensus plan. That document, titled "The Future of the Piers," was presented to the public in February 1987. It made no specific reuse recommendations but instead put forth a common set of six redevelopment goals as well as four illustrative reuse schemes (Webster and Shirley 2018 p. 46). Scheme A emphasized continued or enhanced maritime uses. Scheme B proposed converting the entire site to a public park. Scheme C suggested combining a new public park, a new marina, and a hotel and conference center. Scheme D was similar to Scheme C but also included a substantial amount of new residential development. Perhaps predictably, the Brooklyn Heights Association's membership coalesced around the public park alternative put forth as Scheme B, while the Port Authority and the City announced their support for some version of Scheme C or Scheme D. Anxious to be rid of the contentious pier site and believing no agreement to be possible, the Port Authority announced that it would sell the piers to a qualified developer with or without an approved plan (Webster and Shirley 2018, p. 48). This effort was soon stymied by Community Board 2— before land use proposals are approved by New York's City Planning Commission, they must be OKed by local community boards—which unanimously endorsed the Association's pure park alternative (Webster and Shirley 2018, pp. 54–63). There was just one problem: the Association had no funds with which to implement their plan.

Amidst all this conflict, a consensus was slowly emerging that the piers should be used for a public park and that the park should be financially self-supporting. Realizing that the only way a deal could be done was with a push from the top, a coalition of community groups calling itself the Brooklyn Bridge Park Coalition lobbied New York Governor Mario Cuomo to get involved (Webster and Shirley 2018, p.77). Cuomo, who had started his political career mediating land use conflicts in Queens two decades earlier, convinced the Port Authority to abandon its threatened pier sales plan, and co-sponsor (along with New York State and New York City, and with the participation of the Coalition) yet another planning study to be conducted by the eminent urban design firm of Carr, Lynch, Hack & Sandell. When completed, the results of the new study ended up pleasing no one. It concluded that the piers could indeed be physically developed as a park, but that to make the park financially self-sustaining would require significant new commercial and residential development (Webster and Shirley 2018, p. 79).

Meanwhile, another prominent stakeholder, Brooklyn Borough President Howard Golden, had convened yet another series of community meetings, which, under the guise of being even more comprehensive, enlarged the waterfront planning area to include the area between the Brooklyn Bridge and the Manhattan Bridge (Webster and Shirley 2018, p. 82). Although Golden's working group did not succeed in producing a comprehensive plan, it did reach agreement on what came to be known as the *13 Guiding Principles*, which would continue to govern future waterfront planning and development decisions (Webster and Shirley 2018, pp. 90–92) (Table 15.2). The first principle was that all subsequent planning efforts should be undertaken by a single entity whose only interest would be to design, build, and maintain whatever public park design finally emerged. Trying to get so many disparate parties to agree on a planning process *and* a planning scheme *and* a financing plan was just going to be too difficult. Second of the principles was that whatever scheme finally emerged would have to be "fiscally prudent," which was taken to mean financially self-supporting.

Table 15.2   Brooklyn Bridge Park timeline

1986	The Port Authority (PA) of New York and New Jersey announces its intention to sell the recently closed Brooklyn Piers 1–5 to commercial developers.
1987	The Brooklyn Heights Association (BHA) announces its opposition to the PA's plans and suggests the piers be used as a public park.
1988	Community Board 2 rejects the PA's disposition plan and endorses the BHA's park plan. The Brooklyn Bridge Park Coalition forms to promote the park plan.
1992	The "13 Guiding Principles" for the park are adopted by local elected officials and park advocates.
1997	Local elected officials come together to create the Downtown Brooklyn Waterfront Local Development Corporation (LDC) to develop a practical park plan.
2000	The LDC publishes its initial master plan for Brooklyn Bridge Park with an estimated cost of $150 million. The City of New York commits $65 million to the plan.
2001	The State of New York agrees to fund the remaining $85 million needed to implement the plan.
2002	New York Governor Pataki and Mayor Bloomberg agree to form the Brooklyn Bridge Park Development Corporation (BBPDC) to build the park in accordance with the LDC's master plan.
2003	Landscape architect Michael van Valkenburg is chosen to design the park.
2004	Wendy Leventer becomes president of the BBPDC. Pier 6 is added to the park.
2005	The general project plan and final environmental impact statement are formally approved.
2007	Regina Myer replaces Wendy Leventer as BBPDC president.
2008	Phase 1 park construction activities begin.
2010	The City of New York takes effective control of park planning and construction from the state.
2011	A new study of park financing confirms that housing remains the best source of operating revenues for the park.
2012	Superstorm Sandy strikes the New York City region and the new park facilities perform well.
2014	Amidst continuing disagreements over housingvalign:middle;align:left;, Mayor Bill DeBlasio provides an additional $40 million for the park, but requires that Pier 6 include an affordable housing component.

START, STOP, REPEAT

With New York State, New York City and the Port Authority all struggling under the fiscal weight of the 1991–1992 national recession, no one had serious money with which to get anything started. Finally, on the morning of November 5, 1994, New York State Governor Mario Cuomo, New York City Mayor Rudolf Giuliani, and Brooklyn Borough President Howard Golden all gathered at the Brooklyn anchorage of the Brooklyn Bridge to announce that a local task force under the direction of New York State's Urban Development Corporation (UDC) would be formed to take over planning redevelopment activities for what would become Brooklyn Bridge Park in a manner consistent with the *13 Guiding Principles* (Webster and Shirley 2018, p. 100). Progress was in sight, or so it seemed. Three days later, on November 8, 1994, Cuomo was defeated at the polls by Republican gubernatorial candidate George Pataki.

The new governor was not particularly interested in anything having to do with Brooklyn, so when in 1995, Brooklyn state representative and Assembly Ways and Means Committee member Eileen Dugan earmarked $1 million to support ongoing Brooklyn Bridge Park planning efforts, Pataki's office registered no objection (Webster and Shirley 2018, p. 102). Dugan would pass away from breast cancer a year later, but not before getting her fellow Brooklynite, Senate Minority Leader Martin Connor to take up the Brooklyn Bridge park cause as his own. Although they were in different political parties, Connor and Pataki were friends, so when Connor approached the governor in 1997 about establishing an autonomous local development corporation to consolidate Brooklyn Bridge park planning, financing, and development efforts, Pataki was receptive to the idea. It would take another year to work out all the details, but on March 19, 1998, a certificate of incorporation was filed in the state capital, Albany, establishing the Brooklyn Waterfront Local Development Corporation. The LDC, as it was known, would have a 15-member board of directors, six of whom were to be appointed by elected officials. Seven more were to be chosen by local community groups (including the Brooklyn Heights Association), and the remaining two served as representatives of the local community board and Chamber of Commerce (Webster and Shirley 2018, p. 105).

Despite having political support from both sides of the aisle in Albany and a strong community base, the LDC's success was by no means assured. To ensure the LDC did not waste its time, it sought a formal agreement with the Port Authority promising not to undermine its work (Webster and Shirley 2018, p. 127). A beneficial side effect of all the intervening delays was that there were by now so few remaining maritime businesses in Brooklyn that reusing the piers for maritime uses was effectively off the table. These pressures were further reduced when the Port Authority signed an agreement with the dockworkers union guarantee that their members would have work at other PA facilities.

To develop a master plan for the proposed park, the LDC turned to a team headed by Urban Strategies, a Toronto-based planning and design firm headed by Ken Greenberg, whose previous work had included waterfronts in Toronto, Detroit, Hartford, and Charleston. Along with Greenberg, the Urban Strategies team included noted landscape architect Michael van Valkenburg, who had recently stepped down as chair of Harvard's Landscape Architecture Department to head up his own design firm (Webster and Shirley 2018, p. 129).

After digesting all they had heard at the initial sessions, the Urban Strategies team identified a set of 23 "Core Design Principles" that any final park design would have to adhere to. These included requiring that a "green spine" would extend the length of the park, that the park be organized into distinct districts, and that the park be accessible laterally from the Brooklyn Promenade as well as from surface streets at its north and south entrances. For the most part, the planning process progressed amiably, leading the Port Authority to agree not to entertain any offers for the piers from developers until the LDC's planning process had concluded (Webster and Shirley 2018, p. 139). To keep the LDC's planning process going, the state's Environmental Protection Fund provided it with an additional $500,000 of funding.

Released in 2000, the draft master plan (aka Illustrative Master Plan) reserved 85 percent of the site for open space and 15 percent for recreational and public-use structures. A rebuilt Pier 1 would include a mix of restaurants and recreational facilities such as basketball courts and swimming pools. Pier 2 was to be devoted entirely to open space. Pier 3 would include an earthen amphitheater and fountain. Pier 4 was to be reduced in size and reserved for fishing, and a new indoor recreation center (along with parking) would be built on Pier 5. Graphically, the Illustrative Master Plan, was presented at a large scale and in fairly rough form (Webster and Shirley 2018, p. 138). This was done to forestall debate over specific design details and facility programming. Included in the master plan was an initial cost estimate of what it would take to develop Brooklyn Bridge Park: $150 million (Webster and Shirley 2018, p. 153). Based on this estimate, the team's financial consultant, HR&A, calculated that the completed park could eventually leverage another $400 million in private investment in surrounding neighborhoods.

Where would the $150 million come from? And who would oversee its disbursement? Most participants in the planning process had assumed that the park would eventually be built and operated by the ESDC, a state agency with the statutory power to override local zoning requirements as well as capture increases in neighboring property values. The only problem with this arrangement was that the ESDC was a development and financing agency, not a park manager, and had no experience running a facility as complex and multifaceted as the proposed Brooklyn Bridge Park. With this in mind, LDC and HR&A planners came around to the idea of creating a politically independent non-profit entity which would manage park operations as well as raise additional private funds for park activities.[3]

As to specific funding sources, Brooklyn Borough President Howard Golden started things off with a $14 million commitment from his budget. Hoping to succeed the termed out Golden as borough president, City Councilman Ken Fisher persuaded New York City Mayor Rudolf Giuliani to one-up Golden by contributing another $36 million from the City's budget. Giuliani, who, like Golden, was termed out, was trying to embellish his legacy by funding projects throughout New York City, even in heavily Democratic Brooklyn. With $50 million in New York City funding in hand, Democratic minority leader Martin Conner and LDC President Joanne Witty met with Governor Pataki seeking

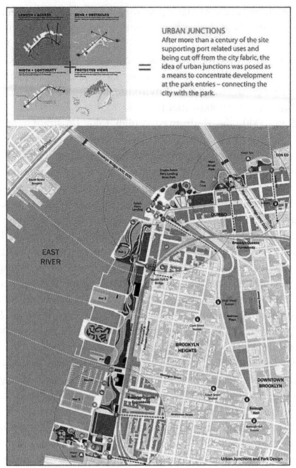

Source:　　Michael van Valkenburgh and Associates.

Figure 15.2　　Brooklyn Bridge Park Illustrative Master Plan

the balance from the state. Their pitch was simple. If the state did not contribute, the new Brooklyn Bridge Park would forever be associated with Pataki's fellow Republican and political rival, Rudy Giuliani. On January 5, 2001, Pataki issued a press release announcing that the Port Authority, an agency he co-headed with New Jersey Governor Christine Todd Whitman, would be contributing $85 million to help build Brooklyn Bridge Park (Webster and Shirley 2018, p. 142). The Port Authority was also prepared to transfer ownership of its Brooklyn piers to the LDC or whatever entity was designated to develop the park. With a credible master plan and sufficient funding now in place, the

LDC scheduled a ground-breaking ceremony for Phase I of the proposed park for July 21, 2001. It had taken 13 years to line up all the players and pieces, but the future of Brooklyn Bridge Park at last seemed assured.

WHO'S IN CHARGE HERE?

Further progress on the park slowed following the 9/11 terrorist attacks and the destruction of twin towers as city and state funds that had been earmarked for the park were reallocated toward rebuilding the World Trade Center site. Having previously agreed that the LDC could serve as the park's developer, Governor Pataki changed his mind and indicated that he now preferred to give the job to the ESDC.

Adding to the uncertainty, New York City had a new mayor, businessman and political novice Michael Bloomberg. Soon after taking office, Bloomberg appointed investment banker Dan Doctoroff as his Deputy Mayor for Economic Development. Only casually acquainted with the proposed Brooklyn Bridge Park, Doctoroff initially saw it as part of a citywide waterfront renewal process. Fortunately, Doctoroff, like his boss, believed in hiring the best person for the job regardless of their political background, and to deal with waterfront planning issues, he hired Joshua Sirefman, who had previously worked on the proposed Brooklyn Bridge Park as part of the HR&A financing team. Sirefman soon joined with LDC President Joanne Witty and Charles Fox, who worked for Governor Pataki on energy, transportation, and environmental issues, to see if they could get the Brooklyn Bridge Park project back on track (Webster and Shirley 2018, p. 146).

To deal with the question of which agency should act as park developer, Sirefman and Fox drafted a memorandum of understanding creating yet another new entity, the Brooklyn Bridge Park Development Corporation (BBPDC) as an official subsidiary of the ESDC to do the job. Importantly, the memorandum also stipulated that no less than 80 percent of the park would remain as open space into perpetuity and thus be precluded from development (Webster and Shirley 2018, p. 147). It also designated the LDC's Illustrative Master Plan as the official document guiding the new agency's efforts. LDC members Joanne Witty, John Watts, and David Offensend were appointed to the new organization's 11-person board. The establishment of the BBPDC was officially announced at a ceremony at Pier 1 on May 2, 2022 attended by both Governor Pataki and Mayor Bloomberg. To advise the BBPDC on community issues, a Citizens Advisory Council was created at the end of 2002. Lastly, HR&A was hired in an expanded role and given the job of integrating the physical design, construction, and financing aspects of an updated Illustrative Master Plan. All of these actions, it was assumed, would hasten BBP's eventual completion.

But instead of speeding up, things slowed down. To get the park through New York City's development approval process, the Illustrative Master Plan would first have to be converted into a land use proposal, or, as it is known in New York City, into a general project plan (Webster and Shirley 2018, p. 151). Only after the project plan was submitted and approved could the ESDC officially change the pier area's zoning from its current industrial designation to park status. Preparing the project plan would require hiring a new design team, which would require a new solicitation process. And despite Michael van Valkenburgh's previous work on the Illustrative Master Plan, the selection of his firm to undertake the project plan was hardly a foregone conclusion. Many teams vied for the job, but in the end Van Valkenburgh's was selected, owing primarily to their knowledge of the site and understanding of what the community wanted.

Concurrently with the Van Valkenburgh team's work on an updated plan, the ESDC and BBDC were required by state law to undertake a detailed environmental impact review (EIR) of the park proposal. This requirement had an "after you Alphonse" quality about it that ended up slowing everything down: the EIR process needed the details of the plan in order to make its findings, and the plan had to mitigate any adverse impacts uncovered in the EIR. Amidst these regulatory machinations, the Jehovah's Witnesses, announced they would be putting their one-million-square-foot warehouse building at 360 Furman Street on the market. Even though it directly abutted Pier 5, no one had thought to include the building in any of the park plans. Nevertheless, it was thought to be important enough to the park's future that some on the BBPDC's Citizen Advisory Board lobbied for the BBPDC to buy it from the Jehovah's Witnesses, a purchase that was well beyond the park's budgeted cost. In the end, the property was sold to a private developer who would later convert it into 434 condominium units.

No one, it seemed, had the big picture or was empowered to take charge. Not until Wendy Leventer replaced James Moogan as BBPDC President in March 2004 would things get firmly back on track (Witty and Krogius 2016, p. 101). Moogan, who had previously headed the New York State Parks Department, had no prior experience running an organization whose mission combined preservation with development. Leventer, by contrast, came to the BPBDC from the Times Square Redevelopment Project, another ESDC subsidiary, where she had gained valuable experience structuring public/private partnerships of the type proposed for the park.

Leventer's first challenge upon taking charge of the BBDC was to deal with the reality that the wooden pier structures and bulkheads below Piers 2, 3 and 5 were too rotted to support the uses they were now designated for. Faced with deteriorating marine structures, Leventer and her planning team decided to demolish them and replace them with a rock berm. This decision had an unexpected silver lining: it reduced the pier area Van Valkenburg had to plan for, and more importantly, reduced prospective park maintenance costs (Witty and Krogius 2016, p. 104).

In late July 2004, Leventer and her team met with the BBPDC Citizens Advisory Council to review van Valkenburgh's updated master plan and the associated cost analysis, which now included maintenance and operation cost estimates. The good news was that it looked like the cost of constructing the park was still within the $150 million construction. The bad news was that prospective maintenance and operation costs were running far ahead of budgeted amounts. With less revenue coming in from revenue-generating activities on the now shrunken area, some additional source of operations revenue would have to be found.

That source would have to be housing. Within the 20 percent of the park area that the Illustrative Master Plan had originally designated for private development, and the only land use guaranteed to generate sufficient tax revenue to pay for park operations was housing (Witty and Krogius 2016, p. 105). Just before Christmas 2004, Leventer and van Valkenburgh presented the BBPDC's nearly completed park plan to Brooklyn elected officials and community leaders. It included a pair of residential high-rise towers on Pier 6 and a third residential structure at the northern end of the park on John Street. The million-square-foot warehouse at 360 Furman Street, which had been sold by the Jehovah's Witnesses to developer Robert Levine was also designated for residential use (Witty and Krogius 2016, p. 118).

The size and intensity of the proposed residential development projects quickly captured the community's attention, and not in a good way. This was partly because until the BBPDC presented its plan, "housing" was just a general land use and not a specific set of building proposals; partly because the housing projects presented in the plan seemed out of scale with the existing waterfront; and partly because a sizeable share of the community had never really bought into the idea that the park should include any revenue-generating activities. Indeed, even though van Valkenburgh's revised plan called for just ten percent of the park to be used for non-public purposes, for many in the community that was still too much. In response to the earlier plan, an anti-housing organization calling itself the Brooklyn Bridge Park Defense Fund sued to block the plan, arguing that it was illegally locating a private purpose in a public park (Webster and Shirley 2018, p. 155).[4]

In July 2005, the BBPDC voted to adopt the general park plan and to certify the adequacy of the draft EIR, setting the stage for one last public hearing (Webster and Shirley 2018, p. 152). Not surprisingly, the debate at that public hearing centered on the housing portion of the plan. Some protesters challenged the BBPDC's park maintenance cost estimates as inflated. Others accused the BBPDC of intentionally promoting gentrification. Still others worried that the proposed residential buildings would block their views, or that the proposed high-rise building styles would gradually spillover into neighboring Brooklyn Heights, undermining its brownstone character. The single required public hearing turned into many, but having drawn the endorsement and funding support of Brooklyn Borough President Howard Golden, State Senator Martin Connor, and State Assemblywoman Joan Millman, the ESDC's rezoning approval and the BBPDC's EIR certification both held. With regulatory approvals and funding commitments now in hand, construction of the Brooklyn Bridge Park could now begin.

THE HOUSING MESS

In 1995, the changeover from Governor Mario Cuomo to Governor George Pataki had put a hold on BBP planning efforts. Now, ten years later, another gubernatorial transition, this time from Pataki to Elliott Spitzer, created a similar slowdown. For one thing, the new Spitzer Administration was slow

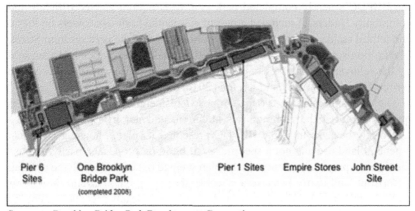

Source: Brooklyn Bridge Park Development Corporation.

Figure 15.3   Brooklyn Bridge Park major development sites

to decide who was properly in charge at the ESDC and, by extension, at the BBPDC. For another, Wendy Leventer, who as BBPDC President had gotten the park planning process back on track in 2004, was falling out of favor with the Spitzer Administration amidst friction with Brooklyn community groups over her insistence that the park accommodate housing, and in March 2007, Leventer was fired from her job. (Witty and Krogius 2016, p. 107). In March 2007, Leventer was fired from her position. Her replacement, Regina Myer, wouldn't assume her responsibilities until eight months later. Five months after that, in March 2008, Governor Spitzer was forced to resign over news that he had frequented prostitutes while New York State Attorney General Spitzer's successor was Lieutenant Governor David Paterson, who had unseated Martin Connor to become Senate Minority Leader. Having represented Manhattan throughout his political career, Paterson had little interest in Brooklyn, and was content to let the Bloomberg Administration bring BBP to completion.

Regina Myer turned out to be the right person to have taken the BBPDC's reins from Wendy Leventer. Early in her tenure, Myer made two decisions that would profoundly impact the park's development (Witty and Krogius 2016, p. 127). First, rather than wait for full funding to complete the park—by early 2008, the cost of finishing the park had risen from $150 million to $225 million—Myer chose to proceed in phases with the funds she already had in hand. Second, Myer overrode her financial consultants and suspended the process of offering development sites to potential bidders. With the New York City economy starting to suffer from the effects of the Great Recession, Myer realized that she would get higher bids from developers once the economy started to recover. To underscore the fact that Brooklyn Bridge Park was soon to be a physical reality, Myer announced a timetable for construction that anticipated opening the park's first phase in the spring of 2011.

Myer's decision to fund phased one construction without having secured funding for later phases provided an opening to those who still opposed building housing in the Park. This opposition coalesced around the candidacy of Working Families Party member Daniel Squadron for the State Senate position held by Martin Connor, who, perhaps more than any other state official, had championed Brooklyn Bridge Park. Whether out of sincere conviction or to better position himself politically, Squadron made opposing housing in BBP the centerpiece of his campaign, and in the 2008 Democratic primary, narrowly defeated Connor (Witty and Krogius 2016, p. 131). Meanwhile, with New York State's economy in worse shape than New York City's, state officials were looking to offload some of their prior financial commitments to other governmental entities. This created an opening for Deputy Mayor Robert Lieber, who had succeeded Dan Doctoroff in 2008, to suggest a deal whereby New York City would agree to take over Brooklyn Bridge Park and nearby Governor's Island Park while the state would assume financial responsibility for the Jacob Javits Convention Center (Witty and Krogius 2016, p. 132). From the state's perspective, the two park projects were likely to be financial losers, while the Javits Center was already making money. To obtain Senator Squadron's approval of the deal, Lieber agreed to reopen the question of whether and how much new housing should ultimately be built in the park.

In March of 2010, Mayor Bloomberg's office issued a press release with the headline that "Mayor Bloomberg, Governor Patterson, Senator Squadron, and Assembly Member Millman Announce an Agreement on the Development,

Funding, and Governance of Brooklyn Bridge Park." The agreement was actually two agreements, the first, a restructuring document transferring control of all Brooklyn Bridge Park properties (and all leases and subleases) from ESDC to a still-to-be-named not-for-profit corporation (Webster and Shirley 2018, p. 174). Essentially the BBPDC would disappear and the LDC would become a city controlled entity with expanded planning and implementation responsibilities. The second agreement was a memorandum of understanding between Mayor Bloomberg's office, Senator Squadron, and Assembly Member Millman promising yet another study of park financing options and the creation of a board committee known as the Committee on Alternatives to Housing, which would look again at alternatives to building housing in the park (Webster and Shirley 2018, p. 177). Lastly, the memorandum gave Senator Squadron and the Assembly Member Millman veto authority over the two housing developments planned for Pier 6 in the south and John Street in the north. Much to the eventual consternation of Senator Squadron, the new study of park financing options and housing alternatives endorsed constructing housing in the park, albeit at a slightly reduced height, as its best source of operating revenues (Witty and Krogius 2016, p. 134). Although motivated by politics rather than economics, the substitution of New York City's much stronger backing for BBP over that of ESDC (and its BBPDC subsidiary) would soon put the park on a sounder financial footing.

Meanwhile, the construction of Pier 1 under Regina Myer's careful direction continued, and on March 22, 2010, with Mayor Bloomberg, Governor Paterson, Brooklyn Borough President Martin Markowitz and other dignitaries all on hand, Pier 1 opened to the public. Bill de Blasio, the newly elected Public Advocate who in 2014 would become the City's mayor, called the Park, "New York's new front yard." Borough President Markowitz called it "Eden on the East River" (Witty and Krogius 2016, p. 138). The Pier 6 playgrounds were opened to the public three months later. It had taken 15 years and the efforts of countless community advocates and public servants, but Brooklyn Bridge Park was now a reality, and still very much consistent with the *13 Principles* put forth 20 years earlier. By the fall of 2012, roughly one-quarter of Brooklyn Bridge Park was open to the public with much more still under construction.

With the end seemingly in sight, nature intervened to create new problems. On October 29, 2012, Superstorm Sandy, the combination of a powerful Nor'easter and a slow-moving tropical storm from the south, hit New York Harbor head on, flooding low-lying areas in New Jersey, Staten Island and Queens, and flooding transit tunnels connecting Manhattan to New Jersey and Brooklyn. All six Brooklyn Bridge Park piers were inundated, but because of sound structural and hydrological engineering, none were destroyed (Webster and Shirley 2018, p. 186). Still, in the wake of Superstorm Sandy, the Mayor's office paused all city construction projects to assess how they might be made more resilient. In the case of the Empire Stores building then being renovated, it was decided that the ground floor would be dug out and that a new concrete slab would be poured. Drains and pumps would be installed, along with an aqua fence designed to make the building watertight in the eventuality of another storm. Similar reinforcements were made to other BBP projects then under or planned for construction.

Meanwhile, Pierhouse and Hotel 1, the two commercial developments at the head of Pier 1 were generating new controversy. As the steel superstructures of the two projects rose to their full heights, it became apparent that they would partially block views of the Brooklyn Bridge from the Brooklyn Heights Promenade. This was in violation of a long-standing agreement between the LDC and the Brooklyn Heights Association and Brooklyn Bridge Park Coalition. The violation was inadvertent rather than intentional: over the course of so many agency and personnel changes, the provisions limiting the two projects' height had failed to make it into ESDC's agreements with the project developers. This explanation did not appease yet another new community group, Save the View Now, which filed suit in April 2015 seeking an injunction to limit the height of the two new buildings. The lawsuit was heard by New York State Administrative Judge Lawrence Knipel, the same judge who seven years earlier had rejected a different community group's arguments against the BBPDC's planned housing projects. Judge Knipel issued a temporary restraining order halting construction on the Pierhouse project, but then, after hearing fuller arguments, allowed the project to proceed (Witty and Krogius 2016, p. 160).

Even with construction still underway, Brooklyn Bridge Park was proving to be a hit with the public, drawing 120,000 visitors on a typical summer weekend, and 25,000 on an average summer day.[5] In 2014, the BBP's Conservancy announced that attendance at its historical and cultural programs had reached 160,000. It had taken more than 25 years to get to the point where the end of Brooklyn Bridge Park's construction period was in sight, but with Mayor Bloomberg finishing up his third term and getting ready to hand things off to a new administration, BBP's future looked secure .

Bloomberg's successor, Bill DeBlasio, supported the park's completion, but with a caveat: 30 percent of the housing units planned for the still-unbuilt residential project at Pier 6 should be "workforce housing," meaning that they would be reserved for households making between $67,100 and $138,440.[6] This new stipulation was just the fuel long-time opponents of housing in the park needed to make their case once again, and this time they were joined by residents of One Brooklyn Bridge Park, the condominium reuse project at the foot of Pier 6 completed in 2008 (Witty and Krogius 2016, p. 180). Even though the prospect of additional residential development had been disclosed in their initial sales agreements, residents cited their lack of involvement in the

Figure 15.4   Brooklyn Bridge Park aerial view looking north

park planning process and concerns that additional residents would overwhelm local services as the basis of their opposition. Characterizing opponents of his affordable housing requirement as NIMBYs, Mayor DeBlasio refused to back down. Fed by social media, new opposition groups quickly formed. Lawsuits contesting the project were filed, leading, as is often the situation when no side is able to prevail, for additional studies. Could the park continue to fund its operations if the height of the proposed building were reduced, or if the required share of affordable units was lowered? No one could say for sure, leading all sides to dig in their heels. Project opponents appealed to New York Governor Andrew Cuomo to intervene on their behalf—Cuomo was known to be at odds with DeBlasio—but the Governor wisely demurred. With the park now mostly completed, there was nothing for him to gain. After two years of ceaseless legal conflict, cooler heads on both sides finally prevailed. The neighborhood conceded on the issue of affordable housing while Mayor DeBlasio agreed to reduce the heights of the two proposed towers from their original 33 stories to 28 stories and 15 stories. The taller building would consist of market-rate units while the shorter one would include 100 affordable rental units. Both sides could claim victory. Opponents claimed they had won the battle over building heights while DeBlasio claimed he had held firm on the number of affordable housing units. Renamed "The Landings," the two-tower project was finally completed in 2018, two years further behind schedule.[7]

Source: Brooklyn Eagle.

Figure 15.5   Photo of the controversial Landings project towers, with One Brooklyn Bridge Park in background

LESSONS AND TAKEAWAYS

Major urban parks don't easily fit into the category of infrastructure megaprojects. For one thing, the cost of developing a major urban park, even a very large one like New York City's Brooklyn Bridge Park, rarely meets the $1 billion cost threshold used to distinguish megaprojects from lesser ones. For another, parks are not usually categorized as infrastructure, but rather as public goods whose benefits are not always easily measured in purely economic terms. Indeed, at no point in the process of bringing Brooklyn Bridge Park to fruition did any major stakeholder suggest that the park be subjected to a cost-benefit analysis that would have weighed its development costs against the combined willingness-to-pay of potential park users.

These differences notwithstanding, Brooklyn Bridge Park offers a number of cautionary takeaways about how not to develop large public-purpose facilities, especially those located in densely-populated urban environments. The first and most relevant takeaway concerns the ability of junior stakeholders to exercise veto power over senior stakeholders in a politically open process, In the case of Brooklyn Bridge Park, the Brooklyn Heights Association was able to use New York City's unique community board-based project approval process to force the Port Authority early on to agree that the overwhelming majority of its Brooklyn waterfront site would be used for a public park and not, as the Port Authority intended, for economic development purposes. This was possible because Community Board No. 2 (the group with veto power over the Port Authority's plans) correctly did not regard the Port Authority as having the community's best interests at heart, and because the Port Authority did not have a coherent plan in place and took for granted its position in the governmental hierarchy. Had the Port Authority made an earlier and more substantial effort to gain the support of local community groups as well senior political players (such as New York's governor) for its development-oriented plans, it very well might have succeeded in getting them approved.

A second key takeaway concerns the importance of initial issue framing. Early on in the process, Brooklyn community groups succeeded in framing the future of Brooklyn's waterfront as an existential conflict between a public park and private development. This early framing stuck, and in subsequent years was used to beat down any and all private development projects, even when all involved conceded there was no vehicle other than private development that might pay for the park's ongoing operation. The BBP's lesson for megaproject sponsors is that early on, they must persuasively frame their projects in terms of delivering public benefits lest those projects come to be seen as primarily serving private interests.

A third key lesson concerns the importance of gaining project support across the political aisle. In the case of Brooklyn Bridge Park, every transfer of guber-natorial and mayoral power from one party to another initiated a one to two year transition period in which all approval and funding decisions were put on hold. In each case, the project ultimately got back on track, but not before losing val-uable time. Had the park's sponsors in Albany and New York City made greater attempts to reach across the aisle to secure wider geographic and bipartisan support, the numerous transition slowdowns would have been less onerous.

These institutional and political problems obscured some otherwise excel-lent planning work. The urban design, landscape architecture, and financial consultants hired by the LDC and BBPDC were all top-notch and consistently produced high-quality and imaginative work. The initial Illustrative Master Plan and later General Project Plan produced by Michael van Valkenburgh's landscape architecture team were particularly noteworthy for their sensitivity to environmental issues and local neighborhood concerns; and required sur-prisingly little modification as the project moved from the conceptual stage to final construction. Likewise, the cost estimates and financing plan produced by HR&A were both accurate and reliable. BBPDC's two presidents, Wendy

Levanter and Regina Myer managed the pre-development planning process and then later the construction process in a straightforward and responsible manner. Myer, in particular, did a thoroughly professional job dealing with two unforeseen contingencies, the Great Recession in 2008 and aftermath of Superstorm Sandy in 2012. Had the political context in which the Brooklyn Bridge Park found itself situated been more reliable and less prone to stakeholder conflicts, instead of characterizing BBP's planning and development process as problematic, we might instead be praising it as a model.

NOTES

1. In its 2009 financial plan, the Brooklyn Bridge Park Corporation listed the full development cost of Brooklyn Bridge Park at "≈$350 million." In a 2015 article entitled, "Brooklyn Bridge Park's finances are being put under the microscope five years after initial opening," the *New York Daily News* reported that estimates of the Park's cost had risen to $370 million.
2. BQE-278 website: https://www.bqe-i278.com/en/about/history (retrieved December 21, 2021).
3. HR&A would later propose something similar for the High Line in Manhattan.
4. The judge who heard the case, Justice Lawrence S. Knipel, eventually ruled against the group on the grounds that until the park plan was finally approved and funded, there was, as yet, no park in which to locate any housing.
5. *Brooklyn Daily Eagle*, December 26, 2017. (https://brooklyneagle.com/articles/ 2017/12/26/millions-and-millions-of-visitors-poured-into-brooklyn-bridge-park -this-summer/).
6. *New York Times*. "City pushes ahead on plan for towers in Brooklyn Bridge Park." May 17, 2016.
7. Curbed New York. "New looks at Brooklyn Bridge Park's Pier 6 rental, priced from $3,100/month." December 22, 2018.

REFERENCES

Unless otherwise noted, all website information was current as of December 2021.

Brooklyn Bridge Park Corporation. 2021a. "About Us" (https://www.brooklynbridgepark .org/about/) retrieved December 21, 2021.

Brooklyn Bridge Park Corporation. 2021b. "Waterfront History" (https://www .brooklynbridgepark.org/about/history) retrieved December 21, 2021.

Flyvbjerg, B. 2014. What you should know about megaprojects and why: An overview. *Project Management Journal*, 45(2), 6–19.

Halcyon, Ltd. 1985. *Development Concepts for the Brooklyn Piers*. Hartford, Connecticut: Halcyon.

Stiles, H. 2012. *A History of the City of Brooklyn*. Applewood Books.

Webster, N., and Shirley, D. 2018. *A History of Brooklyn Bridge Park*. Columbia University Press.

Witty, J., and Krogius, H. 2016. *Brooklyn Bridge Park: A Dying Waterfront Transformed*. Fordham University Press.

16. Powering the future—five clean energy megaprojects

Oscar Serpell and John D. Landis

ABBREVIATIONS USED IN THIS CHAPTER

BCS	Bath County Storage facility.
BOOT	Build–own–operate–transfer—a project delivery method in which a private concessionaire builds, owns, and operates public infrastructure, and later transfers it back to public ownership.
CSP	Concentrated solar power—a system that generates power by using mirrors or lenses to concentrate sunlight onto a receiver or energy transfer medium.
GW	Gigawatt—one billion watts of energy or 1 million kilowatts.
kW	Kilowatt—a unit of energy equivalent to 1,000 watts (a watt is 1 Joule of energy per second).
kWh	Kilowatt-hour—the amount of energy used to operate a 1,000 watt appliance for an hour.
KSPDCL	Karnataka Solar Park Development Corporation.
LCOE	Levelized cost of energy—a measure of the average net present cost of electricity generation for a generating plant over its lifetime regardless of fuel or power source.
MW	Megawatt—1 million watts of energy or one-thousand kilowatts.
MWh	Megawatt-hour—the amount of energy used to operate 1,000 kilowatt appliance for an hour
PPA	Power purchase agreement—a multi-year contract agreement between an energy producer and consumer specifying terms of delivery, payment, termination, and contingencies.
PV	Photovoltaic—also known as a photovoltaic is a non-mechanical device that converts sunlight directly into electricity.
P3	Public–private partnership—a partnership agreement between a government or government agency and a private infrastructure or service provider.
UHV-AC	Ultra-high voltage (alternating current).
UHV-DC	Ultra-high voltage (direct current).

RENEWABLES RISING

If the world's nations are to reach their goal of holding global average temperature increases to between 1.5 and 2.0°C by 2100—as agreed to in the 2016 Paris Agreement and reiterated at the 26th Conference of the Parties in

Glasgow in 2021—they will have to undertake immediate efforts to decarbonize their electricity and transportation sectors. According to a 2021 carbon reduction road map produced by the International Energy Agency, electric vehicles will have to make up more than half of global new car sales by 2030, up from just 7.2 percent in 2021.[1] By 2035, wealthy countries will have to shut down virtually all fossil-fuel power plants in favor of cleaner technologies such as wind, solar, hydropower and nuclear power. By 2040, all of the world's remaining coal plants will need to be decommissioned or retrofitted with technology to capture their carbon emissions and bury them underground.

In 2020, renewable energy sources such as wind, solar and hydropower, together with nuclear power together made up just 40 percent of global electricity production (BP 2021). Between 2000 and 2020, global electricity generation from renewable sources increased at an average annual rate of 4.6 percent (Figure 16.1).[2] This compared favorably with the 2.6 percent rate of increase for non-renewables. Even so, present trends will fall far short of meeting current decarbonization goals.

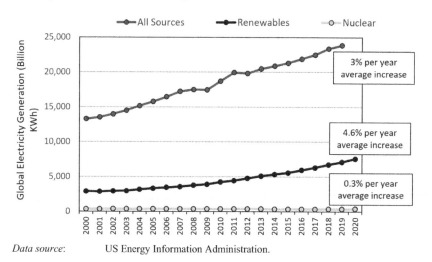

Data source: US Energy Information Administration.

Figure 16.1   *Global electricity and renewable electricity generation, 2000–2020*

These global totals mask wide variations by country. Among the world's ten most populous countries, which, combined, account for 57 percent of the world's population and 70 percent of its energy consumption, renewable energy currently accounts for an average of just 12 percent of primary energy use (Table 16.1).[3] Among countries with populations of 50 million or more, the five that currently derive the highest shares of their primary energy from renewables are Turkey (18.5 percent), Germany (17.5 percent), Italy (16.3 percent), Vietnam (15.2 percent), and the United Kingdom (14.5 percent).

Table 16.1   *2019 renewable energy generation shares in the ten biggest countries by population*

Country	Global population rank	Global population share, 2020	Share of global energy consumption, 2018 or 2019	Per capita electricity use (kWh), 2020	Share of global CO_2 emissions, 2020	Renewable energy share, 2019	Per capita renewable generation (MWh), 2019
China	1	18.2%	32.1%	5,297	30.3%	12.7%	3
India	2	17.5%	10.9%	972	6.8%	7.8%	< 1
United States	3	4.2%	17.1%	12,235	13.4%	8.7%	7
Indonesia	4	3.5%	1.1%	1,039	1.7%	6.1%	< 1
Pakistan	5	2.8%	0.4%	658	0.6%	10.6%	< 1
Brazil	6	2.7%	2.6%	2,850	1.3%	45.0%	7
Nigeria	7	2.6%	0.1%	184	0.3%	n.a.	n.a.
Bangladesh	8	2.1%	0.3%	488	0.3%	0.6%	< 1
Russia	9	1.8%	4.1%	7,026	4.7%	5.9%	1
Mexico	10	1.6%	1.1%	2,349	1.3%	7.2%	3

Data source: US Energy Information Administration.

Renewable energy generation costs have fallen precipitously relative to fossil-fuel generation costs and are expected to continue doing so. A 2020 analysis by the financial analysis firm Lazard of the levelized cost of energy (LCOE), which measures the average lifetime cost for different generating technologies, found the LCOE of solar panel facilities to have declined the most since 2010 (from $360 to $45 per megawatt-hour or MWh), followed by wind (from $140 to $48 per MWh), and natural gas (from $80 to $55 per MWh) (Figure 16.2). A different analysis of 2019 clean energy costs in Europe by Bloomberg Financial found onshore wind to have the lowest LCOE range ($58–$75 per MWh), followed by combined cycle natural gas turbines ($85–$94 per MWh), non-tracking photovoltaic arrays ($86–$104 per MWh), offshore wind ($99–$175 per MWh) and nuclear ($200–$240 per MWh).[4]

If the world is to successfully decarbonize, it will be via a path that combines large- and small-scale projects, individual and collective action, and public and private initiatives alike. Households and businesses will have to look for ways to reduce their individual energy use and produce more electricity from

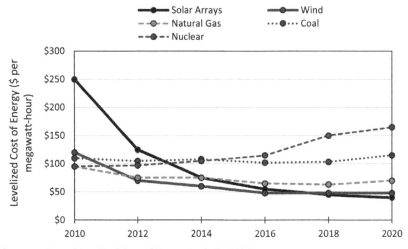

Source: Lazard Levelized Cost of Energy Analysis (2020).

*Figure 16.2   Levelized Cost of Energy trends for different sources,
2010–2020*

distributed sources, such as building-integrated photovoltaics. Governments will have an ongoing role to play in incentivizing energy conservation electric vehicle adoption. Entrepreneurs and companies will have to advance the state of energy storage and emissions mitigation technologies. The share of electricity produced from carbon neutral baseload sources such as nuclear, hydro, or clean combustion will likely have to increase. Most importantly, centralized grid-scale generation will have to shift from fossil fuels use to wind and solar.

This is certain to be expensive, requiring significant infusions of investor capital as well as government spending. How should these funds be spent? Like fossil fuel-based electricity generation technologies, wind and solar projects are characterized by project-level economies of scale. This means that it is generally less costly to produce a megawatt of power at a larger wind or solar facility than at a smaller one (a megawatt of electricity can power between 400 and 900 US homes for a year) (Figure 16.3). Unlike fossil fuel generation projects, however, the economies of scale from renewable generation are less a function of operating efficiency (since farms are generally made up of an array of identical and low maintenance modules) and more from enhanced planning, construction, and procurement.

A 2016 report by Berkeley Labs and the Department of Energy's SunShot initiative, for example, compared the cost per kilowatt-hour between small-scale rooftop residential projects and large- and very large-scale solar parks (Barbose et al. 2016). The median installed cost of a single rooftop photovoltaic installation was determined to be $4.00 per kilowatt hour (kWh). For larger commercial buildings, the cost ranged between $3.00 and $3.50, per kWh and for solar parks generating between 0.5 and 100 megawatts, it fell to between $2.20 and $3.00 per kWh. Costs were higher for solar parks larger than 100 megawatts, rising to about 3.50 per kWh.

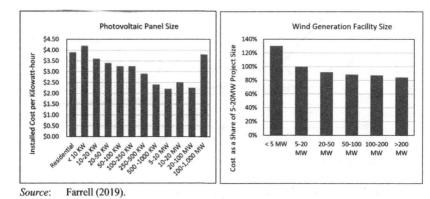

Source: Farrell (2019).

Figure 16.3   Energy cost comparisons for wind farms and solar array
facilities of different sizes

Beyond their lower operating costs, solar parks and wind farms have other advantages over fossil fuel-based power plants. Because they make use of uniform technologies, they do not have to be designed and engineered to match particular site characteristics. This reduces planning and construction times. Likewise, their modular and repeatable design means that projects can be developed incrementally to match demand or financing availability. This reduces their overall risk profile. They do not require water for cooling or access for fuel supplies and can be sited in remote locations. Other than their visual incongruities, they generate relatively few adverse environmental impacts.

Solar and wind projects also have unique disadvantages. The most notable one, of course, is that very few places in the world are always windy, and nowhere is always sunny. This means that they can't continuously generate the same output level, making them poorly suited to supply what is known as baseload capacity. Because customers pay only for the electricity they use and not for reserve or intermittent capacity, this makes solar and wind facilities more difficult to finance. The unique siting requirements of solar and wind generation capacity mean it is often located far from cities and industrial users, necessitating the construction of additional and costly transmission infrastructure. This is especially problematic for offshore windfarms and helps explain the 20 percent cost differential between building off-shore versus onshore windfarms.[5]

How big does a solar park or windfarm need to be before it qualifies as an energy megaproject, costing $1 billion or more to build? Using the US Energy Information Agency's 2018 capacity-weighted average construction cost of $1,382 per kW,[6] an onshore wind farm of 700 to 750 MW of generating capacity currently qualifies as an energy megaproject. Assuming an offshore windfarm costs 20 to 30 percent more per MW to build than an onshore windfarm, the generating capacity starting point for offshore windfarm megaprojects is in the neighborhood of 600 MW. For photovoltaic solar parks in the US, the current dividing line between a megaproject and a non-megaproject (based on the US EIA's cost estimate of $1,850 per kilowatt) is between 500 and 550 MW of generating capacity. Compared with onshore windfarm megaprojects, photovoltaic solar megaprojects are typically 30 to 40 percent larger in terms of generating capacity. Because of their much higher construction and installation costs—currently estimated by the US EIA at about $4,800 per kW—any concentrated solar power (CSP) facility larger than 200 MW in size qualifies as an energy megaproject. The largest CSP megaprojects are only about one-fifth the size of the largest photovoltaic solar parks, averaging between 150 and 280 MW in generating capacity.[7] For comparison purposes, a natural gas power plant would need to have a generating capacity of 1,000 MW or more before being considered an energy megaproject.

As Table 16.2 shows, of the world's ten largest onshore windfarm megaprojects, six are in the United States, two are in India, and one each is in China and Sweden. With the exception of the Alta Wind Energy Center in California, US, wind farm megaprojects are notably smaller than those in China or India. This reflects the fact that US-built wind farms are not subsidized to the same degree by government as wind farms built in Asia and Europe. When fully completed in the mid-2020s at a cost of $17.5 billion, the Gansu Wind Farm near the city of Jiuquan in China is projected to produce 20,000 MW of electricity, making it the world's largest windfarm by far.

Because of their higher construction and operating costs, the biggest off-shore windfarms are generally smaller in terms of generating capacity than the biggest onshore windfarms. Of the world's ten largest offshore windfarms in 2021, five are in the United Kingdom, three are in the Netherlands, one is in Denmark, and one is in Germany. This European focus reflects a number of factors, including a lack of large and sparsely-inhabited sites on which to locate large onshore wind facilities, favorable government financing policies (see below), and the fact that Orsted, the world's largest developer and owner of offshore wind facilities is headquartered in Denmark.

Table 16.2   *Ten largest onshore and offshore windfarms and solar power facilities in the world, 2019*

Facility type and name	Country	Current generating capacity (MW)	Phase I commissioning date
Onshore windfarms			
Gansu Wind Farm	China	5,160	2010
Alta Wind Energy Center (California)	United States	1,548	2010
Muppandal Wind Farm	India	1,500	1986
Markbygden Wind Farm	Sweden	1,120	2010
Jaisalmer Wind Park	India	1,064	2001
Los Vientos Wind Farm (Texas)	United States	912	2016
Shepherds Flat Wind Farm (Oregon)	United States	845	2012
Meadow Lake Wind Farm (Indiana)	United States	801	2009
Roscoe Wind Farm (Texas)	United States	782	2009
Horse Hollow Wind Energy Center (Texas)	United States	735	2005
Offshore windfarms			
Hornsea Project One	United Kingdom	1,218	2019
Borssele 1&2	The Netherlands	752	2020
Borssele 3&4	The Netherlands	732	2021
East Anglia ONE	United Kingdom	714	2020
Walney Extension	United Kingdom	659	2018
London Array	United Kingdom	630	2013
Kriegers Flak	Denmark	605	2021
Gemini Wind Farm	The Netherlands	600	2017
Beatrice	United Kingdom	588	2019
Gode Wind (phases 1+2)	Germany	582	2017
Photovoltaic solar parks			
Bhadla Solar Park	India	2,700	2018
Longyangxia Dam Solar Park	China	2,400	2015
Huanghe Hydropower Hainan Solar Park	China	2,200	2020
Pavagada Solar Park	India	2,050	2019
Benban Solar Park	Egypt	1,650	2019
Tengger Desert Solar Park	China	1,547	2016
Mohammed bin Rashid Al Maktoum Solar Park	United Arab Emirates	1,313	2020
NP Kunta	India	1,200	2021

Facility type and name	Country	Current generating capacity (MW)	Phase I commissioning date
Noor Abu Dhabi	United Arab Emirates	1,177	2019
Jinchuan Solar Park	China	1,030	2019
Concentrated solar power			
Noor-Ouarzazate Solar Power Station	Morocco	580	2018
Ivanpah Solar Power Facility	United States	392	2014
Mojave Solar Project	United States	280	2014
Solana Generating Station	United States	280	2013
Genesis Solar Energy Project	United States	280	2014
Solaben Solar Power Station	Spain	200	2012
Solar Energy Generating Systems (SEGS)	United States	160	1984–1990
Solnova Solar Power Station	Spain	150	2010
Andasol Solar Power station	Spain	150	2008–2009
Extresol Solar Power Station	Spain	150	2010–2012

Source: Assembled by the authors from Wikipedia listings, accessed December 23, 2021.

As a group, Asian and Middle Eastern countries have favored photovoltaic solar parks over windfarms. This is largely because they are located in latitudes where the sun shines for longer periods of the day and where the weather is more consistently sunny. When it comes to the world's ten largest CSP projects, five are in the US, four are in Spain, and the largest, the Noor-Ourzazate facility (profiled in this chapter) is in Morocco. Compared with photovoltaic solar parks, CSP facilities are declining in popularity. Whereas all the largest photovoltaic megaprojects entered service in 2015 or later, except for the aforementioned Noor-Ourzazate facility, all of the largest CSP projects entered service before 2015.

This chapter explores five case study energy megaprojects, including three generation projects and two supporting (transmission and storage) projects (Table 16.3). The case studies include: (i) the Walney Extension offshore wind facility in the UK; (ii) the Noor-Ouarzazate CSP facility in Morocco; (iii) the Pavagada Solar Park in India; (iv) the Bath County (Hydro) Storage facility in Virginia in the United States; and (v) China's 30,000 km of ultra-high voltage transmission lines, which are used to distribute conventionally-generated as well as renewably-generated power around the country. Each case study was carefully selected to present not just a diversity of project types, but also a diversity of financing structures, geographies, and technologies. The chapter will discuss both the specific challenges and circumstances faced by the individual projects, as well as the broader policy and planning lessons that can be learned for the future of what could, in many ways, be considered the largest megaproject of all time: the global modernization of electricity systems.

Table 16.3   Renewable energy case study projects—selected comparisons

Facility name	Walney Extension	Noor-Ouarzazate Solar Complex	Pavagada Solar Park	Bath County Storage Station	Xinjiang-Anhui UHVDC Transmission line
Facility type	Offshore wind farm	Concentrated solar power (CSP) facility	Photovoltaic (PV) solar farm	Pumped hydroelectric storage facility	Ultra high voltage transmissions line
Location	United Kingdom	Morocco	India	United States	China
Entered operation	September 2018	February 2013 (Phase I)	December 2019	1985	January 2019
Generation/ storage capacity	659 MW generation (equivalent of 600,000 homes)	580 MW generation	2050 MW generation	3,003 MW/ 24,000 MWh of storage	1,100 kV transmission
Capital cost	$1.58 billion	$2.0 billion	$2.5 billion	$1.6 billion in 1985— equivalent to more than $6 billion in 2020	$5.9 billion
Ownership form	Private	Public–private	Private ownership via competitive public auction	Private	State-financed and operated
Owner	Orsted Energy (Denmark).	Moroccan Agency for Sustainable Energy (Morocco) and ACWA Power (Saudi Arabia)	Ten companies, each owning a share (includes TATA Power, Azure Power, SoftBank Energy, and Avaada Energy)	Dominion Energy (USA) and First Energy (USA)	StateGrid (China)

Facility name	Walney Extension	Noor-Ouarzazate Solar Complex	Pavagada Solar Park	Bath County Storage Station	Xinjiang-Anhui UHVDC Transmission line
Special siting and entitlement issues			The Pavagada Solar Park required 11,000 acres of land. Instead of purchasing the site outright, the (provincial?) government offered 25–35 year leases to more than 2000 struggling farmers.	Because of the downstream impacts on Bath Creek, an environmental impact analysis (EIA) was required. This added years to the project timeline.	In China, virtually all land is owned by the government. This makes land acquisition for large projects an easier task.
Demand and market issues	To reduce market risk, the UK government guaranteed revenues of £150/MWh for the first 15 years.	Morocco is heavily dependent on imported fuel, making local solar generation an attractive choice, despite its high costs.	Tariffs were set by reverse competitive bids by private developers. The site was leased instead of purchased.	Construction stalled in 1980 because of lower than expected demand, forcing Dominion Energy to sell a 40 percent stake to another regional utility.	?
How financed?	Equity and investment grade bonds.	Build–operate–own–transfer (BOOT) agreement.	Build–operate–own–transfer (BOOT) agreement.	Financed directly by Dominion Energy instead of building a generation facility to meet peak demand.	Financed by StateGrid, a government-owned electrical utility with $380 billion in revenues in 2017.

Facility name	Walney Extension	Noor-Ouarzazate Solar Complex	Pavagada Solar Park	Bath County Storage Station	Xinjiang-Anhui UHVDC Transmission line
Financing sources	PFA and PKA, two Danish pension funds.	ACWA Power, Aries Ingenieria y Sistemas, and TSK.	Tata Power, Renew Power, Fortum Power, Avaada Power, SoftBank Power, Adani Green energy, ACME Solar, Azure Power, Rattan India, and Karnataka Renewable Energy Development Ltd.	Dominion Energy (then Virginia Electric and Power Company) and Allegheny Power (later merged with First Energy).	The Chinese government and StateGrid.
Notable advantages	Reliability and lack of environmental impact	Concentrated solar power technology offers a form of heat storage in addition to daily generation, a notable advantage over PV facilities.	PV facilities provide an inexpensive method of generating carbon neutral energy, are relatively easy to site and build, and can be scale to local demand.	Pumped hydro storage helps balance supply and demand over both daily and longer-term time frames. Although expensive to build, it offers decades of low-maintenance operation.	Higher voltage transports electricity farther and with much lower resistance losses than conventional lines.
Notable disadvantages	Capital costs are notably higher than for onshore wind farms.	Higher capital costs than for equivalent PV capacity.	PV solar power is he most intermittent of renewable energy sources in terms of daylight and cloud cover.	Like all hydroelectric power, pumped hydro storage requires specific geography and is very land and water intensive.	This was an untested technology requiring the entire Chinese electricity grid to be recalibrated.

THE WALNEY EXTENSION—BRINGING WIND POWER TO SCALE

Renewable energy systems harness the earth's naturally available energy by converting it to electricity. One of the most reliable sources of this energy is offshore wind. Because the surface of the ocean is essentially flat, this allows ocean air currents to move more quickly and freely than continental winds, thereby providing a more reliable source of wind turbine power. As a result, offshore turbines operate with less hourly, daily, and seasonal variability than terrestrial turbines. Offshore turbines are also less visually and audibly intrusive than onshore turbines, and don't affect nearby land users.

When the Walney Extension Wind Farm off Britain's west coast—located midway between Blackpool and the Isle of Man—began operating in September 2018, it was the largest offshore wind turbine array in the world. Built at a cost of £1.3 billion (US$1.58 billion), the Walney Extension wind farm delivers up to 659 MW of renewable energy to more than 600,000 United Kingdom households.[8] As its name indicates, the Walney Extension was built to augment the existing 367 MW Walney 1 and Walney 2 wind farms, both completed in the early 2010s and located immediately to its east. All three Walney wind farms are owned and operated by Orsted Energy, a multinational Danish power company that specializes in offshore and onshore wind, solar, energy storage, and bioenergy plants. With ten wind farms off the coasts of Britain and the US, and more planned, Orsted currently owns and operates more windfarm capacity than any other company in the world.

The Walney Extension was financed through the use of investment-grade bonds providing a 50 percent stake in the project. These bonds were purchased by PFA and PKA, two Danish pension funds, and broke new ground in the use of non-bank debt financing for renewable energy projects.[9] Because of its size and track record developing offshore wind facilities, Orsted was able to issue these bonds at a lower cost and with lower coupon rates than would have been possible for a smaller and less-established company, thereby enabling Orsted to undertake a larger and more ambitious project than might have otherwise been possible.

Walney's attractiveness to investors was significantly enhanced by its qualification for the UK's Contracts for Difference (CfD) program for financing offshore wind power projects (UK Department for Business, Energy and Industrial Strategy 2021). The CfD program is organized around a given strike price, such that if the wholesale price for electricity drops below the strike price any time within the 15-year contract, the British government pays the contractor the difference. If the wholesale price rises above the strike price, Orsted and the minority owners are responsible for paying the difference back to the government. This significantly lowers the risk to developers for

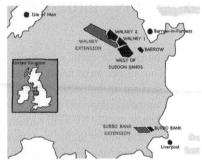

Source: Orsted Energy.

Figure 16.4   Walney Extension Wind Farm

many of the reasons discussed early in this chapter. Orsted's agreement with
the British government effectively guarantees it wholesale revenues of £150
per MWh for the first 15 years of Walney's operation, more than enough to
cover its debt. Because of changes in generation technology and up-and-down
swings in demand, electricity markets are characterized by enormous risk
and uncertainty, which in turn feed back into investment decisions and future
price levels. By offering Orsted a reliable and long-term strike price, the UK
government took on much of this risk for itself while creating an incentive for
Orsted to minimize periods of surplus generation.

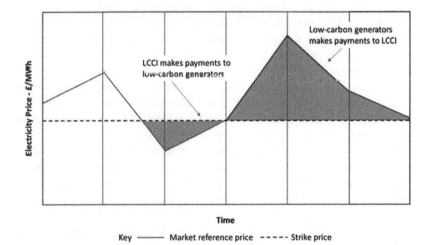

Source: www.itpenergised.com.

*Figure 16.5   How the UK's contracts-for-difference strike price
mechanism works*

Offshore wind is not without its drawbacks. Because the turbine arrays are located miles offshore, they require new undersea transmission lines which can be expensive to install, monitor, and repair. Although generally reliable, the turbines themselves are also costly to repair. Offshore turbine towers are subject to additional stresses from ocean currents and tides, requiring them to be firmly secured to the sea floor or else mounted atop weighted and anchored floating structures. Both require engineering and materials beyond those required for onshore wind. Offshore turbines must also be resistant to corrosion and operate at a higher cut-out speed, the wind speed at which the turbine blades stop spinning and producing power. It is for these reasons that offshore wind turbines use direct-drive drivetrains as opposed to the gearbox drivetrains commonly used on easier-to-repair onshore facilities. (Direct drive turbines use permanent magnets to modulate generator speeds rather than gears.) These design, engineering, and materials factors mean that offshore wind turbines have much higher capital investment requirements than equivalently-sized onshore facilities. Lastly, although wind speeds are more reliable offshore, generation and profits are still dependent on a variable energy source. In the first half of 2021, Orsted and other European offshore wind operators saw their profits slump because of unusually weak winds. Over the long run, however, operators are confident that wind speeds will remain relatively stable.[10]

The largest offshore windfarm facility in the world when it was commissioned in 2018, Walney Extension has already ceded its title to Hornsea 1, another UK–Orsted Energy project located 90 km off the British coast in the North Sea. When Hornsea 1 is joined at full operation by Hornsea 2, perhaps as soon as this year, the two turbine arrays will have a combined peak generating capacity of three gigawatts, enough to supply electricity to more than two million British homes. The increasing size and construction pace of offshore wind projects speaks to their considerable potential as an affordable and reliable source of renewable energy as well as to the benefits of having large and experienced corporate players working in that space.

CONCENTRATED SOLAR POWER IN MOROCCO

Solar power advocates are fond of pointing out that if just one percent of the Sahara Desert was covered with solar panels, it would generate enough electricity to power the entire world. This observation is intended not only to put the land requirements of solar energy into context, but also as a testament to the incredible solar power potential of the world's deserts.

With this in mind, Morocco, an energy-sparse country almost entirely dependent on imported oil and coal, has successfully capitalized on its arid, open geography by undertaking one of the largest solar power megaprojects in the world. Located in the southern Morocco desert 8 km from the city of Ourzarate, Morocco's 580 MW, $2.5 billion Noor-Ouarzazate Solar Complex[11] stands out for both its technology and innovative public–private financing strategy. Completed in phases over the course of five years, the third phase of this project became operational in 2018.

Source: European Space Agency.

Figure 16.6   Noor-Ouarzazate satellite photo showing concentrator tower and collectors

The Noor Complex is the world's largest operational solar farm to use concentrated solar power (CSP). Unlike photovoltaic solar power (PSP), which relies on panels to intercept sunlight over a broad area, CSP uses mirrors to redirect sunlight toward a single focal point where it is used to generate steam which then turns a turbine. Although CSP is less thermodynamically efficient than PSP, it has the advantage of producing heat which can be captured by a fluid medium such as molten salt, as is the case at the Noor Complex. This gives CSP the ability to keep producing power even after the sun goes down. Although CSP projects are more expensive to build and operate than PSP facilities of similar peak output, the technology is getting cheaper. With an initial capital cost of just \$4.3 million per generated megawatt, the Noor Complex is the most affordable CSP projects undertaken to date, able to produce electricity at a price of \$0.19 per kWh (or MAD 1.62/kWh). This is compared with a typical Moroccan household's electricity cost of MAD 1.172/kWh.

Perhaps more significant for future clean energy megaprojects than the Noor Complex's technology is the way in which it was financed (European Investment Bank and The World Bank 2017). The project was designed and developed and is being operated using a public–private partnership (P3) mechanism known as build–own–operate–transfer, or BOOT. BOOT agreements provide an effective means for government agencies to undertake large infrastructure projects by leveraging lower-cost private capital. In a BOOT arrangement, a government or public agency contracts with a private developer or group of private developers to design, finance, and build a project that will benefit the public at large. Once built, the private developer continues to operate the project for a predetermined length of time, earning an agreed upon rate of profit. At the conclusion of the operating contract period, which typically runs for years or even decades, ownership of the project is transferred back to the public entity that originally commissioned its construction. In addition to capitalizing on the private developer's greater access to financing capital, BOOT agreements shift planning, financing, and construction risk from government entities—which typically lack expertise in assessing and managing risk—to private entities who have the required risk management experience.

In the case of the Noor Complex, the BOOT agreement included several power-purchase agreements (PPAs) guaranteeing the project's private developer a stable and reliable revenue stream for 25 years. Should customer revenue fall below an agreed-upon annual amount, the Moroccan government agreed to make up the shortfall. The Noor Complex was initiated and is managed by the Moroccan Agency for Sustainable Energy (MASEN), a privately-owned, publicly-funded corporation founded in 2010 to help Morocco develop six gigawatts of renewable energy capacity by 2030. The private consortium that developed and operates the Noor Complex is led by ACWA Power, a power generation and desalination developer headquartered in Saudi Arabia. Other consortium partners include ARIES Ingeniería y Sistemas, a Spanish engineering company, and TSK, an energy and environmental engineering company also based in Spain. In addition to structuring the 25-year PPA agreement with ACWA Power on behalf of the Moroccan government, MASEN secured additional debt financing for the project and continues to manage it.

In the future, public–private partnership deals like the Noor Complex BOOT agreement will be especially important for small and developing countries that lack the engineering expertise and financing capacity to undertake clean energy projects required to meet their 2015 Paris Climate Accord commitments. Indeed, the fact that the Noor Complex was completed on schedule and is currently operating to its design specification when similar non-P3 CSP projects in the US have run into significant construction, financing and operating difficulties, suggests that the P3 model of financing highly technical solar energy projects may have broader applicability.

INDIA'S PAVAGADA SOLAR PARK

Few countries have adopted as ambitious a renewable energy agenda as India, which in 2016 announced that it planned to install 100 gigawatts (GW) of solar energy generation capacity by the end of 2021, and 280 GW by 2030.[12] This compares with 85 GW of installed solar capacity in the US, a country with a similar electricity demand growth profile. While it remains to be seen whether India will meet these goals on schedule, the progress it has made so far in deploying renewables is noteworthy. Between 2016 and 2019, India added 31 GW of new solar capacity to its grid on top of a prior 18 GW.[13] The country is also ramping up local photovoltaic panel manufacturing in order to cut its dependence on Chinese imports.[14] India also enjoys some of the lowest solar consumer prices anywhere in the world thanks to its relatively low installation costs and high solar potential.

Much of India's new solar capacity has been added using the "solar park" model of development in which multiple private developers bid for, develop, and operate sections (or blocks) of a much larger photovoltaic solar park. The Pavagada Photovoltaic Solar Park in the Indian state of Karnataka was completed in 2019 using this model at a cost of US$2.1 billion.[15] With an installed capacity of 2,050 MW—it is the largest renewable energy megaproject discussed in this chapter, and the second largest photovoltaic solar park in the world, behind the 2,700 MW Bhadla Solar Park in Rajasthan, also in India.

Strictly speaking, solar parks such as Pavagada and Bhadla are not single projects but are instead clusters of independently owned and operated solar farms developed by different industry players. Pavagada, for example, includes separate solar farms that were built and are owned and operated by ten separate companies including TATA Power, Azure Power, SoftBank Energy, and Avaada Energy (Institute for Energy Economics and Financial Analysis 2020). The initial right to develop and operate each farm was allocated through an auction process carried out by the Karnataka Solar Park Development Corporation (KSPDCL), a joint venture established in 2015 by the State of Karnatka and India's national government.

Under the terms of India's solar park auction process, power purchase agreements (PPAs)—the same mechanism used in the Noor Complex case—and access to transmission infrastructure are offered to private developers in exchange for commitments to sell specific blocks of power at "lowest and best" tariff rates. This reverse auction mechanism not only benefits consumers in the form of low prices, but it also benefits individual developers by allowing them to take advantage of construction and operating economies of scale related to the use of government-financed ancillary infrastructure such as access roads and transmission lines. It also relieves developers from the responsibilities and risks associated with assembling the underlying land. That responsibility, in the case of Pavagada, was undertaken by KSPDCL, [16] which assembled the 11,000 acres—an area equivalent to three-and-a-half Heathrow Airports—needed to accommodate the entire solar park. This was achieved by offering 25 to 35-year leases to 2,000 individual farmers. By leasing instead of buying land, KSPDCL was able to prevent individual farmers from demanding exorbitant prices for their parcels. Leasing also gives landowners an annual income source, thus creating a sense of community "buy-in" for what could otherwise be seen as a disruptive technology. In this specific case, many of the farmers who signed leases had recently experienced crop failures due to climate change-related drought. Lastly, should a new technology come along that reduces the need for such a large site, the land can seamlessly revert back to the original owners.

THE WORLD'S BIGGEST BATTERY

Not every renewable energy megaproject is recent. Along the sinuous ridges of the Appalachian Mountains just east of the Virginia–West Virginia border sits Dominion Energy's Bath County Storage (BCS) station, a decades-old facility that, to this day, retains the title of "world's largest battery." The term battery is used loosely since the BCS station shares more in common with the Hoover Dam than it does the power packs of a Tesla. With a maximum generating capacity of 3,003 MW and a total storage capacity of 24,000 MWh, the BCS station has been using pumped hydroelectric power to help balance electricity loads since it entered operation in 1985.[17] Pumped hydroelectric storage is a type of gravity storage in which surplus electricity available during periods of slack demand, such as at night, pumps water uphill to create potential energy. When that water is released and allowed to flow back downhill through powerful generating turbines, the potential energy in the stored water is converted back to electricity. The BCS facility is designed with two storage reservoirs, one located 1,200 feet above the other. Other than through evaporation losses, the BCS facility operates as a closed system, with an overall efficiency of 79%; meaning that more than three quarters of the energy used to pump water uphill is recovered through the downhill flow. All told, the upper reservoir has enough water capacity to keep generating electricity for 11 hours of continuous flow.

The BCS pumped hydro storage station was completed in 1985 by the Virginia Electric and Power Company (VEPCO, now Dominion Energy) at a cost of $1.6 billion to meet the utility's need for daily load balancing (ensuring that the supply of electricity and the demand for electricity remain equal at all times).[18] In VEPCO's case, the need for additional load balancing was born from insufficient "ramping" generation—stand-by generating capacity that can be engaged during periods of high demand. Having started construction on a number of nuclear power plants in the late 1970s, VEPCO expected to be able to generate surplus electricity at night, when most of its customers were asleep. Rather than building additional nuclear or coal power plants just to meet daytime peak demand, VEPCO opted instead to invest in grid-level storage that could begin generating electricity within five minutes and could shift supply from night to day.

Construction of the BCS facility began in 1977 but soon stalled because of a longer-than-anticipated environmental impact assessment process and lower-than-expected peak demand. To complete the project, VEPCO sold a 40 percent share in the facility to Allegheny Power System, another regional utility that had been exploring the potential of pumped hydro storage. Neither utility required BCS's full generating capacity, but by sharing the station's capacity and capital costs, the two utilities were able to finance construction based on their combined customer ratebases over a 30-year intended life. Sean Fridley, BCS station manager during its construction called the pumped storage facility "one of the biggest engineering projects, ever" (Koronowski 2013).

The need for effective load balancing continues today, especially in places such as California where increasing reliance on solar power is creating what has come to be known as the "duck curve." This curve describes a situation where, with many people at work or school during the late morning and early afternoon, there is a surplus of solar-generated power for residential customers and demand for power drops. In the late afternoon and early evening hours, as people begin returning home and the sun starts going down, the situation reverses, with demand starting to exceed supply. It is becoming increasingly clear that the ability to store energy and move it to a time when it is needed will be an essential feature of renewably-powered energy systems.

In the 1970s and 1980s, when the BCS facility was conceived and built, pumped hydro power was seen as the only viable form of grid-scale energy storage and load balancing. Today, other technologies, including lithium-ion batteries and hydrogen storage, are becoming increasingly viable options. Even so, as a "low-tech" solution that makes use of long-established and common technology, pumped hydro storage still remains the most popular approach to load balancing, especially in sufficiently mountainous or hilly regions. Pumped hydro systems also have the advantage of being very long lived: most of the systems currently in the US were built in the 1960s and 1970s. Conversely, pumped storage systems are land intensive, costly to construct, and ill-suited to hot, dry regions where evaporation losses and drought can limit system productivity.

Energy storage systems of all kinds face unique challenges when it comes to recouping costs. Whereas investments in generation facilities can rely on predictable electricity sales to recover costs, grid level storage providers or facilities only make money in markets where electricity generation costs vary sharply by time of day, or where power cannot be economically imported from distant locations (National Hydropower Association 2017). All of this makes financing future grid-scale storage megaprojects like BCS a risky proposition.

Lithium-ion batteries offer compelling advantages over pumped hydro in terms of cost, deployment flexibility, and siting, but become significantly degraded after about seven years and do not function well through periods of intermittent use. Nevertheless, modular and scalable storage technologies are likely to claim an ever-larger share of the energy storage market.

CHINA'S WEB OF POWER

No matter the technology used, storing electricity is expensive. Whenever possible, it is far more economical to use electrical energy as it is being generated rather than to store it for later use. This is where power aggregation and transmission line investment strategies come into play. Instead of storing unneeded electricity at a significant expense, a robust, efficient, and extensive transmission system allows surplus energy to be transported to locations where it *is* needed. Particularly relevant for renewable energy development, an extensive and interconnected grid allows electricity generated in remote locations (such as offshore or in a desert) to be used in distant urban and industrial demand centers where customers may be willing to pay higher prices.

No country in the world has leveraged the efficiency and flexibility benefits of investing in electricity transmission facilities more so than China. Since 2004, China has constructed 22 ultra-high voltage (UHV) direct current (DC) and alternating current (AC) power lines spanning more than 30,000 km throughout the country.[19] Just one of these transmission projects, a 1,100 kV DC line connecting the northwestern autonomous region of Xinjiang to eastern demand centers, cost $5.9 billion. Another line connecting the northern Gansu and southern Hunan provinces cost $3.9 billion to complete.

To complement its existing high-performance grid, China currently has plans to build as many as 30 additional UHVDC and UHVAC power lines as part of a multi-year strategy to improve system reliability by connecting sunny and windy provinces in the west to large cities and demand centers in the east (Fairly 2019). These new power lines will be larger and more technologically advanced than transmission megaprojects anywhere else in the world. In the United States, for example, transmission voltages cap out at about 500 kV. With increased voltage comes decreased resistance and line losses, meaning that China will be able to move electricity further and with greater efficiency than any other country in the world.

In addition to connecting future solar and wind generating megaprojects in China's arid western provinces to coastal population centers, China's high-performance grid will also connect its renewable generation capacity to 21 pumped hydroelectricity storage plants, representing 19GW of electricity storage potential. This secure supply of power will provide additional flexibility to China's economic development planners in terms of where to locate future industrial and infrastructure investments.

China's efforts are not without risk. By connecting regional grids with UHV lines, China has created a single national "supergrid" which requires regional distribution networks to perform with a comparable level of capacity and efficiency. As Qin Xiaohui, the vice director of power system planning at the China Electric Power Research Institute puts it, "The UHV AC power grid is like a deepwater port, and the UHV DC is like a 10,000-ton ship. Only the deep-water port can support the 10,000-ton ship" (Fairley 2019, p. 40). Unless this capacity mismatch is addressed, China's efforts to upgrade its national power system could result in cascading blackouts at the regional level.

China is playing the long game when it comes to these investments. By requiring that at least 90 percent of the equipment needed to build its enhanced grid be produced domestically, China is positioning itself as the world's leader in designing and manufacturing 21st century electricity transmission and distribution infrastructure. China has already led the creation of international UHV standards in collaboration with the International Electrotechnical Commission and the Institute of Electrical and Electronics Engineers; and is putting its expertise to work building two new UHV-DC powerlines connecting Brazil's Belo Monte Dam to Rio de Janeiro's electricity market.

China has only been able to undertake these huge investments because of its highly-controlled political, legal, and economic environment. For one, land rights in China are considerably less robust than in western nations. Unless otherwise specified, land in China is owned by the government, and there is little recourse against the government seizing land for use as a new transmission line right-of-way. Nor do governments in China have to compensate any nearby property owners for any adverse spillovers associated with new power line construction. Furthermore, State Grid, the owner and operator of the system, is a state-owned utility company with direct access to financing from government ministries and banks. In FY2019, State Grid earned revenues in excess of $380 billion, making it the second largest company by revenue in China—after the China Petroleum and Chemical Corporation—and the third largest company in the world.[20] State Grid's sheer size also provides it with immense research, engineering, manufacturing, and operating economies of scale. No US transmission line company can hope to match any of these advantages, a situation which has slowed the construction of new domestic UHV transmission lines.

CONNECTING THE POLICY DOTS

When it comes to understanding the role of individual energy megaprojects, it is important to recognize them as just small pieces of a global and interdependent energy transformation. This is why it is so important to consider not only generation megaprojects such as solar and wind farms, but also energy storage and energy transportation infrastructure such as Bath County and China's UHV transmission lines. To successfully finance transmission lines or storage, you need generation capacity that is producing electricity to move or store. In order to finance generation, you need to assure investors that sufficient storage and transmission infrastructure is available to make efficient use of new generation capacity.

Public policies always have some amount of indirect impact on a system that may or may not have been predicted, wanted, or intended by the policymaker. To the observant and open-minded policymaker, these indirect impacts can be used to create a more conducive environment within which to introduce further policy that directly encourages a desired change. For example, if the goal of policy is to promote investment in solar power, one also needs to ensure that the system (electricity grid) into which solar investment is being encouraged has tools in place to make use of that solar power (demand). Without this feature of the grid, there will be a strong hindrance to a targeted solar policy having its desired effects. The best way to effectively and rapidly increase carbon-neutral generation is to simultaneously encourage investment in both generation and in the systems needed to support it. New generation will increase demand for new balancing systems, which will encourage further investment in renewable generation. By supporting both generation and load balancing infrastructure investments with policies, one is able to shift the system from being stuck in a negative feedback loop to being driven by a positive one.

To promote this positive feedback loop, a suite of coordinated and inter-dependent policy solutions is needed. Direct policies can seek to influence behavior (in this case, investor choice) in three ways: education, incentiviza-tion, and discouragement. Education, in this case, involves making the busi-ness case for investment and offering reassurance that a reasonable return on investment is likely. Incentives and disincentives can be as simple as a new tax or tax credit but can also include policies related to legal bans or unique access according to past performance.

Policies can also work to indirectly influence behavior by changing the system conditions within which the decision is being made. For example, in the case of clean energy investments, a change in market rules or a change in regulatory capacity would indirectly influence the decisions of energy investors. An emissions trading system is an example of a policy that would indirectly influence the decisions and behaviors of energy providers by changing the market conditions of the system within which they operate. This policy does not favor any specific policy solutions but instead simply creates a market mechanism for internalizing environmental and social externalities, thereby creating a much more representative system within which investment decisions can be made. Indeed, ETSs have become one of the most important, accepted, and effective policy methods for encouraging investment and devel-opment of clean energy technology.

However, carbon cap and trade systems do little to influence the system conditions for storage or energy transportation infrastructure. Because these supporting investments in the energy system are not themselves directly responsible for any emissions (beyond the emissions produced during con-struction and maintenance) there is not much opportunity for investors in these sectors to take advantage of an ETS or similar emissions control policy. This begs the question: what are equivalent system-wide, direct or indirect policies that could encourage investors in transmission and storage megaprojects without disrupting progress on clean generation development?

One solution is the streamlining and standardization of the siting and per-mitting process. Permitting, zoning, and approval have already demonstrated themselves to be major challenges to the construction of new transmission infrastructure, particularly in strongly democratic countries such as the United States. While strict environmental and social protections should remain in place and be strengthened, streamlining and standardizing the process for securing necessary approval could reduce uncertainty, shorten the planning period, and reduce costs without sacrificing environmental or community due diligence. Permitting and siting will also become an increasingly large problem for generation and storage as more land is required to meet decarbonization goals. Wind and solar power are much more land intensive than non-renewable energy sources, and while transmission investment would allow much of this generation to be sited outside of population centers, there will undoubtedly be environmental and community concerns that arise.

Another policy solution that could significantly benefit investors in storage and transmission infrastructure is sophisticated demand response and load balancing compensation. This policy would require careful consideration of indirect impacts, as it could adversely impact the business case for renewable generation. In the context of decarbonizing our energy system, transmission and storage play a similar ancillary roll, as discussed in the various case studies above. Both services provide renewable electricity generators with a more reliable source of revenue and help to provide supplemental power when local generation falls short of demand. Currently, these services are supported using legacy patterns of compensation that may prove insufficient in the long run. Transmission operators are paid by distribution utilities, which are in turn funded by consumers who pay a flat grid access fee as well as a usage fee. Storage operators are, for the most part, expected to generate revenue by capitalizing on fluctuations in electricity prices. The problem with both of these systems is that they do not adapt well to a heavily renewable grid.

The best way to incentivize demand side investment in renewable energy is to minimize the flat access grid fee and maximize usage fees. This way, the consumer is able to recoup the maximum amount of their monthly energy bills by selling their locally generated electricity back to the utility. However, this also minimizes the utility's revenue and ultimately weakens the business case for new transmission and distribution investments.

Similarly, when dependent on price fluctuations for their revenue, storage operators are motivated to charge and discharge their systems as many times as possible over a given length of time. However, as discussed earlier, as renewable penetration increases and more seasonally dependent end uses are electrified, storage will also be needed for long-duration load balancing. Therefore, a method of market compensation for idle (charged or discharged) storage capacity is needed. This compensation must come either from the renewable energy providers who use the storage capacity to avoid curtailment, or from the utilities who use the stored energy during supply shortfalls. Imposition of these "stand-by" storage costs on either beneficiary will weaken their own revenue and will become an additional barrier to future financing. Here, a clean energy system could learn from the market systems in place for fossil fuels—for example, storage contracts used to compensate seasonal reserves of natural gas.

Ultimately, a successful suite of energy transition policies will need to weigh the many mutual dependencies and tradeoffs between these three key pieces of the emerging global energy system, and costs should, wherever possible, be shared across sectors. Only by approaching the energy system as just that—a unified and interdependent ecosystem of infrastructure, policy, and market forces—can we successfully promote the financing of a coordinated transition in line with global climate goals.

LESSONS AND TAKEAWAYS

The key lessons that can be learned from the discussed case studies and from the current state of global energy systems as a whole are summarized as follows.

- Renewable generation megaprojects may be somewhat less impacted by many of the challenges that typically hinder megaprojects (e.g. complexity, long time horizons, and investment risks) because they can be completed in distinct and operable phases, they are relatively easy to site, and they have a high degree of uniformity.
- However, they are also constrained by their dependency on the electricity grid into which they feed. The risk to investments in generation megaprojects is directly tied to the robustness of the storage and transmission infrastructure available. Likewise, the investment risk associated with storage and transmission is directly dependent on the availability and demand for temporal and spatial movement of electricity—a feature that is strongly associated with high renewables penetration.
- Because generation projects, storage projects, and transmission/distribution projects are so interdependent on one another, project financing must approach the energy transition with an eye to the entire electricity system as a single ongoing and functioning infrastructure project.
- It appears that clean energy megaprojects stand to benefit significantly from the growing number of large, experienced, and financially secure developers specializing in renewable energy. Because of the relative uniformity of renewable energy projects, this knowledge capacity can grow rapidly and will allow for the financing of larger, and perhaps slightly riskier megaprojects. This should lead to an increase in the rate of renewable energy deployment.
- Public–private partnerships (P3s) appear absolutely essential for the successful completion of renewable energy megaprojects. Because global energy systems are transforming so rapidly and with so much uncertainty, the assurance of government priorities through power purchase agreements, BOOT agreements, strike prices, or other long-term commitments offers private developers and financers a much-needed sense of security for their investments.

NOTES

1. https://www.utilitydive.com/news/global-ev-sales-rise-80-in-2021-as-automakers -including-ford-gm-commit-t/609949/.
2. https://www.eia.gov/international/data/world/electricity/electricity-generation (accessed December 20, 2021).
3 https://www.eia.gov/international/data/world/total-energy/total-energy -production (accessed December 20, 2021).
4. Post-2019 LCOE numbers have been difficult to estimate because of the effects of the Covid-19 pandemic on industrial activity and residential, commercial, and industrial energy demand.
5. Semprius: https://www.semprius.com/onshore-vs-offshore-windpower/ (accessed November 2021).
6. US Energy Information Agency: https://www.eia.gov/todayinenergy/detail.php ?id=45136 (accessed November 2021).
7. These cost estimates do not include the costs of building transmission lines.
8. https://walneyextension.co.uk/ (accessed December 20, 2021).
9. https://www.inframationgroup.com/emea-case-study%C2%A0walney-extension -marks-new-template-non-bank-wind-debt (accessed December 20, 2021).
10. https://www.reuters.com/business/sustainable-business/weaker-winds-slow -progress-offshore-firms-orsted-rwe-2021-08-12/.
11. As reported on the Power Technology website: https://www.power-technology .com/projects/noor-ouarzazate-solar-complex/ (retrieved December 20, 2021).
12. https://www.bloomberg.com/news/articles/2022-02-01/india-to-spend-2-6-billion -on-solar-to-curb-reliance-on-china.
13. Government of India, Ministry of New and Renewable Energy Physical Progress: https://mnre.gov.in/the-ministry/physical-progress (retrieved December 20, 2021).
14. https://www.bloomberg.com/news/articles/2022-02-01/india-to-spend-2-6-billion -on-solar-to-curb-reliance-on-china.
15. As reported on the Power Technology website: https://www.power-technology .com/projects/pavagada-solar-park-karnataka/ (retrieved December 20, 2021).
16. http://www.kspdcl.in/index_eng.htm (retrieved December 20, 2021).
17. https://www.dominionenergy.com/projects-and-facilities/hydroelectric-power -facilities-and-projects/bath-county-pumped-storage-station (retrieved December 20, 2021).
18. Virginiaplaces.org website. Pumped Storage in Bath County: http://www .virginiaplaces.org/energy/bathpumped.html (retrieved December 20, 2021).
19. China Develops $26bn Ultra High Voltage Electrical Grids to Stimulate Economic Recovery. As reported on the Power Technology website: https://www.power -technology.com/comment/china-26bn-uhv-grids/ (retrieved December 22, 2021).
20. https://www.statista.com/statistics/302451/china-state-grid-corporation-revenue/.

REFERENCES

Barbose, G., Darghouth, N., Millstein, D., Cates, S., DiSanti, N., and Widiss, R. 2016. Tracking the sun IX: The installed price of residential and non-residential photovoltaic systems in the United States. Berkeley Lab. https://emp.lbl.gov/publications/ tracking-sun-ix-installed-price.

BP. 2021. *Statistical Review of World Energy Use 2021* (70th edition). Downloaded from https://www.bp.com/en/global/corporate/energy-economics/statistical-review -of-world-energy.html.

European Investment Bank and the World Bank Group. 2017. *Morocco: Noor Ouarzazate Concentrated Solar Power Complex* (October). https://library .pppknowledgelab.org/documents/4689/download.

Fairley, P. 2019. China's ambitious plan to build the world's biggest superguide. *IEEE Spectrum* (February). https://spectrum.ieee.org/chinas-ambitious-plan-to-build-the -worlds-biggest-supergrid

Farrell, J. 2019. *Is Bigger Best in Renewable Energy?* Institute for Local Self Reliance. (2019 re-release).

Institute for Energy Economics and Financial Analysis. 2020. *India's Utility-Scale Solar Parks a Global Success Story* (May). https://ieefa.org/wp-content/uploads/ 2020/05/Indias-Utility-Scale-Solar-Parks-Success-Story_May-2020.pdf.

International Energy Agency. 2021. *Net Zero by 2050.* (May).

Koronowski, R. 2013. The Inside Story of the World's Biggest 'Battery' and the Future of Renewable Energy. ThinkProgress website. https://thinkprogress.org/ the-inside-story-of-the-worlds-biggest-battery-and-the-future-of-renewable-energy -8984e81283c/.

Lazard. 2020. *Lazard's Levelized Cost of Energy Analysis*—Version 14. (October). Downloaded from https://www.lazard.com/media/451419/lazards-levelized-cost-of -energy-version-140.

National Hydropower Association. 2017. *Challenges and Opportunities for New Pumped Storage Development* (https://www.hydro.org/wp-content/uploads/2017/ 08/NHA_PumpedStorage_071212b1.pdf).

United Kingdom Department for Business, Energy and Industrial Strategy. 2021. Policy Paper: Contracts for Difference. (December). Accessed via https://www.gov .uk/government/publications/contracts-for-difference/contract-for-difference

17. Improving megaproject practice and performance

John D. Landis

Having learned what we can from the case studies individually, we now consider them collectively by comparing how each project's planning, engineering, financing, construction and project management practices have contributed to its overall performance. We begin by scoring each case according to a common set of 12 performance measures. We also identify the ways each case study either avoids or falls into Flyvbjerg's megaproject outcome traps. Next, we identify 27 good planning, financing, contracting, project management, risk mitigation, commissioning, and asset management practices, and rate each case-study project on each of them. These ratings are then used to build a series of practice quality indices which are compared to each project's summary performance measures. This enables us to identify which practice measures are most closely associated with successful project performance. Next, we list each case study's good and bad lessons and identify a series of eight good practice takeaways that are common to all the case-study projects. We conclude by identifying the critical choices confronting megaproject sponsors, decision-makers and managers, and offer guidance to help them make the most appropriate choices for their projects and situations.

SCORING MEGAPROJECT PERFORMANCE

The bottom line for any infrastructure project should be how well it performs. In recent years, especially in North America and Europe, there has been a tendency to conflate performance with success, and to define success principally in terms of on-time delivery and adherence to an initial budget. Projects that are delivered on time and within budget are judged to be successful while those that are delivered late and over-budget are branded as unsuccessful or even failures.

This is a shortsighted view. The life of a megaproject is typically measured in decade multiples, so a delivery delay of one, two, or even five years balanced against 40 or 50 years of productive performance probably shouldn't tip the scales from success to failure. Likewise, instead of focusing on cost

overrun amounts or percentages, since most of the societies undertaking megaprojects are either prosperous to begin with, or are on an upward prosperity
trajectory, once the decision is made to proceed with a particular megaproject,
the real issue is which other projects would have to be put off or modified to
cover for any cost overruns. This is not to say that megaproject funders and
project managers shouldn't worry about delivery delays or cost overruns. They
clearly should, especially if the delays and overruns were foreseeable and
avoidable. It is rather that the additional costs should be balanced against the
full set of benefits—properly discounted, of course—that the project delivers
over the course of its life. By this criteria, the two additional years and extra
$250 million it took to deliver the Alaskan Way Tunnel does not automatically
make it a failure. Likewise, the fact that the New LaGuardia Airport has so far
proceeded on time and budget does not automatically make it a success.

In order to create a more balanced definition of megaproject success, we
identified 12 cross-cutting megaproject performance scoring criteria. Nine of
these criteria are what economists call "ex post" or after-the-fact, meaning that
they can only be applied after a project is completed and has entered service.
The other three are input or "ex ante" criteria, meaning that they refer to the
quality of procedures put into place before a project is delivered. For simplici-
ty's sake, all of the criteria follow an ordinal 0 to 4 rating scale, where a rating
of '4' indicates extremely strong performance and a '0' rating indicates
extremely weak performance. In no case are we conducting a formal evaluation which would involve a rigorous numerical tabulation of costs and benefits.

The 12 performance criteria are the following.

1. *Achieves its goals in a timely manner.* Most infrastructure projects are
    undertaken to achieve a particular set of goals or purposes as listed in the
    project prospectus or funding documents. This ex post criteria identifies
    the extent to which a project achieves its stated purposes or goals as
    quickly as possible after it enters service. A rating of "4" on this criteria
    indicates most of the project's goals or purposes were achieved. A rating
    of "3" indicates that a plurality of the project's goals were achieved. A "2"
    rating indicates only a few goals were achieved. A "1" rating indicates
    most goals are not achieved, and a "0" rating indicates no goals were
    achieved. Note that we do not penalize narrowly-conceived projects for
    having only a few goals just as we do not reward broadly-conceived pro-
    jects for having many goals.
2. *Uses appropriate, cost-efficient, and reliable technologies.* When we
    say a project uses an appropriate technology we mean that it uses the
    most modern combination of hard and soft technologies. Hard technol-
    ogies include physical things such as buildings, structures, facilities and
    machines which, for the most part, are designed and engineered to deliver

a uniform quality of service. Soft technologies encompass the use of information and human decision rules to provide a quality of service that caters to the individual user. Because of advances in electronics and miniaturization, the soft technology component of most infrastructure projects has been increasing over time, making it possible for them to deliver more individualized or situation-dependent services.

Cost-efficient technologies are those that use the lowest-cost combination of inputs (i.e., land, workers, services, energy, and investor or borrowed capital) to achieve a particular output level. Once a particular technology has been put in place, it can be very expensive to update. This means that projects using older technologies or those that suffer from lengthy delays between initial engineering and final delivery are likely to be less cost-efficient.

Reliability refers to the average time between service breakdowns. The more complicated a project is, the more components and systems it has that may break down. This is why most megaprojects are designed to the greatest extent possible with backup and redundant systems. Unlike cost-efficiency, which can usually be determined beforehand, reliability is not easy to assess until after a project has been in service for a number of years.

Because of the challenges posed by climate change, there is new emphasis being placed on projects being resilient as well as reliable. The two are similar in some respects but different in others. Reliability refers to breakdowns that occur during normal system operation. Resiliency refers to breakdowns that occur as a result of an external shock or disruption.

Depending on the project there may be tradeoffs between appropriateness, cost-efficiency, and reliability. Older technologies may be more reliable than newer ones but not as cost-efficient. Greater redundancy (and thus greater reliability) may require additional expense. There are also tradeoffs between construction cost efficiency and operating cost efficiency. Consider the differences between an automated metro line and a driver-based bus rapid transit (BRT) line. A metro line can move more transit riders than a BRT line but is typically much more expensive to build. At the same time, because metro systems operate on a dedicated right-of-way, they are easier to automate than BRT systems, making them generally more reliable.

A "4" rating on this criteria indicates that a project uses hard and/or soft technologies in a manner known to be cost-efficient and reliable. A "3" rating indicates that a project's technologies are reasonably cost-efficient and reliable. A "2" rating indicates that a project's technologies may be cost-efficient but not necessarily reliable (or, perhaps the other way around, reliable but not cost-efficient). A "1" rating indicates that a project's technologies are neither cost-efficient nor reliable, while a "0" rating indicates that a project's technologies are cost-inefficient and unreliable.

3. *Avoids significant construction and delivery delays.* Infrastructure projects should be completed and enter service in the timeframe specified when they are initially approved or funded. Delays can occur for any number of reasons. Additional permits may be required or permitting may take longer than expected. Materials and equipment supply chains may be disrupted. Constructors may face unforeseen site conditions or hazards, as it happened in the Seattle Alaskan Way Tunnel case. Subsystem technologies may not work as advertised or different subsystems may be incompatible with one another, requiring time-consuming fixes, as was the case for London Crossrail and the Berlin Brandenburg Airport. Cost overruns or revenue shortfalls may require going back to funders to obtain additional financing. As in the Songdo case, lesser-than-projected revenues during a project's early phases may slow progress during later phases. Testing may reveal unforeseen technical problems.

A timeliness rating of "4" indicates that a project was within 10 percent of meeting its initial completion schedule. A "3" rating indicates that a project experienced unexpected delays of between 10 percent and 25 percent compared with its original schedule. A "2" rating indicates that a project experienced unexpected delays of between 25 percent and 50 percent compared with its original schedule. A "1" rating indicates that a project experienced delays of between 50 percent and 75 percent, and a "0" rating indicates that a project experienced delays in excess of 75 percent. Note that these ratings apply only to project construction and delivery times and do not include planning or approval times. As an example, a project such as the Hong Kong–Zhuhai–Macau Bridge, which took years to plan and fund but which was completed within a year of its construction schedule, scores well on this criteria. By contrast, a project such as the Berlin Brandenburg International Airport, which was approved relatively quickly but took more than a decade to deliver, scores poorly.

4. *Avoids significant design, engineering, construction and delivery cost overruns.* Infrastructure projects should be finalized, built, and delivered within their proposed budgets as specified when they are approved or funded. In addition to all the oversights and circumstances that cause delays, there are other factors that generate cost overruns. These include materials, equipment and labor cost inflation; rising borrowing costs; poor cost estimating during the project planning and engineering phases; poor project contracting and project management practices; contracting disagreements; unanticipated contingencies; and plain old bad luck. Experienced project planners and managers know that cost overruns go hand in hand with project size and complexity and develop contingency

budgets accordingly. They also anticipate sources of construction and financing risk and seek out guarantors or insurers to share in those risks.

A "4" rating on this criteria indicates that a project was completed within 10 percent of its approved construction and delivery budget. A "3" rating indicates that a project was between 10 percent and 25 percent over budget. A "2" rating indicates that a project was between 25 percent and 50 percent over budget. A "1" rating indicates that a project was between 51 percent and 100 percent over budget, and a "0" rating indicates that a project was more than 100 percent over budget. A "U" notation indicates that a project's budgetary performance is or was not public knowledge.

5.   *Generates expected revenues.* Most transportation and energy infrastructure projects require their users to pay some sort of fare, toll or fee which is then used to cover project operating and/or financing costs. Similarly, urban development projects are undertaken based on the presumption that the eventual property user will be willing to pay market prices or rents to own or occupy newly-provided space. Alternately, projects built explicitly for third-party clients or owners are expected to generate commissions and/or transaction fee revenues. In most instances, it takes a few years for a project to get "up and running" and to begin meeting its revenue generation projections.

There are numerous reasons why projects come up short when it comes to generating projected revenues. The most common is that the expected number of project users fails to materialize or is unwilling to pay the required user charge. This was the case for the Hong Kong–Zhuhai–Macau Bridge. In other cases, a project may face unanticipated competition that siphons off expected revenues. Project operating costs may rise unexpectedly, requiring an increase in fares or prices. Or, project planners and funders may simply do a bad job estimating potential project demand, either because they make unsupportable assumptions about the size of the market or because their forecasting methodology is not up to the job. Even when the underlying market and financial analysis is first-rate, politicians and project sponsors may choose to disregard bad news, hoping that once a project is completed, it will somehow create its own market—this is what Flyvbjerg characterizes as "optimism bias." To be clear, this last situation of supply driving demand does occasionally occur, but it is foolhardy not to have a contingency plan in place if it does not.

The best way for project planners to reduce the likelihood that project revenues fall short of projections is to test multiple market demand and/ or pricing scenarios, and to identify the circumstances under which the project is likely to fail economically. This type of economic stress testing is common when financing private real estate projects but is less common when analyzing public infrastructure or redevelopment projects. Instead, analysts too often assume that the project sponsor will have deep enough pockets to make up for any revenue shortfalls.

A "4" rating indicates that a project's operating revenues exceeded its revenue generation expectations as put forth in its initial or updated market and/or economic feasibility study documents. A "3" rating indicates that a project has met its revenue expectations. A "2" rating indicates that a project has come within 10 percent of meeting its revenue projections. A "1" rating indicates that a project has come within between 10 and 25 percent of meeting its revenue expectations. A "0" rating indicates that a project's revenue performance has fallen short of projections by 25 percent or more. A "U" notation indicates that a project's revenue performance is unknown or cannot be reliably assessed.

6. *Makes use of a robust revenue projection and/or financing model.* This success criteria is related to the previous one. Many a megaproject had been completed, only to immediately underperform in terms of its revenues covering operating and financing costs. In the best of cases, the project keeps operating but is financially restructured or requires some form of government subsidy. In the worst of cases, the project is removed from service or shut down. To avoid such outcomes, project sponsors are usually required to undertake careful projections of anticipated project revenues and costs. In addition, in situations where projects are financed with investor equity or bank loans, investors and lenders will almost always require a third-party financial feasibility analysis indicating that they will be fully repaid in a timely manner.

A "4" rating in this category indicates that a project was subject to a rigorous analysis of its likely revenue performance based on the number of likely users or size of the potential market, and the ability of those users to generate the expected revenue stream and repay investors and lenders. A "3" rating indicates that a project was subject to a rigorous market and/ or financial feasibility analysis, but that less-than-favorable contingencies may not have been fully considered. A "2" rating indicates that a project was subject to some type of ex ante economic or financial feasibility but that it may not have been all that rigorous in terms of its market and revenue assumptions. A "1" rating indicates that some type of ex ante multi-criteria evaluation was performed but that economic or financial considerations may not have played the primary role. A "0" rating indicates that no ex ante needs assessment or market study was undertaken. A "U" notation indicates that a needs assessment or willingness-to-pay analysis may have been undertaken, but that its results were never made public.

Unlike criteria 1 through 5 above, this is an input criteria rather than an outcome criteria, meaning that it refers to practices undertaken prior to construction and delivery.

7. *Manages major sources of development and financial risk.* Big projects are by nature risky and face numerous uncertainties. Included among the major sources of risk facing big infrastructure and development projects are: (i) site assembly and entitlements risks—the likelihood that the project sponsor will not be able to assemble all the requisite land and development approvals; (ii) technology risk—the likelihood that a new technology will not work as advertised; (iii) market risk—the likelihood that a project will not draw the anticipated number of users; (iv) interest rate and financing risk—the chance that financing costs will rise and/or that one or more financing partners may withdraw; (v) construction risk— the likelihood that the project will not be completed on time and within budget; (vi) operating and sales risk—the likelihood that actual operating costs will exceed projections, or that an expected buyer for the project may back out; and (vii) inflation and currency risk—for international projects whose construction or financing costs are not pegged to the dollar or euro, the likelihood that exchange rates will change in a disadvantageous direction. As Flyvbjerg properly emphasizes, the longer a project takes to bring to fruition, the more exposed it is to all of these risks.

Properly managing risk requires, first, understanding the sources of risk as they affect a given project (i.e., risk exposure); and then, second, coming up with a series of contingent or contractual arrangements to mitigate risk. This usually involves posting some sort of bond, making payments into a contingency fund, or securing third-party guarantees or insurance. Depending on the types and severity of risks the project is facing, these practices can be extremely expensive, which leads many project sponsors to forego them.

A rating of "4" indicates that project sponsors and managers undertook a robust risk identification and management study prior to undertaking a project, and that they developed a coherent and ongoing risk management plan in response. A "3" rating indicates that a project was subjected to a rigorous risk analysis and management study prior to project approval and construction, but that no ongoing risk management plan was created. A "2" rating indicates that a project was subjected to an ad hoc risk analysis and mitigation study prior to approval and construction. A "1" rating indicates that there was some ex ante identification of risk sources, but no identification of possible risk management approaches. A "0" rating indicates that no ex ante risk analysis or mitigation study was undertaken. A "U" notation indicates that a risk analysis study may have been undertaken but that its results were never made public.

Like criterion 6, above, this is an input criteria, meaning that it refers to practices undertaken prior to project construction and delivery.

8. *Provides for ongoing operations and management activities.* Once completed, projects don't operate or manage themselves. They require adequate staffing, administrative and operations procedures, and funding, as well as information systems to track project performance and anticipate potential problems. A "4" rating indicates that project sponsors have provided adequate funding, staffing, and management systems for the project to operate at peak efficiency on an ongoing basis. A "3" rating indicates that project sponsors have provided sufficient funding and staffing to support project operations for at least 5 years. A "2" rating indicates that project sponsors have provided sufficient funding and staffing to support project operations for 2 to 3 years only. A "1" rating indicates project sponsors have identified the need to support ongoing operations but have not necessarily made sufficient provisions to do so. A "0" rating indicates that project sponsors have not made provisions for continuing operation. A "U" notation indicates that a project operating plan may have been prepared but that it has not been made public.

Like criteria 6 and 7, this is an input criteria, meaning that it refers to practices undertaken prior to construction and delivery. This means that there may be situations in which a project runs into later operating difficulties even though adequate operations and maintenance procedures are in place.

9. *Achieves synergies and positive externalities.* In the best of all worlds, megaprojects have emergent properties, which is to say that they promote positive synergies and externalities—including further innovations—over and above the level initially envisioned. Synergies are beneficial effects that occur in concert with other projects or activities. Externalities are beneficial side effects that benefit parties who may not themselves make use of the project. The effects of synergies and positive externalities can be hypothesized during the project planning process but can only be measured after a project has been in place for a number of years. As a result, assessing the degree to which a project generates synergies and positive externalities must await the completion of some form of ex post, or after-the-fact, evaluation. A "4" rating indicates that one or more ex post assessments was undertaken and identified sizeable positive synergies and externalities. A "3" rating indicates that an ex post assessment was undertaken and identified minor positive synergies and externalities. A "2" rating indicates that a project is associated with some level of external synergies or benefits but they were not carefully documented. A "1" rating indicates that no project synergies or external benefits were identified, while a "0" rating indicates that a project generates external costs and/or

negative externalities. A "U" indicates that the incidence of synergies and side benefits is unknown.

10. *Minimizes social costs.* All large projects generate unwanted side effects, also known as negative or social costs. Sometimes negative externalities are physical or environmental, as in the case of noise or pollution, and sometimes they are social or economic, as in the case of unwanted gentrification or displacement. A "4" rating indicates that a project generates few negative externalities/social costs, and that its development or management program includes provisions for mitigating them. A "3" rating indicates that a project generates few negative externalities/social costs but that its development or management program includes no mitigation provisions. A "2" rating indicates that a project generates unwanted adverse effects but that they don't constitute a physical or health hazard. A "1" rating indicates that a project generates a significant number or magnitude of undesirable side effects and that they constitute a substantial health or social hazard. A "0" value indicates that a project's side effects are almost entirely negative and dangerous. A "U" notation indicates that the incidence of negative side effects and social costs is unknown.

As with the prior criteria, the degree to which a project minimizes social costs can often be anticipated, but exact measurements must await an after-the-fact evaluation.

11. *Promotes sustainability, resilience, and/or equity.* To say that a project promotes sustainability means that it leaves the natural environment or ecosystem better off than before the project was undertaken. To say that a project promotes equity means that it betters the lives and livelihoods of those suffering economic or social disadvantages. To say that a project promotes resiliency means that it leaves a natural or human system better able to cope with external or adverse shocks. Sustainability and equity benefits are similar in concept to positive externalities but whereas positive externalities are typically localized, sustainability and equity benefits are more broad-based. They are also less easy to monetize. Projects may be undertaken for the explicit purpose of promoting sustainability, resilience and/or equity, but as is more often the case, such goals are secondary to promoting economic prosperity.

A "4" rating on this criteria indicates that a project generates measurable sustainability/resilience benefits for natural systems and the natural environment, as well as significant equity benefits for those who are economically or socially disadvantaged. A "3" rating indicates that a project generates significant sustainability/resilience benefits or significant equity benefits but not both. A "2" rating indicates that a project generates some sustainability/resilience benefits and/or equity benefits but that they are relatively small. A "1" rating indicates that a project generates no sustainability or equity benefits, and a "0" rating indicates that a project adversely impacts natural systems or generates negative equity effects. As with previous criteria, a "U" notation indicates that a project's sustainability, resilience, and equity effects are unknown.

As with the prior two criteria, the degree to which a project promotes sustainability, equity or resilience can be anticipated, but exact measurements must await the results of an after-the-fact assessment.

12. *Generates positive and transferable lessons and experience.* Learning saves valuable time and reduces the likelihood that avoidable mistakes are repeated. As with external benefits and costs and issues of sustainability and equity, resolving whether a project generates transferable lessons or experiences is best determined with hindsight. A "4" rating indicates that a project generated valuable lessons that could be productively applied in other situations. A "3" rating indicates that a project generated important but less widely applicable lessons. A "2" rating indicates that a project generated few or exceedingly narrow lessons, and a "1" indicates that a project is strictly a "one-off" in terms of transferable lessons or experience. A "U" notation indicates that one cannot assess whether a project offers useful or transferable lessons, or a project's sustainability, resilience, and equity effects are unknown.

All of these criteria and scores are relative. None are absolute, meaning that they can't be reliably measured using project-independent interval scales or indexes such as benefit-cost ratios.

Table 17.1 scores each case study megaproject or megaproject type according to each performance criteria. It also includes a total score, which adds together the individual category scores, and a percentage score, which divides the total score by the maximum possible score. Note that the scoring categories are unweighted, meaning that each counts the same when determining the total and percentage scores. An alternative aggregation scheme, in which the schedule, budget, and usage projection weights were each multiplied by three, did not substantially affect the projects' comparative performance ratings. Readers who wish to apply their own weighting systems—for example, to give greater weight to promoting sustainability or equity—are encouraged to do so.

Table 17.1 Case study megaproject performance scores

			Rail and transit projects				Bridge and tunnel projects		Airport projects			Urban development projects			Other		
	Performance criteria and ratings: 4 = yes, 3 = mostly yes, 2 = somewhat, 1 = mostly no, 0 = no, U = unknown	Criteria type (pre- or post-delivery)	London Crossrail	Four Chinese metros	China HSR	Six BRT Systems	Seattle Tunnel	Hong Kong Bridge	Jewel Changi	Berlin Brandenburg Airport	New LaGuardia Terminal B	London Canary Wharf	HafenCity Hamburg	Songdo, Korea	Brooklyn Bridge Park	Five renewable energy projects	Average score
1	Achieves project goals and objectives in a timely manner	Post	Project is not yet completed	4	4	3	4	1	4	2	4	4	4	1	3	3	3.2
2	Uses appropriate and cost-efficient technologies	Post		4	4	3	4	4	4	3	4	4	4	2	3	3	3.5
3	Avoids significant planning, engineering, construction and delivery delays	Post		4	4	4	2	4	4	0	4	2	3	1	1	3	2.8
4	Avoids significant design, engineering, construction and delivery cost overruns	Post		U	U	3	3	3	4	0	4	2	3	2	2	3	2.6
5	Operating revenues meet projections	Post		2	2	3	3	1	1	3	3	2	3	1	3	2	2.2

Performance criteria and ratings: 4 = yes, 3 = mostly yes, 2 = somewhat, 1 = mostly no, 0 = no, U = unknown	Criteria type (pre- or post-delivery)	Rail and transit projects				Bridge and tunnel projects			Airport projects		Urban development projects			Other		Average score
		London Crossrail	Four Chinese metros	China HSR	Six BRT Systems	Seattle Tunnel	Hong Kong Bridge	Jewel Changi	Berlin Brandenburg Airport	New LaGuardia Terminal B	London Canary Wharf	HafenCity Hamburg	Songdo, Korea	Brooklyn Bridge Park	Five renewable energy projects	
6 Utilizes a robust revenue projection and financing model	Pre	Project is not yet completed	2	U	3	2	1	U	2	3	2	3	1	3	2	2.2
7 Manages major sources of development and financial risk	Pre		U	U	3	2	1	U	2	3	1	3	1	3	2	2.1
8 Provides for ongoing operations and management activities	Pre		2	3	2	3	1	4	2	3	2	4	1	3	3	2.5
9 Promotes synergies, and positive externalities	Post		3	3	2	4	1	3	1	2	3	4	1	3	4	2.6
10 Minimizes environmental and social costs	Post		3	3	3	3	1	2	1	1	1	3	2	3	3	2.2

Performance criteria and ratings: 4 = yes, 3 = mostly yes, 2 = somewhat, 1 = mostly no, 0 = no, U = unknown	Criteria type (pre- or post-delivery)	Rail and transit projects				Bridge and tunnel projects			Airport projects		Urban development projects			Other		Average score
		London Crossrail	Four Chinese metros	China HSR	Six BRT Systems	Seattle Tunnel	Hong Kong Bridge	Jewel Changi	Berlin Brandenburg Airport	New LaGuardia Terminal B	London Canary Wharf	HafenCity Hamburg	Songdo, Korea	Brooklyn Bridge Park	Five renewable energy projects	
11 Incorporates sustainability, resilience, and/or equity concerns	Post	Project is not yet completed	3	3	2	2	0	2	1	1	1	3	2	3	3	2.0
12 Generates positive and transferable lessons & experience	Post		3	3	3	3	1	3	1	3	2	4	2	3	3	2.6
Total Success Score			30	29	34	35	19	31	18	35	26	41	17	33	34	
Percentage Success Score			68%	73%	71%	73%	40%	78%	38%	73%	54%	85%	35%	69%	71%	

Of the 13 rated projects—London Crossrail is not rated because it opened for service after Chapter 4 was completed—HafenCity scores highest, achieving a total score of 41 and a percentage score of 85 percent. HafenCity's exemplary performance is based on the fact that it achieves high ratings in every performance category. Right behind HafenCity is Singapore Jewel Changi Airport, which earns a total score of 31 and a percentage score of 78 percent. Except for its lack of a robust revenue model and clear risk mitigation strategy, Jewel Changi performs similarly to HafenCity in most categories.

Next up are four projects that earn percentage scores in the low 70s. These include China's high-speed rail system, Seattle's Alaskan Way Tunnel, and the new LaGuardia Airport Terminal B, each of which earns a percentage score of 73 percent; and the six bus rapid transit systems, which collectively earn a percentage score of 71 percent. These four project earn high marks for delivering on their goals and for their on-time and on-budget performance, but don't do quite as well in terms of promoting positive externalities, protecting the environment, or promoting equity and sustainability. The five renewable energy megaprojects also earn a common percentage score of 71 percent, based largely on their superior environmental and sustainability performance.

Two very different projects earn percentage scores in the high 60s. Brooklyn Bridge Park earns a percentage score of 69 percent based on its environmental and sustainability benefits, while falling down on on-time completion. The four Chinese metro systems earn a percentage score of 68 percent. Collectively, they do extremely well in terms of on-time and on-budget performance and meeting their sponsor's goals, but less well in terms of carefully projecting ridership levels and operating costs.

Canary Wharf, which comes next with a percentage score of 54 percent, is an interesting case. Its poor performance during the early 1990s was marked by bad luck and a complete breakdown of its financing model and risk management approach, but since the project's financial re-organization in 1995, it has performed well by most criteria.

The three remaining projects all score poorly. The Hong Kong–Zhuhai–Macau Bridge earns a percentage score of 40 percent, based on the questionable logic of its patronage and financial modeling and its resulting lack of users and toll revenues. The Berlin Brandenburg Airport earns a percentage score of just 38 percent, based on its disastrous project management practices and the resulting time and cost overruns. Picking up the rear is Songdo IBD, which earns a percentage score of just 35 percent. Except for its exemplary land use master plan, Songdo's two chief sponsors, the City of Incheon and Gale International, made just about every market and financial analysis and risk mitigation mistake it is possible to make.

Looking beyond individual project scores, a number of performance patterns are evident.

- *Performance scores vary widely among the megaproject case studies, both within and between project categories.* Compared across all the case study projects or project types, total scores vary from a low of 29 for Songdo to a high of 41 for HafenCity. Percentage scores vary from a low of 35 percent for Songdo (meaning that Songdo's total score amounted to 35 percent of its maximum attainable score) to a high of 85 percent for HafenCity.

  The largest variation in scores is among the three urban development projects, with HafenCity receiving the highest percentage score, 85 percent, and Songdo receiving the lowest with just 35 percent. There was also significant scoring variation within the airport, and bridge and tunnel project categories. Whereas LaGuardia Airport achieved a relatively high 73 percent score, Berlin Brandenburg Airport earned a percentage score of just 38 percent. Likewise, whereas Seattle's Alaska Way Tunnel earned a 73 percent score, the Hong Kong–Zhuhai–Macao Bridge earned a 38 percent score. Excluding Crossrail, all three rail and bus project case studies scored fairly well, with their percentage scores varying from a high of 73 percent for China's national high speed rail network, to a low of 68 percent for the Beijing, Shanghai, Guangzhou, and Shenzhen metro systems when evaluated as a group.

- *Few projects performed consistently well or consistently badly.* Most of the case study projects performed mid-pack in terms of performance consistency across the different scoring categories. (We measured performance consistency by dividing the standard deviation of the score categories for each project by the average score.) HafenCity and the six BRT projects did consistently well across all of the scoring categories while the Hong Kong–Zhuhai–Macao Bridge and the Berlin Brandenburg Airport were the most inconsistent in terms of their cross-category performance. None of the projects performed poorly across all categories. In terms of project types, the rail and transit projects were much more consistent in terms of cross-category performance than the bridge and tunnel, airport, or urban development projects.

Collectively, the case studies performed well using appropriate technologies and achieving their goals, and poorly in terms of promoting sustainability and equity and managing risk. Among individual scoring categories, the case study projects performed best in terms of using appropriate and cost-efficient technologies, earning an average score of 3.5 out of 4. The other category in which most of the case study projects performed well was the goal achievement category, earning an average score of 3.1. At the other end of the performance spectrum, the case study projects earned an average sustainability, resilience, and equity score of just 2.0 (out of 4) and an average risk management score of just 2.1. As a group, the case studies also performed poorly in terms of minimizing environmental and social costs, posting an average score of 2.3; and of providing for ongoing operations and asset management activities, posting an average score of 2.4. In terms of within-category performance consistency (as measured by dividing the standard deviation of the within-category score by the average within-category score), the case studies performed most consistently in terms of their use of appropriate and cost-efficient technologies; and least consistently in terms of avoiding major delivery delays. The other scoring categories in which projects performed inconsistently were the promotion of synergies and positive externalities, and the minimization of environmental and social costs.

- *The project scores are all fairly robust.* Applying alternative weights to the category scores to reflect the greater importance typically attached by project sponsors to goal achievement, and the lesser importance commonly attached to issues of equity, sustainability and transferability, has little effect on the overall or percentage project scores.

AVOIDING FLYVBJERG'S MEGAPROJECT PITFALLS

When it comes to billion-dollar projects, avoiding failure can be as important as achieving success. How do the case study projects perform when it comes to avoiding Flyvbjerg's ten megaproject problem areas? As Table 17.2 indicates, quite well in fact. Three of the four rail and transit cases, including both the Chinese metro and a high-speed rail cases, managed to avoid all ten of Flyvbjerg's megaproject planning and delivery problem areas. The Singapore and LaGuardia airport cases also performed extremely well, as did HafenCity. At the opposite extreme, Songdo fell into nine of Flyvbjerg's ten megaproject traps, and Berlin Brandenburg Airport fell into eight of them. In between these extremes, Brooklyn Bridge Park fell into five of Flyvbjerg's pitfall areas, and London Crossrail, Seattle's Alaskan Way Tunnel, and the Hong Kong–Zhuhai–Macao Bridge each fell into three.

Table 17.2   Avoiding Flyvbjerg's megaproject performance pitfalls

Flyvbjerg megaproject problem areas encountered (Key: N = No, Y = Yes, P = partially, U = unknown)	Rail and transit projects				Bridge and tunnel projects		Airport projects			Urban development projects			Other	Number of case study megaprojects experiencing this problem area
	London Crossrail	Beijing, Shanghai, Guangzhou and Shenzhen metro systems	China's high-speed rail network	Bus Rapid Transit in six Latin America and Asian Cities	Seattle Alaska Way Tunnel	Hong Kong-Macao-Zhuhai Bridge	The Jewel at Singapore Changi Airport	Berlin Brandenburg Airport	LaGuardia Airport terminal B reconstruction	London Canary Wharf	HafenCity Hamburg	Songdo, Korea	Brooklyn Bridge Park (New York City)	
1 A long planning and delivery horizon exacerbates risks of physical and/or financial under-performance.	N	N	N	N	N	Y	N	Y	N	Y	P	Y	Y	6
2 Megaprojects planners and managers may lack "deep domain" experience, creating management problems and adding to the frequency of staff turnover.	Y	N	N	N	N	N	N	Y	N	N	N	Y	N	3

Flyvbjerg megaproject problem areas encountered (Key: N = No, Y = Yes, P = partially, U = unknown)	Rail and transit projects				Bridge and tunnel projects		Airport projects			Urban development projects			Other	Number of case study megaprojects experiencing this problem area
	London Crossrail	Beijing, Shanghai, Guangzhou and Shenzhen metro systems	China's high-speed rail network	Bus Rapid Transit in six Latin America and Asian Cities	Seattle Alaska Way Tunnel	Hong Kong-Macao-Zhuhai Bridge	The Jewel at Singapore Changi Airport	Berlin Brandenburg Airport	LaGuardia Airport terminal B reconstruction	London Canary Wharf	HafenCity Hamburg	Songdo, Korea	Brooklyn Bridge Park (New York City)	
3 Project sponsors and stakeholders are not fully aligned around project purpose, goals, objectives, budget, and construction timetable.	P	N	N	N	N	N	N	Y	N	N	N	Y	Y	4
4 Megaproject technologies and designs are viewed as "one-offs," which impedes learning from the results of other projects.	N	N	N	N	Y	Y	P	Y	N	N	N	Y	Y	6

	Rail and transit projects				Bridge and tunnel projects		Airport projects			Urban development projects			Other	
Flyvbjerg megaproject problem areas encountered (Key: N = No, Y = Yes, P = partially, U = unknown)	London Crossrail	Beijing, Shanghai, Guangzhou and Shenzhen metro systems	China's high-speed rail network	Bus Rapid Transit in six Latin America and Asian Cities	Seattle Alaska Way Tunnel	Hong Kong-Macao-Zhuhai Bridge	The Jewel at Singapore Changi Airport	Berlin Brandenburg Airport	LaGuardia Airport terminal B reconstruction	London Canary Wharf	HafenCity Hamburg	Songdo, Korea	Brooklyn Bridge Park (New York City)	Number of case study megaprojects experiencing this problem area
5 Many megaprojects do not initially undergo a rigorous alternatives analysis, resulting in the wrong technology or scale or scope of project being selected.	N	U	U	P	N	Y	Y	Y	N	N	N	Y	N	5
6 Because of the large sums of money involved in delivering megaprojects, principal–agent and rent-seeking behavior are common, as is optimism bias.	N	U	U	U	N	U	N	N	N	Y	N	Y	N	2

Flyvbjerg megaproject problem areas encountered (Key: N = No, Y = Yes, P = partially, U = unknown)	Rail and transit projects				Bridge and tunnel projects		Airport projects			Urban development projects			Other	
	London Crossrail	Beijing, Shanghai, Guangzhou and Shenzhen metro systems	China's high-speed rail network	Bus Rapid Transit in six Latin America and Asian Cities	Seattle Alaska Way Tunnel	Hong Kong-Macao-Zhuhai Bridge	The Jewel at Singapore Changi Airport	Berlin Brandenburg Airport	LaGuardia Airport terminal B reconstruction	London Canary Wharf	HafenCity Hamburg	Songdo, Korea	Brooklyn Bridge Park (New York City)	Number of case study megaprojects experiencing this problem area
7 The megaproject scope or ambition may change over time.	N	N	N	N	N	N	N	Y	N	N	Y	Y	Y	4
8 Megaproject planners and managers systematically underestimate the potential for adverse-but-low likelihood "black swan" events.	P	N	U	N	Y	P	P	P	N	Y	U	P	N	7
9 Megaproject planners, managers, decision-makers and contractors don't include adequate time or budgetary contingency provisions in project contracts.	Y	U	U	U	Y	U	U	Y	P	Y	U	Y	Y	7

Flyvbjerg megaproject problem areas encountered (Key: N = No, Y = Yes, P = partially, U = unknown)	Rail and transit projects				Bridge and tunnel projects		Airport projects			Urban development projects			Other	Number of case study megaprojects experiencing this problem area
	London Crossrail	Beijing, Shanghai, Guangzhou and Shenzhen metro systems	China's high-speed rail network	Bus Rapid Transit in six Latin America and Asian Cities	Seattle Alaska Way Tunnel	Hong Kong-Macao-Zhuhai Bridge	The Jewel at Singapore Changi Airport	Berlin Brandenburg Airport	LaGuardia Airport terminal B reconstruction	London Canary Wharf	HafenCity Hamburg	Songdo, Korea	Brooklyn Bridge Park (New York City)	
10 — As a result, internal and external misinformation becomes the norm throughout the megaproject development and decision-making process.	Y	N	P	N	N	N	N	Y	N	N	N	Y	N	4
Total problem areas avoided (out of 10)	7	10	9.5	9.5	7	6.6	7	1.5	9.5	6	8.5	0.5	5	
Percentage performance score (from Table PERF-1)	n.a.	68%	73%	71%	73%	40%	78%	38%	73%	54%	85%	35%	69%	

Of Flyvbjerg's ten potential problem areas, the two the case studies fell into most frequently were failing to anticipate low-probability-but-high-cost adverse events—what Flyvbjerg terms "black swans"—and not including adequate contingency funds or delay times in project contracts. This suggests that megaprojects should be subject to more rigorous stress testing than is currently the case, and that the test result should be incorporated as contingency provisions in project contracts.

In six of the case studies, project planners did not adequately anticipate the extent to which an overly-long planning and delivery time horizon might exacerbate downstream physical and financial performance risks. This suggests that megaprojects should be subjected to more rigorous risk analysis than currently, and that prior delivery delays should be identified as an explicit risk factor.

There was also a tendency to view projects as "one-offs," which reduced opportunities for sharing knowledge and learning from past experiences. This suggests there is a bigger role to be had for professional associations in sharing best practices, especially between Asia, Europe, and North America.

Less common but not infrequent problems included difficulties aligning stakeholders around project goals and timetables and finding knowledgeable and experienced senior managers. As a general rule, the more local governments or stakeholders that were involved in the project planning or delivery process, the more problems it experienced.

Because they had fewer resources to deal with market downturns, projects sponsored by private developers (e.g., Canary Wharf and Songdo) experienced more problems than those sponsored by experienced public agencies or clearly-circumscribed public–private partnerships (e.g., HafenCity and LaGuardia Airport). Among the case study projects, new airports were more problem-prone than existing ones, as were ambitious bridge and tunneling projects. Chinese megaprojects undertaken by the central government (e.g., high-speed rail) or by city governments (e.g., metro and BRT systems) experienced fewer problems than those undertaken by multiple provinces or special administrative regions (e.g., the Hong Kong–Zhuhai–Macao Bridge).

All told, the correlation coefficient between the number of Flyvbjerg problem areas a project avoided and its percentage performance score was a relatively high 0.72 (recognizing of course, the small number of observations in play). This suggests that project managers who make efforts to avoid the missteps Flyvbjerg identifies are likely to reap rewards when it comes to project performance.

One intriguing explanation for why many of the case study projects do so well avoiding Flyvbjerg's performance traps is that the field is learning from experience, and that contemporary megaproject managers have learned how to anticipate and avoid the types of pitfalls that characterized megaprojects in the 1980s and 1990s—the era when many of the projects Flyvbjerg based his analysis on were completed.

CONNECTING GOOD PRACTICES TO GOOD OUTCOMES

We turn now to the central purpose of this book, connecting good practices to good outcomes. To identify these connections, we first collected a list of 27 best practices organized by practice category. Next, we rated each case study on each practice and summed the ratings by practice category. These ratings are shown in Table 17.3. Finally, we summarized the ratings by practice category and compared the practice summary scores to the performance percentages scores listed in Table 17.3. Presented graphically, the resulting comparisons are shown in Figure 17.3 and allow us to identify which practices in which practice categories are most strongly associated with overall project performance.

This ratings and comparison approach has both advantages and disadvantages. In terms of advantages, it is simple, straightforward and transparent. On the disadvantage side, since some practice categories include just a few practices, and we have only 14 projects to compare, a change in practice ratings for one or two projects might significantly alter the overall results. With this caveat in mind, we explain our method and results in greater detail below.

Good Practices and Practice Categories

Researchers have identified numerous good practices, activities and conditions that increase the likelihood that a megaproject will perform successfully. We selected 27 of them and organized them into seven practice groupings as follows.

Project planning, design, and feasibility assessment practices category

1. Ensuring that the project sponsor has effective site control and has secured all necessary permits and approvals;
2. Ensuring that the project has a champion in the sponsor's organization who is able to defend it politically and institutionally;
3. Ensuring that all project sponsors and stakeholders are aligned around the project's purposes, goals, budget, and delivery timetable;
4. Ensuring that proper due diligence has been performed with respect to physical and institutional constraints, market demand, cost and financial feasibility, and sources and types of risks;
5. Ensuring that the project's core technologies have been properly tested and vetted; and

6. Ensuring the project delivery process is properly divided into task groupings or phases.

Project financing practices category

7. Project financing has been independently reviewed, underwritten and stress-tested;
8. Project capital stack properly reflects capital source contributions and capabilities; and
9. Avenues for additional financing (if needed) have been identified and secured as necessary.

Contracting practices category

10. Project planners, designers and contractors have experience and a track record of success with respect to similar projects;
11. Contractors are brought onto the project as early as feasible to participate in the planning and design process as appropriate;
12. Project sponsors fully understand the contractors' work program, schedule, and cost structure. Project milestones have been properly identified;
13. Contracts are clear and unambiguous, precisely detailing the responsibilities of sponsors and contractors;
14. Contract incentives and performance requirements are appropriate to objectives and project sponsor and contractor capabilities and roles; and
15. Contract properly anticipates adverse contingencies.

Project management and accountability systems practices category

16. Sponsor and contractor project managers are qualified and experienced;
17. An integrated and robust project management and control system is in place that reflects the budgets, schedules, and obligations of all parties. The project management system explicitly allows for contingencies; and
18. Procedures exist to document and evaluate project scope or design changes with respect to program goals, costs, and delivery times.

Risk management and mitigation practices category

19. Project risks are assigned to the parties best able to manage, control, or reduce them; and
20. Provisions are in place to minimize and manage project-level risks rather than just shifting them about.

Project delivery and commissioning practices category

21. Component systems are tested as they come on line and in concert with other systems;
22. The project and its component systems are tested with regard to redundancy, resilience, and responses to unexpected events or occurrences; and
23. Proper asset management procedures and systems are in place before delivery.

Operations and asset management practices category

24. Ongoing monitoring of usage levels and patterns as regards periodic and preventative maintenance and service;
25. Ongoing monitoring of usage levels and revenue and cost trends to benchmark financial performance and health and identify adverse trends;
26. Monitor positive and negative spillover effects; and
27. Undertake periodic performance evaluations to identify potential modifications, expansions, and investments.

Scoring Good Practice

Next, we reviewed the extent to which each project adhered to each good practice listing, using a nominal 0/1 scoring system where a "1" rating is used to indicate general adherence to good practice, a "0.5" rating is used to indicate partial adherence to good practice, and a "0" value indicates no adherence. In situations where the necessary adherence information could not be assessed, we gave a project a "U" (for unavailable) rating. These good practice adherence assessments are presented by category and project in Table 17.3.

Table 17.3   Case study megaproject adherence to good practice ratings

Practices that ensure or promote megaproject success (Key: 1 = adherence; 0.5 = partial adherence; 0 = no adherence; U = unknown)	Rail and transit projects				Bridge and tunnel projects		Airport projects			Urban development projects			Other
	London Crossrail	Beijing, Shanghai, Guangzhou and Shenzhen metro systems	China's High-Speed Rail Network	Bus Rapid Transit in six Latin America and Asian cities	Seattle Alaska Way Tunnel	Hong Kong-Macao-Zhuhai Bridge	The Jewel at Singapore Changi Airport	Berlin Brandenburg Airport	LaGuardia Airport Terminal B Reconstruction	London Canary Wharf	HafenCity Hamburg	Songdo, Korea	Brooklyn Bridge Park (New York City)
1 Project sponsors have site control and take responsibility for securing necessary permits, approvals, and financing		1	1	1	1	1	1	1	1	1	1	0	0.5
2 The project has a champion in the sponsor's organization who is able to supports the project as necessary	Project is not complete as of this writing	1	1	1	1	1	1	1	1	1	1	1	1
Initial project planning, design and feasibility assessment activities — **3** Project sponsors and stakeholders are aligned around project purpose, goals, objectives, budget, and construction timetable		1	1	1	1	1	1	0.5	1	0.5	1	0	0.5
4 Proper initial due diligence has been performed with respect to physical and institutional constraints, market demand, cost and financial feasibility, and sources and types of risks		U	1	0.5	1	0	0.5	0.5	1	0.5	1	0	1
5 Project technologies have been properly tested or vetted		1	1	1	1	0.5	1	0.5	1	1	0.5	0.5	1
6 Project is properly divided into deliverable pieces		1	1	1	1	1	1	0	1	1	1	0.5	1

Practices that ensure or promote megaproject success (Key: 1 = adherence; 0.5 = partial adherence; 0 = no adherence; U = unknown)

			Rail and transit projects				Bridge and tunnel projects		Airport projects			Urban development projects			Other
			London Crossrail	Beijing, Shanghai, Guangzhou and Shenzhen metro systems	China's High-Speed Rail Network	Bus Rapid Transit in six Latin America and Asian cities	Seattle Alaska Way Tunnel	Hong Kong-Macao-Zhuhai Bridge	The Jewel at Singapore Changi Airport	Berlin Brandenburg Airport	LaGuardia Airport Terminal B Reconstruction	London Canary Wharf	HafenCity Hamburg	Songdo, Korea	Brooklyn Bridge Park (New York City)
Project financing	7	Project financing has been independently reviewed, underwritten and stress-tested	Project is not complete as of this writing	0	0	0	1	0	U	0	0.5	0	0.5	0	0.5
	8	Project capital stack properly reflects capital source contributions and capabilities		1	1	0.5	1	1	1	0.5	0.5	0.5	1	0	1
	9	Avenues for additional financing (if needed) have been identified and secured as necessary		1	1	0.5	0.5	1	1	0.5	0.5	0	0.5	0.5	0.5
Contracting	10	Project planners, designers and contractors have experience and a track record of success with respect to similar projects		1	1	1	1	0.5	1	0.5	1	1	1	0	1
	11	Contractors are brought onto the project as early as feasible to participate in the planning and design process as appropriate		1	1	0.5	1	0.5	1	0.5	1	1	1	1	1
	12	Project sponsors fully understand the contractors' work program, schedule, and cost structure. Project milestones have been properly identified		1	1	0.5	1	1	1	0.5	1	1	1	0	0.5

Practices that ensure or promote megaproject success (Key: 1 = adherence; 0.5 = partial adherence; 0 = no adherence; U = unknown)

			Rail and transit projects				Bridge and tunnel projects		Airport projects			Urban development projects			Other
	#	Practice	London Crossrail	Beijing, Shanghai, Guangzhou and Shenzhen metro systems	China's High-Speed Rail Network	Bus Rapid Transit in six Latin America and Asian cities	Seattle Alaska Way Tunnel	Hong Kong-Macao-Zhuhai Bridge	The Jewel at Singapore Changi Airport	Berlin Brandenburg Airport	LaGuardia Airport Terminal B Reconstruction	London Canary Wharf	HafenCity Hamburg	Songdo, Korea	Brooklyn Bridge Park (New York City)
Contracting	13	Contracts are clear and unambiguous, precisely detailing the responsibilities of sponsors and contractors	Project is not complete as of this writing	U	U	U	1	U	U	0	1	1	1	0	U
	14	Contract incentives and performance requirements are appropriate to objectives and project sponsor and contractor capabilities and roles		U	U	U	0.5	U	U	0.5	1	0.5	1	0	1
	15	Contract properly anticipates adverse contingencies		U	U	U	0.5	U	U	0	U	0.5	0.5	0	U

Table 17.4 *Positive and cautionary lessons from each case study*

Practices that ensure or promote megaproject success (Key:
1 = adherence; 0.5 = partial adherence; 0 = no adherence;
U = unknown)

		Rail and transit projects				Bridge and tunnel projects		Airport projects			Urban development projects			Other
		London Crossrail	Beijing, Shanghai, Guangzhou and Shenzhen metro systems	China's High-Speed Rail Network	Bus Rapid Transit in six Latin America and Asian cities	Seattle Alaska Way Tunnel	Hong Kong-Macao-Zhuhai Bridge	The Jewel at Singapore Changi Airport	Berlin Brandenburg Airport	LaGuardia Airport Terminal B Reconstruction	London Canary Wharf	HafenCity Hamburg	Songdo, Korea	Brooklyn Bridge Park (New York City)
Project management and accountability systems	16 Sponsor and contractor project managers are qualified and experienced.	Project is not complete as of this writing	1	0.5	0.5	1	1	1	0	1	1	1	0.5	1
	17 An integrated and robust project management and control system is in place that reflects the budgets, schedules, and obligations of all parties. The project management system explicitly allows for contingencies.		U	0.5	0	1	U	1	0.5	1	1	1	0	1
	18 Procedures exist to document and evaluate project scope or design changes with respect to program goals, costs, and delivery times.		1	0.5	0.5	1	0.5	1	0.5	1	0.5	1	0.5	1
Risk management and mitigation	19 Project risks are assigned to the parties best able to manage, control, or reduce them.		1	1	0.5	1	1	1	0.5	1	0.5	1	0.5	1
	20 Provisions are in place to minimize and manage project-level risks rather than just shifting them about.		U	1	0.5	0.5	U	U	0.5	0.5	0.5	1	0	1

Practices that ensure or promote megaproject success (Key: 1 = adherence; 0.5 = partial adherence; 0 = no adherence; U = unknown)

	#	Practice	Rail and transit projects				Bridge and tunnel projects		Airport projects			Urban development projects			Other
			London Crossrail	Beijing, Shanghai, Guangzhou and Shenzhen metro systems	China's High-Speed Rail Network	Bus Rapid Transit in six Latin America and Asian cities	Seattle Alaska Way Tunnel	Hong Kong-Macao-Zhuhai Bridge	The Jewel at Singapore Changi Airport	Berlin Brandenburg Airport	LaGuardia Airport Terminal B Reconstruction	London Canary Wharf	HafenCity Hamburg	Songdo, Korea	Brooklyn Bridge Park (New York City)
Project delivery and commissioning	21	Test component systems as they come on line and in concert with other systems	Project is not complete as of this writing	1	1	1	1	1	1	1	1	0	1	0	0.5
	22	Identify resiliency and responses to unexpected events or occurrences		U	0.5	U	0.5	0.5	0.5	0.5	0.5	0.5	0.5	0	1
	23	Ensure proper asset management procedures and systems are in place before delivery		0.5	U	U	0.5	U	1	0.5	1	0.5	1	0	1
Operation and asset management	24	Monitor use patterns and costs to plan for maintenance, upgrading & service changes		0.5	0.5	0.5	1	0.5	1	1	1	1	1	0.5	1
	25	Monitor revenue and cost trends to benchmark financial health and identify how usage patterns are changing		1	U	0.5	1	0.5	1	1	1	1	1	0.5	1
	26	Monitor positive and negative spillover effects		0.5	0.5	0.5	0.5	0.5	1	0.5	0.5	1	1	0.5	0.5
	27	Undertake periodic performance evaluations to identify potential modifications, expansions, and investments		U	0.5	0.5	U	U	U	0.5	1	1	1	U	U
Total adherence score				16.5	17	13.5	22.5	14	20	13.5	23	18.5	24	6.5	20.5

Next, we totaled up each case study project's within-category and total adherence ratings. Projects that adhered to all six good planning, design and feasibility analysis practices earned a maximum score of 6. Projects that adhered to all three good financing practices earned a score of 3. Projects that adhered to all six good contracting practices earned a maximum score of 6. Projects that adhered to the three good project management practices earned a maximum score of 3. Projects that adhered to the three good project delivery practices earned a score of 3, and those that adhered to the four sets of good operations and asset management practices earned a score of 4. A perfect score of 27 indicates a project adhered to every good practice.

Among the 11 case study megaprojects listed in Table 17.3, total good practice adherence scores vary from a high of 24 for HafenCity—meaning that HafenCity's sponsors adhered to 24 of 27 good practice scores—to a low of 6.5 for Songdo. The average good practice adherence score for all 11 megaprojects is 17.2. In addition to HafenCity, the projects that posted better-than-average good practice adherence scores include LaGuardia Airport (23), the Alaskan Way Tunnel in Seattle (22.5), Brooklyn Bridge Park (20.5), Singapore Jewel Changi Airport (20) and Canary Wharf (18.5). Besides Songdo, the projects whose good practice adherence scores were less than the case study average included China's high-speed rail system (17), the four Chinese metro systems (16.5), the Hong Kong–Zhuhai–Macau Bridge (14), the six BRT systems (13.5), and the Berlin Brandenburg Airport. The lower-than-average scores reported for the various Chinese projects are partly reflective of China's centralized decision-making style and general lack of public transparency.

Comparing adherence scores by category instead of project, as a group the 11 case study projects do best adhering to good planning, design and feasibility assessment practices, earning an average percentage score of 83 percent, and worst adhering to good project delivery practices, earning an average percentage adherence score of just 56 percent. Among the other good practice categories, the case study projects do better adhering to good financing practices (earning an average percentage score of 79 percent) but are mediocre adhering to good contracting, project management, risk management, and asset management practices. The average adherence score across all seven good practice categories is also a mediocre 65 percent.

Connecting Practice with Performance

To better connect practices with outcomes, we graphically compared each project's within-category good practice adherence scores as tabulated in Table 17.3 with its performance percentage scores as summarized in Table 17.1. The results of those comparisons are presented as trend-line plots in Figure 17.1. To the degree that a project sponsor followed good planning, financing, contracting, project management, risk management, asset management and delivery practices, and that those practices resulted in a more successful project, the summary trend lines indicated in Figure 17.1 should slope sharply upward. To the degree that following good practice does not necessarily result in better project performance or outcomes, the trend lines in Figure 17.1 will be flat or slope downward. By looking at how well the project datapoints cluster around the trend lines, we are also able to judge the consistency of the relationships between good practice adherence and project performance.

Based on the results shown in Figure 17.1, and subject to all the compromises involved in assigning project success scores and good practice adherence ratings to a small sample of highly diverse megaprojects, we offer the following conclusions about the relationships between megaproject planning, financing, project management and delivery practices and the superior project performance. These results are based on observations of the case study megaprojects summarized in this volume, and great care should be taken in extending them to other projects and situations. Among the case study megaprojects:

- Among the case study megaprojects, there is a strong and positive association between adhering to good megaproject *planning, design, and feasibility assessment practices* and good megaproject outcomes. This relationship is also evident across megaproject category types. Good planning, design, and feasibility assessment practices, it seems, are associated with better project outcomes.
- There is a positive and moderate association between adhering to good megaproject *contracting practices* and good megaproject outcomes. This relationship is strongest among the airport and urban development projects.
- Among the case study megaprojects, there is a positive and moderate association between adhering to good *megaproject risk assessment and management practices* and good megaproject outcomes. This relationship is strongest among the urban development projects.
- Among the case study megaprojects, there is a positive but weak association between adhering to good *megaproject financing practices* and good megaproject outcomes.
- Among the case study megaprojects, there is a positive but very weak association between adhering to *good project management practices* and good megaproject outcomes.
- Among the case study megaprojects, there is a positive but very weak association between adhering to good *project delivery practices* and good megaproject outcomes.
- Among the case study megaprojects, there is a positive but very weak association between adhering to good *project operations and asset management practices* and good megaproject outcomes.

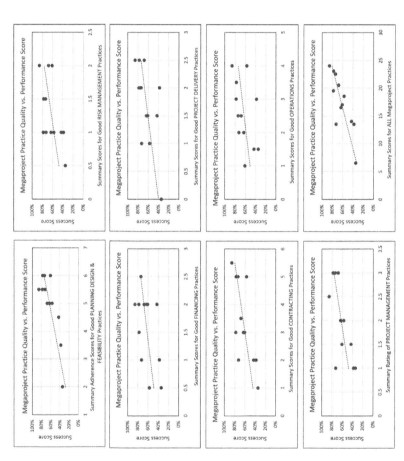

Figure 17.1　　*Comparisons of case study megaproject performance scores with best practice adherence*

Summing up these connections, adhering to good planning, design, and feasibility assessment practices is central to megaproject success regardless of project type or location. Adhering to good contracting and risk management practices is especially important for urban development projects and, to a lesser extent, airport projects. Adhering to good financing, project management, project delivery, and asset management practices is weakly associated with superior project performance. Among the projects set in China, adhering to good planning and contracting practices is more central to project performance than adhering to good financing, risk management, and project management practices. Again, it is worth reiterating that these associations are based on a limited number of projects operating in a variety of international political and decision-making systems so readers should take extreme care when assigning any predictive power to them.

LEARNING FROM THE CASE STUDIES

None of the case study megaprojects was flawlessly executed. Likewise, none of them is completely without merit. Each offers important lessons to future megaproject sponsors about desirable and undesirable planning, financing, and delivery practices.

London Crossrail

London Crossrail entered service in May 2022, after the draft of this book was complete. Even so, it offers a number of positive and negative lessons to those considering undertaking metropolitan-scale transportation megaprojects. On the positive side, the process the UK Department for Transport (DfT) used to identify and estimate Crossrail's likely benefits, was rigorous and thoughtful, and ended up positively influencing the final choice of routes and the mix of financing sources. Although it may slow down the decision making process, other public transportation agencies would do well to review the processes and approaches used in the UK to "make the economic case" needed to justify approving expensive and far-flung infrastructure projects.

On the less fortunate side, Crossrail's government sponsors were so intent on putting in place an innovative and adaptive project management process that they failed to ensure that adequate performance monitoring and accountability provisions were in place. Having weighted their project monitoring efforts toward ensuring that Crossrail's complex tunnel systems were completed on time—an important milestone to be sure—project managers substantially underestimated the difficulties involved in coordinating the multitudes of station construction and passenger control and signaling system contractors. Nor did they have a coherent backup plan to put into place when critical milestones were missed. Finally, the fact that Crossrail had two government agency sponsors whose interests weren't always aligned, the UK Department for Transport and Transport for London, unnecessarily complicated the job of replacing Crossrail's senior management team when they proved incapable of coping with the cascading problems and delays.

The Beijing, Shanghai, Guangzhou and Shenzhen Metro Systems

It is important to acknowledge upfront that undertaking large transportation investments is much easier in China than in most western democracies. As with everything in China, public infrastructure investments are guided by the country's five-year national plans (as well as by city and provincial plans which take their lead from the national plan). Once China's ruling State Council in Beijing approves funding for a project, it goes ahead as approved, notwithstanding any amount of grassroots protest or concern about unintended consequences or temporary funding shortfalls. The fact that political advancement in China is typically dependent on delivering on the Chinese government's priorities—again, popular sentiment has no direct role in determining Chinese investment priorities—means that high-level voices questioning the wisdom of approved projects are entirely missing.

With these important caveats in mind, there is still much to be learned from the metro-building experiences of China's "big four" cities. The foremost lesson concerns the usefulness of standards. At the start of any complex or extensive infrastructure project, Chinese city officials adopt design, engineering, construction, and procurement standards and procedures that must be observed by every contractor, regardless of size or history. And at the conclusion of every job, these standards are reviewed and updated as needed. This standards-based approach has a number of advantages. First, it takes maximum advantage of design, engineering, and construction economies of scale, which means that later projects can be produced more quickly and cost-efficiently than earlier ones. Second, it ensures that improvements in construction or delivery efficiency can be achieved citywide. Third, it ensures technical and physical compatibility between different transit lines and extensions. Finally, it reduces opportunities for corruption since every contractor must perform to the same set of standards and benchmarks.

The flip side to the cost and delivery time efficiency benefits of standards is that they inhibit flexibility and situation-specific adaptations. This is particularly problematic when it comes to locating metro stations. Beijing, for example, has adopted uniform metro station location criteria that focus on consistent station spacing rather than meeting the travel demands associated with above ground activities. This means that metro stations are sometimes located where homes and businesses are not, making it more difficult for travelers to get to them. Similarly, having standardized the design and placement of station access and egress facilities, opportunities to integrate stations into their surrounding land uses are lost. Finally, Beijing's insistence upon using a standard financing model to pay for recent metro line construction has meant that that opportunities to use value-capture techniques to raise needed capital and operating revenues have been missed.

Metro planners in other Chinese cities have learned from Beijing's oversights. Shanghai and Shenzhen's metro stations are more likely to be located near or under major commercial centers, with their entrance and exit facilities better designed for convenience. Both cities have also eschewed Beijing's practice of limiting transfer stations to just two lines in favor of building a few multi-line transfer hubs. Shenzhen in particular has been willing to enter into public–private partnerships with Hong Kong's MTR Corporation to capitalize on their "Rail + Property" approach to locating, building, and financing new metro lines and stations. Guangzhou had gone so far as to overlay a bus rapid transit line atop one of its subway corridors.

Even in a system as controlled as China's, these practice variations are not wholly unexpected. Beijing, being China's capital and political power center, will always take a more hierarchical, and for China, more mainstream approach. By the same token, as China's leading innovation center, Shenzhen will always be looking to experiment. Likewise, Shanghai, as Beijing's traditional economic and cultural rival, has always taken its own course when it comes to rail transportation investments, going all the way back to 2001 and its construction of a mag-lev high-speed rail link connecting downtown Shanghai to the airport.

China's High-speed Rail Network

That China managed to build its 37,000 km high-speed rail system in just 16 years—just four years longer than it took New York City to build its new one-kilometer Second Avenue Subway—is nothing short of astonishing; and is testimony to what is possible when a coherent vision, $600 billion in spending, and the expertise of an army of engineers and contractors is applied in an organized and concentrated manner. The only other transportation project of the last one hundred years comparable in size and national commitment to China's high-speed rail system is the 75,000 km US Interstate Highway system, which took more than 30 years and $600 billion to complete.

Beyond its success as a construction project, China's high-speed rail system has also been hugely popular in the travel marketplace. Between 2010 and 2019, ridership on the new system grew at an overall rate of 26 percent, reaching 2.3 billion in 2019. Indeed, for most non-business inter-city trips in China of less than 600 km, high-speed rail now has the dominant market share.

China's success in building and operating its high-speed rail network offers a number of lessons to other countries and governments pondering their own high-speed rail projects. The first concerns the power of standards and standardization. In much the same way as Chinese cities standardized the engineering and construction of their metro systems, China's Ministry of Railways developed a common set of design, engineering, and construction standards for the country's high-speed rail system, and then used them to pre-certify local contractors. This not only sped up bidding and contracting, but because the standards were continually updated to incorporate on-the-job experience, it meant that that the construction process became more efficient as it progressed. To pay for the new lines, China developed a common joint-venture financing template, but then applied it in a way that was sensitive to local financial capabilities and shifting macro-economic conditions.

Much has been made of the "one-size-fits-all-provinces-and-cities" nature of China's five-year economic plans, but when it comes to building national infrastructure projects, it is doubtful that any other planning and funding approach would have worked as well at aligning so many diverse pieces and priorities. For better and for worse, but in the case of high-speed rail clearly for the better, China's top-down political system ensured a level of project management and decision-making accountability that proved essential to the system's timely completion and delivery. Perhaps most important, the Chinese government's willingness to up its financial and resource commitment to high-speed rail in 2008 when other countries were cutting-back public expenditures in response to the Global Financial Crisis, gave completion of the system a much needed boost and sense of urgency. In short, when it comes to completing national infrastructure projects, there is no substitute for a national commitment.

This is not to say that everything has gone smoothly or that China's high-speed rail system has met all its goals. China's rush to begin service in 2011 on the Yongtaiwen Line resulted in an accident that killed 40 passengers, injured another 192, and was mishandled by government officials eager to avoid responsibility. Of more lasting impact, extending a high-speed rail service to many secondary Chinese cities—which was one of the reasons for building such an extensive network—has so far failed to close the growth and prosperity gap between China's inland and coastal cities. Much the same is also true for France and Spain's high-speed rail systems, suggesting that whatever its success in enhancing inter-city mobility, high-speed rail is of questionable value as a means of balancing regional economic development.

One final note, because of the newness of the high-speed rail service in China, it has taken several rounds of fare and/or service adjustments for China's railway operators to get the balance between passenger capacity and patronage exactly right. This is to be expected, but also serves as a reminder that even in China, providing inter-city travel service is a competitive business, and that travelers are constantly reassessing which services provide the best value for money.

Six Bus Rapid Transit Systems

Megaproject sponsors nearly always assume that their circumstances and projects are unique and that there is little to be learned from past projects and experiences, especially those in other countries. Bus rapid transit (BRT) is the welcome exception to this. From BRT's modern beginning in Lima, Peru, in 1972, most BRT sponsors have made an organized effort to learn from their predecessors, and it is this enthusiasm for sharing experiences that has made the cumulative BRT experience such a success. In addition to lessons about the efficient design of BRT vehicles and stations, BRT system designers have learned important lessons about station spacing and express service and about the integration of BRT with other bus services. More so in Latin America than Asia, cities have learned how to use BRT service to drive development patterns and residential densities. The result of this knowledge exchange is that most BRT corridors implemented in Latin America and Asia have been successful in terms of ridership and revenue generation. This can't always be said for light-rail, BRT's principal modal rival. BRT is also fortunate to have had the services of the Institute for Transportation Development and Policy (ITDP), a non-profit, US-based think tank devoted to promoting sustainable and locally-appropriate transport service.

BRT has had other things going for it as well. Because it doesn't require expensive tunneling or elevated superstructures, BRT is relatively cheap to put in place. This makes it a cost-effective way to move large numbers of people to work and back, even in middle-income cities. Second, BRT's use of conventional bus technology means that additional capacity can be added quickly and cheaply without the usual break-in period required of rail transit. Third, and perhaps most importantly, BRT lives or dies in terms of service quality and convenience. This means that BRT operators must pay constant attention to the preferences and convenience of BRT riders rather than to the requirements of the technology or to what the drivers' union thinks.

BRT also offers a cautionary tale of what happens when infrastructure capacity cannot be added quickly enough to meet surging demand and service quality suffers as a result. This was what happened in the case of Bogota's BRT system and is indicative of the fact that megaproject operating challenges continue once initial construction is finished, and of the importance of putting into place monitoring systems and procedures capable of tracking ongoing shifts in demand, facility use, and service quality.

Seattle's Alaskan Way Tunnel

Seattle's Alaskan Way Tunnel (AWT) is a one-off infrastructure project. As transportation megaprojects go, not only is it on the small side, but it was built for a very specific purpose: to replace a 50-year old elevated highway damaged in a 2001 earthquake. The path to completing the AWT was a bumpy one. Led by planners in the Washington State Department of Transportation, the AWT's initial planning process was too insular and technocratic for Seattle voters, leading them in 2007 to reject its recommendations at the ballot box. The follow-on planning process was more participatory but had trouble converging on a single proposal. The AWT's "eureka" moment came only when one of the planning task force participants proposed building a double-decked single-bore tunnel instead of the usual side-by-side dual bore tunnels, allowing the project to stay within its original budget. Bad luck also played a role. When Bertha, the AWT's huge tunnel boring machine broke after hitting an undocumented pipe early during construction, the project was shut down for two years.

The lesson of the AWT example is that even relatively simple megaprojects—the AWT is just 2.3 miles long and goes through relatively soft soils—can run into unexpected problems; and when they do, having a carefully thought-out contingency plan in place is a must. The AWT's sponsor, the Washington State Department of Transportation, which in other ways was a very competent project manager, had neither set aside sufficient contingency funding or required that the project contractor, have a detailed backup plan in place. The result was a distracting legal fight that prevented the parties from giving their full attention to repairing the broken boring machine and bringing it back on line.

The AWT's other main lesson is more positive. By intentionally expanding the AWT planning process after the public voted down an initial replacement proposal in 2007, Seattle officials created additional citizen engagement space to explore the future of the city's neglected waterfront. Thus, what had been conceived initially as a narrow transportation engineering project grew into a broader discussion of the future of the Seattle waterfront and how best to integrate an improved public realm with new commercial development. The result was an innovative waterfront redevelopment plan that drew support for all sides and could be realistically financed out of the city's budget. This model of using a transportation investment to catalyze a broader discussion about place-based urban futures is one worth emulating.

The Hong Kong–Zhuhai–Macau Bridge

The Hong Kong and Chinese sponsors of the Hong Kong–Zhuhai–Macau (HKZM) Bridge did a diligent job designing and engineering what is now the world's longest bridge-and-undersea tunnel complex. Given the technical and weather-related challenges they faced, the HKZM Bridge contractors also did a creditable job building it at a reasonable (if not inexpensive) cost. The HKZM Bridge connects two high-demand travel destinations, Hong Kong and Macau, and can safely accommodate tourist coaches, private vehicles, and cargo-laden trucks. By all conventional metrics, the HKZM Bridge should be a success.

And yet it is not. Even before the Covid-19 pandemic, vehicle traffic on the HKZM Bridge never came close to meeting projections. This was not because the Bridge tolls were excessive. They were not. Instead, the market the HKZM Bridge was intended to serve was never as robust or free from competition as bridge promoters believed. Instead of flying into Hong Kong and taking a coach to Macau, Asian gamblers now fly directly to Macau. Likewise, instead of the HKZM Bridge being used to transport manufactured goods produced in Zhuhai to Hong Kong ports for export, competing manufacturers in Dongguan are sending their export goods to ports in nearby Shenzhen. The result for the HKZM Bridge is a shortfall in both tourist and freight traffic. Because none of the HKZM Bridge's sponsors ever released the details of the Bridge's usage projections, we cannot know whether the possibility of these outcomes occurring was ever considered; we can only assume they were not. Even if they were, for a provincial or state governments to spend more than $15 billion on a single-mode transportation investment to meet the transport needs of two very specific market segments (Macau-bound tourists and Hong Kong-bound freight shippers) in a highly competitive environment, was just foolhardy. The lesson of the HKZM Bridge is simple: to borrow a maxim from the 1989 movie, *Field of Dreams*, just because "if you build it, they will come."

Singapore's Jewel Changi Airport

Jewel Changi is unlike any other airport terminal in the world. It includes no passenger gates or jetways. What it does include is a five-story waterfall, an indoor nature park, a destination shopping mall, a prestige hotel, and a 2,500 car parking garage. It is the sort of place where first-time and repeat visitors alike pause simply to take in the cleverness and wonder of it all, and to ask why their airport back home has nothing like it.

Jewel Changi offers two important lessons to sponsors of other megaprojects. The first is that for all their size, complexity, and emphasis on efficiency, megaprojects should also function at a human scale, making their use a pleasurable as well as efficient experience. A second lesson is that investing in institutional capacity pays dividends far into the future. Jewel Changi is the end result of Singapore's government having built up its own in-house airport planning and engineering capabilities to the point where they are among the best in the world. Beginning with Prime Minister Lee Kwan Yew's decision in 1976 to give the job of creating the new Changi Airport master plan to Singapore's Department of Public Works, Singapore has continued to invest in its own airport planning and engineering abilities with the purpose of staying a step ahead of the rest of the world. This is not to say that Singapore is intent on always going it alone. Starting with the design of Changi Terminal 3 in 2000 and then with construction of Terminal 4 in 2012, Singapore has made use of some of the world's most capable airport design, engineering, and logistics firms. It has also overseen the partial privatization of its capabilities, spinning them off in 2009 from the government-run Singapore's Civil Aviation Authority (CAAS) into the privately-listed Changi Airport Group (CAG). Throughout this evolution, Singapore's government has insisted that Changi Airport always be a forward-leaning symbol of Singapore itself, and that the principles behind its design and operation be reflective of the government's policy priorities. During the 1980s and 1990s, this meant building airport facilities that were efficient and modern and moved as many people on and off the island as easily as possible. More recently, as Singapore has refocused its priorities on human quality of life issues and protecting the natural environment, Changi Airport's newer facilities have come to represent those priorities as well.

Berlin Brandenburg International Airport

The principal lesson of Berlin Brandenburg Airport, which was finally completed in 2020, nine years late and $3.7 billion over budget, is that developing any sort of major airport facility is a highly specialized endeavor that requires both expertise and experience. When the governments of the German states of Berlin and Brandenburg decided in 1996 to go ahead with building an entirely new airport to replace the obsolete Tegel, Tempelhof, and Schönefeld airports, they substantially underestimated the difficulties they would face. Their first major mistake came in 2001 when, after two rounds of being unable to assemble a public–private partnership to oversee the airport's development, they decided to do the job themselves—despite not having experience developing projects of similar size or complexity.

Their second mistake came six years later when, after two tender processes failed to result in a satisfactory submission from an experienced project management company, the two state governments decided to serve as their own project manager, again, without having had any experience in such a role. This mistake was further compounded by not having a detailed airport design plan ready prior to the start of construction and no clear reporting lines for the job's more than 30 individual contractors. These omissions would continually come back to haunt the project, particularly when individual subsystems repeatedly failed their performance tests. What project managers did not understand was that individual contractors were focused on finishing their particular jobs as opposed to ensuring that their work connected seamlessly to the larger project.

As these various problems came to the fore, instead of implementing an improved project management system, Flughafen Berlin Brandenburg GmbH (FBB), the project sponsor and manager, would swap out one unqualified senior executive for another. The result was that no one was truly in charge so that when FBB officials released periodic updates as to how the project was progressing and when it would be finished, no one believed them. Only after the FBB in March 2017 appointed Berlin Secretary of State Englebert Lütke-Daldrup as its CEO—someone who understood the importance of leveling with the public—did the project finally get back on track. The lesson that emerges from all these travails is that when it comes to serving as a megaproject sponsor and/or manager, there is no substitute for experience and expertise.

The New LaGuardia Airport Terminal B

The LaGuardia Terminal B case offers the same lesson as the Berlin Brandenburg Airport case but from the opposite perspective. In the LaGuardia case, the project sponsor, the Port Authority of New York and New Jersey, had years of experience managing airport expansion and reconstruction projects, and was fully up to the logistically challenging task of redeveloping LaGuardia Airport's main terminal building and surface access facilities. The LaGuardia case also demonstrates the advantages of undertaking difficult projects in discrete phases, especially when a facility must remain in service during construction.

In terms of cautionary lessons, the LaGuardia case demonstrates how credit-seeking politicians can complicate the job of undertaking major infrastructure projects. If, instead of inserting his own independent commission into the LaGuardia planning process, thereby adding an extra year of deliberations that resulted in no changes to the Port Authority's plans, New York Governor Andrew Cuomo had simply lent his political muscle to finalizing project funding, construction efforts possibly could have been completed a year earlier. Cuomo's intervention wasn't a big deal in the final analysis, but if nothing else, it serves to remind us that megaprojects are inherently political and determining who gets the political credit for their success is often a driving consideration.

Canary Wharf

Canary Wharf was unprecedented in so many ways that trying to draw replicable lessons from its success and failures is of questionable value. To begin with, Canary Wharf was conceived of by an American entrepreneur as a way of reusing abandoned docklands as a platform for building back office space that would compete with premium properties in the core of London. When that idea proved too risky to finance, British Prime Minister Margaret Thatcher stepped in to personally recruit Canadian office developer Olympia and York to do the job, giving them complete site and planning control, but no financing guarantees. Flattered by Thatcher's attention, Olympia and York CEO Paul Reichman took on the challenge, figuring he could use an American-style leasing and financing model to complete the project. Reichman's gambit might have worked but for the simultaneous arrival of a major economic recession and a government fiscal crisis. As it was, Olympia and York lost control of the project just as the market was starting to turn around. Over the next 20 years, Canary Wharf would reach and then exceed Paul Reichman's ambitious vision of creating a second London global financial center. Today, Canary Wharf is home to more than 16 million square feet of modern office space and has a daytime population of more than 100,000 people.

Even with the benefit of hindsight, it is not immediately clear what might have transpired differently. Had Thatcher not succeeded in recruiting Olympia and York to take over the Canary Wharf project in 1986, it would have died outright; and with nothing to take its place. Olympia and York's initial Canary Wharf development program and construction schedule were well-considered from a market and cost perspective, and had Reichman not undertaken his project speculatively and waited instead for a market to emerge organically, Canary Wharf would never have gotten off the ground. Had the Conservative government promised to financially backstop Olympia and York, it probably would not have been able to deliver on its promises, or else would have been besieged by similar pleas for assistance.

More than anything else, Canary Wharf reminds us that big urban development projects entail huge risks, that their financial viability always rests on a knife edge, and that the ability of even the savviest of private developers and government officials to overcome once-in-a-decade adverse market conditions is limited. The ultimate lesson of Canary Wharf is simple: great urban development projects may succeed even if their developers do not.

HafenCity, Hamburg

HafenCity's success is the result of both good luck and skill. In terms of luck, the opportunity to redevelop Hamburg's historical docklands arrived just as Germany was beginning to benefit from reunification and Hamburg was re-establishing itself as a major European shipping port. In terms of skill, HafenCity benefited from the political acumen of a far-sighted mayor, from the planning sensibilities and skills of its designers, and from the financial expertise of its public implementing agency, HafenCity Hamburg GmbH (HHG). HHG in particular deserves credit for its flexible land disposition strategy. Instead of selling off land parcels to the highest bidder, or entering into joint-venture partnerships with developers, or subsidizing developers who agreed to provide public amenities, HHG pursued all three approaches at once, choosing a land disposition strategy that combined achieving its long-term development goals and responding to current market realities. In any given month, HHG might make one parcel available to a well-heeled corporation or private housing developer willing to pay full price, while making a second parcel available to university, cultural facility or affordable housing sponsor for next to nothing. In each case, HHG sought to create synergies that would improve and expand use of the public realm, thereby creating new market and social value. It could do so first because, as a city agency, it owned and controlled the entire HafenCity site; second, because the city of Hamburg (and thus HHG) was willing to be patient in terms of achieving its goals; and third, because HHG's senior managers had the technical competence to structure land deals so as to maximize their available capital. Among redevelopment agencies, this combination of patience, commitment to a plan, land disposition and financing expertise, and deal-making prowess is truly rare; and when coupled with a forward-looking land use and building plan, is responsible for HafenCity being perhaps the best waterfront redevelopment project in the world.

Even with all these advantages, HafenCity still fell behind meeting its absorption targets. For all of its good fortune, in the two decades between 2000 and 2020, Hamburg added just 80,000 new residents. In short, even with luck and skill, urban development projects still require growth to be successful.

Songdo IBD

Songdo was the brainchild of the Korean city of Incheon and US property developer Gale International, and its lessons are twofold. First, never undertake a speculative real estate project if you have no real estate development experience or market knowledge (Incheon) or have no knowledge of the political and economic system in which you are operating (Gale International). Large-scale real estate development is such a specialized and risk-laden endeavor that no amount of research, technical analysis, due diligence and, in the end, money, can overcome a lack of experience and local knowledge. Except for situations in which the underlying land is essentially free (e.g., HafenCity) and/or constant population growth is generating what is essentially a limitless market (e.g., many Chinese cities), there is no profitable path to building a very large-scale mixed-use master-planned community. There are just too many things that can and will go wrong. This is as true in Korea as it is in Britain or the US.

Both Incheon and Gale International made unsupported assumptions about the enterprise they were jointly engaged in. Incheon mistakenly thought that by creating a brand—in Songdo's case, as an international business district—that it was also creating market value. For its part, Gale International went into the Songdo deal presuming that if push came to shove, Incheon (and the Korean government) would be willing to renegotiate Gale's debt service payments rather than see the project go under. Meanwhile, Korean homebuyers wondered why they were being asked to pay a 30 percent premium for new homes in an unfinished community compared with what they could pay to buy a home in a completed development a few kilometers away.

The lessons of Songdo are essentially the same as those of Canary Wharf and HafenCity. For very large-scale urban development projects to succeed in the marketplace, four conditions must hold. First, the land must be free or nearly free. Second, the developer must have a robust land disposition and/or financing model that can withstand several years of lower-than-expected market absorption. Third, the interests of all of the project sponsors, investors and lenders must be in alignment. Last, the public sector sponsor must be willing to absorb the initial costs of public infrastructure and amenities. In the case of HafenCity, all of these conditions were met. In the case of Songdo, none were.

Brooklyn Bridge Park

With a cost of roughly $300 million, the 85-acre Brooklyn Bridge Park doesn't properly qualify as a megaproject. Even so, with many cities around the world looking to convert disinvested industrial waterfronts into public amenities, it offers valuable lessons of what and what not to do. Lesson number one is that project decision-making and the funding authority must operate in alignment. In the case of Brooklyn Bridge Park, the power to stop the project from moving ahead resided in a cluster of neighborhood groups who agreed that the waterfront should be converted to a public park but disagreed as to how that conversion process should progress or who should pay for it. Whatever disposition and conversion plan the property's owner, the Port Authority of New York and New Jersey, might come up with, it first had to be approved by the neighborhood-controlled Community Board No. 2. At the same time, because of the site's deteriorated physical condition, whatever park facilities were ultimately built would require spending hundreds of million dollars on construction and remediation activities. As the city and state were only willing to provide partial funding, purchasing the park site would require selling some sites to developers. With state and city officials insisting that some development be allowed, and community groups opposing any development, good-faith efforts to find a middle path were repeatedly stymied. The impasse was finally broken only when newly-elected New York City Mayor

Michael Bloomberg agreed to allow city funds to be used for a compromise plan that included less development than the city wanted but more than the neighbors had previously agreed to. Still, this was not the end of it. Even with an outstanding park design plan and government funding commitments in place, opponent still continued to litigate pieces of the project. By the time construction on the park's first phase finally got underway in 2008, more than 20 years had passed since the Port Authority first notified city officials of their intent to sell the site.

What finally broke the political, legal and funding logjam was a more or less unilateral decision by the president of the Brooklyn Bridge Park Development Corporation—the entity established by the city and state to move the project along—to begin first phase construction even without having funding for later phases in hand. Thus, the second lesson of the Brooklyn Bridge Park experience is that sometimes moving ahead simply to establish momentum is the only way to get projects with contentious histories off the ground.

Five Ultra-large Renewable Energy Projects

Ultra-large renewable energy projects are financially risky. They cost a lot to build, and in the cases of wind and solar projects, there may be slack periods when their operating output falls far short of demand. For private investors to take on these added financial risks, the public sector must provide revenue guarantees for when the sun isn't shining or the wind isn't blowing. In the case of the $1.6 billion 659 MW Walney Extension offshore windfarm, the British government's Contracts for Difference (CfD) program effectively guaranteed Orsted Energy, the project's Danish developer and owner, wholesale revenues at the level of £150 per megawatt hour. In the case of the $2 billion 580MW Noor Ouarzazate Concentrated Power facility in Morocco's Atlas Desert, the Moroccan government entered into a power purchase agreement (PPA) guaranteeing the project's private developer a stable and reliable revenue stream for 25 years. A similar arrangement was used to finance India's 2,050 MW Pavagada Photovoltaic Solar Park, completed in 2019 at a cost of $2.1 billion. Essentially a form of insurance, revenue guarantee contracts have become a necessary means of financing privately-developed large-scale renewable energy projects in both developed and developing countries, and sponsors of other revenue-generating megaproject types would do well to study their uses and limitations.

Table 17.5   *Positive and cautionary lessons from each case study*

Megaproject	Positive lessons	Cautionary lessons
London Crossrail	Economic feasibility case can reliably include secondary and induced benefits if clearly identified.	Beware large and complex projects with numerous contractors and untested project management coordination and accountability mechanisms.
Beijing, Shanghai, Guangzhou and Shenzhen Metro Systems	Standardized planning construction, and procurement practices across lines keeps projects on schedule and budget.	Over-standardization of financing arrangements and related land use and development practices reduces local flexibility and initiative.
China's High-speed Rail Network	Nationally-standardized planning, construction, contracting and procurement practices can help keep projects on schedule.	Achieving secondary economic and spatial development goals is difficult.
Bus Rapid Transit in six Latin America and Asian cities	Sponsors of later BRT systems learned from the experiences of earlier adopters.	It is difficult even in the best of circumstances to match BRT supply and service characteristics to shifting traveler demands and volumes.
Seattle's Alaska Way Tunnel	Large transportation projects create opportunities to think creatively about public realm possibilities and improvements.	It is critically important to plan and budget for adverse contingencies.
Hong Kong–Zhuhai–Macao Bridge		Beware very large highway projects that are principally justified on the basis of economic development, especially in a dynamic and fluid economy (such as China's).
Singapore's Jewel Changi Airport	Singapore's early investments in government airport planning and construction capacity had large and continuing benefits.	
Berlin Brandenburgvalign: middle;align:left; Airport		It is difficult to overstate the importance of having experienced project managers and accountability systems in place.
LaGuardia Airport Terminal B Reconstruction	There are significant redundancy advantages to undertaking and opening complicated projects in phases.	Politics and personalities can complicate even the most thorough of project planning efforts.
London Canary Wharf	Secondary CBDs may make sense for congested and expensive global megacities.	Even the best-planned commercial real estate megaprojects are highly vulnerable to macro-economic downturns.
HafenCity Hamburg	Transformative urban development projects can succeed when thoughtful planning and design initiatives are accompanied by capable implementation.	Even the best implemented of redevelopment projects may take longer to reach build-out than initially anticipated.

Megaproject	Positive lessons	Cautionary lessons
Songdo, Korea	World-class physical development plans may have long-term merit even amidst fiscal or market difficulties.	Beware undertaking projects that are the "biggest" or "most," especially when there is no local precedent. Never hire an outside project developer/manager who doesn't understand local political and performance expectations. Branding alone can't ensure megaproject success.
Brooklyn Bridge Park (New York City)	Big and controversial projects are sometimes best undertaken in smaller increments.	Project approval and funding provisions need to align, especially in political systems with competing power centers.

CROSSCUTTING TAKEAWAYS

Combining the many individual case study lessons yields a number of cross-cutting takeaways, including:

1. *Competence and experience matter above all else.* Nothing matters more to megaproject success than the experience and technical competence of the senior project management team; and nothing makes this clearer than the difference in outcomes between the Berlin Brandenburg and LaGuardia Airport examples. In the Berlin Brandenburg case, Flughafen Berlin Brandenburg GmbH (FBB), a partnership between the German states of Berlin and Brandenburg, had never developed an airport, did not have a staff or senior management knowledgeable about airport development, and had to rely on external consultants for project management expertise. This became serious problem when several airport subsystems serious or failed their operational tests. FBB had no independent expertise and did not know how to move forward. Nor had it inserted the necessary contingency clauses in its contracts to adequately protect its interests. In the LaGuardia example, by contrast, the Port Authority of New York and New Jersey had recently completed two airport redevelopment projects of comparable scale and cost and had developed time-tested in-house procedures for successfully managing contractors and making sure they worked properly together. In the Berlin Brandenburg case, the project was delivered nine years late and at more than twice the promised cost. As of this writing, the LaGuardia project has remained on schedule and within budget.

2. *Learn from experience.* Because of their size and complexity, there is a tendency to treat every megaproject as unique, and to ignore the lessons of comparable projects completed elsewhere. This is a huge mistake. Most modern-day urban rail transit projects use similar technologies and follow similar planning principles. Many use trainset and signaling equip-

ment manufactured by the same companies. Most underground tunnels are dug the same way and most long-span bridges face similar design and engineering problems. Most international airports are designed to accommodate airplane, passenger, and baggage flows in the same way and face comparable landside transportation challenges. All very large-scale urban development projects face market absorption challenges and cost overruns. All public mega-park projects must figure out how to fund their long-term operating expenses, and all large renewable energy projects must provide their customers with power and ensure their investors a competitive return even when the sun isn't shining or the wind isn't blowing. Whatever their type or location, prior megaprojects have much to teach the sponsors of current ones.

The benefits of learning from experience are evident from several of the case studies. When planning the redevelopment and reconstruction of LaGuardia Airport's Terminal B, airport planners at the Port Authority of New York and New Jersey used the knowledge they had gained working on modernization projects at Newark Airport and JFK. BRT planners in Jakarta, Seoul and Guangzhou studied prior BRT planning and delivery practices in Curitiba, Quito, and Bogota, as well as made use of BRT planning manuals developed by the Institute for Transport and Development Policy. Metro system planners in Shanghai and Shenzhen studied Beijing's metro planning practices to learn what to do (standardize construction practices and equipment across lines) as well as what not to do (standardize station location and design practices). HafenCity officials purposely hired senior staff who had prior experience structuring real estate and land disposition deals.

3. *Standardization as a source of cost-efficiency and timely delivery.* The foremost lesson of China's high-speed rail and metro system examples concerns the benefits of engineering, construction, and equipment standardization. In the case of high-speed rail, the Chinese Ministry of Railways' early decision to standardize the design of bridge and elevated track facilities across the entire high-speed rail network ended up saving tens of billions of dollars in design, engineering, and construction costs as well as years of construction time. Similarly, the decision to standardize power, signaling and train equipment across high-speed rail lines paid dividends in reducing testing and delivery times, and in ongoing maintenance costs. Likewise, the adoption of a national joint venture high-speed rail financing model simplified the job of pulling together diverse funding sources. Without such standardization efforts, the though that China could successfully build a 37,000 km high-speed rail system in just 16 years is inconceivable. Similar approaches to standardizing planning, engineering,

construction, and procurement practices have been used to expedite construction of China's major metro systems.

It is also possible to go overboard with standardization, especially when it comes to facility siting and design decisions. The Ministry of Railways decision to locate some of China's high-speed rail stations outside downtown areas may have contributed to reduced construction times and costs, but it also reduced the system's convenience for many business travelers. Similarly, the Beijing government's decision to locate its metro stations at uniform intervals regardless of surrounding land uses and not to build transfer nodes where three or more line connect has made the system much less convenient for transit patrons. Determined to learn from Beijing's mistakes, Shanghai and Shenzhen's metro designers incorporated transfer hubs into their systems and put stations in locations where the surrounding land uses would maximize ridership.

London's Crossrail project and the Berlin Brandenburg Airport demonstrate what happens when construction and procurement standardization opportunities are not pursued. Both projects made use of so many contractors—each with their own procedures and protocols—that in the end, they became too complicated to manage and wound up going years over schedule and billions of dollars over budget.

4. *Senior project leadership should be knowledgeable, capable, and accountable.* Every megaproject runs into problems at some point during its planning and construction. The key question, of course, is how quickly and capably those problems will be resolved. Good leaders not only anticipate problems, they also know how to effectively solve them. Effective problem-solving takes several abilities. First, is the ability to quickly get to the source of the problem. This requires a detailed familiarity with the project's design, engineering, contracting, and construction practices. Project leaders who rely exclusively on mid-level project managers to identify problems are bound to run into trouble. When the Berlin Brandenburg Airport failed its initial fire control tests, there was no one in a senior leadership position in the FBB who knew what to do. Likewise, in the Songdo case, when residential sales fell far short of projections, there was no one in either the Incheon government or Gale International who understood the Korean residential market and could respond accordingly.

Second, effective problem-solving requires an ability to quickly come up with multiple response strategies and not just leave the job up to the contractor. This was the problem in Seattle's Alaska Way Tunnel project when Bertha, the project's giant tunnel-boring machine was unexpectedly disabled by an unforeseen pipe fragment. With no tunnel-boring experience of its own, the project's sponsor, the Washington State Department of Transportation, had to rely on the project's two foreign contractors to come up with a response strategy. Similar problems occurred during the construction of London Crossrail and the Berlin Brandenburg Airport. By contrast, when a problem with the train signaling system caused a collision between two high-speed rail trains in 2011, the head of China's Ministry of Railways acted decisively to upgrade the signaling facilities on all other lines.

Third, effective leaders follow through and are accountable, to project sponsors and funders as well as to eventual users. This is the lesson of the London Crossrail and the Berlin Brandenburg Airport examples. In both cases, it was only after a series of ineffectual senior managers were replaced with project leaders who honestly communicated the problems with each project and the steps being taken to remedy those problems that each project got back on track. The situation was similar in the Brooklyn Bridge case.

5. *Stress test key market and financing assumptions.* Transportation megaprojects are designed to accommodate a specific volume of vehicles or number of users willing to pay the fare or cost of using them. Likewise, urban development projects are designed to accommodate the space demands and rent-paying preferences of particular residential, commercial or industrial market segments. If, for whatever reason, the projected number of users fails to materialize in a timely manner, the project will fail. This is what happened to the HKZM Bridge and in Songdo. In the HKZM Bridge case, a shortfall in tourist and freight demand meant that fewer than half the number of vehicles expected to use the bridge actually did so. In the Songdo case, residential absorption lagged far behind initial projections, generating insufficient revenue for the developer, Gale International, to undertake the project's next phase.

Both of these situations could have been avoided or perhaps ameliorated had the project planners stress tested their initial projections. By stress test, we mean simulate the revenue and/or profitability implications of usage rates set at 20 percent, 40 percent, 60 percent, and 80 percent of hoped for levels. In some cases, a proposed project may not pass its stress test and should be cancelled. In other cases, the project scope may have to be scaled back. In still other cases, stress testing may result in finding additional revenue or financing sources. Had the HKZM Bridge been appropriately stress tested, it most likely would have been cancelled. In the Songdo case, a proper stress testing would have resulted in a very different land takedown strategy and a more flexible land planning and pricing approach. Ironically, of all the projects included in this casebook, the one that was subjected to the most rigorous stress testing was London Crossrail; and because of that, the project could be an eventual success despite its myriad project management and construction problems.

6. *Contingency planning for worst-case situations.* Bad things happen to good projects. Sometimes, this is for reasons of inattention or incompetence. Other times, it is because of a project's size or complexity. Still other times, it simply because of bad timing or bad luck. Regardless of the reason, project planners and managers should expect bad things to happen and prepare worst-case contingency schedules and budgets accordingly. Contingency schedules should pre-identify possible delay-causing events at each step of the project delivery process and identify response strategies to those events. By pre-identifying possible delay-causing events, project managers can put in work-around response strategies that isolate those events and minimize cascading delays. Had London Crossrail managers done something like this, they might have taken the problem-plagued Bond Street station out of the loop and continued working on the other central segment stations. As it was, Crossrail's entire central section work program came to a crashing halt. Similarly, had Berlin Brandenburg Airport project managers pre-identified the integrated ventilation and fire control system as a source of potential trouble, they could have developed back-up protocols that at least temporarily would have decoupled the two systems.

   Proper contingency planning also involves careful contingency budgeting. In most cases, contingency fund set asides are calculated as fixed proportions of the full project budget—10 percent is not an uncommon contingency percentage. Fixed proportion contingencies are reasonable for everyday real estate and capital facilities projects but may not be appropriate for one-off projects making use of cutting-edge construction methods or equipment. Megaproject contingency set asides should be calculated in such a way as to deal with the contingency, not merely limit the financial exposure of the different parties.

   This was the problem with the Alaskan Way Tunnel project. The contingency amounts were determined so that the Washington State Department of Transportation and Seattle Tunnel Partners, could each come in below their allocated budgets, and not, as should have been the case, remedy unforeseen problems.

   By scheduling and budgeting for worst-case outcomes rather than preferred outcomes, senior project officials can prevent significant-but-not insurmountable problems from becoming project-threatening cataclysms.

7. *Contingent financing plans.* If there is one thing to be learned from all three urban development case studies—Canary Wharf, HafenCity, and Songdo—it is that full build-out and market absorption always take longer than originally projected. For project sponsors or developers not wishing to lose control of their projects, this means making plans ahead of time as to how they will restructure their financing arrangements should the need

arise. Contingent financing plans may include provisions to give project investors or lenders additional ownership shares or back-end participation rights. They may include provisions for new parties to buy-out or assume the debts of original investors or lenders. They may include governmental entities coming in with bridge loans to tide a project over until the market recovers. They may include plans for accelerating land or asset sales to third parties. In the worst case, they may include filing for bankruptcy in a manner that guarantees the project will go on. One of the reasons HafenCity succeeded so brilliantly is that its public sector developer developed multiple land disposition strategies and vehicles which could be switched in or out as market and financial conditions changed. By contrast, Gale International wrongly assumed that with so much riding on Songdo's success, when push came to shove, either the Korean government or the city of Incheon would bail them out. When Incheon instead insisted that the original land takedown and payment provisions be honored, the project quickly fell apart.

Having a contingent financing plan also makes sense for transportation megaprojects. In both the London Crossrail and Berlin Brandenburg cases, the project developers were repeatedly forced to go back to their government sponsors, hat in hand, asking for additional funding. Had either CRL or the FBB put a contingent financing plan in place, they could have arranged for bank and/or government lines of credit to help resolve any short-term cash crunches.

8.   *Make the transportation–land use connection.* Transportation investments always affect nearby land uses, usually by making close by sites more valuable and thus promoting their redevelopment. Such effects are especially strong in growing cities with market economies.

Rarely, however, do transport project planners and sponsors incorporate the possibility of achieving positive and concomitant land use change into their initial planning efforts. And yet, at the end of the day, a transportation project's land use benefits may be as important as its mobility or connectivity benefits. This was precisely the case in Seattle, where city planners used the removal of the Alaskan Way Viaduct to undertake a once-in-50-years waterfront revitalization plan. It was also the case in both London and Shenzhen, where the air rights over new rail transit stations were sold to private developers generating additional project revenues. Indeed, Shenzhen and Shanghai's successes integrating metro station transportation and land use planning stand in notable contrast to Beijing's lack of efforts and success in this area. And it's not just rail transit investments. Starting in Curitiba in the early 1980s, and then later in Quito and Bogota, city planners used public sector investments in BRT facilities to promote additional housing construction. By contrast, when

Jakarta began building its BRT system in 2002, it chose not to update its zoning and land use plans, and accordingly, its BRT investments have done little to reduce the city's horrendous traffic.

Few places have connected transportation investments and land use and development plans better than Hamburg. The original plans for HafenCity called for it to connect via a new light-rail line to downtown Hamburg. A few years later, as HafenCity emerged as its own business district, the original light-rail proposal was abandoned in favor of extending the city's metro system. The result has been a development project that devotes far less space to parking and far more space to environmental amenities than comparable projects elsewhere.

CRITICAL MEGAPROJECT CHOICES

Megaproject sponsors, planners, designers, engineers, financiers, managers and contractors must make hundreds of crucial decisions, and the bigger and more complex the project, the more decisions there are to be made. Many of these decisions involve choosing the right option from a menu of choices. When deciding on whether a particular project is merited, planners must decide which project benefits to count and how to value them. Project designers must decide whether the sizeable cost and delivery time advantages of using standardized designs, construction methods and procurement practices outweigh the benefits of being able to customize projects to individual circumstances. Project designers and engineers must also decide whether to gamble on new and unproven technologies in the hope of improved cost efficiencies and project reliability. Project sponsors must decide whether to hire the same firms who design and/or engineer a project to also build it—an approach known as design-build—or whether to separate the job of project design and engineering from that of construction and delivery. When deciding how to finance a project, sponsors must weigh the value of using a joint-venture or public–private partnership (P3) approach, which provides expanded access to private-sector investor capital, or sticking with traditional government or bank financing. Among the many critical contracting choices facing project sponsors are how much contingency funding to set aside and which performance metrics to use. Perhaps most importantly, project sponsors must decide whether they themselves can best manage the project planning, construction, and delivery process, or whether they should hire outside project managers who specialize in delivering particular types of infrastructure and urban development projects.

The case studies included in this volume offer helpful guidance in answering each of these critical choice questions.

In-house or Out-of-house Project Management?

Perhaps no decision is more important than whether project management activities should be undertaken within the sponsoring organization (i.e., in-house), or by an outside contractor or project management firm (i.e., out-of-house), or shared by both the project sponsor and a contractor. The evidence from the case studies is clear. If the project sponsor has an in-house unit experienced in managing projects of a similar type and complexity, the project should be managed in-house. This is evident from the example of the Alaskan Way Tunnel, where the Washington State Department of Transportation served as principal project sponsor and project manager; and from the examples of Jewel Changi Airport and the LaGuardia Airport Terminal redevelopment project. In the Changi case, the recently-privatized Changi Airport Group served as both sponsor and project manager. In the LaGuardia case, the Port Authority of New York and New Jersey was both sponsor and manager. In each case, the project sponsor had experienced in-house project managers knowledgeable about the specific project type. In the HafenCity case, HafenCity Hamburg GmbH (HHG) was created out of public and private sector personnel who had precisely the project development and management experience needed to convert a schematic land use plan into a multi-pronged land disposition strategy.

The dangers of an organization trying to manage a complicated megaproject when it doesn't have an experienced project management team in house are evident from the London Crossrail and Berlin Brandenburg Airport cases. In the London Crossrail case, the two primary project funders, the Department for Transport and Transport for London, gave the project management job to Crossrail Limited (CRL), a brand new entity established to coordinate all aspects of Crossrail's delivery. CRL in turn, went out and hired senior managers who had prior experience managing large transportation projects, but nothing as complicated, or with as many contractors as Crossrail. Crossrail's initial tunneling phases went smoothly, but difficulties subsequently arose when the individual contractors fitting out individual stations and installing the power and signaling equipment ran into difficulty coordinating their work. Would these problems have been less troublesome if someone who had previously dealt with similar coordination and delivery difficulties been in charge? Given Crossrail's size and complexity, it is difficult to say. What can be said is that neither Crossrail's senior managers nor its project management systems were up to the job, resulting in repeated delays and change orders.

The Berlin Brandenburg Airport case provides convincing evidence of what happens when a project is managed entirely in-house by a staff without any prior or comparable experience. Given a choice between hiring experienced project managers or doing the work themselves, the two German states funding the new Berlin Brandenburg Airport chose to undertake the work themselves, despite never having managed anything of comparable size or complexity. The results was a fiasco from beginning to end. Final construction plans and doc-uments were delivered only after construction work had begun. Contractors were instructed to coordinate their operations themselves rather than having a central coordination office to turn to. Government inspection officials would turn up on site to undertake compliance tests on systems that had not been properly pre-tested. A mid-level project manager was fired for having falsified his credentials.

In sum, megaproject sponsors should only undertake project management activities themselves if they can put together a senior management team and project-level engineers who have had experience managing large projects similar to those being undertaken. In all other cases, they should hire an expe-rienced project management contractor.

Conventionally-financed or Public-private Partnership?

Megaprojects have traditionally been financed either directly out of national or local budgets by issuing government or government-backed debt. In recent years, with additional governments wanting to reduce their balance sheet debt and take advantage of private equity and debt sources, public–private partnerships (P3s) have become ever more common. In a P3, a government entity provides a private partner with a concession to build and operate an infrastructure project for a specific period of time, usually between 30 and 50 years, in exchange for the private partner providing an initial equity infusion (or covering initial construction costs) and/or a share of the project's debt. Most operating decisions and practices, including setting tariffs or fees, are consigned to the private partner, who is able to adjust them to cover operating and debt service costs. The other advantage of P3s, at least in theory, is that they will be more economical to build and operate because of the private part-ner's greater financial discipline and experience. Note that projects structured as P3s are almost never entirely privately financed, and typically include large amounts of government funding or debt.

Not including the renewable energy projects (three of which were devel-oped using P3s) or the six BRT projects (which were typically funded out of government budgets or with the help of international aid organizations) or Canary Wharf (which at this point is essentially a private real estate project), six of the projects included in this volume were conventionally funded, three were financed using P3s, and two were financed using a hybrid of conventional financing and a P3.

Of the three P3 projects, two (Jewel Changi Airport and LaGuardia Airport Terminal B) are notable successes in terms of meeting their objectives and staying within their schedule and budget, while the third (Songdo) is a notable failure. Of the two hybrid projects, HafenCity has performed very well, as have the Chinese metro lines that have entered into P3 arrangements with Hong Kong's MTR Corporation. Of the six government-financed projects, two (China's High-speed Rail Network and Seattle's Alaskan Way Tunnel) have performed well, three (Berlin Brandenburg Airport, the Hong Kong–Zhuhai–Macau Bridge, and London Crossrail) have not performed well, and one (Brooklyn Bridge Park) has met its objectives but experienced extreme delays.

Drawing firm conclusions from this mix is a challenge. Of those projects that performed poorly, the form of financing used was generally not the source of their problems. By contrast, of the P3 and hybrid projects that performed well, the additional expertise brought by their private partners and their greater attention to construction and operating details certainly contributed to their success. On balance, this suggests that when appropriate, megaproject sponsors are well-served to look for ways to structure their projects as either full or hybrid P3s. Even in situations where the private partner does not provide a majority of the project financing, their direct involvement in supervising construction and ensuring timely delivery seems to be a benefit.

The Standardization Advantage

For project sponsors wondering whether to standardize their designs, component systems, and construction and procurement practices to take advantage of economies of scale, the answer is yes, they should, especially on spatially extensive projects such as rail systems and highways. As the China high-speed rail and metro examples make clear, standardization offers benefits in terms of staying on schedule and budget and exacts few costs. Had the sponsors of London Crossrail made greater initial efforts to standardize their designs and construction practices across stations, it is likely some of their delays and cost overruns could have been avoided. Similarly, had FBB, the sponsor of the Berlin Brandenburg Airport made greater use of off-the-shelf component systems (rather than specifying their own), it is highly likely that many of the Airport's construction and delivery problems would have been avoided.

The one area where standardization is less appropriate is in siting railway or transit stations and highway interchanges in already built-up areas. Typically, in such cases, the surrounding land use pattern is already well established. Accordingly, facility siting decisions are best made on a case-by-case basis and in a manner that maximizes facility patronage rather than through the use of standardized rules

Single-event versus Cascading Contingencies

Project sponsors always express surprise when a two-month construction delay turns into a six-month delay, or a 5 percent cost overrun becomes a 25 percent overrun. They shouldn't. Most infrastructure megaprojects are constructed more or less linearly, meaning that one set of tasks must be completed before another set can begin. Given the complexity of the individual tasks, what is required is a more considered approach to contingency scheduling and budgeting than is usually the case. Specifically, when developing their initial delivery schedules and budgets, project planners should explicitly consider whether and how a delay or cost overrun in an earlier project phase could result in longer delays and bigger cost overruns later on. This is best done not by preparing a range of possible delay or cost overrun estimates, but instead, by gaming out possible "what if something goes wrong here" scenarios. If, for example, the FBB had seriously considered the possible downstream effects of the Berlin Brandenburg Airport failing its initial fire-safety tests, it would have taken those tests more seriously and insisted that their ventilation system contractor develop their own contingency plans. Likewise, Crossrail's project managers were completely unprepared for the possibility that a delay in completing construction of the Bond Street Station would prevent testing of the entire central Crossrail segment. Had the Washington State Department of Transportation considered the possibility of a breakdown in their one and only tunnel-boring machine, they would have insisted that the contractor have repair and replacement parts on site. Creating realistic delay and budgetary scenarios around adverse events may not prevent those events from occurring, but it will significantly reduce their downstream impacts. Project sponsors and managers should not commence construction until each of their major contractors has developed plans which document their own contingent responses in case of an unexpected adverse event.

Primary versus Secondary Benefits

Most megaprojects are preceded by some type of benefit-cost analysis in which the project benefits are added up and then compared with anticipated project costs. Undertaking this type of analysis involves three sets of issues. The first is how benefits and costs that accrue in different years should be compared. In most cases, this issue can be handled by choosing an appropriate discount rate. The second is how to assign monetary values to each type of benefit (e.g., assigning a monetary benefit to the travel time saved by building a high-speed rail line instead of a conventional rail line). As with discount rates, most government infrastructure agencies have their own well-documented sets of valuation formulas and rates. A third issue is more complicated: which secondary benefits to count and how to value them?

To illustrate the difficulty of this decision, consider the calculations made by Britain's Treasury Department when it was considering whether to recommend going ahead with Crossrail construction. Just counting and valuing Crossrail's primary benefits—the total amount of travel time saved owing to Crossrail's higher speeds and fewer stops—would not have been enough to balance Crossrail's huge construction costs. Adding in a secondary fiscal benefit, the increase in property values and retail revenues likely to occur in and around Crossrail stations, still would not have been enough to make the project meet its required benefit-cost benchmark. Only when Treasury planners developed a convincing narrative about how Crossrail would promote additional business agglomeration economies at selected stations, and how those agglomeration economies would result in greater business productivity and worker salaries could Crossrail planners justify its construction costs.

Should the Treasury planners have considered the secondary project benefits associated with the additional agglomeration economies? In the Crossrail case, because of the importance of the financial sector to the London economy, the decision to include Crossrail's secondary agglomeration benefits was clearly justifiable. If, however, Treasury's bean counters had argued that Crossrail's construction by itself would generate a surge in business employment, they would have been on much shakier ground.

The Crossrail case provides useful guidance as to which secondary economic benefits should be counted and how. To the extent that particular growth or compositional trends are already present in a local economy, then arguing that a particular infrastructure investment will concentrate them or magnify their effects may be valid. If on the other hand those trends are not present or they are uncertain, then arguing for an infrastructure investment on the basis of its secondary economic benefits is questionable. This was precisely the problem with the Hong Kong–Zhuhai–Macau Bridge: its promoters wildly over-estimated the growth in Macau tourists and Zhuhai manufacturing output based solely on the presence of the proposed bridge. In a similar vein, the argument that building high-speed rail lines connecting China's prosperous coastal cities to its lagging inland ones was not only empirically unsupportable, it also ran contrary to the efforts coastal cities like Shenzhen and Guangzhou were undertaking to promote their own growth.

New or Established Technology?

Megaprojects offer opportunities to try out new and often unproven technologies. Should those opportunities be embraced? Perhaps, but with a great deal of care. Three of the four rail and urban transit case studies—China's high-speed rail network, the four Chinese metro systems, and the bus rapid transit cases—made use of existing vehicle and vehicle control technologies. All were completed more or less on time and budget, and, except for a deadly 2011 train collision on the Wenzhou high-speed rail line that was traced back to a signaling system failure, all entered service without incident. The fourth case study, London Crossrail, has suffered from repeated construction delays and cost overruns due in part to the use of a new and more automated train control and passenger boarding system. Among the two tunnel and bridge case studies, both experienced time construction delays and cost overruns due to the use of untried technologies. In the Hong Kong–Zhuhai–Macau Bridge case, contractors ran into difficulties assembling huge pre-cast tunnel segments deep below the surface of Lingdingyang Bay. In the Seattle Alaskan Way Tunnel case, contractors made use of the world's largest tunnel boring machine to drill a double-decked single-bore tunnel rather than drill two smaller side-by-side tunnels as was accepted practice. In neither case was the technology itself at fault. Instead, problems occurred because contractors were not familiar with the new systems. The long-delayed Berlin Brandenburg Airport experienced a similar problem. Never having built a major airport before, the government agency managing the design and construction of the Berlin Brandenburg Airport lacked the necessary engineering experience to oversee contractors installing the airport's state-of-the-art integrated fire control and ventilation system. Technological problems of a different sort contributed to Songdo's many problems. Songdo was the first large-scale development project in South Korea to involve an American partner and be financed using a public–private partnership arrangement, and neither of the two principal participants, Incheon City on the Korean side, and Gale International on the American side, quite realized what they were getting into. By contrast, both Canary Wharf and HafenCity were financed using better-understood and more conventional financing arrangements. The upshot of this discussion is that megaproject sponsors should not necessarily shy away from using new technologies— indeed, in many cases, the use of a new design, construction, financing, or service technology is what makes the project possible—but they should also be aware of the potential for new approaches and new technologies to add significantly to completion times and costs.

Design-Build?

Design-build, the practice of hiring a single contractor to design, engineer, and supervise construction is widely touted in the construction industry as a more efficient and less expensive way to deliver major projects. The theory behind design-build is that designers, engineers, and builders who work together on an everyday basis and are subject to the same set of incentives will be better able to communicate key specifications and instructions. Of the cases profiled in this volume, only one, the Alaskan Way Tunnel in Seattle, was developed using a true design-build process, and except for the problems associated with the breakdown of Bertha, its one and only tunnel-boring machine, the project would have been delivered on time and on budget. Two other case study projects, Jewel Changi and LaGuardia Airport Terminal B, while not technically design-build projects, involved exceptionally close coordination between project designers, engineers, contractors and project managers, enabling both to remain within their in initial schedules and budgets. This suggests that the true utility of the design-build model lies not in its reliance on a single contractor, but rather in its use of tighter and more integrated project management procedures.

Developer or Land Seller?

All developers of large-scale urban development projects face a choice as to whether they should develop the entire project themselves, or, having assembled, master planned and entitled the entire site, sell off individual land parcels to more specialized builders and developers. The sponsors of the three urban development case studies included in this volume each approached this choice differently. Olympia and York, the original developer of Canary Wharf, went the sole-developer route, and then, when the commercial real estate market crashed just as their project was coming to market, was unable to pay its outstanding loans and went into bankruptcy. Gale International, the American developer of Songdo in South Korea, took a similar master-developer approach, albeit within the confines of a public–private partnership with the Korean city of Incheon. It suffered a similar fate when residential sales rates proved much weaker than projected. In Hamburg, HafenCity Hamburg GmbH (HHG), the public sector entity charged with planning and developing HafenCity, took the approach of selling-off or transferring individual land parcels to private and institutional developers in exchange for cash or other financial considerations. HHG's carefully-calibrated land disposition approach enabled it to better insulate itself from short-term market and development risks; and to dispose of parcels when market and financial conditions were favorable rather than just to raise needed cash. Of course, HHG also had the advantage of having obtained its land holdings for free, giving it the flexibility to set its land disposition schedule and pricing in a manner that Olympia and York and Gale International could not.

Index

Printed and bound by CPI Group (UK) Ltd, Croydon, CR0 4YY

16/04/2025

14658378-0005